THE BOAT REPAIR MANUAL

THE BOAT REPAIR MANUAL

George Buchanan

Consultant Editors
Allan Boyd
Harry Spencer
George Chandler

Arco Publishing, Inc.
New York

Published by Arco Publishing, Inc.
215 Park Avenue South, New York, NY 10003

Published simultaneously in Great Britain
by Pelham Books

Library of Congress Cataloging in Publication Data

Buchanan, George.
The boat repair manual.

Bibliography: p.
Includes index.
1. Boats and boating — Maintenance and repair.
I. Title.
VM321.B93   1984   623.8′208   84-11171
ISBN 0-668-06167-7

While every care has been taken to verify
facts and methods described in this
book, neither the publishers nor the
author can accept liability for any loss or
damage howsoever caused.

Typesetting by
Avonset, Midsomer Norton, Bath

Printed in Great Britain by
Purnell & Sons (Book Production) Limited,
Paulton, Bristol

The Boat Repair Manual was conceived, edited and designed by Thames Head Limited, Avening, Tetbury, Gloucestershire GL8 8NB, Great Britain

Editors
Alison Goldingham
Anne Forsyth

Consultant editors
Allan Boyd
Harry Spencer
George Chandler

Art editor
Nick Hand

Designers and illustrators
Tracey Arnold
Nick Allen
Simon Borrough
Barry Chadwick
Dave Chapman
Mark Dempsey
Philip Evans
Jacquie Govier
Bill Padden
Brian Watson

Photography
Nick Allen
Nick Hand

To Allan and Jean Boyd
The reward of a thing well done, is to have done it Emerson

Author's acknowledgements

I am especially indebted to **Allan Boyd, George Chandler** and **Harry Spencer,** who have given so much of themselves in order to make this a better book. It has been a privilege to work with them.

I have turned to many people for technical advice. I would like to thank these people who have helped me in this project.

Mr W F Wetherall and Mr K Payne Wessex Resins and Adhesives Limited, Southampton.
Paul Grigg Hawker Siddeley Marine Limited, Gloucester.
Mr Lennard L T Boats, Taunton.
Dr Roger Berry Princes Risborough Laboratory.
Mr Elliot and Mr Akester MacAlister Elliott and Partners Limited, Lymington.
Mr D K Daniels Hydrovane Yacht Equipment Limited, Nottingham.
Mr N Franklin Aries Vane Gear, Cowes, Isle of Wight.
Mr N J Clegg International Paints, Yacht Division, Southampton.
Mr M Jenkins Hempels Yacht Paints Limited, Southampton.
David Taylor, Peter Buchanan, Derek Johnstone and David Pilch.

My thanks also to the many people who offered expert advice and information.

Mr Ken Watson Avon Inflatables Limited.
Mr R Dyson North London Polytechnic College.
Mr R Wares DuPont Chemical Industries.
Mr Lonton Cranfield Sails.
Mr F Timms Coubro and Scrutton Limited.
Mr A J Kirby E J Bowman (Birmingham) Limited.
Mr Broughton and Mr Waller Racal-Decca Limited.
Chris Jeckell Jeckells and Son Limited.
Andy Charles Kaowool Ceramic, Bristol.

I would also like to thank the following individuals and organizations who have very generously sent me materials on which I was able to base drawings and charts.

Hawker Siddeley Marine, Gloucester.
Munster Simms Engineering Bangor, Northern Ireland.

Lloyds Register of Shipping
Volvo Penta UK Limited Watford.
Simpson-Lawrence Limited Glasgow.
Outboard Marine UK Limited Northampton.
M G Duff Chichester, West Sussex.
Y S Fittings Walsall, Staffs.
Paul Grigg
Freedom Yachts International Limited Southampton.
Lucas Marine Camberley, Surrey.

I am grateful to the following companies for sending me reference material in connection with different chapters in the book.

Avon Inflatables Limited Llanelli, Dyfed, South Wales.
British Seagull Company Poole, Dorset.
Coubro and Scrutton Limited Southampton.
Navigair Limited Southampton.
The Royal Yachting Association.
The Royal Ocean Racing Club.
Outboard Marine UK Limited Northampton.
Jeckells and Son Wroxham, Norfolk.
International Paints Southampton.
Hempels Yacht Paints Limited Southampton.
Walkers Marine Instruments Birmingham.
Lucas Marine Camberley, Surrey.
Pirelli General Southampton.
Hawker Siddeley Marine Limited Gloucester.
Racal-Decca Navigator Limited New Malden, Surrey.
Racal-Decca Marine Radar Limited New Malden, Surrey.
Lewmar Marine Limited Havant, Hampshire.
Hawkins and Tipson Ropemakers Limited Hailsham, East Sussex.
Munster Simms Engineering Limited Bangor, Co. Down, Northern Ireland.
Kemp Masts Limited Fareham, Hampshire.
Simpson-Lawrence Limited Glasgow.
Isaiah Preston Limited Cradley Heath, West Midlands.
R and D Marine Limited Baldock, Herts
Y S Fittings Limited Chasetown, Walsall, Staffs
Volvo Penta UK Limited Watford, Herts.
E C Smith and Sons Limited Luton, Herts.

Contents

Chapter 1

Maintenance Survey

Yacht Maintenance survey

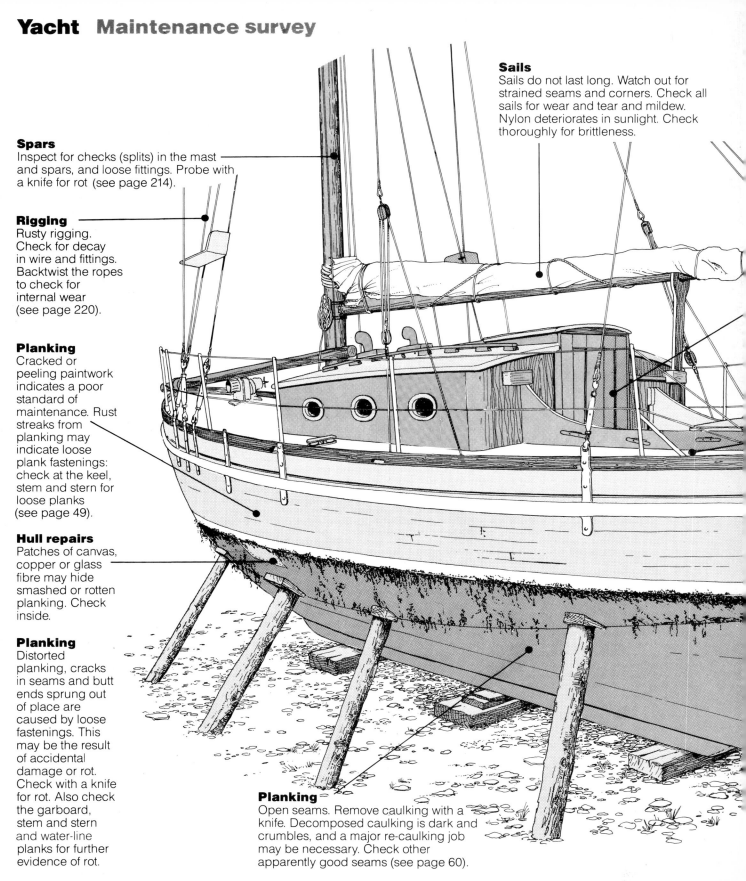

Spars
Inspect for checks (splits) in the mast and spars, and loose fittings. Probe with a knife for rot (see page 214).

Rigging
Rusty rigging. Check for decay in wire and fittings. Backtwist the ropes to check for internal wear (see page 220).

Planking
Cracked or peeling paintwork indicates a poor standard of maintenance. Rust streaks from planking may indicate loose plank fastenings: check at the keel, stem and stern for loose planks (see page 49).

Hull repairs
Patches of canvas, copper or glass fibre may hide smashed or rotten planking. Check inside.

Planking
Distorted planking, cracks in seams and butt ends sprung out of place are caused by loose fastenings. This may be the result of accidental damage or rot. Check with a knife for rot. Also check the garboard, stem and stern and water-line planks for further evidence of rot.

Sails
Sails do not last long. Watch out for strained seams and corners. Check all sails for wear and tear and mildew. Nylon deteriorates in sunlight. Check thoroughly for brittleness.

Planking
Open seams. Remove caulking with a knife. Decomposed caulking is dark and crumbles, and a major re-caulking job may be necessary. Check other apparently good seams (see page 60).

Interior
Stains and flaking varnish may indicate a leaking deck or faulty deck fittings. Check for external damage to deck, and for quality and tightness of fittings.

Deck
Scuffed and torn deck canvas will leak and may cause rot beneath. Check the entire deck for wear and the need to replace canvas. Always check beneath the lino floor coverings for rot (see page 179).

Paint
Marine growth suggests anti-fouling paint has not been used. Check the keel and lower planks for evidence of worm attack. If holes are discovered, poke about with a knife to find the extent of the damage (see page 287).

Rudder
Check the rudder for damage and wear (see page 154).

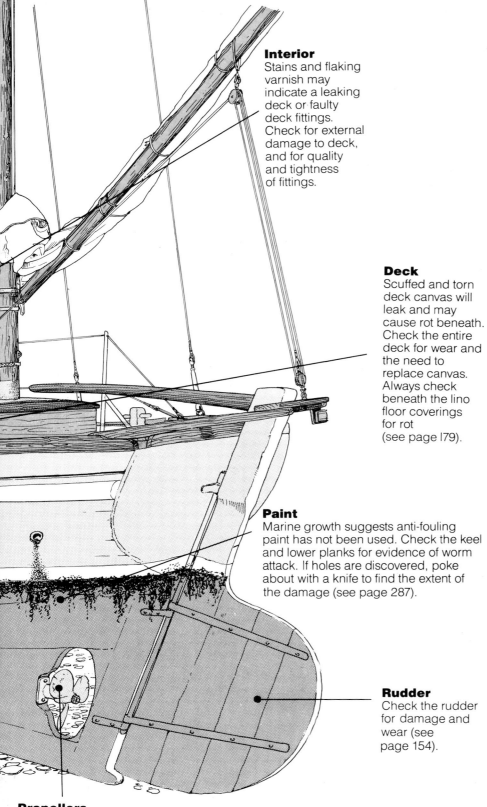

Propellers
Worn or damaged propellers are inefficient. If there is evidence of grounding and shallow water use, check the water cooling system for congestion. Check for play in the bearing by firmly shaking the propeller.

Lifting varnish and discoloured paint in badly ventilated areas may indicate the presence of rot. Check all timbers with a knife point pushed across the grain for soft spots as shown.

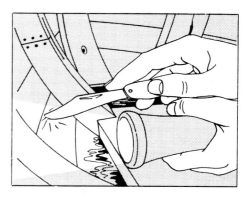

Inspect any checks (splits) in the ribs. Probe for rot and assess the loss of strength. Most sawn frames will split in places. Check for movement of planks as an indication of loose fastenings. Concrete in the bilges may hide decayed planking. Check all timbers, particularly at the keel and around the engine and prop shaft.

Places particularly susceptible to rot are at the stem and stern, under the cockpit, under the cabin floor, the bilges, and any area of poor ventilation where damp and dirt can accumulate. Purplish patches on wood and paint discoloration, indicate dry rot. This can be very serious and is usually expensive to put right.

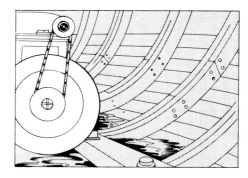

Most boats will have damp bilges but obviously the drier they are the better. Clean water indicates a leaky hull, oily water a badly worn engine. Smelly, wet bilges indicate poor ventilation: ideal conditions for rot and the accumulation of toxic and inflammable vapours. Check the positioning and functioning of engine compartment vents.

Wooden houseboat conversion Maintenance survey

Upholstery
Insulation and ventilation should prevent upholstery, carpets and curtains going mildew. See page 209 for suggestions to help eliminate mildew.

Condensation
Opening windows, cowls, and hatches should help prevent condensation. In addition, insulation with vinyl sheeting or insulation paint will help control this nuisance (see page 192).

Transom and sternpost
Loosened planking at transom and stressed sternpost. As the boat takes the ground, the rudder, particularly large barge-type rudders, will stress the transom and slowly loosen the sternpost. Concrete is often poured into cavities between the sternpost, transom, knee, and planking in an attempt to stop leaks and restore strength. This is not a long-term solution. Repairs are usually very costly and, except in an otherwise sound hull, rarely worth while.

Gas
Gas cylinders should be stored on deck, or in specially designed lockers. An armoured flexible pipe should be attached to regulator and copper tubing to cooker and lamps. Each outlet should be fitted with an isolating valve.

Planking
Cupped planking and opened seams allow water to reach the cloth membrane between plank layers (see page 130). Rot will spread rapidly between inner and outer skin, particularly in a boat moored in fresh water and kept comfortably warm. (See rot, page 287.) Worm-infestation is also likely once water penetrates behind the anti-fouling (see page 307).

Hull
Excessive weed growth suggests a poorly maintained hull. Regular cleaning and anti-fouling is essential to protect hull against marine growth and worm attack. Hauling out, and a thorough cleaning and close inspection of the hull must be a first priority (see page 284).

Books
Keep books neatly in a purpose-made bookshelf. Little can be done to prevent them absorbing moisture, other than by wrapping each book in cling film. The worst effects of swelling and sticking pages can be avoided by allowing warm air to circulate behind and beneath the books. Make shelves from battening.

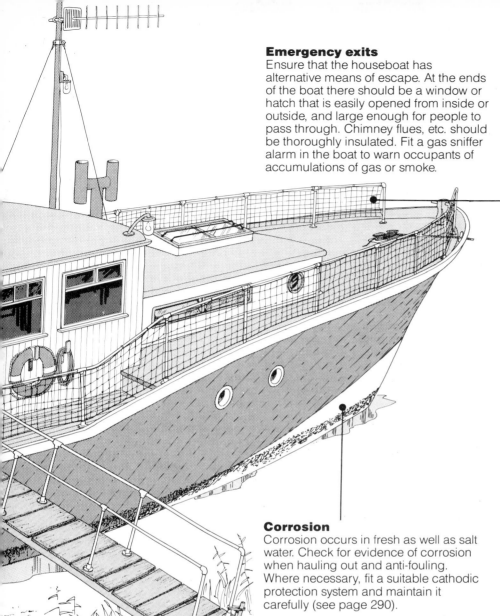

Emergency exits

Ensure that the houseboat has alternative means of escape. At the ends of the boat there should be a window or hatch that is easily opened from inside or outside, and large enough for people to pass through. Chimney flues, etc. should be thoroughly insulated. Fit a gas sniffer alarm in the boat to warn occupants of accumulations of gas or smoke.

Guard rails and stanchions

Houseboats should be fitted with comprehensive guard rails and stanchions around the deck and on the gangplank. Life belts should be provided (see page 297). Where small children live or visit aboard, fit netting against the stanchions as an additional safeguard. In summer guard rails may seem adequate, but for a permanent home, they should be high and strong enough to prevent people slipping from a frosty deck into icy winter water.

Galley

Galley conditions afloat often make it difficult to keep cupboards clean and food fresh and dry. A desiccant in each food cupboard helps to prevent excessive moisture take-up. Smells can be removed by the methods described on page 209. Periodic washing with vinegar will help to prevent mildew.

Wiring

All wiring should be earth return, with wires, switches and appliances suited to marine use. Run all wiring as high inside the cabin as possible and protect it against damp and corrosion (see pages 270 and 290).

Hull

The hull should be well drained and ventilated. Wood will rot faster in fresh water than in salt water. Inspect behind panelling, move furniture etc., to check for the presence of wet or dry rot. Dry rot can usually be smelt by its strong sweet odour. Its fungal growths are purplish and spread across paintwork, etc. Wet rot does not have the same strong smell and is easier to eliminate. (See page 287). Check that all waterways are clear, and even inaccessible parts of the hull are well-ventilated and drained.

Corrosion

Corrosion occurs in fresh as well as salt water. Check for evidence of corrosion when hauling out and anti-fouling. Where necessary, fit a suitable cathodic protection system and maintain it carefully (see page 290).

Hogged or sagged hull

Boats which are moored in tidal waters and occasionally take the ground, may bend their keels and become 'hogged' as a result of inadequate keel support when the water dries out. Very serious damage results from this kind of stressing (which will also happen if a boat is hauled out and incorrectly propped and supported). Hogging and sagging are difficult conditions to detect unless the boat is hauled out and the keel sighted. Fibreglass and large steel yachts may distort if badly supported, but their structure is not significantly weakened.

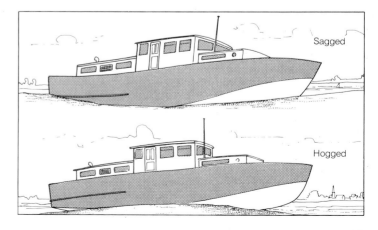

Sagged

Hogged

Steel motor boat Maintenance survey

Interior
The hull's interior should be kept scrupulously clean and dry. Ensure that all drainage and ventilation holes are clear. Check for rust streaks on paintwork, etc. Remedy leaks, and ensure that all surfaces are well protected by paint.

Anchor ground tackle
At least three anchors are required, two main and one kedge anchor, each with sufficient chain or rope separately stored (see page l94).

Vibration
Misfiring will cause excessive vibration in neutral. Otherwise, vibration may be caused by misaligned shaft or damaged propeller (see page 240).

Corrosion
Inspect the rudder, around the prop shaft, and close to through-hull fittings. A professional specified cathodic protection system of zinc anodes, attached to the underside of the hull, will be effective in preventing corrosion outside the hull. Unusually fast erosion of the anode should be investigated, as it may be caused by an earth leak in the electrical system (see page 274).

Denting
Steel hulls are usually extremely strong, and dents have only a cosmetic significance. Hollowing between frames, giving the boat a starved, bony appearance, is often caused by shrinkage during welding, and may indicate heavy construction methods rather than poor handling.

Fuel supply
The filler caps should be clearly marked, pipe runs well-supported and bonded into electrical bonding system. Plastic or glass filters or sight glasses should be changed for metal. Drip trays beneath carburettors and over the air vents should be covered with a fine wire gauze screen, to prevent flash back (see page 260).

Fire extinguishers
Cabins and engine room should be equipped with suitable fire extinguishers that have had regular and recent servicing (see page 296).

Engine
Engine performance can be judged by its power output, colour of exhaust smoke, rhythm of its beat, temperature and oil pressure (see pages 236 and 244).

Aluminium — steel joins
Joint between aluminium deck house and steel deck should be well drained, and above deck level. Fastenings should be compatible with alloy cabin-sides, otherwise severe corrosion will occur (see page 120).

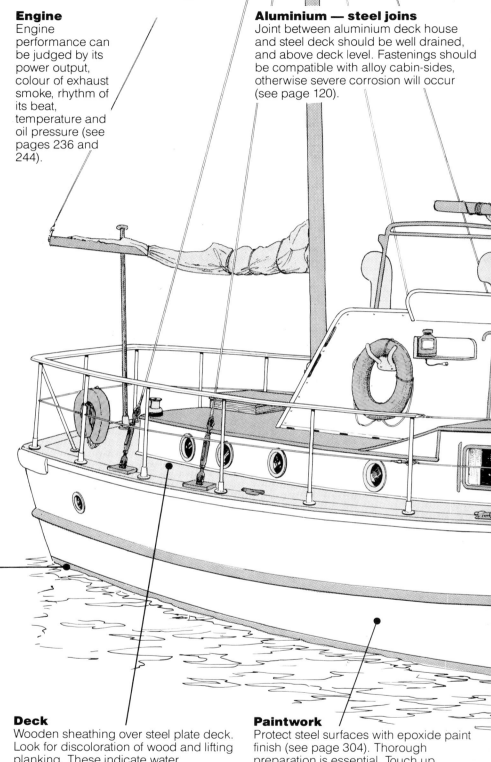

Deck
Wooden sheathing over steel plate deck. Look for discoloration of wood and lifting planking. These indicate water penetration behind laid deck, causing rusting. This is difficult to repair, and without the removal of the covering deck planks, the extent of the problem is often hard to assess.

Paintwork
Protect steel surfaces with epoxide paint finish (see page 304). Thorough preparation is essential. Touch up paintwork immediately before serious rust and pitting occurs. The paintwork covering poorly prepared steel surfaces will lift as rust spreads behind sound paintwork.

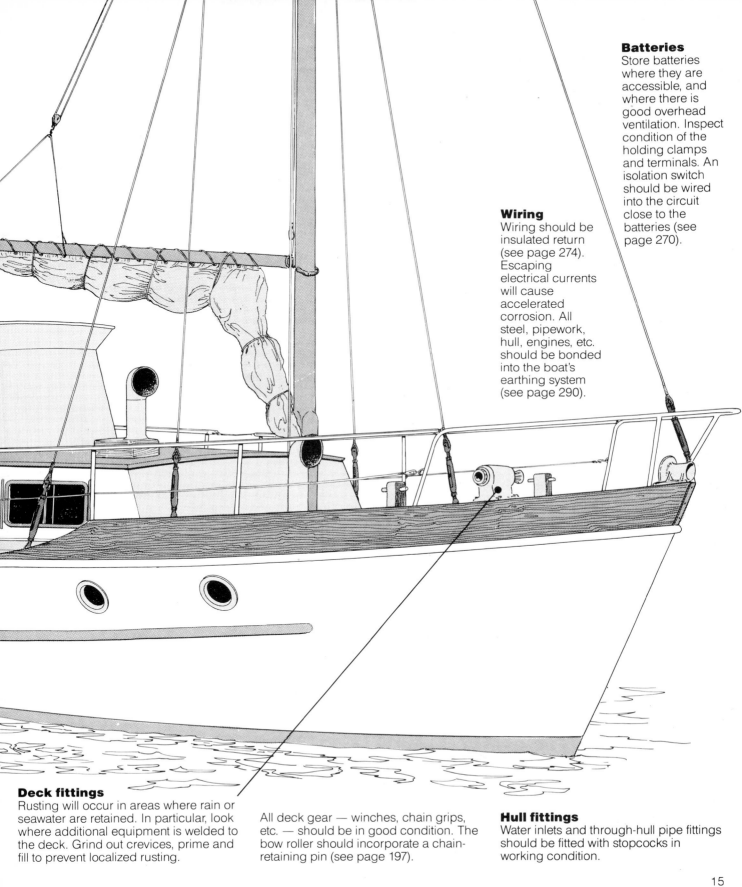

Batteries
Store batteries where they are accessible, and where there is good overhead ventilation. Inspect condition of the holding clamps and terminals. An isolation switch should be wired into the circuit close to the batteries (see page 270).

Wiring
Wiring should be insulated return (see page 274). Escaping electrical currents will cause accelerated corrosion. All steel, pipework, hull, engines, etc. should be bonded into the boat's earthing system (see page 290).

Deck fittings
Rusting will occur in areas where rain or seawater are retained. In particular, look where additional equipment is welded to the deck. Grind out crevices, prime and fill to prevent localized rusting.

All deck gear — winches, chain grips, etc. — should be in good condition. The bow roller should incorporate a chain-retaining pin (see page 197).

Hull fittings
Water inlets and through-hull pipe fittings should be fitted with stopcocks in working condition.

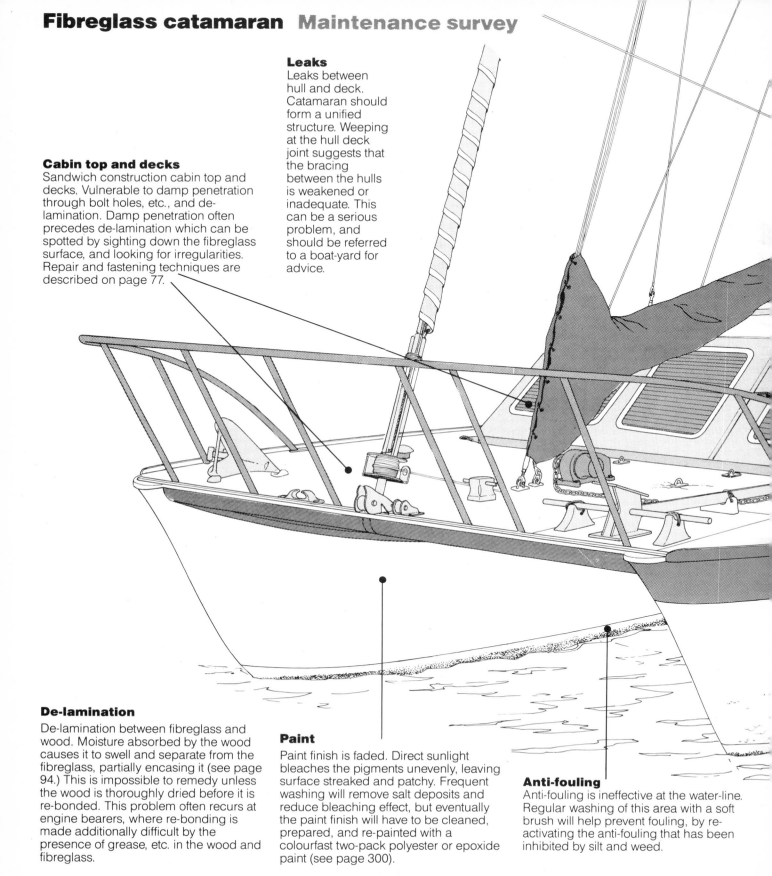

Fibreglass catamaran Maintenance survey

Leaks
Leaks between hull and deck. Catamaran should form a unified structure. Weeping at the hull deck joint suggests that the bracing between the hulls is weakened or inadequate. This can be a serious problem, and should be referred to a boat-yard for advice.

Cabin top and decks
Sandwich construction cabin top and decks. Vulnerable to damp penetration through bolt holes, etc., and de-lamination. Damp penetration often precedes de-lamination which can be spotted by sighting down the fibreglass surface, and looking for irregularities. Repair and fastening techniques are described on page 77.

De-lamination
De-lamination between fibreglass and wood. Moisture absorbed by the wood causes it to swell and separate from the fibreglass, partially encasing it (see page 94.) This is impossible to remedy unless the wood is thoroughly dried before it is re-bonded. This problem often recurs at engine bearers, where re-bonding is made additionally difficult by the presence of grease, etc. in the wood and fibreglass.

Paint
Paint finish is faded. Direct sunlight bleaches the pigments unevenly, leaving surface streaked and patchy. Frequent washing will remove salt deposits and reduce bleaching effect, but eventually the paint finish will have to be cleaned, prepared, and re-painted with a colourfast two-pack polyester or epoxide paint (see page 300).

Anti-fouling
Anti-fouling is ineffective at the water-line. Regular washing of this area with a soft brush will help prevent fouling, by re-activating the anti-fouling that has been inhibited by silt and weed.

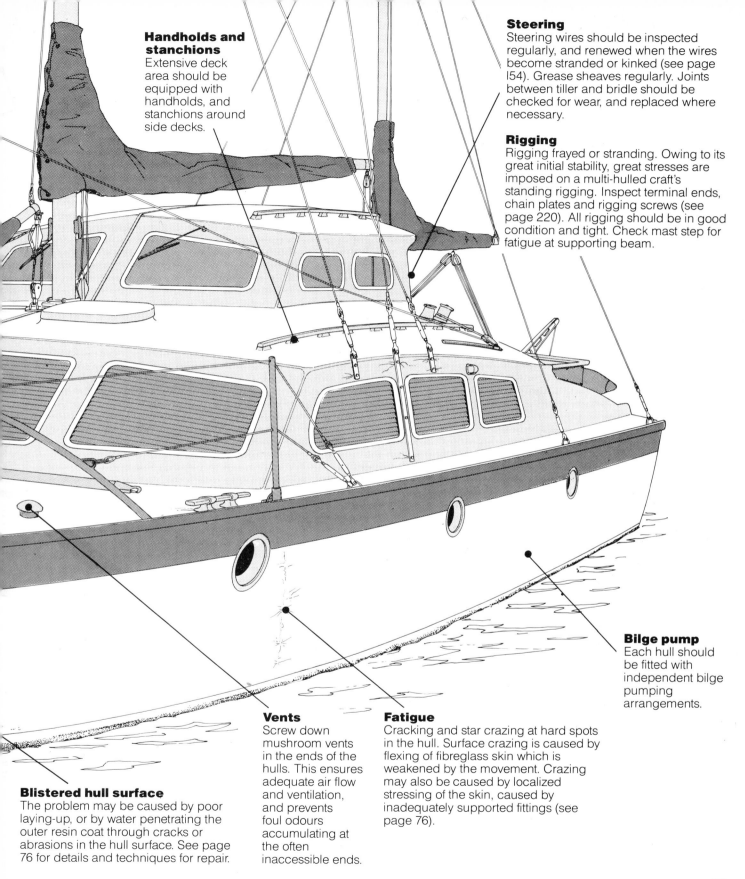

Handholds and stanchions
Extensive deck area should be equipped with handholds, and stanchions around side decks.

Steering
Steering wires should be inspected regularly, and renewed when the wires become stranded or kinked (see page 154). Grease sheaves regularly. Joints between tiller and bridle should be checked for wear, and replaced where necessary.

Rigging
Rigging frayed or stranding. Owing to its great initial stability, great stresses are imposed on a multi-hulled craft's standing rigging. Inspect terminal ends, chain plates and rigging screws (see page 220). All rigging should be in good condition and tight. Check mast step for fatigue at supporting beam.

Bilge pump
Each hull should be fitted with independent bilge pumping arrangements.

Vents
Screw down mushroom vents in the ends of the hulls. This ensures adequate air flow and ventilation, and prevents foul odours accumulating at the often inaccessible ends.

Fatigue
Cracking and star crazing at hard spots in the hull. Surface crazing is caused by flexing of fibreglass skin which is weakened by the movement. Crazing may also be caused by localized stressing of the skin, caused by inadequately supported fittings (see page 76).

Blistered hull surface
The problem may be caused by poor laying-up, or by water penetrating the outer resin coat through cracks or abrasions in the hull surface. See page 76 for details and techniques for repair.

Plywood sailing dinghy Maintenance survey

Safety equipment
Safety equipment should be checked and tested when necessary. Bailing buckets must be tied to the hull with a lanyard. An anchor and anchor rope of adequate length should be carried. Self-bailers and transom flaps must open easily and shut when necessary. Inflatable lifejackets should be tested before use, and those that have a cartridge-type inflator returned to the manufacturer at the end of each year for service and re-charging. Buoyancy equipment must also be of appropriate size. If children are taken sailing, provide them with suitable buoyancy jackets.

Screwed fittings
Loose or missing screws in mainsheet track. End grain holding poor. Replace those which are loose or missing with longer thicker screws. Check all other screwed hull and rudder fittings.

Damp at transom
Blackening indicates water penetration into end grain. Check bond between side and transom. Damp penetration is often followed by failure of glue join. Immediate stripping, drying and re-finishing is necessary, perhaps with application of unthickened epoxy resin and supporting blocks at the transom side joint (see page 54).

Tiller
Tiller retaining pin is bent, and difficult to insert. See page 161 for method of avoiding this problem.

Centreboard or rudder pivot
Blackened wood at centreboard or rudder pivot. Pivot is worn, and perhaps corroded (see page 148).

Varnish lifting
Caused by poor preparation or prolonged exposure to sun. Varnish will have to be stripped off, and the deck re-stained before re-varnishing. (see page 305).

Buoyancy bags
Correct size, securely strapped and well-inflated. Tape or pads should protect bags from bolt ends or sharp corners.

Single bolt
Bends and will fail when under stress in heavy weather. Replace with universal joint (see page 161).

Toe straps
Must be in good condition, tight and firmly fastened at the ends. Replace frayed straps.

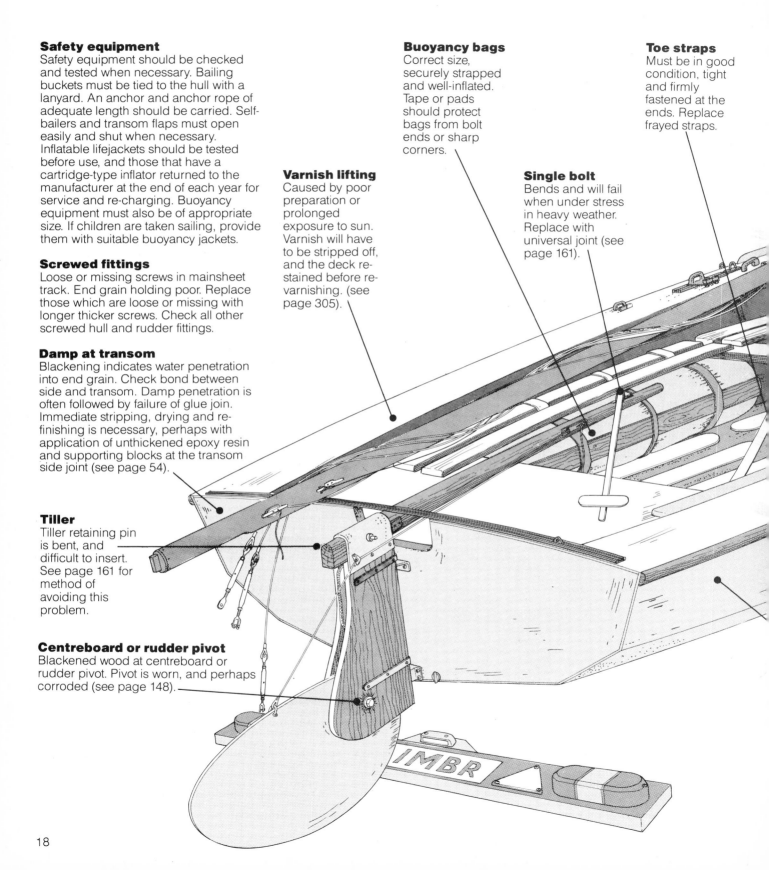

Corroded rivets
Incorrect rivets used. Remove and replace them in turn, fit stainless steel rivets— instead. Check other rivetted mast fittings.

Mast
Slight depressions in the mast are usually not serious, but kinks and larger well-defined dents will probably cause mast failure in strong winds.

Mast step
Wooden mast step split and discoloured by damp. Unscrew and make a new one from teak. utile or larch. Carve a drain hole in the base of the mast step.

Sails and rigging
In order to make a thorough check of the condition and effectiveness of the sails, they should be set and drawing. Each sail should have its own bag in which it is stored. The luff wire of the jib should be free of rust stains. Batten pockets and battens should be checked, and fit easily. These are often the first places where wear appears, and should be inspected and repaired regularly (see page 230).

Check all running rigging. Reverse mainsheet tackle, and replace worn or frayed sheets and halyards. All standing rigging tensioners should be lockable, either with locknuts or wire. Clevis pins and toggles should be of the correct material, size and type. Run a hand lightly down the wire rigging. If the wire is stranded, and the sharp broken ends can be felt, replace it (see page 220).

Towing and launching trolleys
These rarely have the same care and attention lavished on them as the dinghy, yet the safety of the dinghy depends upon the structure, bearings and brakes of the road trailer being in good condition. Look for rust and fractured welds, and check bearings and brakes. When towing, the boat should be firmly lashed to the road trailer with thick pads beneath the ropes to protect paintwork and varnish. Use the truck driver's hitch and pull it tight to hold the boat. Electrical wiring and numberplate board should conform to national requirements.

Paintwork
Bumpy paint finish may suggest damage to ply. Inspect inside woodwork for evidence of filling. Temporary repairs should be removed and holes patched (see page 125).

Bearings
Bearings and over-run brakes must be serviced regularly and in good order.

Chain plate
Paintwork around chain plate fractured by loose fitting. Replace holding bolts with bolts of greater diameter. Protect the ends of the bolts with tape or pads to prevent puncturing the buoyancy bags.

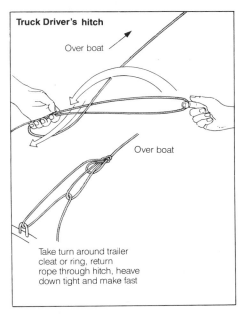

Truck Driver's hitch

Over boat

Over boat

Take turn around trailer cleat or ring, return rope through hitch, heave down tight and make fast

Chapter 2

Tools and Techniques

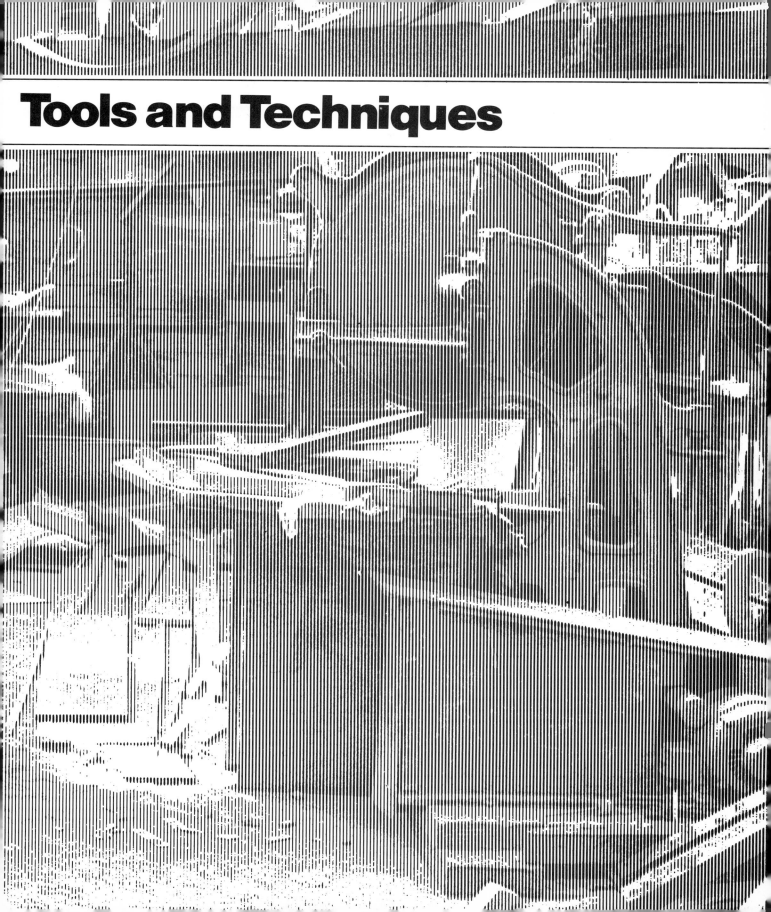

Wood types and identification Tools and techniques

The table lists a number of woods widely used in boat-building and repair, with their densities, appearance and handling characteristics.

Those unfamiliar with these woods will have great difficulty in identifying them, but often an experienced boat-yard worker will be able to help. If the matter is important, the Princes Risborough Laboratory, Building Research Establishment at Princes Risborough, UK, will, for a small charge, identify the wood from a sample sent to them.

Identification problems are made more difficult by the variety of ways in which a timber can be presented. The method of cutting determines which facet of the trunk is exposed, and even similar pieces may weather differently. While one may darken with age and damp, another similar piece left in the sunlight might bleach. Wood that was once painted will appear whiter or greyer than new wood or wood that has been varnished. It usually helps in the first appraisal to remove a small chip of wood from an edge, to establish its true colour and texture.

Seasoning

Seasoned wood is more resistant to fungal decay and worm attack than unseasoned. Timber for boat repairs should be air dried to approximately 20 per cent moisture content. Heavy mainframe timbers — keel, hog, stem, etc — which will be submerged for most of their life need not be thoroughly seasoned. If repair work is carried out in a dry or heated workshop, prevent unfinished wood from excessive drying by brushing with warm linseed oil or varnish.

Only timbers that are to be steam bent are used green, and after bending they should be treated with liberal quantities of preservative. (For moisture content specifications for glueing, see page 38).

For most work an average 15-20 per cent moisture content is suitable, and will be achieved simply by storing sawn wood in a dry, sheltered and well-ventilated stack. Fresh cut one inch (25 mm) boards will reach this figure in about a year, depending on the location of the stack, and the nature of the timber. Add one year for each inch of thickness. Kiln-dried timber will be drier than the 15-20 per cent mentioned above, and unless it is to be glued with epoxy resin glue, it, too, should be carefully stacked for a short while until it reaches equilibrium in the humid waterside atmosphere.

Moisture content can be checked with a moisture meter. These are obtainable from tool shops or through advertisements in woodworking magazines. It may also be possible to borrow one from a boat-yard equipped to repair fibreglass boats, where they are used for testing the moisture content of the inner laminates of fibreglass prior to laying up a repair with polyester or epoxy resin. Although such a meter is unlikely to be calibrated for wood, it is a simple matter to test a known dry sample of the same wood and compare its reading with that of the piece to be used.

Sawing

It is a highly skilled task to saw a log, and obtain from it the maximum quantity of usable timber. It is not a skill that the boat repairer is likely to be called upon to practise. However the cuts are arranged, most trunks will produce a selection of quarter-sawn and slash-sawn planks. The diagrams right illustrate the different strengths and qualities of these boards.

Boards which are slash-sawn are often wider and may, particularly if they have been cut from the edge of the trunk, have considerable quantities of sap wood. These are very prone to shrinkage and associated cupping, and should not be used in a laid deck or at any other exposed location in large widths.

The cupping effect is greatest where the plank is sawn some distance from the heart of the tree, particularly where the end grain reveals an unbroken arc of growth rings on the end of the board.

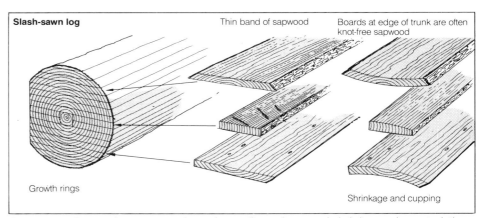

Slash-sawn log and some sample grain configurations and shrinkage characteristics

The tendency to cup can be countered by driving long drift or coach bolts through the board, or by re-cutting the board and reversing alternate pieces before joining. The central planks from a slash-sawn trunk will be cut on the quarter, (radially). Such planks are less prone to distortion owing to shrinkage, (see page 22) and their faces provide a more durable and harder surface. Deck planking ought to be quarter-sawn (unless it is tongue and grooved, or laid over a fibreglass or plywood deck). Quarter-sawn planks are used in steam bending, and in any parts where large surface areas are exposed.

Name and density (kg/m3)	Description
Afromosia 690	Yellow/brown colour, even textured, interlocked grain. A strong, stable, very durable wood. Slightly oily surface can present glueing problems, which are overcome by immediate glueing after preparation, or by de-greasing prior to glueing. Turns black when in contact with ferrous fastenings. A widely used, and attractive boat-building and repair wood.
Afzelia 815	Red/brown, coarse textured, straight-grained wood. Very strong and heavy, stable and resistant to fungal attack. Often used in main structural members of wooden boats.
Agba 515	Straw-coloured golden brown, sometimes with pinkish tinge. Fine textured, lighter wood, with durable heartwood. Used mainly for laminated frames and deck planking, and for marine plywood.
Douglas fir 530	Red/brown, straight-grained, with pronounced grain markings. A strong, easily worked, moderately durable wood, used for stringers, beam shelves, planking and decking, deck beams, etc.
English elm 545	Pale brown, well-defined, but irregular and interlocked grain pattern. A non-durable wood that rots quickly when damp, but seems to last indefinitely when saturated with water. Great resistance to splitting. Used for main frame members below water-line.
Rock elm 705	Pale brown. A hard strong wood, ideally suited for steam bending, where it is used for frames and stringers. Non-durable, and resistant to preservative treatment, must be kept dry and well ventilated.
Wych elm 670	Golden yellow/greenish yellow. A close-grained wood, similar in appearance to English elm. Very strong and flexible. Used in main frame members, as well as in planking for clinker-built fishing boats, particularly where ends are full, requiring considerable curvature in the planking.
Gurjun/Keruing/Yang 735	Brown to dark brown, straight-grained wood. Coarse resinous texture. A strong wood that is moderately durable, resinous to work. Used for main frame, and planking — particularly below water-line.
Iroko 640	Yellow/brown to deep brown, interlocked coarse grain. Very durable. General all-purpose wood. Cheaper than teak, and almost as good.
Kapur 735	Yellow or red/brown, even-textured, similar to Gurjun in appearance, but without the resin. A very durable wood with many boat-building applications. Grain contains grit which makes it difficult to keep tools sharp.
Larch/Hackmatack 560	Red-orange timber, with pronounced grain pattern. Resinous and frequently knotty. A fairly durable wood, but difficult to obtain without bark-encased knots. Planking and stringers. The roots of the larch tree are used for grown knees.
African mahogany 530	Pink to rich brown, with fine, interlocked grain. A stable, moderately strong and durable wood. Many boat-building uses including main frame, planking, and laminated frames.
Honduras mahogany 545	Pink, turns rich brown after exposure. Fine, even, interlocked grain. A durable, easily worked wood, with general application. May stain when glued with two-part urea-formaldehyde glues.
Makore 625	Pink to deep red, with fine straight grain. Stable strong and very durable. Dust can be harmful, breathing mask and goggles should be worn when machining. Used in main frame construction.
Oak 770–720	English and American. White — yellow/brown colour. Straight-grained, coarse-textured wood, with figure on quarter-sawn faces. Oak is durable, and except for decking, has a large number of boat-building uses. Darkens when in contact with ferrous fastenings which will in time be corroded by the tannic acid in the timber. Can be steam bent. Best wood for boat building comes from forest grown trees. May stain when glued with two-part urea-formaldehyde glues.
Opepe 735	Orange yellow, coarse-textured, and variable grain pattern. Latter quality must be watched when choosing plank, as strength is reduced if large proportion of cross grain is present. A very durable wood, used for main frame, and hull and deck planking. This wood, more than most, is resistant to marine borers.
Pitch pine 705	Yellow or red/brown. Resinous with conspicuous growth rings. A strong, resilient durable wood, used for planking and stringers. Often difficult to glue due to high resin content. Resin accumulates on plane soles etc., which need frequent cleaning and waxing.
European redwood (Scots pine) 515	White-yellow with darker, red, heartwood. Marked growth ring pattern. Best timber comes from higher lattitudes (i.e. northern Russia) Strong, stable, takes preservative better than most shipbuilding woods. Used for planking and stringers.
Robinia 720	Pale yellow, darkens to dark gold colour. Coarse and straight-grained wood, with conspicuous grain markings. Durable. Main frame, floors and frames. Bends well.
Sapele 625	Darker and harder than African mahogany, otherwise similar. Very strong, moderately durable and because of interlocked grain is difficult to work. Main frame, planking, stringers and marine ply but not bent or laminated framing.
Sitka spruce 450	Only use best quality, clear grained wood. White, with lustrous surface. Grain markings show, but less pronounced than in redwood. Lightweight and high strength (for weight) make this suited to spar making, and planking where lightness is its principal advantage. Non-durable, and resistant to preservative impregnation. Ensure good ventilation, and thorough protection.
Teak 655	Golden to dark brown. Coarse straight grain, with conspicuous grain markings. Very durable. Oily texture makes it sometimes difficult to glue (see afromosia). Apart from bending, has general applications. Expense is its main drawback. Collect offcuts, or visit schools or hospitals being re-built or demolished, where large planks will be found as laboratory surfaces, etc.
Utile 655	Similar to sapele, but with a coarser texture. Interlocked grain makes it difficult to work. Used mainly for planking. Durable.
Yacal 990	A heavy, yellow/brown to dark brown fine textured wood. This wood has a wide range of uses — although it is not used for spars or planking where its great weight would be a serious disadvantage.
Yellow pine 990	Pale yellow — light brown. Straight-grained and even-textured. Lacks the grain markings of the European redwood described above. Non-durable. This wood has general application in boat-building, but only highest quality, knot-free boards should be used.
Port Orford cedar	Pale brown/yellow, straight-grained and even textured wood. Moderately durable, and easily worked. Has a distinctive aromatic odour. Used for decking and planking, but dwindling stocks make this wood difficult to obtain.
Ash 710	White straight-grained wood, with distinctive rich musty odour when worked. Best wood comes from wood or forest-grown trees that have grown vigorously. Very strong and resilient. Ash bends well, and is suited to steam bent frames and floors. Is however a non-durable wood, which must be thoroughly treated with preservative each year if rot is to be prevented.

The chart on the previous page sumarizes the qualities of some of the boatbuilding timbers, and the brief description of the seasoning process should assist in selecting wood for boat repairs.

There are other considerations to take into account and they are of equal and sometimes greater importance than that of obtaining the correct species of seasoned wood. A well seasoned piece of oak which has incipient rot, which is fitted into the joinerwork or hull planking of a boat, will cause more harm than a weaker but uninfected wood.

The following paragraphs point to some of the qualities to look for when choosing your wood, and will assist in sorting the desirable wood from the dross left in the woodyard by other, more experienced, buyers.

Grain

Unless wood is being chosen for a particular location where, for maximum strength, a curved grain pattern is required, the grain should be straight, and parallel with the sides of the board. The end grain will confirm whether the log has been slash or quarter-sawn. Quarter-sawn timber will be more stable, and is less likely to cup as it shrinks. It is unlikely that quarter-sawn timber for decking will be available in small quantities. Both teak and iroko planks, which are slash sawn from boards close to the heart are almost as good as quarter-sawn counter parts.

Sight down the plank

Reject pieces that are kinked or warped, unless the curve suits your purposes and is not caused by internal stressing within the wood (see page 25).

Inspect the ends of the plank

Most timbers of more than 6 inches width stored out of doors will end check.

Sap wood

Scrutinize the sides and faces of the plank, for evidence of sapwood. On some timbers, such as beech and elm, it is hard to distinguish the sap wood from the heart wood, but it is usually identified by a change in the colour and texture of the wood. Sap wood is often lighter in tone, and softer. A wany or bark covered edge will confirm your suspicions. Discount the sapwood when calculating the size of the board, and do not use it for repairs.

Faults to watch for

Rot

Wood that has been stored lying on the soil is likely to carry with it minute rot spores, which are potentially lethal to the structure of the hull. Wood that appears blotchy, where parts are spongy and refuse to dry out, and logs that have fungal growth clinging to them, should not be used.

Knots

Plan the work to avoid knots. These form a discontinuity in strength, which might cause the piece to fail when under stress. Where great strength is not at issue, reject the planks which have knots surrounded by bark. As the plank works or dries, the knots will drop out. Knots on quarter-sawn timber are particularly troublesome, as they radiate across the face of the board, and weaken it.

Look for indications of hidden knots. A slight turbulence of the grain in a part to be incorporated into a joint, may be the only sign of an enormous knot deeper in the heartwood. Plan the joints to avoid these questionable areas. It is often better to buy more wood, and to use the rejected piece for other, smaller repairs, than to press ahead, and find that the wood and labour spent in fashioning the plank have been wasted.

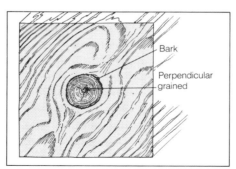

Encased knots will drop out

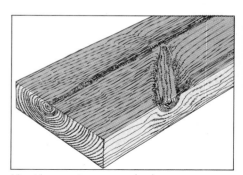

Knot in quarter-sawn plank

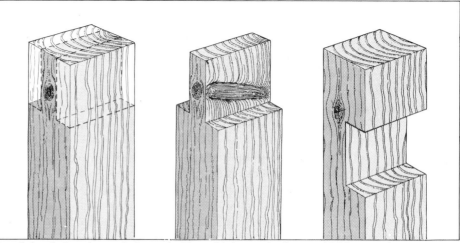

Scrutinize timber for grain irregularities which may indicate a hidden weakness

Reaction wood

The wood from trees which have grown on a slope or have been bent or stressed is often unsuitable. Grain configurations should be regular and balanced. If, for instance, the heartwood is off-centred from the plank, and the grain pattern on one side is much denser than the other, it is likely that the plank will be weak, and will warp and twist as it is being worked. The surface of reaction wood is often characterized by a fibrous, furry appearance in the open grained part, while its opposite side may appear brittle, dense and polished.

Typically, the instability reveals itself when a board is being sawn, and the plank separates or clamps against the saw as the cut progresses. This wood is unreliable, difficult to work, and has the dangerous quality of breaking without warning under very moderate loads.

Brash failure

The grain on some hardwood planks is intersected by a line, almost at right angles to the grain. The line may be similar to a watermark or stain, but indicates the existence of a serious fracture, probably caused during felling. The wood at each side of the line should be sound.

Achieving the maximum strength from wood

Match the strength of the wood with the joints and fastenings. In general, timber is strongest along the grain, although end grain and short grain will break out. Use the wood to gain the maximum possible strength and resilience. Do not force it to perform bends that are too sharp, or to hold fastenings that are too large. Given time, and an average measure of common sense, things will not go far wrong. The illustratons right show some of the more typical errors.

Short grain

(See section on fastening, page 30). Splices and scarfs should be planned to gain maximum strength. Some correct and incorrect positions for scarfs are shown right. Those which are incorrect will break at the short grain. Bent timbers should be cut out with the annual rings arranged to remain parallel to the axis of the curve when the wood is bent. Timbers with knots or wavy grain should not be bent. Where greater rigidity or strength is required than can be easily handled with the steam bending operation, laminate instead. Use wood from the same plank (to ensure identical moisture content). Use resorcinal or epoxy resin glue (see page 39).

Avoid inserting short replacement sections into long planks. Greater strength is achieved if the weakening and stiffness of the joints is spread over a greater distance.

Protect all exposed end grain. It is particularly vulnerable to damp penetration, rot, marine borer and woodworm attack.

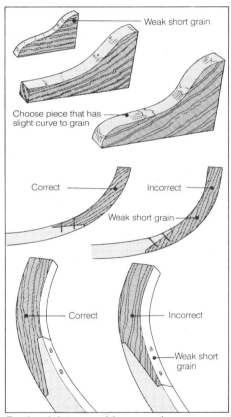

Design joints to achieve maximum strength

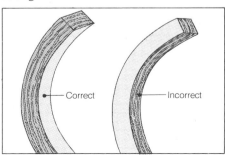

Ventilate the hull

Always plan repair work to improve or retain the ventilation in the hull. Design repairs to facilitate drainage.

Preservative and bedding compounds

Treat all woodwork (except marine plywood) with preservative before refinishing. Preservative applied warm will penetrate deeper than cold, but beware of the considerable fire hazards involved in warming wood preservative fluids over a naked flame.

Unless joints are glued, coat their touching faces with a bedding compound of some kind. This will seal the timbers and prevent moisture penetration.

Some recipes for home-made compounds are listed below. Commercial products are also available.

Luting compound

Cover the touching surfaces with a thick application of marine quality paint or varnish and close the joint before it dries. Where joints are of considerable area, some muslin or flannel, soaked in paint or varnish, can be laid on to one surface before the joint is assembled and fastened.

A thicker compound can be mixed by mixing two parts putty (linseed oil putty) with one part of white lead. Mix to a smooth paste and then add a small quantity of turpentine, red lead or a good quality oil-based primer. Mix again and store ready for use.

Select straight-grained wood for bending and position growth rings parallel to axis of curve

Basic hand tools
Some of the repair procedures
described in this book assume a
certain level of proficiency in the
use of woodworking hand tools.
The following pages outline
some suggestions for using and
sharpening a number of hand tools.
Cutting tools must be sharp. It is
much easier and quicker to produce
good results with keen-edged tools
and sharp saws.

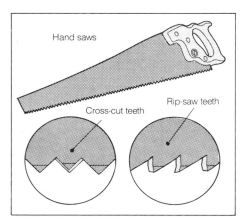

Hand saws

Cross-cut teeth

Rip-saw teeth

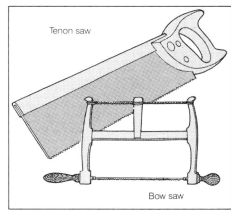

Tenon saw

Bow saw

Saws

Rip-saw for cutting with the grain. Cross-cut saw for cutting across the grain. Bow saw for cutting curves. Tenon saw for general small work.

Use

Use the biggest-toothed saw that can conveniently be handled without damaging the work. Use the rip-saw for cutting tenons and large dovetails. Use the tenon saw only where cuts are short. Use the cross-cut saw for all cross-grain sawing and for cutting plywood.

The bow saw will cut curves but use it only when it is certain that the rip-saw is too large to follow the curve.

Holding

When holding hand saws or tenon saws, keep the first finger of the right hand along the line of the blade.

Do not press the saw into the wood to accelerate its cut, as it will be driven off course. Develop a regular and relaxed action that is easy to maintain. Support the workpiece and make sure that the timber does not close on to the blade as the wood is cut. Some woods, because

of their inner tensions, will clamp the saw as it cuts through the wood.

If there is a tendency for this to happen, wedge a slip of wood in the saw cut to keep the pieces apart, and lubricate the blade with candle wax. (See section on reaction wood, page 25). It is useful to be able to reverse the saw and cut away from the body when cutting into large sheets of plywood. Gentle pressure is all that is required.

Tenon saws

To ensure a clean edge to a cross-grain saw cut, mark the cutting line with a sharp knife and cut a shaving on the waste side with a bevel-edged or paring chisel. Start the saw cut below the surface of the wood. Guide the saw with the thumb and first finger.

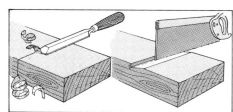

Sharpening

All teeth must be the same height. Their length is not so important, but should as far as possible be the same. Top the teeth by levelling them with a file.

Saw teeth are offset to provide clearance for the blade. Set for the minimum possible clearance, otherwise effort is wasted in making sawdust. Use a saw setting tool, adjusted for the correct number of teeth per inch. Saws that are used to cut green or wet wood need a greater set than those cutting seasoned timber. Set alternate teeth. The set on each side must be the same, otherwise the saw will cut out of true.

Use a new triangular file to sharpen the teeth. For sharpening rip and bow-saws, the file is held at right angles to the blade. The teeth of a cross-cut and tenon saw are sharpened alternately, with the file angled as shown. Start from the tip, giving each tooth the same number of passes with the file. Tilt the file at the angle illustrated to give the teeth a knife-edged sharpness. Complete one side before changing the faces of the file, perhaps by moving the handle to the other end of the file, and, starting from the tip, filing the teeth from the other side.

View the saw teeth in a strong light. Flattened tips will glitter. File them to a point, and test the saw by cutting through a piece of waste wood. Inspect the saw cut. If it is rough, place the saw on the flat bench, and rub a sharpening stone down each side.

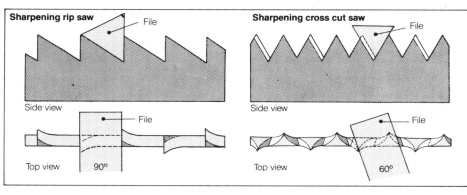

Sharpening rip saw File

Side view

File

Top view 90°

Sharpening cross cut saw File

Side view

File

Top view 60°

Chisels

An old, roughly sharpened 1¼ inch (32mm) chisel may also be used for removing paint and splitting out old planks, etc. All other chisels must be kept extremely sharp. Bevel-edged chisels should be handled gently, as their blades are ground away to allow the tip to reach into corners inaccessible to firmer and mortise chisels. The latter are powerful tools that should withstand fairly heavy malletting but cutting edges will last longer if small cuts are made.

Two-handed chiselling

Hold the chisel as illustrated. The right hand controls the handle and transfers the person's weight to the cutting edge. The left hand is always behind the cutting edge, and it controls, guides and opposes the force of the right arm. Thus, the left arm is always ready to brake the movement of the chisel.

Care

Keep chisels sharp and strop them. Buy or make a tool roll for carrying the chisels to prevent their edges chipping against other tools.

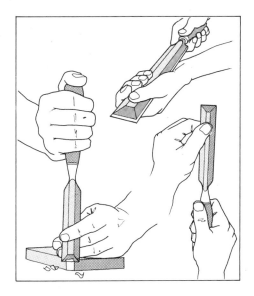

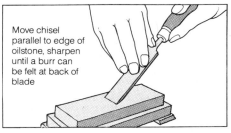

Move chisel parallel to edge of oilstone, sharpen until a burr can be felt at back of blade

Sharpening

Hold the chisel as illustrated, and move it parallel to the sharpening stone. Start with a medium-coarse stone, lubricated with oil, and grind its edge until a burr can be felt at the back of the blade.

Remove this by placing the back of the chisel flat against the oilstone. Raise a second burr and remove it as before. Change to a finer stone and repeat the grinding and de-burring procedure a couple more times.

Move to a stropping board made by rubbing stropping compound or the oil and dust collected from the oilstone on to a flat softwood board and strop the chisel. Strop the bevel five times for every one or two passes with the back of the chisel flat on the stropping board. Repeat this several times, using less pressure each time. To maintain a keen edge, strop the chisels between cuts.

Other tools

Planes

Hold the plane with two hands, one pushing, the other providing downwards pressure and guidance. Because the blades are sharpened to a very slight curve, the angle of the planed edge can be altered, by adjusting the position of the blade relative to the centre of the edge being planed. Thus, by moving the plane from side to side as it passes down the edge of the plank, a true and accurate square edge can be planed. When shooting joins, use a long-soled plane.

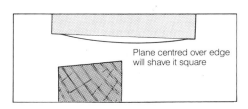

Plane centred over edge will shave it square

Plane blades are sharpened in exactly the same way as chisels. When replacing the blade, make sure that the cap iron is screwed tightly. To reduce blade wear, lift the plane for its return stroke. To ease its handling, rub candlewax on to the sole of the plane.

Spokeshave

These are held with both hands, and when sharpened properly, will remove a lot of stock quickly. Sharpen as for the chisel. Always work to a pencil line when using a spokeshave, as the sole is too short to keep the cut fair and regular.

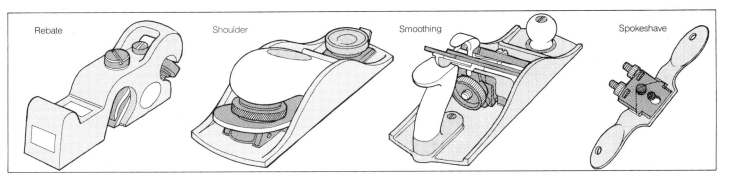

Rebate   Shoulder   Smoothing   Spokeshave

Tools use and care **Tools and techniques**

Squares and winding sticks
Mark squared and tested edges clearly and use them as a reference point for other measurements. Winding sticks are used to check whether an edge is straight. The adjustable bevel is used a great deal, and it is sometimes necessary to record the angle on a piece of timber to enable the tool to be used for other work.

Dividers
Dividers should be the lockable type with a span of about one foot (304 mm). Use these for transferring measurements and shapes.

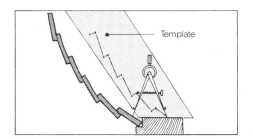

Template

Dumbstick
This is also used to transfer shapes, by resting a pencil against one edge of the stick while the other is pressed against the shaped surface that needs to be copied. Note that when using a dumbstick, the recorded shape will be smaller by the width of the stick, which must be used again against the marks to find the original shape.

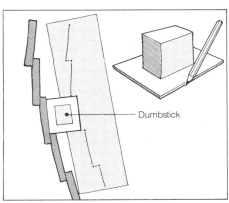

Dumbstick

Gauges
Keep a couple of marking gauges, and make others as required. Avoid measuring by eye, as it is easy to waste time and wood. Two homemade marking gauges are illustrated, which will simplify some of the marking work involved in boat repair.

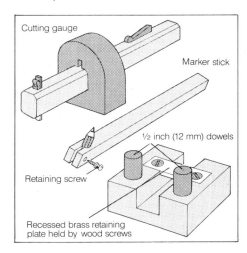

Cutting gauge

Marker stick

½ inch (12 mm) dowels

Retaining screw

Recessed brass retaining plate held by wood screws

Drills and augers
A range of drills and augers may be required, although most work can be achieved with ⅜ inch (9mm) and ⅝ inch (15mm) brad point drills, and one or two lengthened twist drills. Buy others as they are needed. A ⅜ inch (9mm) and ⅝ inch (15mm) cross-grain plug cutter is invaluable for cutting short dowel plugs to cover screw and nail fastenings.

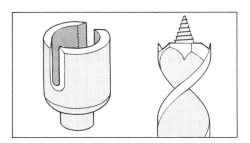

String line
Any thin garden string will do. It can be used without chalk, stretched between two points, and the line recorded with a pencil mark beneath the string. Alternatively the string can be rubbed against a block or stick of chalk, then pulled and snapped against wood. Either way the line will need to be pencilled over with a soft pencil and a straight batten.

Batten
Several battens will be needed. They should be straight-grained and straight-edged battens of even thickness, and clear of knots or splits. When drawing a fair curve, bend the batten against nails hammered into the plank. Where the curve is slight, use the edge of the batten as this gives greater stiffness, and is less likely to introduce kinks into the shape.

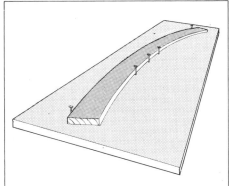

Clamps
Clamps of all kinds will be needed to hold pieces together. A good supply of carpenter's G clamps, and some of the simple homemade clamps illustrated will be found to be useful.

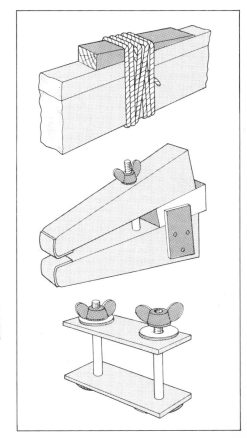

Power tools

Safety
Clamp work firmly before commencing. Always wear a mask if grinding or sanding fibreglass or if the work creates a lot of dust. Wear goggles whenever high speed cutting, routing or grinding. Keep the electric cable of the power tool and out of puddles, and protect it from passing traffic.

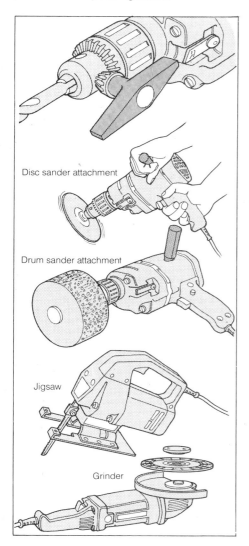

Disc sander attachment

Drum sander attachment

Jigsaw

Grinder

Hand-held circular saw
Grip tightly with both hands, keeping the fingers well clear of the blade guard. Start the motor clear of the wood, and control every movement of the saw. Use the fence whenever possible and where necessary tack a batten to the timber to form a temporary edge for the tool to bear against.

Electric drill
Ensure that the drill or arbor is held firmly in the chuck and use all three key positions to tighten it. Keep the motor running at full speed when drilling deep holes into wood, and rub the drill bit with a wax candle each time it is inserted. Withdraw and clean the bit frequently.

Without assistance, it is difficult to bore long, accurate holes. One way is to bore a small diameter pilot hole and place a dowel in the hole for sighting. Adjust the direction before re-boring with the correct size drill. Use a metal work twist bit when drilling end grain wood.

Disc sander
Wear a breathing mask. Hold the drill with both hands and cut the surface with the edge of the disc. Paint or rust will be removed quickly, but the finished surface will appear scored and uneven. Do not prepare topsides or brightwork with a sanding disc.

Drum sander
Wear a breathing mask. Keep the sander moving, otherwise the quick biting edge will leave a depression that will show when the surface is varnished or painted.

Jigsaw
Quality jigsaws have the facility to control the speed of the cut. Hold the saw with both hands and start cuts in the centre of a panel by tilting the saw forwards.

Grinder
Wear a mask and goggles and hold this high speed tool firmly in both hands. A variety of discs and wire brushes are available for grinding and cutting different materials. Move the grinder against the direction of the wheel's rotation. When removing rust, make certain that the burnished surface left by the wire brush or abrasive wheel is bare metal and not polished rust or scale. Chip the surface with a sharp cold chisel to check if the rust and scale have been removed. Prepare welded seams with a resin-bonded abrasive disc.

Orbital sander
This is a relatively slow cutting tool that will produce a fine, flat, smooth finish. Inspect the condition of the sandpaper attached to its moving sole. Accumulations of dust will inhibit the

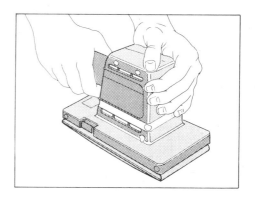

abrasive action of the paper and may score the surface. Work through a range of sandpaper grits (the sanding marks of the previous paper will be covered by the next, finer grade). Only stop sanding when all marks have been removed, or small circular scratches will mar the smooth surface.

Router
Wear goggles for eye protection. Routers are used for moulding, mortising and graving. Pull the router against the direction of the tool's rotation. When mortising, set the fence parallel to the side of the mortise and tack strips of wood at each end of the mortise to prevent the tool over-running. When starting a mortise in hard or resinous wood, step plunge one end, and remove the remaining wood in small stages. High speed steel cutters wear out quickly and should be replaced with tungsten carbide-tipped tools.

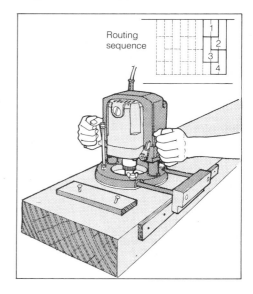

Routing sequence

The position of a fastening must always be planned to obtain the maximum strength at the joint, with the least possible weakening of the pieces being joined. When adding extra fastenings to reinforce a join already loosened through wear or stress, it is important to realize that the additional holes might seriously weaken the remaining structure. It is often better to remove and replace weak fastenings, than to insert additional ones.

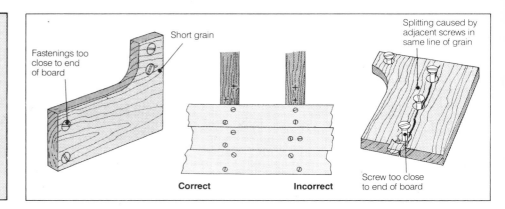

Wood

Do not place the fastenings close to the end of the board, or in short grain. Avoid placing two or more fastenings in the same line of the grain. The position of the fastenings is often pre-determined by the number of fastenings to be used, and the size of the pieces to be joined. There are, for instance, only a few points where through fastenings holding a plank to a frame can be drilled. If there are planks each side of the one being replaced, the choice of position is even more limited.

Ply, steel, alloy and fibreglass

Positioning of fastenings is equally critical in these materials, although considerations of grain do not apply. However, when working with the above materials, ensure that the fastenings are staggered to prevent a line of weakness developing which might fracture when the joint is under stress.

Nails

A variety of nails are illustrated. Most of them are available in mild steel, galvanized iron and silicone bronze. Barbed nails are available in silicone bronze, steel and stainless steel.

Nailing

Bore a pilot hole before nailing, and when driving large-headed nails, counter-bore the pilot hole to enable the head to be recessed and plugged with a wooden dowel. Support the pieces being nailed to make certain the nails bind the joint together. Dip iron nails in red lead paint before hammering them into the wood.

Copper nails

Copper nails for rivetting are usually square-sectioned, and the pilot hole is slightly small so that the nail is firmly held against turning or bending. Because they have not the strength to withstand heavy hammering, and do not therefore hold themselves tightly into the wood, copper nails should be chosen which pass right through both pieces to be joined, with sufficient additional length for clenching or rivetting.

Clenching

Drill a pilot hole slightly smaller than the

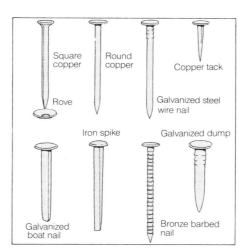

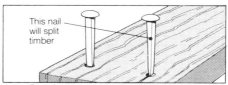

Correct alignment prevents splitting

diameter of the copper nail, and prod a bradawl into the timber close to the pilot hole to take the tip of the nail as it is bent into place. Drive the nail from the outside, supporting the timber on the

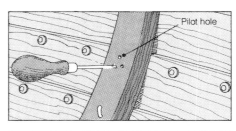

inside with a hammer tilted to form the nail into a hook as it emerges. Support the nail head while the hook is hammered into the previously bradawled hole.

Rivetting

Instead of clenching, copper nails can be rivetted. Drive the nail right through the timber until the head is flush with the outside planking. Slip a small copper washer (a rove) over the point of the nail and, using a small tube punch, tap the rove over the point and down the shank until it rests against the inside timber. Use a fairly blunt pair of wire cutters to snip off the tip of the nail, leaving sufficient protruding through the rove for rivetting. Blunt cutters squeeze the nail as it cuts and often prevent the rove slipping off.

Hold a weight against the head of the nail and use the ball pein of the hammer to burr the end of the nail over the rove.

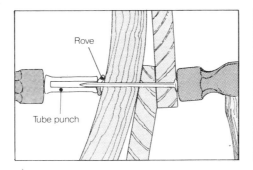

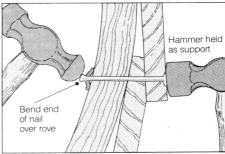

The most common problem with clenching or rivetting is that the soft copper nail bends in the wood either as the hook is formed and hammered home, or when the rove is rivetted on to the nail end. In time, the join will loosen as the nail pulls straight. To avoid bending the nail, drill a pilot hole no larger than is absolutely necessary, and use very light taps for all but the finishing strokes when clenching or rivetting.

Bolts

Several different types of bolt are illustrated. Some are available in galvanized iron, and others in silicone bronze, stainless steel and monel, but the choice of metals is often very limited. Try to avoid using galvanized or uncoated ferrous fastenings in oak, and stainless steel fastenings below the water-line. Lag bolts should never be used for holding down engines. It is better to fit a captive nut in the engine bearers, as they allow the bolts to be tightened as the bearers shrink or wear.

Always use a washer beneath the nut. If the fitting is likely to vibrate loose, use a locknut, or a spring washer. Standardize the thread type and nut sizes, then the same spanners, washers, locking washers and nuts can be used, and stocking the spares locker becomes much simpler.

Drift bolts

These are made in the workshop from lengths of copper, galvanized or bronze rod. Washers may be available from a chandler, or drilled and then cut from a sheet of suitable metal.

Drift bolts are used blind, or can be rivetted at both ends. Whichever method is used they are very efficient fastenings and extremely difficult to remove.

Drill the pilot hole for the drift bolt. Because drift bolts are used when extra long, or non-standard bolt sizes are needed, it may be necessary to make a

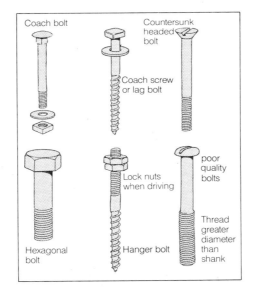

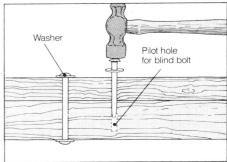

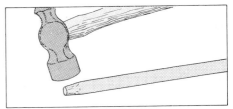

simple drill bit to fit into the chuck of an electric drill before boring the pilot hole. Use tool steel rod, slightly narrower than the diameter of the drift bolt. Flatten the sides of the rod, and file a cutting edge at the tip. Unless many of these long holes need to be drilled quickly, this homemade drill will cut its way through the timber quite well.

Start the drilling with a normal twist drill, and finish with the homemade drill, lubricating it with wax, and withdrawing it frequently as it works deeper.

Cut the drift bolt rod to length, and hammer a slight taper at one end. Oil or wax the rod, and slip the first washer over it. Slow, regular blows will succeed in driving the bolt into the wood. Keep the bolt moving. Its top will burr over and the washer will form a head as the bolt is driven home. If the bolt is driven blind, that is all there is to do, but if it passes right through the timber, a second washer should be rivetted on.

Screws

Roundhead, countersunk and self-tapping screws are illustrated. Roundheads should be used when attaching fittings to a wooden spar.

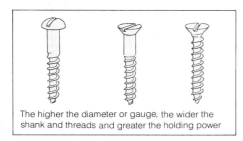

The higher the diameter or gauge, the wider the shank and threads and greater the holding power

Most yacht chandlers will supply marine grade screws, but do not choose brass screws unless they are for interior cabin work, where the head will be protected by paint or varnish. Brass corrodes, and although the screw may appear sound, its zinc content may be removed by galvanic corrosion, leaving a shell pitted with minute holes and very weak.

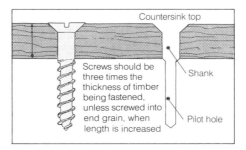

Screws should be three times the thickness of timber being fastened, unless screwed into end grain, when length is increased

Countersink top

Shank

Pilot hole

Clamp the work before screwing, and drill a pilot hole the full depth of the screw. Enlarge the hole for the shank. A drill combining the functions of boring the pilot and shank clearance hole and counterboring at the same time is illustrated. If a number of identical screws are being driven in one operation, one of these drill bits will save a lot of time.

Self-tapping screws are fitted in the same way. Even though the screw thread reaches right to the head of the screw, it

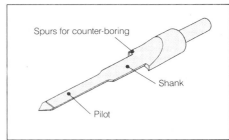

Spurs for counter-boring

Shank

Pilot

is necessary to drill the shank clearance hole before inserting the self-tapping screw into the pilot hole. These have poor holding power in soft wood and should only be considered for hardwood or plywood.

Always match the screwdriver to the size of the screw. The tip of the screwdriver should be ground flat, and fit snugly into the slot in the screw. Too large, and the screwdriver will tear the surrounding wood. Too small, and it will damage the head, and not give satisfactory torque.

Trenails

These are not often used, but where the wood is of sufficient size they can form a cheap, durable and strong means of fastening wood to wood.

Choose straight-grained, knot-free, partially seasoned wood for the trenail, and split it roughly to size. Half an inch diameter is usually considered the smallest practical size. To form the nail, the roughly-shaped stick is driven through a hole bored through a piece of steel, or into a homemade cutter. Allow half an inch (12mm) at each end of the trenail for wedging. Bevel the head of the nail. Bore the hole for the trenail, and ream out its ends with a reamer or gouge.

If the nail is driven blind, cut a very thin saw cut down the end of the trenail, insert a small wooden wedge, and drive the nail home. Where the nail passes

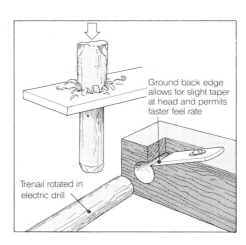

Ground back edge allows for slight taper at head and permits faster feel rate

Trenail rotated in electric drill

right through the timbers, drive it home before cutting the slots for the wedges.

With the trenail in place and standing proud on each side of the timber, saw

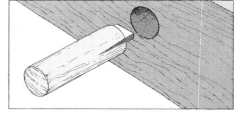

and then wedge the ends. Drive the hardwood wedges while supporting the nail on the outside. Cut the trenails flush when both the inside and outside wedges are home.

Rivetting (metal to metal)

Most readers will be familiar with the technique of pop-rivetting, which is a

well-tried and successful means of rivetting where there is access to only

one side. Metal mast fittings are usually held with pop rivets. Rivets should be marine grade stainless steel or monel, and the pilot hole should be the precise size recommended by the rivet suppliers. All rivet holes should be staggered to prevent forming a line of weakness where stress concentrations may cause fatigue failure.

Very few boat-yards are now equipped to hot rivet a boat, but the technique of cold rivetting is straightforward, and will provide a strong, permanent fastening between metal plates and girders avoiding the problems of heat distortion and fire associated with welding.

Rivets can be bought, or fabricated from any suitable rod. Drill the hole for the rivet, and cut the rivet to length. It should stand proud on the inside by approximately two thirds of its diameter. Hold the head of the hammer against the head of the rivet while a helper burrs its other end.

Increased force can be used once the head is formed, but the rivet must be supported at all times to prevent the hammering from working it loose. Finish the rivet with the flat face of the hammer, moulding the head into a smooth dome.

If flush-rivetting is needed, the hole on the exposed side should be countersunk

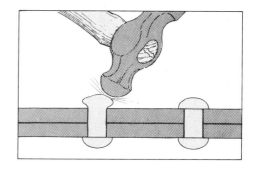

before rivetting. The rivet head is then formed, and fills the recess cut by the countersink bit. File the head until it is level with the surrounding surface.

Corrosion

Choose metal fastenings with care. Try not to introduce new metals where previous fastenings have survived unaffected by the wood or seawater. In most cases, corrosion is easy to identify unless the fastenings are made from stainless steel. Corroded fastenings appear wasted, and the surrounding paintwork lifts, or is smeared with traces of rust, etc. Stainless steel fastenings may appear to be in good condition, but, particularly where they are used below the water-line, or positioned where they lie in puddles of water, they should be

tested for pitting and crevice corrosion. Place a few sample fastenings in a vice, hit the head with a cold chisel, then try to bend them. These tests should reveal any inner corrosion that is invisible from close inspection of the metal surface.

Look closely at the material through which the fastenings were fixed. Wood that is darkened, softened, or which has a white deposit around the hole, has decayed due to the presence of the fastening, and it is best to replace it with a fastening of a different material. (See

page 290). Where the fastening passes through metal, the condition of the surrounding metal must be balanced against the strength and bulk of the fastening. Unless they are of identical chemical composition, one or other will corrode, and it is important to decide which of the two metals can least afford to be weakened by corrosion. See the section on corrosion (page 290), and aluminium and alloy hulls (page 120) for details of insulation and protection against corrosion.

Removing fastenings
Some of the tools and techniques described below should be useful when trying to remove stubborn fastenings.

Bear in mind, however, that a well-bedded fastening may do less harm and cause less inconvenience if left undisturbed, than if removed.

Plugging and re-fastening
Once a fastening has been removed, the hole must be plugged to prevent decay. Bore out the hole with a metalwork twist drill, and soak surrounding wood and the hardwood peg with unthickened epoxy resin. Add thickeners to the resin, and smear it inside the hole before pressing in the peg. Leave the resin to cure before re-fastening through the peg with a longer screw to give additional holding power for end grain screwing.

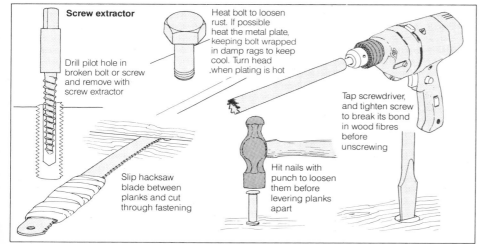

Screw extractor

Drill pilot hole in broken bolt or screw and remove with screw extractor

Heat bolt to loosen rust. If possible heat the metal plate, keeping bolt wrapped in damp rags to keep cool. Turn head when plating is hot

Tap screwdriver, and tighten screw to break its bond in wood fibres before unscrewing

Slip hacksaw blade between planks and cut through fastening

Hit nails with punch to loosen them before levering planks apart

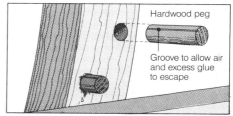

Hardwood peg

Groove to allow air and excess glue to escape

The illustrations show a variety of woodworking joints used in the making and repair of wooden boats. Each joint has its own strength and shrinkage characteristics and in choosing a join these qualities should be borne in mind. The advent of resin glues, which can be thickened with fillers until they form strong and brittle substances, often tougher than the wood itself, has simplified the task of making some joints and virtually eliminated the need for some others. However, solid timber is unstable, and glued joints between pieces which are immersed in water, subject to severe strains and sudden stresses, and which may occasionally dry out, are not always strongest. The differential rates of swelling and shrinkage coupled with the twisting and racking strains imposed upon the piece may open a joint. It is no safeguard to drive a couple of screws to hold the joint in case the glue fails. Joints should be planned so that they do not fail. If it appears that glue alone will be insufficient, plan and cut a mechanical joint and hold it with bolts or wedges. Glue it as well, but in doing so, consider the possibility that the wood will be better protected by preservative and some thick flexible bedding compound instead.

Mechanical joints will also open or move when subjected to periodic drying out. Some joints are more prone to loosening than others. The beam to shelf joint is often subjected to alternate drying and soaking. A deck beam which is notched into the shelf with a half-lipped dovetail or a variation of that joint will move apart as the dovetail shrinks.

The movement of the beam, perhaps assisted by the twisting of the hull and the wedge-shaped dovetail, may further open the joint, which, when it is later saturated, may never close up to its previous tightness. The notched or dowelled joint however, will not pull apart under these conditions, and is generally more suited to this particular structure. These are the qualities that should be considered when choosing a method of jointing.

Mark and cut the joints with great care. Time spent marking and checking will save time later. Always cut on the inside or waste side of the marks, and trim the joint to fit.

Edge to edge joints
A simple edge-to-edge butt join, carefully shot and true, and glued with epoxy or resorcinal resin glue, will be stronger than an alternative mechanical joint. To assist alignment, short stub dowels can be driven into one face prior to glueing. Their position can be established by taping pins to one face before pressing the other against it. The impressions of the heads give the centre point for the dowel drill holes.

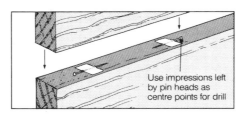

Use impressions left by pin heads as centre points for drill

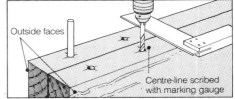

Outside faces

Centre-line scribed with marking gauge

The butt joint of a naturally oily timber such as teak can be further strengthened by the use of bronze rods which are drilled and then drifted into the face of one joint before the two planks are glued and tapped together.

Loose tongue
This joint is no stronger than the simple glued butt joint, but it has a mechanical strength, and with the use of supporting cleats behind and bedding compound between the planks, permits large areas of flat board to be built up, which can dry out or swell without cracking or splitting individual planks. This joint can be made waterproof with bedding compound and caulking if necessary, and it permits movement.

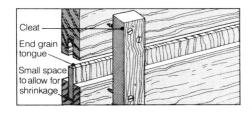

Cleat

End grain tongue

Small space to allow for shrinkage

Lengthening a beam or plank
Three scarf joints are shown. The first, a straight splice, is easy to make. Strength is provided by the glue. The bedding faces must be a close touching fit, and roughened prior to glueing. A peg or dowel, even brads, can be used to locate the scarf whilst being clamped.

The two jogged scarf joints illustrated below obtain their strength from their fastenings. Scarfs must be very carefully marked. The method of marking varies with the location of the scarf. It is often best to cut a cardboard template and use it for both parts of the joint. Where space permits, cut one table and use it as a template from which the line of the other can be drawn. It is most important with work of this type, that all cuts are square and true, otherwise inaccuracies will result which will be difficult to remedy. Do not mark or cut the second part until you are absolutely certain that the first is square. Where the beams are tapered or do not provide a flat surface against which a set square can be rested, use winding sticks (see page 27).

The tabled hooked scarf has the advantage over the plain scarf because it can be tightened with wedges. A variation which gives the joint additional stiffness is to notch its ends. A template is used for the notches which are positioned along the centre-line of each table. Tighten with opposing wedges prior to bolting.

Deck planks and covering boards are often butt jointed. The joint is watertight, but has no mechanical strength other

Steam bending

Although timbers under half an inch (12 mm) thick can be bent cold, and in time will adjust themselves to the new shape, it is usually necessary to steam, boil or laminate thicker pieces into place.

The choice between laminating and steaming is not always easy to make. Provided the equipment is available, steaming is often quicker and easier, but there is always the risk, often as high as 20 per cent, that the wood will break or splinter, wasting time and money. When laminating, the thickness of the veneers can be cut to suit the flexibility of the wood, so this hazard is eliminated. Never replace a laminated with a steam bent frame.

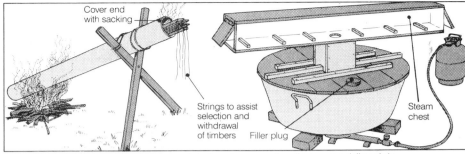

Simple steaming apparatus — watch for danger of collapse and fire risk

Steaming and boiling are similar techniques. A boiling tube is usually the simplest to arrange, but for wide, flat stock it may be necessary to construct a steam chest. Both require heating.

The following descriptions apply to both methods.

Most species of timber can be bent. Rock elm, oak, ash, hickory, and robinia are considered best for marine use. Wood is used green, or partially seasoned. Dry timber should be soaked in fresh water for several days before bending.

Select straight-grained, knot free timber. Grain irregularities weaken the wood and make it difficult to bend into a regular curve. If frames are bent, and wherever timber is bent to a small radius, choose a piece with the line of the growth rings parallel to the axis of the curve.

Plane and sand the wood before bending. Wait until the water boils before placing the timber in the steam chest or boiling tube. Leave the timber until a test piece is supple enough to take the desired bend. Approximately one hour of heating for each inch of thickness is required, but this figure varies enormously. Nothing is lost by leaving the timber for a long while, and it is less likely to fracture if thoroughly heated.

Bending over a mould

This is easier than fitting the hot wood straight into the boat. Make a substantial mould, perhaps by nailing a number of wooden blocks to the workshop floor or, if several pieces of a particular shape are required, by constructing a framework on which they can be clamped.

Because the timber will spring back a little after it is released, the curves of the mould should be tighter than the curve of the template.

Handle the hot wood with leather gloves. Work quickly, moving the timber swiftly from steam chest to mould, and spring it into place in a single slow movement. A bending strap will prevent the outer edge of the timber from splintering. It can be made from a strip of galvanized iron, no more than 1/16 inch (1mm) thick. Rivet a hook at one end and bolt a wooden block at the other. Slip this on to the hot timber the moment it is taken from the heat. Provided the timber fits tightly between the hook and stop, the strap will compress the inner fibres, and prevent the fibres on the outside of the timber from stretching and splitting.

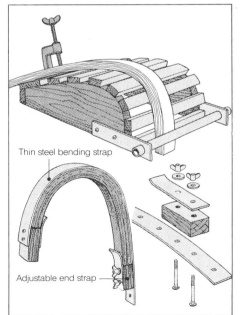

Thin steel bending strap

Adjustable end strap

Bending strap and simple mould

Straps are easy to use in conjunction with a mould, more difficult when bending frames or other parts directly into the hull. They cannot be used where compound or reverse curves are required.

Working without a mould

Work quickly. You will almost certainly need help to bring the wood from the steam box, and press it into position before it has a chance to cool. Although the amount of time varies according to the air temperature, there is usually no more than 3-4 minutes in which to work. Extra time can be gained by pouring boiling water directly on to the plank, or by wrapping the hot wood in a towel soaked in boiling water, while it is eased into position.

A combination of the above methods, which is useful where thick stock has to be bent into position, is to use the boat itself as the mould, exaggerating its curve by tacking blocks in appropriate positions. The timber is sprung in place and left to cool. Later it is released and the blocks removed. It is then shaped and fastened in position, its initial spring-back having been anticipated by the additional curve produced by the blocks.

There are three stages to a glueing operation: preparation, application and clamping. Of these, the first and the last frequently demand skill and ingenuity. Mixing and applying the glue is a straightforward mechanical operation which is bound to succeed if the instructions are followed.

It is important to choose the right glue. There are few situations more hostile and destructive than the marine environment. Most boat repairs should be carried out with glues that have been formulated for marine use.

Safety
The resins used in the synthetic glues described below may cause skin irritation. Follow the manufacturer's suggested safety precautions to avoid unpleasant side effects. Until the injury is done, there is no way of knowing whether skin is sensitive to the particular resin being handled.

Take sensible precautions: use a recommended barrier cream and disposable gloves where necessary. Wipe away splashes of glue with a clean damp rag. Never use thinners except for cleaning clothes and tools.
If glue gets into the eyes, splash them with water and seek medical advice.

Preparation
Surfaces should be clean, dry and slightly rough. Machined wooden surfaces can be sealed by the beating they receive from rotary cutters and spindle moulders. This is generally called case-hardening. Such surfaces need to be sanded to open the grain. Draw a fine-toothed hacksaw blade across the joints to leave a rough but level surface. Remove all dust before applying the glue.

Dense hardwoods and woods with a greasy or oily texture are sometimes difficult to glue. When glueing the former, watch for smooth surface case-hardening. If present, lightly sand before glueing, and then assemble, but delay clamping to permit the glue to penetrate. Apply clamps before the resin sets. In some cases elevated temperatures must be used when curing the glue. The joints in oily or greasy woods must be glued immediately after they are cut and tested for fit, and before the oil or resin has an opportunity to exude on to the jointing faces. Where this is impractical it will be necessary to degrease the joints with carbon tetrachloride or acetone.

Moisture content
The moisture content of most air dried wood is between 15-20 per cent. To ensure satisfactory glued joints it is usually recommended that the moisture content be reduced to 12-15 per cent, although up to 20 per cent has been used with some resins. The use of certain epoxy resins used for wood stabilization calls for moisture content of 10-12 per cent.

Moisture content can be accurately gauged by a meter, but for most purposes wood that has been seasoned and then taken into a warm room for a week or so will be dry enough.

The moisture content of larger pieces can be modified by drying with a convector heater, space heater, heat gun, and even a hair drier. To bring the moisture content down without distorting the wood, apply the dry heat over trays of water, so that the humidity drop is not too great or too sudden. When working outside, rig a canopy or tent over the work area to protect it .

If the wood has been saturated with seawater, residual salt crystals in the grain will prevent it drying. Rinse away the salt with hot fresh water before drying.

Temperature
The setting time of the glues listed below is affected by temperature, and the rate at which resin cures can be changed and controlled by altering the temperature in the work place, and by warming the surfaces to be glued. Curing can be delayed by wrapping a cold wet towel around the glue container, or placing it in a pan of ice-cold water. These techniques are useful when working with epoxy resins in hot conditions.

Once the glue joint is clamped, it is most important that the glue is hurried to its fully cured state, otherwise the clamping pressure could squeeze out the glue and leave a weak, starved joint. Arrangements must therefore be made to keep work warm for the duration of the curing period.

Urea-formaldehyde glues

Uses
Wood, plastic laminates. Interior cabin joinery, small dinghies and tenders. Not for structural repairs on larger boats. While these glues are waterproof — they will withstand immersion in cold water — they are not weatherproof so glued joints must be protected against weathering by painting, varnishing etc.
There are two types: Cascamite wood glue has the resin and hardener pre-mixed, and requires only the addition of water to initiate curing. This eliminates the possibility of errors caused by inaccurate measuring of the components. An alternative wood glue is purchased as a powdered resin, which must be mixed into a syrup by dissolving it in water. It hardens when the resin is applied to one face of a joint and comes into contact with an acid hardener, brushed on the other. When using glues of this type, it is important that the components are mixed and applied correctly. Some woods will discolour when painted with the acid hardener.

Temperature and moisture
Temperature conditions are not critical, but below 50°F (10°C) additional heating will be required to speed curing. Moisture content 12-18 per cent.

Application
Apply with a brush, stick or roller. Leave glue to sink into the surface before assembling. Clamp before the glue sets. Full strength is reached some time after the glue has cured and the clamps are released (usually 5-7 days).
While the glue is still liquid, clean the excess glue with a damp rag. Rinse brushes and spreaders with warm soapy water. Use plastic mixing containers, leave excess glue to harden; later it can be released by flexing the container.

Safety
Use a barrier cream, and wash glue from skin with a clean wet rag.

Resorcinal resin glue

Uses

Wood, plastic laminates, sealing and bonding expanded polystyrene foam. Weatherproof and waterproof, extremely durable. Ideal for most structural and incidental repairs to wooden hulls.

This is a two-part (liquid resin and powder catalyst) glue which is very easy to handle. With the addition of 10 per cent fillers, gaps up to .050 inch (1.3 mm) can be filled without loss of glued strength. The proportions of resin to catalyst are specified by weight, but a couple of measuring jars, calibrated with the volumes of weighed quantities of the resin and catalyst, will simplify achieving a correct mix.

Temperature and moisture

Temperatures are dependent upon the species of wood involved. Do not glue dense hardwoods such as oak or teak at temperatures below 15°C (59°F). Lower temperatures are quite acceptable when glueing more porous woods such as African mahogany. Moisture content from 12-18 per cent.

Appplication

As for the urea-formaldehyde glues. Rough and porous surfaces need additional quantities of glue. Wherever practical, apply glue to both touching surfaces. Allow resin to remain on the wood surface to ensure thorough penetration, then clamp. Do not release clamps until curing time has elapsed and allow an additional period for the glue to reach full strength (5-7 days). Clean tools in soapy water before the glue has a chance to cure.

Epoxide resin glues

Uses

Glass, aluminium, steel, wood, fibreglass, plastic laminates, and many other porous or rigid materials. With fillers it can be used as a gap filler (applicable by trowel) or fillet. It can be cast and, in its thixotropic form, can be applied in thicknesses up to 1/4 inch (6mm) thick on vertical surfaces.

The resin forms a complete weather and waterproof bond, often stronger than the material being joined. Unlike the glues above, it combines these qualities with glass-like clarity, making it ideal for sealing cold moulded and plywood edges. It will not bond to flexible and stretchable plastics or to polystyrene. These are two-part resin glues, mixed in proportion by weight. In some cases pump dispensers are available to facilitate the mixing.

Epoxy resins are exothermic — they generate their own heat during curing. When mixed in large quantities the resin cures faster than when small quantities are mixed. When disposing of uncured resin, rags, or wood saturated with wet resin, take care to prevent fire caused by the exothermic reaction.

Temperature and moisture

At lower temperatures, the glue takes longer to cure, and as with the other glues, there is a danger of glue starvation at the joint. Although temperature itself is not as critical as with resorcinal or urea-formaldehyde, beware of changes in air temperature that cause condensation to form on a hard cold glueing surface just before they are glued. Moisture content of wood or other porous substances should be 12-15 per cent.

Application

Mix resins in proportion by weight. This is especially important with thixotropic resins where trapped air may cause an incorrect relation between the resin and hardener which results in a weaker glue join. Where pump dispensers are used with liquid resins and hardeners, ensure the pumps are primed and the air is expelled. Mix the resin in a cardboard or plastic container, do not use expanded polystyrene cups. Apply with roller, brush or flexible plastic spreader. Only moderate pressure is required to form a strong bond. Clean equipment with acetone or cellulose thinners.

Safety

Use barrier cream to protect the hands and arms. Wear disposable gloves.

Which glue?

Resorcinal or epoxy resin must be used for structural repairs and repairs to the exterior of the boat. Resorcinal is cheaper and easier to apply over large areas than epoxy resin, and the timber may not need to be so dry. Epoxy is more expensive and may be less exacting in the conditions in which it is used, but its versatility will enable surplus liquid adhesive to be used for other purposes — filling, filletting, casting, bonding a non-slip surface etc., which may ultimately save money.

Old glues

Urea-formaldehyde and all glues developed before the Second World War should be carefully protected from the weather, otherwise the joints will fail. Protein-based Casein glues have, in the past, been used for joining the component parts of wooden masts, and this type of glue has also been used in plywood construction. Protein glues have a short life once the glue line is exposed to the weather, and they are susceptible to mould and worm attack.

Clamping

Plan the clamping procedure before applying the glue.

A polythene sheet beneath the pads used to distribute the pressure of the clamps will prevent them bonding to the workpiece. Withdraw staples and pressure pads before the glue is hardened. All staple holes must be filled with resin, varnish, or stopper, otherwise moisture will penetrate beneath the surface, causing localized discolouration and perhaps rot.

It is necessary to have some simple and effective means of locating the pieces that are to be joined, and also a means of preventing them from slipping when pressure is applied. A dowel or some brads cut short, and tacked into the face of one part will usually supply sufficient grip. In other cases, longer tacks or screws may have to be used.

To prevent building stresses into the joint, clamp from the centre outwards. When laminating, ensure that the veneers are able to move against each other as the clamps are drawn tight.

Chapter 3

Carvel Hulls

Carvel hull construction

The diagram below shows the framework and planking of a typical carvel hull. The planks are fastened to the framework of the boat and the seams between them are stopped with caulking cotton above the water-line, spun oakum below the water-line, and a sealing compound to make the hull watertight. High quality hulls are sometimes splined with a tapered sectioned batten, usually only above the water-line, instead of being sealed with compound. The batten is glued and then driven into the seam, and planed flush with the hull when dry.

The soundness of a carvel and other conventional wooden hulls depends upon the entire centre-line framework (keel, stem, sternpost etc.), the frames, the planks, and all the structural fastenings being maintained in first-class condition.

Planking

Planks are often made from several pieces of timber, butted or scarfed together. Butt blocks to support the joins can be easily identified on the inside of the planking. They are invariably spaced between frames and overlap adjacent planks by at least half an inch (12mm). There should always be sufficient space between the blocks and the frames for drainage and ventilation.

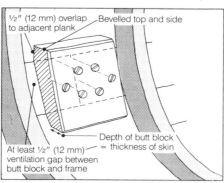

½" (12 mm) overlap to adjacent plank

Bevelled top and side

Depth of butt block = thickness of skin

At least ½" (12 mm) ventilation gap between butt block and frame

Scarf joint

Scarf joints may be used instead of butt blocks. These are in the form of a plain stepped scarf, the outer edge of which should point aft. Scarfs should be at least four times longer than the plank thickness, and be located over and fastened to a frame.

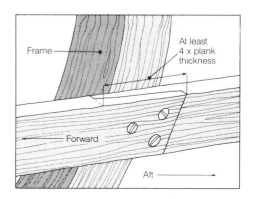

Frame

At least 4 x plank thickness

Forward

Aft

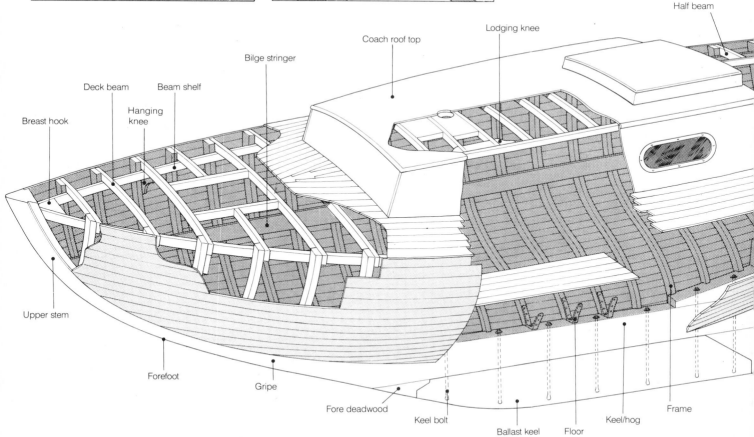

Half beam

Lodging knee

Coach roof top

Bilge stringer

Deck beam

Beam shelf

Hanging knee

Breast hook

Upper stem

Forefoot

Gripe

Fore deadwood

Keel bolt

Ballast keel

Floor

Keel/hog

Frame

Frames

Frames can be made from steel or from bent, laminated or sawn wood and a single hull may be framed with a combination of these. Frames are usually aligned at right angles to the centre-line of the boat. In canoe-sterned vessels, and at the ends of cold-moulded multi-skinned hulls, the frames are sometimes perpendicular to the planking. This is called cant framing.

Floors

Most frames are cut and notched against the keel. Floors are fitted to tie the frames together and fasten them to the keel. They vary as illustrated. Floors should have at least two fastenings to the keel, and three on each part of the frame. Sawn frames often incorporate the floor in the structure of the frame. Where laminated frames are used, floors are incorporated, with laminates running across the centre-line.

Shelf

The shelf is fitted inboard against the frames, and ties the planking, frames and deck beams together. When the shelf is bolted to the frames the heads of the bolts are likely to be concealed by the sheer strake. The shelf is butted against the ends of the boat, and held by knees (breast hook in the bow, quarter knees in the stern).

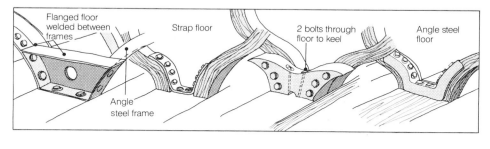

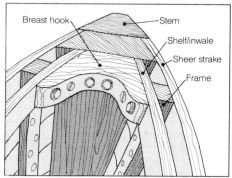

Detail of stem

Bilge stringers

These run the length of the boat, and support the hull at the turn of the bilge. Sometimes other stringers are fastened against the sides of the hull to add strength.

Degradation

Degradation occurs in damp, poorly ventilated conditions. The ends of the boat below decks and the bilge areas should always be kept as well ventilated as possible. Keep limber holes clear, and vents open, to give a through draft of fresh air inside the hull.

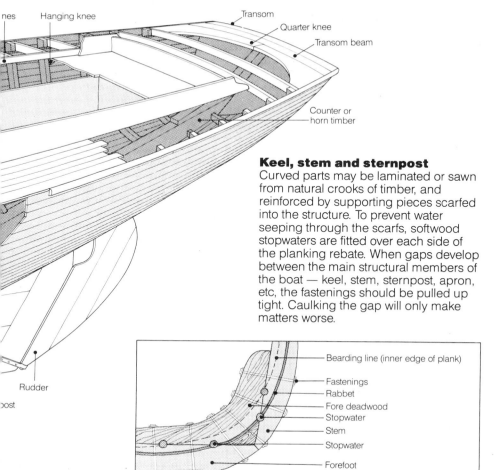

Keel, stem and sternpost

Curved parts may be laminated or sawn from natural crooks of timber, and reinforced by supporting pieces scarfed into the structure. To prevent water seeping through the scarfs, softwood stopwaters are fitted over each side of the planking rebate. When gaps develop between the main structural members of the boat — keel, stem, sternpost, apron, etc, the fastenings should be pulled up tight. Caulking the gap will only make matters worse.

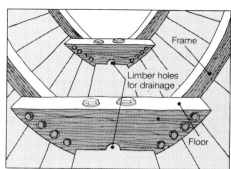

Limbers

Metal fittings

All shipboard fittings and metal parts used in the hull are subject to corrosion. Inspect bolts and fittings below the water-line for galvanic corrosion.

Detail showing stop-waters and plank rabbet

Minor repairs to planks Carvel hulls

All holes, scratches, or areas of damaged wood should be repaired promptly. Wood that is left exposed to the weather will invite decay, and become more difficult to repair as the moisture content of the wood increases.

Where fittings have been removed, bolt or screw holes should be stopped and the paintwork re-touched. Larger dents which do not penetrate more than half the thickness of the plank can be stopped with an epoxy filler, or

plugged with a wooden patch (known as a graving piece). Wood that has been soaked in sea-water will be difficult to dry, due to salt impregnating the fibres. Rinse the wood with hot, fresh water and allow it to dry before applying glue.

Plugging screw and bolt holes

Holes should be cleaned before being plugged. This is best done with an electric drill, fitted with a drill bit slightly wider than the original hole. Drill to the depth of the previous fastening, and then gently work the drill around, scraping and cleaning away the traces of rust

and decayed wood from the edges of the hole.

Whittle a straight-grained hardwood peg to fit the hole and soak it in epoxy glue. Mix some of the same glue with fine sawdust to make a thin paste, and force

the paste into the hole. Hammer the peg well home.

Clean around the peg to remove any drips of glue, and when the glue has set, cut the stub of the peg away and trim with a paring chisel or small block plane.

Repairing surface scratches and dents

Clean and dry the area to be filled and remove the paint or varnish. Roughen the wood and remove loose splinters with coarse sandpaper. Where surface damage is deeper than ¼ inch   6mm), drive in small copper tacks so that the heads are below the level of the outside surface. These nails will help to reinforce the bond between the filler and the wood of the hull.

Surround the damaged area with masking tape. Mix a quantity of epoxy resin glue and brush this unthickened glue into the cavity so that it penetrates the timber. This will seal the surface of the wood and make a good bond with

the filler. Make this by mixing the glue with fine sawdust of a suitable colour, or ground coconut shell, until it has the consistency of toothpaste. Stir the mixture very thoroughly and apply it — working it well into the hole and forcing it behind the heads of the copper tacks. Leave the surface proud, and allow it to cure. Remove the masking tape and sand down the filler.

Graving pieces

These are small wooden patches inserted into the woodwork of the boat. Where the damaged area has a varnished finish, care will be needed to select and position the wood patch.

Fitting a patch
Clean around the damaged area, removing any rotten wood or crushed

and broken fibres. Once the limits to the damage have been discovered, square the outline to a more regular shape. Place a piece of card over the area and press around the edge of the hole with a thumbnail to define it. If the timber is varnished, take the opportunity to check the reflective qualities of the wood. Mark these on the template before cutting.

Pencil in the thumbnail mark, and then draw a clear outline around it for the patch. A diamond-shaped grave does not present any end grain glued edges, and so is particularly good for patching.

Cut around the template and pin it to the timber selected. Cut out the patch.

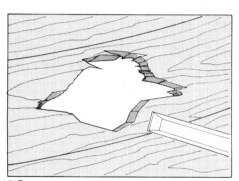

1 Square up rough edges

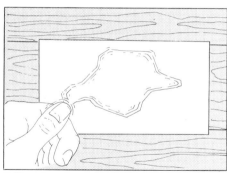

2 Transfer shape to thin cardboard

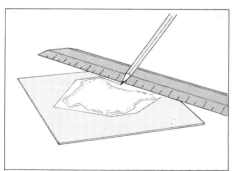

3 Design pattern for graving piece

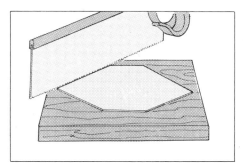

4 Undercut sides of graving piece

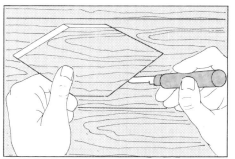

5 Position and mark round edge of piece

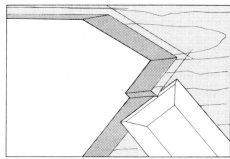

6 Rest part of blade against finished line

Bevelling the patch

Cut a slight bevel around the edge of the patch. Hold the patch over the damaged area, and draw around it with a knife. Cut out the recess for the patch, working from the centre (which can be bored with a brace and auger bit to remove most of the waste) outwards to the marked line. Clean and smooth the bottom of the hole before making the final cuts at its edge.

Soak the patch base and hole in epoxy glue and then hammer the patching piece into place. Fair the patch with a block plane and scraper.

Fitting large graving pieces into the hull planking

Where the new piece will extend nearly to the full depth of the plank, a scarfing joint should be made at each end to enable it to be glued and through-fastened, without seriously weakening the plank.

For ease of fitting, longer graving pieces should have parallel sides, and square edges, and the shape should be marked on to the damaged plank before the scarfs are cut.

The length of scarf for a repair greater than one third the depth of the plank should be about four times the plank thickness. The leading edge of the scarf should be stepped.

Cut the scarf on the graving piece with a hand saw. Mark the space on the plank between the scarfs which will have to be routed to the full depth of the graving piece. Clean out this area with a router, or brace and bit, finishing with a chisel.

Using a mallet and firmer chisel chop out the scarf ends to the depth of the step, and then carefully cut away the slope to match the scarfed piece.

Fit the scarfed repair in place, using chalk to expose the high spots. Shave these down until the joint is a good tight fit. Take great care when fitting the scarf, and remove only the smallest amount of wood with each cut. Make adjustments to the recess first. Never trim both surfaces without checking for a tight fit between cuts.

Bed the patch in thickened epoxy resin, and glue and screw the ends. Once the glue has cured remove the screws and fair the repair. Replace the screws, stop their heads, and apply paint.

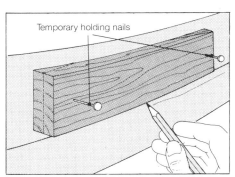

1 Mark outline before cutting scarfs

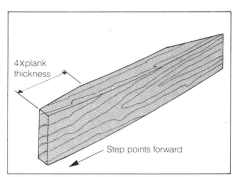

2 Leading edge of scarf should be stepped

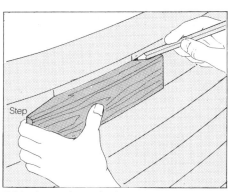

3 Mark scarf on plank

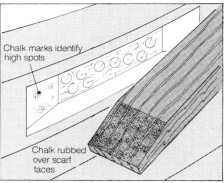

4 Shave down high spots until repair fits snugly

Replacing a damaged carvel plank Carvel hulls

Always investigate the full extent of damage or rot before purchasing repair materials.

Avoid using short planks, they tend to weaken the hull, put more stress on fastenings than longer planks, are more difficult to fair. They should only be used at the ends of the boat and in parts where there is very slight curvature.

Equipment
These tools will be useful:
Straight edge; dividers; pencil; marking knife; handsaw; keyhole saw; hacksaw; 1 inch (25mm) firmer chisel; plane; spokeshave; brace; ½ inch (12mm) bit; nail cutters; punch; hammer; clamps; fastenings; luting; paint

See pages 278-9 and 286-7 for painting and varnishing.

Locating the butt end joints
Locate and clearly mark the butt end joints on all planks adjacent to the damaged area. The position of the frames can be determined from the plank fastenings and should also be marked. Plan the length of the replacement plank by allowing at least two frames between butts on adjoining planks. Butts should be midway between frames. Remember that a long replacement plank is less likely to weaken the hull than a short one.

To remove the damaged portion of a plank, mark the line for the butt ends with a marking knife; drill a starter hole through the plank against the waste side and use a keyhole hacksaw or jigsaw to cut the plank. Repeat this at the other end, and with a heavy chisel or mallet, split the plank away from the fastenings.

Removing the fastenings
Copper rivets are removed by supporting the frame with a hammer,

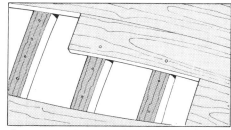

Two frames between butts on adjoining planks

driving the rivet in, cutting off the rove and pulling it out by the head. Drive nails in a fraction to release them, then withdraw by the head. Turn screws clockwise to release, anti-clockwise to withdraw. If they cannot be moved, saw them off and paint over with a rust-inhibiting paint.

Check all adjacent woodwork for fractures and signs of rot and remedy all faults in the framework before replacing the plank. (See pages 70).

Fitting butt blocks
To support the joins, butt blocks should be fitted inside. These are usually oak, about twelve times the plank thickness in length and should overlap adjoining planks by about 5/8 inch (16mm) Touching surfaces should be painted with luting compound (see page 25). Use the same number of fastenings at the butt end as for holding the plank to the frame.

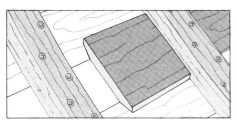

Butt blocks should not impede drainage or ventilation

Selecting new timber
The approximate size of plank can be measured with a tape measure, and a piece of suitable straight-grained timber should be selected. If knots are unavoidable they should be graved (see page 24). Allow for a reduction in thickness if the plank needs hollowing on the inside to fit against the frames.

Fitting a fairing batten
If more than one plank has been removed, a fairing batten will be needed to re-establish the line of planking. This is aligned to the edge of one row of planks and nailed in place. Sight along the edge to check that it is fair with the remaining planks.

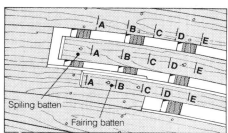

Spiling and fairing battens in position

Tacking on the spiling batten
Take a thin batten, a little narrower than the required plank, cut the ends short and nail it in place. This is called a spiling batten. With a straight edge, mark and number stations every 12 inches (300mm) on the fairing batten, spiling batten and plank.

Marking off stations
Set the dividers to the maximum gap between the spiling batten and plank. Open them a further 3/8 inch (10mm) and lock them. At each station the fixed distance to the plank will be marked on the spiling batten. At the ends dividers can be used to scribe a line parallel to the butts and a known distance away, or a parallel-sided piece of timber can be used instead. Remove the spiling batten

from the frames and lay it on the new timber. Tack the spiling batten in place and mark the stations clearly. With the dividers at their previous setting, transfer the end lines to the new plank (or use the same piece of timber as before to do this). Lock the dividers at a convenient setting, transfer the marks to the plank from the spiling batten at each station and remove the spiling batten.

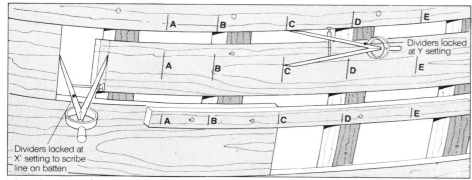
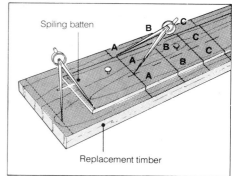

Dividers locked at Y setting

Spiling batten

Replacement timber

Dividers locked at X' setting to scribe line on batten

'x' setting must be transferred directly to new plank 'y' is constant for each run of measurements.

Drawing the line between stations

With a straight batten sprung edgeways to the marks and tacked in place, pencil in the line. Remove the batten and saw the ends and side of the plank. Check the plank for a correct curve by holding it against the boat (remembering to align the stations). Any minor adjustments to this edge should be completed before the second stage is cut.

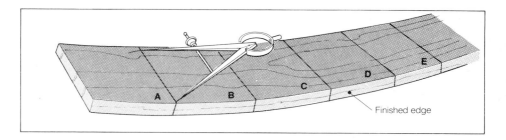

Lining batten

Sawing the new plank

Transfer the stations to the inside face of the plank, squaring round the edges and marking across with a straight edge. Number them as before. Use dividers at each station to transfer the accurate inside width of the plank from the hull to the new plank. Check and then draw a line as before. Saw this line, keeping well on the waste side of the line.

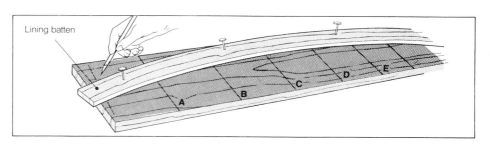

Finished edge

Shaping the plank to fit

Hold the plank in place and mark the width and location of the frames. If the plank needs hollowing in order to fit against the frames, make cardboard templates for each frame and chop out the inside of the plank, using a mallet and chisel. Use a round soled plane and spokeshave if the inside planking is exposed. With the plank in place, plane the newly sawn edge until the inside edges for a drive fit and the plank lies snugly against the frames. The plank can be held in place using a bridge and wedges. It should not be forced to fit. Excessively tight repairs will cause distortion and leaks when the wood swells in the water.

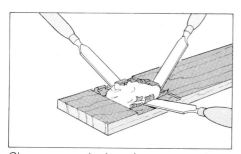

Chop across plank and remove waste

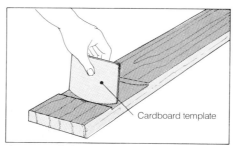

Cardboard template

Accurate fitting at this stage essential

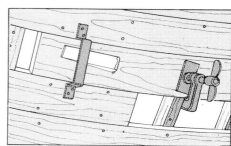

Plank held by wedges and clamps

Replacing a damaged carvel plank

Marking the caulking bevel
Before removing the plank, mark in the caulking lines. The space between the outside edges of the planks should be a little more than one tenth (.15 is correct) of the plank thickness. Mark the bevel lines in pencil on the new plank. Remove the plank and place it in a vice, edge up.

Use a pencil to mark a line along both edges of the plank, a quarter of the plank thickness away from the inside edge, and parallel to it.

The bevels should be planed to this line, and down to the marks on the outside of the plank. If two adjacent planks are being fitted, the second bevel can be planed at a similar angle to the first.

Applying preservatives
Treat all inside woodwork with preservative, and when dry, paint all

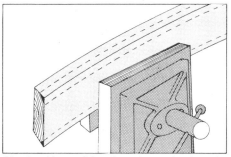

Plank with caulking bevels marked

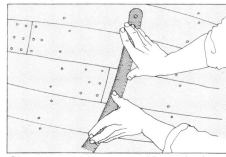

Check for unfair curves with steel rule

interior and touching surfaces with bedding compound or paint. Before the paint dries, replace the plank with wedges and fasten it. If the original plank was clenched or rivetted, drill from the frame outwards, using the same holes.

If several planks adjacent to each other are being renewed, postpone fairing

until they are all fastened in place. Shape the plank with a plane, and finish with a scraper and sandpaper. Use a steel rule bent around the hull to check for high spots.

Replacing a carvel plank at the ends of the boat

Planks fitted at the ends of the boat, or at the garboard, require a considerable degree of force to bring them into place. The traditional method involves boiling or steaming the replacement plank overnight, and then clamping and hauling it into position, with chain, jacks, and clamps. This is an extremely skilled operation, because not only must the plank be a good fit the first time it is sprung into place, but it must also be fitted quickly, before the wood cools and resists the bending and twisting imposed upon it.

The task is more difficult when repairing a boat, as the adjacent planks make direct clamping to the frames impossible. The difficulty is compounded when a relatively short piece of wood needs replacing, and more localized force must be exerted.

Laminating a plank
This is a method which results in a new plank at least as strong as a steamed plank, but which does not impose any stress on the hull, (or workers!) as it is fitted.

This is a great advantage, particularly where there is a great deal of curve, and where the frames and ends of the boat are old or slightly rotted, and will not hold fastenings as well as they once did.

Equipment
The tools normally needed for fitting a plank: hand saw, cross cut saw; keyhole hacksaw or jigsaw; brace and bits; dividers; chisel and mallet; smoothing plane; set square; screwdriver; hammer etc. A supply of thixotropic epoxy resin glue (see page 39 for details). Some bridging clamps and, if the work is to be performed outside or in conditions below 10°C (50°F) an efficient space or convector heater. Two sheets of thin wrapping film.

Preparation
The laminates for the plank should be knot-free and straight-grained, and, if possible, cut from the same board and laid in the order in which they were cut. Laminates should be between ½ and ¾ inch (10 and 20mm) thick, (thinner for very small boats) and bend easily into the curve required. However if they are cut too thinly, they may take up unfair curves, which will make laying and fairing additional laminates more difficult.

Technique
The laminates are cut and fitted without glue so that the clamping arrangements can be tested, and any problems encountered in the glueing process resolved.

Trim the first, inner laminate so that it rests snugly against the frames. Make no attempt to cut the caulking bevel — the laminates should rest tight up against the adjacent planks.

Remove the laminates, and lay two sheets of thin wrapping film over the space for the new plank. This is to ensure that the laminated plank can be freed without difficulty once the glue has cured. Place the first laminate in position over the film against the ends and frames.

Clamp it with the minimum of clamps necessary to keep it from falling out, and apply a thick coat of thixotropic (non-drip) epoxy glue to the spaces between the wedges and clamps. Give the second laminate a generous coat of glue, and work it into place, covering the unglued parts of the first piece as the clamps are removed. Wedge the second laminate in place. Keep clamping pressure light so as not to distort the planks, but sufficiently great to cause surplus glue to ooze from the interface of the two surfaces.

Leave to cure (keeping the glue and wood at the required temperature for the entire curing period), and clean away excess glue. Fit the subsequent laminates when the glue has hardened.

When all the laminates are in place, and the glue thoroughly cured, remove the clamps, the laminated plank, and wrapping film.

Trim the caulking bevels and refit the plank. Fasten, plug the fastening holes, and fair the plank as described on Page 44 and 46

Traditional method

The shape of the replacement plank must be spiled and cut very accurately. It will be necessary to spring a thinner batten into the final position for the plank, and take the dimensions from that. Plank ends must also be cut very precisely. Where the planks are lapped at the transom, this final trimming can be left until the plank is securely in place.

A variety of strong and basic clamping devices should be prepared for use, some examples of which are shown in the main illustration.

If the plank is to take a considerable degree of curve, it may be helpful to bore through the plank at the end, and fit a ring bolt with a heavy steel plate on the outside of the plank to spread the load when the ring is winched into place.

When all the preparations are complete, recruit as many helpers as possible, and carry the freshly steamed plank to the boat. First clamp the end that is the most difficult to pull up, and then winch in the other, fitting bridges across the plank and wedging the plank tightly in place as it is heaved in. Work very quickly, and keep the wood moving, a slow steady

bending action is more likely to succeed than a series of sudden jerks.

If the plank is too big, mark the high spots before removing it and shaving them down, replace the plank in the steam chest for a few more hours before making a second attempt.

Once the plank is in position, leave it to cool and set, before releasing it and making final adjustments to the inside or to the bevels. If the plank is clamped and released in the same order as before the small degree of spring back should not make the subsequent refitting difficult.

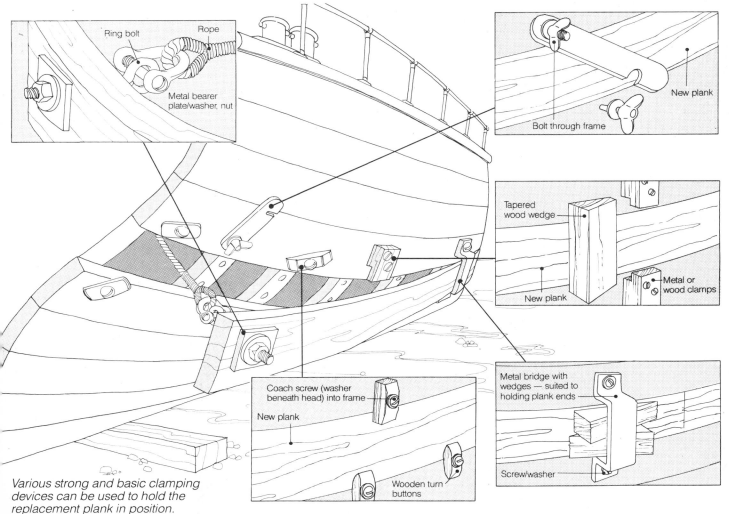

Various strong and basic clamping devices can be used to hold the replacement plank in position.

Replacing a damaged sawn frame   Carvel hulls

Remove all the fittings and cabin furniture close to the frame so that the full extent of the damage can be established.

If the damage or rot extends up the frame and behind the shelf, it will be necessary to remove and replace the top part of the frame. This may involve dismantling part of the bulwarks, removing the covering board, and some deck planking.

Before undertaking work on this scale make careful drawings of the deck, side and frame arrangements, and in particular note the precautions taken to prevent water seeping below.

Sawn frames are made up of several pieces of timber, known as futtocks. These may be paired and their joints staggered to give a very solid and heavy structure, or they may be end-butted and supported by a cleat at each joint.

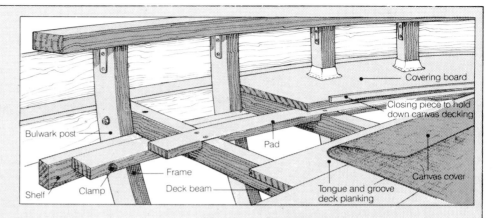

Covering board
Closing piece to hold down canvas decking
Bulwark post
Pad
Canvas cover
Shelf
Clamp
Frame
Deck beam
Tongue and groove deck planking

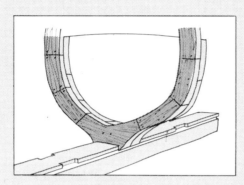

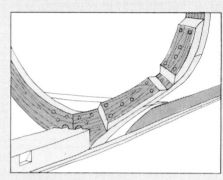

Technique for removing a damaged futtock

Try to remove futtock fastenings. It is impossible to withdraw trenails, but where room permits it may be feasible to partly drill them out.

Splitting out the damaged futtock
Use an old, heavy chisel, striking it with a mallet or lump hammer, to split out the futtock piece. Work with the grain, starting close to the side of the futtock piece and splitting down its length.

Removing plank fastenings
Spikes and nails need several smart blows with a light hammer to dislodge the wood plug or stopping on the

outside of the hull. Wood plugs can then be removed with an old chisel or screwdriver. Nails and spikes should be hammered back from the inside. Ask a helper to hold a lump of pine against the plank, over the head of the nail, while it is being driven out. This will prevent the plank from splitting as the fastening is driven back.

Cleaning the futtock ends
Once the damaged futtocks have been removed, the area should be cleaned up. Exposed butt ends should be straightened and squared up with a chisel. Take the opportunity to inspect the area for rot.

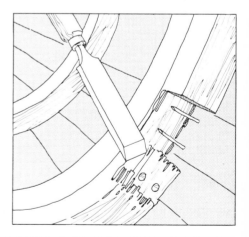

Fitting a new futtock

Making an accurate template
Cut a hardboard template roughly to shape and hold it against the remaining parts of the frame. Work on the midships

side of the frame to allow for the cutting of the standing bevel at the edge of the futtock piece. Spile the shape of the hull on to the template, and cut. Hold the

template against the frame and mark one butt end. Cut to the line, mark the second, check it carefully and then cut.

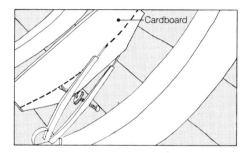

Marking the bevel

Hold the template against the hull and mark on it stations for taking bevel measurements. Mark and number the same stations on the inside hull planking.

Remove the template and position a light, stiff, board across the space to be fitted with the new futtock. Clamp it to the sides of the frame. Use an angle bevel to find the angle at each station on the hull, and mark it off on a piece of straight-sided stock. Number the angles to correspond with each station number.

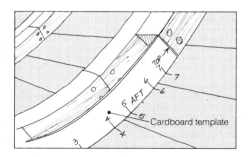

Cutting the replacement piece

Place the template over the new wood, and align the grain to give the least cross-grain over the length of the futtock. Mark around the template and then cut it to shape with a band saw or bow saw. Cut the butt ends of the futtock well on the waste side.

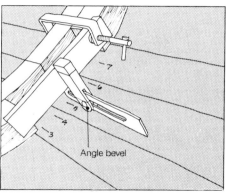

Measure angles between frame and planking

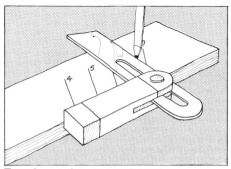

Transfer angles on to a board

Shaping

Transfer and number the stations for the bevel on to the edge of the face side. Make sure that the futtock piece is correctly orientated, or the bevel will taper the wrong way. Transfer the bevel angles from the block to the futtock. Fair in the marks, and cut down the bevel using a chisel and spokeshave.

Fitting the futtock

Introduce the new piece gradually. It should be slightly too long. Do not force it into position, but ease away at the ends, or if the bevel needs some adjustment, at the bevel, until it fits.

Fastening

Considerable problems can occur at this stage if the adjacent frames are too close to allow for the use of a straight drill or auger bit. Where this is not a difficulty, the faying edges (touching surfaces) should be treated with a preservative followed by a bedding compound, and then clamped and bolted into place. Alternatively trenails can be used. Fair the inside bevel with a spokeshave and treat the inner faces with preservative. Replace the plank fastenings.

Fastening futtocks in confined spaces

Clamp the futtock into place and mark the correct position for the new hole. Either use a pencil, or sharpen the end of a suitable dowel, and drive it through the existing fastening hole, so that its point leaves an imprint on the new wood. Mark the angle of the dowel to help guide the drill. Remove, and bore the futtock. Brush on preservative and then, when dry, smear bedding compound or weather-proof glue over the futtock piece, and fit it into place. If glue is used, slip polythene sheeting between the frame and planks to prevent these bonding together.

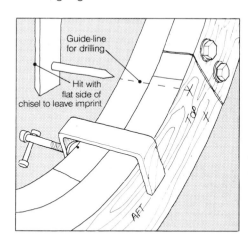

Repair and removal of a complete frame

Replacing the entire frame is a similar operation to the replacement of part of the frame. Draw the position of the frame on the inside of the planking. Release the floor bolts, if necessary by sawing through the bolts with a hacksaw blade slipped between the frame and the floor. At the head of the frame the futtocks will have to be split and the bolt holding the shelf to the frame sawn in the same way. A full-sized template should be cut from hardboard, fitted in place, and used to plan the size and location of the futtock pieces. Make sure that the template is drawn on the midship side of the frame and allow for the bevel.

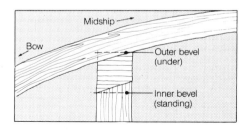

Replacing a damaged sawn frame Carvel hulls

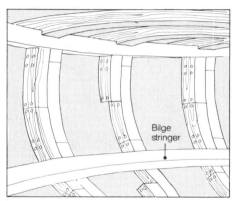

Install futtocks from ends, working towards middle of frame

Once the size and position of the futtocks have been decided, they can be built up in the workshop, and fitted. Fit them from the floor upwards, and from the shelf downwards. Hold them in place with temporary fastenings while the remaining pieces are fitted. Do not trim the last pair of futtocks to length, until the final fastenings are in place.

Soak the futtocks in a tub of preservative after the bolt holes have been bored.

Build up the frame as before, bolting the pairs together progressively towards the middle. Make the final length adjustments to the closing pieces before boring, soaking in preservative and fastening them in place.

Fastening the frame to the beam shelf

Unless the sheer strake is removed or cut, it will be impossible to fit a bolt at the head of the frame, to hold the shelf and frame together. Where only a single frame is being replaced, a pair of coach screws with washers under their heads will make a satisfactory alternative to bolting. If several frames need to be bolted, follow the procedure below.

Bolting the frame heads

Bore through the shelf, frame head and sheer plank. Use a chisel to enlarge the hole in the sheer plank. Smear the bolt with old paint or varnish and drive it into the hole from the outside. Draw it tight

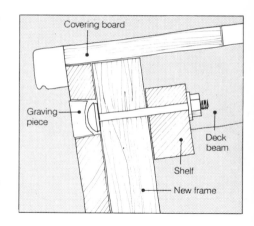

(with a washer beneath the head and the nut). Fit a graving piece over the hole in the sheer plank.

Finishing

Once the frame is securely held in place, and supporting the planking across its entire bearing surfaces, fasten the planks. Fair the inside bevel on the frame, brush preservative over the new wood and replace the cabin fittings.

Laminating a new frame

A laminated frame can be substituted for a sawn frame, and will be stronger and just as rigid as a sawn frame of equal size. The problem with fitting a laminated frame is that unless a midship frame is being replaced (lying perpendicular to both the hull planking and the centre-line), it must be moulded, glued and bevelled outside the hull and fitted in one or even two pieces.

Selection of laminating wood

The wood should be straight-grained and knot-free. It is best if the strips are all taken from the same piece of timber, to ensure a similar moisture content. Each piece of the lamination should be of an adequate length: if joins have to be made, these should be scarfed with the slope not greater than 1:10.

Saw the strips to a thickness which is easily bent to the required shape.

Laminating a frame in place

This is only possible where a short length of frame is to be laminated, or where the frame lies perpendicular to the hull side and to the centre-line. Very

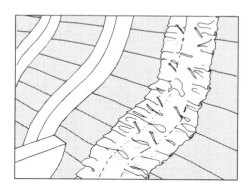

careful fitting of the laminates is essential to avoid an ugly repair.

A strip of light polythene sheeting should be stapled to cover the area where the laminating will take place. Drive a row of nails down each side of the proposed new frame; these can be aligned against a strip of laminate.

Fit the first two strips of timber into place. Apply a resorcinal glue to the join between them, and press into position. Hold in place with roundheaded screws (and washers) screwed into the hull

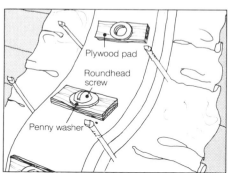

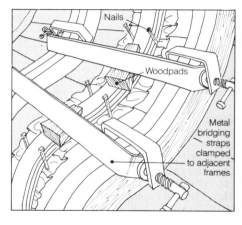

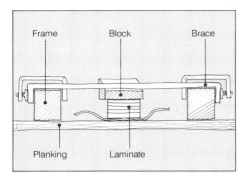

Frame Block Brace

Planking Laminate

planking. Wash away the excess glue and allow it to dry. Remove the screws and prepare a third strip for glueing. A small degree of spring back should be expected at first, but as the additional strips build up and are glued in position,

this will be reduced, and the laminate will become stiffer.

Temporary clamps

Simple clamps may help to hold down subsequent strips. Glue the third in place, hold it with the clamps, and staple or screw the strips together. Continue in this manner until the full thickness of the frame has been built up. Always be assiduous in cleaning away the excess glue, and in removing the temporary fastenings once the glue has dried. (If epoxy glue is used it is best to remove the fastenings once the glue has partially cured). Clean the frame with a sharp chisel and a scraper. Fasten the floor, shelf and plank fastenings to it, after removing the polythene, and applying preservative.

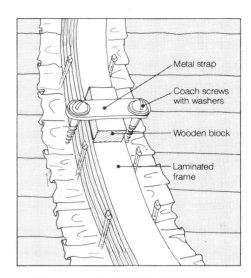

Metal strap

Coach screws with washers

Wooden block

Laminated frame

Laminating off the hull

The same rigorous conditions apply to the selection, joining and preparation of stock as for the previous example. An accurate and rigid mould which allows for easy clamping will need to be made. When laminating is done off the hull more strips can be applied in one glueing session, provided that the mould is sufficiently well built to withstand the stress of the bent laminates. Bevelling and fairing should be left until after laminating is complete. A fair amount of wood will be lost in the bevelling, so provision for this should be made when calculating the amount of wood required.

Fitting and bevelling is the same as for the fitting of the sawn frames. Take care to make accurate station and bevel marks.

Where, despite careful planning, the frame will not fit in its place, a straight scarf join will have to be sawn (see illustration). This should be reinforced on the midships side by a cleat extending beyond the ends of the scarf, and fitted closely to the planking.

Drill the bolt holes through the frame before sawing the straight scarf. Re-assemble the frame, using bolts to pull it together, fit and drill the cleat. Dismantle, glue and re-assemble the frame in place. Once the frame is bolted into position, replace plank fastenings.

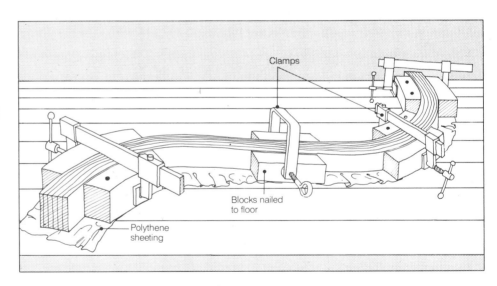

Clamps

Blocks nailed to floor

Polythene sheeting

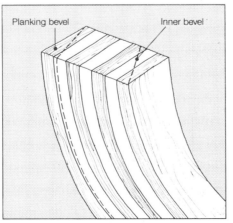

Planking bevel Inner bevel

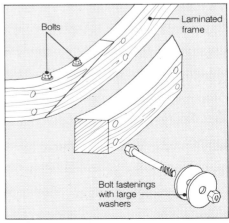

Bolts

Laminated frame

Bolt fastenings with large washers

Repair of plank ends Carvel hulls

Seriously weakened or loosened fastenings at the stem or stern of a carvel built hull may be caused by a weakness in plank-to-frame fastenings, allowing the planks to move as the boat flexes in a seaway.

Inspect the fastenings, the wood surrounding the fastenings, and the frames. If there is any evidence of corrosion, electro-chemical decay, or softness in the wood surrounding the fastenings refer to the section on corrosion (pages 286 and 290).

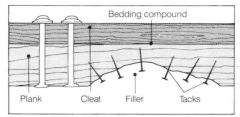

Section through plank

Remove old paint and loose splinters from the outside of the plank, and sand it with coarse sandpaper. Prime the damaged area with unthickened epoxy resin glue and follow this with a layer of thickened epoxy filler or glue mixed with dust collected from a belt sander.

Where damage extends across a caulked seam, each plank should be supported with a cleat, with bedding compound between cleats.

Remove the old caulking material from the seam with a hook, and whittle some wedge-shaped pieces of softwood to fit the seam. Wrap these in thin polythene or wrapping film, and apply the filler to the damaged areas. When the epoxy filler has cured, remove the wedges, fair the repair, caulk and paint the surface.

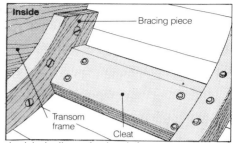

Inside hull — plank reinforcement at transom

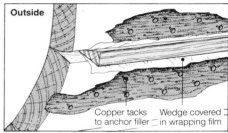

Wedge protects seam and facilitates filling

Where the cavity is more than ¼ inch (6mm) deep, drive copper tacks into the planking to help reinforce the bond between the filler and the plank. Sand and make good.

End repairs

Crushed or broken planking as a result of wear or accidental damage, can be repaired in the following ways.

Damage that is confined to a single plank can be made good by through-rivetting a cleat behind the plank. This should extend well beyond the area of damage and, where possible, brace it against the transom. Bevel the edges of the cleat, to avoid creating a water trap.

Replacement and repair

Where plank ends are damaged or degraded to the extent that strength has been lost, small parts may be replaced. This is permissible at the ends of the boat, though it is not good practice to insert short plank repairs in the midship sections. Take care to ensure that joints in adjacent planks have at least two frame spaces between them.

Before replacing the plank, check the condition of the frames before attaching the new fastenings. Where the holes are already enlarged due to corrosion, they should be drilled, and a dowel, glued with epoxy resin, driven into the hole. Smear some glue into the opening of the hole before inserting the dowel.
If new fastenings are driven into old holes, or into the end grain of the hardwood dowel plugs, a thicker gauge and longer screw should be used.
As with every repair job, all degraded parts should be removed and new wood inserted prior to correcting any further problems.

Repairs to worn ends
The most satisfactory repair in this case is to add new fastenings into sound wood further in from the ends. Where the transom is made from very thick timber, or has a considerable bevel, this is a straightforward task. It is not necessary to remove the old fastenings, but new ones should be positioned, drilled, and attached with great care so as not to weaken the timber at the ends.

Where the transom is too thin to allow extra, staggered fastenings, a doubling piece should be fitted hard against the transom. The procedure for shaping and fitting is similar to making a replacement frame. Transom frame parts are usually cross-halved rather than butted together. Cut and fit all parts of the frame, before marking and cutting the halving joints. Set the sides of the frame in bedding compound, and glue and screw the frame to the transom, before fitting the new fastening through the planking.

Scuffed and worn plank edges should have the worst of their roughness removed and then be soaked in unthickened epoxy resin glue. Sand the plank ends when the glue has saturated the end grain and torn fibres, and is completely cured.

The epoxy glue will not restore the wood to its original strength, but it will create a hard surface capable of taking a protective layer of paint or varnish, and help prevent further deterioration.

If much of the damage at the stern is the result of abrasion and collision, fit a rubbing strip around the corner of the transom.

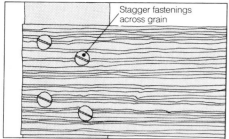

Stagger screws for maximum strength

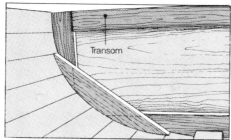

Transom frame

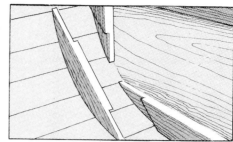

Cross-halving frame joint

Sprung planks at the stem

Similar techniques to those described for the stern can be used at the bow. The simplest solution is to remove the holding screws at the stem, replacing them with longer screws after removing the accumulations of putty, caulking material etc, that may have helped ease the end from its bedding.

Where the weakened condition of the plank ends prevents use of the same fastening holes, it is sometimes possible to screw and glue a holding cleat to the stem and screw the plank ends into that. Fill all air pockets. Where the apron of the boat is rounded, set up a separate nailing bulkhead behind it. This should be made in two parts, each bearing closely against the planking. Brace the two parts of the bulkhead together. Fasten knees to the shelf at each side, and between the keel and the new bulkhead.

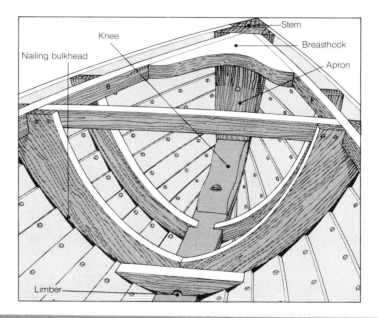

Cut limber holes at the base of the bulkhead and allow ventilation at the top. Fasten each plank to the new bulkhead

Bilge stringers

Bilge stringers are normally held with two fastenings per frame. Sometimes these fastenings are driven in from the outside, but it is more common to find them screwed or spiked from the inside of the hull.

The stringer is usually longer than the boat itself, and needs to be sprung into place. Its replacement will involve removing most, if not all of the internal hull fittings, as well as part of the deck, to allow room for it to be braced, shored and wedged into place.

Fractures are easier to repair, although part of the interior fitting will still need dismantling in order to reach the damaged part. However, fractures or breaks in the stringer are unusual without associated damage to the framing and planking. Inspect both sides of the hull for evidence of this. Seek professional advice if the frames or planking have been affected by the breakage or if seams have opened up.

Laminating a brace

Mark the position of the bolts or nail heads on the side of the stringer. Clean up the top surface of the stringer around and between the fastenings, so that the brace can be glued against it.

Cut the laminates to length, place the first one over the stringer and tap it with a hammer to locate the position of the fastening heads. Remove the laminate

and carve out depressions to allow it to sit easily over them. Cover the frames and planking beneath the stringer with polythene to catch the excess glue, and build up the brace. Some useful temporary clamps are illustrated on the following page.

Fractures are likely to be associated with extensive frame and plank damage

Repairs to bilge stringer Carvel hulls

Bracing a bilge stringer
Before it is tapered and faired into the line of the stringer, the bracing piece should be cut so that it overlaps the fractured part by at least six times the thickness of the stringer.

Fairing the brace
Trim the ends of the brace so that it fairs into the line of the stringer, without introducing a localized stiffness.

Fitting bolts through the brace
These will have to be fitted between the frames. Check the marks on the side of the bilge stringer to avoid cutting into the existing stringer fastenings, and drill down through the brace and stringer. Pour preservative down the holes and around the sides of the stringer before

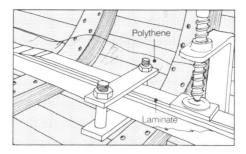

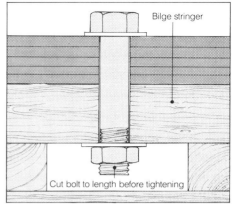

cutting and fitting bolts. Hold the washer and nut on the underside of the stringer with a ring spanner. Tighten up the head with a washer beneath.

When the bolts are tightened and the preservative is dry, mix up a thick epoxy glue and trowel it into the sides of the

stringer to seal any open cracks. Sand when dry and apply more preservative before painting.

Replacing a section of stringer
Make a straight saw cut across the stringer and release the rotten part by splitting it free. Remove the fastenings and plug the holes with dowels.

Saw a straight scarf at each end of the stringer. A small, portable, circular saw, with the blade set to cut no deeper than the stringer, is ideal for this. Alternatively a floor board saw can be used. Tack a batten to the face of the stringer to guide the saw cut, and take care not to cut into the frames.

Cut the replacement part to length, adding the length of scarf at each end. Position this carefully, shoring and bracing where necessary. (A beam clamped to the side of the stringer and used to pull and hold the replacement in place may make this awkward task a little easier.)

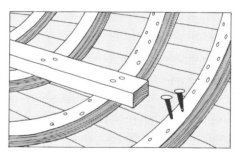

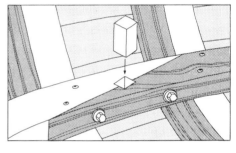

Soak the underside of the new wood, and the bearing faces of the frames, with preservative, and re-position the replacement piece. Screw the new piece to the frames before brushing epoxy glue on to the faces of the scarf joins and clamping them together.

When the glue joins are dry, leave the shoring in place, and drill through the side of the bilge stringer to take a pair of bolts at each end of the scarf join. It may

be necessary to drill these with a large gimlet if a brace cannot be worked into the turn of the bilge. Tighten the bolts before drilling a half-inch (12mm) hole down the seam of the scarf to take a hardwood peg. Stop the hole before it passes right through the stringer, square its shape with a bevel-edged chisel, and trim a hardwood peg to fit. Soak this in weather-proof glue before driving it into position and fairing off the top. Repeat this at the other scarf.

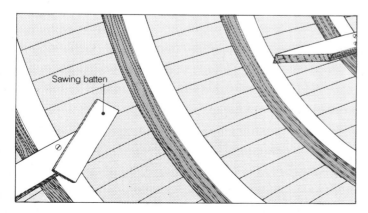

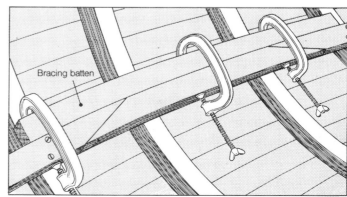

Repairs to the beam shelf Carvel hulls

The beam shelf and clamp are tucked into the side of the hull where the deck beam and the frame heads meet. Deck beams are usually half dovetailed into the shelf and are supported by the clamp bolted beneath. Several different methods of joining the deck beams to the shelf are illustrated.

Inspect the shelf and clamp fastenings annually, especially the areas where air cannot circulate freely. These are particularly vulnerable to rot.

If rot is discovered, seek professional advice. Replacing the shelf, for example, is a major undertaking, often involving the complete removal of the deck and deck beams.

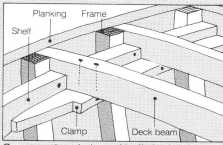

Constructional view of hull deck join

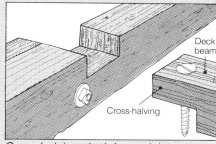

Cross-halving deck beam joint

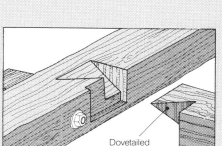

Dovetailed beam fastening

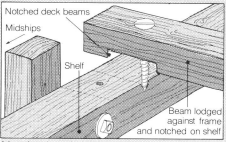

Notched and screwed beam

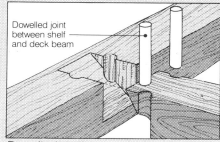

Dowelled deck beam joint

Replacing short lengths of shelf

The technique is the same as for the bilge stringer, except that the deck beam joints need to be cut before the shelf is finally fixed into position. In order to mark these joins, the replacement piece must be fitted snugly below the beams, before the positions of the beams can be marked. Transfer the exact shape of each dovetail with a cardboard template before cutting. This is a very tricky fitting operation and if it is undertaken, the dovetail housings and beam ends should be doused with preservative, and bedded in compound or thickened epoxy glue when slotting the shelf into place.

When repairing both a shelf and a clamp, stagger the end scarfs so that there are at least three frame spaces between joints.

Curing leaks at the shelf bolts

This is likely to occur at any of the bolt fastenings through the shelf, but it is most common where the fastenings pass through from the outside of the hull, as in the case of the chain plates. Rust-streaked or speckled paint, perhaps lifting and cracking around the bolt end, will indicate trouble. Outside the boat, there may be traces of rust running down the paintwork, and perhaps evidence of movement at the edge of the external fastenings.

Strip away the decayed paintwork and flush the wood with warm water to clean away the salt. If possible, withdraw the bolt, and check it for corrosion. Paint it with a rust-inhibiting paint before replacing it in the hole with a twist of cotton beneath the head. When the wood is dry, soak the area with wood preservative, finish with paint or varnish.

This treatment will inhibit the corrosion of the fastening and the decay of the timber, but it will not restore strength to the fastening. Where necessary, insert an extra fastening below and to one side of the original to reinforce the frame and shelf.

Hanging, lodging and quarter knees

It is worth while checking these periodically to see that they are correctly supporting the fittings. There should be at least three fastenings spaced at approximately eight times their diameter on each bearing face. All fastenings should be sound and tight.

Transom construction and repair Carvel hulls

To fit a replacement knee

Knees can be cut from curved or straight-grained wood, but a laminated knee is both the strongest and the most resistant to rot. Laminations should be moulded around a sawn centre support.

To ease clamping, make the knee laminations before sawing the support to shape. Once the knee is made, it should be spiled and bevelled to fit. In awkward corners it is often best to fit a cardboard template before cutting the knee to shape.

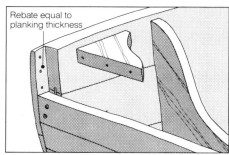

Position for maximum strength

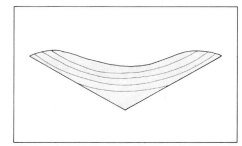

Laminate on to solid wood former

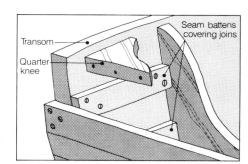

Shape knee after glue is cured

Transom construction

The drawings show some of the most common ways in which a transom for a carvel hull is constructed.

Most transoms are made from edge-joined boards, supported by vertical cleats and perhaps a transom frame. The latter is usually made from several pieces of timber cross-halved together, and screwed or bolted to the inside face of the transom. This will not only stiffen the transom, but will also present side-grain holding for the plank fastenings.

Transoms constructed from more than one board are edge-joined, splined or dowelled, and those made with narrower planks are often drift-bolted together. A seam batten may be fitted behind the join. Plywood transoms are either braced against a substantial frame or are screwed and glued against an inner planked transom of thicker wood.

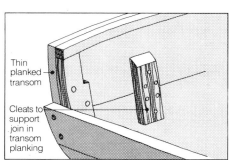

Planks rebated into transom

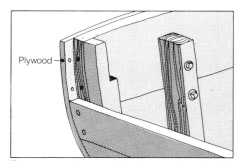

Flush-planked transom

Transom reinforced with frame

Transom enhanced by decorative veneer

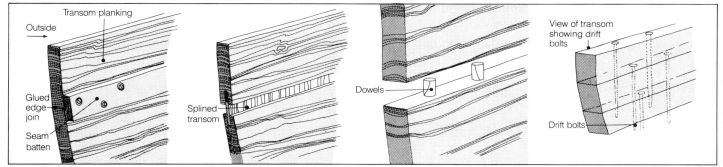

Four common ways of building up a planked transom

Curved transoms

Each plank is bent and fitted to a sawn frame. Usually the planks can be fitted cold, but they should be steamed when there is a sharp curve.

A mould with a radius roughly 1/25 less than the inner radius of the transom is used to hold the plank while it cools; the reduction in radius compensates for the spring back of the plank when it is released. Sometimes it is possible to bend the boards into place by wrapping them with towels soaked in boiling water.

The grooves for the loose tongues are normally worked in the edge of the transom plank before bending.

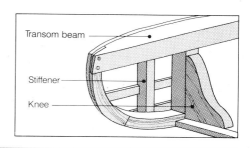

Damage to transom at planking

The areas at the very ends of the boat are almost always poorly ventilated and prone to rot. This usually originates at metal fastenings, and in the end grain of the boards where they butt against the outer planks. Graving pieces can be inserted into the transom to repair small areas of rot, but longer areas adjoining the planking should be repaired in the following manner.

1 Probe the transom with a thin steel spike to discover the extent of the rot. Rot travels across the grain as well as with it. Spike well in towards the centre of the transom, until sound wood is reached.

2 Where possible, remove the screw or bolt fastenings holding the frame and planks to the rotted area of the transom. When working inside the hull remove any fittings or wires that may be damaged in the repair process. Make a hardboard template of the part to be replaced, including the width of the planking at the edge of the transom. Hold the template against the outside face of the transom, and draw round it. Remove the rotted part, cutting well on the inside of the line. Use hand tools — a brace and bit and a keyhole saw — so that the condition of the wood can be assessed as the rot is removed.

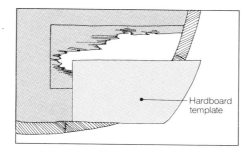

Hardboard template

3 Push back the plank fastenings. Use the template again to make a replacement piece. Cut the sides of the replacement square, check for accuracy before holding it against the transom, and marking round it with a knife. Remember to allow the new piece to overlap the planks at the sides.

4 Support the inside edge of the butt join with a temporary block to prevent the timber splitting as the bevel is cut.

5 Take an angle bevel and measure the angle between the transom face and the planking. Establish the greatest angle, and move the bevel slightly to increase this. Cut this bevel on a small block to make a chiselling guide, then cut this bevel at the butt join. It is important that the angle at the butt should be a little greater than the bevel at the edge of the transom, otherwise the replacement will not fit tightly against the planks. Remove the temporary butt block.

6 Make a cardboard template of the shape of the hole from the inside of the transom, and mark and cut this shape square on the patch. Calculate the bevel for the outer edge of the patch from the angle between the transom and planks measured from the outside.

7 Cut this accurately, then trim the butt join to the correct bevel. Cut it back, until the patch slips into place.

8 Support the butt with a block, and screw and glue seam battens to support the edge join. Apply preservative to all the wood and, when dry, screw and glue the patch to the butt block and battens. Re-fasten the planks.

9 If drift bolts have been sawn away when trimming the edge joins, fit one or two cleats on the inside of the transom and notch them over the battens.

10 Plane up and finish the repair, replacing any wires that may have been moved on the inside.

To prevent a recurrence of rot, improve the ventilation at the ends of the boat.

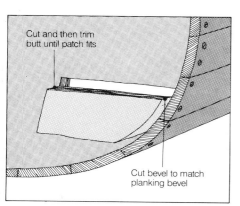

Cut and then trim butt until patch fits

Cut bevel to match planking bevel

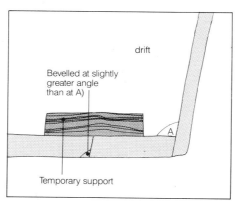

drift

Bevelled at slightly greater angle than at A)

A

Temporary support

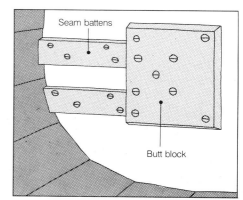

Seam battens

Butt block

Caulking Carvel hulls

The traditional method of stopping the seams of a conventionally constructed wooden boat is to caulk them by forcing a twisted rope of cotton or oakum into the tapered crevice between the planks. The seam is then primed and the remaining 1/8-1/4inch (3-6mm) seam sealed with a flexible compound which protects the caulking and levels the seam in preparation for painting the hull.

The hull of a carvel boat and also the seams at the stem, keel and between the planks of a laid wooden deck, are normally caulked.

Oakum, which is hemp fibre impregnated with Stockholm tar, should be used below the water-line. Cotton is best above the water-line and wherever very narrow seams have to be caulked.

When caulking absorbs moisture, it swells, and the hard-packed fibres form a watertight seal. If the planking is dry when the caulking is driven, great care must be taken not to force too much caulking into the seam, otherwise the combined swelling of the caulking and wooden planks may pull the planks from the framework of the boat.

Caulked deck seams

First signs of decay are often near engine

Caulked stem rabbet seam

Caulked garboard/keel seam

Caulked plank seams

The degree of force required to drive the caulking varies with the hardness and thickness of the planking. The effect of caulking is always to wedge planks apart. New boats are rarely caulked until all the planks are in place. When replacement planks are fitted, caulking is normally left until at least two planks above the seam are fully fastened.

Seams must not be caulked if the wedging action of the caulking drives

the fastenings apart, otherwise the leaking seam will be opened, further weakening the fastenings.

When re-caulking small sections of seam, care is needed to prevent the new work from loosening the original caulking adjacent to it. It is best to work cautiously, soak the seam in priming paint or varnish, and twist the tails of the old caulking into the ends of the new, before driving the caulking rather more gently than one would for a full length seam.

Caulking should last about ten years, although towards the end of the period small lengths of seam may need raking out and replacing. Cotton, which is white when new, turns black or brown when decayed and its condition is easy to see. Oakum, which is brown or black, must be hooked out and tested. In good condition both materials are flexible,

fibrous, and resilient. They both turn friable with age.

As a rule, caulking first deteriorates at the keel to garboard seam, at the stem rabbet, and perhaps beneath the engine, where oil from the inside may penetrate between the planks and decay the caulking fibres. Complete replacement, however, may not be necessary. Before raking out the seams, make a few spot checks at other parts of the hull, both above and below the water-line, to find the overall condition of the caulking. Use a fine awl to open up short lengths of seam, and hook out portions of oakum or cotton for inspection. It is quite common for a re-caulking job to be limited to one or two areas, perhaps where the planking has worked loose.

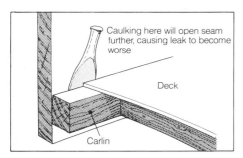

Caulking here will open seam further, causing leak to become worse

Deck

Carlin

Tools

The tools illustrated below cover most caulking needs. The making iron is normally home-made, and the others can be adapted from suitable household and carpentry tools. A good chandlery store that stocks oakum and cotton will probably sell or lend a set of professional tools or recommend a supplier.

A small bricklayer's bolster, ground to the correct seam angle will make a good reamer, and a floorboard lifting tool, old firmer chisel, cold chisels, and even a thick-bladed kitchen knife can be ground and used in the manner described below.

It may be impossible to duplicate the grooved firming iron, but its effect can be achieved by hitting the caulking with a fine-edged making iron before following with a thick-ended making iron for the final hardening strokes. Never use wooden wedges for caulking; if they break, the end will be very difficult to retrieve from the seam without damaging its edges. Any wooden mallet will suffice. The traditional beetle has the advantage of being finely balanced, and is handy when working in awkward corners. Do not use a hammer.

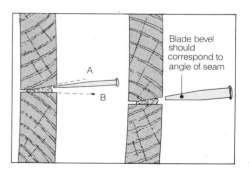

Blade bevel should correspond to angle of seam

Seam rake

The sides of the rake are ground to enable them to scrape the sides of the caulking seam. The point of the rake is blunt to prevent it from cutting the caulking seam deeper than necessary. Fit a large, comfortable handle on to the raking iron, and use it by drawing it towards you. Control the pull and the pressure on the back of the rake to prevent it slipping out of the seam and scoring the planks. Brittle sealing putties can be chopped out by hitting the back of the rake with a light hammer, or loosened by tapping them with a making iron, before raking out.

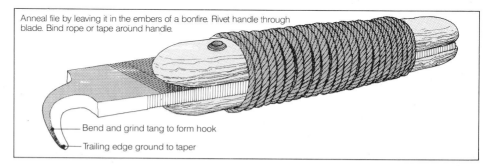

Anneal file by leaving it in the embers of a bonfire. Rivet handle through blade. Bind rope or tape around handle.

Bend and grind tang to form hook

Trailing edge ground to taper

Reamer

This is used to widen a narrow groove. It is driven into the seam compressing the planks. Do not force too much caulking into a reamed seam, as the wood will eventually swell and return to its previous size. Soft wood may compress, but the planks on a well-made hardwood hull are more likely to squeeze some of the caulking from between the planks.

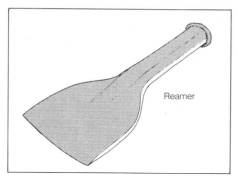

Reamer

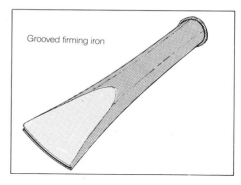

Grooved firming iron

Irons

The making iron is tapered to a flat edge, between 1/16-1/8inch (1-3mm) wide, while the firming iron has one or two shallow grooves filed down its edge. The making iron is used to press the loops and tucks into the seam. This is then hardened up with the firming iron, hit with heavier strokes until the caulking is compressed. A variety of irons is illustrated; their size and shape make them suitable for working in awkward corners or wide seams. Irons are held as illustrated. They are rocked very gently as they are struck to prevent them from wedging tightly. Gentle pressure is used to start and finish the caulking. Heavier pressure is

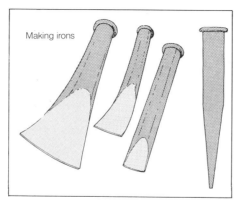

Making irons

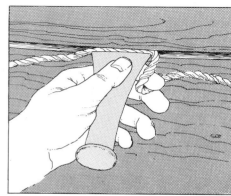

applied during the initial firming strokes. Dip the irons in paraffin, or in a tub filled with cotton waste soaked in linseed oil, to help lubricate them.

Caulking Carvel hulls

Caulking wheel
The caulking wheel is tapered to conform to the caulking groove, and forces the cotton into the groove as it is rolled down the seam. This is a quick method of caulking suitable for narrow seams between thin planks [¼ inch (6 mm) or less].

Seam brush
These are generally of two types, although any brush which will successfully work the paint into the

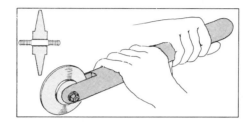

Tin lid for holding paint

narrow seam will do. Priming is often left until after caulking, but a coat of paint in the seam before caulking will help bind

the caulking, and protect the edges of the planking.

Preparation
Remove paint or varnish from the hull before raking out the old caulking. With the stopping and caulking in place, the plank edges are better protected from the scorching, splitting and minor damage resulting from burning and scraping paint. Use the rake to ensure that all previous sealant and caulking is removed before priming and re-caulking.

Where only a small area of caulking needs to be removed, clean away loose paint, etc. before working on the seams.

Before re-caulking, check the condition of the planking and fastenings. Replace loose fastenings, rotten planks and

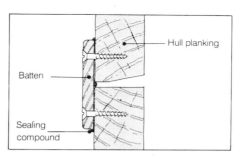

Hull planking

Batten

Sealing compound

broken frames. All seams should be tight on the inside. If they have opened, close the inside with a batten bedded in flexible compound. Where a plank edge is badly split, rout out a new edge, and glue a tapered batten into the seam.

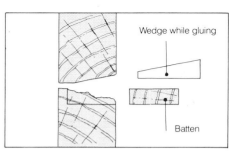

Wedge while gluing

Batten

Where the seam has opened, but it is not bad enough for battens or splining, soak some strips of calico in marine glue and press them into the seam. Follow with paint or varnish, and caulk while the seam is still wet.

Caulking narrow seams
Cut a length from the ball of cotton equivalent to about 1 ⅓ the length of the seam to be caulked. The additional length compensates for the losses due to twisting the strands into a rope. Separate two or three strands and twist a short length together until they form a loosely wound string. Force a short sample length of the twisted cotton into the seam with the caulking wheel. If the cotton is the correct width, it will be easy to start in the seam, but increased pressure will be needed to firm it up as it goes deeper.

Remove the cotton and correct its size by adding or removing a strand. Run varnish or paint into the seam with the seam brush.

Cut, fit, and press the butt join caulking first, and bring the tails of the cotton into the longitudinal seam.

Tack a small nail in the plank at each end of the seam. Tie one end of the caulking strand to the tack, and hook the other end over a bent nail held in the chuck of an electric drill. Use the drill to wind the strands together until they form a loose

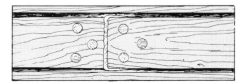

rope of the correct thickness. Tie the other end to the second nail. The caulking cotton should then lie along the seam. By running the wheel along it, it is easily pressed into position.

Work the caulking into the end seams of the plank, and then finish with sealing compound.

Caulking-cotton wider seams
Separate enough strands from the roll and twist together to form a loose rope of sufficient size to caulk the seam. With old planking, the size of the seam will vary, as the seams are enlarged each time the boat is re-caulked. If there are noticeable

variations in the width of the seam, choose an average size, and twist extra cotton into the roll wherever necessary. Never try to hammer in a second layer of caulking, as it will not help to make a watertight seal.

Where seam width is fairly constant, the electric drill can be used to twist the strands into a suitable rope. Otherwise the cotton will have to be twisted as the seam progresses, with additional cotton wound in when necessary.

Caulk the butts first, bringing the tails into the longitudinal seam and hold them in place with a few light taps with a making iron. Then with the same narrow making iron, tuck the cotton into the seam. Hold the iron in the left hand, with the thumb closest to the planking. Guide the cotton with the first finger and the end of the making iron. Use the making iron to lift the cotton and tap it lightly into the groove, allowing the cotton to fall into small loops between tucks. These loops provide additional cotton for filling the wider seams. Their size will be determined by the width and the depth of the seam.

Once 2-3 feet (600-900mm) of cotton has been tucked, work back over the seam, collecting and tapping the loops and driving them in.

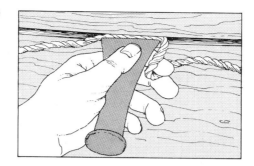

When the seam is filled, change to the firming iron, and work this along the seam, rocking the iron as it is hit, but taking care not to damage the caulking. Try to establish a rhythm and listen to the resonance of the iron as it strikes. This, with its movement, will help you to gauge the amount of force needed to maintain

Leave a tail hanging down to mark incomplete seams

Making — Firmed in

an even caulking pressure along the seam. Initial tucking and final firming blows should be lighter than the hardening up strokes. Make sure that there is sufficient space for the sealer to cover the caulking. A gap of 1/8-1/4 inch (3-6mm) is usually large enough.

Oakum

This is purchased in a bale. The fibres must be teased and separated into strands, and then rolled into a rope before they can be used. No special tools are required. A handful of oakum is picked from the bale and any sticks or stalks discarded. Roll the strands to form a loose cord, about 1 inch (25 mm)

diameter, and when it is 2-3 feet (600 — 900 mm)long, roll it tightly across your knees until the strands compress to make a rope the thickness of a pencil.

Coil this in a box to retain its shape until needed. Caulking is then the same as for the cotton described above. Use the

loops to give additional fill when required. Add extra thickness by twisting more into the rope. Join lengths of oakum by partially unlaying each piece and twisting them together.

Sealing

With the caulking hammered in, use the seam brush to prime or varnish inside the caulking groove. With the seams still wet, apply the sealing compound, using a knife or gun to press it firmly into place. Various flexible compounds are available. The new polysulphide varieties are very convenient and adhere well to the planking.

Flexible sealers are used below the water-line, finished off with the side of a small diameter bent tube, or a shaped stick, to leave the seam slightly hollow. For the topsides, a harder seam composition can be used, usually applied slightly raised, and sanded or scraped flush after it has partially cured.

A flexible seam putty can be made by adding white or red lead paint to linseed oil putty and mixing it into a workable paste. The mixture can be made harder by reducing the quantity of white or red lead, or by adding whiting or some other fine powder. The addition of raw linseed

oil will help the compound to remain flexible. The same effect can be achieved by saturating the inside seam with priming paint, applied with a pump or oil can, and leaving it to dry before sealing. This will prevent the oils in the sealing composition from being leached into the planking.

Press the compound into the seam with a springy flat-bladed knife. Keep the knife clean by wiping it with oil. Scrape away excess sealer from the seam. Run the rounded stick along the seams below the water-line. After several days, the topsides can be sanded or scraped clean, and the boat primed for re-painting.

If re-caulking a section of deck which has marine glue in the seams, it will be necessary, especially in cold weather, to remove a large quantity of glue from adjacent seams, and repay together with the re-caulked section, due to the shattering of the glue which occurred during the hammering.

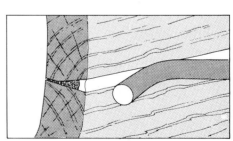

Seams below the water-line should be finished slightly hollow. Topsides can be finished flush, while deck seams should be left proud and 'trodden in' for a few weeks before levelling (see page 170)

Chapter 4

Clinker Hulls

Clinker hulls

The illustration below shows the main features of a clinker built hull. Wide, thin planks, usually of mahogany, wych-elm, larch, spruce or cedar, are overlapped and fastened to each other with rivets or clenched nails. Because of their width, these planks can only be bent in one direction and are therefore shaped to take the curve of the hull. Planks at the turn of the bilge are often so banana-like that they have to be cut from two planks and scarfed together.

The upper outside edge of each plank is bevelled, so that the plank above can rest flat against it. This overlap is called the land, and it remains constant along the length of the plank, and for all planks (except perhaps for those at the turn of the bilge, when the overlap is likely to be slightly less). The lands run into rebates at each end of the boat, so that the planks lie flush at the stem and stern. The rebate is cut in both the planks and does not usually extend for more than l0 inches (250mm) from the ends. The rebates at the stern are sometimes omitted where the planks are bevelled to fit against each other, or are notched into the transom.

Frames are usually steam bent, pairs of frames overlapping and fastened at the hog. They are spaced at approximately twelve times the thickness of the plank, but this varies according to the nature of the boat.

Boats that are worked from open beaches need the extra support of jogged frames fitted to the planking.

Floors are steamed or sawn. They are usually fastened to the planks and not to the frames. The resulting hull is light, strong and resilient.

Only the keel and stem rabbets are caulked. The plank seams seal together as the wood absorbs water and swells (this is known as taking up). Clinker boats that are left out of the water and allowed to dry will take two or more days to take up properly. If the planks have been distorted by exposure to dry heat, they may never be watertight again.

Places to look for damage

Check the condition of the frames — invariably some will be cracked or broken. Look particularly at the turn of the bilge, and at the fastenings to the hog for fractures and localized rot. Check the ends of the boat for evidence of caulking which may indicate that the plank ends are beginning to spring out.

Caulking at the stem may also indicate a developing crack between the apron and the stem, made worse by the caulking and almost certainly not watertight.

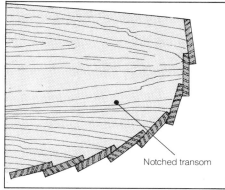

In this example the bevel is run out at the transom

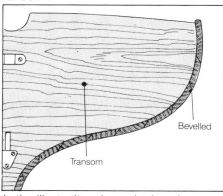

In the illustration above the bevels are cut on both plank edges

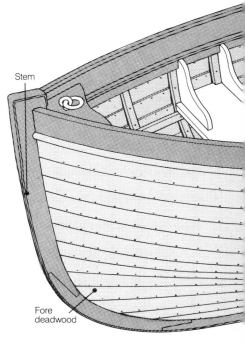

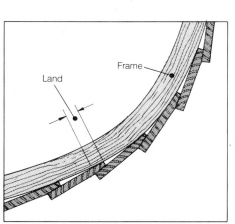

The overlap between planks is called the land. Planks and frames are rivetted together through the lands.

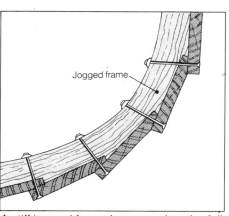

A stiff jogged frame bears against the full width of the planking, giving greater support. Jogged frames and floors are often fitted to beach launched fishing boats.

Turn button to hold plank end in place while it is screwed to stem

At the stem the planking bevel is changed to a rebate worked into both plank edges. This allows planking to lie flush at the stem without any serious weakening. Rebates are usually a standard length, and, unless planking is very thick, the rebated lengths are kept to a minimum.

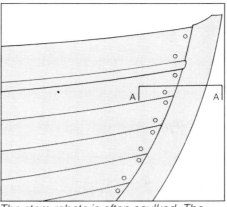

A

A

The stem rebate is often caulked. The addition of caulking to the seam will eventually loosen the plank ends, and may also wedge stem and apron apart and it is then often difficult to make the stem and planking watertight once the fastenings have loosened.

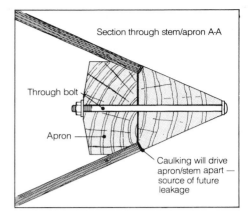

Section through stem/apron A-A

Through bolt

Apron

Caulking will drive apron/stem apart — source of future leakage

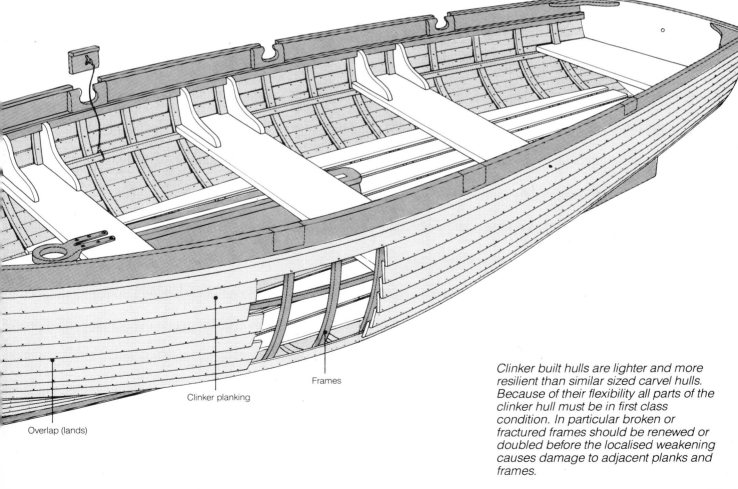

Overlap (lands)

Clinker planking

Frames

Clinker built hulls are lighter and more resilient than similar sized carvel hulls. Because of their flexibility all parts of the clinker hull must be in first class condition. In particular broken or fractured frames should be renewed or doubled before the localised weakening causes damage to adjacent planks and frames.

Repair to collision damage at the stem Clinker hulls

Serious structural repairs to a one-piece stem entailing the release of the plank ends and the removal of the stem should be left to a professional shipwright. However, many stems are made from two or more pieces, the back rebate being cut into the stem while the planks are fastened to an 'apron' bolted or rivetted to the inside of the stem.

Replacing a damaged stem

Remove the metal stem band, release or saw through fastening bolts, and punch them free. Release the fastenings between the stem and the breasthook, and any stem head fittings and pry away the outer stem.

Make an accurate copy of the old damaged stem, and hold it in place on the boat. To improve the fit, rub chalk on to the seating, scarf and plank ends and ease away high spots marked by the traces of chalk.

Clamp and shore the new stem in position and drill down into it through the bolt holes. Remove the stem and paint the touching surfaces with large quantities of wood preservative. Pour preservative down the bolt holes also.

Cut a strip of flannel, soak it in marine paint or varnish, and press it against the face of the stem. Clamp and shore the stem into place and insert the bolts. Before tightening, dip short lengths of cotton wicking into the paint or varnish, and twist them around the bolts and beneath the bolt washers. Drill and refit the stopwaters.

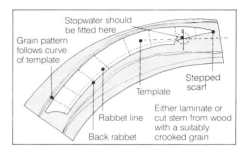
Stopwater should be fitted here
Grain pattern follows curve of template
Stepped scarf
Template
Rabbet line
Either laminate or cut stem from wood with a suitably crooked grain
Back rabbet

Repairing a one-piece stem

Although the complete removal of a one-piece stem is a skilled task it is quite possible to renew much of the stem without disturbing the planking and the plank fastenings.

Small areas of damage can be repaired by scarfing-in replacement wood, but avoid introducing weak points into the stem structure.

Where the damage is extensive, mark the area to be removed, and withdraw any fastenings that might obstruct the saw cut. Saw away the damaged part, and level the surface with a plane, spokeshave, and paring chisel.

Cut straight-grained replacement laminates to the required width and length. Laminates should be thin enough to bend easily into place, but not so thin that they take an irregular or unfair curve. Straight stems can be built up with one or two thick pieces.

Laminating

Thixotropic epoxy glue has the right gap-filling qualities for the laminating process to ensure a sound glue bond without the need for massive clamping pressure. Fit the first laminate into position, glue, screw or staple it in place, and leave it to cure. Remove the fastenings before the glue is fully hardened. Build up the laminate until the profile of the stem is restored.

Fair the new work. Drill and re-fasten the stem fittings, finish with paint or varnish, and refit the stem band.

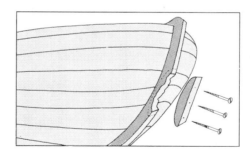

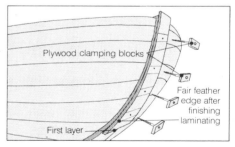
Plywood clamping blocks
Fair feather edge after finishing laminating
First layer

Fitting replacement wooden bilge keels

These take a lot of punishment and occasionally need to be replaced. However, seek advice before extending or fitting new bilge keels to a boat. They can exert considerable stress on to parts of the hull not designed to take the extra loading.

Remove the bilge runner

Release the holding bolts, remove the bilge keel, and use it as a pattern for the new one. Position the new keel beneath

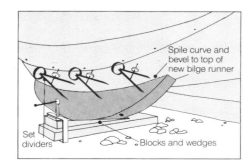
Spile curve and bevel to top of new bilge runner
Set dividers
Blocks and wedges

the hull, and check its angle to the hull by dropping a bolt through the bolt holes. Chock the keel so that it rests against the hull at the correct angle and is positioned over the bolt holes.

Set the dividers to the maximum gap between the top edge of the keel and its bedding on the hull. Spile along both sides of the keel.

Remove the keel and work the bedding face back to the spiling marks. Chock it back into position and bore through the bilge keel from inside to take the bolts.

Remove the keel and treat it with preservative. Paint both facing surfaces, then bolt the keel in place. Before tightening the bolts, slip a couple of turns

of wicking soaked in paint beneath the bolt washers to make them watertight.

Replacement frames

Inspect the inside of the hull. If one fractured frame is found, look along the plank and check the adjacent frames. Do not stint on this kind of reinforcement work. If there is an evident line of weakness, strengthen the entire part, otherwise the local repair will almost certainly fail again.

Fitting doubling frames

Remove the bottom boards and other fittings and select straight-grained, knot-free ash or oak for the doubling pieces. Orientate the wood so that its annual growth rings (revealed at the end of the piece) lie parallel with the hull planking. Chamfer the showing face, and taper the ends. Place the frame into a boiling tube or steam box.

Wear thick rubber gloves to handle the hot, wet wood. Take one of the strips which have been steamed or boiled, and lift it into the boat. If one end is fitted behind the bilge stringer, it should be tucked and worked into place. Press it down on to the frame, pushing it against the hull with your knee or foot. Pull the loose end back, snap the frame into place, move your weight along the doubler, and pull the frame back again.

Repeat this, moving along each time. Work quickly, and position the frame before it has cooled and begun to resist bending. If the boat has a reverse turn at the bilge, this operation should start with the frame positioned and wedged against the keel, and bent and slipped under the bilge stringer.

Rivetting the frames in place

Frames should be drilled from inside, through the centre of the frame and through the plank lands. Where the doubler is positioned close to another frame, stagger the rivet holes slightly, to prevent splits occurring in the plank edges.

Fit wedges beneath each doubling frame where it rises from the planking to lie flush with the keel or hog. Cut them to shape and soak them in preservative before fitting and rivetting. Remember to cut the wedge short of the keel so that it does not obstruct the flow of bilgewater through the limber holes.

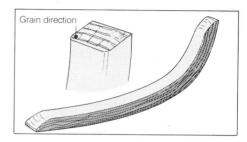

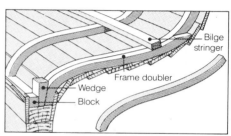

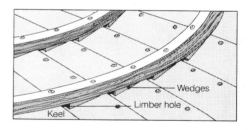

Fitting a new frame

A new frame is made and fitted in the same way as a doubling frame. It may, however, be impossible for the frame to fit into place without cutting through the bilge and other stringers. Sometimes it is possible to tuck the hot frame under the stringers and push them up to the shelf.

Where there is only a single frame being replaced, and the bilge stringer, riser, and perhaps other stringers too make installation difficult, it is better to cut the frame, and fit it in sections. Butt the ends behind a stringer (after soaking them in preservative), and then slip in a doubling piece to brace the join. This should extend to four planks each side of the butt join. Make sure that the rivets are

slightly staggered to reduce the likelihood of the planks splitting.

Jogged frames

Where extra framing strength is required, frames and floors are jogged. To fit a jogged frame, a deeper section frame is steamed and bent into position, and

shored in place until cold.
The inside shape of the side is then scribed on both sides of the frame, which is removed, trimmed to shape, and fitted. When fitting jogged frames, remember to cut the limber holes at the side of the keel.

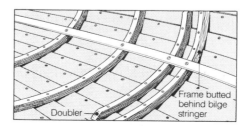

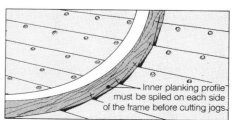

69

Replacing a broken or rotted plank   Clinker hulls

Always choose materials that are of equal or superior quality to those used originally. In clinker construction, there is no caulking forced between the planks to make the hull watertight. Workmanship must be accurate and thorough and it is essential to use extremely sharp tools when cutting scarfs and bevels.

Releasing the damaged plank

Mark the location of the scarf joins for the replacement plank. The joins should be centred between the frames. At the forward end the mark for the saw cut making the rear edge of the scarf should be aft of the midpoint between frames, and at the stern, the saw cut should be forward of the midpoint between frames.

Mark the line of the saw cut so that it is perpendicular to the outside lower edge of the plank.

Release all the plank fastenings between the marks, and about 10 inches (250mm) beyond them. Copper rivets can be cut free by slicing between the plank lands with a steel kitchen knife with saw teeth filed down its edge.

If necessary, force the lands apart with soft wood wedges to enable the knife to move freely. Where the rivets are too thick to saw through, lodge a sharp chisel against the side of the rove and lift it to allow a pair of nail cutters underneath. Clenched nails which cannot be cut must be pried up with a spike, then nipped off with nail cutters, and punched out.

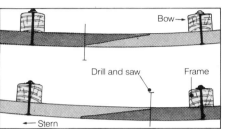
All feather edges should trail to avoid snagging or tearing

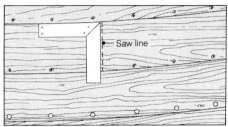
Saw-cut should be perpendicular to line of planking

Cutting out the plank

Drill through the plank on the waste side of each cutting line. Slip a thin sheet of ply or formica beneath the plank to protect the bevel, and saw the lower part of the plank with a keyhole saw. Move the sheet, placing it between the upper lands, and finish the saw cut.
Repeat this at the other end of the plank. Remove the plank and use its shape and bevel as a master for the new plank.

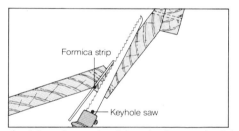

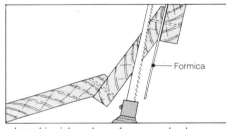
Avoid cutting or bruising the lower plank bevel and inside edge of upper plank

Cutting the scarf joints

The length of the scarf should be about eight times the thickness of the plank. Make a cardboard template for use at all of the joints and cut the position for the step in the scarf with a marking knife.

Slip thin wedges between the planks at the lower edge, to make room for a chisel. Trim the scarf with a bevel-edge chisel. Repeat this at the other end, remembering to cut the scarf on the outside face of the rear join.

Take the old plank, lay it on the new wood, and mark round it. Remember to add on the scarf lengths and a fraction extra at each end. Cut the top edge and ends, and smooth the faces and edges with a spokeshave and block plane. Cut the lower edge, but allow about half an inch (10mm) extra for trimming later.

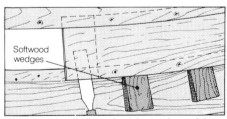
Trim the scarfs from inside and outside

Transfer the marks for the bevel to the top edge of the new plank. Pencil in the lower line of the bevel and cut it with a chisel, finishing with a small block plane (a plane with a slightly convex iron is ideal for this job).

Cut the scarfs on the replacement plank. Hold the plank in position, and trim the scarfs where necessary. It is vital that the plank should rest easily in place: if it is difficult to fit without fastenings, it will

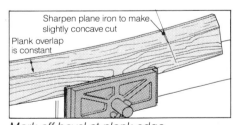
Mark off bevel at plank edge

be impossible to pull home with the fastenings. While the plank lies in position, hold a batten along its lower edge and on to the edges of the original plank, to test the lower edge for a fair sweeping curve. Pencil in any adjustments, remove the batten, and trim the new plank to its finished shape.

Apply preservative to the new plank, and to any timber exposed in the removal and refitting operations.

Cut two rectangles of brownpaper to the size of the scarf faces, soak them in glue, and place one on each scarf face. Using the same holes, drill through from the inside on the lower edge of the plank and from the outside on the upper edge.

Where there is difficulty in manoeuvring a drill into position, a bicycle spoke, flattened and sharpened at one end and held in the chuck of a hand drill, makes a very useful flexible drill bit.

Drive all the nails in before fitting and rivetting the burrs, and clenching the scarf joint fastenings.

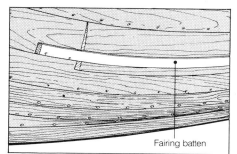

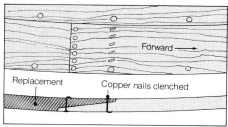
Clench scarf joint

Trim lower edge after fitting and before fastening

At the after end of the repair a straight rather than a stepped scarf can be used. This is quite satisfactory provided its feather edge trails aft.

Fitting a plank at the ends of the boat

At the ends of the boat the bevel runs out and, instead, a short rebate is worked into the top outside and bottom inside edge of the plank. Generally, the upper rebate is a little longer than the rebate it slides behind. The landing dimension (overlap) remains the same. The plank is then slotted up and under the rebate of the upper plank and into the rebate on the lower plank.

After removing the damaged plank, and before cutting the rebates on the new plank, measure their lengths, and check the angles at which they are cut. Two types are used: one square and one bevelled,

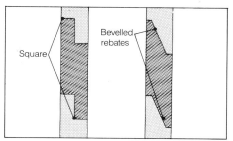
Section through planking and stern

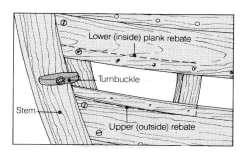

and the appropriate one must be worked. Screw a turnbuckle at the stem to hold the plank while it is being fitted.

This will restrain the plank and prevent it from springing out and damaging the rebate of the upper plank.

Fitting a new garboard

This is probably the most difficult plank to fit on the hull, because it has to incorporate a severe twist at each end.

It is necessary to take out the first plank before removing the garboard and when refitting it you may need to screw a

temporary reinforcing cleat to the end to prevent the garboard from splitting as it is twisted into position. If the plank is very difficult to fit, wrap towels around it, soak them with boiling water, and manipulate the plank when it is a little more pliable.

Fastenings to the garboard
Plug the old fastening holes, and fix the garboard to the keel with countersunk screws about four times the plank thickness, and between 1 and 3 inches (25 and 75mm) apart.

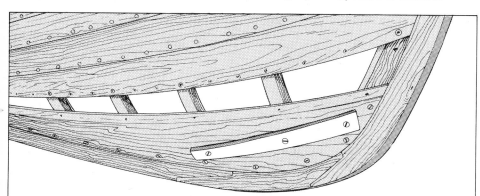
The cleat is removed after all fastenings are in place

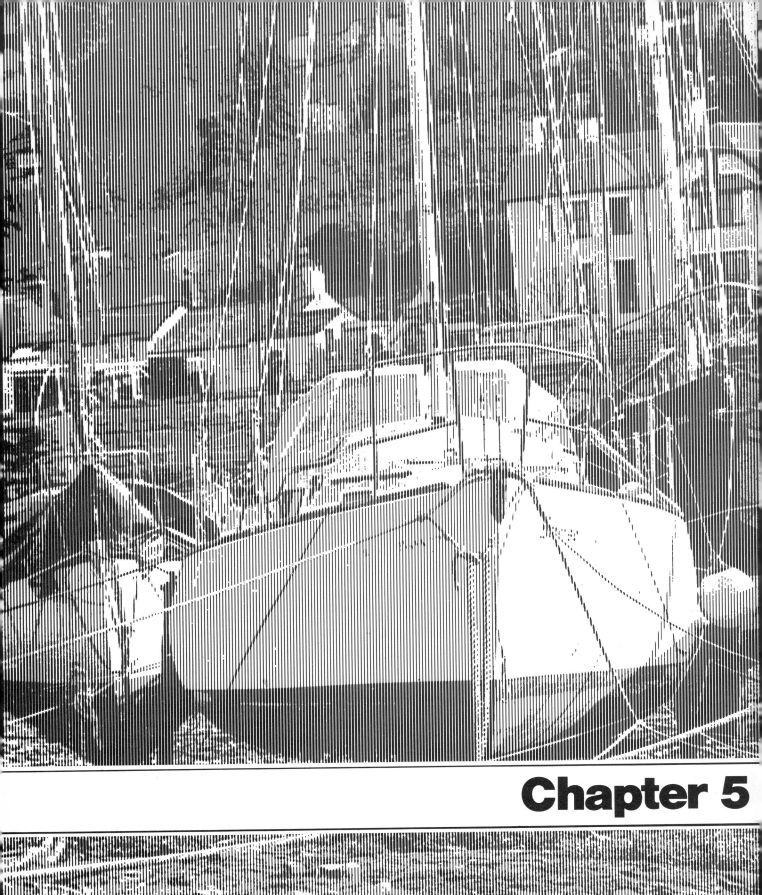

Chapter 5

Fibreglass Hulls

Fibreglass hulls

Fibreglass hulls are made from laminations of glass fibre matt or cloth, impregnated and bonded together with polyester resin. The most common method of laying up a hull is to build the laminate against a female mould, covering the mould first with a releasing agent, like furniture polish, then a thick layer of resin (the gel coat), prior to bonding on the inner cloth laminates.

The gel coat is backed and supported by a fine surfacing matt, and the heavier layers of glass fibre random matt or woven rovings are bonded to it. For convenience in handling, the glass fibre sheets are laid in fairly small sections. Adjacent layers are overlapped to maintain consistent strength.

Areas in the hull that are under most stress and require greater strength can be laminated more thickly. Additives can be mixed into the resin to increase its hard-wearing and abrasion-resistant properties, to enable it to be used as a filler, or to create a non-slip deck finish.

Frames, floors and bulkheads are normally built into the hull, before it is removed from the mould. Decks are usually moulded separately and bolted and bonded to the hull.

Fibreglass boats are not maintenance free. Good quality hulls, purchased new and handled with care, may not require painting for the first four or five years of use, but even where the gel coat is in good condition, (without surface pitting, bubbles or scratches), there are other parts that will deteriorate or show signs of wear.

When assessing the condition of your craft, bear in mind the points indicated in the illustration. Some of them relate to simple cosmetic problems. Others which are easily overlooked may be the only warning signs before part of the hull fails or the boat deteriorates to the point where expensive repairs are required. Repairs to the hull should be well bonded and faired, with no evidence of de-lamination between the new repair and the hull.

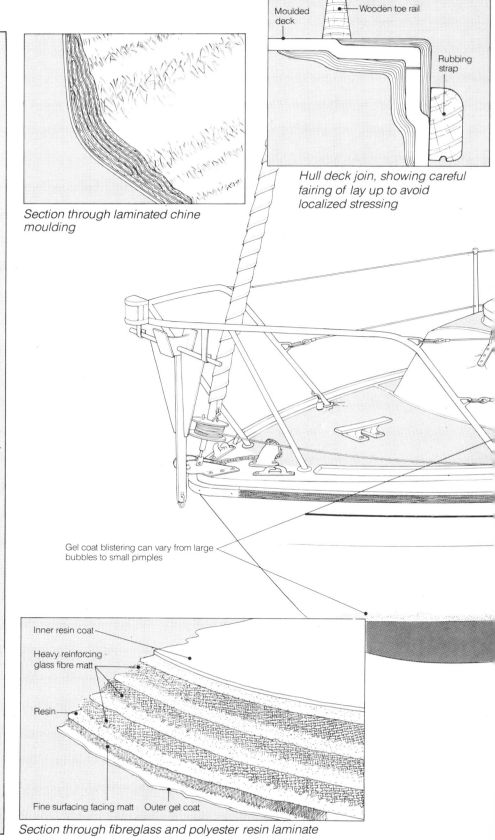

Section through laminated chine moulding

Moulded deck — Wooden toe rail

Rubbing strap

Hull deck join, showing careful fairing of lay up to avoid localized stressing

Gel coat blistering can vary from large bubbles to small pimples

Inner resin coat

Heavy reinforcing glass fibre matt

Resin

Fine surfacing facing matt   Outer gel coat

Section through fibreglass and polyester resin laminate

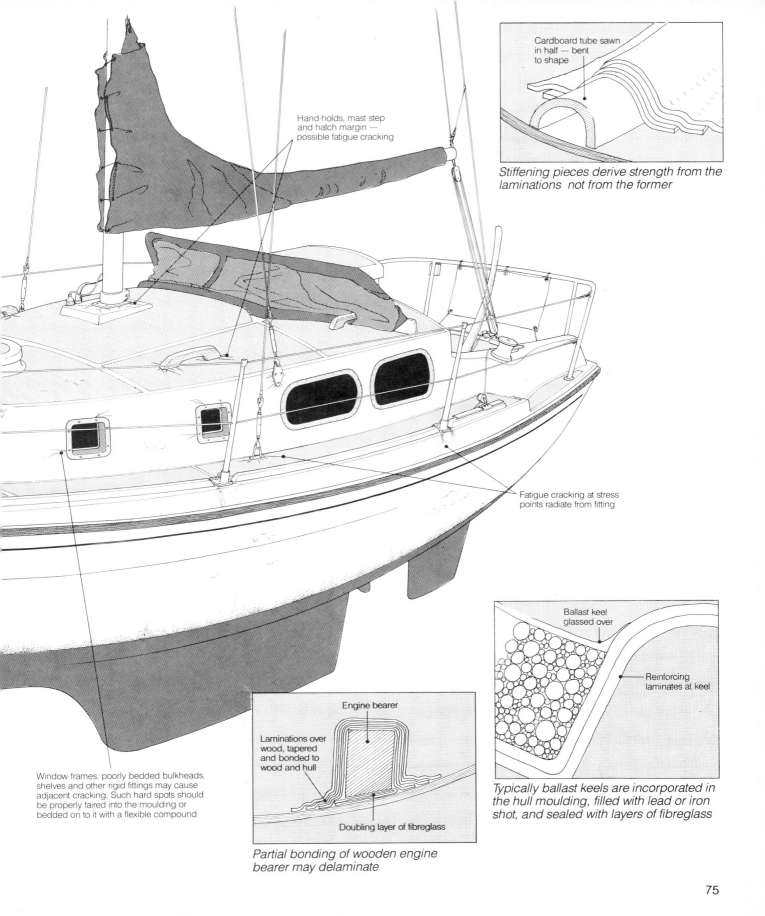

Hand-holds, mast step and hatch margin — possible fatigue cracking

Cardboard tube sawn in half — bent to shape

Stiffening pieces derive strength from the laminations not from the former

Fatigue cracking at stress points radiate from fitting

Window frames, poorly bedded bulkheads, shelves and other rigid fittings may cause adjacent cracking. Such hard spots should be properly faired into the moulding or bedded on to it with a flexible compound

Engine bearer

Laminations over wood, tapered and bonded to wood and hull

Doubling layer of fibreglass

Partial bonding of wooden engine bearer may delaminate

Ballast keel glassed over

Reinforcing laminates at keel

Typically ballast keels are incorporated in the hull moulding, filled with lead or iron shot, and sealed with layers of fibreglass

Outer hull surface   Fibreglass hulls

Staining and bleaching

After two or three years unpainted white topsides begin to yellow, and look dirty. This may be caused by the gel coat yellowing with age, or it may be the result of oil and dirt lying in minute cracks and pit holes in the gel coat. Additives mixed into the resin of a white gel coat will prevent new hulls from yellowing, but for older hulls the only solution is to paint the hull with a two-pack polyurethane paint. Where staining is the result of dirt and oil penetrating the gel coat, the hull should be cleaned and

inspected very carefully. On most craft the gel coat thickness is no more than .6mm thick. Once this is penetrated, water can enter the laminations and even where there are no air traps between the layers of fibreglass, seepage may cause serious problems. Inspect the hull closely for signs that the gel coat has been breached. Wash the stained parts with a detergent, soap or paraffin, to try to remove the stain. Minor scratches can be rubbed back with a car polishing wax. If the staining is deeply ingrained into the hull it will have to be painted.

Where a colouring pigment has been added to the gel coat, some fading of the colour will occur. This may only be noticeable when the boat is viewed from head on, or where shaded parts of the hull are compared to those normally in direct sunlight. Darker colours fade more quickly than lighter ones; dark blue hulls are the worst of all in this respect. Fading, in itself, is not necessarily a problem. Difficulties arise, however, in matching new fibreglass work to the old colour when repairs are carried out.

Blistering beneath the gel coat

This can occur shortly after the moulded hull leaves the mould or long after the boat has been fitted out and is in use. Pockets of air or water are trapped between the laminations, and swell or contract in response to changing temperatures outside. This problem can be serious, particularly where water is trapped, and it might indicate poor laying up procedures. If unchecked the bubbles will enlarge and the condition of the hull will deteriorate further.

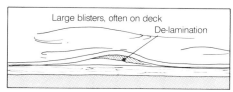

Blistering is usually found below the water-line where opened blisters, exposing the fibre, may permit water to enter the laminate and are difficult to dry

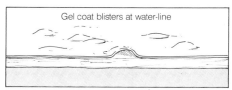

out. Seek such blisters, particularly at laying up time, when they should be opened to dry out before sealing with thickened epoxy resin

Stress cracking

Fibreglass is a brittle material and will not adapt itself to new distortions or stresses. Once the hull and deck mouldings have cured, it will not be possible to ease or spring them into new positions. If there is any tendency to resist the pull, the bolts holding together the deck to hull mouldings should not be used forcefully. Internal stresses will be established in the fibreglass that will result in splitting or fracturing. At best, the tensions within the glass fibre will be locked in, causing localized weakness in high stressed areas. Look around the deck-to-hull join for cracking at the fastenings. Check also where any fitting is drawn up tight to the fibreglass.

Fibreglass hulls are made as a monocoque unit. Load bearing parts of the hull or deck being built up with extra laminates. All points of stress should be reinforced with a thickening of the moulding and, if necessary, extra pieces of wood or steel moulded into the hull to help to dissipate the load. If this is not done, hard spots will form in the moulding, weakening the areas around them. At such points the hull will appear

to be slightly kinked, and fine cracks may occur around the stress point.

This is typical at a poorly fitted bulkhead. Where the fitting is done correctly, the load will be spread over a large area of the hull by laminating a doubler into the moulding, and then placing layers of fibreglass tape, carefully graduating their overlap, so that the bonding tapes taper into the line of the hull. Frequently the doubler is omitted, and the bulkhead is fitted directly against the hull side, with one or perhaps two narrow layers of tape to bond the two together.

All deck fittings, hand holds as well as cleats, winches and fairleads, should be well supported by load-spreading supports in the inside of the moulding. Evidence of stress fracturing should be noted and attended to quickly.

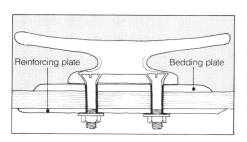

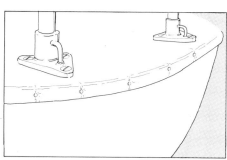

Rubbing strip removed to expose cracking around deck fastening bolts

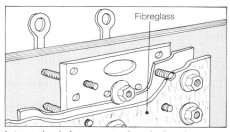

Internal reinforcement for chain plates

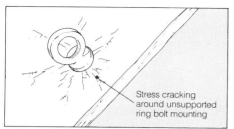

Fine cracks radiating from a fastening may indicate stress fatigue

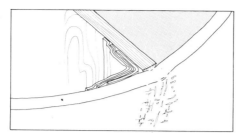

Distortion in hull and cracking reveal fatigue weakening at bulkhead hull joint

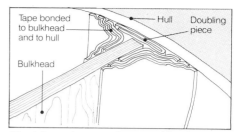

Doubling piece and tapered laminate help eliminate stress points at bulkhead

Fastenings in fibreglass

Although pop-rivets will hold fibreglass, the compressing effect of the pop-rivetting gun tends to crush the fibreglass moulding immediately behind the head of the rivet, weakening its own anchorage point. Screws should not be used to hold any stressed fittings: these should be held by bolts which pass through the fibreglass moulding and tighten against a reinforcing plate incorporated in, or pressed tightly against, the moulding. A large diameter washer with bedding compound beneath, is a suitable reinforcement for bolts not holding stressed fittings.

All fittings that bear directly against the hull or deck moulding should be bedded in a load-spreading, flexible, sealing compound. This ensures a thorough bedding which compensates for the slight irregularities in the surface of the fibreglass, and also prevents seepage of water into the hull.

Cracks in the gel coat surrounding the fastenings, and perhaps a slight looseness in the fittings, indicate unsatisfactory arrangements.

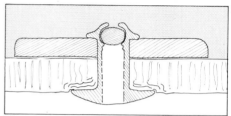

Pop-rivet compresses laminate

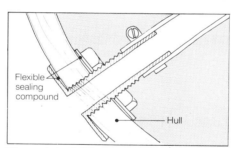

Through-hull fittings need bedding compound inside and out

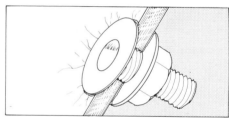

Inadequate bedding compound causes cracking and leakage

Hinge effect

Other signs of fracturing may be evident close against any moulded flanges — surrounding a deck hatch for instance, or at the edges of the cockpit floor, where the fibreglass has been moulded into an abrupt angle. Intermittent stress concentrations along the corner of the

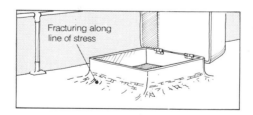

moulding can form a 'hinge' and, in extreme cases, lead to the parting of the moulding at that point.

Wood

Wood is often embedded in the moulding to provide a strong and easily attached anchorage for fittings, engines etc. Moisture sometimes penetrates through the glass fibre to the wood, even if it does not seep past the bolts and other fastenings. Inspect the laminates enclosing the wood for evidence of water penetration. Withdraw one or two screws to check the condition of the wood.

Wood that is partly embedded in fibreglass must be carefully inspected to see whether the bond is sound. Polyester resin is a poor adhesive and, unless the wood is primed with thinned resin prior to bonding, the fibreglass will begin to peel away from the wood.

Superior bonding will be achieved with epoxy resin and a compatible fibreglass cloth.

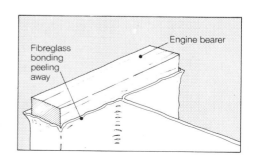

Sandwich construction Fibreglass hulls

The illustration below shows the main features of a sandwich fibreglass hull. The inner and the outer skin are each thinner than the single skin hull, and between them is a core of end grain balsa wood or polyurethane foam. The resulting hull is no heavier than the single fibreglass skin hull, but is considerably stiffer.

It is unusual to use a female mould for a sandwich construction hull. Most hulls are built over an unpolished but fair male mould. The application of the core against the inner skin leaves all the open joints of the core on the outside, where they can be filled prior to applying the outer skin.

Sandwich construction is used for deck mouldings, because it gives a lighter and stronger unit for the equivalent weight of a single skin deck. These are laid in a horizontal female mould, and as there is no violent shape in the surface of the deck, the core is easily cut to shape and glued into position.

After gaps between core segments have been filled, the interior skin is applied to seal the deck structure.

Sandwich hulls need to be treated with care. The outer skin, being thinner than that of a normal fibreglass boat of similar size, punctures more easily. Water that enters the inner core of the hull is difficult to dry out and may, in the enclosed conditions of the hull, produce rot in the wooden core. Also, denting, and quite minor impacts or collisions with other craft, may result in the separation of the inner core and the inside face of one of the skins. Good quality hulls are fitted with cross braces to tie the skins together, and limit the spread of de-lamination, but where these are not fitted, the constant working and twisting of the hull in the water will encourage de-lamination. The more the core separates from the skins of the hull, the greater is the stress on the remaining bonded parts, and the more likely they are to fail at the bond.

Evidence of de-lamination is difficult to spot. Some parts may visibly bulge away from the inner core, and compress when trodden on. Other parts may become completely separated from the core, (negating the structural advantage of the construction) without any superficial indications of failure.

Special fastening and working techniques must be adopted when fitting out or repairing a sandwich hull. Drilling, sawing, and filing must be performed so that the inner and outer skin are not forced away from the inner core. Fastenings must be fitted so that the tightening action of the bolts does not compress the core and distort the skins. For details on handling, repairing, and fastening new fittings, see page 95.

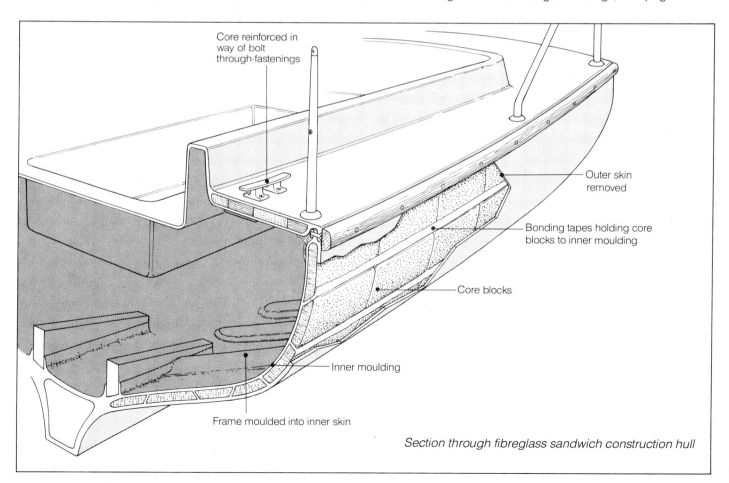

Core reinforced in way of bolt through-fastenings

Outer skin removed

Bonding tapes holding core blocks to inner moulding

Core blocks

Inner moulding

Frame moulded into inner skin

Section through fibreglass sandwich construction hull

Glass fibre is a brittle material. New parts or repairs are better bonded-in than bolted or jointed. Bonding can be reinforced with bolts where appropriate. When it is partially cured or 'green', fibreglass is easily cut with a sharp knife, but once hard, hacksaws or jigsaws will be needed to cut the laminate.

Because of its brittleness and tendency to shatter, sawing, drilling and filing fibreglass should, wherever possible, be directed from the smooth gel coat side towards the rougher inner surface. Where this is impossible, sawing and filing strokes should be light, and at an angle to the surface. Hacksaw and keyhole saw blades can be reversed in the blade holder so that they cut on the return stroke. When drilling from the inside towards the outer skin, place a pad of wood against the outside to support it as the drill breaks through. Sand polyester resins with 'wet and dry' paper, lavishly lubricated with water. When building up a repair that will need rasping and sanding back, add about 10 per cent french chalk (obtainable in bulk from most chemists) to the resin mix. This will ease the sanding operation and reduce the tendency of the resin to clog the tools.

Repair materials

Polyester and epoxy resins can be stored for long periods provided that they are kept cool. The shelf life for a polyester resin is at least one year even if it is stored at above 21° C (70° F) and epoxy resins can be kept longer. Both types of resin are usable provided that they are still liquid, easily mixed, and easily poured or brushed. Once the resin becomes difficult to apply it should be discarded. Thorough impregnation of the glass fibre matting or cloth is essential; if the resins are too thick it will be impossible to guarantee adequate saturation.

The detailed contents of a repair kit depend upon the scale of the work being undertaken. Seek professional advice before assembling the materials. Each kit should include the following items in varying quantities.

Resins
Epoxy resin with hardener, fillers and syringes for measuring quantities.

Polyester resin
The accelerator should be purchased pre-mixed with the resin to simplify mixing. Thixotropic additives, or a separate supply of thickened resin, will be required for saturating fibreglass on vertical or sloping surfaces in order to prevent the resin draining away.

When repairs are to be carried out in cold conditions, it may be necessary to add extra accelerator to the resin before mixing in the catalyst. Always ensure that the accelerator is mixed into the resin before adding the catalyst. Use separate, well marked utensils for each, and store the accelerator well away from the catalyst.

It is dangerous to mix the accelerator directly with the catalyst

Gel coat resins
These should also have the accelerator pre-mixed with the resin. A separate coloured resin will be needed for each moulding colour. A gel coat resin that is painted over the outside of a repair will remain tacky, and will not cure properly unless an evaporation inhibitor is added to the gel coat resin mixture. An alternative method is to press a sheet of polythene against the face of the freshly applied gel coat, and remove it when the resin has fully cured. These precautions are unnecessary when the gel coat resin is painted against the inside face of a mould.

Catalyst paste
Suitable catalyst paste in sufficient quantities for the above resins will be required to harden the resins. A proportion of 2 per cent catalyst to resin is about normal, but more catalyst will be needed when working in cold conditions. Always follow the manufacturer's instructions.

When the catalyst is supplied in paste form, and dispensed from a tube, the quantity of catalyst paste can be measured by the length of squirt. If the catalyst is in liquid form, a simple and, as far as possible, foolproof system should be devised. As quantities of catalyst are so small, it is best to measure the catalyst by volume rather than by weight. A disposable eye dropper can be used; between six and twenty-four drops of catalyst per ounce (25g) of resin will give a usable proportion. Measuring can be simplified if the dispenser is graduated. Add more catalyst for cold conditions, less for hot.

Glass fibre
Some 7 ounce (198g) glass cloth, and some lighter (1 to 1½ ounces (30g) per square foot) glass matt will be needed. Matt is cheaper than cloth, and can be moulded into shape more readily.

If an epoxy resin is used for the laying up of glass fibre, check that the glass fibre is of an appropriate type.

Repair equipment
As well as the supplies listed above, have some paper cups handy for mixing the resin, some stirrers, several cheap ½ to ¾ inch (12 to 20mm) paint brushes, french chalk, masking tape, various thin wooden battens, pieces of card, wire and string.

Safety
Apply barrier cream to the hands and arms before starting work. Apply it also to the face, neck and other exposed parts if moulding is performed in difficult or awkward places. Wipe hands clean and dust them with french chalk or talcum powder whenever they get messy or sticky.

Used rags should be taken away from the workshop. Do not pile them together, as the heat generated in the curing of the resin may cause a fire.

Never allow the catalyst to come into contact with the accelerator. Use resins which are pre-mixed with the accelerator. If working conditions are very cold and an accelerator boost is recommended, keep it away from the catalyst and make sure it is well mixed into the resin before adding the catalyst.

Clean tools in acetone, but do not wash resin away from the skin with the acetone. This will remove the natural oiliness in the skin, increasing the likelihood of more resin adhering to the hands once work is resumed.

Boat repairs are rarely carried out in ideal conditions, but the following guidelines, if followed, will help in achieving a satisfactory repair.

1 Try to keep the working area dry and warm. Avoid working with fibreglass on wet or very humid days if the boat is outside. Where conditions are difficult, arrange temporary sheltering. Use heaters to warm and dry the work. Space heaters, convector heaters, an electric heat gun (used with caution), even hot water bottles pressed against the resin (with a layer of polythene interposed to prevent it bonding) will help to keep away the damp. Do not use paraffin stoves, as these add moisture to the atmosphere.

2 Clean the area to be repaired. Greasy marks (even those left by sweaty hands) will prevent resin from bonding, and should be scrubbed.

3 Chip away the gel coat to expose the glass fibre laminations and vacuum away the dust before building up the new work.

4 Work with small sheets of glass fibre, and small quantities of resin.

Make sure that each layer of glass fibre is very thoroughly saturated with resin, that it is well into position, and lies flat against other layers. Do not lay up the laminate too quickly. Build the laminations to about 1/4 to 3/8 inch (5 to 10mm) thick, and leave to cure. The heat generated (exotherm) as the resins cure in thicker laminates may crack and weaken the structures. Pour away unused resin as it begins to go lumpy.

5 Use a thicker thixotropic resin, or add appropriate fillers, when working on a vertical or sloping surface.

6 Where superior adhesion is required use epoxy resins rather than polyester resins. If wood is to be bonded to the fibreglass it is best to use epoxy resin, especially where the surface areas are small, or where the wood will be regularly soaked in water, or under stress. If the bonding area of the wood is large, warmed polyester resin can be used instead to prime the wood surface, and glass fibre then laid up as normal. Bulkheads are fitted in this way.

Polyester resins will bond to hardened epoxy resins and vice

versa, they should never be used together when both are wet.

7 Use paint brushes to apply the resin, and to prod and stipple the resin into the glass fibre. If the brush begins to pull the glass fibres away from the work, add more resin. After the brushes have been used for a while they should be left to soak in acetone (with a polythene bag placed over the containers to inhibit evaporation). The brush should be wiped dry before using, but it is not necessary to remove all traces of the acetone, as this is compatible with the resin. Brushes washed in detergent, should be dried and then soaked in acetone and wiped to ensure no moisture is introduced to the glass fibre lamination.

8 Clean hands with an emulsion hand cleaner. Do not use solvents to clean the skin. If solvents have been used to clean resin from working clothes, change the overalls before standing near an open fire.

Repairs to gel coat blemishes

At the end of each season, and during very hot weather, the outer (gel coat) surface of the moulded hull should be inspected for signs of blistering and cracking. Most hulls over eight years old, and newer ones that have been left in the water over the winter, will begin to show signs of surface deterioration.

Slight surface irregularities that do not penetrate the gel coat (very small blisters, scratches and pimples) may

hold the dirt and be difficult to clean, but are not problems requiring immediate attention. However, the dirt and uneven surface may hide cracking which, if it penetrates through the brittle gel coat, may allow water into the inner laminates and cause a weakening in the structure.

It is often very difficult to detect these cracks. The only way in most cases is to scrub the surface clean, and then to check to see if the scrubbing and

scouring has removed the dirt from the crack. If it has, the crack is unlikely to be deep, but if in doubt, warm the area with a heat gun or hair drier, and run polyester resin into the crack. Burnish the surface with a clean rag once the resin has soaked in, and before it begins to cure. This procedure will seal the gel coat, but if there is an underlying structural weakness causing the gel coat to crack, this should also be attended to (see pages 96-9).

Blistering of the gel coat
It is essential that liquid found trapped behind blisters is washed out with fresh water, and then left to dry.

Most gel coats will have small blisters somewhere on the surface. If they are less than 1/16 inch (2mm) and scattered

over the hull they do not constitute a serious problem and do not require immediate attention. In time they may enlarge, and then will need filling. Where small blisters cluster, or form a line, they should be noted and included in the winter maintenance list, when they should be opened, vacuumed, and filled

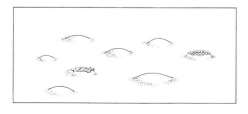

with resin or epoxy putty. If the problem is widespread, the gel coat should be gently sanded and then painted with a suitable two pack polyurethane paint. (see page 306)

Larger blisters
Blisters between ¼ and ¾ inch (6 and 20mm) should be inspected with care. They are often quite easy to see, and obvious to the touch. Open a few sample blisters with a pricker, and flush out any liquid that may have accumulated beneath the bubble, with fresh water. Dry

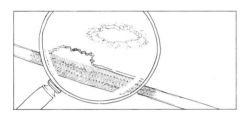

the cavity thoroughly. If the blistering occurs between the coats of a double gel coat, the base of the cavity will be sealed. These bubbles can be left and corrected at any convenient time. There may even be an advantage in leaving the pricking and filling for a while, to allow the formation of bubbles to cease before remedial action is taken.

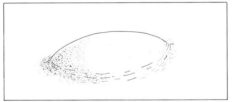

If the broken blisters expose an inner glass fibre laminate, thoroughly impregnated with resin (this will be hard, shiny and wet looking) the bubbles can

be left to the end of the season when they should be opened, dried, cleaned, and vacuumed, before being filled and levelled with epoxy filler.

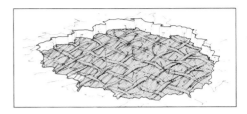

If the opened blister reveals dry glass fibre without a coating of resin to bond the fibres into a solid and almost impervious surface, the blisters should be attended to at once. If they are allowed to remain, water will enter the glass fibre laminate. The technique for cutting back and filling these blisters is described below.

Swellings beneath the gel coat
These can appear as low oval humps anywhere on the moulding. Sizes can vary from between ¾ inch to over two inches (20 to 50mm). They are the result of inadequate saturation of the glass fibre during the lay up of the laminate, and although not in themselves serious, numbers of these swellings may indicate a poorly constructed moulding. Swellings should be opened, flushed and dried if necessary, and injected with epoxy resin, or cut back and built up with glass fibre.

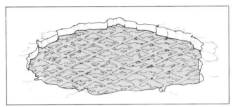

Blisters swell in the heat – mark when seen

Most of the blemishes mentioned above can be remedied by breaking back the blister, cleaning and drying the cavity, and filling it with an epoxy resin filler.

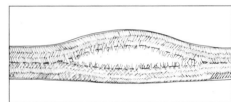

Separation of laminates

Where unbonded glass fibre is revealed at the base of the cavity, the following technique should be used.

Repairing blisters
Break open the bubbles. As each bubble is broken, mark around it with a marker pen so that it is not overlooked during the filling process.

Use the handle of the pricker or bradawl to tap the surrounding gel coat. If the coat cracks, or falls away, continue tapping until a sound bond between the gel coat and the resin is reached.

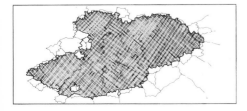

Inspect the glass fibre laminate. Glass should be saturated and thoroughly bonded by the resin. Areas of dry, unbonded fibre should be ground back until solid resin and fibreglass is reached. Wear goggles and a mask for this dirty work. Use a resin bonded sanding disc mounted in an electric drill for quick cutting. Vacuum away the dust and flush the area with warm water. Dry it very thoroughly.

Apply polyester resin to the cavity and lay in a shaped piece of glass fibre matt. Saturate this with resin, and stipple it into position. Continue to build up to the level of the outer surface. Shallow depressions can be filled with epoxy putty. Apply a thick coat of epoxy resin to this, and leave it to cure. File and sand back the

finish, dry the surface, and apply more resin if necessary. Finish with fine 'wet and dry' paper, and then burnishing cream. Because of its superior strength and adhesive properties, epoxy resin should be used to build the finish when the subsurface is rough or irregular.

Filling cavities in the lamination
Sand back the gel coat. If there is evidence of water penetration, the outer surface of the lamination will need sanding back. After drying, rebuild the structure and thickness as described above. Where there is no evidence of moisture, drill several holes through the surface, stopping the holes as they reach the cavity. The holes should be sufficiently large to accept the nozzle of a plastic syringe. Inject epoxy resin glue

into the cavity, forcing glue down each hole until no more can be forced in. Press the swelling down, and wipe away any resin that wells up the holes.

Lay a sheet of polythene over the area and place weights on top of the swelling to hold it down while the resin cures.

Note: the curing time for epoxy glue cannot be accelerated by adding a

Do not overfill swelling with resin

greater proportion of hardener. A reduction in curing time can be effected

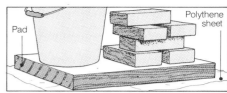
Leave weights until resin is cured

by pre-heating the glass fibre before injecting the resin.

Drying the inner laminates
If surface defects have allowed water to saturate the inner laminates, the gel coat covering the affected area should be removed, and the laminate exposed so that it can dry outside. This may take at least 3 months outside, and it would help to bring the boat into a controlled environment. Flush the area with warm

water to rinse away any salt that may prevent drying, and leave the hull for about 4 weeks to dry out. To speed drying, the area can be warmed with a hair drier; heat gun, or convector heater, but avoid excessive heat (it should never be too hot to touch) which may damage the laminate. Solvents can be used to speed up the drying process, but seek

professional advice first.

Where blisters are close together, and large areas of gel coat are falling away to reveal resin-starved glass fibre laminate, ask a professional surveyor to assess the condition, and the possibility of repair.

Hull repairs

Wherever possible, try to work from the inside, as well as from the outside of the hull. There are several reasons for this:

1 Impact damage to a fibreglass hull ruptures the resin and fibreglass laminations adjacent to the point of impact. As well as repairing the more obvious damage, this area of weakened resin will need restoring to its former strength. The extent of the cracking and buckling of the hull will be evident from inside the hull, and can be ground back, and reinforced with fibreglass.

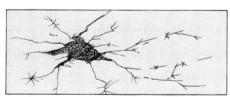
Impact and associated fracturing

2 The repair will be stronger if the lay-up of the glass fibre is on the inside of the hull. The wider the bevel on which the new fibreglass is laid, the greater will be

the strength of the repair. Not only will the bond between the new and the original fibreglass be stronger, it will also be possible to fair in the new repair from the inside. This is very important, as a well-bonded patch that fits abruptly to the fibreglass hull will introduce a localized stiffening around the repair that may cause weakening of the hull, and even the separation of the new repair from the hull.

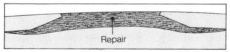
Section through satisfactory repair

Abrupt joints form hard spots in hull

3 If the repair bevel is ground, and then laid up on the inside, finishing work on the outside of the hull is kept to a

minimum, and the problems of matching the gel colour across a wide margin is also avoided.

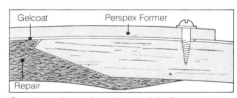
Section of repair with outside former

4 Where there is access to the inside of the hull, a sheet of formica or thin perspex can be screwed to the outside of the hull and used as a former, against which the fibreglass can be laid.

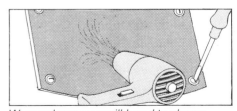
Warmed perspex will bend to shape

Patching damaged fibreglass
It is sometimes necessary to make the initial cuts into the hull without knowing what fittings, wires or other

obstructions lie behind the damaged part. Use a trepanning cutter to cut a circular plug from the hull, about 3 to 4 inches (80 to 100 mm) diameter. The

plug should be sufficiently large to allow a hand into the hull to check for obstructions.

Wherever possible cut all patches with curved sides and large radiused corners. These are easier to fit and fair than straight sided patches, and are less likely to introduce hard spots into the hull, which may result in fatigue failure at the edge of the repair.

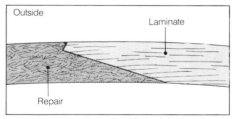

Trepanning cutter

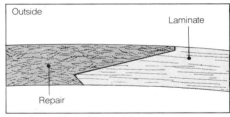

Section through hull with inside access

Section with only outside access

Cutting the bevel

The repair bevel should be cut at as an acute angle to the line of the hull as practical. Where the lay up bevel is on the inside of the hull, the outer bevel can be short and nearly at right angles to the surface of the outer skin. If the main lay up bevel is on the outside face of the hull, then it is necessary to grind a shallow step at the edge, so that the new gel coat can be butted against the existing coat, reducing the amount that the original gel coat is rubbed back.

If, in the course of cutting back and bevelling the edges of the damaged area, dry glass fibres are encountered in the laminate, they should be ground out into a shallow 'V', and saturated with resin, prior to laying up the repair patch. An electric hand grinder should be used for this operation. Goggles and a breathing mask must be worn.

Laying up the patch

Where a patch is to be grafted into the hull, or where there is a large built-up repair to the hull, it is good practice to lay up the repair patch (either on the female mould, or on the former pressed against the outside of the hull) thinner than the hull thickness. Once the patch is in position, or partially laid up, its thickness is increased by laying larger sheets of glass fibre behind the patch, overlapping it onto the undamaged hull. The resulting thickness at the join will be about 25 per cent thicker than the normal hull and patch thickness. Patches grafted into position in this way are easier to fit, and will readily take the shape of the existing hull. By building the join slightly thicker than the patch or hull, hard spots, with their resulting stresses, are avoided.

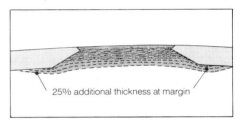

Taper repair into line of hull

Matching the gel coat

It is very difficult to achieve an exact colour match between the original hull and the new patch. This is because the colour of the original finish will have faded. Burnish back the surface of the gel coat near to the damaged area, in order to discover the original tone and colour of the gel coat. Match the new gel coat as closely as possible to the original.

Try to burnish or sand away as little of the gel coatings as possible, otherwise, as the coloured gel is removed, a 'halo' of lighter toned resin will appear to surround the join.

Remember to mix an evaporation inhibiting additive to the gel coat resin, or cover the gel coat with polythene to ensure thorough hardening of resin.

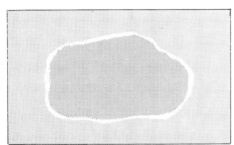

A 'halo' will appear at the margin of the join when sanding has thinned gelcoat finish.

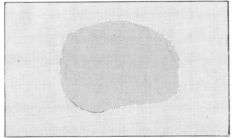

If perfect match is unobtainable, leave patch slightly darker. In time it may fade to correct tone.

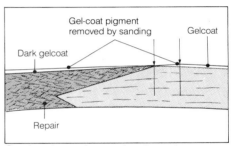

Section through margin of repair, to show cause of 'halo' in polished finish.

Cracks and small holes 1-8 inches

1 Cut the edges of the laminates with a keyhole saw, to make the hole a regular shape, and file the edges to a 'V' so that the laminates will effectively clamp themselves into the hole. Wherever possible file from the outside gel coat towards the inner laminates.

2 Chip away the gel coat from the inner, rough face of the moulding to expose the glass fibre reinforcements. Brush away the sanding dust and wash the area with white spirit or acetone. Wipe the surfaces dry.

3 Cut a strip of fibreglass cloth, sufficiently large to cover the hole, and mix a small quantity of polyester resin. Apply the resin to the inside edges of the hole, and press the cloth into position. Stipple more resin around the edge to bond the cloth securely to the hull. Brush resin on to the cloth and leave it to harden. As the resin begins to cure, mix a very small quantity of new resin and brush it on to the inside of the repair. This will gently mould the cloth into the shape of the hull. Leave the resin to cure.

4 Cut several pieces of glass matt, and mix up a small quantity of resin. Lay up the repair patch, both on the inside and on the outside. Each layer should extend a little beyond the layer beneath.

5 Build the repair in stages. If the hull is more than 3/8 inch (10mm) thick, at least two stages will be needed, so that heat build-up does not crack the laminate. Continue adding the layers of reinforcing matt until patch is slightly raised, both on the inside and outside of the hull.

6 Leave to cure. File and sandpaper the outside back to shape and finish with one or two layers of epoxy resin and paint, or with some suitably tinted gel coat resin. Finally sand with very fine 'wet and dry' paper, followed by burnishing cream.

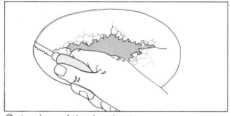
Cut edge of the laminate

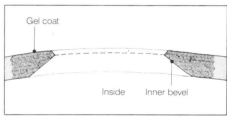
Section showing inner and outer bevels

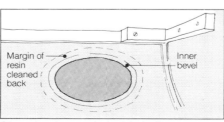
Clean back margin inside hull

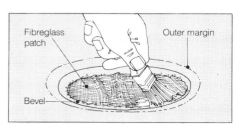
Use plenty of resin when stippling

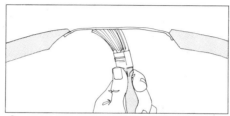
Once first layer is partially cured, brush more resin inside, pressing into curve of hull

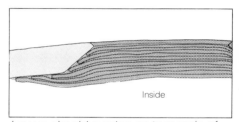
Lay up should overlap on to margin of hole with additional 25% thickness on inside

Finished patch

Repairs to fibreglass hulls are more conspicuous by their poor finish than by their poor bonding. Bonding failure is usually the result of laying up the fibreglass in damp conditions, or inadequate sanding and de-greasing before the resin is applied.

A common fault is that the sides of the laminate are bonded out of alignment. This is a very difficult fault to hide, and care should be taken to prevent the problem from arising.

The surface of the hull should be held with improvised clamps. Resin-impregnated tapes are laid between them and allowed to cure before the clamps can be removed and the hole covered and built up. Where clamps are needed it will probably be necessary to build up the repair from the outside.

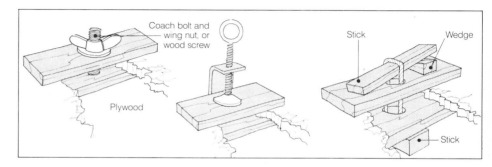

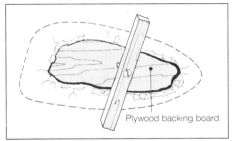
Clamping to hold backing pad

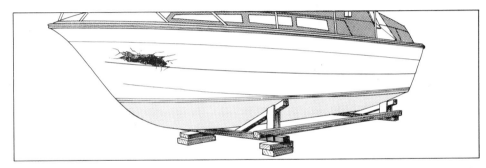

Repairs from the outside

1 Shape and bevel the hole as described above.

2 Sand around the outer edge and scrape away the gel coat from the inner rough face, to expose the glass fibre reinforcements.

3 Devise and fit a plug to act as a backing board to hold the glass fibre matt as the layers are built up. It need not be strong, but it should be screwed, tied, or wedged into place so that it does not move when the first laminating coats are worked into position. Do not use materials that will rot or rust in the enclosed hull and make sure that the fibreglass not only bonds to the hull, but also to the supporting piece, to prevent this from rattling about once the repair is complete and the fastenings released.

4 Cut a piece of fibreglass matt to shape, and mix a small quantity of resin. Apply resin to the backing board, and to the inside edges of the hole. Work the matt into position. A cut may have to be made to allow the matt to fit around the holding screws or wires. Alternatively the matt can be cut into sections and laid separately, each overlapping the other by about 2 inches (50 mm). Stipple resin on to the matt, and work it tightly into the corners of the hole. Add more matt to build up the repair.

5 Allow the first few layers to cure before cutting or removing the fastenings holding the backing board, then build up the repair to its final layer.

6 File and sand back the repair, until it lies fair with the hull. Backing pads sometimes introduce distortion, and the area should be carefully levelled.

Use an epoxy filler to level the surface of the hull before finishing with coloured gel coat or two-pack polyurethane paint.

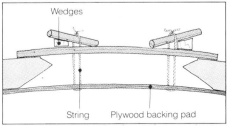
Backpad held by string and wedges

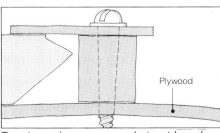
Toggle and screw may obstruct bevel

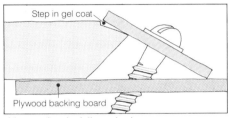
Alternative holding device

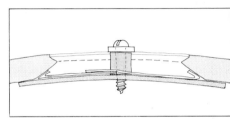
Laying up avoiding clamp

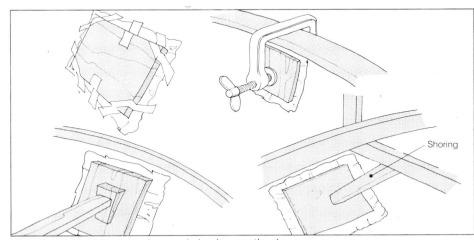
A variety of inside clamping and shoring methods

This repair method is, of course, equally suited to repairing patches accessible from the inside, particularly if the damaged part of the moulding is flat, or nearly so. Where there is easy access to the inside, the board should be wedged, shored or taped into position, with a sheet of polythene taped to its outer face to prevent the resin bonding to it. Once the repair is cured, the board and polythene can be removed.

Repairing large areas of compound curvature

There are two ways in which repairs of this type can be carried out. Where the curvature is fairly gentle, battens can be fixed to the inside of the hull and the fibreglass repair built against them. This method is described on page 89. Where the damage extends to parts that have moulded-in features, the only satisfactory method is to find or make up a suitable female mould, and lay up a new section of hull, which is then bonded in. This procedure is described below.

Making a mould
Sometimes the owner may be able to locate and obtain permission to use the original mould in which the boat was made. This greatly simplifies matters, as the new part can be made under ideal factory conditions, and simply cut to shape and fitted to the hull. Unfortunately, manufacturers are often unwilling to withdraw a mould from the production line in order to lay up a small repair patch, and, instead, the owner will need to make a female mould from a similar boat.

Whether or not the original mould is used, the exact location and extent of the damaged area should be ascertained. This is often far from simple, as the damage may be some distance from any readily identifiable part of the boat's structure, yet the dimensions must be clear and easily interpreted.

Tidy up the shape of the hole and make up a thin cardboard template to fit over the hole. Cut and tape together gores in the edges of the template to help it to lie snugly against the hull. At least two separate pairs of positioning lines should be devised for locating the patch in the female mould, or against the same part of a similar hull. Take dimensions from moulded features, not from fittings whose position may vary from boat to boat. Some ingenuity will be needed, but time spent measuring and checking this vital information may prevent expensive and embarrassing mistakes.

Where an original mould is available, the procedure for laying up the new laminate is quite straightforward, and will be found on page 87. If it is necessary to make the female mould from another hull, the following technique should be used.

Using the template and measurements, mark off the area of the hull from which the mould will be taken. Clean that part of the hull very thoroughly. If the repair is to the topsides of the boat, polish the hull with a slightly abrasive car burnishing cream. Scratches and pits do not need to be filled, and may, in any case, be very difficult to merge into the finish of the hull. These blemishes will appear in the female mould as small bumps or ridges, and can be sanded out before the repair patch is laid up.

Coat all those parts of the hull that may come into contact with the polyester resin with a wax furniture polish,

and then a thin coating of a PVA (poly-vinyl-alcohol) release emulsion.

Check that every part of the area is covered with the emulsion, and also that there is no obstruction to prevent the mould's release. Lay up the fibreglass and resin laminate in the order described on page 87. Mould the reinforcing pieces around and across the mould to hold it rigid when it is released from the side of the boat. This is explained on page 101.

When the laying up of the mould is complete, and the bracing pieces are bonded across, release the mould from the side of the boat. Polish the inner (moulding) face of the mould until it is smooth and free from ridges, pimples and scratches.

Laying up fibreglass

Wherever possible, fibreglassing work should be carried out in a warm and dry environment. When working outside, arrange adequate rain shelter, and take the lay up and curing time into account.

Do not, for instance, leave a freshly applied laminate to cure overnight if it is likely to be shrouded in evening river mist, and then covered with morning dew. Moisture will become trapped in the structure and weaken it. Extra catalyst to ensure that the laminate cures more quickly, shelter, and overnight background warmth, may all be required to ensure a satisfactory result.

Preparing the mould

The inner face of the mould should be smooth and shiny. This is particularly important if the new part is to replace a section of the topsides of the craft.

If a lot of sanding and smoothing down has been involved, improve the overall finish by brushing the inner face of the mould with a coat or two of shellac. This is an alcohol-based, quick-drying sealer, obtainable from most paint shops. Allow the shellac to harden (about 30 minutes)

before rubbing down the surface with very fine sandpaper. Wax the face of the mould with a good quality, slow drying, furniture wax, which will cover the mould, and fill any remaining scratches and holes.

Prepare the fibreglass matt by tearing or cutting it into suitable sized pieces. If there are moulded-in features on the mould, have a supply of smaller pieces that can be worked into the shape. Bear in mind when cutting or rough-shaping

the pieces that, although matt can be worked into curves and odd shapes, the resulting stretching of the matt often leaves lines of weakness. It is better to avoid this by making the pieces smaller, and overlapping them by about 2 inches (50 mm).

Paint on the release agent. Follow the manufacturer's instructions, apply it thinly and very thoroughly, and leave it to dry.

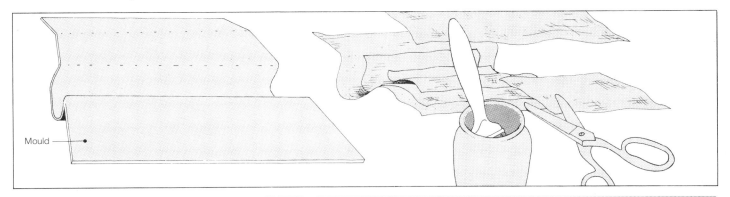

Mould

Moulding fibreglass

Coat hands and wrists with barrier cream, and arrange adequate ventilation if you find the fumes released by the resins unpleasant.

Read and follow the manufacturer's instructions before mixing the resins. If working in cold, or hot and humid conditions, slightly increase the proportion of catalyst.

If the repair patch is a large or complicated shape, make sure you allow adequate working time to saturate the glass fibre thoroughly before the resin begins to go lumpy and unworkable.

1 Paint the inside of the mould with the appropriate gel coat resin, and leave it to go hard. No further coats of resin should be painted on to the mould until this is set, otherwise they will pull the gel coat

into wrinkles. Test for dryness at the edges of the mould, not at the middle, where grease or finger-marks may weaken the bond between the gel coat and the lay up resin.

2 Mix up a suitable quantity of resin, and paint it thickly on to the gel coat. Press the first layer of matt against the resin, and work it into the contours of the mould. Overlap pieces by about 2 inches (50mm). Press the glass matt well into the resin, leave it for a few moments

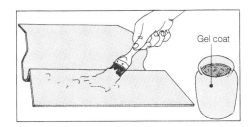

Gel coat

to soak up the resin before pouring or brushing on more resin. Stipple the matt with a paint brush, used with a prodding action, to ensure a thorough impregnation of the resin in the fibreglass. There must not be any gaps between the mould and the glass fibre, and no 'dry' glass fibre. If the stippling action of the brush tends to pull the matt apart, add more resin.

3 The moulding process can be interrupted between layers, but should never be left with glass matt partly wetted out. A second and third layer of glass fibre laid into the mould should be very thoroughly stippled into place.

Do not discontinue moulding for more than a day, otherwise the bond between the new polyester resin and the hardened laminate will be weaker than it should be.

Repairing large areas of compound curvature (continued)

Stagger the joints between the layers, and where there are lines of weakness over sharp or awkward corners, experiment with different, narrower pieces of cloth, laid in different patterns to overcome and compensate for the weakness in the initial layers.

4 Continue to build up the layers of laminate. Stop before the laminate is much thicker than ¼ inch (6mm) to prevent the exotherm (a result of the resin curing reaction) from damaging the laminate.

5 Finish laminating when the repair patch reaches the required thickness and leave to harden. It is best if the patch is thinner than the hull moulding, as it will flex into position more easily. The overlays on the inside will strengthen the patch to the original hull thickness and make the thickness at the edge about 25 per cent greater than the original.

6 Clean up the inside of the mould. Snip off, or sand down, areas of frayed stranding. Sand down the bigger, unnecessary bumps and uneven areas.

7 Brush or vacuum out the inside of the moulding, and apply a couple of pure resin coats to seal the surface.

For details of workshop practice, cleaning brushes, and measuring resin mixtures etc, see page 80.

Take the trouble to prepare the right working conditions, mix the resins to the manufacturer's instructions, and apply the resin to the glass fibre generously.

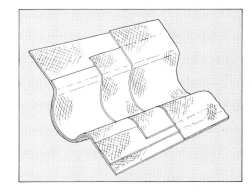

Poor results are often caused by skimping the resin, or overlooking gaps between laminations. If the mould is left overnight to cure, the inner face of the moulding can be trimmed and sanded before subsequent layers are added.

Releasing the mould
This is very unlikely to be a problem if the initial precautions of waxing and then painting on the PVA release emulsion have been taken. Work from the edge of the mould, prising it away, and the new patch will suddenly come away. (It is sometimes a help to pour warm water between the mould and the moulding.)

Fitting the patch to the hull
The patch must be very carefully shaped, and its edges bevelled to a point. Make the patch over-size, to allow for slight errors in measurements when making the initial female mould.

Hold the patch against the hull, and draw round it. If this is impractical, use the same cardboard template that was used for transferring the shape of the break to the hull of the boat from which the female mould was taken. Draw round this, and cut the broken part of the hull away to allow for the fitting of the patch. If it is obvious that there will be problems in aligning the patch, trim and position the most critical direction before cutting that dimension to fit.

Cut round, and fair up the hole. Bevel the sides, clean away the inner resin until the glass fibres are exposed, and sand a constant one inch (25mm) margin around the outside edge of the hole. Once the patch is positioned and held by clamps, the exact location of the patch can be adjusted, and its fairness with the curvature of the hull checked with a springy batten. If, because of excessive curvature, the patch tends to lie proud, inset it slightly, so that the bonding laminates can fill the depressions by the joins, and the high spot can be sanded without seriously weakening the laminate. This, however, is an unfortunate circumstance, which accurate measuring at the outset would have prevented.

Tape across the gap between the hull and the patch. Build up the strength of the tapes, and allow them to cure, before removing the clamps and bonding in the new patch.

Polyester resin can be used for this repair, but because of its superior adhesive qualities, it is better to use epoxy resin. This has the advantage of strength, but is more difficult to handle, and the humidity and temperature conditions of the work area are also more critical.

Wear disposable polythene gloves, and follow the manufacturer's instructions, when mixing and using the resin. Check that the glass fibre matt selected to bond the patch to the hull is compatible with the epoxy resin. (The binder that holds the fibres of a random matt cloth should dissolve in the resin, or the bond between the fibre and the resin will be impaired).

Do not increase the proportion of hardener to accelerate the curing process. Proportions are determined to give the optimum strength to the resin mix, and adding more hardener will only result in a weaker bond.

Bond in the patch. Add suitable fillers to the outer resin coats to ease the sanding down and levelling of the patch. Finish with a polyurethane paint.

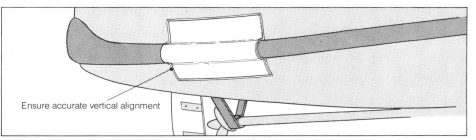

Ensure accurate vertical alignment

The vertical alignment of the patch is more critical than its horizontal location

Repairs to the hull without using a mould Fibreglass hulls

These repairs can be successfully completed, provided that the shape to be rebuilt is not too complex and does not include moulded-in features which break up the line of the hull. The instructions below assume that access to the inside of the hull is, for the purposes of repair, impossible. Where the working area can be reached from both sides, the making, fitting and removal of the moulding battens is much simpler.

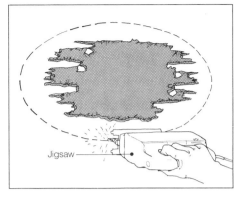

Jigsaw

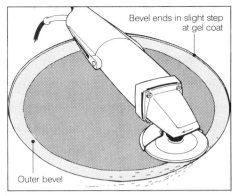

Bevel ends in slight step at gel coat

Outer bevel

1 Cut back the damaged area until the frayed and cracked fibreglass is cleared away, to give a firm edge on which to bond the repair. Bevel the edges of the

hole, remove the resin coating around the hole on the inside of the hull, and sand a one-inch (25 mm) margin on the outside. If the hull is a sandwich

construction, the inner core will have to be scooped out with gouges, to facilitate the movement of the rasp.

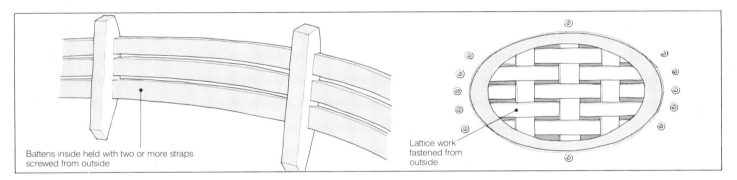

Battens inside held with two or more straps screwed from outside

Lattice work fastened from outside

2 Assemble a selection of thin, straight-grained battens that are long enough to span the break in the hull. These will be fitted into the hull, and used to support the initial layers of glass fibre cloth. Some suggestions for holding and fastening the battens in place are illustrated above. The operation is simplified if no attempt is made to remove the battens once the laminate is partly rebuilt. However, the battens should not be left to loosen and rattle about in the hull, or to rot or rust.

3 Use an epoxy resin for this repair; it not only has a greater bonding strength, but also, with suitable fillers, makes a very stable and strong fairing paste. For full details on using epoxy resins, see page

38. Add a thixotropic filler if the resin is to be used on sloping surfaces, or if there is a chance that it may drain from between the glass fibres. If the battens are to remain in the hull, cover them with resin. Brush resin on to the inner edge of the hole.

Wet the strips of glass cloth with the resin, and press them into the hole, manipulating them to lie between the battens and the hull on the inside, and overlapping each other as they bear against the battens bridging the hole. Add a second layer of cloth strips, at right angles, or parallel to the first layer. If the strips are laid parallel, stagger the joints between them to maintain the unity

of strength in the laminate. Press the cloth gently against the battens and stipple more resin on to the cloth, to ensure that it is thoroughly saturated, and leave it to cure.

4 Continue to build up the layers of fibreglass. After the first two layers of cloth strips, random matt can be used instead. Level the area by sanding and filling with epoxy filler, and small pieces of matt, as each layer cures. Each layer should be levelled before adding the next. Finish the final coat with fine 'wet and dry' paper and then burnish it with abrasive cream.

Removing the battens from within the hull
A layer of polythene should be interposed between the battens and the first layer of fibreglass where it is thought desirable to remove the wooden supporting battens.

The technique for building up the repair is the same as described above, except that the repair must be built up in stages. Remove the battens from behind the cured first section before laying up the area above. It will be necessary to fit the

shutting strip of cloth with a supporting batten behind it.

When working in this way check that the symmetry of the hull is being accurately maintained as the repair is built up.

Repairing moulded-in features Fibreglass hulls

Accidental damage can occur at almost any part of the hull, and in many cases, where the curves are fair and regular, repairs are easy (see page 84). However, moulded parts of the hull that stand proud from the skin (such as moulded rubbing strakes,) and the corners of the hull (like the stem, chine, and edges of the transom) are particularly vulnerable to damage, and are often rather tricky to repair.

This section explains two methods of repairing moulded-in features. It is often the small careless repairs that mar an otherwise well-maintained and smart hull. They deserve the same attention to fairing and finish as the larger repairs.

The illustration shows a moulded rubbing strake, holed to the extent that the new part will need to be sculptured into shape.

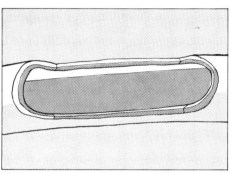

1 Moulding opened and bevelled

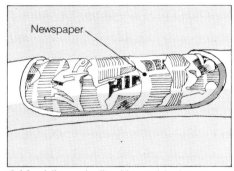

2 Moulding rebuilt with wadded paper

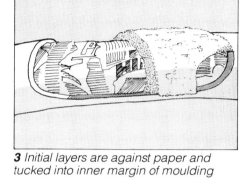

3 Initial layers are against paper and tucked into inner margin of moulding

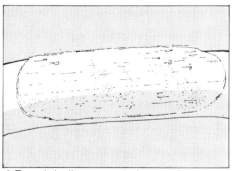

4 Repair built up, ready for rough shaping

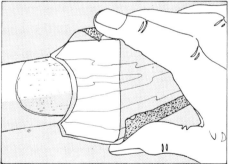

5 Final shaping with shaped block and sandpaper

before commencing to round the edges. At this stage of the repair, work with rough shaping tools, — surform, rasps and very coarse 'wet and dry' sandpaper, a hand grinder (see page 8l) with a suitable resin-bonded sanding disc, etc. More layers of resin will need to be applied after the initial blocking in of the shape has been completed. It is important to cut down the repair to size so that the next layers of resin can be pasted on and smoothed to give the final sealed resin finish. Once one has gained familiarity with the materials, rough shaping can be completed with a knife, while the resin is in a partially cured, rubbery state.

5 Dust and then wash the repair with white spirit and allow it to dry. Apply a thickened epoxy resin filler paste over the repair and leave it to cure. Rasp, and then sand the repair. Support 'wet and dry' paper with shaped wooden backing blocks to ensure that the profiles of the moulding are retained. Finish with polyurethane paint.

1 Clean up the area of damage, prepare the edges of the moulding to a 'V' as for the other repairs. Where access is possible from the inside, the repair can be completed as described on page 84. Otherwise use the following technique.

2 Fill the cavity with wads of paper, card, or any other suitable packing to support the initial layer of fibreglass.

3 Build up the repair from the outside, using a polyester resin with the method

described on page 85. Use plenty of resin, to ensure that the matt is thoroughly saturated. After the first ¼ inch (6mm) thickness has been laid up, leave the resin to harden, and then continue to build up the repair until it is proud of the adjacent surfaces.

4 When the laminate has hardened, file and trim back the new part until it approximates the shape of the feature. It is a good idea to block in the major outlines of the part with flat filed surfaces,

More complex shapes, such as those illustrated below, are relatively simple to reproduce in an easily-worked material such as plaster, but are very difficult to finish cleanly in hardened polyester or epoxy resin. If there is a chance that the repair method described above may not prove satisfactory (this is likely to be the case if the shaping includes hollows as well as the rounding of convex features), then use the following technique.

1 Leave the frayed and torn fibreglass around the damaged area. This will help the plaster to key into the fibreglass, and will strengthen the bond. Devise a means of bridging the space between the edges of the glass fibre. Tight supporting wires, woven through holes drilled into the skin further back from the repair can be used if necessary.

2 Spread some wet hessian over the wires, and tuck it behind the edges of the break in the hull. Build a layer of plaster of Paris (obtainable from most large chemist stores) on to the hessian. Add more plaster to the first layer, and leave this to set. Do not try to model any features while the plaster is still wet.

3 Once the plaster is dry, it can be cut and shaped with normal woodworking edge tools and finished with sandpaper. Perfect the plaster repair; do not overlook holes or pimples on the surface, and add more plaster if necessary. It is far easier to achieve a smooth finish on the plaster than on the hard surface of the fibreglass patch.

4 Once the plaster has been modelled to the desired shape, brush on three or four coats of shellac. Allow the shellac about 30 minutes to dry between coats. This will seal the plaster, and improve its finish. Rub the shellac down with fine wire wool, or with very fine glass paper dipped into linseed oil. Then rub a coat of slow-drying furniture wax on to the patch, and the adjacent fibreglass.

5 Follow the procedures for laying up the mould, and then making a patch as described on page 87. However, before commencing to make a female mould of the plaster repair, consider the problems of clamping and fitting the repair to the hull. It is often easier to align and clamp a large section than a small one, and it is very difficult to bond around pieces that are cluttered by clamps etc. Plan the shape of the repair patch before applying

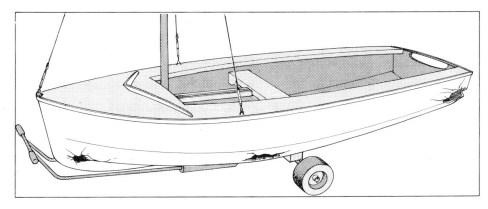

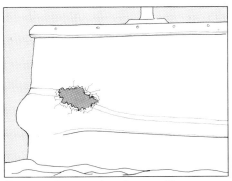

Damage to complex shape with compound curvatures

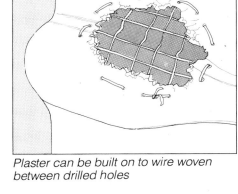

Plaster can be built on to wire woven between drilled holes

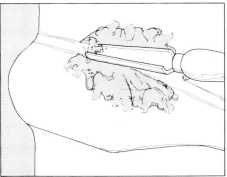

Gouge and chisel plaster to required shape

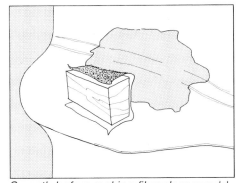

Smooth before making fibreglass mould

the release agents (wax and poly-vinyl-alcohol) and laying up the mould.

6 Once the female mould has been made, break out the plaster, and remove the reinforcing wires. When the patching piece has been made up and positioned against the damaged part of the hull, cut back, clean up, and chamfer the edges of the hole.

Leave room to work between the patch and the hull. If the patch fits too closely,

it will be difficult to hold, and it may also be difficult to bond to the hull. Use epoxy resin and finish with polyurethane paint. As with all hull damage of this type, if parts are known to be vulnerable and easily damaged, take precautions to prevent a similar accident occurring again. Fit wooden or rubber rubbing strakes — consistent with the overall appearance of the boat — and have an adequate number of well-situated fenders to toss over the sides and protect the hull when they are needed.

Sandwich construction Fibreglass hulls

These hulls, with their relatively thin outer skins, are easily punctured. Repairs to the outer skin should be undertaken immediately to prevent water seeping into the inner core, where it will be trapped, and very difficult to dry out. Punctures on the outside of the hull often put stress on the bond between the inner skin and the foam or balsa filling. Localized de-lamination of the inner skin may result from a bump that at first appears to do no more than shatter the gel coat.

Slightly different techniques must be used when repairing sandwich hulls. Both the skin damage and the consequential damage to the bond must be attended to. The outer hull should be repaired with care, and with woven cloth where possible, to give the maximum strength for the minimum of laminate thickness.

Repairing small holes in the hull

1 Cut back the damaged fibreglass, scoop away the crushed inner core, so that the edges of the hole are accessible from the outside. Bevel the edges of the outer (damaged) skin. Dry out the area to be repaired.

2 Cut, and fit into the recess behind the outer skin, some segments of a suitable core material. Small pieces will be readily available from most boat-yards. If the core piece is cut into several pieces, these can be fitted and pressed home with a tapered final closing piece. Cover the inner faces of the core pieces with a generous layer of epoxy resin, and press them against the inner skin using just enough pressure to hold them in place.

Where most of the inner core appears to be intact, it will still be necessary to scoop out the core material immediately behind the edges of the broken outer hull, but the rest of the core material should be left at its normal thickness. Before commencing the outer repair, locate the position of the damaged area on the inside of the hull. If necessary drill a hole from outside through the centre of the damaged part, to pinpoint its position. Wad small scraps of random matt glass fibre, soaked in epoxy resin into the scooped out areas, before laying in the first strip of woven fibreglass.

Cut a piece of woven glass fibre cloth cloth, soak it in epoxy resin, apply more resin to the outer face of the core material, and to the inner edge of the bevel, and tuck the cloth into the hole. Work it into position with a blunt but springy kitchen knife or strip of tin.

3 Build up the repair from the outside of the hull and fair and finish it.

After completing the repairs on the outside, clear away the fittings from

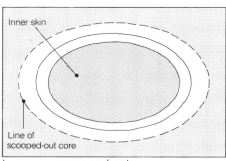
Inner core scooped out

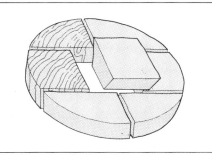
Use tapered closing piece

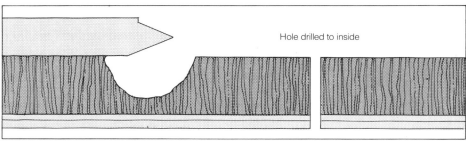
Core mostly intact with scoop at margin and locating hole

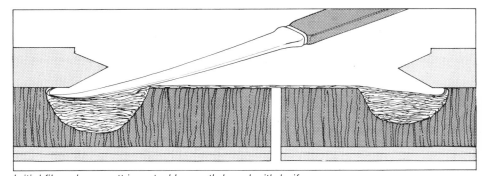
Initial fibreglass matt inserted beneath bevel with knife

around the area of impact on the inner skin, and re-bond it to the core in the following way:

4 Mark the approximate extent of the damaged area on the inside of the hull.

Add a 1½ inch (40mm) margin all round to allow for errors. Select a ¼ inch (6mm) masonry drill, with an electric drill, fitted with a depth stop set to cut through the inner skin, but not to pass into the core material. Drill a pattern of

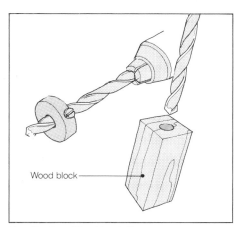

Wood block

Depth stop fitted to drill

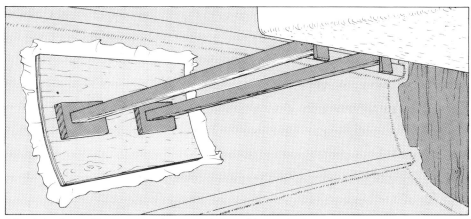

After injecting with epoxy resin, press inner skin against core

holes within the limits marked on the inside of the hull. Holes should be approximately one inch (25mm) apart, and spaced regularly. Inject epoxy glue into each hole, and then press the inner skin outwards. An arrangement of internal temporary shores is best for this, and the ends of the shores should bear against a sheet of thin plywood to spread the load and prevent distortions occurring in the inner skin. Seal all holes not already sealed with an application of epoxy resin filler.

Repairing large holes in the hull

Provision must be made for the replacement of the core material between the skins, and great care should be exercised in re-establishing a sound bond between the core, and the inner and outer skins.

In all fibreglass repairs, matters are greatly simplified if there is adequate access from the inside of the hull. With sandwich constructed hulls, where the outer skin has been crushed or punctured over an area greater than a 4 inch (100mm) radius, it is essential to have access to the inside hull behind the damaged part. Obstructive fittings, wires, and pipework must be moved.

Draw round, and then cut out, the damaged portion of the outer skin. Remove this and drill through the core to locate the centre of the damaged area on the inside. Working from the inside, cut out a section of the inner skin. There should be at least a 1½ inch (40mm) margin overlap between the inner and the outer skin, the hole in the inner skin being the larger, to allow for the laying up of the fibreglass outer skin and the

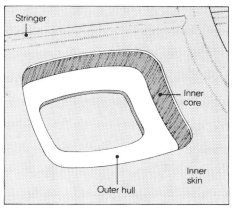

Stringer

Inner core

Outer hull

Inner skin

Inner skin cut, core removed

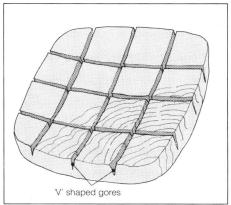

'V' shaped gores

Replacement of inner core

re-positioning of the core behind it. Leave the hull and the remaining core to dry. (See page **38** for approximate drying times and moisture content) Bevel the edges of both skins, and lay up the outer skin laminate. Wherever possible use technique described on page **88** to obtain the desired outside shape.

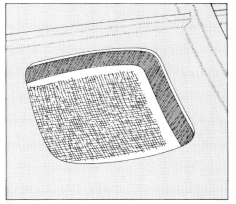

Repair of outer skin

Fit the replacement inner core. If there is difficulty in bending the core material to lie into the curve of the hull, either cut it into smaller sections or slice gores on the inner face, and then shore it into position. Once a good fit is obtained, apply a thick coating of thixotropic epoxy resin to the inner face of the outer skin, and press and shore the core in place.

Note: do not lay epoxy resin on to uncured polyester resin.

Once the resin has cured, fair the inner face of the core. Fill any gaps between this and the original core. Cover the face of the core with epoxy resin, and lay up the inner patch. All of the above processes can be simplified if a large tank cutter, or a trepanning tool is available to cut the holes and plugs of core material to a regular shape.

93

De-lamination will almost certainly occur where the hull has suffered a heavy bump. It is less likely to be a problem if it happens close to a bulkhead, deck, or at the ends of the boat where the increased curvature of the hull gives added firmness to the fibreglass panelling. Other places to check for de-lamination are around the fastenings to the hull (particularly where they are only fixed to one skin of the laminate) and at points on the hull that have been carelessly drilled or clamped.

Problems of de-lamination between the core and the inner and outer skins, will to a certain extent be related to the constructional sequence used in the manufacture of the sandwich hull.

Where the inner skin is laid up against a male mould, stiffened with an end grain balsa or polyurethane foam core, and covered with the outer laminate, the weakest internal bond is likely to be between the inner skin and core — especially at the sides of the hull where resin drainage may have occurred while the core was being applied.

The outer skin, on the other hand is likely to be very well bonded, because the glass fibre outer skin is laid and wetted out, resting against the core material.

Alternatively, the core material may be bonded to a fairly thin outer skin,

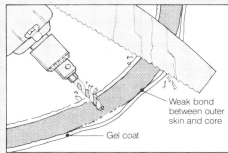

Drilling or sanding from inside to outside is likely to cause de-lamination

while it is still resting in a female mould, with the inner lamination laid directly on to the core material.

This latter type can be distinguished from the former by the unfinished, rough appearance of the inner surface of the hull. The weave of the glass fibre cloth will be apparent beneath the covering coat of resin. In this type of construction the bond between the core and the inner fibreglass laminations is likely to be strong, while that between the outer skin and the core may be weaker. Where the inner and outer skins are both pre-moulded, it is possible that both bonds may be weak in places. These possibilities should be borne in mind when drilling or sawing a sandwich constructed moulding.

Whichever method is used, the resulting hull will be light, and stiffer than an equivalent single skin hull. Its stiffness relies upon the bond

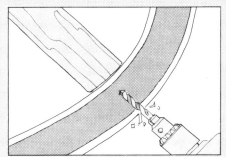

Drill or saw from either side, support opposite side

between the two skins, and is reduced when the bond is broken, increasing the stress on those parts still securely bonded.

Serious de-lamination can be spotted fairly easily. Even if the fibreglass does not lift from the core to form a large, low swelling in the line of the hull, the separated panels will 'give' when pressed, and if the panel crunches when pressed down, this will be further confirmation that the skin has de-laminated.

Minor de-lamination is a fairly common failing with most sandwich constructed hulls, and although extensive and obvious faults should be referred to a boat-yard for assessment and repair, localized separation of the core can quite easily be re-bonded by the owner.

Repairing a de-laminated hull

In most sandwich hulls the core and the inner and outer skins of the vessel are bonded with polyester resin. This is the same resin that is used for laying up the laminated skins and, although it readily combines with the resin of the skin, it makes a very poor adhesive. The technique for repairing the de-laminated section is to inject a superior adhesive (epoxy resin) into the cavity between the skin and the core, and then to apply pressure to the fibreglass to ensure a satisfactory re-bonding of the skin. The procedure for this is as follows:

1 If both skins appear to have separated from the core, re-bond each skin separately, and wherever pressure used to re-bond the skin seems likely to weaken or distort the hull or deck, shore the other side to support it.

2 Define the area that needs re-bonding. Err on the side of caution, and include doubtful parts at the margin of the repair area. Fit a depth stop to a ¼ inch (6mm) masonry drill bit, fit it in an electric drill, and bore a regular pattern of holes spaced 1 inch (25mm) apart over the entire face of the piece. The depth stop

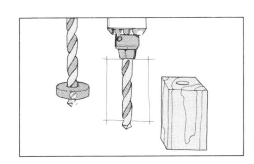

should be adjusted so that only the skin is pierced, deeper holes would merely waste epoxy resin.

3 Check the moisture content of the core with a meter. Test several of the holes, particularly at points where moisture may have penetrated the outer skin. Any holes made through the fibreglass skin are likely to introduce moisture into the core (cleats, winches, stanchions, etc.) and the area around them should be checked carefully. Drying can be accelerated by playing a hair drier or heat gun over the holes, but avoid damaging the fibreglass skin by overheating it.

For a satisfactory bond with epoxy resin, the moisture content of the core and the laminates should be below 15 per cent. If there is no evident moisture penetration into the core, pre-heat the core until its temperature is over 50°C (122°F) before injecting glue.

4 Mix up a sufficient quantity of unthickened epoxy resin, and inject it into the holes in the skin. Work in a sequence, ensuring that no holes are missed. This initial priming with pure epoxy resin will be absorbed into the core, and will serve as a foundation for

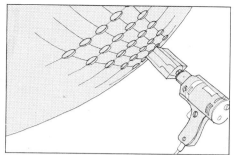

Grid pattern ensures even coverage

the thicker resin used to bond the core and the skin together. Before following with an epoxy resin thickened with collodial silica, depress the surfaces of the de-laminated section together, to spread the resin onto the fibreglass.

Inject the thickened resin into each hole. Do not stint the resin, but do not use it to fill voids that may occur in parts of the core material. Cover the area with thick, polythene sheeting and arrange weights or shores to press the laminate together.

Dry core before injecting resin

Sand down the surface and finish with polyurethane paint.

This technique can be used to restore the bond between parts that have suffered extensive de-lamination. Epoxy resin, in comparison to polyester resin, is more expensive, and the conditions in which it is to be used are critical.

The success of this repair depends upon the copious use of the epoxy resin in conditions where the temperature and moisture are carefully regulated.

Bolting fittings to a sandwich constructed deck or hull

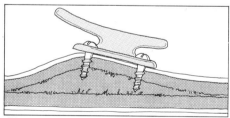

Cleat screwed to outer skin

Incorrect fastening practices can cause local de-lamination, and should be remedied whenever they are found. All fittings should be through-bolted, with spacers set into the core to prevent it from being crushed as the bolts are tightened. Cleats and other deck fittings should be bedded upon a load spreading plate, with a similar, or larger plate positioned beneath the deck.

Alternatively, the inner skin can be cut out, and the core removed from behind the position of the proposed fitting. Re-bond the core, adding an extra thickness of fibreglass in the recess and around the lip of the cut-out, and then bolt the fitting, bedding it on to a load spreading

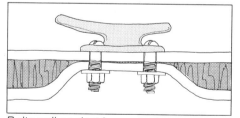

Bolts pull against large washers bedded in flexible compound

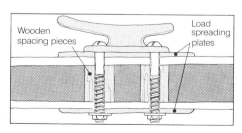

plate, with nuts and penny washers beneath. In both of the methods described above, a non-hardening sealing compound should be spread beneath the plate and under the washers, to prevent leaks and moisture seeping into the core material.

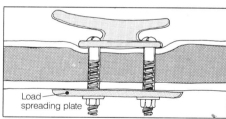

Bolts compress core material and leaks occur through bolt holes

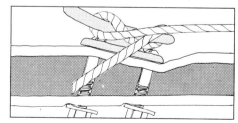

When working with sandwich mouldings remember that the thinner fibreglass laminate, with a soft, compressible core packed behind it, is easily damaged. It is liable to separate from the core if too much pressure is used when drilling, or with too vigorous sawing of the laminate.

No hulls, even those that are largely maintenance free, can be expected to survive indefinitely the stresses that conditions at sea impose upon them. The natural degradation of the construction material is recognized and compensated for in wooden and steel ships, by designing and building the hulls up to four times stronger and heavier than is structurally necessary.

Fibreglass hulls are an exception, simply because the fibreglass and resin laminate does not degrade in the same predictable way as steel or wood. Fibreglass boats are therefore frequently built to a minimum thickness consistent with safety and durability in the circumstances in which they are likely to be used.

This practice is justified by the large numbers of fibreglass boats, more than ten years old and still in regular

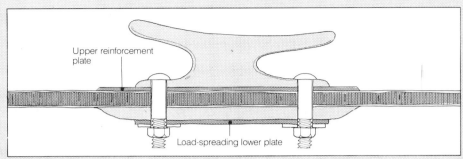

Upper plate reinforces moulding against pressures from above

use, maintaining their value and appearance at an age when many wooden and steel boats, will be in need of major maintenance work.

However, because fibreglass hulls are generally lightly made and slightly flexible, problems occur when rigid interior structures and stressed deck fittings are installed in the hull. The correct practice, to

avoid localized hard spots in the hull, is to swell the laminate thickness at these points. Where this has been done badly, or where new fittings have been fastened to the hull without the appropriate thickening of the laminate, stress concentrations will cause cracking of the gel coat which could, in extreme cases, lead to the failure of the laminate behind the cracking.

Identifying stress cracking

The first, and sometimes the only, sign of stress fracturing within the fibreglass laminate is hairline cracking in the gel coat. These cracks may follow a line of weakness, such as at a junction between the cockpit sole and the sides of the seating, or they may radiate from centres of localized stress. Cracks in the gel coat may also be evident on the outside of the hull at the point where the hull has suffered impact damage.

Stress cracking penetrates the full depth of the gel coat, and is easily distinguished from surface abrasions and scratching by the fine definition and regular pattern of the cracking. Once dirt

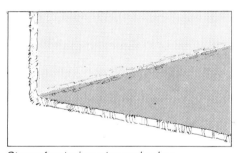

Stress fracturing at panel edge

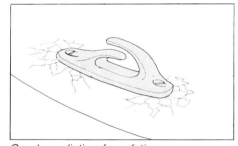

Cracks radiating from fatigue

or grease enter the cracks, they are very difficult to clean. Surface abrasions rarely score as deeply, and can be burnished out. It is likely, however, that

any accident causing serious surface damage may also cause associated stress cracking.

Causes of stress cracking

Much of the gel coat cracking may have occurred during the construction of the hull. Bolts drawn up tightly between the hull moulding and the deck moulding, for instance, will often be surrounded by a web of fine radial cracks. So, too, will any hard metal deck fitting that is drawn up tight without bedding compound or load-spreading plates interposed between the fitting and the moulding.

Any fitting bolted through a sandwich moulding, without spacers to prevent the core from being compressed, will also be a focus of stress cracks.

Apart from cracking built into the hull, many more areas of stress cracking are the result of poorly fastened fittings being put under stress.

Stanchions, for example, can exert very powerful forces on to the deck moulding which will crack if the stanchion is poorly fastened, or if the surrounding part of the deck is inadequately thickened. This fracturing is associated with stress and movement and may be serious, as fibreglass is a brittle material. Constant or intermittent flexing at one point will have a cumulative weakening effect.

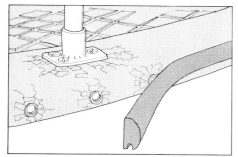
Fracturing at hull deck joint

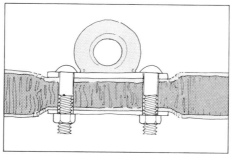
Fitting compressed and weakens skin

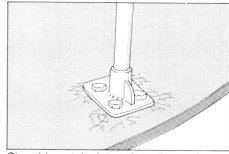
Stanchions take intermittent heavy loads

A third cause of stress fracturing is similar to the one mentioned above. Here, too, it is the flexing of the fibreglass that is the cause of the weakening. Glass fibre will twist or bend to a small extent without loss of strength. However, where there are hard spots in the hull (where for instance, a bulkhead is bonded to the hull, or where a deck fitting is bolted to the deck upon a poorly designed and badly bonded load spreading plate) the flexing of the fibreglass moulding will be concentrated at the abrupt border between the thin moulding and the hard spot. A stanchion may be put under severe stress perhaps ten or twelve times a year, but a badly supported hull section that is flexing at the edge of a hard spot may pant in and out hundreds of times both day and night, while the boat is at sea or moving at her moorings.

Cracking at border between thin moulding and hard spot

This weakening, due to flexing at the borders of a hull fitting or at the interface between a flexible and a stiffer part of the hull, is often known as the 'hinge effect'. (see page 77). This is just as likely in a steel or cold moulded wooden hull, and the warnings in those are perhaps less obvious. It is important, however, to be aware of the problem, and to be able to make some assessment as to whether the tell-tale signs on the hull or deck are insignificant marks left by the manufacturer and are merely sources of persistent but trifling leaks, or are serious faults that require attention.

Assessing gel coat crazing

First establish whether the cracking

1 occurred during the manufacturing process

2 is caused by poor mounting of hull fittings

3 is the result of weakening of the laminate at the border of a hard spot.

Hull and deck mouldings are often held together with bolts before they are bonded with fibreglass. In some cases, however, the bolts form the only bond, apart from a weak and brittle fillet of epoxy putty that is forced into the spaces between the mouldings to seal any remaining gaps. Where the latter is the case, and the holding bolts are associated with gel coat crazing it is wise to seek professional advice. The number and size of the bolts, the size and

bedding of the washers, and the conditions in which the boat will be used, will all help determine whether work is necessary.

Where the hull deck join has been carefully bonded with glass fibre and resin, the cracking at the bolt-holes is unlikely to be structurally significant (although it is possible that they may be the source of troublesome leaks).

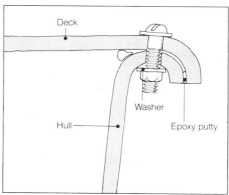
Unsatisfactory hull deck join

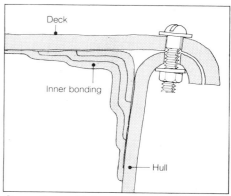
Strengthened join

Hard fittings

Hard fittings that are bolted to the moulding without bedding compound or load spreading plates will certainly be the source of leaks, and, if the fitting is stressed, are unlikely to be very secure All such fittings should be removed and bedded upon an ample layer of flexible bedding compound. This will prevent water seeping beneath the bolt holes, and will, to a certain extent, prevent further cracking.

If, however, the fitting comes under constant or occasional loads, proper fastening and bedding arrangements should be made.

At such fittings, the moulding should be thickened, and reinforcement plates added where necessary. Poorly fastened fittings are inclined to break away at the moment when they are most needed. Apart from the stress cracking, fibreglass shows no outward signs that the inner fibres are severed, so it is better to attend to suspected weak points before they fail. Guidelines for attaching fittings to a sandwich construction hull are detailed on page 95. It is a simpler matter to fit them to a single skin hull, as the spacer pieces can be omitted. The repair procedure is as follows:

Remove the fitting from the hull, clean the underside of the fitting and the area of the hull upon which it is bedded.

Cut and fit a metal or plywood backing plate. The plate should be larger than the seating of the fitting, and should have curved edges and radiused corners. Where the fitting is highly stressed, such as a winch or the end to a mainsheet horse, the edges of the plate should be tapered so that it fairs into the thickness of the glass fibre laminate. Hold the plate in position, on the inside of the hull, and draw around it. Clean away the dirt or grease from the bedding area.

Seat the fitting in flexible bedding compound, insert the bolts through the moulding and either add more compound on to the touching face of the plate or cover it with a layer of thickened epoxy glue. Press the plate into position, and bolt the fitting and plate together.

Where there is a possibility that the strains imposed upon the fitting may be

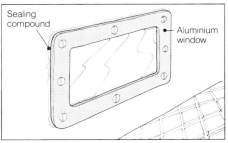

Bed rigid fixtures in flexible compound

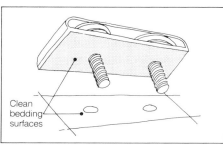

Clean bedding surface before installation

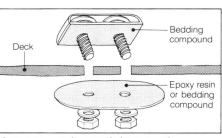

A strong, and watertight mounting

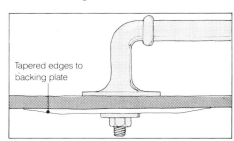

Taper plates to avoid hard spots

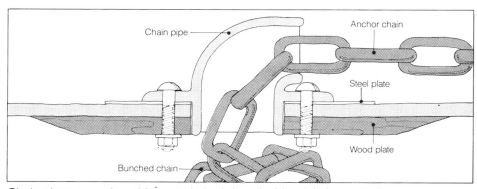

Chain pipes are vulnerable to strain both from inside and above deck

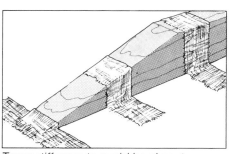

Taper stiffeners to avoid hard spots

reversed, stiffening plates may be needed both inside and outside the moulding. This applies to the chain pipe, which will occasionally be highly stressed from the inside when the anchor chain bunches against the pipe as it is run out. The pipe is also

subjected to considerable stresses from the outside, where it is in a vulnerable position on the foredeck.

If a fitting has been installed correctly, it is unlikely that stress cracking will be evident in the surrounding glass fibre moulding. However, it will occur, despite attempts at shaping and fairing in the reinforcing plate, where the fitting and its stress dissipating plates still form an abrupt border between the hard fitting and the thinner and more flexible moulding. Such hard spots must be eliminated in the following way.

Where fittings are causing local distortion, it is often possible to trim or fair the backing plate or to change it for a larger one. Struts that are bonded into or are pressed against the hull should be tapered, and where there is inadequate room or length to taper the strut, a dissipating pad should be fitted at the end. Bulkheads, which because of their stiffness, often cause stress cracking on both sides of their position in the hull, should be bonded-in with wide tapered flanges at each side. Where the flanges are omitted it is often worth while installing them.

Both the inside of the hull and the surface of the bulkhead should be cleaned of paint, varnish and surface resin, prior to laying up strips of woven cloth saturated with epoxy resin, to tie the bulkhead to the hull. Start with narrow strips and build up the flange with wider strips. A triangular cardboard or wooden fillet can be fitted in the corners between the bulkhead and hull. If these are well bonded into place they will reduce the amount of glass cloth used, and increase the flange efficiency.

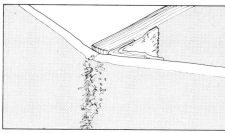

Plate dissipates load

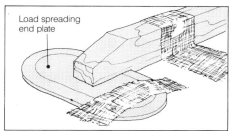

Fatigue fractures at hard spot

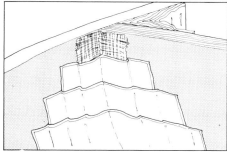

Lay up helps spread load

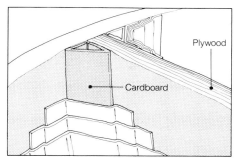

Fillets give additional bearing area

Stress at the bulkheads

If a decision is made to remove and re-bond a bulkhead, make sure that there is a gap at the perimeter of the bulkhead. This should be filled with a foam insert, before applying the fibreglass attachment flanges. This ensures that in the event of a severe localized impact the hull is supported by the flanges, and not by the rigid bulkhead. It does not however, inhibit the primary function of the bulkhead, which is to maintain the strength and symmetry of the hull.

A problem which sometimes occurs where there is pronounced hull stress cracking at the bulkheads is that other stiffeners (or fitted units, berths etc.) are inadequately bonded together. This concentrates the flexing at a very narrow band of unsupported glass fibre. All interior fittings that bear against the side of the hull should be bonded together to prevent this occurring. It may be necessary to build in a shelf or two, or a working surface, to bridge the gap between pieces of cabin furniture.

However, any additional cabin furniture that is fitted into the hull should be sufficiently strong to withstand the stresses that it was installed to help dissipate. A weak or poorly bonded

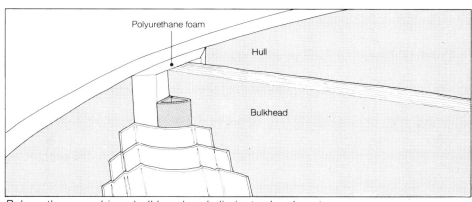

Polyurethane cushions bulkhead and eliminates hard spot

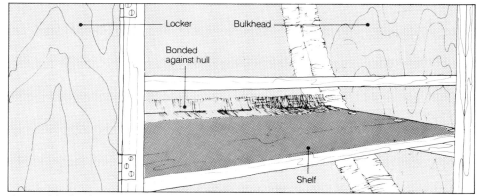

Any cabin furniture bonded to hull may introduce hard spots

Stress at the bulkheads (continued)

fitting could harm existing structures and create more problems than it solves.

In some cases, the bulkheads are installed before the fore and aft stiffeners are fitted to the hull. This is a poor practice, as the bulkheads being the most rigid members should support and brace the stiffeners. However, it is easier to fit the bulkheads first, and this method is difficult to detect once both the stiffeners and the bulkheads are bonded into position.

Inspect the joints carefully. If there is any possibility of movement between them they should be bonded together. This is not always a straightforward task, as working conditions are likely to be cramped. If it is impractical to cut through the bulkhead, and to pass a beam through the bulkhead and bond it to the stiffeners, a satisfactory strengthening can be achieved by making, and then bonding-in, steel brackets. These should be bolted to the bulkhead, and then bonded to the stiffeners and the whole then bonded over with glass fibre cloth soaked in epoxy resin.

Fatigue failure can also be found at angles in the deck moulding. A typical place where this occurs is illustrated opposite. Usually the reason is that the change in angle of the moulding forms a pivot point, against which the panels flex. Another cause is often that sharp corners can be difficult to lay up in a female mould and there may be a resin or glass fibre starvation at the very edge of the bend.

This type of fatigue weakening is unusual in the hull which is normally composed of fair curves and is reinforced on the inside with struts and bulkheads. However, lightly constructed sailing dinghies sometimes suffer from this type of fatigue at the line where the thin, flexible, and often unsupported bottom of the craft meets the vertical side of the internal buoyancy tanks. Here, stress cracking can develop quite swiftly into a serious weakness.

Stress cracking along a feature of a cabin deck, or cockpit moulding, is not unusual. The join between the floor and sides of the cockpit is a case in point.

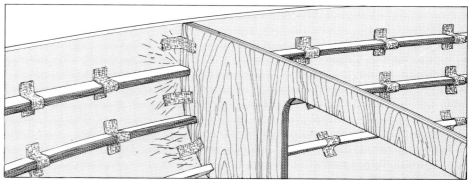

Fatigue failure caused by incorrect fitting of longitudinal stiffeners

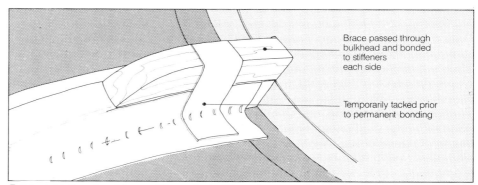

Brace passed through bulkhead and bonded to stiffeners each side

Temporarily tacked prior to permanent bonding

Brace transfers load from stiffener to bulkhead

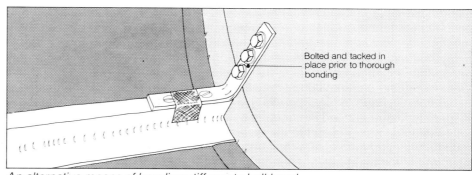

Bolted and tacked in place prior to thorough bonding

An alternative means of bonding stiffener to bulkhead

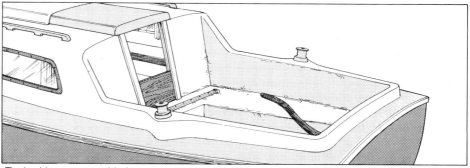

Typical instances of fatigue weakness at abrupt angle in deck moulding

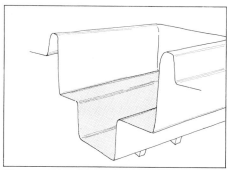

Stress reversals weaken laminate

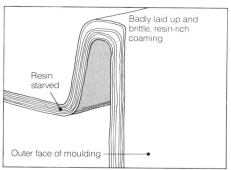

Hidden causes of weakness

Badly laid up and brittle, resin-rich coaming

Resin starved

Outer face of moulding

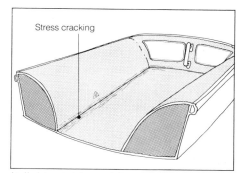

In lightweight mouldings, failure is likely to be sudden, with very little warning

Stress cracking

It is difficult to assess to what degree the structure has been weakened by the cracking, but if the cockpit floor withstands the impact of a burly crew member jumping into the cockpit, then it is unlikely that a heavy sea will cause it to fail!

Reinforcing struts

Fibreglass can easily be reinforced, the problem in doing so is that by changing the pattern of stresses within the hull, there is a danger of overstressing another perhaps equally weak part. This aspect must always be considered with care before altering the internal arrangements of the hull.

The illustrations below show some of the ways in which formers can be used to help mould stiffening members against a fibreglass panel. In all of the examples, the formers are not themselves structural, and it is often best if those that are retained have a negligible inherent strength.

All reinforcing pieces should be bonded on to ground-back glass fibres, and epoxy resin used to lay up the new strut. The first layers of woven fibreglass should be narrow, followed by wider strips to fair in the moulding. Those formers that are to be removed after use should be coated with wax and a poly-vinyl-alcohol release agent, or wrapped in polythene. If the strut is to meet with other stiffeners, plan the intersection to achieve maximum strength.

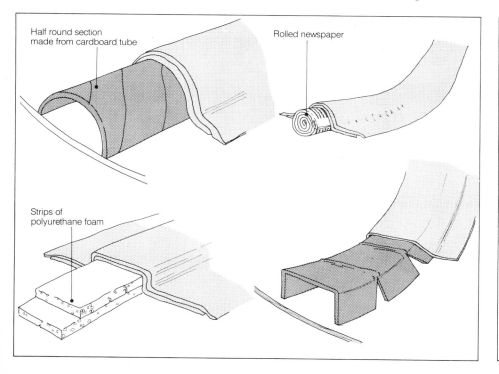

Half round section made from cardboard tube

Rolled newspaper

Strips of polyurethane foam

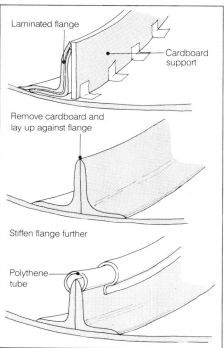

Laminated flange

Cardboard support

Remove cardboard and lay up against flange

Stiffen flange further

Polythene tube

Chapter 6

Other Hull Types

Steel has great strength and an inherent flexibility that makes it an ideal boat building material. Most small steel boats (apart from some river craft which are constructed from the thinnest gauge steel with no margin for corrosion) are built with heavier gauge steel than either the structural integrity of the design or their likely use demands. This is partly because of the difficulties in welding and fairing steel plate thinner than 1/8 inch (3 mm), and also to compensate for the inevitable loss of strength due to corrosion (see page 290).

Apart from its obvious stiffness, a steel hull has a high degree of residual strength; unless nearby welds are fractured, it will not be weakened by a heavy impact. Puncturing of a steel plate hull is unusual, and where it does occur it is likely to be in an area already weakened by corrosion. Denting is far more common (and more difficult to repair) but this is a consequence of the bold way in which steel boats can be handled.

A steel hull will corrode whether it is kept in fresh or salt water, but with the use of a planned cathodic protection system (see page 290) and modern rust inhibiting and epoxide paints, external hull corrosion below the water-line can be reduced or even eliminated. However, cathodic protection will only work where metal surfaces are immersed in water. Areas of the hull at and above the water-line, and the entire inside steel structure of the boat, are more difficult to protect.

To keep the corrosion to a minimum, the internal framework of the hull is designed and built so that any sea and rain-water that finds its way below, drains to the bilges, where it can be pumped out. Careful planning is needed in order to prevent puddles of water being trapped. Large limber holes are cut into floors, frames, and struts, often with other lightening holes and 'mouseholes' which facilitate drainage and the circulation of air inside the hull.

However, because the attitude in which a boat lies in the water is ever changing, it is impossible to prevent the formation of small puddles. A hairline crack in a welded seam, or an area where slag is trapped in the weld, are sufficient to allow the water to seep through the unprotected steel, and start to corrode it.

Corrosion is not necessarily gradual. It can, in certain circumstances, be very localized and swift, and if it isn't spotted, the blocked limber holes cleared, and the offending parts cleaned and painted, the serviceable life of the hull may be curtailed quite dramatically.

Apart from regular inspection and replacement of the cathodic protection system, (where signs of unusually severe degrading of the zinc sacrifical plates must be investigated without delay) the hull should be regularly inspected for corrosion, and corroded parts tested for strength.

Checking the hull

Limber holes should be checked regularly to make sure that they are clear of obstruction and that bilge water is reaching the pump inlet. It may be worth fitting a thin steel chain, running through the floor limbers, which can be tugged to clear any blockages. These are particularly useful where parts of the bilge are inaccessible for most of the year.

Apart from the floor limbers, there will be many others that should be checked. Most of the stringers that run longtitudinally, and are welded to the transverse framing members should have limbers cut in them. These can usually be found at the intersection of the stringer with the frames, where a notch will be cut in the stringer to avoid the frame plate weld meeting the stringer plate weld. Engine bearer brackets and tank supports will also have limbers cut in them which, because they are generally situated low down in the hull, are often found to be blocked by accumulations of debris.

All horizontal stringers, flanges and brackets should be inspected for indications of corrosion. Check particularly welded seams, especially at the ends of discontinuous welds. Areas of high condensation, (at the deck/hull join for instance), cluttered arrangements of beams and brackets, and any points where wood floors, fittings or bulkheads have been bolted to the metal hull, should all be thoroughly explored.

Above deck, rust spots will form in the welded angles between the deck and the bulwarks, and around and beneath deck fittings. It is very difficult to prevent moisture seeping beneath a laid wooden deck, and rust spots often occur at the edges and below the seams. Discoloured, or lifting planking will indicate this fault, which is unfortunately very difficult to remedy.

A powerful waterproof torch, a cold chisel, and a light hammer are required for this type of quick survey. If more information is needed, a plate-thickness

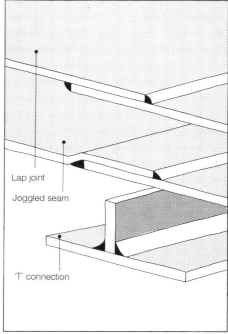

Lap joint

Joggled seam

'T' connection

Fillet welds

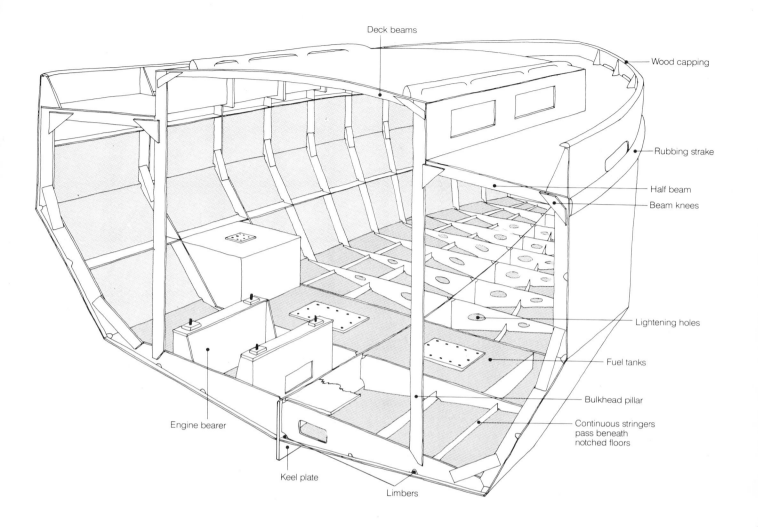

Deck beams

Wood capping

Rubbing strake

Half beam

Beam knees

Lightening holes

Fuel tanks

Bulkhead pillar

Continuous stringers
pass beneath
notched floors

Engine bearer

Keel plate

Limbers

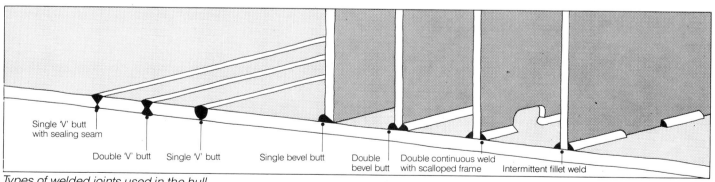

Single 'V' butt
with sealing seam

Double 'V' butt

Single 'V' butt

Single bevel butt

Double
bevel butt

Double continuous weld
with scalloped frame

Intermittent fillet weld

Types of welded joints used in the hull

gauge, sometimes used in combination with an electric drill, can determine the thickness of the framing members. However, for most purposes, all that is needed is a hard whack with a hammer to find a weakness in the framework — if frames dent, or their welds fracture, some local stiffening will be needed.

The illustration above shows the construction details of a section of a typical steel hulled motor boat. Note the care with which the stringers are positioned to prevent trapping moisture, the large limber holes, and the efforts of the designer and builder to keep the weight of the hull down without reducing its strength.

Working steel Other hull types

Cutting
Mild steel can be cut with a hacksaw, jigsaw, or machine hacksaw. Plates can be cut with a guillotine or a powered nibbler. Boat-yards equipped with tools for repairing steel hulled vessels are likely to have these tools at hand. Where the owner is undertaking repairs it is best to keep the cutting and shaping to a minimum, and to select suitable sections of steel angle or plate from the stockholder or from a scrap metal merchant.

Bending
Compound shaping should not be undertaken by an amateur. Heavy section steel is usually rolled or pressed into shape and the facilities required for handling the metal put this subject beyond the scope of this book. However, smaller section steel can be bent cold and, in the majority of small steel craft, most of the hull plates are fitted without compound curvature.

Angle bar is almost impossible to bend unless it is pre-heated, or mechanically rolled, and all shaping of angle bar should be possible by cutting the flanges and re-welding them when the bend is achieved. This simplifies the task of bending and also enables a lot of the prefabrication to be performed off the hull, in workshop conditions.

Flat bar can be bent by either hammering against an anvil, or by holding the ends between posts fixed to the floor or embedded into the ground and heaved into shape. If the bar can be heated at the bend it will be much easier to manipulate.

As a general rule, it is better to keep shapes simple and work in small units, welding the pieces together, rather than to spend a lot of time and energy cutting and bending the steel into shape with inadequate tools.

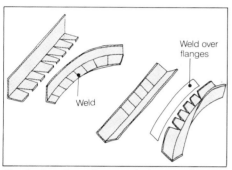

Cut before bending angle iron to shape

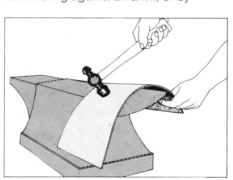

Beating at one side to form a curve

Leverage needed to bend heavy steel

Drilling
Small holes can be drilled with very little difficulty. A morse metal working drill should be used in the chuck of a powerful low speed drill. Centrepunch to start, and lubricate the drill with oil. Where holes greater than 3/8 inch (10mm) are required, wide handles should be fitted to the drill to give control.

Drilling should progress in steps. Start with a 3/16 inch (5mm) drill, stepping up in size in 1/8 inch (3mm) stages. Take care to hold the drill straight, otherwise the larger drills will tend to dig in.

Where pieces are being prefabricated, and need to be adjusted while they are held by bolts, drill one hole the diameter of the bolt, and drill the other with a drill that is about 1/4 inch (6mm) wider. This gives some play in the joint, and enables the seam between the two plates to be welded over, once the bolt has been removed.

Bolting
Steel bolts should be used in steel boats. Touching surfaces should be free from scale and rust, painted and then coated with a flexible bedding compound. Place heavy washers below the head and nut, with bedding compound beneath. Where a flush fastening is required, countersunk bolts should be used.

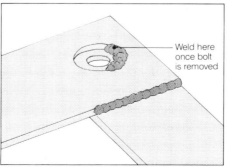

Take up adjustment with both holes of differing sizes

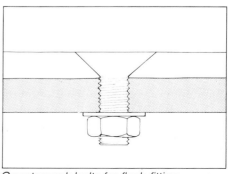

Countersunk bolts for flush fitting

Rivetting

Fittings to the hull should either be welded or bolted. Rivetting can be used in the construction of the prefabricated sections made in the workshop. Rivets are easily made from mild steel rod, and are cheaper than bolts. The illustrations show the technique involved.

Countersink the holes for flush rivets, and crop the rivet closer to the surface of the plate. Coat the surfaces to be rivetted in paint before joining them. Because rivets cannot be tightened once they are in place, ensure that their positions are well planned, and that their size and number are adequate.

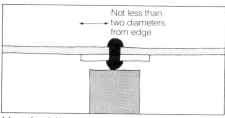

Light taps bind rivet in place

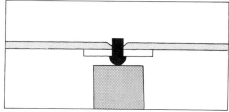

Heavier blows shape rivet head

Countersink rivet

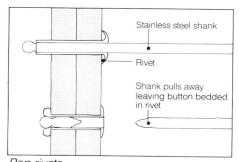

Pop rivets

A pop-rivetter provides a quick and simple means of permanently securing fittings. Apart from the speed with which fastenings can be inserted and pulled up tight, the great advantage of a pop rivetter is that it is only necessary to have access to one side of the panel. Pop rivets have a central core of stainless steel, most of which pulls out as the rivet is drawn tight, leaving the outer shell which is made of aluminium or monel to hold the pieces together. Monel rivets are more expensive than aluminium, but they are stronger and much less likely to be corroded. This is an important point, as a hollow pop rivet is particularly vulnerable to water seepage, and has very little reserve strength.

The specified diameter drill must always be used in conjunction with the pop-rivetter. Rivets should be the correct length for the task in hand. Where a fitting is stressed, ample rivets should be used, as a precaution against one or two of the rivets failing.

Prefabricating

Wherever possible, prefabricate fittings, reinforcements etc. away from the boat. Use cardboard templates to find the shape and curves required. Bolt prefabricated parts together, making allowance for adjustment in the bolt holes (see page l06) before welding everything together at the work bench. There are many advantages to working in this way. Most welding can be down hand, metal working equipment stays in the workshop, rather than being scattered between the boat and the workshop. Working conditions are easier and the remoteness of the boat ensures that adequate dimensional control is practised.

Preparing steel for welding

Cracked welds, or those that incorporate lumps of slag and other impurities, are weak and a source of future corrosion problems. Careful preparation of the steel is a prerequisite for good welding. Rust and scale should be removed, and rust pitting completely ground out before welding commences. If the pieces are to be arc welded, another area, close to the weld, should be ground free of rust or paint so that the clamp which takes the power from the arc welding unit to the steel has a good electrical contact.

An electric hand grinder is an ideal tool for cleaning back the steel, and for bevelling the corners to be welded. This should be fitted with a resin bonded abrasive disc that is suited to the work in

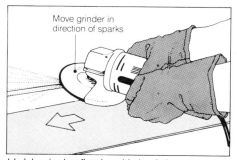

Hold grinder firmly with both hands

hand. For grinding steel, a carborundum disc is normally used. Discs are fitted to the high speed head by releasing the clamping nut with a special lever, while the head is prevented from rotating with another, thin, spanner.

Wear goggles when using a grinder, and if the work is in a confined or poorly ventilated space, a breathing mask as well. For maximum control, hold the tool with both hands and work it against the direction of rotation of the disc. The sparks should fly ahead, in the direction in which the tool is moving. Do not skimp on the work, only stop grinding when all of the rust and pitting have been removed and the steel looks smooth.

Clamping

Prefabricated parts should be held together prior to welding. Spring grips and wood-working clamps are useful. It is also convenient to have an assortment of thin metal straps which can be bent into place and tack-welded to support the work.

Hull plating and frame damage

Straightening out dented plating is often a very difficult task and, unless the damage is quite severe, it is worth while considering cutting back the paint layers, and levelling the dent with a trowelled epoxide filler (see page 304). Dents that have distorted the plating by 1/4 inch (6 mm) or more, and which the owner finds impossible to overlook, will need to be pulled back into shape. This is often a problem, because the steel plate will have stretched slightly on impact, and will not return to its original shape. Use a hand grinder to cut a narrow slot across the face of severely dented plates to allow the excess metal an escape route when it is forced back to shape. Weld over the slot once the plate has been forced into position. It will be necessary to weld a stringer between the two frames that lie each side of the dent in order to hold the dented plate in place.

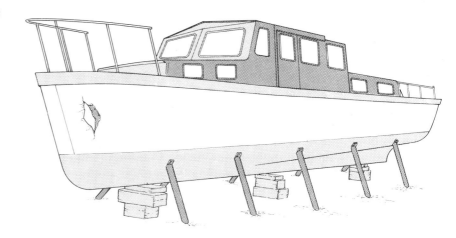

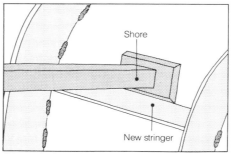

Shore holds plating while welding

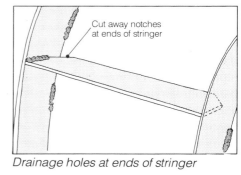

Drainage holes at ends of stringer

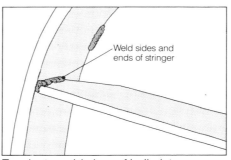

Terminate weld clear of hull plate

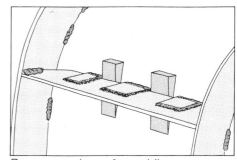

Remove wedges after welding.

Before welding the stringer into position, remember to cut limber holes at the ends. These will serve to drain any water that might otherwise lie trapped between the stringer and the frame, and also prevent welds meeting at the stringer, hull plate and frame intersection.

Shore the dented plate so that the ends of the stringer can be welded into place. Fully weld the ends, and then release the shoring. Inspect the hull from the outside. If the plating lies fair, it can be continuously or intermittently welded to the stringer. This will have a slight shrinking effect on the plate which should be taken into account before welding commences.

If the plate needs to be pressed out further, knock a couple of steel wedges between the stringer and the hull plate,

until the plate lies fair. Weld some spacing pieces on to the stringer and against the hull plate, and remove the wedges. If a slot has been cut in the outer plating, weld over it, and clean up

and paint the new stringer and freshly welded seams very carefully, to prevent future corrosion problems. The outer hull plating will still need to be faired in with epoxide filler and then painted.

Frame damage and corrosion

Frame damage is usually associated with serious hull plate and internal structural damage beyond the skill and facilities of the average boat owner. Repairs usually entail cutting out and rebuilding the damaged framework, and replacing the dented plating.

The lower ends of the frames, and the floors that tie the frames and keel plate together, frequently suffer from serious corrosion problems. This is particularly the case in the after end of the ship, where bilge water and water-saturated debris accumulate. Check each frame and floor with a hammer, testing for

weakness. Where steelwork has corroded to the extent that there is no strength left in the structural members, seek advice. In most boats, even though the rusting may be quite advanced, there is sufficient strength for bracing pieces to be fitted without the total renewal of the frame ends and floors.

Work on one frame and floor assembly at a time. Chip away the rust and scale, and use a handheld electric grinder to prepare the surface for painting. Prime it with rust inhibiting paint.

Design and cut cardboard templates for the prefabricated supporting pieces.

These supporting pieces should incorporate bolts to the keel plate, and to the floors and frames. They should extend well beyond the area of severe corrosion, and taper into the frame line.

Prefabricate the assembly, using bolts to hold it in position, and check that it

fits against the frames and sits on the keel plate before taking it to the workshop for welding.

Clean and paint the assembly before bolting it into place.

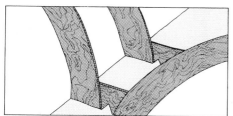
Corroded frame ends and floor

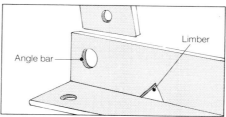
Prefabricated supporting piece

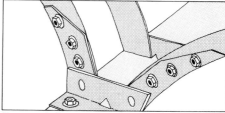
Taper reinforcements into frame

Shaping and bending plates

Sometimes it is necessary to reinforce or repair parts of the hull seriously weakened by corrosion. Where two dissimilar metals are placed together and immersed in seawater, the less noble (see page 290) may corrode,

In steel hulled boats this is likely to occur where a seacock or water inlet of bronze, or other metal more noble than steel, is fitted to the hull. As the paint cover deteriorates, the steel close to the rim of the fitting will seriously corrode, and eventually need attention.

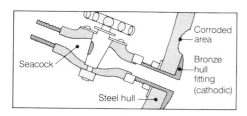

This is a task that will have to be undertaken when the boat is out of the water, but the operation need not take long if the reinforcing plate is cut and bevelled, and bolt holes are drilled through it, prior to starting work on the hull.

Do not cut out and replace the weakened plating. This is a job that should be undertaken by skilled shipwrights accustomed to this type of work. It is better to remove the hull fittings, bolt a plate over the weakened area, and replace the fitting with a slightly longer internal pipe if necessary.

Remove the hull fitting and wash it in warm water. Replace any perished seal so that it is ready for re-installation later. Mark out and cut a plate of steel to cover the damaged area. The new plate should extend beyond the corroded part, so that the bolts holding it are tightened into sound metal. Where there is even the slightest degree of compound curvature needed, cut out a second patch of thinner steel. Experiment with this, before hammering the thicker plate into the correct curves. Do not practise on the thicker plate.

If this has not already been done, bevel the edges of the hull plate so that it will lie fair with the hull, and drill bolt holes around its edge. If the plate is more than 3/16 inch (5mm) thick, the bolts can be countersunk, and should be spaced

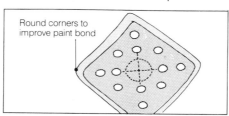
Prefabricated doubling plate

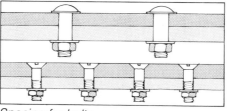
Spacing for bolts

closer together than is necessary with round-headed or square-headed bolts.

Hold the plate against the hull, and drill all of the bolt holes. Hold the plate in position with three or four bolts, and then, from the inside, draw or scribe round the edge of the hole cut in the original hull plate to take the fitting. Remove the plate and cut the hole.

Clean both the inside of the plate and the part of the hull to be covered. Use a grinder to dig out the rust crevices and pitting. Bed the plate in copious quantities of thixotropic epoxy glue (pre-heat the area if necessary (see page 38), and bolt it into place. Clean the resin, paint the plate and the inner edges of the hole. Replace the fitting, with suitable seals beneath the flanges. (A couple of twists of caulking cotton, wound round the thread, and covered in bedding compound makes a good alternative sealant.) Connect the internal pipework, and paint inside and outside the hull in the area of the repair. Although strength will be restored to the weakened hull plate, the corrosive action between the steel and the fitting will resume once the hull is immersed in sea-water. To prevent this, it is necessary to bolt or weld a small sacrificial anode to the new plate, close to the fitting. Studs to hold the anode can be welded on before fitting the plate, and should be painted. Fit the anode after painting is finished. Dab paint on to the nuts and threads still exposed, but do not allow paint to fall on to the anode or its effectiveness will be reduced.

Preparation

All surfaces that require welding must be ground back until they are free from rust, scale and paint.

The localized and concentrated heat at the weld will cause the steel to move or buckle. Holding jigs should be used. Bolt prefabricated pieces together, prior to welding. Large pieces of steel can be tack-welded to make a temporary but secure bond between them. Before running a permanent weld over this, it should be ground back to bright metal, and the adjacent edges prepared to the standard of the rest of the seam.

It is often possible to hammer light gauge steel together, and then continue welding if the items separate while the welding is in progress. This is easy to do when gas welding, but if an arc welded seam cools, it will be necessary to chip away the slag, and then grind back to bright metal before continuing the process.

The illustrations below show the main types of seam used in boat building. The dotted lines indicate the shape of the weld. Note how the edges of the joining pieces are prepared and ground prior to welding. It is good practice not to let welds meet. Where this is unavoidable — run the short weld, grind back its end, and run the long weld across it.

Joints should be as closely fitting as possible. If the fit is poor, it is easier to bridge the gap by gas welding than by arc welding.

In general, arc welding is suited to welding heavy gauge plate; steel that is thinner than 1/8 inch (2 mm) must be gas welded.

In both gas and arc welding it is important to heat both surfaces to an equal temperature. This is a fairly straightforward matter where pieces of equal thickness are to be edge joined. Where they are of unequal thickness, or where the edge of one piece abuts on the centre of another plate, it will be necessary to direct the torch or the arc welding rod towards the greater mass of metal. Wherever possible, try to arrange the conditions in which the welding takes place, so that neither piece dissipates the heat. It is better not to rest the items flat on a heat-conducting surface that will dissipate the heat generated by the flame.

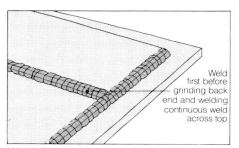

Weld first before grinding back end and welding continuous weld across top

Weld short seam first, before grinding back and running continuous weld across its end.

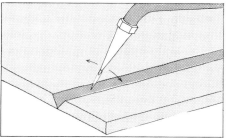

Heat from torch or electrode should be played evenly between pieces

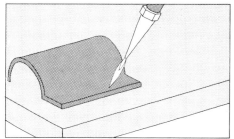

When welding metals of unequal thickness, play more heat onto the thicker piece

Arc Welding

Safety

It is essential to use a purpose-designed arc welding visor conforming to BS1542 and BS679 which gives protection from infra-red and ultra-violet radiation. This incorporates a dark glass screen to reduce the glare of the arc light, and a wide curved shield that prevents sparks, slag and molten metal falling on to the face. On no account should one look directly at the arc light, unless it is through a darkened glass screen as even a very small exposure to the arc light will cause arc-eye, which is a very painful experience.

Make sure that the earth clamp and the hand clamp never touch. Switch off the arc welding unit before handling the earth clamp, keep the runs of electric cable tidy between welds, place the visor face up on top of the welding unit, and place the stick clamp upon it.

When arc welding on board, remember that electrical installations will be damaged or affected by the current passing through the hull, and consider what is behind the surface being welded.

Wear a breathing mask when welding steel that has been painted, sprayed or galvanized, dust masks will not be satisfactory.

Wear overalls of a flame retardent material, a hat with a peak and an apron. Trousers should be without turn up.

Precautions against electric shock should be taken particularly when working in confined and wet spaces.

Keep a fire extinguisher handy.

Tools

The arc welding unit, a supply of appropriate rods, a grinder fitted with an abrasive disc, a wire brush, and a cold chisel and hammer to chip away flux and slag will be needed, also a supply of clamps and some wire cutters.

Arc welding rods should be stored in a warm, dry place. They should not be allowed to get wet or damp before use.

There are many different types of rod available, if overhead or up hand welding is involved, seek advice before selecting the appropriate rod for the job. The diameter of the rod is usually selected to suit the thinnest of the pieces to be welded. There will be a table of reference and a power adjuster on the arc unit, and once the rod has been selected, the correct power setting should be chosen. Again, if in doubt, seek advice: If the amps are set correctly the flux deposited by the rod will clear itself as it cools.

Technique

Fit the earth clamp to a clean part of steel as close to the location to the weld as possible. Place the rod in the electrode clamp, take up the visor, and switch on the power.

Look carefully at the electrode clamp, your hand and the rod tip. Until a spark is struck, it will be impossible to see anything through the blackened glass, so it is necessary to get used to the balance of the clamp and the position of the end of the rod. Strike the rod against the steel a little away from the prepared seam, and bring it away in the same bouncing movement. Tapping like this cleans away any flux that might be adhering to the tip of the rod, preventing a spark. Once a spark strikes up, move the rod across to the seam and commence welding.

Problems

Until a steady spark burns at the end of the rod it will be almost impossible to see what is happening. Practise striking with the power off, and without the protection of the visor. However, once the power is switched on, the visor must be used. If the rod sticks or doesn't spark, release it from the hand clamp, and then break it free. Inspect the end of the rod. The initial tapping may have broken away the coat of flux that surrounds the rod. Clip back the rod.

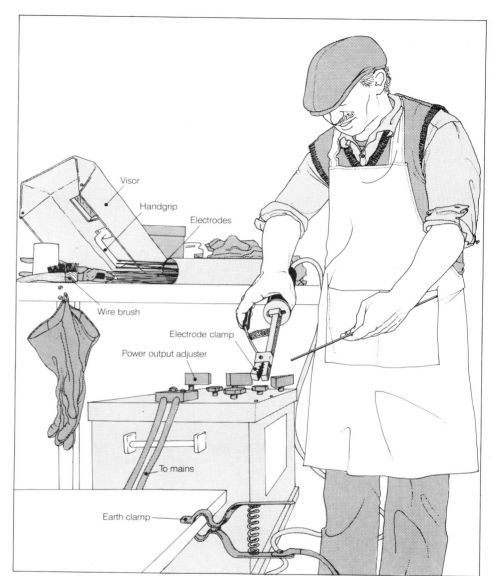

Visor

Handgrip

Electrodes

Wire brush

Electrode clamp

Power output adjuster

To mains

Earth clamp

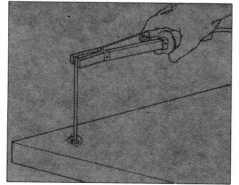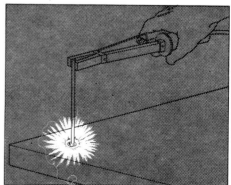

Tap rod against steel to strike a spark. It will be virtually impossible to see anything through the blackened glass of the visor until a spark is struck.

Problems (continued)

The steel against which the rod is tapped may be rusty or dirty: either clean away the dirt, or try tapping another part.

The earth clamp connection may be poor, or there may not be a continuous bond between the clamp and the steel. The power may be set too low. Turn up the power setting on the arc unit.

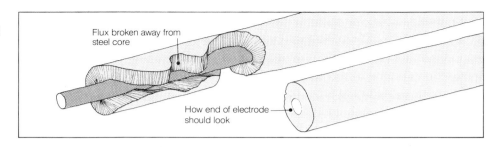

Welding

Once the spark is struck, skip the rod across to the weld, which should be illuminated in the bright glare of the arc. Hold the rod at 45° or slightly less, and move the tip in small circles just above the weld. (It is unnecessary to play some rods over the weld, they need only to be held in the weld and pulled along.) As the arc burns, a puddle of flux will form. A steady and careful wrist action is required to lay a clean and continuous weld, as this will be hidden beneath the flux.

As the rod burns away, move the hand slowly towards the weld, so that the end point of the rod (which is growing shorter) gradually moves along the seam. The following illustrations show how the welding rod can be held for welding different types of join and for up hand and overhead welding.

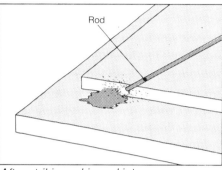

After striking, skip rod into seam

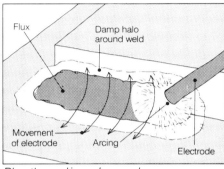

Play the rod in a slow and even movement

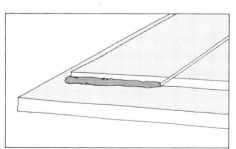

Running a seam feed rod into arc, and allowing weld to build up slowly

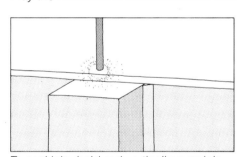

To seal join, hold rod vertically over join, allow it to arc, molten steel will drop into joint

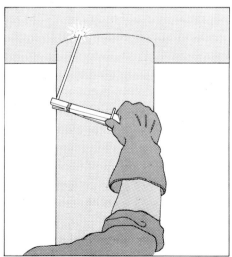

Use minimum power. Keep rod almost perpendicular to steel, so that blast of arc will keep back flux. Small stabbing strokes will bridge join and form weld Wear gloves

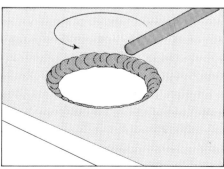

To fill a hole. Hold rod at low angle (so as not to burn hole any larger). Work around edge once. Chip away flux

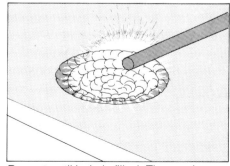

Repeat until hole is filled. Thorough cleaning between each layer is necessary to clear away all flux

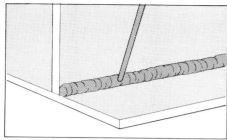

When the electrode is held at a steep angle to the seam it deposits more metal

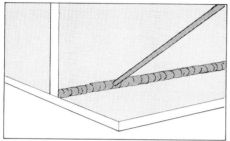

When the electrode is held at a shallow angle to seam it deposits less metal

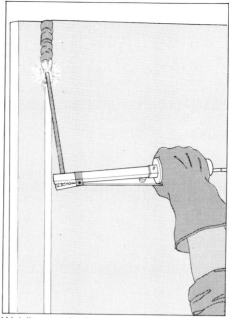

Welding vertical seam — increase power and hold rod at acute angle to seam

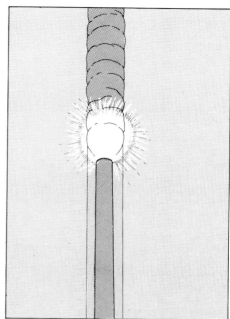

Use rod to blast back flux. Hold it at acute angle to seam. Rest rod in seam, if necessary, to achieve satisfactory weld

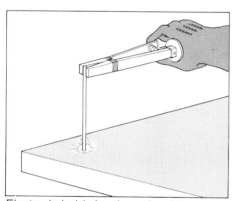

Electrode held closely and at right angles to steel will burn through it

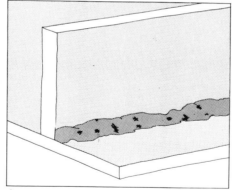

Appearance after flux has cleared away. Rod moved too quickly — poor fusion of weld. Drops of metal scattered along seam. Do not confuse flux with molten metal when looking at weld

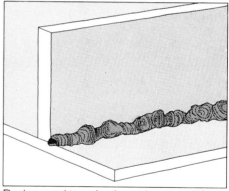

Rod moved too slowly and unsteadily. Corner burnt away, uneven accumulations of weld material. Thinner stock may have burnt through

Problems

If the rod sticks: check the earth clamp connection, ensure that there is adequate flux at the end of the rod. Increase the power slightly.

If it burns holes in the steel: check that the correct rod and power level has been selected for the thickness of the steel being cut. Keep the rod at an angle of about 45° or less to the welded seam.

Removing the slag. Once a seam has been run, the weld will be covered by a hot, brittle layer of slag. As it cools it will drop off, or it may need to be chipped clear. The slag on a good weld will fall away easily. On an unsatisfactory weld all debris must be removed, and any that is embedded in the seam must be ground out prior to re-welding the joint.

A considerable degree of practice in welding is needed. Do not experiment on the boat. Master the techniques in sheltered workshop conditions and, unless it is absolutely necessary that the welding be carried out on the hull, prefabricate parts in the workshop, and bolt them into place on the hull.

Oxy-acetylene welding is a slower and more controlled operation than arc welding. The state of the welded seam is visible, and it is possible to return to areas previously welded, to build them up, without chipping away slag and grinding back to bare metal. Up-hand welding and gap filling is also easier.

Gas welding is also more versatile. Very thin steel can be welded, as well as the heavier plates used in boat building. However, as the thickness of plate increases, there is a corresponding increase in the quantity of weld to be deposited. For most purposes, therefore, gas welding is suited to limited fabrications and for welding plates less than 3/16 inch (5mm) thick, while arc welding is best for extensive welding operations where greater speed is an obvious advantage.

Equipment

All gas welding equipment must be maintained with great care. The cylinders and attached equipment remain a potential hazard even after the blowpipe is turned off and the equipment is put away. Anyone contemplating purchasing or borrowing a set should consult the supplier's safety manuals, and follow the recommendations concerning safety and storage. It is most important that the equipment is not tampered with, and that only approved attachments are fitted to it.

Oxy-acetylene equipment must always be well maintained.

It is unwise to store cylinders on board a boat, unless there is a special storage room designed for the purpose, with low and high level ventilation ducts, flash proof electric switches etc. Again, for full details on maintenance and safety, refer to the makers of the equipment, or the suppliers of the bottled gas.

In brief, the following precautions should be taken.

1 Store gas bottles vertically in a cool, dry place out of direct sunlight.

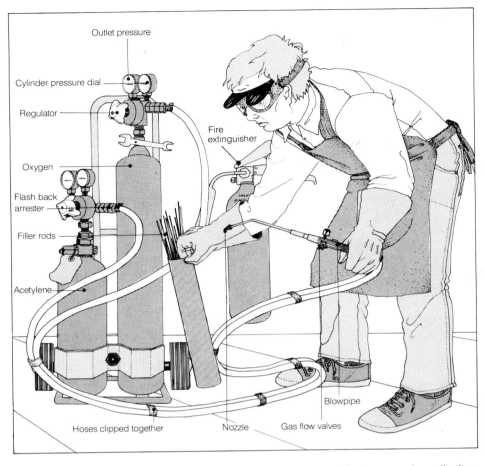

Outlet pressure

Cylinder pressure dial

Regulator

Oxygen

Flash back arrester

Filler rods

Acetylene

Fire extinguisher

Blowpipe

Hoses clipped together

Nozzle

Gas flow valves

2 Keep the cylinders away from oil drums, oily rags, or puddles of oil. Do not use oil or grease for lubricating or Cleaning oxygen cylinders, as a violent reaction is possible.

3 Make sure that cylinders are isolated from any fires, naked lights, and live electrical wiring.

4 Check the cylinders for leaks by brushing soapy water around the screw joints and look for bubbles of escaping gas.

5 Make sure that the equipment used in conjunction with the gas cylinders is compatible and well-maintained and does not leak. Install flash back arresters immediately downstream of each regulator (oxygen and acetylene). For added safety, fit a hose check valve between the hose and blow torch.

The above illustration shows a portable set of welding equipment.

There are two cylinders, one (usually the smaller) containing acetylene, and the other oxygen. The valve and regulator fittings at the top of the cylinders cannot be interchanged.

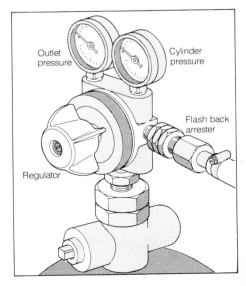

Outlet pressure

Cylinder pressure

Flash back arrester

Regulator

Cylinder pressure is reduced and adjusted by a regulator fixed to the top of each cylinder. One dial registers the cylinder pressure, the other measures the outlet pressure. The regulator can be adjusted by turning the wing nut in the centre. Whatever the pressure needed for welding, the outlet pressures at each cylinder should be the same.

An isolating valve is fitted in line with the outlet pressure dial. Flexible hoses take the gases to the blowpipe where another set of valves regulate the gas flow. It is a sensible precaution to fit a flashback arrester to each gas line. It should be clamped in the low pressure pipeline on the outlet side of the low pressure outlet valve as close to

the torch as possible. If it is not fitted, it is possible that a serious blowback might occur, which may ignite the gas in the acetylene tank and cause an explosion. As well as the basic oxy-acetylene welding apparatus, a selection of filler rods of varying diameters, goggles and gloves will be needed. A hammer, and a few clamps may also be required.

Safety

Keep a fire extinguisher handy. Goggles (with darkened lenses, made from a non-inflammable material) and gloves should be worn where necessary. A breathing mask should be worn if painted, electroplated or galvanized surfaces are being heated. Dust masks are not suitable.

Emergency procedure in event of a blow back

At the first sign of a blowback, turn off the gas supply at the cylinders, or bend the hose back on itself to constrict the flow of gas. If the hose has ruptured and burnt at the regulator valve, extinguish the fire with a CO_2 dry powder or BCF extinguisher before closing valves, or spinning off the pressure adjusting

screw. If the cylinder begins to heat up, close valves, take it outside, and hose cold water on to it until it cools. This may take several hours. If, in the unlikely event that the heat build-up is sufficienct to cause the cylinder to vent itself, shout a warning and keep well clear.

Notify the fire brigade and the gas suppliers when they collect the cylinder.

Procedure

Select an appropriate filler rod, and a suitable nozzle for the blowpipe. Most blowpipe boxes will have tables from which it is possible to calculate the sizes necessary but, if in doubt, seek professional advice.

Take a single length of filler rod, and make a right angle bend at one end. This is partly to render the loose end less dangerous and partly to make it easy to

distinguish the hot (straight) end from the end that is cool and safe to handle.

Check that all the valves are turned off and release the pressure on the regulator screw by turning it anti-clockwise.

Slowly turn on the main cylinder valves, and wind in the regulator wing nuts until the correct pressure (which should be

matched with the rod diameter, and blowpipe nozzle size) is reached on the dials. Outlet pressures must be equal. When welding thin steel, low pressure will be needed, and it is wise to tap the dials to ensure that they are responding to the small adjustments in pressure.

Turn on both outlet valves, and pick up the blowpipe.

Lighting the blowpipe

Turn on the acetylene gas valve first (usually marked with an A, or painted red), and light the gas with a spark from a flint lighter. Acetylene burns with a smoky orange flame.

Turn on the oxygen valve slowly. As the oxygen flow increases, the flame

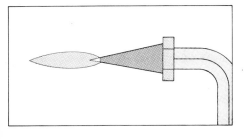

will become noisier. Balance the oxygen flow so that the flame has a well defined, tapered blue cone, which burns with a quiet hiss.

Problems

If the flame blows out, turn off the oxygen, and light the acetylene again. When lit, slowly turn up the oxygen gas and start again.

If the flame continues to blow out, or even blows back, switch off the valves. Check the dial pressures and adjust them to bring them level.

If the flame blows back as it is lit, switch off the acetylene supply and start again. This time allow time for the gas flow to become established.

Excessive noise or a ragged flame indicate a worn or dirty jet. Switch off the gas supply and clean the nozzle. Wide diameter nozzles will roar more than smaller ones.

If the flame is too hot, turn down the oxygen before turning down the acetylene. Set the oxygen at a new, reduced level.

Technique

Hold the blowpipe in one hand and the filler rod in the other. Hold the nozzle of the blowpipe close to the part to be welded. The tip of the short conical blue flame should play across the surfaces.

Heat the metal until it glows a bright orange, and then dab the filler rod into the centre of the hot spot. Withdraw the rod, and play the flame across the heated area. The very smallest movement is all that is needed to brush the weld into a neat seam.

As with arc welding, where pieces of different thicknesses are being welded, or where the edge of one piece is joined to the centre of another, the flame should be directed towards the greater mass of metal.

Work the seam slowly, adding only sufficient rod to the molten metal to build up the weld. Keep the gas jet gently playing over the seam, and use it to move and smooth the weld into position.

The finished seam should appear even, and apart from small surface ripples, smooth.

Because of the heat used during welding, pieces that are being joined tend to pull apart, and any resulting crevice is susceptible to corrosion.

To avoid this continue welds around the ends, and if small crevices remain, fill them with an epoxide filler before painting.

Because of consequential shrinkage after welding, long continuous welds between plating and framework are often avoided, and step-welds are used instead. These reduce plate distortion.

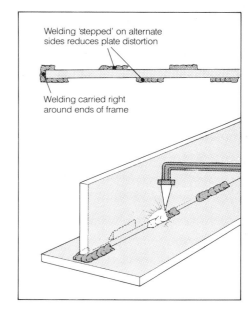

Welding 'stepped' on alternate sides reduces plate distortion

Welding carried right around ends of frame

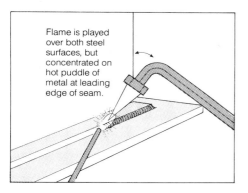

Flame is played over both steel surfaces, but concentrated on hot puddle of metal at leading edge of seam.

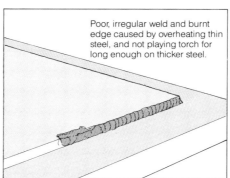

Poor, irregular weld and burnt edge caused by overheating thin steel, and not playing torch for long enough on thicker steel.

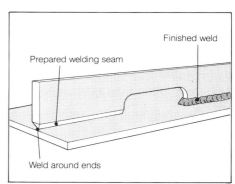

Prepared welding seam

Finished weld

Weld around ends

Problems

If the flame blows out, turn off the oxygen, turn down and re-light the acetylene. Turn on the oxygen supply and check that the dials are functioning, and reading the same outlet pressure on each dial. Sometimes, particularly after a number of small blow-outs, the regulators will need re-adjustment.

Inspect the shape of the flame. After a blow-out, small pieces of dirt and soot, and sometimes molten metal, will cling to the nozzle of the blowpipe. This will result in an irregularly shaped flame. Without extinguishing the flame, wipe the nozzle across some clean steel to remove the obstruction. If this doesn't work, turn off the gas, plunge the nozzle in cold water, remove the nozzle and clean it thoroughly.

If the heat output of the flame seems to be reduced, (this becomes apparent when the seam takes longer than usual to heat up), check to see if there is a localized thickening of the metal absorbing the heat. It may also be necessary to re-adjust the regulators. Point the flame away from the cylinders and check the dial settings.

Turn up the pressures if necessary.

Flame burns away one edge of the seam before the other is hot enough to fuse with the welding rod. This is the result of careless use of the blowpipe. Do not allow it to play for too long over one piece but move it across the seam heating them equally.

If the metals move apart as the weld commences, strike the seam a few times with a hammer while it is still hot, to bring the metal together.

Procedure for turning off

Follow this procedure before leaving the welding equipment: turn off the oxygen, then the acetylene, at the blowpipe. Turn off the outlet valves and the main cylinder valves. Slacken the regulator screws.

Because there will still be gas under pressure in the gas lines and in the regulator and dial assemblies, it is necessary to open up the valves again to flush out the remaining gas. Open the acetylene valve in the blowpipe, and in the low pressure outlet, (not the main cylinder valve). Close them again. Repeat this with the oxygen valves.

The tender Other hull types

The tender is often a much abused and poorly maintained workboat, receiving only cursory attention at the end of the season and an occasional wash. Tenders are easily neglected, yet they are often less stoutly constructed and much less durable than the parent craft.

The following section does not aim to encourage boat owners to lavish care and love upon their tenders. Instead, it outlines some practical arrangements that will make the tender a useful, reliable and safer little boat.

The maintenance and repair of collapsible and inflatable boats is described overleaf. Make repairs at the earliest convenient moment. Repair any faults before the tender becomes unsafe.

The drawing illustrates the parts of a tender requiring regular maintenance and inspection. Without exception, the tasks are easily accomplished, but they are important and should not be overlooked or postponed.

Strap prevents rudder lifting off

Fenders
Fit a rope or rubber fender along the sides and around the corners of the transom. A simple fender can be made by lashing a length of old rope around the boat. A 'D' section rubber strip makes a smarter and more durable fender, and looks particularly striking if it contrasts with the colour of the hull.

Painter
The painter should be made from good quality new rope, about twice as long as the tender, and securely fastened to the ring bolt at the stem. One end should be whipped, the other spliced with a thimble seized into the splice and shackled to the ring bolt. If the tender is towed, a ring bolted to the forefoot makes a better anchorage point for the painter. The inner ring bolt can then be used to fasten a reserve tow line to hold the tender, should the painter part.

Rowlocks
The rowlock pins should be greased or

smeared with tallow, with a light lanyard attaching them to the hull.

A bailer or bucket, tied to the boat with another lanyard, should be stowed aboard the tender. Equip the tender with adequate reserve buoyancy. Polystyrene blocks can be cut and fitted beneath the thwarts. Paint them with resorcinal resin glue, then tape into place. Bottom boards should be held in place with one or two turn-buckles.

A thin plastic preventer strap should be screwed to the transom to stop the rudder floating off the pintles when the

stern is pushed deep into the water. Fit a ring bolt in the stern, to take a mooring line. Drainhole bungs should be tied to the boat.

Cleaning out the dinghy
The easiest way to clean out a small tender is to pull the boat out of the water, remove the bottom boards, roll her on to her side and sluice buckets of water over her. A rinse with fresh water will clean away the salty residue which might leave thwarts, etc., slightly sticky.

If the dinghy is to be stored for the winter in an exposed position, place it upside down on some form of support which allows plenty of air to circulate round the inside of the hull.

Oars and rowlocks
The diagram illustrates the dimensional relationship between the thwart, rowlocks and stretchers. Because of the space they occupy, stretchers are not fitted in most tenders. However, a thin batten 1 inch x ¼ inch (25 x 6 mm) screwed across the bottom boards or notched into a brace fixed to the skin, will provide a measure of heel support when rowing.

Rub tallow into the oar leathers each year, and use what is left over to lubricate the rowlock pins. Oars should be sanded and varnished each season.

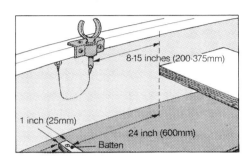

8-15 inches (200-375mm)

1 inch (25mm)

24 inch (600mm)

Batten

If the transom is sufficiently strong, cut a semi-circle into the upper edge, and line it with leather. Alternatively, fit a rowlock

Sculling — greater speed is achieved by altering the angle of the oar in water

in the centre of the transom, so that the boat can be sculled with a single oar.

Tenders Other hull types

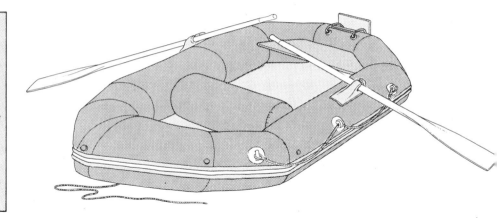

Inflatables

Inflatables make excellent tenders. They are easily stored, and when inflated they have a high load-carrying capacity. Lack of space, rather than lack of buoyancy, is the main cause of overloading. Their low centre of gravity and separate buoyancy compartments make them safe and reliable tenders.

Maintenance is simple. The points to look for are illustrated below.

Abrasions
Look at the bottom of the tender. This area is often scuffed where the boat has been pulled up the beach or hard. Scuffing marks are usually not serious, unless the inner woven fabric has been exposed. Badly scuffed parts should be patched as described below.

De-lamination
Occasionally the hull fabric of a poor quality inflatable will de-laminate, the outer layer of rubber having peeled away from the inner cloth. When a boat is in this state, it is best to buy a new one of better quality.

Patches should lie fair with the contours of the inflated chambers. Bulging patches have been badly glued, and should be replaced.

Wooden fittings
Check the bottom boards, thwart, and transom, and look for fractures and sharp edges. If left, these will endanger the craft. Broken bottom boards should be replaced, and sharp edges rounded to protect the fabric of the craft.

Ropes, handholds, and painters
These should be in good condition, and well-secured to the hull. A lanyard should tie the outboard motor to the tender should the transom clamps work loose.

Inflating
Inflate the hull chambers until they are difficult to depress with your thumb. Pressure varies according to the temperature. Seven psi is usually sufficient and the foot bellows will be difficult to operate beyond this pressure.

It is common practice to inflate the dinghy in the cool of early morning, invert in on the foredeck, lash it down, and leave it in the sun. The increase in temperature and pressure strains the joint between the bottom of the craft and the side buoyancy tanks, particularly at the corner where the side tube joins the bow tube. If dinghies are left on deck, they should only be partially inflated

Storing
Inflate the tender to full pressure and hose it clean. In particular, flush the crevices between the side tubes and the bottom. Make sure all grit and sand is removed before leaving the inflatable to dry. After a couple of hours, return to check the pressure. If temperature conditions have remained constant but pressure has dropped, check for leaks. If it does not leak, deflate and store.

Checking and repairing leaks
First check the valve of the deflated chamber. These are self-sealing and the seal can often be improved simply by re-inflating the chamber. Air flow dislodges the sand particles that may have prevented the seal. Reflate the chamber and test the valve with soapy water. If the valve continues to leak, dismantle and clean but do not grease or oil.

If the valve is found to be airtight, brush soapy water over the buoyancy chamber. Mark the puncture with a ballpoint pen or piece of chalk, and deflate the chamber. Leave it to dry on a smooth, flat, working surface. Select a patch of a suitable size. For cuts or tears of less than 2 inches (50mm), a patch with 1½ inch (37mm) overlap is usually

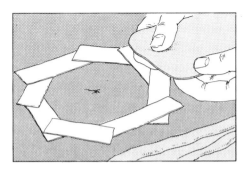

adequate. Round the corners of the patch, and then place it over the puncture. Draw round it with a ballpoint pen, and lightly abrade the surface of the patch and the area around the puncture with fine sandpaper. Take care not to roughen the surface beyond the

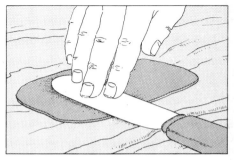

marks. Mask off the border of the repair area and apply a thin coat of repair adhesive to both the face of the patch and the damaged chamber.

Leave to dry and repeat. With the second coat just tacky, press the repair patch into position and flatten it with a smooth hard tool — a knife handle, rolling pin or piece of dowelling are suitable. Ensure that there are no folds or air bubbles between the patch and the fabric being repaired. Leave the patch for 12 hours, to cure before re-inflating. Larger tears can be sewn together, using the herringbone stitch described and illustrated on page 230 before glueing the patch in place. Remove the masking tape from around the repair before the glue has cured.

Punctures in the bottom of the inflatable can be located by raising the inflatable off the floor, and covering the bottom with an inch (25 mm) of water. Leaks will be noticed on the workshop floor beneath the puncture. Dry thoroughly, and fit a patch on both sides of the puncture.

Manufacturers of quality inflatables operate a network of service centres around the coast. More serious problems should be left to them to remedy.

Collapsible boats

The illustrations show a 7 foot (2m) 'Sea Hopper' dinghy, which weighs no more than 60 pounds (27.2kg), and collapses into a portable and easily-stowed unit, that can be lashed to the coach roof, or slung beneath the fo'c'sle deck beams. The 'Sea Hopper' is easy to stow, simple and quick to assemble, as well as being a safe and handy boat. The sides and bottom are made from ¼ inch (5mm) marine plywood, with hinges made from reinforced PVC. The main hinges, at the chines and keel, are strengthened by interlocking flanges which give additional rigidity when the boat is unfolded. The thwarts and bow transom are the only pieces that have to be inserted into the hull once the sides have been opened. These latter, with the folding plywood transom, keep the boat in shape.

Construction is straightforward, with hinges and ends glued to the unfinished plywood sides and bottom with a two part ethyl acetate adhesive. They are further reinforced at the hinges with the plywood flange strips which are glued and through-rivetted to sides and bottom.

The faired panels virtually eliminate chafe or abrasion of hinges and transom, and the entire woodwork of the hull is painted or varnished with a conventional oil-based marine finish.

Safety
Collapsible boats do not, as a rule, incorporate their own built-in buoyancy. Provision is made for fastening buoyancy bags beneath the thwarts on the 'Sea Hopper' and these should always be inflated and fitted before the tender is used. In addition, the tender should be equipped with a paddle, and a bailer which should be attached to the seats.

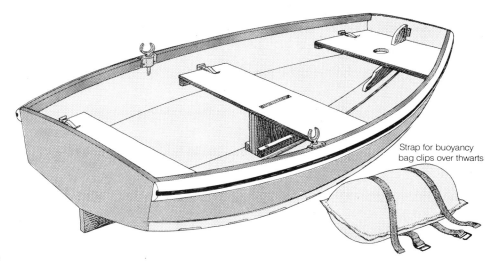

Strap for buoyancy bag clips over thwarts

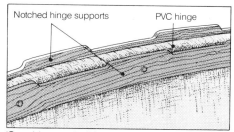

'Sea Hopper' chine hinge

Notched hinge supports   PVC hinge

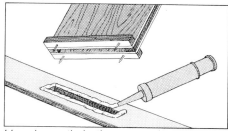

Use domestic bathroom sealant

Storing
Before storing for the winter, wash the boat thoroughly in fresh water. Take care to direct the hose into the hinges, and make sure that sand and grit are washed clear. Dry thoroughly before folding.

These small boats are durable, and require very little maintenance. Most of the repair and maintenance work is cosmetic. After several years, the varnish will need to be sanded and re-finished. Paintwork should also be touched in. The mast and spars of the sailing version should be waxed to protect them against corrosion, and the running rigging checked for wear.

After two or three seasons, the rivets holding the hinge flanges to the plywood panels oxidize. They should be scraped clean, and covered with hard epoxy filler and re-varnished.

The centreboard box, which is fitted to all models, is screwed to the keel, with a flexible sealing compound between the box and the keel to prevent leaks. Once leaks occur at the base of the centreboard, it should be unscrewed, and the bedding faces cleaned. Apply a film of flexible sealing compound around the slot in the keel, and position the centreboard box. Hold it in position with the woodscrews, and tighten them when the sealant has cured.

Aluminium hulls are more prone to denting and cracking than steel hulls, because the resistance of modern aluminium alloys to corrosion in sea-water makes it possible to construct the hulls from thinner plate than would be used on an equivalent steel hull.

Aluminium is easily worked, drilled and filed. It can be cut with a grinder, hacksaw or jigsaw, and fairly thick plate can be cut with hand shears. It hardens when hit, and so rivetting should be completed with the minimum of hammer blows.

Aluminium can also be very successfully bonded with epoxy resin, and where this is combined with pop-rivets or bolts, a very strong joint results.

It is possible to weld aluminium alloys, however, the equipment and the training required are not normally available to members of the general boat-owning public. Instead of venturing into this rather specialist field, it is probably better to use alternative jointing methods.

When working with aluminium in a metal-work shop, it is very important that tools and surfaces that come into contact with the aluminium are carefully cleaned of any iron or steel filings, swarf etc. Aluminium is (in contrast to steel) a soft metal, and small pieces of steel which become embedded in the surface of the aluminium will be the source of severe localized corrosion when fitted to the boat.

A well made boat constructed of aluminium alloy will not seriously corrode in conditions at sea. The surface of the aluminium will oxidize, and very slight pitting will occur, which, in the absence of other corrosive influences, will stabilize once the oxide film is established.

However, inter-craft electrolytic action will occur when an aluminium boat is moored in close proximity to a boat coated with a copper based anti-fouling, or sheathed in copper. The aluminium, being less noble than the copper, will suffer from this electrolytic activity. The welds are the first areas to be attacked, particularly in heavily welded areas — as at the stem, and centre-line aft of midships.

Aluminium is rarely used exclusively, and serious corrosion problems can also occur when other metals and materials are used in conjunction with aluminium.

Using aluminium alloys

When deciding to repair or alter an aluminium alloy hull it is essential to choose an alloy suitable for use at sea. Duralumin, although very strong, corrodes quickly, and should not be used. The alloys that are used successfully in ship building are generally aluminium/magnesium, and aluminium/magnesium/silicon alloys. Do not use alloys that contain copper. Seek advice before purchasing stock, fittings or fastenings.

Even the boat building alloys will corrode if they are covered with permanently damp lagging — such as asbestos insulation, or are faced with damp wood (decking, hand-rails etc), without a protective barrier of zinc chromate, bitumin, PVC, or anti-corrosive paint interposed between them. Permanently damp accumulations of debris in the bilges of an unpainted alloy hull will also start this form of poultice corrosion and may result in serious pittings, and even holes, developing in the aluminium.

With the exception of zinc, marine grade aluminium alloys are nearly all anodic to other metals used in shipbuilding. Great thoroughness must be exercised when fastening repairs, reinforcements or fittings to an aluminium structure, and if the additions are made from aluminium alloy, care must be taken to isolate them from the steel or other more noble metals used in the boat.

Various means can be adopted to insulate the dissimilar metals, or to

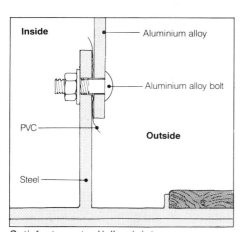

Satisfactory steel/alloy joint

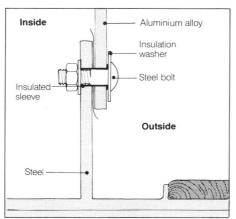

Insulation inhibits bolt corrosion

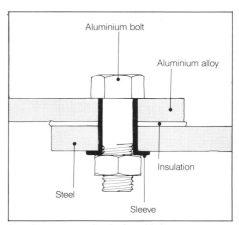

Insulate at poorly drained joints

reduce the potential difference between them. The cathodic metal can be sprayed or painted with an aluminium paint composition, or an insulating barrier can be interposed between them.

Where dissimilar metals are rivetted together, it is impossible to isolate them completely. Instead, it is best to design the joint so that the dissimilar metals are placed in a sheltered and self-draining situation, to inhibit the corrosion, while the similar metals (rivet and outer plate) are exposed to the weather.

The configuration of the joint will determine which metal should be used for the rivet. Where it is inevitable that corrosion around a rivet will occur, make sure that the rivet is cathodic to the surrounding plate. In general, where galvanic corrosion is likely to occur, the fastening should be cathodic to the mass of metal.

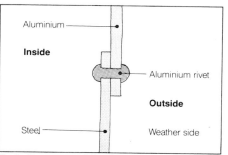
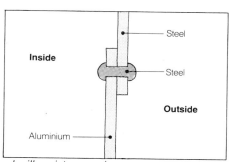

Both these combinations are well planned and will resist corrosion

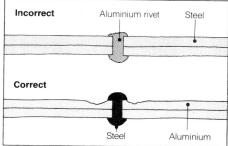

Use cathodic or similar fastenings

Fittings below the water-line

Wherever possible use plastic or nylon skin fittings through an aluminium hull. However, if these fittings are unavailable, and a metal fitting is used instead, take every precaution to prevent electrolytic activity from occurring between the aluminium hull and metal fittings.

There are several methods to protect the hull and fittings. Because none of the safeguards will ensure total protection, it is best to use a combination of the methods described below.

1 Fasten the fitting with aluminized steel bolts, and coat all touching surfaces with several coats of zinc chromate paint.

2 Fit a non-metallic gasket and sleeve between the dissimilar metals. The minimum thickness for the gasket, which can be made from Delrin, or other suitable insulating material, should be about 1/4 inch (6mm).

Note: Nylon is hygroscopic and should not be used to insulate dissimilar metals immersed in sea water.

3 Bed the gaskets in flexible compound, to which a quantity of zinc chromate paste has been added.

4 Where the through-hull fitting is made from copper, or from a nickel-based alloy, take these precautions in conjunction with a sacrificial anode bolted close to the fitting.

If in doubt, seek professional advice before making alterations or additions to the hull involving dissimilar metals.

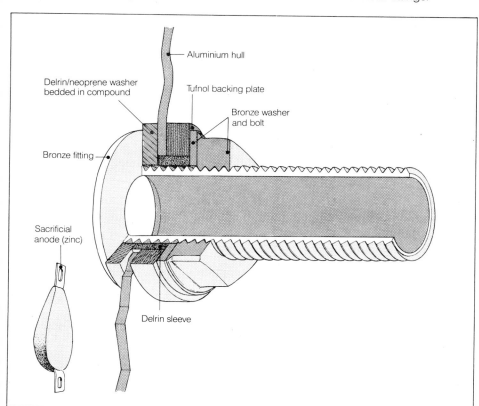

Insulated through-hull fitting below water-line

The illustration on the right shows the constructional details of a ferro-cement hull. The cement is reinforced by a framework of rods, pipes, and wire mesh. A very thin (1/8 inch [3mm]) layer of cement fairs and seals the reinforcement against the entry of water off the hull.

In most ferro-cement hulls the keel is hollow and filled with ballast before being grouted over. Rudders are made either from steel plate or timber. Decks can be built into the structure but, in many cases, a plywood deck is laid upon laminated wooden deck beams bolted or bonded into a reinforced cement beam shelf.

Structural bulkheads and floors are usually built into the concrete reinforcing, and laid up with the rest of the hull. Timber bulkheads in small boats under 35 feet (10m), and non-structural bulkheads in larger ferro-cement craft, are attached to lugs or flanges integral

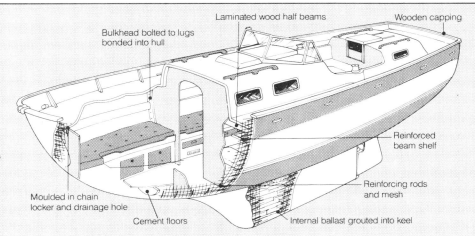

with the hull reinforcement. Repairs are generally straightforward, and do not require more tools or technical knowledge than the average handyman possesses. Repairs have been successfully carried out to some vessels so badly damaged that large sections of hull were missing.

Particular attention should be paid to any cracking in the thin surface cement. These cracks should be sealed at once, before moisture penetrates into and starts to corrode the reinforcing matrix. The procedure for doing this is described below.

Repairing cracks in the cement skin

Dry the area very thoroughly with a heat gun or portable electric heater before filling the crack with thixotropic epoxy resin. Press the resin into the crack with a piece of flexible plastic or a palette-knife. The degree of re-finishing required will depend upon the extent to which the surface of the paintwork has been disturbed. Where it has been necessary to rub back to the cement, a thin coat of resin, followed by two coats of epoxy primer will be required. Finish with a suitable marine paint.

Larger cracks and flaked areas
Remove loose flakes of cement, and chip open the larger cracks. Dry the area thoroughly. Mix a small quantity of ordinary portland building cement into some pre-mixed epoxy resin. Add sufficient cement to bring the mixture to a putty-like consistency. Prime the crack with a brush coat of epoxy resin, and then press the putty into the holes and level it.

Rub down the surface with 'wet and dry' paper, and re-paint it. Rubbing down is the most arduous part of the operation,

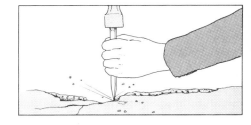

and every effort should be made to level the putty and fair it into the line of the hull before the resin starts to cure. Prime the repair and adjacent hull surfaces with epoxy resin, before final painting.

Repairing holes or dents
As with the previous examples, it is very important that the damaged area should be completely dried out. Where salt water may have entered the cement, the whole area should be thoroughly washed with fresh warm water.

Remove any loose fragments of cement, and clean back the friable edges so that the new cement composition has a sound foundation.

Punch back the distorted reinforcing until it is fair with the rest of the hull. Check this by holding a flexible batten against the hull. There should be at least 1/8 inch (3mm) between the reinforcement and the batten. Anything less than this will result in a lump in the hull when the cement is faired in. Depressions less than 3/4 inch (20mm) deep can be filled with a low density epoxy filler once the major repair is complete.

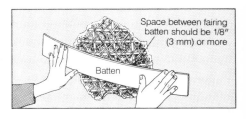

Do not separate the reinforcing mesh in order to bring it fair with the line of the hull. It is the closely spaced mesh of wire and rod reinforcements which give the hull its strength. Large volumes of unreinforced cement will weaken the hull.

Once the general profile of the hull has been restored, inspect the cement bonded to the reinforcements, and remove any pieces that are loose. Flush the repair with warm, fresh water and leave it to dry. Brush away surface dust, and then stipple on a coat of epoxy resin, thinned with 20% epoxide thinners.

Follow with a couple of coats of full epoxy resin, leaving a full day between coats for the resin to cure properly.

Mix up, and make good the repair with an epoxy resin and dry cement putty. Apply this with a trowel, and fair it with small sheets of flexible plastic. Leave it to cure, then fair, and build up low spots with a second coat. Make sure that the epoxy resin-cement mix is well pressed into the reinforcement matrix, and that all voids are filled.

If the repair is undertaken while the boat is laid up, the patch can be repaired with a cement and aggregate mix (in proportions of about 1½:2) instead of using dry cement and epoxy resin.

Fresh cement should always be used. There is a wide variety available, and it is sensible to seek help in choosing a type suited to the weather conditions. A quick-hardening cement is to be preferred when working outside in cold weather. Aggregate should be fine and even textured and graded with a 3/16 inch (5mm) mesh sieve. Mix the cement and aggregate thoroughly before adding the minimum amount of water necessary to make the mix workable.

Before plastering up the damaged area, brush or stipple a cement grout or other bonding agent, to improve the bond between the dry cement skin and the wet cement repair.

Lay up the repair with a trowel or float. Finish with a wooden float. Fair the patch with a light wooden batten. Do not try to press the repaired section into shape once the cement has begun to cure. This might cause serious internal fracturing, that will be a source of weakness and corrosion.

As the cement begins to cure, rub it down with a damp sponge to remove the trowel marks. Use very little pressure, and work the sponge in small circles over the repair.

Cover the repair with a sheet of polythene, and tape around its edge. This is to prevent evaporation of the water, and is a necessary precaution to take if the reinforced cement is to reach maximum strength without cracking. After leaving the repair for twenty-four hours, open up the polythene, and drape a rag saturated with water over the repair, then replace the polythene. Maintain this routine for about a month. In cold, wet weather the cement will take longer to cure. Dry, windy weather will accelerate curing and the rag may need more frequent replenishment with water.

Grind back the hull with a grinder fitted with a carborundum disc. Use the grinder cautiously and avoid cutting through to the reinforcements. Brush off the dust, and apply a wash of diluted hydrochloric acid to the freshly cured cement. When it is completely dry, wire brush it, then apply an epoxy resin sealing coat. Fair in the surface with an epoxy resin filler, and finish with paint. (Details of a ferro-cement paint scheme can be found on page 305).

Ferro-cement decks are sometimes prone to surface crazing which, if left unattended will continue to deteriorate, particularly in frosty weather. Cracks should be filled with an unthickened epoxy resin, and burnished smooth in the manner described on page 80. If the problem persists, the deck will need to be laid with a glass fibre cloth.

Bond this to the hull with epoxy resin. Lay up the woven cloth with polyester resin once the initial epoxy has cured. Seal with epoxy resin, and finish with traditional deck paint.

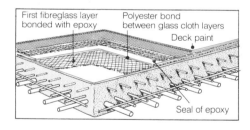

Fastenings to a ferro-cement hull

Unstressed fittings can easily be fixed to the inside of the hull by glueing them with an epoxy resin adhesive. Stressed fittings should be bolted. Use a masonry drill to bore through the skin. Steel bolts should be bedded in sealing compound and have large washers, with a load spreading plate where necessary. Press the fitting into a bedding of thickened epoxy resin, and tighten the nuts. Clean away the resin squeezed from the join.

Where new bulkheads or major stressed fittings need to be installed, the cement skin must be drilled and then chipped back with a hammer and cold chisel to expose the reinforcement rods. Wire in a

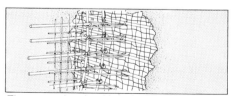
Flange rods wired into hull mesh

suitable reinforcement mesh. Load-carrying bulkheads should be supported by a continuous flange; lighter structures can be fixed against lugs bonded into the reinforcement.

Before trowelling on the cement, arrange suitable wooden shuttering. Ensure

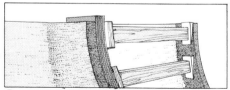
Press cement against rigid shuttering

that it is wedged firmly into place, as a thorough impregnation of the reinforcement requires a considerable degree of force and vibration. Fill in the cavities in the hull, and lay up the flange with either an epoxy resin and cement mix or, if time allows, cement and aggregate.

Plywood hulls Other hull types

The illustration below shows the framework of a typical plywood single chine hull.

Plywood panels are cut to shape and bent cold over rigid frames and battens. The plywood is glued and fastened to these and to the chine stringer — a thicker batten that runs the length of the hull at the turn of the bilge.

The edges of the plywood sheets are usually protected by a covering batten glued and screwed once the ply panels are in place. No caulking is applied at the joins between the plywood, instead plenty of resorcinal or epoxy resin glue is used to fill any gaps between the ends. Plywood panels can be scarfed (with a joint not less than eight times longer than the thickness of the ply). Alternatively they can be butted with very large butt straps of similar ply,

glued, and screwed, or through-fastened, to support the join.

In comparison with traditionally constructed hulls, plywood hulls are generally lighter, their frames tend to be spaced further apart and the skin thickness is often over 40 per cent thinner than on a similarly sized carvel hull.

It is therefore very important that the hull is built and maintained to the highest standards.

Plywood is subject to the same afflictions which beset other wooden craft with the added concerns that all fastenings fitted to the plywood skin must bear against doubling pieces to spread the load, and that every part of the framework must be functional and in good order.

Only marine grade plywood should be used for boat building or repairs. Marine ply is designated with the British Standard 1088 mark. Marine grade plywood in the USA is sold as 'marine ply', and is further graded by the quality of the facing veneers and the core material used between them. De-lamination (the separation of the plywood veneers) is not a serious problem in boats made from marine grade ply; however, many plywood boats have their decking, and sometimes their topsides, made from exterior ply, which does not stand up to the conditions afloat. Where surface buckling occurs (revealed in cracked and lifting paintwork, or undulations along the direction of the grain beneath the finish) it is essential to discover whether the cause is the stressing, or freezing of waterlogged marine ply, or the inevitable deterioration of exterior grade ply.

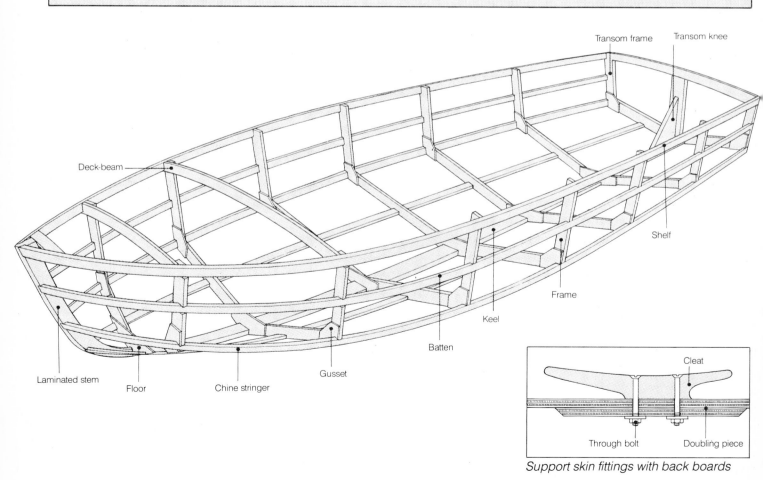

Support skin fittings with back boards

Cutting and working ply

The face plys tear and splinter when sawn. Cut plywood with its face side uppermost using a small toothed cross cut saw.

Where both the inside and the outside of the sawn edge are going to show, clamp a thin board behind the ply to prevent it from splintering. Plane the edges with a low angle block plane, held askew to the line of the board.

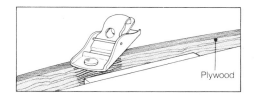

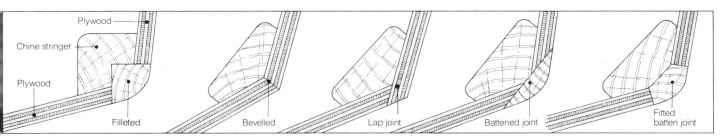

Edge protection

Marine grade ply can be used with or without the protection of an edge batten. Badly fitted battens which permit the water to enter the end grain of the plywood core also prevent the panel from drying out thoroughly. Moisture trapped in the core can cause internal rot that may not spread to the outer veneers, and is therefore difficult to detect. Rot is indicated by a dead, muffled sound when the panel is tapped with a light hammer and, possibly, by a discolouration of the face plys. Explore rotted areas with a bradawl, probed through the outer veneers. The weakness of the inner core will be apparent by the ease with which the bradawl passes into the ply once it has penetrated the outer layer. Rotted parts must be cut out and replaced.

Repairs to de-laminated areas of marine ply

Marine ply that has become de-laminated is not usually seriously weakened by the slight lifting of the surface layer of veneer, but it looks ugly, and is impossible to re-finish well without rectifying the fault.

Open the veneer bubbles with a knife, and dry the inner core with a hair drier, or a heat gun. Mix up a small quantity of thickened epoxy glue, and work in the glue with a palette knife or syringe.

Cover the area with a sheet of polythene, and hold the de-laminated parts down with staples, fired through a thin plywood board.

Remove the staples and polythene once the glue is cured, but before it is fully hardened. Sand and re-finish when thoroughly dry. (All working conditions for epoxy glues must be strictly followed - see page 79.)

Fill the staple holes before refinishing.

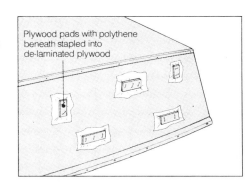

Plywood pads with polythene beneath stapled into de-laminated plywood

Repairing small areas of accidental damage

Fill small scratches and areas of localized damage with epoxy putty or a resin filler. Deep scratches and dents should be cleaned and sanded and backed with a butt block of marine ply, through-fastened to the outer skin. Anchor the filler with copper tacks embedded in the recess below the surface level of the outer veneer. For varnished hulls make the filler by adding an appropriately coloured sanding dust (taken from the bag of a belt sander, for instance) to unthickened epoxy glue. Surround the damaged part with a coat of strippable paste or masking tape, and apply the filler, pressing it well in behind the heads of the tacks.

The anchorage of the filler can be improved if a little unthickened glue is brushed over the recess and allowed to partly cure before the filler is added.

Patching

Repairs to small holes

Cut back the damaged wood, and shape the hole to a regular rectangle or oval with a jigsaw or keyhole saw. Clean around the border of the hole on the inside, and cut a large oval or rectangular backing piece of ply. Chamfer the edges, and drill two small holes through the centre. These holes are to take a holding wire to brace the patch against the inside of the hull — more can be drilled if it is to be braced against a curved part of the hull.

Paint thixotropic epoxy glue on to the inside of the ply, and also on the bearing face of the inner patch. Slip the patch through and position it behind the hole. Pull the wires tight, and leave the glue to harden.

Cut another patch, slightly larger than the hole in the side of the hull. Align the wood to match the grain of the hull and mark round its edge while holding it in place.

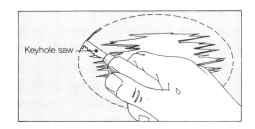

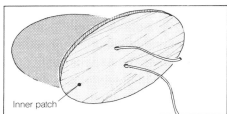

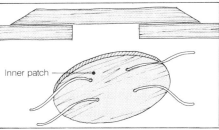

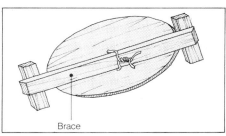

Apply glue before inserting patch and pulling tight

Outer patch should fit snugly, and match grain etc. if varnish finish

Fit the patch. Bed it in glue, and hold it in place with staples. Remove the staples

and fill any seams between the patch and the plywood hull.

Repairs to large holes

Holes greater than 4 inches (100mm) square — caused by collision or grounding — are repaired by cutting out the damaged ply and inserting a well-fitted patch of marine ply. The procedure for doing this is rarely straightforward, as battens or frames often need to be cut back or removed entirely, before the inner bracing piece can be fitted.

1 Make a template of the insert needed, and hold it against the hull to check that it covers all the broken or splintered ply. Draw round the template and check that the area on the inside of the hull is clear of fittings, wires and pipework before

cutting. Use a jigsaw fitted with a short, fine-toothed blade. Square up the edges of the hole with a rasp or bullnose plane.

2 Ask a helper to hold the ply for the replacement patch against the hull. Position it over the hole and align the grain to match that of the skin. Mark round the inside edge of the hole to give the exact shape of the new patch. Cut it out and trim it to fit.

3 Check inside the hull. A backing piece to brace the patch will need to be inserted. This must lie flush against the inner face of the ply. Battens or frames must be removed or cut back, close to

the line of the plywood. If this is impossible, or impractical, fit a bracing piece to the side of the frame, and notch the butt strap into it, bedding it in epoxy glue and filler.

4 Cut the larger inside brace from a single piece of marine ply of the same thickness as the outer skin, or from four strips of ply, mitred at each corner. The width of the butt support should be at least 6 inches (150mm) wide for ¼ inch (6mm) ply, and 8 inches (200mm) for 3/8 inch (10mm) ply. These are minimum sizes. A wider butt strap should be fitted at the bows and to the underside of the

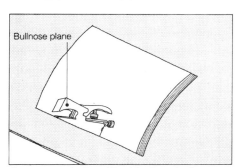

Square up hole with chisel and plane before cutting repair patch

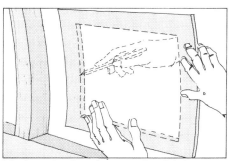

Mark and cut replacement patch by holding ply against hole and drawing around its edge

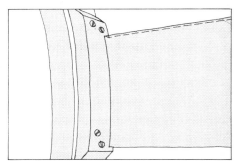

When damaged area is adjacent to stringer or frame, fit bracing piece to hold patch

hull. Clean away the finish on the inside, to take the butt support.

5 Glue, and screw or rivet the brace to the inside face of the plywood. Fastenings should be spaced not more than 2 inches (50mm) apart, in two rows.

6 Spread glue on to the bedding faces of the brace and fasten the patch into position.

7 Add a thickener to the epoxy glue,and fill and level the joints. Clean up with 'wet and dry' paper prior to finishing.

8 Replace any battens and frames that have been removed and pack and seal any spaces with epoxy filler to restore the support behind the frames.

Splicing and doubling frames

The most common forms of framing used in the construction of a plywood hull are illustrated below.

Frames are constructed from straight-grained, often parallel-sided timber. Stress concentrations occur at the keel and at the chines, where frame members are butted or cross-halved together. Chines should be supported by gussets, faired into the line of each frame timber.

The plywood planking of the hull is glued and screwed to the framework so that, even after fracturing or splitting, the frame is very difficult to remove without damaging the plywood. Where fracturing occurs, it is usually best to repair the damage frame and then support it with a doubling piece.

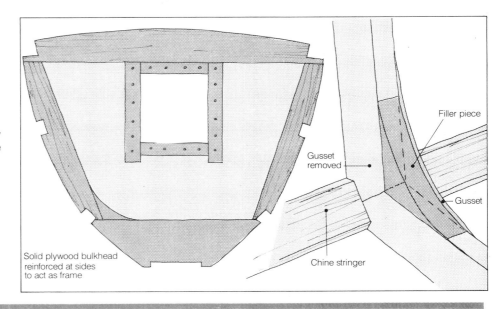

Solid plywood bulkhead reinforced at sides to act as frame

Filler piece

Gusset removed

Gusset

Chine stringer

A damaged frame
All interior fittings close to the frame, including those that cover the keel, should be removed and the entire frame inspected closely. Serious impact at the side of the frame will be transmitted to the keel and to the deck beam and shelf, and may even cause weakening at the chine on the opposite side of the hull.

All glue joints and fastenings should be checked for movement and weakness.

Repairing a fractured frame
Mix a thickened epoxy glue, wedge open the splits in the frame timber, and squeeze the glue into the crack with a plastic syringe.

Shore the frame together and hold it with screws. Scrape the glue and paint away from the ply and the side of the frame. Clamp a bracing piece against the side of the frame and spile the curve of the ply skin on to its side. Cut this line, refit the brace, and make a second spiling for the bevel.

Cut the inner face of the brace flush with the frame. Taper the ends of the brace, unless they rest against the chine stringer, shelf or keel. Set the brace in thickened epoxy glue and through-fasten it to the frame.

Serious breakages should be repaired with reinforcement pieces glued on both sides of the frame. Where the damage has occurred close to the chine, gussets should be removed and the bracing pieces brought right down to the chine stringer. A new larger gusset should then be fitted.

As with all boat repairs, where damage has occurred which reveals a localized weakness in the hull, the repair should remedy the damage and attempt to rectify the weakness. Seek professional advice before undertaking major or time-consuming alterations.

Note: Do not countersink screws — let them recess themselves under the pressure of the screwdriver.

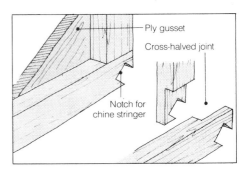

Ply gusset

Cross-halved joint

Notch for chine stringer

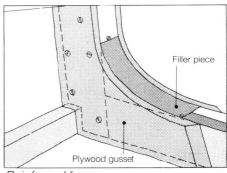

Filler piece

Plywood gusset

Reinforced frame

The illustration of the moulded plywood hull shows its essentially simple construction. The hull is constructed over a mould to which strips of veneer are fitted and tacked. Several layers of veneer are laid, the grain direction of each layer at an opposing angle to the layer beneath. Small voids between veneers are filled with epoxy filler and the surface is planed smooth before subsequent veneers are added. The resulting hull is extremely strong and resilient and, because the laminates are impregnated with epoxy resin; they are virtually rot-resistant and stable.

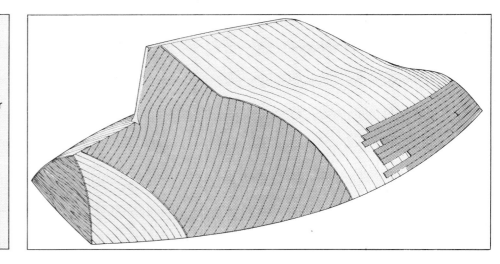

Damage to a moulded hull

Minor surface abrasions can be repaired using the techniques of filling and sanding described on pages 44-5. Large areas of damage must be cut back and new veneers laminated to restore the original strength and shape of the hull.

Repairing a moulded hull
Assemble a collection of veneers suited to the repair. Wider veneers can be used at the ends of the boat, narrower ones at the middle of the hull where there is more compound curvature. Keep the veneers that best match the colour and the grain pattern of the outside skin for the last layer.

Ideally the replacement strips of veneer should be fitted and the layers staggered, as they build up to the outer finish layer. However, this means that such a very large outer area of veneer is removed and replaced that the technique, although sound, is often impractical. An alternative is to insert a plug into the hull skin to make up most of the required thickness, and to laminate over this.

No internal mould is needed for this repair. Fashion a plug a trifle larger than the hole or break in the hull. Fair the outer and inner face of the plug to conform with the curvature of the hull. Working from the inside of the hull, cover the damaged area with the plug, and mark round its edge. Remove the waste inside the marks, so that the plug lies flat and below the inner surface of the hull skin.

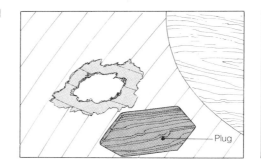

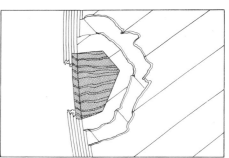

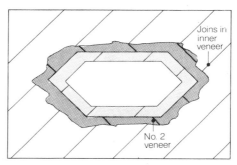

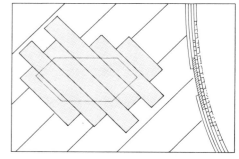

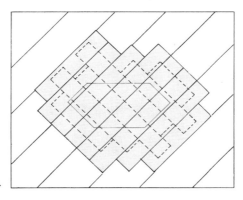

There is little advantage in choosing a complex shape for the plug. A simple square rectangle, diamond, or a combination of these shapes, is quite suitable, provided it fits well into the recess. Insert plug and lay up veneers on inside. When the glue has cured, use the same technique for the repairs to the outside.

Glue the plug in place. When the epoxy resin has hardened, fair it flush with the groundwork of the second layer of veneer on the inside.

Trim, fit, and glue the inside veneers in place, staggering the ends of each layer by the width of the veneer strips, and overlapping the layer beneath also by a width equivalent to one veneer strip, or 2 inches (50mm). Staple the veneers into position with holding pads placed beneath the staple to spread the staple pressure.

If after the inner plug is fitted more than five plys need to be built up on the outer layer, a small outer plug should be fitted and glued, to bring the face of the plug level with the groundwork for the final three layers. Finish as for the inside, choosing the outer layer of veneers with care, and laying them on a groundwork free from bumps or depressions.

Twisting veneers into awkward corners

Most problems of this kind can be overcome by building the laminate layer with narrower strips of veneer. However, in parts of the hull where there is a sudden and awkward curvature, the solution is to cut the veneer so that its grain is on the bias to the line of the strip. This short-grained strip will bend readily into the required shape and, provided that it is lapped into the strips of laminate in the normal way, and is well soaked in epoxy resin, it will not reduce the strength of the repair significantly.

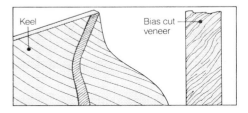

Fitting and shaping veneers

As the outer veneers are replaced, they will need to be fitted accurately to each other. Fit the ends of the veneers first, so that they lie within the recess. Fit one veneer in the centre of the repair, keeping both of its sides straight and parallel. Slip the adjacent veneer beneath the side of the centre veneer, and trim its end to butt closely into position. Draw down the overlap to mark the profile of the edge joint, remove the second veneer, cut it to the line with a knife, and trim with a block plane. Apply glue to both the veneer and to the recess, once the veneer has been fitted.

Where there is a large number of veneers to be laid, it is worth while making up the spiling jig. This enables the veneer to be glued and stapled into place before its edge is transferred to the new veneer. Cut the veneers to the spiled line before trimming the ends to fit into the recesses cut in the hull.

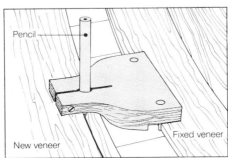

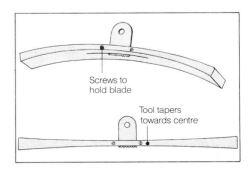

Finishing the veneering

Cut back the groundwork for the final veneer very carefully. Before cutting and fitting the final layer, chisel and rasp away any high spots, and fill any depressions revealed by a toothed depth gauge. The finish veneer should lie flat and very slightly proud of the surrounding skin.

It is impossible to make any but the most modest adjustments to the surface of the repair at this point, otherwise plane cuts or sanding and scraping may cut through to the layers of veneer beneath, marring the finished appearance.

Planing the veneer

Do not plane the final veneer unless it is more than 1/8 inch (3mm) thick. Sub-surface veneers can be planed. The risk of tear-out is reduced if the blade is sharpened to a very steep angle.

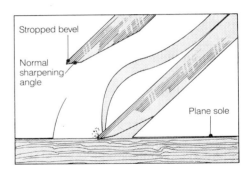

The insert shows the fastening arrangements for each type of planking. Planking thickness is equivalent to that of a carvel hull of the same size, but it may be lighter if a durable but lightweight wood is used for the inner planking.

A waterproof membrane of calico or muslin soaked in boiled linseed oil (or other oil-based compound) provides a watertight seal at the intersections of the inner and outer planking. In example C, muslin soaked in resorcinal or epoxy glue can be used to bond the planks.

The inner and the outer layers of a double skin hull are screwed or clenched together. Both layers are through-fastened to the frames. The planks on the fore and aft double skin are screwed at the seams and through-fastened to the frames.

The planks are planed to fit tightly together without any caulking bevel. Caulking is used only at the garboard seam and at the stem. Some thin strands of caulking cotton are usually laid in the stem rabbet and around the edge of the transom before the planking is nailed in.

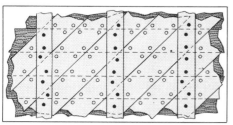

A Outer fore and aft, inner diagonal

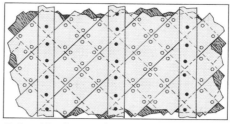

B Double diagonal

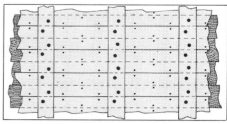

C Both plank layers fore and aft

Damage to a double skin hull

Repairing damage to a double skin hull is relatively straightforward, provided that it is limited to the outer planking.

Planks can be removed by releasing the fastenings holding the outer plank once they have been identified on the inside. This operation is best performed by drilling four pilot holes from the outside at the corners of the damaged part and releasing all fastenings that fall within the area defined by the four holes.

When only a very small part of a plank is damaged, release the fastenings holding the plank a little beyond the damaged part. Chop a deep groove across the width of the damaged plank, taking care not to penetrate right through to the calico membrane. If the membrane is impaired, slip a strip of calico soaked in boiled linseed oil over the damage. Slide a thin sheet of ply beneath the

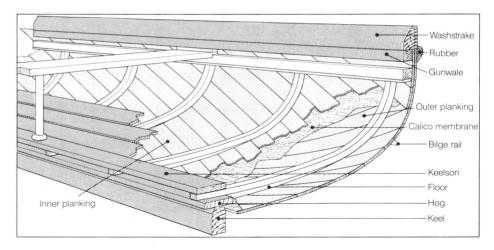

Inner planking
Washstrake
Rubber
Gunwale
Outer planking
Calico membrane
Bilge rail
Keelson
Floor
Hog
Keel

broken and loosened end of the plank. Mark across and chisel the butt square, using the ply as a chopping board. When replacing planks that expose large portions of end grain, stand the planks in preservative before fitting them to the hull. Always brush boiled linseed oil or compound on to the cloth membrane before replacing the plank. Fit, paint, and then screw or rivet plank in place.

Locating leaks

The eventual deterioration of the membrane between the inner and outer skins will cause the hull to leak. Although the leak may not, in itself, be serious, the result may cause the inner planking to rot. It is extremely difficult to trace the exact source of a leak. The best solution is often to remove the outer planking and renew the membrane.

If a close inspection on the inside of the hull reveals signs of rot or dampness behind the paintwork, drill through from the inside to identify the outside planks that need to be removed. Release all fastenings on the inside in the area of rot. Follow these down the line of the outside planks, releasing all the outer planks from the inner layer. Remove the fastenings holding both layers of planking to the frames. Work very thoroughly: one or two missed fastenings will prevent a plank from being removed and more time will be lost returning inside the hull to hunt for the overlooked nails.

The condition of the watertight membrane will be evident once one or two outer planks are removed. If it is rotted and friable, more outside planks should be removed until sound cloth is reached. Cut or tear away the decayed fabric, and inspect the inner planking.

Repair to the inner planking of the hull

In order to make a thorough repair to even a small area of rot, large numbers of extra outside planks will have to be released. The operation is straightforward, but extremely costly and time consuming.

An alternative to removing all of the overlapping outer planks is to cut out the

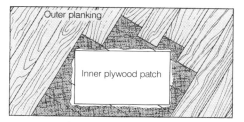

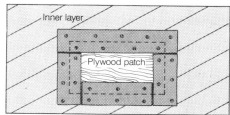

rotted inner planking and replace it from the outside with a plywood patch of the same thickness as the original planking. Screw and glue plywood butt blocks behind the patch also, to brace it to the inner planking.

Replacing the decayed calico

Before replacing the outside planking,

tear a length of calico into strips a little wider than the outer planks, and soak them in boiled linseed oil. Overlap the edge of the old, sound, membrane with the calico, and re-fasten the first plank. Continue in this way, laying the calico over the inside planking, with its edge overlapping the previous strip, before each plank is added.

Fitting new planks to the outside

New diagonal planks are spiled and fitted in the same way as for a normal carvel hull (see page 46). Before fastening the new planks in place, put plywood plates beneath the heads of the fastenings at the edge of the original plank. These hold the new plank firmly while it is fitted; remove the plates before tightening the fastenings. In most parts of the hull it is only necessary to spile and shape one edge of each plank, although the curve on each plank will vary, depending upon the part of the boat being planked and the degree of curvature at that part of the hull. As each plank is fastened into place, make sure

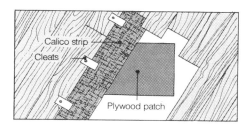

that the nail or rivet heads are punched well below the surface of the timber, and that the screws are countersunk. The hull can then be planed fair without damaging the plane iron.
Once the outer planking is in place and fastened, return to the inside of the hull.

Complete the repair by drilling two rows of through-fastenings to tie the butt blocks to the inner planking and to the plywood. Remove the screws holding the butt blocks, and replace them with fastenings driven through from the outside, and rivetted on the inside.

When the hull has been restored and the rotted parts have been removed and replaced by new wood, consider the possibility of sheathing the hull with a nylon cloth impregnated with resorcinal glue, to protect the planking and the remaining tired, old, membrane from further deterioration.

Double skin

Double skin hulls with both layers of plank running fore and aft, are generally easier to repair than the double or single diagonal planking. Access to each inner plank is obtained by removing two outer planks. However, where the planks are bonded together with a layer of muslin and marine glue between them, the hull will have to be repaired as for a single skin boat, replacement lengths of plank being stepped and laminated into place. Remove screws and through-fastenings prior to cutting out the damaged planking with a router, set to the same thickness as the plank.

Ashcroft

This is a similar construction to that detailed above, except that the planking is set at a raking angle to the keel. A

calico or muslin membrane is interposed between the double planking.

The first, thinner, layer of planking is tacked to the keel, stringers and gunwale. The outer planking is nailed or screwed at the keel and stringers, and through-rivetted or screwed at the gunwale. The two layers are rivetted together once the hull is fully planked.

Inner planks can be exposed and renewed by removing the two overlapping covering planks. Replace the calico as described above for the double skin hull. Spile replacement planks after springing them into place. Do not fasten the inner and the outer planking together until all the main fastenings to the keel stringers and gunwale have been made.

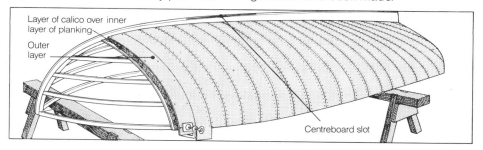

Strip planking Other hull types

The main methods used to strip plank a hull are illustrated below. In example 1, the strips are narrow and parallel-sided, and run out to the gunwale where they are trimmed. 2 is built with strips faired and tapered, as in carvel construction. Example 3 combines both techniques.

The strips are edge-nailed with either glue or bedding compound betweeen them. Galvanized nails are normally used, their length apppproximately two and a quarter times the width of the strips.

Edge seams are either bevelled to a close fit or radiused with a spindle moulder or set of moulding planes. Scarf joints equivalent in length to two nail spaces are made down the face of the strip.

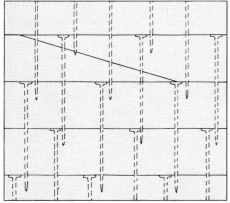

Staggered plank fastenings

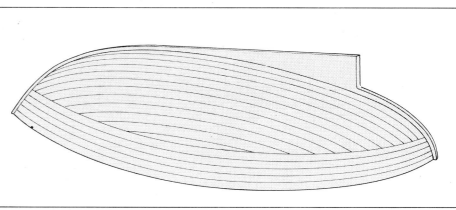

1 Strip planked hull made from parallel strips run-out at gunwale

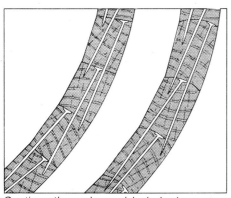

Sections through moulded planks

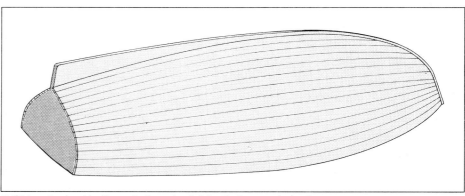

2 Strip planked hull made from individually tapered planks

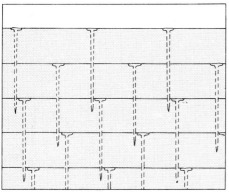

Vertical scarf joint

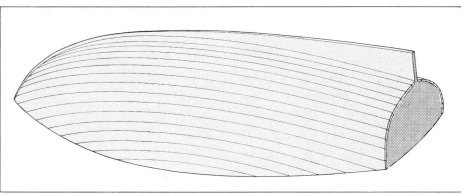

3 A combination of above

Framing

Frames are steam bent and, because of the inherent strength of the hull, are more widely spaced than on a carvel or clinker hull. The edge-nailing of the tightly fitted strips creates a structure that, when wet, will swell to the point where frames pull away from their fastenings, or fracture because of the tensions in the hull. These frame

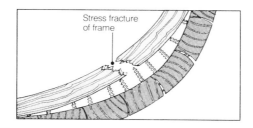

breakages can occur at any point, but are most common at the turn of the bilges. New part frames or doubling pieces should be rivetted to strengthen the weakened area.

Repairs to the hull planking

Even where planking is damaged close to the sheer-strake, cutting out strip planks and replacing them with new wood is a far from straightforward operation. In practice, it is unusual to be able to re-use a plank once it has been forced apart from the strips below, and keeping intact the strips that are nailed and glued is nearly impossible.

Remove interior hull fittings and square up the damaged area. Saw out the broken ends of the strips, and chop out the wood between fastenings. Saw away the fastenings flush with the strip seams.

Mark on the side of the hull the approximate position of each fastening. Plan the sequence of repairs, with the position of the fastenings in mind. To avoid cutting a scarf through a nail, butt the final closing strip at each end. Steep scarf joints can be used at the ends of the other replacement pieces. Cut and trim the butts and scarf joints using a power jigsaw fitted with a metal cutting blade. Remove and replace the minimum planking necessary.

Fit and rebuild the hull planking. Set each strip on thixotropic epoxy resin and glue and wedge it in place. If there is room, nail each strip as well.

Force the final closing piece into place after the glue holding the other strips has cured. Make the closing piece a little thicker than necessary so that it can be pressed right through to lie flush, or just raised, on the inside.

Leave the repaired planks to set in the resin, and then fair the inside and the outer planking. Fit short, steamed ribs across the inside of the repair and blocks at the butt joints and scarfs.

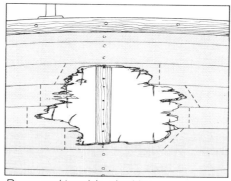

Damaged topside planking

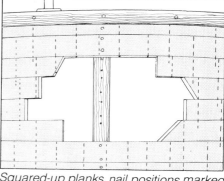

Squared-up planks, nail positions marked

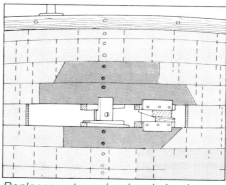

Replacements wedged and glued

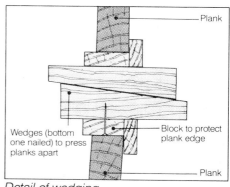

Detail of wedging

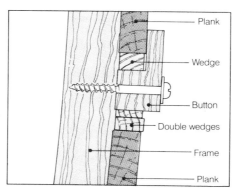

Alternative wedging method

Closing piece into place

Chapter 7

Keels, Ballast and Rudders

A ballast keel, bolted against the main keel, serves to lower the centre of gravity of the hull. This will increase the ability of a boat to carry sail and, when fitted to a motor boat, will compensate for the weight of the superstructure.

The precise weight of the keel will be decided while the boat is still in its design stages. Trimming the boat after the hull is completed and the engine and all other fittings are aboard is accomplished by stowing inside ballast.

The ballast keel is therefore not the only stabilizing factor in the hull. The engine, hull fittings, water and oil tanks and anchor chain are all included in the calculations before the weight and location of the ballast keel is decided.

A ballast keel that is too heavy will give the boat a stiff, cranky feel that will make her uncomfortable in moderate sea conditions and dangerous in rough weather. A boat fitted with a keel that is too light, will roll and seem top heavy. Both faults result in a vessel that is unseaworthy and uncomfortable, and it is not always easy to distinguish between the two sets of symptoms. Proposed

alterations to the weight and situation of the keel should be referred to a naval architect.

There are several different methods of fastening a ballast keel to the keel of a boat.

The following descriptions and techniques relate in particular to traditionally constructed wooden hulled vessels, but as the method of bolting is similar in fibreglass, steel, and ferro-cement hulls fitted with outside ballast, the information is broadly relevant to all these boats.

The ballast keel is bolted against the underside of the keel. Fairing in pieces, known as deadwoods (fore deadwood and aft deadwood) are fitted against the leading and after edge of the ballast keel. At the after end, the joint between the ballast keel and the aft deadwood is usually stepped or scarfed. This permits at least one long keel bolt to pass through the aft deadwood and the rear end of the ballast keel, effectively tying them together.

The ballast keel is held against the keel with closely spaced bolts. A lead keel will normally be bolted with bronze bolts, with lead grommets

placed beneath the head and beneath the nut and bronze washer on the inside. Two methods of bolting are used, they are through bolts and galleried bolts. The use of galleried bolts is usually limited to ballast keels which are wide in relation to their depth, and therefore the bolts can be fitted in pairs without being too close to the edge of the lead or wood keel on the inside. Galleried bolts are usually found about a quarter of the way in from the top of the keel on each side. They can be very difficult both to locate and to extract. If galleried bolts are suspected, the anti-fouling will have to be removed from the outside of the keel in the approximate position of the bolts and the surface of the lead closely examined for the 'plugs' filling the galleries which house the nuts. A cast-iron keel should be held with galvanized iron bolts, with galvanized washers bedded in cotton wicking and bedding compound.

Cast iron keels are sometimes drilled and tapped to receive threaded steel studs which pass through the keel and are tightened with nuts on the inside.

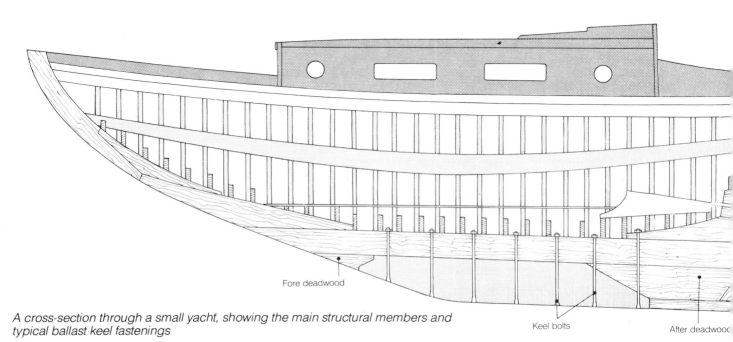

Fore deadwood

Keel bolts

After deadwood

A cross-section through a small yacht, showing the main structural members and typical ballast keel fastenings

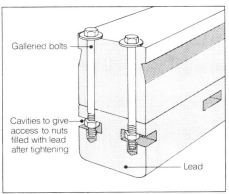

Galleried keel bolts

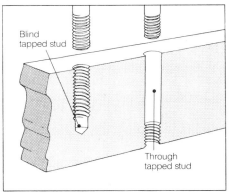

Iron keel held by studs

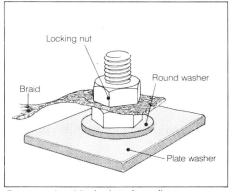

Connect keel bolts into bonding

Corrosion and leakage at the keel bolts

Keel bolts must be made of a metal which is compatible with the metal of the ballast keel. This obvious precaution is to minimize the corrosive reaction between the metals immersed in seawater. However, corrosion will occur, particularly with galvanized steel bolts. Because keel bolts are often inaccessible from both the inside of the boat and from the outside, the first indications that corrosion is taking place might be that the hull begins to leak at the keel bolt holes. Blackened wood, lifting paint, and rust marks around the keel bolt washers on the inside of the hull, are tell-tale signs that the bolts are beginning to corrode. In boats with an oak main frame, there is a higher risk of keel bolt deterioration when steel bolts pass through the wood of the keel.

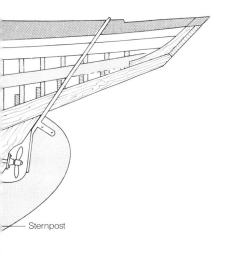

Sternpost

Checking the keel bolts

Withdrawing the keel bolts is, in most cases, impossible, unless the boat has been hauled out and chocked clear of the ground. Generally when they are laid up, boats rest on their ballast keels and this prevents access to the bolt heads, and prevents the long bolts from being dropped out. There are more difficulties inside — cabin floors are usually installed with a view to periodic removal, but keel bolt nuts are sometimes completely concealed by installations that are extremely difficult to move. The nuts to at least two keel bolts are likely to be found tucked beneath the motor sump, others may be hidden behind the companion steps, or even beneath the mast step.

It is not practical to remove and inspect the bolts every year. Instead, a thorough inspection around the washers on the inside of the hull, coupled with a vigorous wrench on the nut, will have to suffice. If all seems well, sample bolts can be withdrawn every four years, and it is sensible to keep a note of the location of the bolts and their condition to ensure that different bolts are withdrawn and, if necessary, replaced each time.

Where there is evidence that the keel bolts are being weakened by corrosion, there are specialist firms who can be engaged to x-ray the keel and ballast keel area, and who will be able to assess the condition of the bolts without disturbing them. The value of the x-ray is that it can tell you not only which bolts are corroded, but also which have been replaced recently and do not need to be withdrawn.

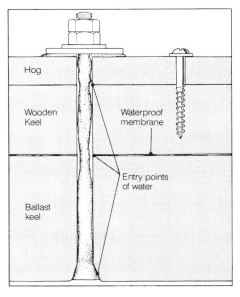

Removing a keel bolt

Unless the ballast keel is bolted with captive bolts, which can be withdrawn from the inside, the boat will have to be hauled out of the water before the keel bolts can be removed. There is very little cause to tamper with the bolts during the sailing season so, for the purposes of this and the following procedure for removing the ballast keel, it is assumed that the boat is hauled out, and supported by blocks and shores.

Clear a space beneath the ballast keel so that the keel bolt can be dropped out. It may be necessary to dig a small pit if there is insufficient space between the boat and the ground.

Remove as many fittings as possible from the area close to the keel bolt nuts. It may also be necessary to have clear access to the space above the bolts.

Unscrew the locking nut, and remove any electrical bonding etc. that may be held beneath it. Place a ring spanner or socket spanner over the head of the nut, and wrench it in a counter clockwise direction. If the nut is misshapen, use a stillson wrench. A badly corroded bolt is likely to sheer off, but most nuts won't be moved so easily. Soak the nut in penetrating oil, and devise an extension to the spanner handle to increase its

leverage. Heat the nut and bolt with a blow torch, or drill and split it free where necessary.

Take a mild steel rod, slightly narrower than the diameter of the keel bolt and drift it out. If the drift tends to jump off the head, file a point at the end of the drift rod and centrepunch a recess in the end of the keel bolt. This will be more effective than hollowing the end of the drift to sit over the bolt.

If the bolt refuses to move, first check outside to make sure that there are no blocks or wedges preventing its movement. Re-position any that are, and then screw a nut on to the end of the bolt until it lies flush with the top of the bolt. Hit this down with a lump hammer. It is very unlikely that a keel bolt will resist this kind of force for very long. However, if

there is no obvious movement and the bolt resounds with a clear ring each time it is struck, it is probable that it is a stud that is being hit (which will be impossible to withdraw), and not a bolt at all.

When the bolt begins to move, remove the nut and continue to drift it out. Remember to hit the drift in the line of the bolt. Occasionally keel bolts are canted diagonally across the keel, and the drift should be held and hit at the same angle.

Once the head of the bolt emerges from the underside of the ballast keel, a friend who can be persuaded to hold a wrench on the bolt head and twist it, while the end of the bolt is being drifted from the inside, will make the task of driving it out much easier.

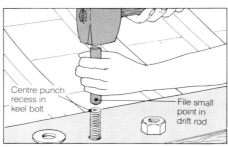
Loosen bolt with short, heavy blows

Centre punch recess in keel bolt

File small point in drift rod

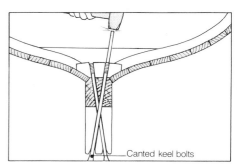
Always align drift rod with keel bolt

Canted keel bolts

Replacing the keel bolt

This is often as difficult as the removal of the bolt, and every effort should be made, prior to replacing it, to make sure that it will slip into position with as little trouble as possible. A new bolt may well be slightly wider than the bolt that has been withdrawn. This can be checked by clearing the bolt hole with an auger or drill, then testing the bolt for a fit by pressing it in from the inside. Grease the bolt before experimenting, and do not hammer it or insert it to its full depth. If the hole in the wooden keel is worn, borrow a shorter, but similar diameter, bolt and try to press it into the hole in the underside of the ballast keel.

Re-bore the hole if the bolt cannot be inserted. Before fitting, bind a twist of wicking around the heads of conical-headed bolts and smear them with bedding compound. With conventional bolts, a plate washer will be needed beneath the head. Wicking should be

twisted around the shank on the underside of the washer before the bolt is driven home. Spread the ends of the wicking across the full width of the washer to complete the seal.

Bronze bolts should be fitted with lead grommets under the washer before the cotton is wound around the bolt. Spread plenty of bedding compound beneath the washer and then pull the bolt tight.

Line up the bolt and work it into position. Tap the head with a lump hammer, and if necessary twist the bolt to ease its passage. Draw up the bolt with a nut tightened with a socket spanner and bearing against a pair of greased washers.

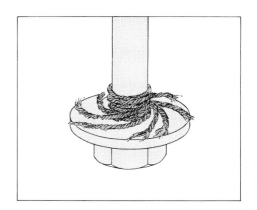

Release the nut, remove the greased washers, and fit the heavier plate washers, cotton wicking and bedding compound. Refit the nut and tighten it. Replace bonding or other fittings that were anchored to the keel bolt. Paint the nuts and thread with a rust inhibiting paint, or smear them with waterproof grease.

Rot between the keel and deadwoods

Areas of wet rot are often found at the joints between the wooden keel and the deadwoods and the ballast keel. These parts will remain damp long after the planking of the boat has dried out, and rot will be evident by the darkening behind the paintwork, which will often be cracked or lifting.

Rotted wood will offer little resistance when a spike is driven into the fibres. Small areas of rot can be repaired without the removal of the ballast keel. Rotted wood should be scooped back, flushed with fresh warm water, dried, primed with unthickened epoxy resin and then filled with an epoxide filler.

However, where it is evident that the waterproof membrane between the metal ballast keel and the wood has deteriorated, and that other, at present sound, parts are in danger, it will be necessary to remove the ballast keel, and to repair and seal the wood with a new waterproof barrier.

Removal of the ballast keel

Most ballast keels are designed for removal at some time, and can be dropped straight down. Even so, this is a major undertaking, requiring planning and a little ingenuity. Do not attempt it, unless you are assured of success. When handling a ballast keel that may weigh between one quarter to five tons, there is no place for bodged, make-do supports, or cobbled together lifting arrangements.

The modern boat hoist makes the removal of the hull from the ballast keel a relatively easy matter, as the keel can be left in its support and the hull parked elsewhere until the repairs have been accomplished. If such facilities are not available, and there is a likelihood that the keel may need removal, arrange with the boat-yard to rest her on chocks rather than on the ground when she is hauled out, and invest in the few components necessary to make the installation bolts illustrated right.

Position the shores with care. They must keep the hull upright both with the ballast keel in place and, if the work is undertaken without the assistance of a boat hoist, after the keel has been dropped out. Remember that without the ballast weight, the centre of gravity moves upwards and the hull, already a difficult shape to prop upright, becomes more unstable.

Extra supports should not prevent access to and removal of the ballast keel which, after lowering, can usually be withdrawn sideways, or moved a little sideways and then pulled clear.

Clear away blocks and supports beneath three keel bolts. If the bolts are canted at an angle to the keel it is important to remove three bolts angled in the same direction, otherwise it will be difficult to lower the keel with the devices illustrated

Insert the installation bolts through the keel bolt holes from the inside, trapping a thrust bearing sandwiched between

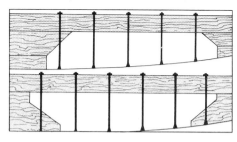

two heavy washers at the head of the device.

Before screwing on the nut, slip a heavy plate washer, then a thrust bearing and another washer over the threaded end of the bolt when it protrudes beneath the keel. Insert a split pin to prevent it from unscrewing.

Tighten the nut on the inside of the hull. There must be sufficient length of threaded bar above the nut to allow the ballast keel to be lowered into its cradle. Fit and tighten one of these devices into each of the three keel bolt holes, and

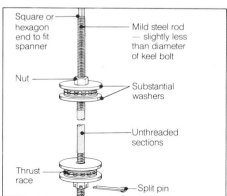

Square or hexagon end to fit spanner — Mild steel rod — slightly less than diameter of keel bolt

Nut — Substantial washers

Unthreaded sections

Thrust race — Split pin

Installation bolt lowered from inside

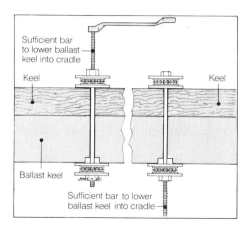

Sufficient bar to lower ballast keel into cradle

Keel — Keel

Ballast keel

Sufficient bar to lower ballast keel into cradle

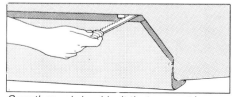

Saw through keel bolt that cannot be unbolted

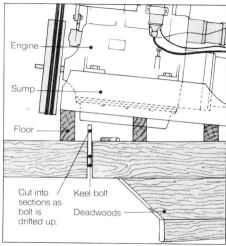

Engine

Sump

Floor

Cut into sections as bolt is drifted up.

Keel bolt

Deadwoods

remove the other keel bolts. Where installations in the hull prevent the bolt from being drifted out, the nuts should be removed and, provided that there are very few such bolts and that they cant in the same angle, the weight of the ballast keel will probably be sufficient to pull the bolts free. If the bolts prevent the ballast keel from being lowered, they should be cut off at a crack between the keel and the ballast keel, then drifted back into the boat and cut into sections as they near the internal obstruction.

Once all of the bolts are removed, the keel will be held in place by the installation bolts, and by the adhesion of the bedding compounds used when the keel was installed. Slacken all three lifting screws and free the keel with a set of wedges or a masonry bolster.

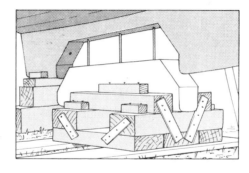

Gradually wind down the three installation bolts until the ballast keel lies in a sturdy cradle resting on greased planks positioned beneath it.

Remove the split pins, cage nuts and thrust races, and withdraw the lifting screw. Pull the ballast keel free.

An alternative to the lifting and lowering devices outlined above is to use reversible lifting blocks, or hydraulic jacks available from tool hire centres. Two or three of these would take the weight of the keel, and all operations could be carried out close to the keel to allow a close watch to be kept on progress. The design of the cradle and lifting straps will vary according to the shape of the ballast keel.

Once the ballast keel is detached from the hull the centre of gravity of the hull becomes very high, and it becomes top heavy. Rearrange the shores, and take great care in moving about the deck until the ballast keel is replaced.

Preventing rot and replacing the ballast keel

Clean the surfaces of the keel and the deadwoods and all other exposed wood. Cut out all rotted parts, and insert graving pieces. Where these cover a keel bolt hole, glue the piece in place and re-bore the hole from the inside. Small areas of rot can be filled with epoxy filler mixed with glass microspheres or ground coconut shell. All areas of rot should be entirely removed and replaced with sound wood or filler. There will be no significant loss of strength, unless a large part of the keel is rotted — in which case you should seek professional advice.

Apply several brush coats of preservative, and allow several days for it to dry.

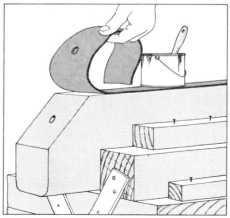

Insulate with a waterproof membrane

Prime and paint the faying surfaces prior to refitting the keel. Touching surfaces on the ballast keel are likely to be encrusted with dried paint and tarred paper, and should be cleaned back to the metal. Lead ballast keels do not require priming, steel ballast keels should be cleaned back, shot-blasted if possible, and prepared in accordance with the painting schedule on page 303. Fit a strip of tarred roofing felt to the edge of the ballast keel where it will be touching against the keel and deadwoods. Hold it in place with hot tar or wet paint. This will serve to insulate the metal keel, and prevent the formation of wet spots which occur where large areas of metal are in close contact with wood.

Fitting the ballast keel
This operation needs a great deal of care and attention.

Slide the cradle holding the ballast keel beneath the boat, and align the bolt holes. Drop the installation screws through the keel and ballast keel, and slip the washers, thrust races and cage nuts into place. Tighten the bolts in the sequence shown, until a 3 or 4 inch (100 mm) gap remains between the ballast keel and the deadwoods and keel. Brush copious quantities of paint or hot tar over the top of the tarred felt, and stipple the paintbrush on to the

faying wood surfaces of the keel and deadwoods.
A bedding composition can be used instead of tar or paint. Whatever form of seal is used, it is important that there is a

satisfactory barrier between the ballast keel and the wood, which is sufficient to fill any irregularities.
Pull the lifting bolts tight, and insert and tighten the keel bolts (see page 138).

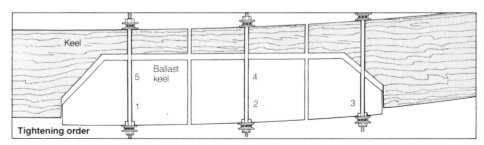

The principles governing the weight and distribution of ballast are discussed on page 162. Except in river boats, small dinghies and some multi-hulled craft, there will be a quantity of internal ballast battened beneath the cabin sole and tucked into convenient spaces at the turn of the bilge. Most boats will also carry an outside ballast keel, positioned along the centre-line of the hull and slightly aft of midships.

The care and maintenance of the external ballasting arrangements are described on page 136. Ballast keels are normally built into the structure of the hull and their weight and position is determined at the design stage. Internal ballast is placed in the boat to alter the trim, and to improve the handling characteristics of the boat. Most of the internal ballast will be concentrated in the midships section with a gradual reduction of weight towards the ends. Ballast should be spread transversely across the frames and floors out to the turn of the bilge.

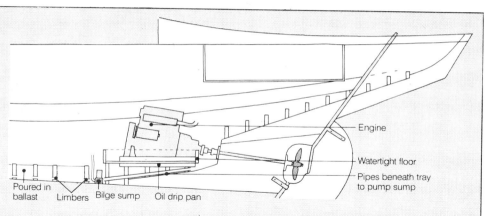

Engine
Watertight floor
Pipes beneath tray to pump sump
Poured in ballast
Limbers
Bilge sump
Oil drip pan

The longitudinal positioning of the ballast, with the weight concentration set approximately amidships, reduces the tendency of a hull to pitch and plunge in a head sea. The transverse distribution enables a hull to roll and recover, rather than stagger and snatch in a beam sea.

Internal ballast can be moved to any part of the hull, provided that it is held fast. Boats that are very stiff and cranky may well benefit from internal ballast bolted beneath the beam shelf, well above the water-line. Wherever ballast is stowed it must be prevented from damaging the hull, fittings or furniture. Where major alterations to the ballast distribution are made, especially when iron ballast is moved and re-positioned in close proximity to the compass, the boat should be swung, and tested for compass accuracy.

Materials for ballast

Many different materials are used as inside ballast. Their relative densities are listed below :

Concrete 130 to 145 lbs/cu ft (65kg/m³)
Rock 150 to 170 lbs/cu ft (77kg/m³)
Iron 450 lbs/cu ft (204 kg/m³)
Lead 700 lbs/cu ft (317 kg/m³)
* **Iron shot** 340 to 350 lbs/cu ft (158kg/m³)
* **Iron/concrete** 230 to 300 lbs/cu ft (136 kg/m³)
* Iron shot bonded with epoxy resin
* Iron cast in concrete

Concrete, rock, and scrap iron bedded in concrete are cheap and readily available forms of ballast. The density of the concrete/iron mix is only approx-imate as much depends upon the size and the distribution of the iron. In general, smaller units of iron will lie more closely and give a denser ballast than a few large pieces. The relatively high density of the cold cast epoxy shot system, is due to the very small size of the graded iron/lead shot used, which virtually eliminates cavities in the casting.

Lead ballast is stowed in the form of bars or 'pigs'. Lead is the most dense form of ballast normally used, and a considerable weight of inside ballast can be distributed about the hull without serious loss of space. Lead ballast in pig form must be very firmly bolted or strapped down, to prevent it working loose. Iron ballast is also stowed in this way, and needs to be well secured.

Fitting and stowing arrangements

Fibreglass hulls
Fibreglass hulls are frequently moulded with a hollow keel which is filled with pigs of lead ballast. These must be positioned carefully to achieve the correct weight distribution and then sealed with a plywood sheet bonded to the hull, or with a lay up of glass fibre. Minor adjust-ments can be achieved by positioning movable lead or iron ballast, or by cold casting internal ballast with epoxy bonded iron or lead shot.

Steel and wooden hulls
These hulls use the entire range of ballasting materials. Pig iron ballast, carefully bolted or strapped to the floors or frames, and concrete, cast in place or pre-cast into movable blocks, being the most popular. The density of the concrete can be increased with the addition of steel scrap, or reduced with polystyrene blocks.

Positioning ballast
Apart from the considerations of trim and seaworthiness, a number of factors should be borne in mind when planning and experimenting with the position of the ballast. Each ballast pig should be

Positioning ballast (continued)

secured and held in such a way that if one bolt or coach screw fails, whole sections of ballast will not come adrift. Each separate piece must have its own holding device, which should be strong enough to restrain the ballast if the boat is knocked down on to her beam ends.

Pig ballast should not rest against the outside planking of a wooden boat. The weight of the ballast must be supported by the frames and floors and, where necessary, beams should be placed across the frames to support the ballast. The keel, frames and floors are the strength points in the bottom of the boat and any weight resting directly on the planks will tend to loosen the fastenings between the planking and framework.

Ballast should not obstruct the flow of bilge water down the planking between the frames and from the keel or hog to the pump sump. Waterways and limbers

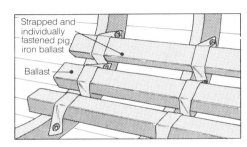
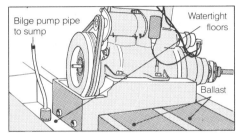

should be kept clear; this will allow for satisfactory drainage, and prevent rot from occurring in the poorly ventilated areas between the ballast and frames and planking.

The ballast should be protected against corrosion. This is not a problem that arises when lead or cold cast epoxy is used as inside ballast. Iron cast into cement, and cement on its own in certain conditions, will all have a harmful effect on the ferrous fittings of a wooden boat and should be painted in epoxy

resin or bitumen before being placed in the hull.

Where moulded-in epoxy/shot or concrete is used, the flow of bilge water to the pump must be kept clear, and if an oil drip pan is fitted below the motor, precautions should be taken to prevent the bilge water flowing into the sump and mixing with the oil. It may be necessary to arrange a high bulkhead around the sides of the sump, or to channel the bilge water underneath the sump through large diameter plastic pipes.

Removing ballast

In most cases it is easier to remove the inside ballast from a boat before hauling her out, than to wait until she is blocked and shored in the boat-yard. Keep a note of the position of each piece removed, and mark it so that it can be easily identified and replaced. An aerosol paint spray is ideal for this purpose.

Installing ballast

Clean and paint the inside of the hull before installing the inside ballast. If loose ballast pigs are used, a coat of thick bitumen paint on the inside planking and frames will help to protect the woodwork, and also help to hold the ballast. All loose debris, shavings, rags etc, should be removed, and the limbers

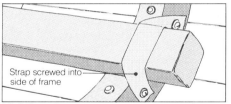

Holding-down arrangements must be secure and prevent all movement

cleared. Wash the bilges with fresh water to remove traces of salt and mud before replacing the ballast.

Loose pigs must be positioned and held, using whatever holding devices seem suitable. If each pig is painted with bitumen, the weight of the ballast will tend to soften the tar and help to hold

the pigs together. This will make the battening down of the pigs a little easier.

Straps and holding-down boards are the normal methods for securing inside ballast. These must be bolted or screwed into the keel, frames and floors, so that excessive loadings do not concentrate at any one fastening.

Installing cast ballast

Cold cast iron or lead shot with epoxy resin

Once the weight distribution of the ballast has been decided, shot is mixed with epoxy resin and bitumen and poured into the keel cavity, or into simple moulds positioned inside the hull. Mixing is best done with a cement mixer. The epoxy bitumen coating protects the iron from corroding, and also binds the shot into a dense cohesive unit.

Instructions for mixing and pouring are supplied by the manufacturers of the cast epoxy ballast system. It can be laid directly on to the inner face of a fibreglass hull. However, in wooden and steel boats, inside ballast must be removable, and a suitable casting method should be devised before mixing the ballast.

Every effort must be made to prevent the ballast from resting against the planking or plating of the hull. In order to prevent this, boards or sheets of polystyrene foam should be laid against the planking to lift the ballast clear. Mould the ballast in large polythene bags or over a heavy gauge polythene sheet. Shutter the sides of the bags or sheets with thin plywood to give the ballasting sections a regular shape, and to facilitate their removal.

A wire or nylon rope with large plate washers moulded deep into the ballast block will allow it to be lifted clear of the hull. Holding down arrangements can also be cast into place where necessary.

Cold cast epoxy ballast is extremely heavy (340 to 700 lbs/cu ft—154 to 317 kg/m3) so avoid making units of ballast too large. Not only should it be feasible for one man to lift the unit, it should also be possible to restrain the mass of ballast with normal coach screws, bolts and straps. The heavier the individual units of ballast, the more difficult it is to fasten them to the hull securely.

Leave the cast units to cure overnight, and then lift them in turn, removing the boards or polystyrene foam from beneath the ballast, and the plywood shuttering from between the sections.

Replace and secure the ballast. The cold casted epoxy and iron shot system ensures that the iron shot is protected from corrosion by the epoxy and bitumen coating. However, the blocks themselves are permeable, and those parts of the ballast in a wet or poorly drained position should be painted with waterproof paint.

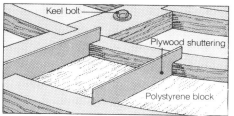
Shuttering before casting

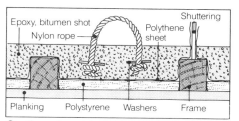
Section of cast ballast

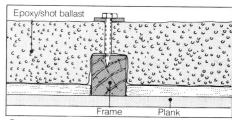
Section with shuttering removed

Cast concrete ballast.

This is a cheaper alternative to the cold cast epoxy ballast and, if undertaken with care, will produce satisfactory results. It is a poor practice to cast the cement directly into the bilge frame spaces. Even where every effort is made to ensure a bond between the wood and the cement (by painting the wood with cement screed improver, and by brushing a slurry of cement over the wood before pouring in the concrete and vibrating it into every crack and fissure in the inside of the planking) water will eventually find its way between the wood and the cement.

Rot will occur close to the upper edge of the cement ballast, where the wood is not permanently saturated with water.

Apart from the problems of rot, the solid cast ballast, which is intimately bonded to the skins and framework of the hull, will prevent the boat from working and flexing as it passes through the water. This causes an increased stressing of the framework and planking just above the level of the concrete, and results in strained fastenings and, in extreme cases, broken frames. Whenever poured-in ballast is used in a hull, the casting should be divided into sections

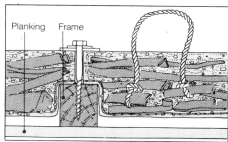
Regular shapes facilitate later removal

no more than 3 feet (900mm) long, and not more than a third of the bilge width, to allow the hull to flex.

Casting concrete.

Arrange similar shuttering systems to those described for the epoxy cold cast system above. If assorted scrap iron is used instead of carefully graded iron shot, it is necessary to bend a sheet of thin wire mesh (chicken wire) into each section to prevent the heavier or sharper scraps from passing right to the bottom of the concrete block, where they will be exposed and corrode in the bilge water.

Add a waterproofing additive to the cement, which should be a 1 : 3 mix of portland cement with sharp sand. Use plenty of water. Pour a first layer of cement over the wire mesh, so that it presses the polythene against the packing pieces resting on the planking. Then add a layer of large pieces of scrap iron. Pour more concrete over the iron,

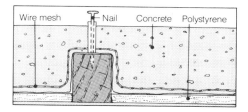

and press smaller pieces of iron between the larger pieces to fill all the voids and bring the centre of gravity of the block as close to the bottom of the boat as possible.

Install rope handles — tying each end of the rope to a piece of metal. Large sections of ballast should have two or more handles embedded in them to enable the block to be manoeuvred into position.

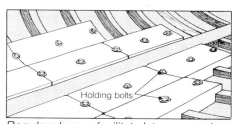

Add more cement until all of the metal is covered. Trowel it flat and lay wet sacks over the surface to prevent the blocks from drying too quickly. Leave the blocks for a week or so to cure, and then lift each in turn, and remove the polythene, plywood and packing. Paint the blocks and replace them. Finally, fit the holding-down clamps.

Maintenance, removal and repair

The illustrations show three typical methods of fitting a fin keel to the hull of a sailing boat. Figure I illustrates a section across the keel, floors and frames of a wooden boat fitted with a deep fin keel, with a lead or iron ballast bolted at its base. The wooden keel structure is usually laminated and faired prior to assembly. The entire unit is tied to the keel and hog with long keel bolts bored from the inside passing through the floors, hog, keel, fin and ballast weight at the bottom. Each floor is bolted with one floor bolt and one keel bolt, which are sometimes canted across the centre-line of the keel. Keel bolts are fitted to each or to alternate floors depending upon their spacing.

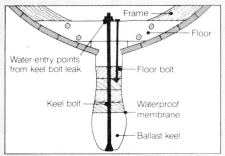

Figure 1

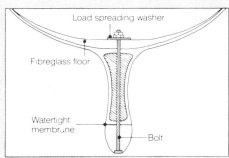

Figure 2

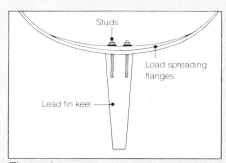

Figure 3

Fin keels are designed and built to withstand considerable and continual sideways stresses, which are at their greatest when the boat is beached or aground, but are never entirely absent. A keel bolt leak in such a hull is extremely troublesome to cure. Water which seeps into the keel bolt hole will emerge either from beneath the keel bolt washer, or from the floor/keel join.

The latter point of seepage is particularly difficult to cure. It is generally impossible to stop such leaks from the inside of the hull and it is impractical to remove and re-bed the floors in flexible compound. The only solution is to remove the keel bolts (changing them where necessary), and then to wrap the heads and the lower shank in cotton wicking and canvas saturated with wet paint and bedding compound.

Tighten the keel bolts and the floor bolts when they are refitted.

Illustrations 2 and 3 show alternative means of fastening a fin keel to a fibreglass or cold moulded hull. In both cases the likeliest source of leakage will be at the keel bolt holes. If the keel bolt leaks, it is a fairly straightforward matter to replace the washers with larger plate washers and to bed them in flexible compound before pulling them tight.

This method will work, provided that the bedding face of the fibreglass is reasonably level. On an irregular surface, the bedding washer is likely to

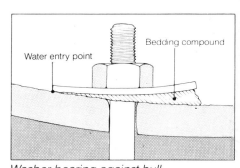

Washer bearing against hull

squeeze the flexible compound from around the bolt until the bedding plate touches the brittle fibreglass. A leak will start from this point once the boat is in regular use.

Levelling the bedding surface

Remove the nut and load-spreading washer from the keel bolt. If the washer is cupped or distorted, replace it with a more substantial washer. Clean away the dirt, grease and any compound still clinging to the fibreglass hull. Chip back the resin covering the fibreglass reinforcements, and dust off the area.

Wrap masking tape around the screw thread of the bolt where it emerges from the hole and smear grease over the rest of the screw thread.

Prepare a flat moulding plate that can be slipped over the keel bolt. Grease the under-side of the plate, or cover it with a thin layer of polythene.

Warm the cleaned area with a heat gun, and mix a quantity of unthickened epoxy resin. Brush this over the bedding area.

Add colodial silica to the remaining resin, until it makes a firm paste. Pile the paste around the bolt shank, and over the previously primed bedding area.

Slip the moulding plate over the end of the keel bolt, and press it firmly onto the epoxy resin paste. Add the heavy bearing washer and the nut. Tighten the nut sufficiently to squeeze the resin from beneath the edge of the moulding plate and maintain slight pressure while you clean the excess from around the edge of the plate. Leave the resin to cure.

Remove the nut, washer, moulding plate, and polythene sheet. Apply bedding compound to the flat surface of the cast epoxy resin-bearing pad. Refit the heavy washer, and nut, and tighten.

Seepage from the keel bolt holes is often associated with keel bolt corrosion. Inspect, or X-ray, the bolts at the first opportunity, and replace them where necessary.

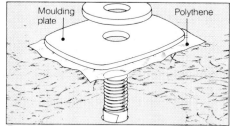

Preparation for moulding level bedding surfaces

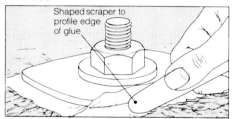

Apply epoxy resin. Tighten nut and clean away excess glue

The illustrations on the right show an alternative method of fitting a fin keel to a fibreglass yacht. The keel is prefabricated from steel plate and hardened lead, and painted with an epoxy-bituminous paint. The flange plate at the top of the keel is bolted into a recess in the fibreglass hull moulding with short bolts or studs.
Leaks at the bolt holes are not easy to remedy, as they are usually caused by water seeping behind the flange plate. Generally the most satisfactory solution is to unbolt and lower the keel, and clean away the old bedding compositions. Refit the plate with new flexible compound and perhaps one or two layers of canvas, saturated with wet paint, interposed between the steel and the fibreglass. A sealing fillet of flexible compound should be run at the edge of the metal flange. Do not use a brittle epoxy putty. This will crack as the fibreglass hull flexes. The thinner and deeper ballast keel (figure 3) is usually fastened by studs cast into the top of the keel, in conjunction with a reinforcing bar which spreads the bolt loads over a larger area of the top of the lead. These studs are usually bonded into the hull, and cannot be withdrawn. Bolts sleeved and fastened over the keelson with nuts and load spreading washers, can be unfastened once you have removed the resin covering the nuts. Take great care when attempting to remove a fin ballast keel. Unlike a traditional ballast keel it is inherently

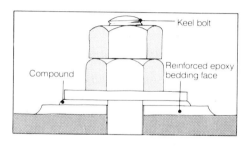

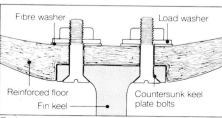

Bolt and flange keel fastening arrangement

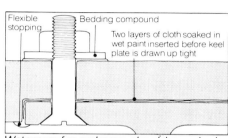

Waterproof membrane should cure leaks at keel bolt

unstable, and once freed from the hull will be top heavy and difficult to control.

Repairing scratches and dents in the keel

All underwater parts of a boat should be fair and clean, and every effort should be made to keep the hull clear of weeds, and encrustations such as barnacles. The annual cleaning and anti-fouling programme should take care of the condition of the paintwork and prevent marine growth from adhering to the hull. However, lead ballast keels are very vulnerable to scoring and gouging when they rub against underwater obstructions. The repair technique is described below.

Clean back the area with a knife or chisel to flake off paintwork, filler and any small stones that might be embedded in the lead. Finish off with a wire brush.

Attempt to rebuild the line of the keel by hammering back bulges, and cleaning and trimming smaller irregularities with a surform file or other woodworking tools. Plane blades should be adjusted to a minimum cut and it is helpful if the lead is smeared with petroleum jelly prior to trimming.

Wipe the area clean, and scrub it with a wire brush dipped in epoxy solvent, so that all the jelly, grit, dirt and grease are washed clear. Dry with a clean rag.

Mix up a small quantity of unthickened epoxy resin glue, and stipple it on to the damaged part of the keel. Agitate the epoxy with a wire brush, making sure that none is flicked over the hull or into the eyes.

Mix some more resin and add sufficient thickeners to give it an easily worked, putty-like consistency. When working on a vertical surface, low density fillers are best as the mixture will have less tendency to sag. Build up the shape of the keel with the epoxy filler. Rebuild the shape in stages where necessary, and fair the keel with a separate application of filler. Sand with coarse sandpaper, and repaint.

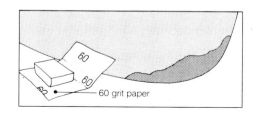

Centreboards Keels, ballast and rudders

The centreboard trunk, or case, is situated close behind the mast step. It contains a keel that can be lowered to improve a boat's performance when sailing into or across the wind, and retracted when sailing down wind. Where centreboards are fitted in full displacement yachts they are invariably involved with the ballast keel, do not protrude above water-line level and are virtually impossible to get at without rebuilding the boat. Repairs should only be tackled by professional shipwrights.

Dagger boards are fitted to smaller craft, and in small yachts where cabin space is at a premium. Unlike centreboards, they do not pivot at the forward edge, but are dropped down a vertical or near vertical slot. Some cruising yachts incorporate

a pair of dagger boards, each weighted with a hard lead ballast tip. These are set in the bilges and are raised by tackles operated from the cockpit. See the illustration opposite.

Centreboards and dagger boards can be subjected to quite considerable stresses, particularly when the boat is run aground, or the centreplate is used by the crew as a platform and lever with which to right the boat. Centreplates and their cases need to be strong enough to withstand this kind of pressure. Boats are designed so that the centreboard fails before the case is torn out of the hull. Repairs to centreboards are described on pages 150 and 151. The maintenance and repair of centreboard cases is described below.

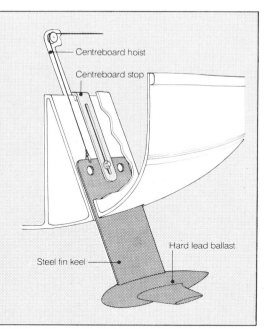

- Centreboard hoist
- Centreboard stop
- Hard lead ballast
- Steel fin keel

Fibreglass centreboard cases

Fibreglass hulls are moulded with an integral centreboard case.
Pivot bolts are either fitted through the case and keel, or suspended from a thin internal frame which braces against the insides of the case.

Most problems with fibreglass centreboard cases are associated with leaks at the bolt hole, or obstructions in the case preventing the board from being lowered or raised. Annual maintenance will include re-varnishing or painting the keel, replacing the watertight grommets between the bolt and the case, and replacing the rubber centreboard flaps screwed beneath the half-round metal shoe that passes down each side of the centreboard case. If

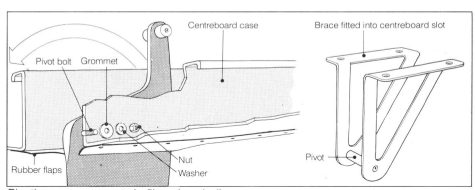

- Centreboard case
- Brace fitted into centreboard slot
- Pivot bolt Grommet
- Rubber flaps
- Nut
- Washer
- Pivot

Pivoting arrangements in fibreglass hull

fitted, raising and lowering devices and wires should be inspected annually. Wires are subject to both corrosive and

electrolytic action, and in larger boats the latter is by far the worst. Degraded or chafed parts should be replaced.

Plywood centreboard cases

There are several different methods of making and fitting a centreboard case to a plywood hull. Two are illustrated. The joint in figure 1 between the trunk and the bottom is made by bonding the plywood with layers of glass fibre saturated with polyester resin. If this method of construction has been used, the seams should be checked each year in case the fibreglass bonding tapes are

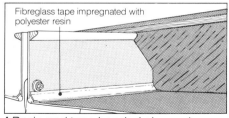

Fibreglass tape impregnated with polyester resin

1 Resin and tape bonded plywood case

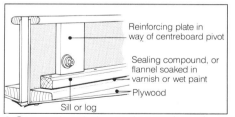

- Reinforcing plate in way of centreboard pivot
- Sealing compound, or flannel soaked in varnish or wet paint
- Plywood
- Sill or log

2 Conventional plywood centreboard case

beginning to pull away from the wood. Where this occurs, the old tape should be removed and new tapes bonded in with epoxy glue. Figure 2 utilizes traditional construction and fastening techniques.

The repair and maintenance procedures described below will apply here.

Conventional wooden cases

The illustrations show the typical construction details of a conventionally made wooden case. Note that the stopwaters are fitted at the joint between the ledges and the keel, and that the sides and keel are bolted or screwed together with a layer of compound in between to prevent leaks. Centreboard sides are either rabbeted into the ledges or lie flush against them and the ends capped with fairing pieces.

The centreboard case in the illustration above right is well braced, with knees and brackets bolted to the floors and frames. The logs and floors are also bolted together to provide more lateral stability. The example centre right, however, is without any evident lateral support. This type of case is used in lightweight hulls which are too flexible to provide adequate stiffening to brace the case. Strength is achieved by running the sides of the case beyond the ends of the slot and fairing them into the keel. Packing pieces are inserted into the space between the sides, and bolted to the keel to which the sides and the ledges are then glued and bolted. Additional support may be provided by a low thwart fastened to the after end of the centreboard trunk.

A dagger board case (illustrated bottom right) has a much shorter slot than a centreboard and, apart from the lateral braces, a substantial knee is positioned against both ledges. These ensure that the case structure is undamaged if the boat hits an underwater obstruction while travelling at speed.

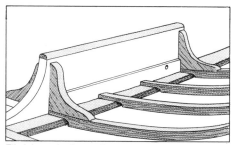
Rigid centreboard case

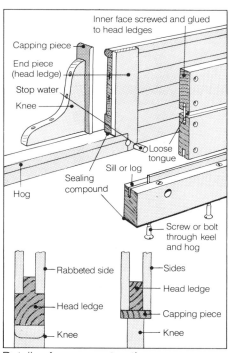
Details of case construction

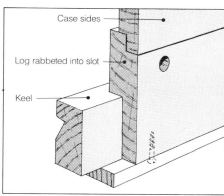
Inside case

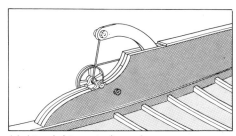
Lightweight centreboard case

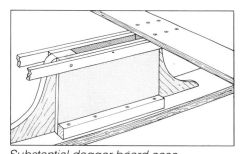
Substantial dagger board case

General maintenance of the centreboard case
The outside of the centreboard case should be kept clean and well painted. This is a simple task as the case is readily accessible, and its finish can be assessed at a glance. The inside of the case is a different matter. Centreboard slots are too deep and narrow to permit any worthwhile maintenance, and in many cases, do not even allow for satisfactory inspection.

Assessing the condition of the case
Examine the case for leaks. Varnished wood will darken and the paintwork will tend to lift or crack. The seam at the log and the area around the pivoting bolt are the most vulnerable to leakage. Other places to look are at the ends of the sides, where they butt against the ledges, and at seams between side planks at or below the water-line.

From the under-side of the hull, check the condition of the rubber flaps (if fitted) and the state of the paintwork on the inside of the slot. The end-grain of the end ledges should be well coated with paint and protected by a strip of half-round bronze.

If there is evidence of serious rot or worm attack, the centreboard case will have to be dismantled, and rotted parts carefully replaced.

Centreboards Keels, ballast and rudders

Curing leaks in the centreboard case

Leaks at the pivot bolt
The normal fastening and sealing arrangements for a centreboard pivot are illustrated below.

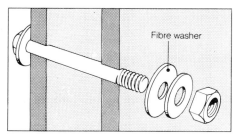

Bolt, fibre and load-bearing washers

A leak at the pivot bolt cannot be cured by tightening the nut. The only satisfactory cure is to remove the bolt and fit a new fibre washer. This is a straightforward operation, although the re-positionining of the keel may prove rather difficult. Take the oppportunity to clean and paint the keel, and wait until the paint is dry before replacing it.

Rot at the pivot hole
Satisfactory repairs here will have to wait until the boat is taken out of the water, and has dried out. A temporary means of stopping the leak is to screw a hardwood cap, bedded in sealing compound, over each end of the centreboard pivot. It will be necessary to hollow-out the inside of each cap so that the ends of the bolt will lie flush against the centreboard trunk.

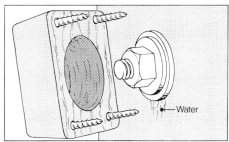

Hardwood capping piece

Bushing the pivot hole
Once the centreboard trunk adjacent to the pivot begins to rot, it will be very difficult to prevent further leakage problems, as the wood holding the ends of the bolt will tend to give slightly with the movement of the centreboard, and new leaks will start.

Remove the pivot bolt and centreboard, and allow the wood to dry out. (This can be hastened by scraping back the paint

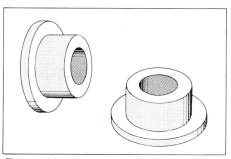

Flanged bushes

or varnish and playing a heat gun over the damp wood.)

Ask a local engineering shop to fabricate two flanged bushes, bored to take the centreboard pivot and whose outside diameter is a standard drill size.

Drill the pivot holes to accomodate the bushes, and fit the bushes to the centreboard case with the flange against the outside of the trunk. Check inside the trunk to make sure that the flanges do not obstruct the centreboard slot.

Remove the bushes, and soak the newly exposed wood of the centreboard trunk with epoxy resin. Add thickeners to the resin before bedding the bushes in place. Grease the pivot bolt, and use it to hold the bushes in place until the resin is cured.

Re-hang the centreboard and fit new grommets beneath the head and nut washers.

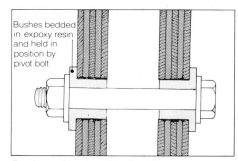

Bushes glued and bolted in place

Leaks at the centreboard trunk

Centreboard case leaks are not uncommon, occurring mostly at the joint between the trunk sides and the keel/hog. Leaks need to be stopped from the outside of the centreboard trunk. The usual method entails screwing a quarter round wooden batten to cover the joint.

Shave both flat faces of the moulding to increase the angle between the sides to slightly more than 90°, and plane a bevel at the apex. Bed the batten in flexible compound and fasten it in place with closely spaced wood screws.

A similar batten seam technique can be used to stop leaks at joints in the trunk sides and at the ledges. In general, it is best to avoid glued repairs to faults of

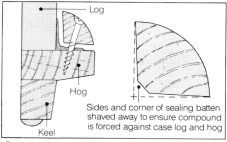

Quadrant moulding

this type, as further movement is almost certain to occur which will destroy the brittle seal.

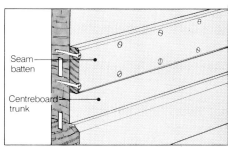

Seam batten

Maintenance of the drop keel

Centreboards are particularly vulnerable to damage and they must be maintained with as much care as the rudder and other, more visible, parts of the boat. A racing dinghy should have its centreboard removed several times each season so that it can be cleaned, smoothed and waxed. Periodic maintenance, and some quick and easy repairs, will also improve a racing dinghy's windward and across the wind performance.

Cruising dinghies and small yachts should have their centreboards removed at the end of each season. It will also be necessary to remove the board, replace the rubber flaps, and clean the case and centreboard whenever the plate becomes stuck or difficult to raise or lower.

Sailing boats that are left at tidal moorings during the season, if fitted with a galvanized steel centreplate of the type that slots on to the pivot bolt, should have a steel wire attaching the centreplate to the boat to prevent it from working free and dropping into the mud.

Renewing the centreplate lifting wire of a full displacement cruising boat is often a difficult task, which may involve lifting the boat and resting it on blocks. Because of these difficulties it is worth while considering electrolytic protection for the wire and other fittings normally submerged in the centreboard case.

Centreplates in small dinghies are made from either plywood, hardwood, or sheet metal. Cruising dinghies are often fitted with a 3/8 inch (10 mm) galvanized steel

plate. Racing dinghies have a lightweight aluminium alloy plate which is a little thinner, and a fraction of the weight, of the steel. A shock cord is used to hold the centreplate in the down position as the plate tends to retract due to water pressure when the boat travels fast.

Plywood centreboards are thicker and require a wider slot in the case and keel. Leading and trailing edges are faired to reduce drag. Larger dinghies and small yachts that are fitted with wooden centreboards, sometimes incorporate a lead weight at the lower tip of the board to counteract the buoyancy of the wooden board. Occasionally a centreboard fitted to a yacht will be constructed from edge-joined boards, drift bolted together.

Raising and lowering the centreboard

In the simplest form, the top forward edge of the board is shaped to form a handle which is pulled back to lower the plate. Heavy plates have a tackle fitted to the end of the handle and carried forward to a ring bolt in the hog. Jam cleats to hold the tails of the rope are screwed on each side of the after end of

the centreboard case, where they are within easy reach of the helmsman.

Some heavier centreplates are also equipped with a winch. The tail end of the adjusting rope is fitted with a toggle, and held by a jam cleat. The other end passes through a fairlead and is wound around, and fastened to, the large diameter wheel at the side of the winch.

By pulling the toggle, the centreplate can be raised or lowered quickly.

Most dagger boards are held with a shock cord, that either slips over the top of the board, or pulls the board so that it rests against a peg set into the top of the case. Notches cut in the trailing edge of the dagger board allow the depth of the board to be adjusted.

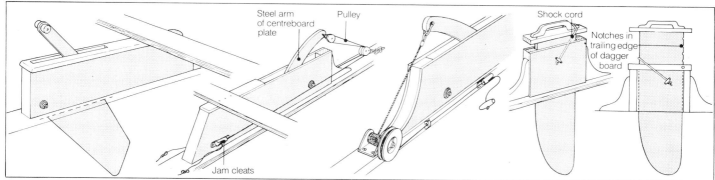

Centreboard and dagger board lifting and retaining devices

A jammed centreboard

Mud or shingle that enters the centreboard case is likely to restrict movement. Obstructions can usually be hosed clear, or hooked out with a wire or thin batten. The rubber flaps screwed to each side of the centreboard case

should prevent the worst of the dirt and stones from entering the case, and must be renewed if they are perished or torn.

This is a very simple job, requiring only a pair of scissors, a screwdriver and a

length of replacement rubber tape. When replacing the flaps, position them so that they touch each other at the centre of the slot. If the rubbers overlap, they may wedge themselves against the board and prevent it from being raised.

A jammed centreboard(continued)
A metal centreboard will also jam if it becomes bent. All but the lightest of alloy plates will need to be removed from the hull before they can be straightened, and even in workshop conditions this is very difficult to do well.

Clamp the top of the plate against the top of a solid bench, with the bend directly over the edge of the bench. Lever down the bent part. If it is necessary to beat the plate flat, use a copper headed hammer.

It is unlikely that the plate will ever be perfectly true once it has been distorted. Straighten it to prevent jamming, but do not attempt to restore the plate to its original, perfectly flat, state. The more the plate is bent and hammered, the weaker it will become, and small, additional distortions will be harder to rectify than the original bend.

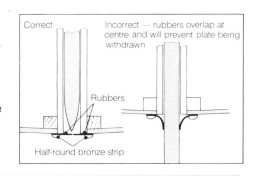

Repairing a damaged wooden centreboard

Wooden centreboards are very simple to repair; and those that are broken can easily be rebuilt from a suitable piece of marine plywood.

Surface abrasions should be sanded back, and re-finished with paint or varnish. Grooves in the sides, or dents in the leading edge can be cut back and filled with epoxy resin mixed with a suitable filler. Repair more serious damage with a graving piece let into the plywood, shaped so that the clamping pressure improves the surface contact between the centreboard and the repair. It is difficult to fit a patch into the edge of a piece of plywood, so it is best to keep the design of the join as simple as possible.

Re-bushing a centreboard
A centreboard with a worn pivot bolt will vibrate, increasing the turbulence created by the centreboard. To overcome this problem you can either remove the plate, and ream the bolt holes to accept a larger bolt, or you can cast or fit a new bearing surface.

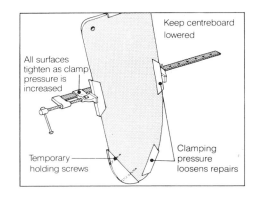

Casting a new pivot bearing in a wooden centreboard

Remove the centreboard, and dry the area around the pivot hole. If necessary flush with fresh warm water to remove salt, before drying the area with an electric heat gun.

Work on one side of the centreboard at a time. Cut back the worn wood at the edge of the hole. Take a new bolt of the same diameter as the pivot bolt, wax its shank with car wax, and arrange it so that it passes through, and is perpendicular to, the hole in the centreboard.

If there is a space between the bolt and the wood where resin might seep through, seal it on the under-side with a stopping of Plasticene or a similar compound.

Wet the wood around the pivot with unthickened epoxy resin, and then add thickeners (50 per cent colodial silica, 50 per cent graphite powder) until the mixture reaches a paste-like consistency. Inject or run this into the cavity between the bolt and the face of the centreboard, and leave it to cure.

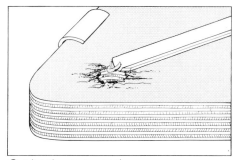

Cut back worn wood

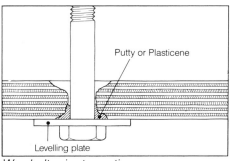

Wax bolt prior to casting

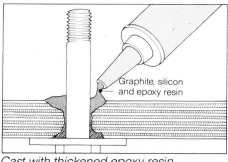

Cast with thickened epoxy resin

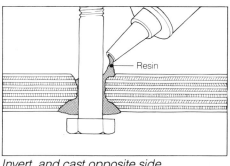

Invert, and cast opposite side

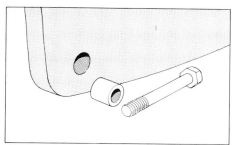

Centreplate pivot bush

Remove the bolt and cut back the frayed edges of the pivot hole on the other side. Re-insert the bolt, and repeat the procedure from the opposite side.

When the resin has thoroughly cured, sand or grind back the excess until the plate can be inserted into the centreboard case. Finish with varnish before refitting the centreboard.

Fitting a nylon, Delrin or metal bush to the centreplate

Use a drill press to bore out the hole in the centreplate to take the metal or nylon bush. The bush should be chosen so that it is compatible with the metal of the centreplate, and also with the pivot bolt. Do not, for instance, choose an aluminium bush to insert into a galvanized iron centreplate. If a similar metal bush is not available, select one that is slightly higher in the galvanic series.

Wire brush the outer surface of the bush, and paint epoxy resin on to it. Agitate the resin with a wire brush or with rough sandpaper to improve its adhesion. Prime the centreplate hole in the same way, and insert the bush. Grease the pivot bolt and sides before re-hanging the centreplate.

Fitting a lead weight to a wooden centreboard

Wooden centreboards are not built to take a ballast weight at the tip, and to add sufficient weight to alter the trim or stability of the boat would overstress the case and keel slot, or result in the board breaking off. Ballasting a centreboard boat is either the work of the helmsman and crew, or is achieved by the careful positioning of inside fixed ballast. (See page 141). However, a weight fitted to a wooden centreboard prevents the keel from floating back up once it is lowered.

Bore a hole through the plywood close to the tip of the centreboard. Bevel the hole from both sides so that the lead will stay in position. Drive some tacks into the inner edge of the plywood to help anchor the lead once it is cast into place.

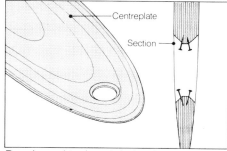

Bevels and tacks retain lead

Paint the exposed wood and the surrounding board with water-glass. This will protect the wood from the molten lead and prevent it from being burnt.

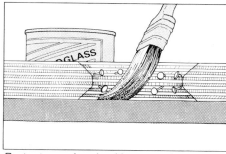

Protect woodwork with water-glass

Clamp a board against one side of the board, to act as the back to the mould, and paint the exposed face with water-glass. Lay the plate horizontally, with the hole facing upwards.

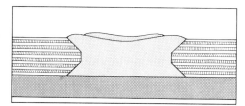

Add lead to give level surface

Casting the lead

Place some scraps of lead in a steel saucepan or ladle. Heat this with a blowtorch until the lead melts. Pour the lead into the hole in the centreboard until it is level with the plywood surface. Continue to heat the container and add a little more lead if necessary. Make sure that the extra lead is perfectly dry before adding it to the melting pot.

The lead will shrink as it cools, and a low depression will form in the centre of the

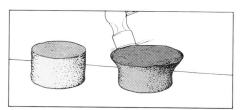

Setting one edge of lead slug

casting. Fill this with a second application of lead, after scraping off the film of lead oxide.

Remove the wooden backing piece and clean both surfaces with a chisel, or a plane set for a fine cut. Sand the lead down and cover it with unthickened epoxy resin. Wire brush the lead to improve the bond and paint on a second coat of resin before sanding and finishing with paint or varnish.

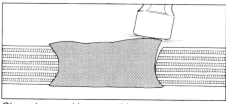

Slug dressed into position

An alternative method is to cast the lead slug in a mould of the same diameter as the inside diameter of the centreplate hole, but to make the lead slug project on each side. One edge is 'set' before the plug is inserted in the hole, and then with the centreboard lying flat on one face, the edge of the plug is dressed out to the larger diameter. The centre of the plug is planed flush when the plug is tight in the hole.

Maintenance and adjustment

> Many yachts can be balanced so that they sail themselves with the tiller lashed, allowing the crew a short respite from steering. Movements below, wind shifts or an increase in wind strength, and even the unpredictable effect of the waves striking the hull, however, may cause the boat to change heading and wander off course.

Two different types of vane self-steering gear are illustrated. They are designed to maintain the yacht in a constant attitude to the wind. The plywood or framed canvas vane is feathered, so that it is pointed directly into the wind. As the yacht yaws or slews off course, the vane presents an increasing area to the wind and is deflected downwards. The force of the deflection is used to alter the direction of the boat until she is once more on course, when the vane will return to its neutral position.

The vane gear illustrated utilizes a pendulum-type oar which is feathered when the boat is sailing on course, but is twisted by the vane when she yaws. The deflection, combined with the forward movement of the boat, causes the oar to sweep to one side, pulling on one of the steering ropes. These, by a combination of pulleys, adjust the main steering tiller or wheel until the course is resumed.

The gear illustrated has its own integral balanced rudder, and operates when the main steering is lashed or the wheel locked. The movement of the vane is transferred by a simple system of forks and pivots enclosed in the body of the casting to the auxiliary rudder which automatically corrects the course. Larger models of the latter type of vane gear have a ratio control to increase or reduce the movement of the rudder to suit all weather conditions. The drawings below explain in detail how these systems work.

Vane gear is usually mounted in the stern, where it is unobstructed and unaffected by turbulence or backwinding from the sails. Where a mizzen boom is lower than the vane, it is normal to lower the wind vane or remove it when going about or gybing.

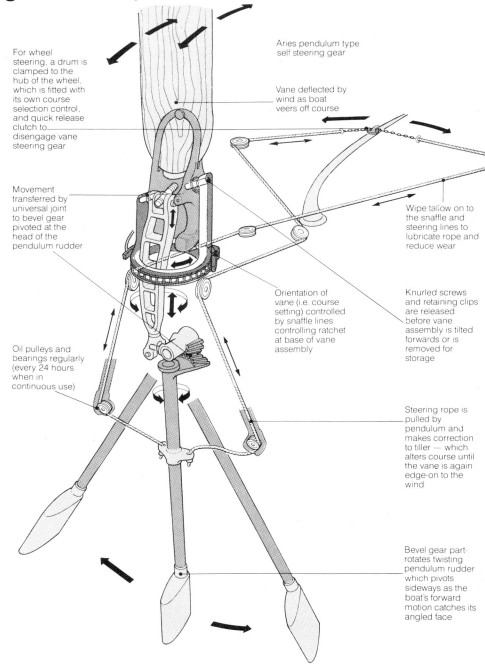

For wheel steering, a drum is clamped to the hub of the wheel, which is fitted with its own course selection control, and quick release clutch to disengage vane steering gear

Movement transferred by universal joint to bevel gear pivoted at the head of the pendulum rudder

Oil pulleys and bearings regularly (every 24 hours when in continuous use)

Aries pendulum type self steering gear

Vane deflected by wind as boat veers off course

Wipe tallow on to the snaffle and steering lines to lubricate rope and reduce wear

Orientation of vane (i.e. course setting) controlled by snaffle lines controlling ratchet at base of vane assembly

Knurled screws and retaining clips are released before vane assembly is tilted forwards or is removed for storage

Steering rope is pulled by pendulum and makes correction to tiller — which alters course until the vane is again edge-on to the wind

Bevel gear part-rotates twisting pendulum rudder which pivots sideways as the boat's forward motion catches its angled face

Both forms of vane gear generate considerable turning force and are capable of maintaining a heading even when there is heavy lee or weather helm. However, in these condtions, energy is wasted by constant yawing and correcting. For efficient functioning, the sails should be balanced before engaging the vane steering gear.

Trim the sails until the balance is such that when the tiller is released, or is held steadily with as little pressure as possible, the boat sails herself without rounding up or bearing away. The steering gear will then keep the boat on a steady wind-related heading until the helmsman resumes control.

Maintenance (Aries)
Vane steering gears are solidly constructed from carefully chosen materials. In most, the castings are anodized aluminium, the tubes are hard-drawn aluminium or stainless steel. Bolts and retaining pins are also made from

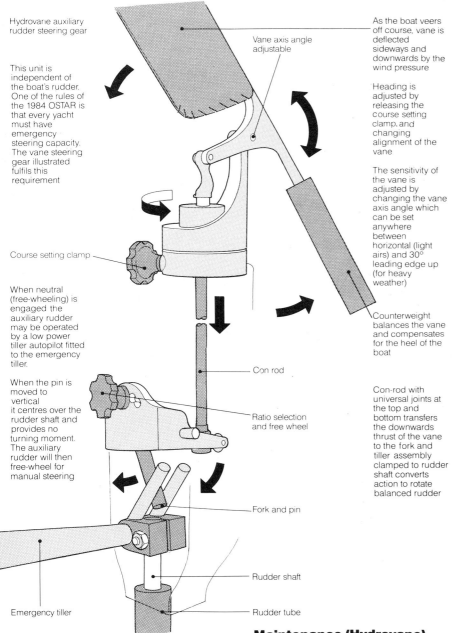

Hydrovane auxiliary
rudder steering gear

This unit is
independent of
the boat's rudder.
One of the rules of
the 1984 OSTAR is
that every yacht
must have
emergency
steering capacity.
The vane steering
gear illustrated
fulfils this
requirement

Vane axis angle
adjustable

As the boat veers
off course, vane is
deflected
sideways and
downwards by the
wind pressure

Heading is
adjusted by
releasing the
course setting
clamp, and
changing
alignment of the
vane

The sensitivity of
the vane is
adjusted by
changing the vane
axis angle which
can be set
anywhere
between
horizontal (light
airs) and 30°
leading edge up
(for heavy
weather)

Course setting clamp

When neutral
(free-wheeling) is
engaged the
auxiliary rudder
may be operated
by a low power
tiller autopilot fitted
to the emergency
tiller.

When the pin is
moved to
vertical
it centres over the
rudder shaft and
provides no
turning moment.
The auxiliary
rudder will then
free-wheel for
manual steering

Con rod

Counterweight
balances the vane
and compensates
for the heel of the
boat

Con-rod with
universal joints at
the top and
bottom transfers
the downwards
thrust of the vane
to the fork and
tiller assembly
clamped to rudder
shaft converts
action to rotate
balanced rudder

Ratio selection
and free wheel

Fork and pin

Rudder shaft

Emergency tiller

Rudder tube

Encrustation with salt and dirt is the most common cause of loss of efficiency. In their exposed position, they are often doused in spray, which in warm and relatively calm conditions evaporates, leaving salt caked to the moving parts. This is a particular nuisance in the tropics where regular and frequent sluicing with fresh water will help to wash away the salt deposits. Once dry, a light brushing with engine oil or a spray of light oil will remove salt residues and protect the surfaces for a while.

Mounting
The mounting points for the steering gear should be sufficiently strong to take the loading imposed on them. In many boats the mounting points will be at the base of the counter and at deck level. Both these areas are strong and unlikely to need additional reinforcement. Where mounting brackets are positioned in the middle of a wide, flat and unsupported surface, load-spreading plates should be fitted inside the hull and securely bedded in epoxy or polyester putty.

Sometimes through-hull bolts have to be inserted and tightened in almost inaccessible places. In these cases, fit and weld metal straps beneath the heads of pairs of bolts before inserting them from inside. Then the holding nuts can be tightened or released from the outside.

Manoeuvring
Under most circumstances, the steering gear can be left in place. Both types can be feathered so that they free-wheel and do not affect the steering of the boat. However, in crowded anchorages or where there are warps lying beneath the surface which might snag on the underwater parts, the rudder can be tilted clear of the water or removed.

When under power, the auxiliary rudder of the vane steering can be locked amidships. If this gives the boat a directional bias, the rudder may be fixed at an angle to compensate. This may result in a slightly larger turning circle.

When manoeuvring in reverse, the handling characteristics of the boat may also be affected. This will depend upon the relationship between propeller, rudder and steering gear. The boat can often be controlled better with the rudder of the vane steering gear than with the main rudder.

stainless steel. Some collars are nylon, but precision bushes are made from either PTFE or Delrin. Delrin bushes are black to prevent ultraviolet degradation. Galvanic corrosion is rarely a problem, as most of the parts are above the water-line and dissimilar metals are isolated by plastic sleeves. Care should be taken, however, to insulate mounting brackets bedded against a steel hull.

Although vane steering gears are sturdily constructed, their mechanisms are balanced and must operate freely.

Maintenance (Hydrovane)
Apart from regular washing in water (preferably fresh water) and oiling, very little maintenance is required. The steering gear assembly is easy to strip down. Pivots and bearings are retained by allen screws and axles are isolated from the castings by plastic sleeves. Re-assembly is best started at the bottom end, fitting first the rudder tube shaft and fork, then the lower lever. Adjust the horizontal location of the lower lever until the rudder can move freely when the pin is locked at neutral with the ratio knob.

Steering Keels, ballast and rudders

The drawings below illustrate some of the more typical forms of rudder fitted to yachts and motor boats. There is such a great variety in rudder design, that many boat owners will find a feature of their particular steering system in each of the illustrations. Some of the problems and maintenance procedures mentioned below are relevant only to a single type of rudder, but many of them are common to all.

The condition of the steering gear should be checked frequently. Examine the rudder and rudder bearings when the boat is hauled out of the water. The rudder and steering gear — central to the safety and seaworthiness of the hull — are subjected to high stresses and continual movement. Corrosion and fatigue are very common problems which must be detected and remedied at an early stage, before the safety of the boat is jeopardized.

Transom hung rudder

Gudgeons and pintles bear the weight of the rudder, and also any other stresses that may result from fouled ropes or grounding. They should be through-bolted to the sternpost or transom and fixed to the rudder. The very small pintle-bearing surfaces wear quickly, causing the rudder to drop slightly. This may cause the tiller to wear as it rubs across the top of the transom.

A simple expedient to restore the rudder to its correct height is to unship the rudder and slip a couple of greased washers over each pintle. This raises the bearing surface and, provided that the washers are of the same material as the rest of the metal fitting, will serve until the pintles themselves require replacement.

Rudder fittings often work loose. The most common cause is that the through-fastenings corrode, sometimes degrading the surrounding wood at the same time. Test the fittings very thoroughly.

Use a spike to check the condition of the wood and attempt to tighten screws and

bolts. Weakened fastenings can be replaced without unshipping the rudder, either by withdrawing and replacing the old fastenings, or where space permits, by drilling and inserting new ones. However, where the wood of the rudder is degraded, it will be necessary to unship the rudder and remove the straps in order to expose the full damage.

If it is found that the wood is sound, apart from the areas immediately surrounding the through-fastenings, there are one or two options.

The first is to raise or lower the strap to a new position on the rudder, where the fastenings can be fitted through sound wood. In addition, the gudgeon or pintle fitted to the stern of the boat must marry with the rudder bearing. Make good the recesses in the rudder and the holes in the stern, and accurately fit the old parts into new wood. Apart from the need to keep gudgeons and pintles in line and avoiding driving fastenings through existing bolts or dowels, this is a straightforward but lengthy operation. Difficulties in positioning the fittings on

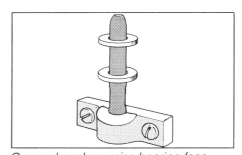

Greased washers raise bearing face

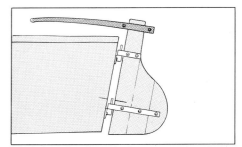

Mark bearing face before removing fittings

the rudder and the transom can be avoided if the rudder is rehung and the new bearing face marked on to the stern and rudder before the gudgeon and pintle are removed.

The alternative technique is to sleeve the through-fastenings where they pass through the rudder, and bond the sleeve to the rudder with epoxy resin glue.

Sleeves must be prefabricated in a compatible metal, bored to take the strap fastening bolt, while the outer surface is threaded or grooved to increase the hold of the resin glue.

Once the sleeves are cut to length, bore suitable holes in the rudder to accept them. There is no advantage in the holes being a tight fit and, in any case, the decayed wood surrounding the original hole will probably make a close fit impossible. Gouge out any remaining decayed wood and leave the rudder to dry out.

Sleeve bored to accept gudgeon bolt

Mix up a quantity of epoxy resin glue, and prime the wood surface. Add enough colodial silica to the mixture to thicken it to a toothpaste consistency. Fill each hole that needs to be sleeved with the resin, then press the sleeves into position. Pack more resin into cavities in the strap groove or around the sleeves before sliding the straps of the rudder fitting into place and inserting the bolts. Tighten the bolts before leaving the resin to cure.

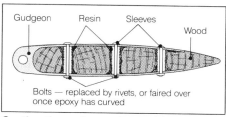

Section through wooden rudder

Provided that the moisture content of the rudder is below 15 per cent and that the overall strength of the rudder has not been seriously reduced by the decay surrounding the original bolts or rivets, the repair will be quite as strong as the original fittings when new, and may in fact be slightly less prone to corrosion and degradation because of the sealing and insulation effect of the epoxy resin.

Rebuilding a rudder

A rudder is not difficult to make, but it is very awkward to repair. Surface abrasions, minor cracks, and breakages can be repaired with bolts, resin glue or graving pieces as described on pages 44-5. It is often a different matter to replace large sections of a wooden rudder, because of the number of bolts and heavy spikes buried in the timber.

The suggestions below are included to help those who opt to make a replacement rudder, as well as those who are lucky enough to be able to dismantle their rudder and prepare the sound parts for rebuilding.

Wood
Make the rudder from narrow sections of quarter-sawn timber. These must be edge-glued together, and then drift bolted or spiked once each glue line is cured. This is more time-consuming than glueing and drift bolting in one operation, but unless the rudder is made from very thick stock where slight inaccuracies in drilling and fastening do not matter, it will be more satisfactory.

Plan the positioning of the metal spikes and bolts. They must be lined down the centre-line of the rudder, not interfering with its fairing. Use a template to plan and position drift and bolt positions.

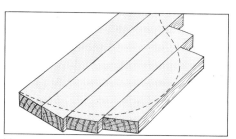

Use narrow quarter-sawn boards

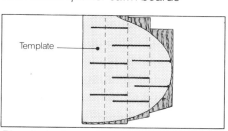

Plan fastenings on card template

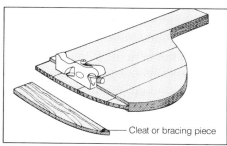

Cleats protect and brace end grain

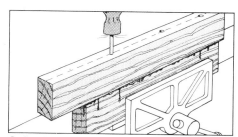

Spike boards after glue has cured

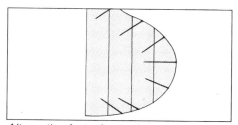

Alternative fastening pattern

Once the profile of the rudder has been cut, counterbore and drive drift bolts at an angle into the rudder blade to tie the structure together.

Sight and mark a centre-line down the rudder stock and around the trailing edge of the rudder, before fairing. If the lower edge of the rudder is straight, and exposes a lot of end grain. Rebate each side and glue adequate stiffening pieces into each rebate.

Steering Keels, ballast and rudders

The tiller

The tiller is the simplest form of steering arrangement. Check that the tiller bolts are tight and in good condition, and ensure that there is no slop in the tiller-rudderpost joint. Any looseness at this point adds considerably to the stresses at the joint, and accelerates wear on the gudgeons and pintles. Packing pieces can only be a temporary solution to the problem. Badly worn tillers should be replaced.

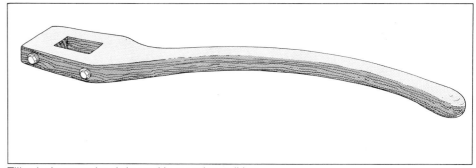

Tiller bolts must be tight and in good condition

Spade rudder

There are many varieties of spade rudders, from the short balanced rudder of a motor cruiser to the dagger-like rudder of an ocean-racing yacht. The feature they share is that the lower pivoting point is dispensed with, and stresses are concentrated at the two bearings on the rudder stock. Spade rudders are made from a variety of materials, including glass fibre and carbon fibres, as well as bronze and galvanized iron.

Modern fin and skeg boats with a short base to the keel and propped in the normal manner, have very little longitudinal stability. Before testing or working on the rudder of a fin keeled boat, shore the ends of the boat to give additional support.

Before the rudder is removed, it should be tested in a number of ways. By

grasping the lower edge of the rudder and pulling it sideways the state of the top bearing can be assessed. With the steering gear held or locked, the play in steering lines can also be checked. Also, where it is possible to see the joint between the rudder stock and the rudder, the joint should be inspected for small hairline cracks that might indicate metal fatigue.

Unlike the transom hung rudder, spade rudders can be withdrawn only once the boat is hauled out of the water. Once the steering and clamping devices at the head of the rudder stock are released and the watertight bearing at the hull is unscrewed, it is a simple matter to lower and remove small and lightweight rudders for inspection and maintenance.

Before removing the rudder, however, make certain that there are sufficient

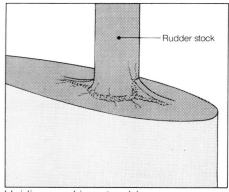

Rudder stock

Hairline cracking at weld

assistants to hold and control the rudder as it is dropped out.

Heavier rudders should be lowered from above, by fitting an eyebolt into the top of the rudder stock, and rigging a simple gantry over the cockpit. Slip a strop through the eyebolt, and rig a block and tackle between the gantry and the strop.

All major repairs to the rudder or the rudder stock should be carried out professionally. Many rudders fitted to production boats are stock items, however, and can be replaced with little trouble, and often with less expense than would be incurred by engaging a professional marine engineer to rectify the fault.

Bearings in the rudder stock tube can be removed and replaced with professionally machined bearings to fit the new rudder stock. Worn bearings should be removed and new ones, ground to fit the worn rudder stock, fitted in their place.

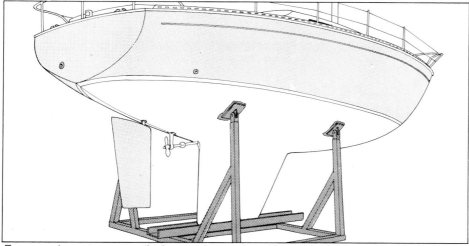

Ensure adequate support before testing and working on rudder

Epoxy cast bearings

Before attempting to cast a new bearing surface for a lightweight rudder, ensure that the sideways movement in the rudder is a result of sloppiness in the bearings and not a failure in the bearing mounting or a weakness in the supporting brackets.

Remove the rudder and rudder stock assembly and clean the rudder stock. Wipe away all grease, and polish the stock with a car polishing wax.

Inspect the top bearing faces. These, too, must be thoroughly cleaned. The repair procedure involves casting an epoxy bearing surface between the rudder stock and the bearing face, and if there seems to be insufficient room for a satisfactory casting, file a bevel at the top edge of the top bearing. Clean the bearing very thoroughly before casting. If the bearing is positioned at the end of a trunk, stuff rags up the trunk, and afterwards push them out from below to catch the metal filings and to keep the lower bearing clean.

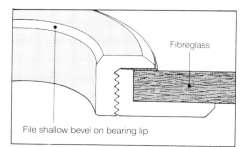

File steep bevel in edge of bearing

Insert the rudder and align it with the centre-line of the keel. Arrange firm holding devices to keep it in position while the bearing is cast.

Mix a small amount of epoxy resin and add equal parts of colodial silica and graphite powder. Blend the mixture before injecting a fillet of resin into the space between the upper bearing and rudder stock. The resin mix is viscous and will require steady firm pressure on the syringe to ensure that there is adequate penetration of the resin.

Leave the resin to cure, then rotate the

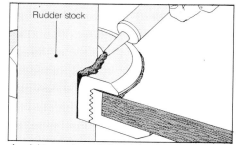

Avoid trapping air bubbles in casting

rudder to release it from the bearing. If the rudder is stiff, smear waterproof grease on to the rudder stock. Should this fail to ease the movement, withdraw the stock and apply a little abrasive rubbing compound to the end of the stock or to the bearing, before refitting the stock and swinging the rudder from side to side. Do not swing the rudder more than 30° each side of the centre-line. Thirty degrees from centre is enough movement for purposes of steering, and slight distortion in the rudder stock when swung 180°, will result in excessive wear in the newly cast bearing.

Packing the rudder shaft bearing

The rudder arrangement illustrated below is typical of many modern and more traditional craft. The rudder stock passes through two bearings in the hull, while the heel bearing pivots and supports the main weight of the rudder.

The rudder stock is usually encased in a trunk which is sealed at the hull opening to prevent water entering the hull. Sometimes as an additional safeguard a watertight bearing is fitted at the base of the trunk.

The lower rudder stock bearing usually incorporates a packing gland to prevent water entering the hull. Whether or not this bearing is enclosed in a trunk, access is usually difficult. Packed bearings are sometimes fitted with a locking device that locates into a knurled screw which, when tightened, compresses the washers or packing against the rudder shaft.

Remove the locking clip and screw and hook out the packing washers. If one is

being replaced, replace them all. Collect the old washers and cut new pieces of gland packing to length before twisting each one around the shaft and pressing it into the bearing socket. Stagger the joints. Replace the knurled tightening screw and tighten. After several days' use, the packing will have bedded in. Tighten the knurled screw.

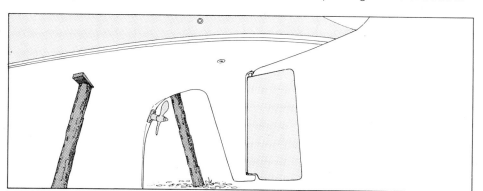

Configuration incorporating heel bearing and two rudder stock bearings

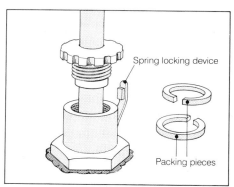

Watertight rudder bearing

Steering   Keels, ballast and rudders

Heel bearing

In a design of this type, the heel bearing supports much of the weight and over half of the sideways stress of the rudder, and it wears quickly. The heel bearing of a traditionally constructed wooden boat will often be a massive affair, badly worn, but retaining plenty of reserve strength, and requiring only a greasing with waterproof grease at the beginning of each season.

The rudder bearings of a modern yacht should be maintained in good condition and renewed where necessary. This is particularly important if steering wires are attached to a quadrant on the rudder stock, as the smallest lateral movement in the rudder stock will wear the wires and may, in extreme conditions, cause them to jump off the quadrant.

Various types of heel bearings are fitted, and the maintenance for each will be different. In some, it is possible to gain access to the heel bearing by raising the rudder. With others, the shoe fitted to the skeg which contains the bearing has to

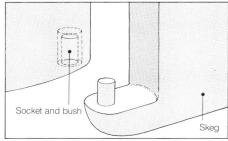

Heel bearing incorporated in skeg

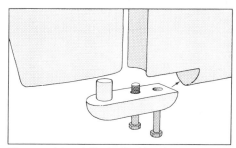

Removable pintle bolted to skeg

be unbolted and dropped from the keel before the bearing bush can be inspected or replaced.

Seek the manufacturer's or other professional advice before fitting new bearings. Nylon and Tufnol are hygroscopic and swell when saturated with water. A bearing that slips smoothly around the heel pintle when the boat is hauled out, may stick when the boat is back in the water. Some bearings are designed and manufactured with this quality in mind, so that the bearings are

easy to fit, and swell to a predetermined size once the boat is afloat.

In the absence of any professional guidance, fabricate the heelbushes from Delrin, which has high strength and wear resistance properties, and is not significantly hygroscopic. Delrin, which is a homo-polymer, is manufactured by Dupont Chemical Industries, and can be machined, drilled and cut, etc. Arrange good ventilation, as the material smells unpleasant while it is being worked.

Trunk leaks

This fault can only be properly cured with the boat pulled out of the water. Whether the trunk is made from wood, metal tubing or fibreglass, the most satisfactory cure is to dry the area, and prepare the surfaces for fibreglassing. Hook out bedding compound and caulking, and any other materials that have been used to seal the trunk. Brush unthickened epoxy resin over the entire trunk, horn timber, etc. Apply a second coat of resin, and then stop all crevices

with epoxy putty. Sand the surfaces until they are fair, before laying up fibreglass matt and tape, bonded with epoxy resin, to encase the trunk. Build up sufficient strength of matt and resin so that the fibreglass trunk becomes the structural part, and the original trunk acts as a mould. This is necessary because if the fibreglass functions merely as a gap filler, further movement in the trunk will certainly lead to more leaks.

For instructions on handling epoxy resins and glass fibre cloth and matt, see page 80. When working in a confined space, arrange plenty of ventilation to disperse the fumes. Wear goggles and a breathing mask, and gloves when handling or sanding the resin.
The joint between a tubular trunk and fibreglass hull and deck can often be resealed by renewing the bedding compound.

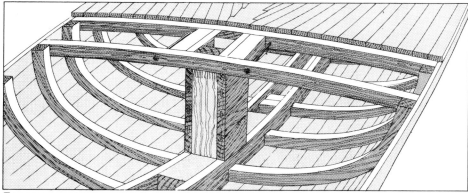

Encase wooden trunking in fibreglass to prevent leaks

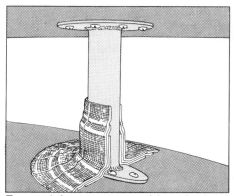

Taper reinforcement to avoid weakening

Rudder and propeller clearance

In many yachts the propeller shaft from an auxiliary motor is bored through the sternpost and the propeller itself rotates in a recess cut partly from the sternpost and partly into the leading edge of the rudder. Deteriorated resilient engine mountings or wear in the rudder bearings might bring the rudder too close, or even into contact with the revolving propeller. The clearance between the propeller and the rudder should be checked, both with the rudder lined up fore and aft, and with it swung about 30° to each side.

With the rudder in any of these positions, or in any point in the arc, there should be a space equivalent to $\frac{1}{12}$ the propeller diameter between the propeller and rudder. If the clearance is less than this,

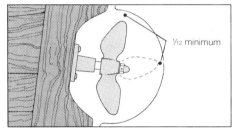

Ensure adequate rudder clearance

the efficiency of the rudder and the propeller will be impaired, and, in bad cases, they may both be damaged.

Check the rudder pivoting arrangements as well as the propeller and prop shaft itself. The propeller may have moved slightly aft, due to excessive packing or

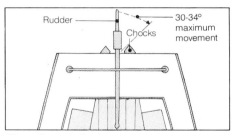

Plan view of deck at stern

the fitting of a flexible coupling at the inboard end.

Where there is a possibility that the rudder and propeller may touch when the tiller is put hard over, screw chocks to the sternpost or transom, just above the water-line, to reduce rudder movement.

Remote steering

The remote steering gear is typical of the kind of wire and linkage arrangements found on yachts and cruisers. When inspecting the steering gear, it is worth bearing in mind that the forces that are generated at the rudder are carried to the more remote mechanisms, and that even the weakest part should be capable of withstanding the worst kind of stresses that the steering gear is likely to experience.

Steering arrangements must be regularly inspected with attention to the smallest detail. Frayed wires and worn bolts, evidence of wear on the sheaves and quadrants, or movement in the rudder's stock fitting and quadrant must not be overlooked. The steering gear is only as strong as its weakest point.

Routine inspection and maintenance
All wires must be tight, to prevent them from jumping off the quadrant. Rigging

screws or screw bolts provide adjustment, and should be locked or wired after tightening. Tension the wires so that the wheel is centred with the rudder fore and aft.

All wire runs must be fair. Sheaves should be oiled regularly and positioned accurately so that the wire runs freely around the pulley without rubbing or twisting the sheave. Kinks will weaken the wire and extra sheaves of adequate strength should be installed wherever necessary.

Inspect the condition of the grease on the quadrant. Small metal fragments in dirty black grease indicate that wear is occurring. Clean off the old grease, and check the condition of the wire.

Rod linkage systems must be greased and maintained according to the manufacturer's instructions. Movement in the mounting bolts will impair the

efficiency of the steering gear. Loose bolts should be tightened.

The linkage bolts should be removed and inspected annually. These are subjected to severe strains and wear quickly. Carry replacement bolts aboard.

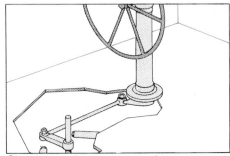

Check wear in remote steering

Preventive maintenance
Renew steering wires regularly. Inspect the wires, particularly at the sheaves, quadrants and endings. Where the wire has begun to strand, it is almost certain that the inner strands are fatigued or may have failed. Stranded or rusty wire should be replaced. Because of the

difficulty of estimating the degree of corrosion, stainless steel wire should be renewed regularly.

Secure wire ends with patent terminals or wire clamps fitted in pairs. Clamps or terminals should be clear of the quadrant or sheaves, so as not to

introduce kinks in the wire. Wherever possible, thimbles should be used at wire ends. The exposed parts of sheathed wires should be greased, and thinner penetrating oil used to lubricate the wire where it runs in the sheathing.

Steering Keels, ballast and rudders

Sheaves

As described, sheaves must be carefully positioned to ensure a fair run with the minimum deflection of the cable. All sheaves must be substantial and securely bolted to the hull. Screws are not suitable in most cases, partly because they may pull out when the wires are in tension and partly because the wire runs are often installed in damp, poorly ventilated places, where the screws and timber are vulnerable to electrolytic degradation. Bolts will also degrade, but the evidence of deterioration will be more apparent and the bolt is unlikely to fail without warning.

Quadrants

These are fitted over the rudder stock, and locked in place with a key. Quadrants are subjected to continuous movement and considerable stresses. Inspect the bolts holding the top clamp and, with the rudder locked or held from below, check for play between the quadrant and rudder stock. There should be no movement at all between them. Slight looseness will cause the wires to slip off the quadrant. Seek advice before dismantling the quadrant. A boat-yard engineer will find it easier to advise on the need for repair or replacement with

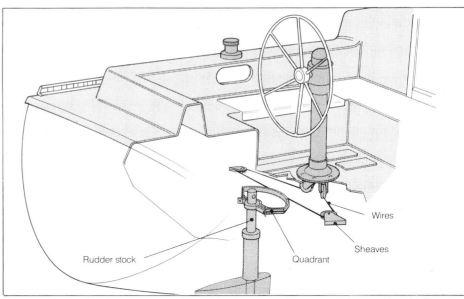

Wire configuration imposes considerable stress on sheaves and mounting bolts.

the steering arrangements intact. Apart from inspecting for play in the quadrant/rudder stock joint, look for signs of metal fatigue. This is unusual, unless the fitting is undersize or has been very well used. Clean the top and sides of the quadrant and look for small cracks at the

bolting and fastening flanges, and at the web supporting the rudder stock clamp.

While this part of the steering gear is being inspected it is always worthwhile checking that the wire tensioning bolts are tight, and that a lock nut is fitted.

Pedestal or bulkhead steering positions

These should be opened and greased regularly. The manufacturer's instructions will recommend the type of grease and how often it should be used.

The pedestals themselves are subjected to considerable stresses, quite apart

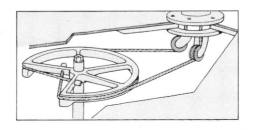

from those transferred by the steering linkage. The structure supporting the pedestal must be firmly braced and the cockpit floor reinforced. Where pedestals are fitted to a fibreglass floor check for evidence of fatigue failure, and reinforce if necessary.

Spare and emergency steering arrangements

All boats used at sea should have aboard some kind of emergency steering gear, which should be tried and tested before putting to sea.

In the event of the rudder carrying away, spars, bottom boards, and sweeps may have to be called into service. However, equipment for using the rudder after the steering gear has broken down can be installed and stowed away, ready for use in an emergency. Arrangements vary, and are usually of an individual nature. Access to the rudder stock has to be

gained by cutting a small hatch in the cockpit floor. Emergency tiller devices range from pipes swaged out to fit over an octagonal or squared end to the rudder stock, to a more sophisticated tiller that locates over the stock and is bolted to the quadrant.

To be of any use, the emergency tiller must be capable of being used when the leverage on the rudder is at its greatest. The tiller must therefore be as rugged a device as possible, with sufficient arm length to give adequate leverage.

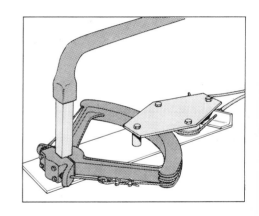

Sailing dinghy rudders   Keels, ballast and rudders

The drawing shows the construction details of a typical dinghy rudder. The rudder is pivoted by a pair of pintles bolted through the transom, which locate on to two gudgeons strapped to the rudder cheeks.

The blade is pivoted at the cheeks to enable it to be raised when running the dinghy ashore. A shock cord fitted to the leading edge of the blade and clipped on to a cleat on the tiller, serves to hold down the rudder blade and gives if the rudder hits a submerged obstruction. To raise the rudder, a line attached to

the trailing edge of the blade is tugged, and locked in a jam cleat.

The tiller is held between two small jaws in the top of the rudder, and retained by a stainless steel split pin. It is best if the pin goes through the tiller only and not through the rudder head. The tiller can be prevented from sliding aft by chocks fitted forward of the rudder head. The reason for this is that the tiller to rudder fitting has to be operable when the timber is wet and swollen. Otherwise excessive movement between rudder and tiller imposes a

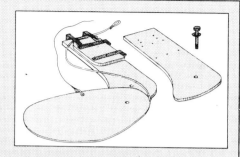

bending strain on the clevis pin, which usually causes distortion, and makes the pin ultimately very difficult to insert and withdraw.

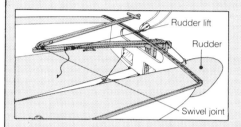

Rudder lift
Rudder
Swivel joint

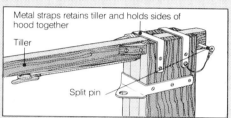

Metal straps retains tiller and holds sides of hood together
Tiller
Split pin

Clevis pin and tiller hood

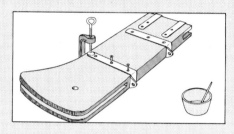

Maintenance

The lower gudgeon straps are almost invariably screwed to the rudder cheeks. In time, the marine ply or mahogany cheeks will blacken at the screw holes and the screws will loosen. Once the wood has started to degrade, larger replacement screws will soon loosen, and need further attention, and it is impractical to fit bolts.

The procedure for restoring the strength of the fastenings is as follows:

Remove the gudgeon strap and bring the rudder indoors and leave it to dry. Once the wood is dry, use a penknife to remove frayed and decayed wood fibres from all the screw holes. Prime the holes on one side only with some unthickened epoxy resin.

Add colodial silica to the resin until it forms a smooth paste. Fill each hole in turn, pressing the paste well in with the side of a penknife blade, and slip the gudgeon into place. Tighten a clamp at

each end of the strip to hold it, and then screw in the self-tappers with only the slightest pressure, or the resin will well up the hole and starve the screw of adequate resin to hold it in place. Press the screws in tight, and cramp a batten across the top of the self-tapping screws until the resin cures. Repeat this procedure on the opposite side, working through the screw holes in the gudgeon strap.

Rebushing the rudder plate

This is a very simple operation which will prolong the life of the rudder once the pivoting holes has ovalized. A metal bush (usually bronze or Tufnol) should be obtained and cut to length. Drill the rudder blade slightly oversize to hold the bush, which is bonded into place in two stages.

1 Mix a very small quantity of hard car body filler and wedge it against the bush. Insert the rudder blade between the cheeks and fit the pivot bolt.

2 When the car body filler is hardened, remove the blade and fill around the bush with thickened epoxy resin. Once one side is cured invert the blade and repeat on the other side.

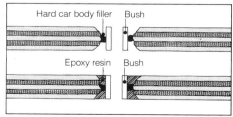

Hard car body filler   Bush
Epoxy resin   Bush

Section through rudder plate

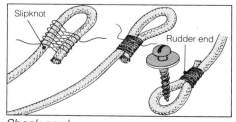

Slipknot
Rudder end

Shock cord

The two factors governing a boat's stability are the hull shape (including those parts submerged when the boat is heeled), and the distribution of weight. Alterations to a completed hull shape are seldom undertaken to improve the boat's stability, but small changes to the position of the major weights aboard can affect stability and handling characteristics.

The buoyancy of a hull is dependent upon its size, shape and weight. The amount and disposition of reserve buoyancy (the watertight part of the hull above the water-line) affects load bearing capacity, the safe degree of heel, and the ability of the boat to right herself. Boats with very little beam will be slow to recover from a roll while those with ample, full, sides will recover quickly. The drawings below illustrate these points. It will be noticed that example A with the flared sides will have an increasing resistance to heel, while example B, which has a pronounced tumblehome, will tend to roll badly.

All boats carry a quantity of fixed and movable weights. The fixed weights — hull, engine, ballast, fittings, decks and coachroof etc. can be added together and resolved at a single point which is the centre of gravity. This will remain constant unless major alterations to weight distribution are carried out. The movable weights — crew, stores, portable equipment, etc. will vary. The fixed weights are positioned so that the centre of gravity of the hull is lower than the axis point around which the hull rolls. If the centre of gravity were higher than the axis point, the boat would capsize.

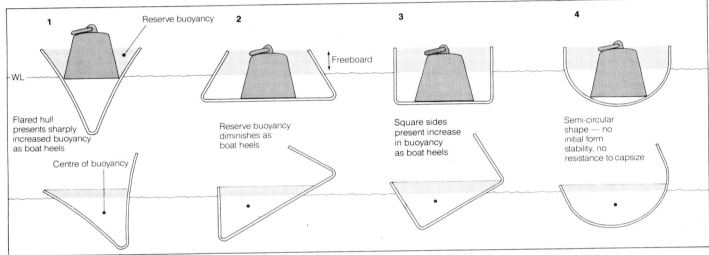

1
Reserve buoyancy

WL

Flared hull presents sharply increased buoyancy as boat heels

Centre of buoyancy

2
Freeboard

Reserve buoyancy diminishes as boat heels

3
Square sides present increase in buoyancy as boat heels

4
Semi-circular shape — no initial form stability, no resistance to capsize

These exaggerated hull forms will have different freeboard and stability characteristics

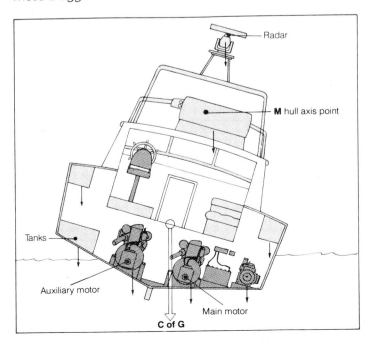

Radar

M hull axis point

Tanks

Auxiliary motor

Main motor

C of G

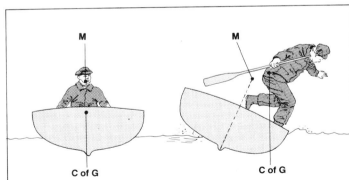

M

M

C of G

C of G

Centre of gravity is directly below axis point M. When centre of gravity rises above M, boat becomes unstable

All weight acts downwards, but can be resolved at a single point, referred to as centre of gravity

The distance between the axis point M and the centre of gravity (C of G) determines the boat's stability. When the boat heels, the centre of buoyancy (which changes as different parts of the hull are immersed) will move sideways. The horizontal difference between the new centre of buoyancy (B) to a line plumbed from the C of G will be the righting lever. The longer the righting lever, the more powerfully the hull resists being heeled and the quicker she rights herself.

The length of the righting lever will vary according to the angle of heel. The righting lever will be powerful while there is ample reserve buoyancy at the sides, but as the side deck is submerged, the centre of buoyancy will remain fairly static, while the centre of gravity rises above the axis point.

By plotting the length of the righting lever on a graph, it is possible to predict the recovery characteristics of the hull at different angles of heel. The plotted curve is known as a stability curve.

At sea, other variables including the wind direction, hull windage, steepness and frequency of the waves, will make a critical difference to the actual performance of the boat.

Extreme stability may be desirable in a navigation buoy or a fisherman's float, but it is undesirable in a pleasure craft. An excessive concentration of low weight will make a boat's movement very short and jerky, particularly in a beam sea.

Alternatively, a boat which rolls heavily is neither comfortable or reassuring (although it might be quite safe). The correct distribution of weights must be a compromise between the need for low weight to ensure stability and recovery, and higher weights to ease the roll of the boat. A long righting lever results in a stiff cranky boat, a short lever in a boat that rolls badly.

Alterations to the engine and fuel tanks, or the additional weight of a dinghy slung in davits over the stern, may have a detrimental effect on the handling and sea kindly qualities of a boat. Alterations should be undertaken with these consequences for the stability of the boat in mind. Compensate for heavier engines by placing ballast or tanks higher in the hull. The top-heavy effect of a dinghy in davits may be countered by additional ballast weight or the removal of other high-up weights and their relocation in the lower parts of the hull. The effect of re-distributing fixed weights about the hull will be enhanced where the boat is constructed of fibreglass or aluminium or cold moulded veneers. The likely effect of such changes on a lightweight hull should be considered before alterations are made.

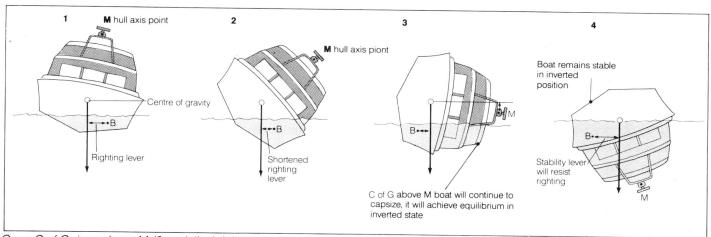

Once C of G rises above M (3 and 4), righting lever tends to maintain boat in inverted state

Trim and hull shapes

Trim is altered by the longitudinal re-distribution of weights aboard the boat and, with sailing boats, by wind direction and the type and size of sails set.

The quantity of ballast that each section of the boat should carry is calculated from the lines, from which the displacement of the hull can be determined. However, boats that have fine ends tend to be very wet in rough weather or when working into a head sea, and for these it is better if the ballast weights are concentrated at the longitudinal centre. Excessive weight forward or aft in a full-ended boat will have the same effect and will also lead to violent pitching.

Hull shape has a profound effect on performance. The variety of sizes and uses for small boats results in many different shaped hulls, adapted to the conditions in which they are to be used.

In general there seems to be an overall advantage in hull efficiency with respect to speed and carrying capacity if large displacement boats have full ends and uniform hull sections. Smaller displacement hulls are probably best designed with fine ends and full sections amidships, giving a clean entry and the minimum degree of turbulence aft.

Bow and stern shapes affect hull performance and seaworthiness. Hollow sections aft and flat or raked transoms create turbulence and increased drag, particularly at higher speeds. Canoe and pointed sterns are strong, but have less reserve buoyancy, or usable deck space than a transom or counter stern.

Trim and hull shapes (continued)

Flush decked boats and those with reverse sheer have greater reserve buoyancy but also slightly increased windage. Open boats worked at sea benefit from the added forward buoyancy of a pronounced sheer. Decked boats benefit from the protection from spray that the sheer gives, but suffer from the windage.

Speed

Displacement boats have a maximum speed which is largely dependent upon water-line length. As the boat passes through the water it displaces a volume of water equivalent to the weight of the boat and the volume of the wetted surface. The displaced water forms a bow wave and a quarter wave.

At low speeds other waves will form between them, but as the speed of the boat increases, the bow wave becomes steeper and the stern wave higher, and the space between forms a single trough. At maximum speed the wavelength is slightly longer than the water-line length of the boat. Additional power will give a small increase in speed and massively increased turbulence.

Water-line length imposes a maximum speed limit on a displacement boat. By reducing weight, fitting more efficient motors and rigs, and by polishing or painting the hull to minimize hull friction, boats can be tuned to reach their maximum speed with less energy.

The maximum speed imposed by the water-line length and displacement of a hull is exceeded when the boat planes. Boats with suitable planing hulls and favourable wind and sea conditions will ride on to the bow wave. The reduction in displacement and wetted area enables the hull to accelerate until the maximum planing speed for the hull (dependent upon weight, hull shape, length and sea conditions) is achieved.

At optimum hull speed, bow and quarter wave may be barely discernible

As speed is increased, energy is wasted in wave formation and turbulence

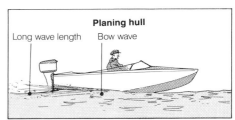

At high speeds, hull rises and friction is reduced

Heeling

It is now generally accepted that for most sailing boats the optimum angle of heel in rough weather is about 22°, and at most 25°. When a yacht heels a number of changes occur which affect its speed and handling. The sail area presented to a beam wind will be at its maximum with the mast vertical and falls off sharply as the boat heels.

The underwater profile of the boat becomes asymmetrical while the windward side presents increased windage. Rudder and keel efficiency is impaired. Control characteristics will change as the boat heels. Modern boats are sufficiently well balanced to remain controllable but increased angles of heel beyond 25° usually lead to lower speeds and less directional stability. The planing hull reaches its maximum speed in the vertical position. Most displacement yachts reach theirs at 22° of heel or with the lee rail just awash, whichever comes sooner. Beyond this point the hull makes excessive leeway and forward speed is reduced, as a result of diminished rig efficiency and increased drag caused by applied helm.

As the angle of heel is increased, the force of the sails acting to capsize the boat may be diminished. However at a certain point the power of the hull to resist the capsizing force also diminishes. This point depends upon the disposition of the ballast and hull shape. The righting action of an outside ballast keel becomes more efficient as the angle of heel reaches 90°. A flat bottomed or centreboard yacht or powerboat however, will be without this outside balancing factor, so that the righting lever will be shorter at the same angle of heel.

Coach roof size and shape and its watertightness as well as the quantity of movable ballast (including the bilge water) will be reflected in the boat's ability to resist a capsize and to recover from one. A stability graph gives the length of the righting arm for any given angle of heel, and can be obtained from the designers or manufacturers of modern yachts. Reference to the graph and to a clinometer attached to the cabin bulkhead will indicate strength of the righting arm for the given angle of heel.

Three stability curves are drawn on the graph on page 165. The first is of an open

sailboat, the second a catamaran, and the third a fin-keeled displacement yacht.

It will be seen from the graph that beyond a certain angle of heel a boat will lose its vertical stability, and will develop an inverted stability with the keel uppermost. The time that a boat will remain upside down is dependent on hull shape, weather conditions, position and security of the ballast, and the quantity of free flowing bilge water aboard. In general, the more water aboard the hull the more likely she is to right herself.

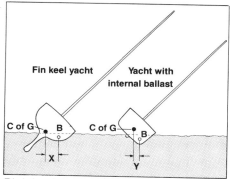

Righting leverage of keel increases with angle of heel

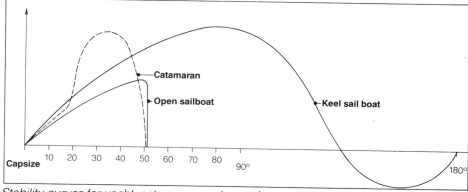

Stability curves for yacht, catamaran and open boat

Multi-hulled craft have a very high initial stability, which increases as the weather hull rises. When the hull comes clear of the water the centre of gravity moves to windward, while the centre of buoyancy moves to leeward, thus increasing the righting arm. In strong winds, multi-hulled craft should be handled with extreme caution as the tendency of a lee float to dig in when the weather float lifts due to the reduction in buoyancy, will increase the chance of a sudden capsize.

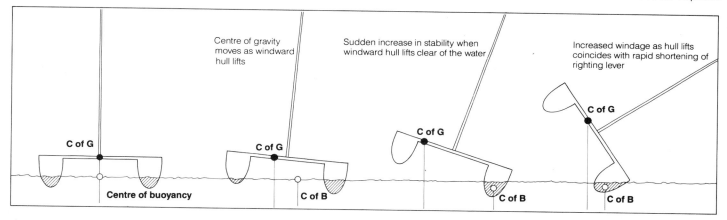

Bilge water

Excessive quantities of moving bilge water will de-stabilize a boat. The centre of gravity of a free flowing liquid changes as the liquid surges about the bilges and cabin floor. As a boat heels or rolls the water will alter the boat's centre of gravity by moving to the lowest part of the hull. The closer the water moves towards the side of the boat, the shorter the righting lever becomes, and stability is reduced.

Fuel and water tanks incorporate baffles and compartments to control the surge of the liquid. When large amounts of water which cannot be readily pumped out flood aboard, internal doors should be shut and obstructions wedged across the cabin floor to impede the flow of the water. If the water can be collected and restrained in buckets and drawers etc., the dangerous surging effect can be minimized, otherwise pump or bail the bilges as soon as possible.

This de-stabilizing effect works to advantage once a boat is overturned. A yacht with an outside ballast keel will not remain inverted for long, as flood water, coupled with the leverage of the keel will return her to an upright position.

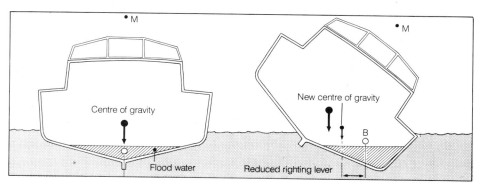

165

JACK

Chapter 8

Decks and Cabins

Wooden decks   Decks and cabins

The drawing below illustrates the framework of a typical wooden deck. Cambered deck beams rest against the frame heads and are bolted to the beam shelf. The deck beams supply the transverse strength which completes the structural unity of the hull. Apart from the functions of providing shelter and a level working surface, the deck serves to brace the topsides so that the wracking stresses, which occur when sailing, are absorbed by the structure as a unit, and do not overstress any particular part of the hull. Undecked craft obtain this strength from bulkheads or thwarts fitted across the boat. In some fibreglass boats, moulded stiffeners are incorporated into the skin moulding instead.

The decks are built after the main hull and framing is complete. The sheer strake is often fitted after the deck beams and half beams have been installed to facilitate joining the beams and the beam shelf.

A traditionally laid deck, illustrated below, will flex with the movement of the boat, and will begin to leak after a number of years.

When planning repair work, the option is either to strip off the old decking and replace it with marine plywood, or to re-lay the original deck, and renew rotted and damaged planks where necessary.

In terms of overall cost, and as a long-term cure for leaks, the first option must appear the most attractive. However a carvel or clinker hull may not benefit from a rigid plywood deck which will inihibit the flexing of the hull and concentrate the movement in the framing and outside hull planking. This can lead to seams opening, and fastenings and lighter frames working loose or breaking. Seek professional advice before undertaking this type of alteration.

Deck framework

Deck framing is added once the basic hull is complete and sometimes after the engine and storage tanks are installed. This makes the removal or inspection of these fittings, and the hull beneath, very difficult. The beam shelves are fitted first and their top edges are bevelled to allow the deck beams to rest upon them. Alternatively deck beams can be notched or dovetailed into the beam shelf.

The beam shelves are bolted or screwed to the frames. In some vessels clamps are then bolted in, giving added strength to the topsides and providing greater bedding and bolting surfaces for the deck beams. Spaces between the beam shelf and frames and planking are either packed with wood or adequately ventilated to prevent rot.

Transverse deck beams are fitted so that they rest agains the frames, and are notched, dovetailed or bolted on to the shelves. Stronger beams are used at deck openings and at each side of a highly stressed part.

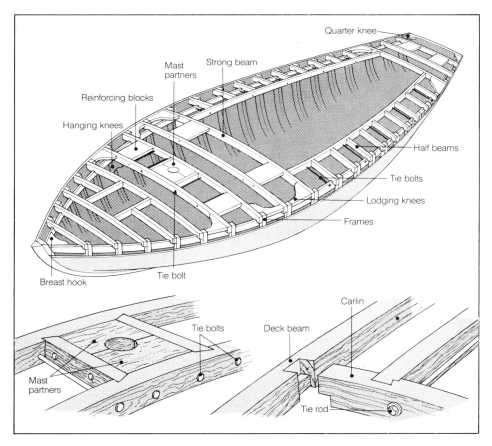

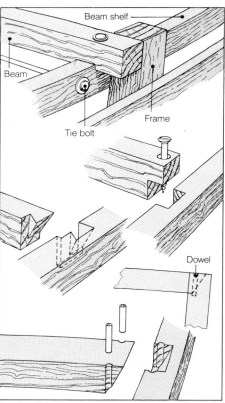

Examples of beam shelf joints

Deck framework (continued)

Carlins are temporarily braced into position and their ends are notched into the beams. Half beams between the carlin and the beam shelf are then jointed into place. Before the temporary braces are removed, long tie bolts are positioned to hold the shelf and the carlins together. Other tie bolts placed about the hull give added strength.

Knees are placed against the frames and beneath the deck beams. Vertical knees are known as hanging knees, which, in the absence of bulkheads, provide the necessary diagonal support for the hull. Six fastenings per knee is usual, all must be tight, and the knee should be properly bedded against the members it is intended to brace.

Horizontal knees are incorporated into the deck structure when a laid wooden deck is fitted. These are situated against the beams at large deck openings, and also against the beams supporting the mast. These lodging knees are often omitted if a plywood deck is laid.

Extra reinforcing is necessary where the mast passes through the deck. Blocking pieces are cut and fitted between the deck beams and are through-bolted in place. Mast partners are notched at the outside edge of the blocks to resist sideways movement. Blocking and mast partners are normally as deep as the deck beams.

When the framework is completed, it is painted, and the upper faces are coated with bedding compound before the deck is nailed or screwed down.

A variety of deck types exist, the main types are described below.

1 Laid decks. This is the traditional method of deck planking. Planks are laid over the deck beams, and notched into the king plank at the centre-line of the deck, and into the covering board at the side. They are fastened with screws or nails, and the seams between the planks are caulked and then payed with a stopping compound or with hot marine glue. Best quality decks are laid with teak which turns white when scrubbed and weathered. Iroko, pitch pine and other less durable woods can be used, and these are sometimes sheathed with fibreglass or covered with canvas.

2 Canvas covered decks are usually laid with tongue and grooved boards. Each plank is laid with its tongue on the outboard side, and the centre plank is fitted with a loose tongue at one side. Canvas is stretched from the centre-line to the sides, where it is tacked and hidden by a toe rail or rubbing strake, or is pressed into a rebate in the side of the covering board and closed with a wood fillet, after the board has been fitted.

3 Plywood decks are lighter and stronger than the above mentioned decks. Joins are supported at the underside with butt blocks.

4 A laid deck over plywood combines the beauty of a traditional deck with the strength and watertight qualities of a plywood deck. Where thin plywood is used, deck planking is fastened through the ply and into the beams. Butts are centred over a heavy beam or supported by a butt block. Where the deck is made from thicker plywood, thinner planks are laid on to thixotropic epoxy resin.

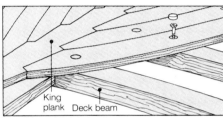
Traditional laid deck

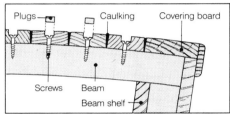
Section through laid deck

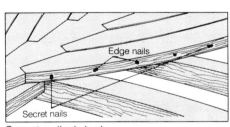
Secret nailed deck

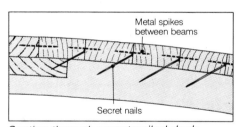
Section through secret nailed deck

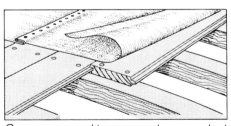
Canvas-covered tongue and groove deck

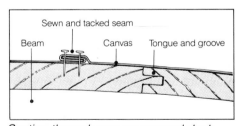
Section through canvas-covered deck

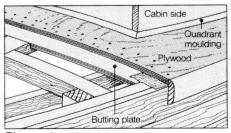
Plywood deck

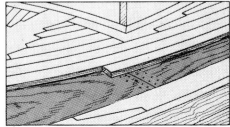
Laid deck over plywood

Cleaning wooden decks

Laid wooden decks are normally left unfinished, requiring regular scouring and washing to keep them looking clean and smart. The traditional method of cleaning a bright wooden deck is to rub it with a sandstone block lubricated with detergent or wood cleaning fluid mixed with water. The sandstone cleans and abrades the surface, leaving the wooden deck flat, smooth and free from splinters. Hard edges are rounded off, and the finish provides a sure foothold, whether wet or dry.

After rubbing down, the decks are flushed clean with seawater. Parts of the deck that are difficult to reach with the sandstone block will have to be cleaned with a scrubbing brush dipped in a detergent solution.

In modern boats and some less expensively built older ones, the decks are not made from close grained quarter-sawn timber. If such a deck is scrubbed in the direction of the grain, it will quickly become ribbed as the soft summer growth wears away and the harder growth remains. Too much scrubbing also tends to loosen the dowel plugs covering the deck fastenings.

Teak and other laid decks should therefore be scrubbed with a 'soft' scrubber across the grain, or with the traditional holystone block, to prolong the life of the deck.

There are many commercial teak deck revivers and finishes available from boat chandlers and marine paint manufacturers, and these cut down the amount of labour required to obtain a satisfactory finish. Manufacturers' instructions should be carefully followed when applying these revivers and finishes. After washing and scrubbing, a teak deck will dry to a bleached grey-white colour. A very thin application of deck oil, well rubbed into the surface of the deck, will restore colour to the teak without making it slippery. These natural oil finishes are sold as deck sealers, and are available from most marine paint and varnish specialists.

Deck seams

A repaired, or newly constructed, traditionally laid deck will leak slightly until the planking has settled and the seams have taken up. This is particularly true of a deck that has been left to dry out and the planks have shrunk excessively before caulking and sealing

Due to this expected movement, traditional marine glues and the polysulphide varieties of sealing compound should be left raised for 2-3 weeks, and cleaned up after the planking and caulking have settled and the sealer has been trodden in.

In older boats where the deck seams give as the boat moves, it may be

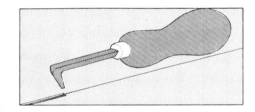

necessary to remove the compound at a later date from some seams and firm up the caulking before re-sealing.

The technique for renewing the caulking and paying is described below. Removing the composition can be a tedious and frustrating business. A hooked scraper fitted with a comfortable

handle will be needed. This can be made from a piece of tool steel or the tang end of a file. The tool is drawn along the seam, rocking and lifting out sections of the paying compound. Where the composition is old and brittle, it will have to be broken up into small pieces and cut out with a coarse-toothed saw. Once the sealing compound has been removed, inspect samples of the cotton or oakum. If the caulking is dry and crumbly, it will have to be hooked out and new caulking hammered into the seam. The procedures for this are described on page 60. Work in small sections of the deck at a time. This enables the deck to be made watertight if the job has to be left for a while.

Sealing the decks

Paying
The traditional and cheapest method of sealing the caulking is to pay the deck seam with hot marine glue. This is bought in cake form, and is heated gently until it melts and can be poured from a ladle or lipped saucepan.

The deck must be completely dry before paying, and all dust and debris vacuumed from the deck and seams. Use a gentle warmth to heat the marine glue. Some forms of glue can be heated in a double boiler; others can be

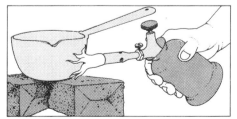

Avoid over-heating marine glue

warmed by playing a blowtorch flame over the side of the saucepan. Whichever method is used, it is

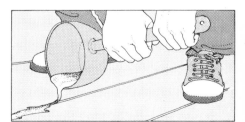

Fill the seam in two stages

important that the temperature increase should be gradual, and that the glue should not get too hot, otherwise bubbles will form in the marine glue. These bubbles will be enclosed in the liquid, and trapped in the seams, where they will become the source of leaks.

Work backwards down the seam, pouring the melted glue into the seam as you progress along the deck. Partially fill each seam, then return to the end of the seam and fill it to the top. Marine glue shrinks very little, but it is best to leave the payed seams rough and raised for 2-3 weeks so that they can be trodden down. Clean away the excess marine glue with a heavy steel scraper held diagonally across the seam, and pressed hard against the deck.

Sealing compounds can be used to fill the seams instead of marine glue. There are various types available, some of which are two-part, and are applied with a trowel or knife. Others are pre-mixed and applied with a gun. Various colours of compound can be purchased and used to striking effect on a teak or iroko laid deck.

Take care to keep the compound away from the face of the deck planks. Masking tape laid on each side of the seam, or a sealing coat of shellac or varnish will enable any accidental stains left by the compound to be cleaned off.

Two-part deck sealing compounds are mixed as needed, and applied with a palette-knife or trowel to force the paste into the deck seam. Work across the seam, cleaning and levelling each part

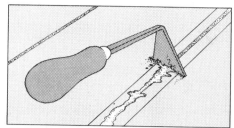
Clean seam with scraper

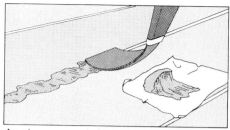
Apply compound across seam

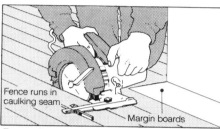
Preparing seam for compound

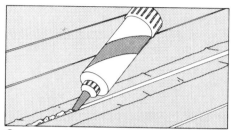
Compound squeezed from dispenser

and wiping away any excess from the deck before progressing.

One-part seam fillers are squeezed from a simple tubular gun. Techniques for using these vary. In some cases, special preparation of the seam is required. This involves removing all the caulking and opening up the seam into a slot before injecting the compound. The quickest way of doing this is to adjust a hand-held circular saw so that the depth of cut is equal to the seam depth. Run the saw down each seam. The ends of the seams will have to be chopped out using a small chisel.

Where the planks are straight and laid parallel to the centre-line of the deck, the saw fence can be adjusted to fit into the adjacent seam, and will help to guide the saw when widening the seam.

Take great care to control the saw. Do not overrun the seam and cut into the covering board, king plank or margin boards that surround the breaks in the deck. To safeguard against this, tape markers on to the sides of the saw to mark the position of the leading and trailing edge of the saw blade. Apply the sealing compound as instructed by the manufacturer.

Deck repairs

Fit graving pieces into small holes in the deck. The technique for fitting is described on page 44. Renewed planking must be given time to settle before further attempts are made to prevent leaking (see page 63).

It is possible to apply small quantitites of marine glue to a seam by holding an electric soldering iron against a lump of marine glue, and dripping the glue into the seam. Where the extent of the repair is known to be very limited, this can be a satisfactory technique, but in most cases

it is simpler to handle the glue in the normal manner, and pour it from a ladle or lipped saucepan. Preheating the area to be repaired with an electric heat gun improves the bond between the original and the newly applied glue.

Non-slip decks
For full details of preparing and painting a non-slip deck see page 308.

For best results, old non-slip finishes should be removed prior to renewal. Those finishes that depend upon the

paint to bond the grit to the deck can be removed with paint stripper or a heat gun.

Fibreglass decks that incorporate a non-slip tread moulded into the surface are rarely very effective. These may have to be ground smooth, and painted with

two-pack polyurethane paint before being painted as described on page 308, or covered with a self-adhesive textured fabric.

The source of a steady, entirely predictable leak, which drips into the cabin when it rains or when the decks are awash, is fairly simple to discover. Other leaks may be more elusive. Some are intermittent, others occur when parts of the boat's equipment are under strain. By isolating the occasions when the leaks occur, it is possible to detect the causes and location of the leaks without recourse to desperate and often unsuccessful means of testing, such as hosing, or standing pails of water on the deck and watching for leaks dripping below. Such methods are often a waste of time and, where successful, will soak the wood, and prevent any remedial action until it is thoroughly dried.

Steady leaks

Apart from the ever-present possibility of water finding its way into the cabin, there is the problem of internal condensation. Glass fibre boats are particularly prone to condensation, especially boats with large windows and a single skin hull and deck. Condensation occurs at the interface between the warm, moisture-laden cabin air and the cold surface of the cabin and deck. In the absence of good insulation or ventilation, large quantities of water can accumulate overnight, drip from the cabin-sides and run down the hull.

Check the small gutters and drain holes channelling off the water that enters the cabin or condenses against the windows, etc. Very small obstructions will dam the waterways which will then overflow.

Holes in the outside deck covering will lead to leaks. Water will seep into the cabin, and its course is often marked by lifted or discoloured paintwork and staining beneath the varnish. Water will often travel some distance beneath the deck planks before accumulating at a deck beam or carlin and dripping. Trace the source of the water before lifting the deck covering and sealing off.

Breaks in the structure of the deck (at the deckside joint, and all the seams between the cabins, hatches etc., and the deck) are very difficult to keep entirely watertight. Wherever quadrant mouldings are fitted at a suspect joint, they should be removed, and the old bedding scraped out and replaced. Do not try to caulk the opened seam, as the wedging action will tend to force the pieces apart, and will result in an increase in the degree of flexing between them. Instead of caulking, tighten the fastenings, or remove the piece and fasten it properly.

The joint between the covering board and the planking of a laid deck often leaks. All parts at the edge of the deck are prone to leakage, and the wider the covering board, (and the stiffer it is) the more deck flexing will be concentrated at the joint. Also, covering boards, being flat sawn, will warp and break their seal to the adjacent planking. Before new caulking is driven home, the covering board will have to be securely held flat. Soak the top face with fresh water until it lies flat before adding more bolts to the deck beam and sheer-strake, and recaulking.

Leaks where the bulwarks pass into the covering board can be wedged and caulked, or fitted with a lead coat, wrapped around the fitting and closely tacked in place.

Some fibreglass decks leak at the joint between the deck and the sides. In some the only seal is made by a brittle polyester putty forced into the crevice between the two mouldings after the bolts holding them together have been pulled tight. These putties have poor adhesion and should be scraped out and replaced with epoxy putty. To prevent a recurrence of this trouble, the joint should be properly bonded across with a lay-up of glass fibre cloth, bedded in epoxy resin. (See page 96.)

Intermittent leaks

Leaks at deck fittings
Fittings that are through-bolted to the deck may work slightly when in use, and will allow water to seep below. Fastenings should be withdrawn, the bedding renewed, and new grommets fitted beneath the washers where necessary.

A very common source of leaks is where the chain plate anchorages pass through the deck. These are very troublesome to cure. Movement in the bolts holding the chain plates must first be prevented, before flexible compound is packed around the deck openings.

Unattributable leaks
Far more detective work is needed to discover the source of an intermittent leak unrelated to any through-deck fitting. The characteristics of the leak should be noted and pondered before any attempt is made to locate and deal with its source. Think about changeable factors such as the direction of the wind or rain and spray, angle of heel, and movement of the boat (a boat that 'works' at the deck seams will leak when being sailed, but might remain watertight when at a sheltered mooring). The attitude of the boat, and the presence of people standing on the deck may also be factors that determine whether the deck leaks or not. Sometimes the smallest clue leads to the location of the trouble.

The following guide-lines may help in the maintenance of a leak-proof cabin.
1 Keep the deck covering and paintwork in good order.
2 Keep waterways unobstructed.
3 Remove beadings and renew compound when the deck is repainted.
4 Strip off and repaint when the paint film (or varnish) begins to crack or peel.
5 Aim to cure leaks permanently. Temporary cures sometimes exacerbate problems. Look for the cause of the leak and deal with it at source, before stopping the hole.

Deck beams

Evidence of rot in a deck beam or in the deck planking above the beam should be investigated promptly. Rot occurs when the moisture content of the wood rises above 20 to 30 per cent, and is caused by poor ventilation or a leaking deck.

Clean back the paint or varnish covering the rotted part and increase the cabin ventilation to allow the wood to dry. For suggestions that may help in locating leaks in cabin and deck, see page 172. If the rotting is serious, and the beam has lost more than 25 per cent at its centre or 30 per cent at the sides, a doubling piece or a replacement beam will have to be fitted.

If the rot is not serious, saturate the weakened wood with preservative and, when it has dried, re-finish it with paint or varnish. Where there are indications that the rotting is widespread, or that other members of the hull, such as the beam shelf, covering board, or frame head are rotten it will be necessary to remove the deck planking and work from the outside of the hull. (See page 176.)

Bracing a deck beam

Provided that the ends and major parts of the deck beam are sound, it is a fairly simple matter to restore the strength of the beam by bolting a brace to its side. Fractures and splits in the beam must be wedged open and injected with epoxy resin glue, and shored together. Wood screws driven across the fracture will help hold the joint until the glue cures.

A glued repair may restore the beam to its original strength but if the beam needs reinforcement, a brace must be fitted.

Make a template of the inside camber of the deck. Mark on the template the thickness of the beam, and the limits of the damaged area. Select a piece of straight-grained timber, one third the thickness of the deck beam, to use as the brace. Mark the board with the shape of the template. Where the deck camber is pronounced, cut out the curve from the under-side of the board and glue it to the top. Trim the top of the supporting piece so that it lies flush against the deck planking and bevel the

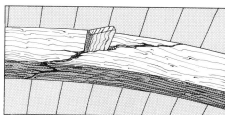

Insert glue in opened crack

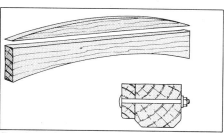

Bracing piece

under-edge on the side furthest away from the deck beam.

Scrape away the paint or varnish from the side of the beam. Apply copious quantities of bedding compound to the

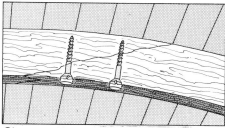

Close and hold with wood screws

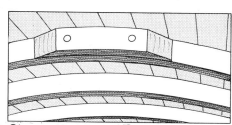

Glue and bolt brace against beam

top of the brace. Glue the brace to the beam, and clamp it in place.

Remove any excess glue, and fit bolts through the brace and beam. Finish with paint or varnish.

Fitting a replacement deck beam

1 Check the beam for any fastenings that might make its removal difficult. Where screws holding the deck planking are accessible from the outside, remove them. Also remove any hand grips, cowls or other fittings that may be screwed to the beam.

2 Make a plywood template of the beam. If the top of the beam is bevelled, make the template on the highest side. Mark in the ends — if the beam is jointed into the beam shelf at the sides, mark the position and angle of the join on the template also.

3 Saw the beam into short lengths and split it free from the deck planking and beam shelf.

4 Cut off all those fastenings that cannot be withdrawn.

5 Where the beam is dovetailed into the shelf, drill out the dovetails and chisel out the remains of the deck beam. Square up the notch so that the replacement beams can be inserted from the side rather than from above the shelf.

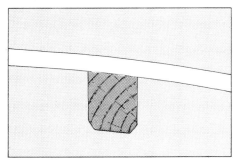

Bevel the beam to fit beneath deck

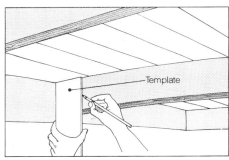

Mark shoulder of joint with template

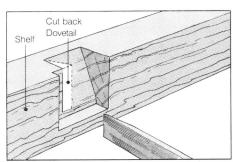

Square dovetail to give side access

6 The new deck beam needs to be scarfed into place. Select suitable timber for the two parts of the beam, cut it to size and shape each piece to lie against the deck planking and fit into the notches in the shelf. The two parts should overlap each other by approximately three to four times the beam thickness.

7 Square the end of the longer beam. Use a parallel sided piece of card to mark in the length of scarf, and scribe in the steps with a marking gauge.

8 Cut out the scarf joint, planing the scarf true with a rebate plane if necessary. Paint or varnish the top face,

and cover it with a strip of calico soaked in varnish. Pump gap-filling glue into the notch in the shelf, and shore the part beam into position. Check that it lines up exactly with the notch for the other end of the beam before fixing it into place. Use screws from the outside, or long, small diameter screws from the inside.

9 Fair the top edge of the second part beam, until it lies flat against the decking and cut the notch for the shelf joint.

10 Slip the part beam into place and mark off the end of the scarf. Cut this away very cautiously, shaving the end with a shoulder plane until it fits tightly into the opposing step in the beam.

Once the end step has been cut, the inner step can be marked off with the same cardboard template that was used before. Mark and cut the scarf in the second piece. Trim and fit it.

11 Varnish and lay a strip of calico over the top of the beam before pumping glue into the notch and spreading it on to the scarf face. Shore the beam section into position and clamp it. Drill and fit holding bolts through the scarf.

12 For added strength, a bronze or galvanized iron knee can be screwed to each end of the beam, and bolted to the beam shelf.

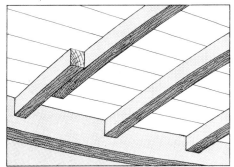

Fit beams and check overlap

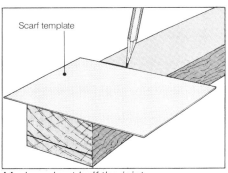

Mark and cut half the joint

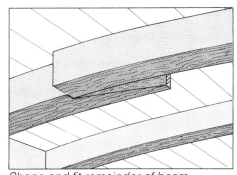

Shape and fit remainder of beam

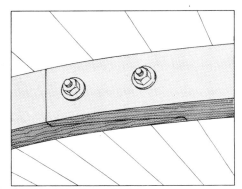

Glue and bolt scarf joint

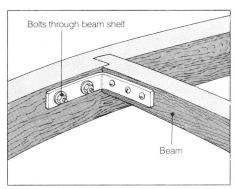

Fit knees at beam shelf joint

Carlins can be replaced in a similar manner. However, this is a more complicated task owing to the number of joints into the half beams and the additional nuisance caused by the tie bolts which tie the beam shelf and the cabin sides to the carlin.

1 Remove as many fastenings and fittings as possible. Make an accurate pair of hardboard or plywood templates. One template should record the curve of the side of the carlin, the other, its lateral bend. Mark on the templates the exact location of the tie bolts and half beams.

2 Where the carlin has curvature in two planes, set up a double string line beneath it, and mark offsets to record the curve. Using the offsets, cut out two pieces of timber to make the replacement carlin (as described opposite). Remember to add extra length at each end for the joint into the deck beams, and scarf joint. Laminate the carlin sections if it seems likely that force will be needed to bend them into the correct position.

3 Release all tie bolts and any other accessible screws. Saw the carlin into short lengths and split it away from the remaining nails, screws and joints. Saw away those fastenings that remain, but leave the tie bolts intact.

4 Trim the dovetails at the ends of the half beams, and square up the notches that take the ends of the carlin. Saw the scarf on the side of the carlin. Position the cut so that it does not coincide with a half beam joint.

5 Fit the end into the notch in the deck beam and mark off the positions for the half beams and tie bolts. Cut out the joints and drill the bolt holes.

Fit the longer section of the carlin first. Bend the beam shelf tie bolts down and insert them into their holes in the carlin. Locate the cabin-side bolts as the carlin is eased into position. Fit the shorter section of carlin and cut the stepped scarf at its end (see page 172). This is the time to deal with installation problems before the glue has been applied.

6 Dismantle the carlin and prepare the surfaces for glueing. A clamp to hold the scarf and several shores will be necessary to hold the carlin in place

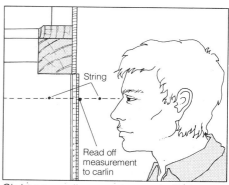
Tie parallel string lines beneath carlin

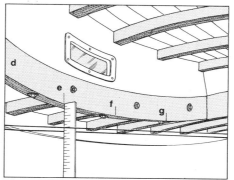
Sight across lines and record offsets

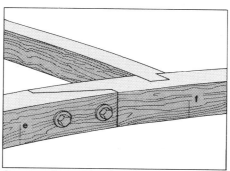
Saw scarf on side of carlin

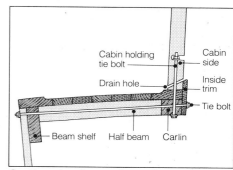
Section showing carlin and tie-bolts

while the glue cures. Do not overtighten the tie rod nuts. The carlin has only to be pulled against the shoulders of the deck beams. Excessive tension on the rods will distort the carlin.

7 Clean away the excess glue and finish with paint or varnish.

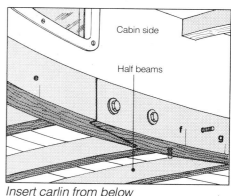
Insert carlin from below

Replacing cabin-side tie bolts

Where cabin-side holding bolts have been severed, new long bolts will need to be inserted.

Borrow a long drill or auger to suit the diameter of the new bolt. Bore through the carlin and up the cabin side, checking for signs that the auger is about to break out of the wood.

Bore the hole for about 2 to 3 inches (50 to 75 mm) into the side, and then chisel

out a slot on the inside of the cabin to receive the nut and washer. Insert the bolt through the carlin and tighten it. Block the hole in the cabin side with epoxy putty or with a small graving piece.

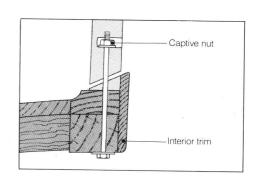

Re-laying deck planks Decks and cabins

Wooden decks

The drawing below shows the construction details of a laid deck. The ends of the deck planks are snaped into each side of the king plank, which is usually slightly thicker than the deck, so that it can be faired with a slight crown once the decking is complete. The king plank is either recessed into the deck beam, and rebated at its sides, or blocking pieces are inserted between the deck beams to support the under-side of the decking where it fits into the king plank.

A covering board is fitted at the outer edge of the hull. Narrow covering

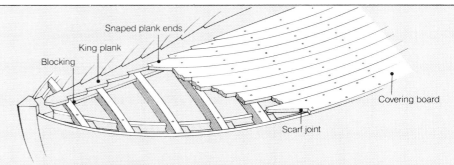

boards are cut from one piece and sprung sideways into position. Wider boards are made from sections, and scarfed or butted together. The ends and side planks of a straight laid deck are shaped to fit against the covering board. Instead of being

tapered to a feather edge, they are cut off and snaped into the side of the covering board. A batten set into the deck beams or blocking positioned beneath the edge of the board provides firm support for the ends of the deck planks.

Deck fastening

The planking of a traditionally laid deck is either screwed or nailed. Screws are normally driven through the plank into the deck beam, and are counter-bored and stopped with a cross-grain wood plug. Cross-grain plugs may also hide heavy iron nails or barbed nails. The same fastening pattern is applied to nails but removal of a deck plank is far more troublesome and sometimes impossible.

With a secret nailed deck the planks are skew nailed as they are laid, with a nail driven from about the middle of the side of the plank diagonally into the beam below. Additional stiffness is achieved by edge-nailing planks together in the spaces between deck beams. The resulting deck is light and strong and very difficult to repair.

Tongue and groove decking is laid with wider soft wood boards laid parallel to the centre-line of the deck, and cut flush with the outside of the sheer strake. Feather ends of the planks are nailed down to the top of the sheer strake and also into the side of the adjoining plank. To allow for the timber to swell, planking is not butted up tight.
All timber decks are planed and sanded prior to caulking or covering.

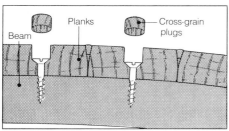

Section through laid deck

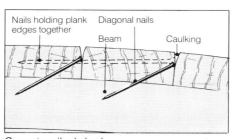

Secret nailed deck

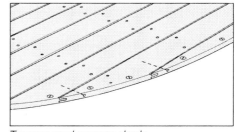

Tongue and groove deck

Removing parts of the deck

Cross-grain plugs are removed by driving an old screwdriver into the plug and levering the broken parts free. It is best to tighten the screw to break its hold in the wood before withdrawing it. Use a brace and screwdriver bit for this as plenty of weight can be exerted over the screw head and ample leverage is provided by the cranked handle.

Planks that refuse to move after all the holding screws have been withdrawn, may be edge-dowelled together. One

plank will have to be sacrificed, by splitting it apart, before the other planks can be unscrewed and wedged clear. Nailed planks can sometimes be lifted by inserting wedges between the deck beams and the under-side of the plank. Tongue and grooved planks are normally quite easy to lift in this way, as long as the adjacent boards are tilted to allow the tongue and groove joint to separate.

Secret nailed and edge nailed deck planks are best broken up and removed in small sections. Use a brace fitted with

a wide diameter bit to bore boles through the plank along its centre-line. Split the plank with an old chisel struck with a mallet and withdraw the nails once the plank has been removed.

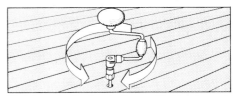

Tighten clockwise before withdrawing

Replacing a laid deck

Deck timber should be quarter sawn and air dried and follow the sectional dimensions and length of the original planking. Where it is necessary to fit a shorter plank, plan the location of the butt joints or scarfs to allow at least three beam spaces between butts on adjacent planks.

A caulking seam will need to be planed on the top two thirds of each side of the plank (unless the deck has a pronounced camber). Experiment before planing by placing offcuts of planking on to the beam.

Butts between lengths of planking should be centred over a beam, or a blocking piece inserted between deck beams. A caulked lip scarf is simple to cut once standard lengths and depths of cut have been established. Where new planks are straight butted together over blocks, or situated over a heavy beam, cut the planking runs to length and then fit them before removing them, drilling for stopwaters then replacing the planks.

Snaped ends must be cut with care, using an accurate cardboard template to eliminate errors. If, after the snaped end is fitted, the plank is found to be a little too long, remove the excess from the square butt end, or from the snaped end if the other end is scarfed.

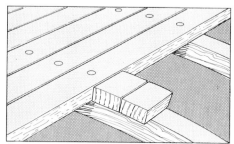
Spare plank to check bevel

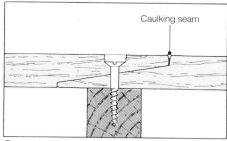
Centre scarf over deck beams

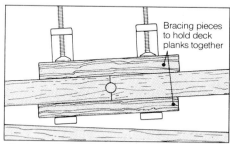
Jig for drilling stopwater

Fitting the planks

It is only at the bow in small boats, and on very large boats, that much force is needed to bend the deck planks into position. Until the closing piece is fitted, clamps and wedges are moved across the beams as the planks are replaced. The last plank is shored into position using strategically placed baulks of timber so that it can be trodden down once it is correctly positioned. If the foredeck is free of handy supports to brace the timber baulks, a few simple variations of a tyre lever lodged against the inner curve of the planking will restrain the plank while it is fitted.

Smooth down the deck with a plane and sander before driving caulking cotton into the seams. Follow this with hot marine glue, and scrape off the excess when the glue has cooled. If a synthetic sealing compound is used, the seam must be prepared and filled according to the manufacturer's instructions. This normally involves cutting the seam into a deep groove, and pumping compound into the joint with the nozzle at the base of the groove. Clean off excess compound as directed.

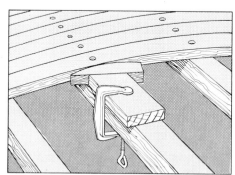
Wedging plank

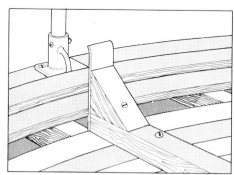
Fitting closing plank

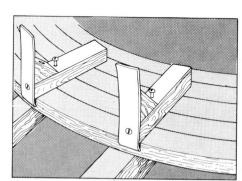
Guides for fitting planks

Replacing tongue and groove planking

This type of replacement presents few problems. Wide boards should be positioned close together with provision for the boards to swell. If a plank is being fitted to the middle of the deck, it will be necessary to lift adjacent planks. Butt joins should be cut with a straight scarf, and supported underneath with a butt block. Where a simple butt join is used, ample fastening should be fixed to prevent the plank ends lifting and working through the canvas covering.

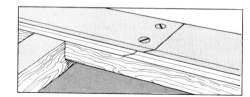

Replacing the covering board

The joints between the deck, beams, planking and beam shelf are often highly stressed. The wood there being vulnerable to leaks and occasionally rot. Satisfactory repairs can only be carried out with the covering board removed. Unless this is screwed down it will be virtually impossible to remove intact.

Unscrew or split out the covering board. It is not necessary for the entire length to be replaced, particularly if the joints between the sections are straight butts. Adjacent side deck planks may have to be removed in order to gain access to the space beneath. Once repair work to the structure below the covering board is complete the new board will have to be made and fitted.

Select a straight-grained board slightly longer than necessary and sufficiently wide to permit the curved shape to be sawn. Mark up from the sheer plank the outside curve of the board, and saw it out. Position the board, spring a batten around the edge of the existing covering board and draw the inner curve. Saw this, and, before replacing the board, run some wide masking tape down the edge of the scarf or butt joints. Run the line of tape on to the adjacent planking. The tape will give a clear reference point to allow the shape of the scarf or the angle of the butt to be transferred to the new board. Place the covering board over its position, and use a straight-edge to mark the end joints. Cut one end and fit it, before trimming the other. Once the covering board is fastened in place, drill into the side of the plank at the butts, to fit stopwaters where appropriate.

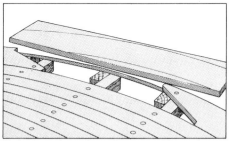

Select and mark replacement board

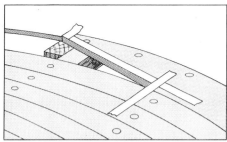

Extend scarf edge with masking tape

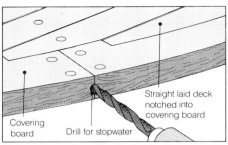

Straight laid deck notched into covering board

Covering board

Drill for stopwater

Drive stopwater after fastening

Repairing plywood decking

Plywood decking is normally glued and nailed with barbed nails. When repairs are necessary it is best to cut out the damaged part and replace it with a new patch, scarfed or reinforced by butt straps underneath. (See page 126.) If a large section of deck needs replacing, try to rebuild the deck with the largest possible pieces of plywood. If the compound curvature of the deck makes it difficult to bend the sheet into position, plan the cuts so that they do not cross or lead toward stress points in the hull. Lodging knees are usually omitted in a deck framed for plywood.

Once the plywood replacement panel is cut to fit, remove it and mark the location of the beam and batten centres at the edges of the adjoining deck. Glue the beams and battens, then press the deck section into position. Use a string line stretched between the marks at the edge of the new panel, to establish the centre-lines of the beams and batten. Screw or nail the panel in place, fastening at centres no further apart than 2 inches (50 mm). Gaps between the plywood panels should be filled with epoxy putty before the deck is covered or painted.

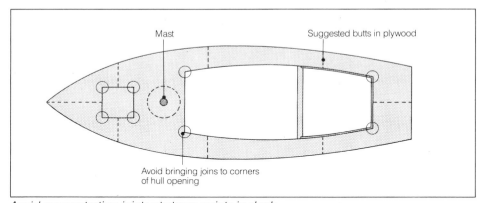

Mast

Suggested butts in plywood

Avoid bringing joins to corners of hull opening

Avoid concentrating joints at stress points in deck

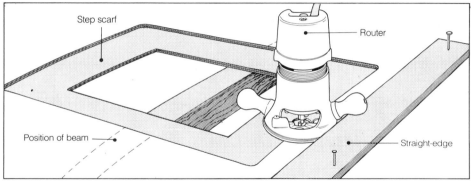

Step scarf

Router

Position of beam

Straight-edge

Use a router to cut a step scarf for inserting small repairs

Canvas and sheathed wooden decks

A fabric-covered deck will remain watertight and look smart for many years, provided it is correctly fitted and properly maintained.

The most common causes of a leaking covered deck are listed below:

1 Abrasions and tears in the deck covering. Joins in the canvas and lumps beneath the covering will be subjected to greater wear than the rest of the deck. Tears, which are particularly common on the foredeck, will also allow water to seep in beneath the deck covering.

2 Abrasions will also occur where the deck planking beneath the covering has swollen, causing the canvas to stretch over a sharp edge, where it will be vulnerable to increased wear. Tongue and groove planking often lifts in this way, because the boards are wider than those used on strip laid decks, making them more prone to cupping.

3 Tears will almost certainly occur where the deck covering is bonded tightly to the deck planking. Provision must be made for the movement of the deck when the boat

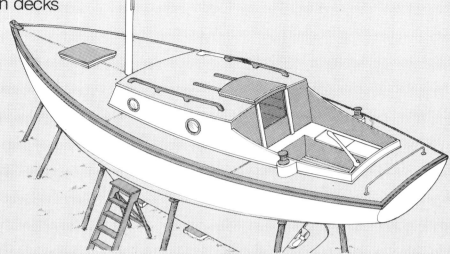

is in the water, and for shocks and shakes that she will receive when in use. A rigid, tightly-bonded covering will be unable to resist the stresses that cause the decking to move, and will tear. This problem is common with sheathed laid decks, but a fabric glued to a well-fitted plywood deck will normally be satisfactory, until the time comes to replace the deck covering.

4 A paint finish which consists of numerous layers of assorted paints will crack. Indiscriminate use of hard

marine paints will leach out the oils from the paint and from the canvas waterproofing, leaving a wrinkled, dry, fissured finish. Apart from the cracks caused in the leaching and drying of the top coat, the finish will be further crazed by engine vibration and temperature variations.

5 Water which seeps between the fabric and the deck will cause rot — which will degrade both the covering and the deck planking. Decayed covering will tear up when pressed or stretched.

Fitting a canvas deck covering

The illustrations show details of the methods used to hold down and seal the edges of the canvas. The canvas is bedded in thick wet paint and tacked in place. The raw edge of the canvas is concealed by a batten or moulding which should be fastened so that they can be re-used when the canvas is replaced.

Preparation
Remove all deck fittings that can be unscrewed or unbolted. Plank fastenings must be countersunk or punched below the level of the deck, and stopped with filler. Smooth and sand the deck. Shave down the high spots, and fill the hollows with commercial filler, or with epoxy resin mixed with fine sawdust. Seams between planks should be caulked and payed, or filled level with a flexible compound. Paint the deck with a priming paint, followed by an oil-based undercoat.

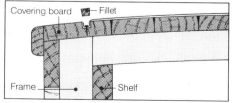

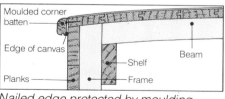
Nailed edge protected by moulding

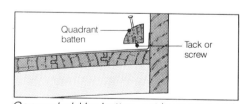
Canvas held by batten, set in compound

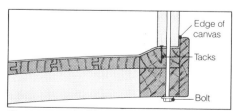
Canvas carried beneath cabin sides

Canvas deck with exposed covering board

Canvas used for deck coverings should be 10 oz (280 g) weight. Lighter canvas will not withstand rough usage, and a

heavier grade is difficult to stretch and lay flat. Plan the laying of the canvas so that minimum joins are required. In

Preparation (continued)

practice it is impossible to avoid joining sections of canvas owing to the number and position of pieces of deck furniture, cabin-sides, etc. Allow about 2 inches (50 mm) overlap for tacked joins, add 3 inches (75 mm) for sewn seams between pieces at each join. Foredeck canvas is subjected to very hard wear: arrange joins so that parts of the foredeck can be renewed without cutting into the side deck covering.

Cut the canvas sections to the correct size — remembering that the fewer the joins, the better will be the result. Leave sufficient canvas at the inboard side for tacking, and at the outboard edge for tensioning.

There are two methods of laying the canvas. Some boat-yards lay the canvas on to the dry deck, and paint it once it is in place. Others lay the canvas on to wet paint, and press it into position, adding further coats of paint once the canvas is secured. The latter method is a rather messy business, but has the advantage that the canvas is lightly bonded to the deck and looks, perhaps, a little smarter.

Stretch the canvas in a fore and aft direction, before pulling it across to the sides of the boat. Tack the inboard seams before working on the outboard edge. To eliminate wrinkles, follow the

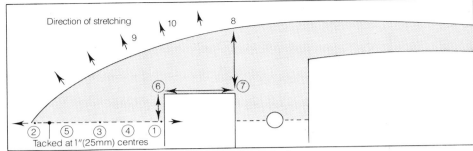

Stretch and tack canvas covering in order illustrated

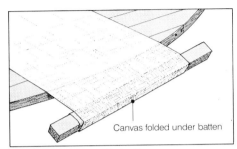

Tension canvas with batten . . .

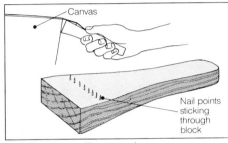

or with device illustrated

stretching and tacking sequence shown in the diagram.

Start at the stern, centre the canvas and tack each end of the centre section with ½ inch (12mm) copper tacks. Pull the canvas to the side and tack it, then work the wrinkles out by pulling and stretching the canvas tight before each

tack is driven home. A square section batten makes a useful tensioner. An alternative tensioner (illustrated) holds the canvas with short nails, rather like an upholstery webb strainer. Only enough tension is needed to eliminate wrinkles. Techniques for folding and seaming are illustrated below.

Making a seam

Once the canvas sections have been cut to size, and positioned on the deck, with an overlap of approximately 3 inches (75 mm) between sections, the centre-line of each seam should be clearly marked with a ball-point pen and straight-edge. The canvas will need to be taken to a

sailmaker or tent and tarpaulin manufacturer who will join the pieces with a double seam. Be sure to explain the significance of the centre-line before leaving the canvas pieces to be joined.

Alternatively, the seam can be tacked directly on to the deck. Punch down the

first row of tacks before the canvas is folded over. Use the tacks to help tension the fold as it is driven into the deck.

Whichever seaming method is used, take great care to centralize the middle seam, and to keep it straight while the edge tacks are hammered in.

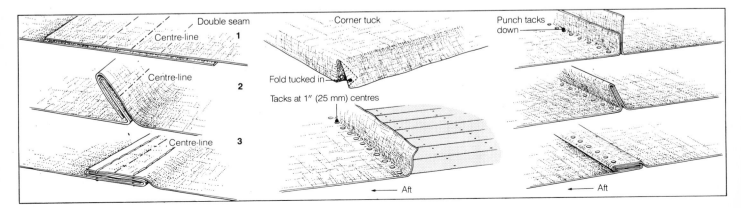

Once the canvas deck covering is complete and tacked, it should be damped by lightly brushing water over it. This shrinks the canvas and opens the weave. Paint the canvas while it is still damp with an oil-based undercoat, thinned with boiled linseed oil. Brush the paint on vigorously, using a short-haired brush, to force the paint into the canvas. A second, unthinned coat of paint can be applied once the first coat has dried. Use a wooden block to smooth and press the paint into the weave of the canvas. Finish with a purpose-made deck paint.

Once the deck is painted, fit the finishing battens over the edges of the canvas and replace the deck fittings. Battens and fittings should all be well bedded in flexible compound before fastening.

Repainting a canvas deck

To maintain their smart appearance, canvas decks need to be repainted every year. After two or three years, the build-up of paint on the canvas will become too thick, and the addition of more paint will lead to cracking of the paint film and the eventual deterioration of the canvas. It is necessary, therefore, to strip off some of the old paint before repainting.

Use paint stripper to soften the paint film and clean away the softened paint with a scraper. Neutralize the stripper and wash the surface of the deck with number two wire wool, dipped in methylated spirits. Sand the surface lightly, then repaint as described, starting with a linseed oil thinned undercoat.

An electric heat gun can be used instead of stripper. This makes the operation less messy and simpler to control. Do not overheat the canvas. Only sufficient heat is needed to soften the paint, to allow it to be scraped away.

Repair of torn canvas decks

Once the wooden deck and canvas are thoroughly dried, small tears can be repaired by cutting the area of degraded covering to a square or oblong shape. Fold under the edges of the original covering. Insert the patch under the edge of the original covering, and tack all round. Glue a filling patch of canvas over the slight recess formed at the repair, or use other suitable fillers — paint or trowelling cement — to level the repair. Re-finish the patch as described above.

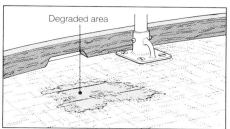
Cut away decayed canvas

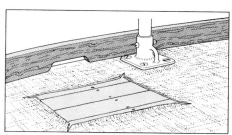
Mitre corners and fold under edges

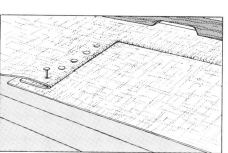
Insert repair and tack edge

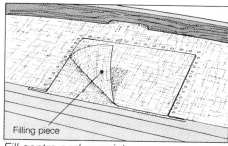
Fill centre and re-paint

Sheathing a deck

Seek professsional advice before attempting to sheath a planked deck. Plywood, steel and ferro-cement decks can be sheathed successfully, but it is often necessary to spline a laid wooden deck to prevent the planks swelling and breaking the bond between sheathing and deck. This operation involves cleaning out the seams of the deck with a hooked scraper or a carefully adjusted portable circular saw, then glueing tapered splines into the groove with epoxy resin or resorcinal glue.

Once the deck is prepared and level, all fastenings have to be punched down and stopped with epoxy putty. Sand the deck and mask off all vertical and horizontal faces where sheathing is not wanted. Prime the deck with a coat of unthickened epoxy resin. Cut the sheathing material to shape, taking the edge about an inch (25 mm) up the cabin-side and coaming, and then overlapping the edge of the deck by the same amount. Lay the sheathing material — nylon or fibreglass — on to a thickly applied layer of epoxy resin. Paint on a second coat of glue and stipple the cloth flat. Work from the stern, so that the cloth overlaps face aft. Subsequent coats of sheathing material can be applied once the epoxy is cured. Carry the cloth a small way up the side of the cabin and coaming, etc., and fair it with a hand-held grinder once the resin has cured. Finish with deck paint.

Basic wooden construction   Decks and cabins

Making a cabin involves simpler woodworking techniques than constructing a wooden hull. Most planking runs are straight, or nearly so. The joints are straightforward, many of them being used in cabinet work and carpentry as well as in boat building. Varnished work, however, requires a high standard of precision in jointing and skill in finishing, and the quality of the hull construction is often judged by the construction details revealed in the cabin work. The accompanying illustrations show the main features of a typical cabin construction. More detailed sketches show variations in construction, and a closer view of the joints.

Traditional cabin construction with laid deck

Cabin-sides rest on rebated mouldings and are through-bolted to the carlins and deck beam. The sides are also rebated and screwed into the corner posts which are notched to fit into the intersection of the carlin and deck beam. Roof beams are mortised into the ends of the corner post and dovetailed into the cabin-side or bracing piece. Planking is laid over the beams. The canvas covering is secured behind edge-nailed mouldings screwed to the cabin-side and trunk.

Corner posts

1 Close-up view of the top of a corner post, shows mortise to take the end of a roof beam, and a dovetail housing for a beam end cut into the cabin side. The curved outer face of the post is faired once the sides and front have been fitted and fastened.

2 Bottom end of the corner post, notched and bolted to both the carlin and beam.

3 Lighter corner construction. The front plank is lapped or mitred against the side plank, and screwed to triangular corner post.

4 Heavy deck house construction. Edge-nailed boards are cross-halved at corners, and bound by long bolts or drift bolts driven at the corner. Better quality structures are dovetailed at the corner. Deck beams are slotted into the cabin-side.

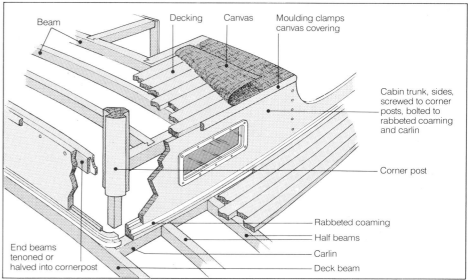

Constructional drawing of typical wooden cabin

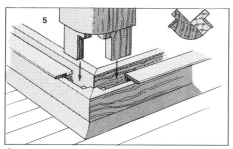

Corner post for glazed deck house

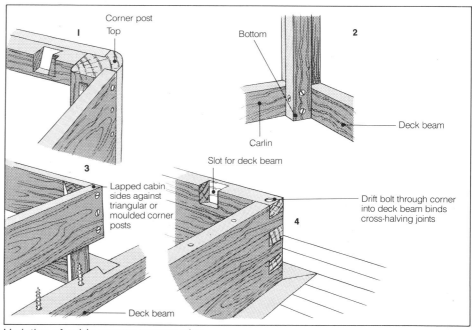

Varieties of cabin corner construction

5 High quality joinery at corner post for a glazed deck house. The corner post is made from two pieces of timber, glued together and tenoned into the framework on the deck. The base framework is mitred and joined with a stopped mortise, and braced by the tenons of the corner post. All joints should be held with weather-proof glue.

Sides and deck joints

6 Sides are bolted against the carlins and deck beams. This is simple to construct, but prone to leaks at **A** which can be cured by renewing sealing compound beneath a quadrant moulding.

7 and 8 An alternative arrangement where the cabin-sides are tied to the carlin by a facing strip or framework member. **6, 7,** and **8** suffer from the defect that the fastenings do not pull the woods together at the entry point of the water, and so are difficult to keep watertight.

9 Cabin-sides are fitted on to rebated strips, mounted over the carlin and deck beam. Cabin-sides more than 1⅛ inches (29 mm) thick are through-bolted to the carlin; thinner sides are held down with long screws or bolts fitted with captive nuts. This is a sophisticated arrangement which, when properly maintained, gives little trouble.

Cambered roofs

10 Cambered roof, covered with plywood and canvas. Moulding strip at the edge holds the canvas in place. Handholds etc., should be bolted to beams, and not to the roof.

11 Deck house roof with changing curvative at the sides, and normal camber in the middle. Shaping at the edge is accomplished by building up curves with strips of wood, edge-nailed and planed to the desired profile.

12 Framed and glazed cabin. Windows fit against rebates, and are sealed with quadrant mouldings inserted from the outside.

Doorway and hatch apertures. Carlin and half beams are mortised into posts at the doorway. These are rebated for tongue and groove planking. Corner posts at cabin-sides are rebated on the inside, but planed flush where the side runs into the cockpit coaming.

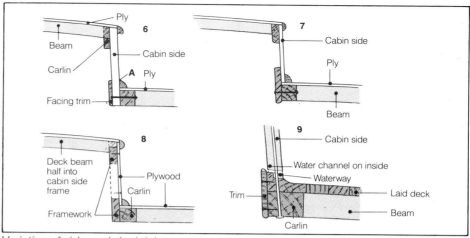

Varieties of side and deck joints

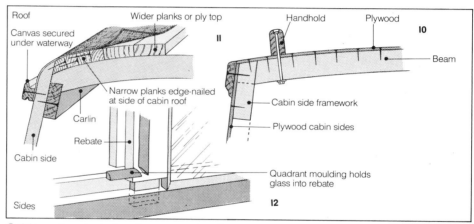

Cabin roof and window frame construction

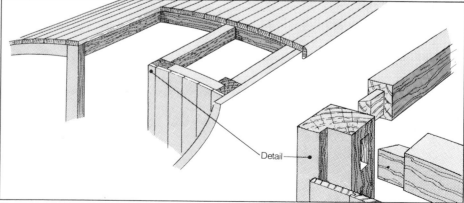

Doorway and hatch openings

Most deck structures are now glued as well as bolted or screwed to the deck beams, and a leak may well be the result of a glue failure, either through age or stressing. This can often be corrected by minor modifications or the addition of one or two battens bedded in epoxy resin, and massive replacement and repair are rarely required. Leaks at corner posts etc., can often be cured by drilling holes and injecting thickened resin into the joint.

The diagrams surrounding the illustration in the centre of the page show the correct method of fastening the stanchions, pulpits, and other handholds and lifelines to the deck and superstructure of the boat, and suggest means of checking their condition.

All of these vitally important fittings should be bolted through the hull. Fibreglass hulls should be reinforced with load spreading plates beneath the fittings to help to brace the anchorage point against sudden severe loads.

All fastenings should be designed and fitted with the safety of the crew in mind, and should be strong enough to support the weight of the heaviest crew member. They should be included in the list of deck fittings to be inspected regularly, and tested annually.

Handholds

a Handholds should be bolted through the deck or cabin-side, with load-distributing pressure pads fitted where necessary.
b Pressure pads, washers, and outside flange fittings should be bedded in sealing compound.
c Bolts should be free from corrosion and drawn up tight.
d Testing: handholds should be tugged away from the anchorage point and rocked sideways. Slight give is likely. Excessive movement should be corrected by tightening bolts or renewing compound. Evidence of cracking at the bolt holes in a fibreglass skin should be noted, and larger load spreading plates fitted.

Wooden handholds
a These must be bolted and bedded in sealing compound, with pressure pads fitted where necessary.

b Handles should be inspected for splitting, as indicated. Discard split or broken handholds, and make and fit new ones. Smooth rough edges with a rasp and sandpaper. Finish with varnish.

c Testing: As for the above handhold. Corrosion in the bolt fastenings is

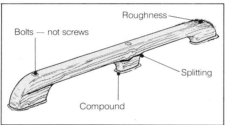

Handholds

common with wooden handholds. Withdraw and inspect a sample bolt at the end of each season.

Guard rails

Stanchions should be substantial, and spaced not more than 7 feet (213 cm) apart.

a Anchorage plates must be through-bolted to the deck, or to the deck and hull, with load spreading plates where necessary. Fibreglass decks should be protected with a pressure pad beneath the anchorage point where the base flange is less than 2 inches by 3 inches (50 by 75 mm).

b Anchorage plates should rest on a bedding of flexible compound that will prevent water penetrating the hull and corroding the bolts.

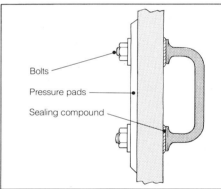

Handhold fitted to fibreglass stern

c Withdraw sample bolts annually. Corrosion of galvanized bolts is easy to assess. Stainless steel bolts should be held by the head in a vice and bent, to check for crevice corrosion.

d Drain holes in the bottom of an anchorage point should be clear.

e Inspect the welds for fracturing and cracking.

f Clevis pins or bolts should be fitted to hold the stanchion in the anchorage plate. All must be made of compatible metals, with no excessive corrosion.

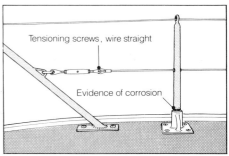

Pulpit, stanchion and lifelines

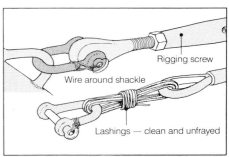

Rigging screw

Wire around shackle

Lashings — clean and unfrayed

Lifeline tensioning arrangements

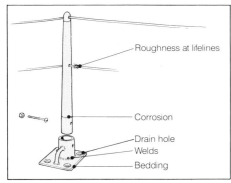

Roughness at lifelines

Corrosion

Drain hole
Welds
Bedding

Lifelines

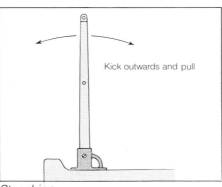

Kick outwards and pull

Stanchion

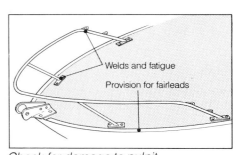

Welds and fatigue

Provision for fairleads

Check for damage to pulpit

Stanchions

a Stanchions should be straight and free from corrosion — look particularly carefully at the point where it rest against the top of the anchorage plate.

b Apertures to hold the lifelines should be smooth and bushed if necessary, so that wires are not kinked or worn.

c Testing: stanchions should be designed to withstand severe and suddenly applied loads. Test them when you have the opportunity to repair or reinforce them. Pull the top of the stanchion inwards, and press it outwards with your foot. Check for flexing and cracking at the anchorage point, and for evidence of loose fastenings at the deck.

Pulpits

a The pulpit should be anchored to the deck with bolts and load spreading plates wherever necessary.

b Inspect the condition of the anchorage plates, and check for bends in the pulpit tubing. Evidence of collision damage should prompt inspection of the welds and anchorage points.

c Check the condition and suitability of the fairleads and anchor cable fittings on the foredeck. These should be designed to prevent the cable jumping out of the fairlead and pulling against the pulpit supports.

d Pulpits should be tested in the same

vigorous and thorough manner as the fittings mentioned above.

Lifelines

a Check for fatigue and corrosion. Plastic-coated or stainless steel wire is just as likely to be weakened as galvanized wire. Check particularly the point where the wires pass through the stanchions.

b Tensioning screws should be in line with the wires, and wired up or locked to prevent them from unscrewing. Shackles should be wired, and cotter pins held with a split pin or clip.

c Lanyard tensioning lashings should be tight, and in good condition.

d Test wires by forcing them down towards the deck. Apply downwards pressure midway between stanchions.

The mast and rigging of a sailing yacht or dinghy are the focus of many forces which exert considerable strain on hull and decking. The motive power supplied by the action of the wind on the sails is transferred to the hull by the mast, and to some extent by the standing rigging. More power is usually generated than is utilized directly for forward motion, as many of the forces are racking, pitchpoling and capsizing moments that the keel, ballast, and hull form have to counteract in order that the boat may function efficiently.

Most of the forces generated by the mast and sail arrangements are transmitted to the hull through the mast step. The standing rigging also serves this purpose, as well as fulfilling its primary function of keeping the mast straight. Note that the lee shrouds play no part in supporting the mast or the transmission of power to the hull.

Wind

Deck beam pushed upwards and sideways

Windward coaming and chain plates forced upwards and inwards

Lee side is pushed outwards

Each side of the rig must be more than capable of dealing with all the loads imposed on the rig by the combination of righting and capsizing forces. This highlights the importance of fitting adequate rigging wire, and maintaining it to the highest standards.

There are, in general, two methods of stepping a mast. The traditional method is to step the heel of the mast, which is cut with a stub tenon, in a slot, resting on the floors of the boat. In fibreglass boats such a mast step rests against a reinforced pad, which is bonded to load spreading flanges set across the centre-line of the hull. Often the slot in the mast step is longer than required by the tenon at the heel of the mast. Adjustments in the rake of the mast can be made by placing small wooden blocks in the mortise to prevent fore and aft movement. Once the optimum degree of rake has been established, the blocks are nailed or screwed into position.

The mast is also restrained where it passes through the deck. Mast partners are bolted between strong deck beams, and are cut to accept the mast, which is wedged in position. Fibreglass decks are also reinforced with top hat section beams or extra internal stiffening. Minor adjustments to the rake of the mast can be made when the mast is wedged into position. The mast and deck aperture is sealed with a canvas or PVC mast coat to minimize corrosion and rot at this vulnerable point.

Provided that there are suitable reinforcements below decks, stayed masts can be stepped on deck, with the advantage that the cabin space remains uncluttered, and the difficult-to-seal mast coat is dispensed with. There are other, less obvious, advantages to this method of stepping the mast. The mast is shorter, its position and rake are easily altered, and it is a simple matter to arrange the mast so that it can be rotated to improve the airflow over the mainsail. Also, if a shroud carries away, the boat is unlikely to suffer structural damage as a result of the mast breaking at the deck, and the mast, unless it falls against a hard obstruction, may also be recovered without serious damage being incurred.

Where the masts are stepped on the deck, the under-side of the deck must be braced to take the compressive loads exerted by the mast. There are many different ways in which this load can be dissipated. Some boats, particularly those that have the mast step on the cabin roof, fit a bulkhead, or a pair of bulkheads, beneath the mast step. These take the stresses to the side of the boat, and down the hull to the centre-line. A simple alternative to the bulkhead is a vertical steel or aluminium prop placed directly beneath the mast step.

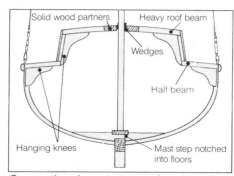

Conventional mast step and partners

Solid wood partners — Heavy roof beam — Wedges — Half beam — Hanging knees — Mast step notched into floors

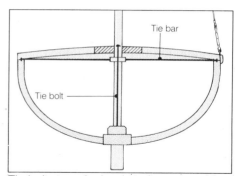

Tie bolts transfer loads to frames and keel

Tie bar — Tie bolt

Where these are fitted, the deck structure is also reinforced in way of the mast. A third method of supporting the step leaves the cabin clear, and transfers the mast weight and stresses directly to the beam shelf. This is accomplished by fabricating steel or alloy U-section beams, bending them to conform to the deck and cabin section, and bolting the ends to the beam shelf. Additional strengthening frames are added where necessary. The mast is then stepped on a channel girder set across the top of the deck and bolted through the beams.

The illustration shows the forces acting on a sail boat. The exaggerated bending and buckling indicate the degree of stress etc., experienced at that point. The sections drawn show some of the means adopted to accommodate the stresses at the mast step.

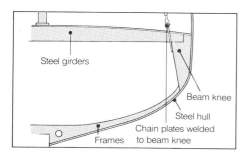

Steel girders
Beam knee
Steel hull
Chain plates welded to beam knee
Frames

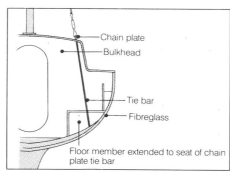

Chain plate
Bulkhead
Tie bar
Fibreglass
Floor member extended to seat of chain plate tie bar

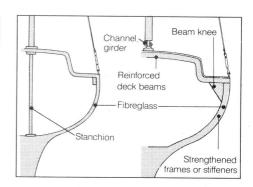

Channel girder
Beam knee
Reinforced deck beams
Fibreglass
Stanchion
Strengthened frames or stiffeners

Through-deck fitting

Mast step

The mast step is a substantial timber, notched on its under-side to sit over the floors, which are themselves notched to accept the step and to prevent sideways movement. The mast step is bolted or spiked to the floors, and often incorporates two or more bolts to bind the timber and prevent it from splitting. Drain holes should be bored at the bottom of the mortise.

Once the mast is unstepped it is very easy to renew a mast step, except for those fitted with tie rods to the deck beams. In this case, the mast step will

probably have to be split out, and the tie rod replaced with a wire and rigging screw.

Before cutting and shaping the step, inspect the heel of the mast. If the tenon is worn or rotted, cut it away and fashion a new tenon, before making a mast step from thicker timber to compensate for the slight loss of length. If more than 1⅛ inches (29 mm) of wood needs to be made up as a result of the new tenon, make the mast step from several pieces of wood, glued and bolted together with the step slot cut in the top piece. This will reduce the chance that the new step will split once it is in place.

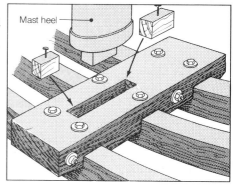

Mast heel

Mast partners

Mast partners are fairly prone to rotting. They can, in less severe cases, be chiselled back to sound wood and new wedges cut and fitted. In severe cases, it will be necessary to remove the partners from below decks, often by splitting them free. Remove or cut away deck plank fastenings and unscrew the tie bolts before making and fitting a new set of solid wood partners. This is a tricky job, best accomplished by completing most of the work off the ship, including boring the holes for the tie rods, and leaving fitting and fastening the partners until last. Use the same tie rod holes in the deck beams, and bend the rods

beneath the adjacent beams while they are inserted. Be sure to align both ends of the hole while the partner is being bolted. Once the tie rod is started at one end, it will be self-aligning, but the far end of the hole, at the intersection of the deck beam, should be kept in alignment

by resting a loose-fitting bolt through the beam into the hole. If the ends of the tie rod are rounded and greased before driving, it should enter quite freely and drift out the bolt at the opposite beam as it works through.

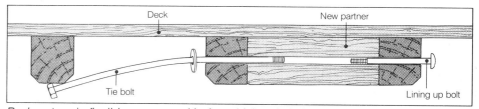

Deck
New partner
Tie bolt
Lining up bolt

Bed partner in flexible compound before driving tie bolts and deck fastenings

Wedging

Wooden masts are held with shaped wooden wedges. The mast is wedged after it has been set up and its rake and verticality have been established. Wedges should be driven firmly into the space between the deck and the mast, but they should not compress or distort the mast. The usual method of fitting is to drive the wedges at opposite sides of the mast, and then continue to place them in opposition to each other, to prevent the mast creeping out of position. Once the wedges are tapped home they should be sawn off below the partners and the ends painted.

Alloy masts are held with rubber chocks which are thicker than the space between the mast and the mast ring bolted to the deck. They must be slipped into position while the mast is winched aft to compress the after chock. The rubber chocks will be easier to fit if they are made up from one or two thicknesses of rubber and smeared with detergent before insertion.

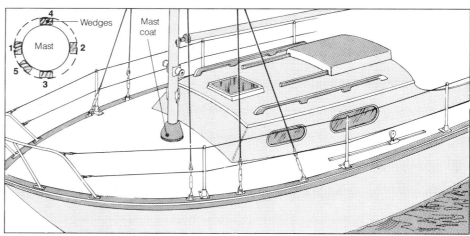

Order for fitting wooden wedges

Mast chocks, deck rings, mast coats and clips are usually supplied by the manufacturers of alloy masts and their fitting and adjustment instructions should be followed.

As all mast rubbers, unlike wedges, tend to work when the boat is being sailed hard, it is good practice to put a large jubilee clip round the mast and wedging, usually below deck, to hold the rubber in position.

Fitting a mast coat

Mast coats are lashed or clamped around the mast, and fastened to the adjacent decking to make the joint between the mast and deck watertight. Mast coats can be bought ready made, and are slipped over the heel of the mast as it is stepped or they can be made and sewn into position once the mast is in place.

Where a wooden mast is fitted to a boat, it is useful to be able to lift up the mast coat in dry weather, to ventilate and dry

the deck beneath it. The traditional method of securing the mast coat to the deck was to cut out a ring of sheet lead and, having folded the mast coat on the deck, to fit the lead ring on top of the canvas coat and copper tack it to the deck. Lifting the mast coat to ventilate the deck and wedges is impractical in these circumstances.

The fastening holes in the deck are likely to lead to rot, and it is best if the mast coat can be fastened to a flange or batten, fitted close to the mast and screwed to the deck.

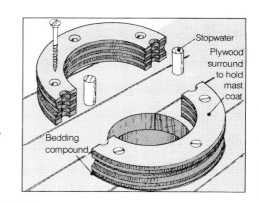

Making and fitting a mast coat

The mast coat must be a very tight fit against the mast, and make a watertight seal at the deck. However, the fabric of the coat should be loose enough to permit slight movement between deck and mast. Cut a paper template of the mast coat. The example illustrated is of a pole mast. Square masts should have a square hole at the centre. The mast coat must be sufficiently large to allow the section that is lashed or clamped to the mast to be turned back and brought down to the deck, where there should still be ample fabric to lash it to the flange or batten.

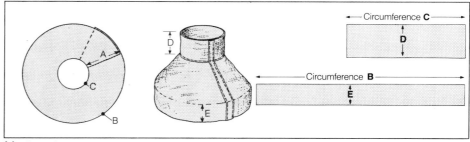

Mast coat components

Cut the mast coat from heavy canvas or nylon-reinforced PVC, fit it around the mast, and sew the seam joining the two

sides. Bond the seam with rubber-based impact adhesive, before sewing.

Position the seam on the centre-line of the boat, facing aft. Lift the mast coat and lash or clamp it to the mast. Turn down the coat and lash or clamp it to the flanges or fillets of wood at the deck. Run sealing compound around the top edge of the mast coat, and brush a warmed mixture of linseed oil and varnish over the canvas to make it waterproof.

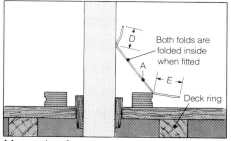

Measuring for mast coat

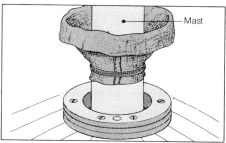

Fasten mast coat to mast

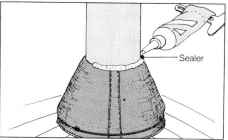

Lash and seal its top edge

Tabernacle

The illustrations below show methods of stepping a mast in a tabernacle. A tabernacle allows a mast to be raised and lowered, and enables sailing boats to pass below bridges, etc., without unstepping the mast. The illustrations show some typical arrangements. In one example a counterbalance is fitted at the heel of the mast to facilitate lowering.

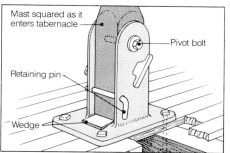

Wedge relieves pivot of mast thrust

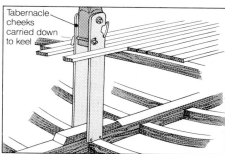

Thrust transferred downwards to keel

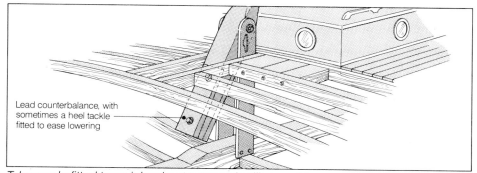

Tabernacle fitted to an inland water type of sailing yacht

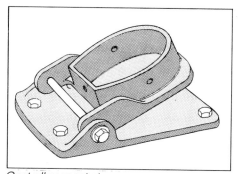

Cast alloy mast step

Deck mounted mast step

Except on small dinghies, the mast step is usually made from steel or aluminium alloy, with provision included for fore and aft adjustment. It is most important in fitting deck-stepped masts to ensure that the mast cannot be bounced out of step in extreme conditions. Most manufacturers make provision for a through-bolt somewhere in the assembly and, as the heel fittings are usually cast alloy, they will break at the bolt if the mast goes over the side. This usually prevents structural damage to the step and its immediate support structure.

A variety of deck mounted mast steps are available, and it will be noted that the mast steps and masts are often incompatible, unless purchased from the same manufacturer. All fittings should be snug and tight, and inspected annually for corrosion and wear.

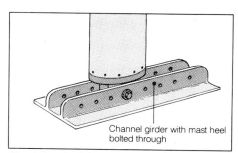

Retaining bolt vulnerable to corrosion

Cockpit construction and motor access   Decks and cabins

The illustration shows the constructional details of a cockpit designed and built to withstand offshore conditions. The cockpit provides a degree of shelter, combined with a good view of the sails and the way ahead, and ready access to the deck. The floor of the cockpit is raised above the level of the water-line and is self-draining. The floor is also canted towards the stern. Water that comes aboard drains out through the drainage holes. Seats are provided along both sides of the cockpit, and double as locker lids, covering the storage spaces below. Liquid gas cylinders are stored in one of the lockers which is fitted with a low-level vent to drain escaping gas overboard.

A hatch cover is concealed in the cockpit floor, which gives rather limited access to the stern tube and the auxiliary motor. The hatch cover is sealed and provision is made to channel water which seeps past the seals away from the engine and into the bilges.

Apart from the engine hatchway, the bottom and lower sides of the cockpit are free from fittings and any controls, etc. that may cause injury or leak water into the bilges. Engine controls are fixed to the main cabin bulkhead.

Removable washboards are fitted into grooves behind the open door to the cabin. These support the door when it is closed and prevent an unexpected sea that floods the cockpit floor from entering the cabin when the door is open.

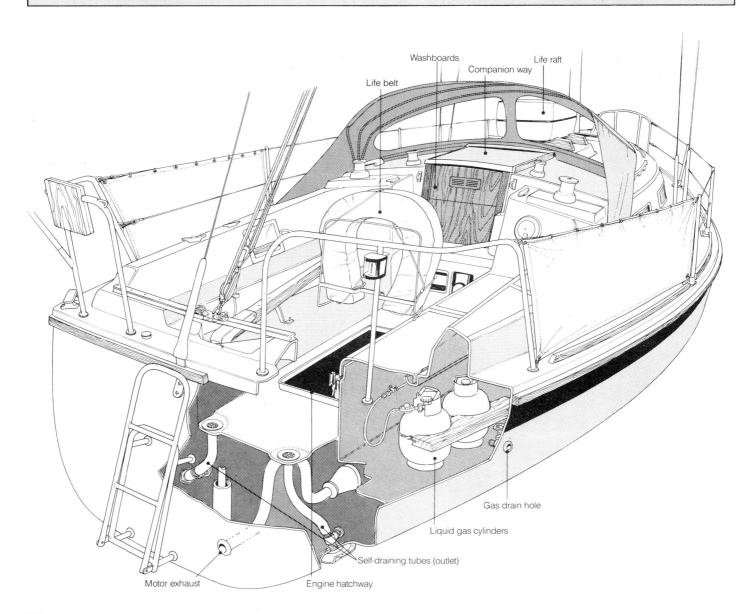

Washboards

Companion way

Life raft

Life belt

Gas drain hole

Liquid gas cylinders

Self-draining tubes (outlet)

Motor exhaust

Engine hatchway

Self-drainage system

The floor of a self-draining cockpit must be above the level of the water-line. The simplest form is to run the cockpit to the sides of the hull, and arrange breaks in the bulwarks so that water that enters the cockpit can leave through the freeing ports. This arrangement is fairly common on large sea-fishing motor cruisers where the cockpit doubles as a sun deck and fishing platform. With smaller boats such a large cockpit would be vulnerable to breaking seas and would afford very little shelter to the crew.

Smaller cockpits that are set well inboard are usually drained by a pair of 2 inch (50 mm) diameter pipes that are positioned at the after end of the cockpit floor. Outlets in the hull sides should be at or slightly above the water-line. A small clam shell cowl fitted over the outside of the cockpit drain skin fitting will very effectively pull the water out of the cockpit when the boat is sailing. Seacocks should be fitted where the outlet is below the load water-line. Drain holes in the cockpit floor should be fitted with a grating.

In some yachts, the bilge pump outlet is either plumbed into the self-draining tubes or outlets directly into the cockpit, close to the drain grating. These arrangements are unsatisfactory and should be altered if there is any possibility that the boat will be making a sea passage. Difficulties with this arrangement arise when the hull has shipped so much water that the loaded water-line has risen until the self-draining facility ceases to function. Bilge pump

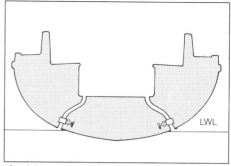

Avoid cross-connecting cockpit drains

and self-draining arrangements should be separate, and where heavy seas are expected, it is sensible to carry in the cockpit a strong plastic bucket attached by a lanyard to supplement the self-draining system.

Engine and floor hatches in the cockpit

These are normally fitted so that the opening catch is operated from above. Water seals are fitted at the lip of the hatch which should prevent serious leaks. It is virtually impossible to seal floor hatches completely. Small gutters are therefore cut into the beams and carlins surrounding the hatch. These carry the water to the small diameter copper pipes which are plumbed into the guttering to carry the water to the bilges. Excessive leaking at the floor hatch is usually a sign of flimsy hatch construction which distorts when it is trodden on. Catches should be such that the hatch will not fall out when the boat is knocked down or capsized.

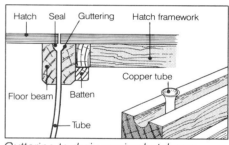

Guttering to drain engine hatchway

Washboards

These fit into grooves and each board should be capable of being locked into position. Washboards serve a vital role as they allow movement and communication between the cockpit and the crew below, while preventing water entering the cabin from the cockpit. Boards should be substantial and interlock with each other. Where the companion way widens towards the hatch, a centre clip to a ring bolt should be set in the companion steps, and similar arrangements fixed in the centre of each washboard to tie them together independently of the catches at the side. These fittings are necessary because tapered washboards cannot be retained by a fastening at one side only. In the absence of secure fastening arrangements, a spare set of washboards, each clearly numbered, should be carried aboard.

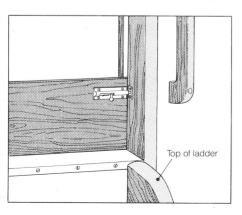

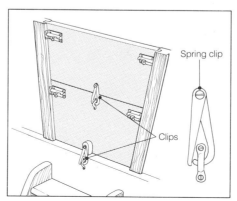

Number washboards and fit them with individual fastening bolts

Washboards which slot into a tapered companion way opening should have an additional centre clamp

Ventilation Decks and cabins

It is essential for the well-being of the crew, boat and stores, that the hull is adequately ventilated. The dank, musty smell indicating poor ventilation will be immediately apparent when opening the hatch of a boat that has been left with its hatches screwed down and cowls plugged or obstructed.

Air circulation is necessary to enable the hull to dry out, and to prevent accumulation of smelly and sometimes poisonous pockets of gas in the bilges.

Boats taken to sea should be provided with ventilation facilities that function when windows and hatches are battened down. Severe weather conditions which prevent airing of the cabins may last for several days, and the replacement of foul air should also be considered.

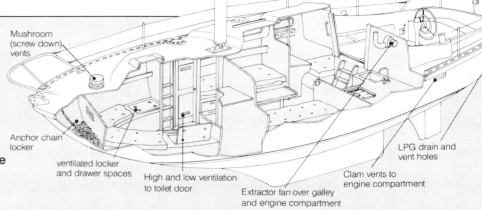

Mushroom (screw down) vents

Anchor chain locker

ventilated locker and drawer spaces

High and low ventilation to toilet door

Extractor fan over galley and engine compartment

Clam vents to engine compartment

LPG drain and vent holes

Ventilation arrangements need to be planned with care. A few well-placed ventilators combined with minor alterations to the cabin furniture can improve the flow of fresh air through the hull.

There is a wide variety of easy-to-install hull and cabin ventilators, some of which will operate efficiently in all but the most extreme weather conditions. A range of ventilators is illustrated opposite. Deck and coach roofs are often fairly cluttered, and although it may be desirable to add to the number of ventilators to increase the air flow through the hull, it is often impossible to fit extra ventilators without further obstructing the deck.

Cabin

Doors
The only accommodation hatchways or doorways that need to be airtight are those that give access to the engine room or battery compartment. Others should be altered when necessary to provide both high- and low-level ventilation. Doorways can be pierced with drilled patterns or with shaped holes cut with a power jigsaw. Where privacy as well as ventilation is desired, angled louvres can be slid and glued into place. Decorative motifs at the top of the doors should be combined with an aperture cut at the foot of the door. These can simply be cut back.

Arrange the floor boarding so that the bilge spaces beneath are ventilated. Boards can be positioned a small distance apart, or drilled to allow air to circulate.

Drawers and lockers should be provided with high and low ventilation. Deep lockers that are difficult to ventilate can be fitted with false bottom gratings to facilitate air flow.

Plywood mattress and cushion supports should be drilled, both to ventilate the under-side of the upholstery and to allow air to circulate in the storage spaces beneath, when the boat is laid up.

The ceiling
The light tongue and groove ceiling which lines the inside framing of a traditionally constructed wooden boat should be open at the keel and at the beam shelf to allow air to circulate and to channel bilge water away from the cabin fittings and lockers when the boat heels. It is very important that cabin alterations in traditional wooden hulled boats do not close the space between the ceiling and the beam shelf.

The air flow through the cabin is normally from aft forward. Extractor ventilators should duct foul air from the bilges of the boat, via wooden trunks or large diameter plastic hoses.

Hatches and cabin windows can be opened in fair weather to improve ventilation. A wind sail fitted over the hatchway will increase air flow through the boat. It will also, however, channel water into the hatch and should not be left rigged unless dry weather is forecast.

Most of the arrangements illustrated function well if the boat is in motion or if there is a good breeze. Electric extractor fans should be fitted to the engine compartment to ventilate the boat whatever the wind and weather conditions. Make every attempt to ensure that air is circulated.

Mushroom ventilation cowls at the ends of the boat are essential for this purpose.

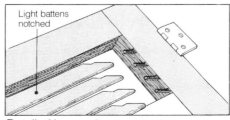

Light battens notched

Detail of louvre door

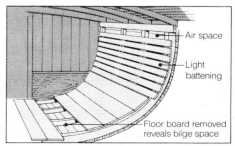

Air space

Light battening

Floor board removed reveals bilge space

Do not obstruct ceiling vents

Cowls

The illustrations show a variety of cowls that can be fitted to the deck or the coach roof of the boat to improve ventilation. All except the mushroom ventilator will allow water below, when the ventilator is submerged by a breaking wave. The use of water traps will prevent spray and waves from flooding the cabin, but all the ventilators fitted to sea-going yachts should be fitted with plugs that can be used in severe weather conditions. Some of the ventilators are of a venturi type, designed to extract air from the hull. Most of the ventilators illustrated can be rotated to face into or away from the wind.

Fitting a cowl ventilator

Cowls are normally supplied with full fitting instructions. Sandwich moulded decks and coach roofs must always be reinforced and, where necessary, sleeves should be inserted to prevent the compression and saturation of the core material.

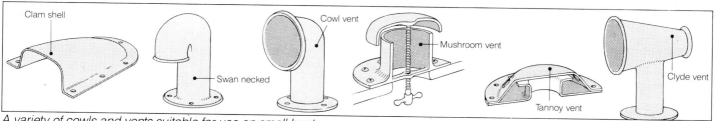

A variety of cowls and vents suitable for use on small boats

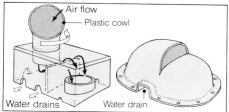

Dorade-type ventilators

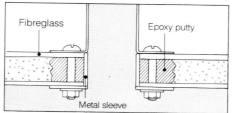

Protect core when fitting cowl

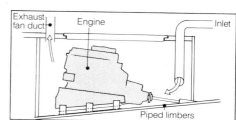

Engine room ventilation

Ventilation of engine and battery compartments

The engine compartments of both diesel and petrol engines should be well ventilated. Engines consume large quantities of air when they are in operation. They are also the source of unpleasant and potentially explosive gases. The engine compartment should, wherever possible, be separated from the accommodation by a gastight bulkhead through which the bilge limbers are piped, to prevent heavy gases seeping into the cabin.

Clam shell and cowl ventilators arranged with water traps are usually fitted in the engine compartment, supplemented by an electric extractor fan connected to a high-level air outlet duct, which works in conjunction with low-level inlet ducts.

Where an extraction fan ventilator is fitted in the engine space, the induction due to manifold depression is considerably greater than the fan can produce and there is therefore little to be achieved by switching on the fan while the engine is running. In petrol engined boats, the fans servicing the engine compartment should be of spark-proof type to avoid the possibility of explosions should a gas concentration be present.

Battery compartments must have high- and low-level ventilation ducts. Liquid gas bottles should be stored in a separate compartment, also with high air inlet and low gas outlet. LPG is heavier than air, and should be prevented from leaking into the limbers where an explosive air/gas mixture can accumulate in the bilges (see page 271).

Ventilating when leaving the boat at moorings

Arrangements should be made to allow air to circulate through the hull when the boat is unoccupied and left at moorings. The enclosed parts of the hull aft of the cockpit and forward of the mast are often badly ventilated, and are the first to suffer from damp and mildew.

Lift mattresses on to their sides and partially open lockers and drawers. Remove one or two cabin floorboards and prop open internal doors with adequate restraint to prevent them swinging about.

Where ventilation cowls are not fitted at the extreme ends of the craft, open the hatches slightly. Fit locks that secure the opening against the entry of thieves, but permit air flow.
For hints on ventilation arrangements when laying up see page 283.

It is impossible to over-stress the importance of equipping a sea-going boat with adequate ground tackle, and maintaining it in first class condition. All parts of the equipment should be inspected, including the anchor and its shackle attachment to the anchor cable, the entire anchor cable, the fairlead or stemhead roller, devices for holding the chain and preventing chafe, as well as ensuring that the drainage holes in the chain locker are free and that the end of the anchor cable is made fast.

The equipment must also be of a type suited to the boat and the conditions in which it is to be used. A wide variety of anchors can be bought, in all sizes. Different anchors are suited to their own favoured holding grounds, and may be quite ineffective elsewhere.

Sea-going boats should be equipped with at least two independent anchors and cables, with a partitioned chain locker, and separate navel pipes for each. It is common practice for the bower or main anchor to be stowed and veered from the port side, and the kedge to starboard. A third anchor, known as a stream anchor, may also be carried. This is usually stowed near the stern, where it is shackled to a cable when required. Many modern production boats are fitted with anchors that are too small, and shackled to cables that are too short. Although one hopes never to be in a situation where the inadequacy of the equipment is all too apparent, there will may be occasions when, because of the boat's skimpy ground tackle, owners will spend harrowing and exhausting nights listening to the scrape of the dragging anchor, and watching lights on the quayside loom closer.

Lloyd's-approved high holding power anchors include: Bruce, CQR, Danforth, Meon and Stokes.

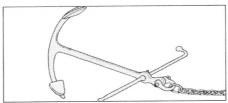

Fisherman
Use Usually carried as reserve anchor

Fouling Fouling can be avoided by using anchors in pairs and lying between them. Otherwise anchor cable is likely to catch on to and foul second fluke as boat swings with the tide

Holding Can be improved by filing flukes to sharp point. Good in rocky or coral bottoms, or when seabed is covered with layers of kelp or weed

Storage Stock disengages, and anchor can then fold flat

Remarks A useful stream anchor to have in reserve. Weight for weight, and in most conditions, less efficient than high holding power anchors

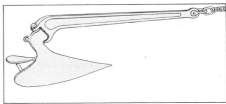

CQR
Use All sizes and types of small craft

Fouling Bites quickly and thereafter buries itself. Not susceptible to fouling

Holding Excellent. A Lloyds designated, high holding power anchor

Storage Does not fold, usually lashed on chocks on deck, or held in stem head roller

Remarks Excellent quality anchor, although less effective on weedy bottoms. Copies of CQR probably less efficient

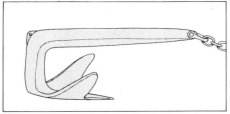

Bruce
Use All sizes and types of boat

Fouling Buries itself, not vulnerable

Holding Lloyds designated, high holding power

Remarks A simple one-piece anchor, no moving parts and good holding power. Will not lie flat. Stowed, usually clamped, on stem head roller

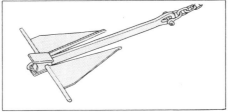

Danforth
Use All sizes and types of boats

Fouling Buries itself, not susceptible to fouling

Holding Lloyds designated, high holding power anchor

Remarks Very popular anchor but not very efficient in weedy or kelpy bottom

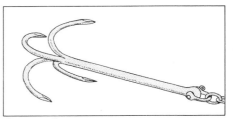

Grapnel
Use General purpose anchor

Fouling Vulnerable to fouling

Holding Flukes do not fold. Anchor usually suspended on bow

Remarks Still in use amongst fishermen, where its ability to hold in rocky and weedy inshore waters is a great advantage

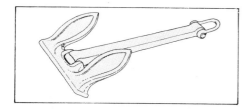

Stockless

Use Heavy anchor. Usually limited to boats over 60 feet (l8m)

Fouling Buries itself. Not susceptible to fouling

Holding Good, provided that it is sufficiently heavy to obtain initial bite

Storage Can be drawn up hawsehole where it will lie flat against ship's side

Remarks Unsuitable for small craft

Calculating anchor and cable size

A number of factors need to be taken into account when selecting a new anchor, or checking the suitability of an existing system.

Whether a boat is purchased new or secondhand, the anchor is quite likely to be the minimum necessary for the size of the boat. Boat owners sometimes grow very fond of their anchors and will transfer tried and tested ground tackle to a new boat, perhaps leaving a new, cheaper and untested anchor in its place. For years the inadequacy of this essential equipment may remain undiscovered. It is sensible to look to the equipment, and be confident in its quality and ability to hold the boat.

The hull shape, superstructure and draught are all factors to be included in a calculation which enables a boat's 'equipment number' to be computed. Once a boat's equipment number is known, refer to table for anchor and cable weights and strengths appropriate for the boat. The formula and appended table are based on the 'Rules and Regulations for the Classification of Yachts and Small Craft' issued by Lloyd's Register of Shipping, and reproduced with their permission.

For a stocked anchor, the weight without the stock is to be not less than 65 per cent of a stockless anchor up to EN 500. When the equipment number exceeds 500, seek assistance in choosing an appropriate anchor.

Examples

From the two examples given, it will be evident that the hull shape plays a significant part in determining the weight of the anchor and the breaking strain of the cable.

Equipment number	Bower anchors		Chain cable		Hawsers and Warps	
	Mass lb (kg)		Diameter inch (mm)		Breaking load ton f (tonne f)	
	Stockless	High holding power	Short link	Stud link	Hawser	Warp
200	30 (14)	25 (11)	5/16 (8)	—	2.00 (2.03)	1.40 (1.42)
300	40 (18)	30 (14)	5/16 (8)	—	2.00 (2.03)	1.50 (1.52)
400	50 (23)	35 (17)	5/16 (8)	—	2.00 (2.03)	1.60 (1.62)
500	60 (27)	45 (20)	5/16 (8)	—	2.50 (2.54)	1.70 (1.72)
600	70 (32)	50 (23)	3/8 (9)	—	2.90 (2.95)	1.80 (1.83)
700	80 (36)	60 (27)	3/8 (9)	—	3.40 (3.46)	1.80 (1.83)
800	90 (41)	65 (30)	3/8 (9)	—	3.90 (3.96)	1.90 (1.93)
1000	110 (50)	80 (37)	7/16 (11.2)	7/16 (11.2)	4.70 (4.77)	2.00 (2.03)

$$\text{Equipment number} = 10.76L \left(\frac{B}{2} + D \right) + 5.38A$$

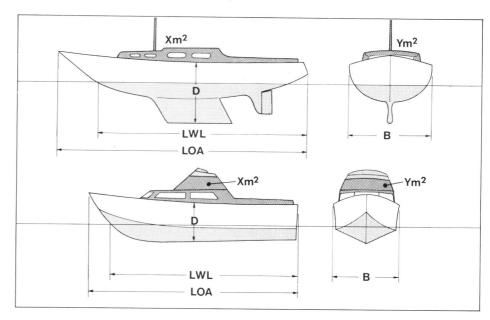

$$A = Xm^2 + Ym^2$$

D = distance, measured from amidships from bottom of keel to top of the upper deck or gunwale at the side. Where centreboard is fitted, **D** is depth to keel increased by l5 per cent

$$L = \frac{LOA + LWL}{2} \text{ metres}$$

A = projected area (length x height) of all deck structures which have a length or breadth greater than $\frac{B}{2}$ square metres

Chain or rope

Anchor chains are expensive and very hard and heavy to handle. Against these disadvantages are the considerable benefits of the chain's weight, reliability and durability. In order to hold, an anchor should be veered on a chain at least three times the maximum depth of water. The more chain veered, the better will be the hold and the less the boat is likely to snub at the chain. The weight of the chain is usually such that the pull on the anchor stock is horizontal, causing the anchor to dig deeper.

Fasten the inboard end of the chain (the bitter end) to the boat with synthetic rope long enough to allow the end of the chain to be on deck, so that the chain can be slipped without having to go below.

Rope cables have all the advantages of light weight, ease of handling, and immense strength, but they suffer from wear: the lightness, which is such an advantage when heaving the anchor aboard, is a liability when the anchor is veered. In order to hold, an anchor rope should be at least 5 times the depth at high water.

To overcome the tendency of a lightweight rope to snatch and break out the anchor, it is normal practice to shackle five or more fathoms of chain between the anchor and the end of the anchor rope. This will weight down the stock of the anchor and allow the anchor rope to keep clear of the ground where it would otherwise be abraded by rocks and sharp-edged debris. If there is no chain between anchor and rope, a small float attached to the rope, about a fathom back from the anchor, will lift the anchor warp off the bottom, and prevent chafing damage.

The anchor cable

Chain

At the end of each sailing year, range the chain on a well-drained gravel or concrete surface, hose clean, and inspect for wear and kinks before locking it away in a safe store.

Most wear usually occurs at the anchor end. Prolong the usable life of the chain by reversing the ends at the start of each season. Where more than 25 per cent of the link thickness has been worn away, the worn section of chain should be removed. Badly worn chain can be sold for scrap, or used to make permanent moorings for small boats.

Galvanizing should be in good condition, although after a year or two it will wear away in places and rust marks will stain the links. There is no point in painting the anchor chain, as it is rarely possible to prepare the links properly, and, in any case, the paint wears away very quickly. Re-galvanize the chain only after seeking professional advice, as galvanizing may not prolong the life of the chain by more than a couple of years, owing to the degree of wear already present.

Stud-linked chain does not distort under stress and is less likely to kink or bunch than short link chain. Study the links, both for wear, and for evidence that the chain links have stretched or bent. These are likely to be the only signs of weakness a chain will give before parting. If in doubt, arrange with a boat-yard for a sample of chain to be tested by the manufacturer or a specialist testing company.

Rope

Rope anchor cables require regular and frequent inspection. Unless the cable is adequately protected against chafe, the part where the cable passes through the fairleads or over the stemhead roller will wear rapidly. The anchor end is very vulnerable to wear against submerged obstacles, as well as the more subtle internal wear caused by the entry of sand particles into the twist of the rope which severs the fibres.

It is always a good idea to buy about 30 per cent more anchor rope than necessary, so the worn ends can be cut off. Remember that the splices at the end of the rope — for the anchor shackle and the ringbolt in the chain locker — will reduce the strength of the rope by as much as one-eighth. Do not discard good rope at the first sign of wear. Instead, change ends so that the working end originally shackled to the anchor or short length of chain remains most of the time in the chain locker, while the relatively unused portion bears the brunt of the remaining use. Cut out and renew frayed parts. Use a long splice for joining lengths of cable, and a short splice for the eyes.

Protect the rope against chafe. Apart from the small float mentioned previously, little can be done at the anchor end, except to ensure that there is a galvanized thimble seized into the eye splice at the very end. Chafe at the fairleads and roller can be minimized by slipping a length of garden hose on to the rope to sheathe it, and by arranging rope runs to avoid kinks and sharp corners. High pressure water hose (with

a fabric reinforcement) is available in a variety of diameters and lengths to be used on heavier ropes.

Anchor rope is not self-stowing, so there will be plenty of opportunities to check its condition as it is paid out or hauled in. The cable should be free of knots or kinks. Both will permanently weaken the cable and must be cut out. The rope should be reasonably clean without signs of chemical staining or UV degradation. Back-twist small lengths of rope to inspect the condition of the inner lay. Severed fibres, whether at the inside or outside of the rope, are an obvious indication of weakness. Such cables should be clearly marked, and relegated to less exacting uses.

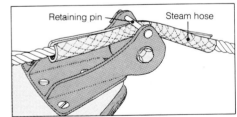

Protect rope passing through stem head roller

Marking the anchor cable

It is a useful practice to mark the anchor cable every 5 fathoms (30 feet [9 m]), so that an accurate estimate may be made of the amount of cable veered, and the amount held in reserve. Methods vary, and depend to some extent on the foredeck lighting and winch arrangements. Where no winch is used, anchor chains and ropes can be marked by tying small lengths of knotted lanyard to the link or by weaving thin ribbon into the rope lay. The knots indicate the fathoms (in multiples of 5) and can be felt in the dark, as well as read in daylight. Where chains or ropes pass through a gypsy or windlass, the ties are likely to be torn off. Coloured adhesive tape around the rope and paint on the chain will serve instead.

Even if the windlass is equipped with a meter, it is worth while painting or tying a prominent marker to indicate when the cable is almost completely paid out.

Deck and chain locker
There are a number of deck and chain locker configurations, from the simplest triangular stem head hatch concealing the anchor and anchor rope ready to slip over the roller, to the complex arrangements of chain locker, chute, navel pipe, windlass, and fairleads on a larger yacht.

Many chain lockers are situated in the forepeak, sealed from the rest of the accommodation by a watertight bulkhead, and fitted with drainage holes above the water-line. To improve the ventilation and drainage, fit a small grating that lifts the anchor rope above the narrow floor.

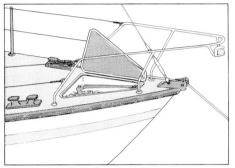

Anchor and chain stowage

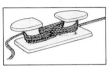

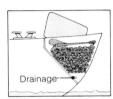

Drainage

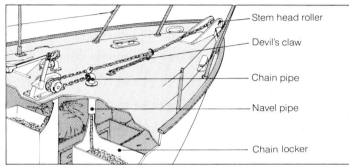

Stem head roller

Devil's claw

Chain pipe

Navel pipe

Chain locker

Complex foredeck and chain stowage arrangements for larger craft

Anchors

Anchors should be lashed to chocks secured to the deck. CQR and Bruce anchors are best lashed over the stem head roller or to cat-davits at the side.

Anchors require virtually no maintenance. When the pivot pin of a CQR (plough) anchor wears thin, it should be returned to the supplier or manufacturer, who will either repair the anchor or recommend a new one. The flukes of a grapnel or a fisherman's anchor can be sharpened to improve its holding power. The chain and wedge of a fisherman's anchor should be periodically checked to make sure that the stock does not release itself once the anchor is assembled and lowered over the side.

It is worth while making sure that the wooden retaining pin in the anchor shackle is in good condition.

Chain or navel pipes
These should be secured to the deck, with reinforcing pieces beneath the deck where necessary (see page 98). Chain pipes are connected to a large diameter plastic pipe that feeds the chain to the chain locker. Sometimes a wooden chute is used instead. Both the plastic pipe and the chute should be positioned so that the chain passes up and down the system without snagging.

Chain pipes are difficult to keep watertight. On long sea passages it is often worth while unshackling the anchor and bunging the pipe with a large cork. Pipes that face forward are often troublesome. A good way of securing a bung in the chain pipe is to put a large hook on the underside of the bung, and hang the chain on it. The chain weight holds the bung in place.

Stem head rollers
These are usually substantial cast pieces of equipment, which act as a fairlead for the anchor cable. A Tufnol roller is pivoted between two cheeks. The anchor cable passes over the rollers and is retained by another pin or bolt slipped across the assembly. The pivot bolt is easily withdrawn for inspection. The upper retaining bolt or pin should be attached by a short lanyard to the boat, to prevent it from being lost.

Some roller assemblies are fitted with a chain pawl which, when slipped into position, will hold the chain and prevent its running out. The pawl and pivot bolt take a lot of wear. A worn pivot will usually cause excessive play in the pawl and should be replaced.

There are many companies specializing in galvanizing and re-galvanizing marine fittings. Ask at the local boat-yard for the names and addresses of the nearest companies.

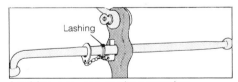

Lashing

Lashing ensures anchor remains assembled

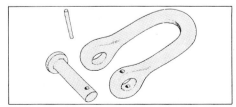

Check condition of wooden pin in anchor shackle

Hatches Decks and cabins

Not only must hull and cabin opening be secure against the entry of water, but also against the entry of thieves and unwanted visitors. Since the 1979 Fastnet Race Enquiry, an additional and very sensible recommendation to safeguard the crew is that it should be possible to open or close hatches and cabin doors from inside and outside the cabin.

These hatchway and door arrangements prevent a situation arising where the crew below decks are unable to secure and make watertight the companion hatch and doorway. They also ensure that crew members on deck, or the rescue services, can open the hatch from the outside whenever necessary.

These points also have a general application to boat owners who never venture far out to sea, or who limit their cruising to inland waters. It is an obvious and, in some areas, statutory precaution to have at least two cabin entrances or exits. One of these should be able to be opened from both inside and outside.

Security against theft, etc. is nevertheless an important feature of any cabin-locking devices. It is, however, not advisable to fit Yale type locks wihout an opening handle on the outside. Locking bars should not be swung into position, even without the padlock, once the boat is occupied.

Hatchways

Hinged hatches and lifting hatches

A variety of hatchways is illustrated. Most will be positioned on the centre-line of the boat, well clear of any likelihood of submersion when the boat heels. For a sea-going boat, the hatchway ought to be able to sustain the weight of a crew member, or of a breaking sea that might crash into it. It is more likely that the hatch will be damaged by the butt end of a dropped spinnaker pole, or a spanner or pair of pliers dropped from aloft, and suitable precautions should be taken to strengthen and protect it.

Lightweight fibreglass hatchway covers often leak when trodden on, and also when the clamping nuts or toggle fasteners are over-tightened. Alterations to make it watertight may involve strengthening the hatch, increasing the number of tightening clamps, and re-seating the rubber seal.

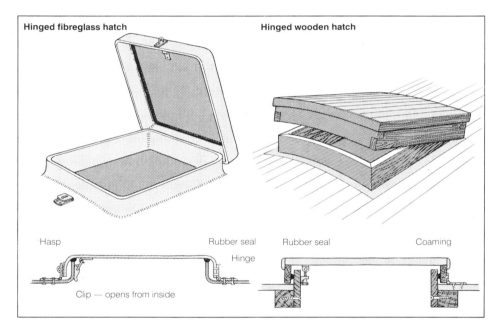

Hinged fibreglass hatch

Hinged wooden hatch

Hasp

Clip — opens from inside

Rubber seal

Hinge

Rubber seal

Coaming

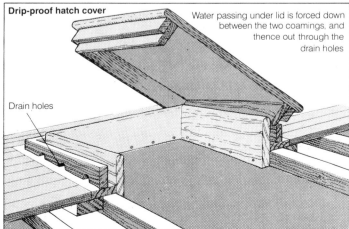

Drip-proof hatch cover

Water passing under lid is forced down between the two coamings, and thence out through the drain holes

Drain holes

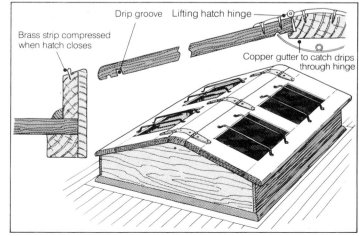

Brass strip compressed when hatch closes

Drip groove

Lifting hatch hinge

Copper gutter to catch drips through hinge

Sliding hatches

Typically, these are fitted over the companionway of smaller yachts to give headroom for those leaving the cabin, and to provide access to the cabin when the washboards are in place. Sliding hatches are very difficult to keep watertight, but unless they are particularly poorly made they do not leak badly either. A transverse beam should close the space between the two hatch bearers at the forward end of the hatchway and the hatch should hold against, and bear on, a brass strip or fibreglass moulding.

In the light of the Fastnet Race Enquiry report, arrangements should be made to lock and unlock the sliding hatch from both inside and outside the cabin. A vertically-mounted mortise lock set into or against the companion door or top washboard, turned by a ring on the outside and a handle on the inside will provide the necessary security in the absence of a simpler alternative.

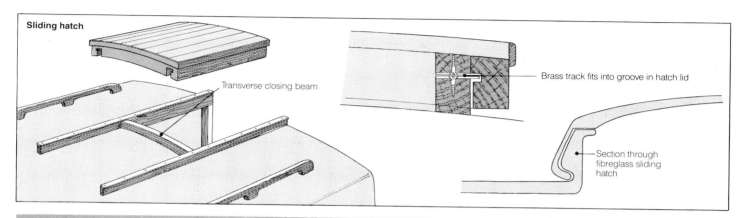

Sliding hatch

Transverse closing beam

Brass track fits into groove in hatch lid

Section through fibreglass sliding hatch

Cabin doors

For sea-going boats, the sill height for the cabin or deck house door should be at least 5 inches (125 mm) above the level of the deck or cockpit floor. In practice many boats have sills fitted much higher than this minimum. If the boat is only occasionally at sea, a storm board should be carried which fits into a recess behind the door to support it, and acts as a sill when the door is opened.

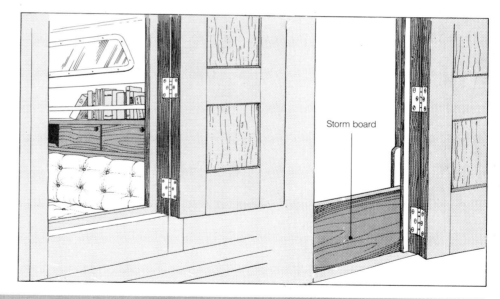

Storm board

Windows, portholes, deadlights

These are normally ready-made fittings that give little trouble and require virtually no maintenance. Perspex windows are easily scratched and can be cleaned with Brasso wiped on with a clean, soft rag. Large windows, and those retained with a rubber strip, should be fitted with removable shutters to seal the window aperture in rough weather.

Leaks at windows and doors are most successfully cured by careful positioning of additional compressible compounds, or the fitting of watertraps. However, it is important not to overlook the existing structure, hinges and catches. A window hatchway or door that leaks badly may also be poorly constructed with flimsy hinges and inadequate support. It is worth taking a look at the hardware and perhaps comparing it to quality fittings of a similar type and size on display in a reputable chandlery. Leaks are a nuisance, but if the forehatch or other openings fail when the boat is caught in rough weather, the results can be catastrophic.

> Procuring adequate quantities of uncontaminated drinking water, keeping it sweet, and keeping the plumbing working are problems that are likely to confront a boat owner.

Water supply

Two gallons (9 ls) of fresh water per person per day is generally considered to be sufficient to provide minimum daily requirements. This figure will vary according to the temperature conditions inside and outside the boat. The range of a sailing yacht will be limited by the amount of water she can carry.

Tank capacity can be supplemented with water-filled plastic bottles, stored wherever there is space for them. Paint the bottles or keep out of direct sunlight and in the cool to prevent green algae growing on the inside. This looks unpleasant, but is harmless.

Water tanks

The location of the water tanks is a matter which is decided by the naval architect. Water tanks and sometimes fuel and waste water tanks are built into the bottom of a fibreglass hull. Prefabricated tanks will be positioned in accordance with the needs for stability and space available.

Apart from the filling inlet, a vent hole of at least 3/16 inch (4mm) is needed. This is often incorporated into the filler cap. In other installations, particularly side tanks, a vent pipe is fitted at the top of the tank. This rises to deck level where an 180° bend prevents dirt and dust entering the water supply. Vent holes must be clear otherwise water flow will be impaired.

Baffles to prevent the de-stabilizing effect of surging water should be positioned across the tank. An inspection cover, in the top or side of the tank, will give limited access for cleaning and inspecting the inside of the tank.

Calibrating the tank

Tanks that have been tested are fitted with a small plate detailing their capacity. If there is no indication of size, fill it with water from a 5 gallon (22 ls) water can. Make a dip-stick to insert down the inlet pipe to check the water level. Fit a soft pad at the end of the dip-stick to avoid damaging the bottom of the tank unless a thick striking plate is fitted beneath the inlet pipe. Calibrate the stick in units of 10 or 25 gallons (112 ls) as the tank is filled.

Water contamination

It is tempting to make compromises with one's normally high standards of hygiene when there is a shortage of fresh or hot washing water and accommodation is confined and rather intimate. This is obviously a grave and selfish mistake, which can easily upset the rest of the crew. Scrupulous cleanliness is essential. To help conserve fresh water, seawater soap should be supplied for all the washbasins equipped with seawater outlet taps.

Tanks and pipework

Every two years, flush the pipework. Inspect plastic pipes to see if they have growths of algae clinging inside. Flush the pipes with a mild bleach and clean them with plenty of fresh water. Replace badly affected hoses. Perhaps because they are warmer than the water tanks, hoses tend to become contaminated and impart an unpleasant taste to the water long before the tanks themselves need thorough cleaning.

Tanks must never be positioned close to a heat source such as an engine or its exhaust, nor should they share a common single skin barrier with a fuel or waste water tank. Osmosis between tanks is quite a common occurrence in poorly built boats and can only be prevented by keeping tanks separate. Badly constructed fibreglass tanks often allow styrene (which is released from the fibreglass laminate) into the drinking water. This is a poison, which in sufficient quantities will cause nausea and headaches. Flush the tanks with acetic acid or vinegar and water solution. If the presence of styrene is thought to persist, the top or side of the tank must be cut away, the inside cleaned, dried and coated with two thick coats of epoxy resin. Add a thixotropic additive for painting the sides and top of the tank. Bond back the removed part, after coating it in resin.

Metal tanks and some fibreglass tanks are equipped with hand holes which are covered by plates bolted to the sides or top of the tank. When these are opened, it is possible to reach into the tank and scrape out the accumulations of scale and sediment. Brush or vacuum the tank clean before washing it with a hose. Calcium carbonate deposits can be removed with a weak solution of caustic soda, but take care to protect hands, arms and face as it will burn if it splashes on to the skin.

It is sometimes impossible to ensure that the water taken aboard is clean. If there is any doubt, separate the tanks by closing the taps on the levelling pipe, and boil the suspect water before use. If the water supplies cannot be separated, drop some tablets of calcium hypochlorite in the tank. This should disinfect the water. It is nevertheless safer to boil all water that is thought to be contaminated.

Chlorine tablets are available which will disinfect water and prevent it going bad, even after it has been stored for a week or so. Other tablets can be added later to remove the taste of chlorine.

Clean out the fresh water system as soon as possible, and flush it with a mild bleach. Open all the taps etc. so that the entire system is washed clean. Rinse with several tankfuls of fresh clean water.

Dirty water

Filters in the tank and at the pumps should be cleaned or replaced regularly. Those caked in calcium deposits can be cleaned by soaking them in vinegar or acetic acid.

Fresh water supplies are often delivered through a translucent plastic hosepipe. Small black organisms will cling to the walls of these hoses and are washed into the water tank of the boat. Very little can be done to prevent this, other than changing the dockside hosepipe and storing it in the shade, filtering the water as it comes aboard, or using your own hose, specially reserved for this purpose, stored dry and in the dark.

Smells

It is usually easy to locate the source of unpleasant odours emanating from the plumbing. Look for a cracked or fractured pipe, leaking contaminated water, or sniff the drainage system. Sometimes a smell comes from a sink drainage pipe. This will be more difficult to trace, as the smell occurs only when a passing wave pumps or moves the air in the pipe, releasing the odours of the organic decaying matter lodged inside. These can be cleaned by blocking the outlet hole and filling the drain pipe with a mild bleach or washing soda.

Toilets

Chemical (bucket-type) toilets require regular emptying. The chemicals should be of the correct type, mixed in the right proportions. Other toilets incorporate a waste tank for harbour or inland water use, and a pumping facility, which allows waste to be pumped overboard when at sea.

These units smell when the packing gland at the pump shaft is worn, or if the valves in the system are wedged open. Clearing a toilet unit is an unpleasant task, both because of the smell and mess involved, and also because the toilet compartment is situated in a very tight space. If some degree of dismantling is required, make sure that the seacocks are closed. Dismantle the wide diameter pipe, because this is where the obstructions are found.

Pumps

There are a great variety of water pumps that are used to lift the water from the storage tanks. Many are either hand- or foot-operated. If an electric pump is fitted, water consumption will almost certainly exceed 2 gallons (9 ls) per day. The most common reason for a pump not working is that there is an airlock in the water feed to the pump. The slightest crack which allows air into the suction pipe will prevent the pump from operating. One of the advantages of using semi-transparent plastic hose is that it is easy to see if the water has drained from the pipe. Pumps which are not self-priming can be prevented from draining by arrranging the flexible hoses into an S-bend, ensuring water in the pump.

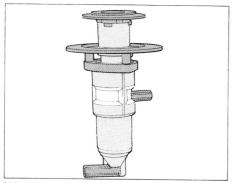

Whale tiptoe pump

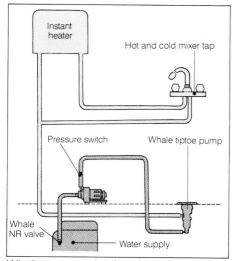

Whale accessories for galley pumps

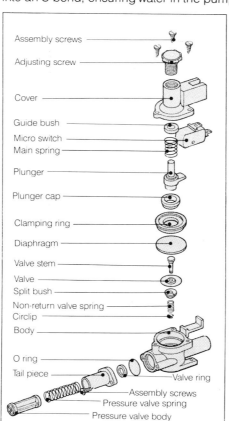

Whale pressure switch

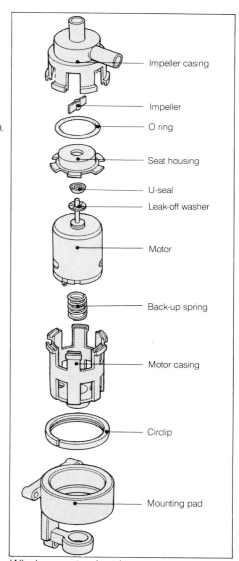

Whale remote electric pump

Plumbing Decks and cabins

The drawings show two simple, reliable and sturdy water pumps and an automatic pressure switch. The plumbing diagram illustrates how they might be plumbed into the system of a small boat. Pumps generally give very little trouble. Small hand-operated pumps are often easier replaced than repaired, but it is a sensible precaution to take spare diaphragms or washers for the pumps when embarking on an extended cruise.

Waste tanks

At the end of each season, empty the waste tank and flush it with a mild bleach or a proprietary brand cleaning fluid before laying up. Remove and clean the toilet and change the valves and washers every five years. Renew the gaskets when rebuilding the toilet, and ensure that the touching surfaces are clean and smooth.

Ensure that easily-understood operating instructions are posted where they can be seen. Provide a lidded bucket to take nappies and items which might block the toilet. Use toilet paper that does not disintegrate too readily when wet.

Bilge pumps

Bilge pumps should be sturdy and reliable. It is a good practice to have more than one pump aboard. They must drain overboard, and one should be operable from below.

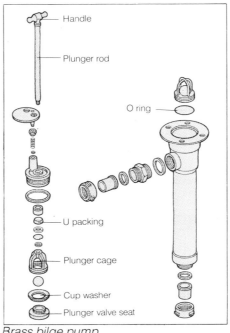

Brass bilge pump

Labels: Handle, Plunger rod, O ring, U packing, Plunger cage, Cup washer, Plunger valve seat

Sometimes the pump in the toilet can double as a bilge pump. If electric pumps are fitted, have a standby pair of hand-operated bilge pumps in case of emergency.

The bilge pump lift pipes should be fitted with strum boxes of much greater surface area than the cross-sectional area of the pipe. To ensure that the strum box remains clear, position it where there is an access hatch to enable it to be cleaned whenever necessary.

Plumbing

Copper, galvanized iron and also plastic flexible hose are all used in the plumbing systems of pleasure boats. Frequently boats are found which incorporate a combination of these in their plumbing.

Soldered and compression fittings are used to join copper piping. Unless flexible copper piping is used, plumbers' bending tools will be needed. Gentle curves can be achieved without the proper tools, and sharper bends can be made if the pipe is filled with fine sand before bending the pipe around a beam or post. A cork in one end of the pipe will prevent the sand running out. Clean out the pipes before fitting them in place if sand is used for the bending.

Galvanized iron piping must be made up from lengths of straight pipe. The ends of the pipe are threaded to screw into elbows, T-s and other fittings.

After soldering or tightening, the entire pipework system must be supported to prevent vibration. This is particularly important with copper piping, which workhardens, and fractures when subjected to continuous vibration. Plumbing procedures are standard. There are no special skills required that cannot be learnt from the local plumber. If soldered fittings are used take precautions to prevent fire. Remember to connect the completed metal plumbing into the earthing system of the boat.

Plastic piping is ideally suited to installation in boats. When alterations or replacements are needed, fit plastic hose rather than replacing with pipes of the original metal. Plastic piping of the correct quality is easy to install, is electrolytically neutral, does not transmit sound or pump vibrations, and is very strong. Run the pipework in straight lines or gentle curves. Kinks will distort the tubing and inhibit the water flow.

Joints

Fit the flexible hose on to a short length of standard diameter copper waterpipe. The copper pipe allows the fittings to be anchored by brackets or pipe clips. In order to get a watertight fit, slip a stainless steel hose clip over the pipe, soak the end of the plastic tube in hot water until it is supple, and then press it on to the end of the copper pipe. Tighten the hose clip.

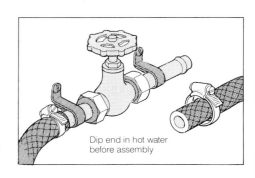

Dip end in hot water before assembly

Repairing or breaking into existing copper pipework

Plan the route for the pipework carefully. Pipes must be well-supported. Install mounting battens where necessary. Keep the pipework out of the bilges, and avoid introducing traps in the piping that are impossible to drain. Fabricate and brace all new pipework, and position the unions before joining the pipes. Avoid brass fittings. Whenever possible, use fittings made from non-brass alloys.

Cutting
Use a tube cutter. Centre the cutting wheel over the mark, and rotate the tool around the pipe. Give the handle a slight clockwise twist to force the cutting wheel into the pipe. A small hacksaw will also be needed. Saw cuts should be de-burred with a file or penknife.

Soldered joints
Clean the inside of the pipe fitting and the outside of the pipe end with wire wool, and smear them with soldering flux before assembling. Once the joints have been prepared, avoid touching them. Press the joints together and give each joint a slight twist to distribute the flux. When all the pipework is in place, and supported with a suitable number of clips or brackets, light the gas blow torch and play the flame over the joint. Too little heat is better than too much. Stop heating when a tell-tale ring of bright solder appears at the edge of the joint.

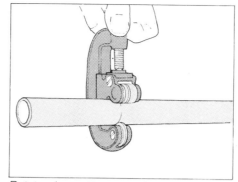
Rotate pipe cutter around tube

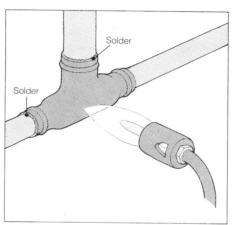
Heat each joint in turn, taking care not to overheat pipework

Take sensible fire precautions, and remember that copper is an efficient conductor of heat. Ensure that parts close to woodwork and other inflammable materials are lagged with wet rags. Place an asbestos insulation board behind the pipework where the torch is being used. Do not use a blow torch near a fuel tank.

Problems

Solder will not melt Water standing or flowing through the pipe will make it almost impossible to heat the joint sufficiently to allow the solder to melt and fuse with the copper. Drain the pipe before soldering, or use a compression fitting instead.

Solder forms lustreless droplets on the side of the pipe Poor preparation of the copper pipe, or excessive heat causes this problem. Separate the pipes and try again.

Pipes pull apart as they are heated This is the result of the air expanding in the piping as it is heated. Open the taps in the system to allow pressure to escape.

Compression fittings
A section through a compression fitting is illustrated. Pipes must be clean, round, and without scoring or other marks that may permit water to seep past the olive. Compression fittings are simple to install, but they have a tendency to self-centre as they are tightened up, and leak if they are twisted. Assemble the plumbing with the joints slightly tightened, and correct any mis-alignments before pulling them tight.

Ends must be cut at right angles and, if flexible copper pipe is used, the ends should be reamed out round before assembling the joint. Before the joint is assembled, wipe silicon rubber over the olive to ensure that the joint is watertight.

Problems
Most problems with these joints occur because the pipework is pressed to an insufficient depth, or is out of round. New pipework correctly assembled will not leak, unless the pipework is twisted, and works when the boat is in motion.

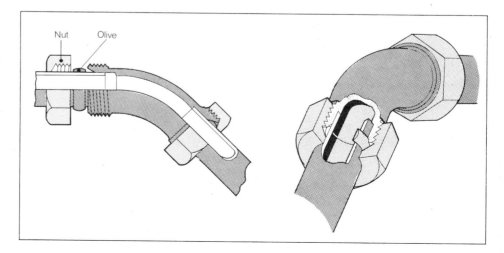

Keeping Warm

Sensible precautions

It is always a good idea to ensure that a dry change of clothes is available; if necessary, they can be stored in sealed polythene bags.

Change into dry clothes immediately after getting wet. Dry the wet ones as best you can, in order to have dry clothing at hand when you need it.

Activity will also keep you warm. As soon as you have changed, get busy, pump out the bilges, re-organize the cabin, or do some exercises. Any physical task will help generate body heat. Wear a hat and a windproof smock if going on deck.

Cabin heating

Install only heating units specifically designed for use in small boats. Normal domestic heaters, either gas or paraffin, are quite unsuitable — they are difficult to install securely, are likely to corrode, and will be without the safeguards necessary on a marine unit.

Except for heating systems that obtain their heat from the engine cooling system, and electric fires that are plugged into shore-based power supplies, most heating arrangements depend on combustion to generate heat. These take oxygen from the cabin, and replace it with carbon monoxide, a heavy, odourless and poisonous gas. Ventilation arrangements must allow sufficient fresh air into the cabin for both the heater and the occupants.

Heaters must be well fastened with mounting brackets strong enough to restrain floor-bolted stoves against the very considerable reversing stresses which develop as the boat rolls. Any movement is potentially serious, as even slight movement between the flue and the stove may fracture a joint, and allow poisonous gases to escape.

Correctly installed, lightweight Liquid Petroleum Gas and paraffin burners are unlikely to break free but, when fitting them, consider the possibility that the unit may be struck or fallen against, and even grabbed when the boat is heaving and pitching. Mounting bolts should be able to prevent it from coming adrift even under these difficult conditions. If the unit is fixed to a bulkhead, it is sometimes sensible to provide a grab handle for people adjusting it, or warming themselves, and a guard to prevent the possibility of a crew member accidentally grabbing the flue pipe to retain his balance.

Flue pipe insulation

There must be adequate insulation behind the heater, and around the flue where it passes through the coach roof or cabin-side. Rockwool or mica, covered with brass or aluminium sheeting, make efficient and easily-cleaned insulation. Do not lag the flue, except where it passes through the boat. The heat radiated from the flue often constitutes a fair proportion of the heater's overall output.

When the heater is in use, fit a cowl or chimney on to the flue. Protect sails etc. from carbon deposits that collect on most things above or downwind from the flue. Never use the heater with the exhaust outlet blocked.

Heat exchanger systems

The cooling system of the motor can be used to heat the cabin or the water supply. Hot air is easily directed from an air-cooled diesel engine into the cabin. Cowls or portholes should be opened to allow the stale air to escape, and to prevent a build-up of heat in the engine compartment. The water from a water-cooled engine can be passed through a heat exchanger. This is a cylindrical tank, with copper tubing coiled inside it, through which the cabin heating water is piped. These systems are often efficient, with the water circulated through cabin radiators by a low power electric pump.

Problems sometimes arise as a result of galvanic corrosion between dissimilar metals in the heat exchanger and engine. This is difficult to detect as the waterways in the engine block are not open to inspection or measurement. The engine and pipework can sometimes be protected by installing sacrificial anodes in the heat exchanger, which should be removed and inspected from time to time (see pages 257 and 290).

As with all engine cooling systems, provision must be made to bypass the heat exchanger when the engine is warming up, or is operating in low temperatures. In most systems, a thermostat incorporated in the pipework will do this automatically, but always try to ensure that the motor is operating at its optimum running temperature when the central heating system is in use. If the engine is running cold, switch off some of the radiators or the circulating pump until it warms up. If the engine is being run while the boat is in dock, it will achieve working temperatures more quickly, and do the machinery less harm if the propeller is engaged and the engine works under load, but first check the mooring lines.

Paraffin and liquid fuel heaters

Liquid fuel heaters are the most common, and probably the safest form of heating for yachts.

Some modern bulkhead-mounted heaters incorporate a heat exchanger which enables the exhaust gases to be separated from the hot air, which is circulated via flexible lightweight ducts to the cabin. In these heaters, the fuel is usually pumped from a small tank in the bilges. Before installing a heater which requires electrical power to drive the fan or pump, check the electrical consumption required to operate it. Other liquid heaters incorporate their fuel tanks at the base of the burner. These units must never be refuelled when the heater is burning. Turn them off, and take them on deck, where spillages are less hazardous. Paraffin has a strong smell so, after topping up the tank, wipe it dry to prevent evaporation when the tank is brought into the cabin.

Very little maintenance is required to keep these stoves operating efficiently, other than draining the drip pans, and trimming the wicks whenever necessary.

Always follow the manufacturer's instructions when operating and maintaining the stoves and heaters. The exhaust gases of a paraffin heater contain a large proportion of water, which will condense on the cabin roof and any other cold surface. Unless the heater has its own sealed exhaust flue, make sure that there is adequate ventilation.

Bottled gas

Bottled gas appliances require little maintenance; many are now fitted with a piezo spark lighting system which has a virtually unlimited life, and is extremely reliable.

If a number of heaters are intended to be run from a single gas cylinder, it is as well to check the evaporation rate of the cylinder at the ambient temperatures likely to be experienced at the gas bottle storage. There is a contradiction between the need for well-ventilated storage, and protection of the bottles from the low temperatures in which heaters are likely to be in demand, and in some circumstances a larger, or an additional cylinder may be required. Gas heaters burn the oxygen in the cabin and, like the paraffin heaters mentioned above, require adequate ventilation when in use. Floor-mounted heaters can successfully be supplied with air through grills placed in the cabin floor in front of the heater. These grills will take air from the bilges (which should, in any case, be well ventilated), and the low-level air inlets will help avoid the worst of the draughts that result from keeping lots of portholes open. Liquid gas units are only safe if stringent precautions against gas leakage are taken.

Escaped propane and butane gas, being heavy, will collect in the lowest part of the boat (often in the engine compartment if it is poorly sealed from the accommodation) where it will remain until ignited by a sparking electrical appliance, or naked flame. There does not have to be much gas in a small space to make an explosive mixture, and it is not sensible to rely upon smell to detect a gas leak. Boats equipped with liquid gas appliances must have the equipment installed correctly. It is recommended that an electronic gas sniffer alarm is fitted in the cabin to give an early warning of a gas leak.

Installation

The storage arrangements for a gas cylinder are described on page l90. Further guidance on recommended practices can be obtained from the suppliers of the gas, from the British Standards Institute, or from the US Coastguard. Cylinders that are not in use should be stored on deck, or in other purpose-built storage lockers.

The pressure regulator and tap should be connected to the gas pipeline by an armoured flexible hose, which is clipped to both the seamless copper pipework and the regulator outlet.

Copper piping should be fixed at approximately 4 inches (10cm) intervals, and prevented from vibrating or sagging. Connections between copper pipes should be kept to a minimum. Joints are usually made with compression fittings, sealed with a flexible compound manufactured especially for use with LPG pipe connections.

The pipework at each outlet should have a tap which can be switched off to isolate the supply. These taps must turn easily and should be checked regularly. Taps that are difficult to turn may not only seize when you need to turn them off, but may also cause the pipework to fracture when efforts are made to close them down.

Leakage of bottled gas

It is the duty of the boat owner to ensure that his boat is safe, and unless the gas pipelines are well installed and regularly inspected, they will constitute a considerable risk to the safety of the crew. Inspect all copper and flexible pipework for looseness or signs of fatigue. Leaks at the connections can be identified by brushing soapy water over the suspect connections, where escaping gas will cause it to bubble.

When gas appliances are not in use, switch off the supply at the cylinder. This relieves the pipeline and appliance of gas pressure, and reduces the danger that a faulty control switch might leak gas into the cabin.

Expelling accumulations of gas

It is impossible to pump out accumulations of gas with a normal bilge pump and, if a pump is electrically driven, it is dangerous to try.

When a gas leak is suspected, switch off all electrical installations, but do not try to disconnect the battery, in case it sparks.

Turn off the gas cylinder, open the companion hatch, and bail the gas with a large plastic bucket. To a casual onlooker it may seem a rather silly exercise, but there is no other safe way of removing large quantities of gas from the floor of the cabin. When it is thought that most of the gas is overboard, sniff the contents of the bucket; if the gas concentration is low, open the cowls and windows, and channel fresh air to the bilges.

Coal and other solid fuels

Installations must be fitted with adequate floor-mounting brackets, and an insulated collar for the flue. Most stoves are at their most efficient when they burn slowly. Stop draughts in the firebox by sealing them with fireclay, and keep the firedoor windows clean to benefit from the radiant heat.

Insulation

Heating problems cannot be overcome by efficient insulation without unacceptable loss of cabin and storage space, but thin, thermally efficient, plastic and fibre covering materials can be bought which are either self-adhesive, or easily glued to the underside of the deck and exposed hull sides. These will not only reduce the amount of heat lost from the cabin, but will also tend to reduce condensation. The edges of the insulation can be sealed with a varnished wood strip.

Carpeting will also make the cabin warmer and more comfortable, but its use should be limited to those boats which are normally dry, and where there is adequate room aboard for people to remove wet clothes and boots without standing on the carpet.

This important area should be well planned and carefully organized.In sea-going boats, the galley will be needed irrespective of the weather conditions, and crew must be able to prepare hot food or drink whenever necessary.

The galley is often small. If it is functional and tidy, this will probably be an advantage. In a compact galley, the cook can have stove controls and working spaces within easy reach. This can be a great help when the boat is at sea.

The galley should be well-ventilated and light. Air flow through a cabin is usually from aft, forwards. An electric extractor fan, fitted into the coach roof above the galley, will prevent cooking smells from percolating through to the accommodation.

Good lighting is also essential, and is best provided by portholes or decklights, and neon strip lighting.

Many new boats are equipped with fully fitted out galleys, and with well-planned stowage for cutlery, plates and cups. Even in these, the fiddles that restrain the pots and pans and prevents spillages from dripping on to the cabin floor are sometimes too low or are badly fitted.

The following section suggests some ways in which the galley can be improved, particularly for use at sea.

Working surfaces

The provision of decent-sized fiddles around the working areas will allow maximum use of the available working space. One or more removable partitions set between the fiddles will enable sections to be reserved for food preparation, while other parts are piled high with plates and pots.

Slides fitted beneath some of the working surfaces will provide additional surface space. These do not need to be wide, and are best without any kind of fiddle around them. They can then slide out of the way when not in use. They are easily made, and usually involve cutting

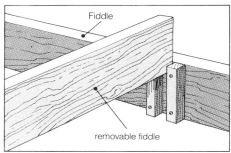

Removable fiddle partition

down the top of the cupboard or drawer immediately beneath, and fitting a substantial top and bottom channel to

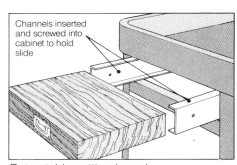

Retractable cutting board

give the board support. A peg fitted into the centre of the slide will prevent it from falling out when the boat heels.

Sink Units

Sinks should be at least as deep, and preferably deeper, than they are wide or long, with foot-operated pumps for water supply and sink drainage. Foot pumps are an advantage in heavy weather as they allow the cook to have a hand free.

Like all other boat furniture, the sink unit should have rounded corners. Fitting rounded fiddles to the top edge of the sink unit is a time-consuming task, which manufacturers often avoid by rounding off the fiddles short of the corner. A gap in the corner of the sink fiddle will

shoot sink water on to the floor when the boat heels. A hard metal border screwed to the edging pieces will be ugly, uncomfortable to lean against, and difficult to keep watertight and clean. A rounded wooden corner is easily fitted: a method of making one is illustrated.

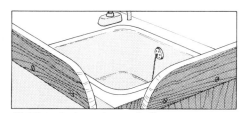

Fiddles drain water on to floor

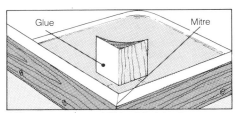

Mitre corners and fit inside block

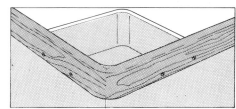

Radius outside and top edges

Handholds

Sometimes the cook will have to forsake his pans, and hang on with both hands. Provide substantial handholds for the

cook to grab. Simple turned pillars look attractive, and are easy to see. Most joiners or cabinet-makers will be happy to turn up a suitable post or two, which

should be secured with concealed coach bolts or coach screws.

A heavy canvas webbing strap, clipped across the galley opening, will enable the cook to continue work with both hands, while bracing himself against the movement of the boat with his feet and back. The clips should be simple hooks, not the self-locking clips fitted to safety harnesses. One or two additional ring bolts inside the galley space will enable the cook to adjust his supporting strap to suit the job in hand.

Refrigerators

Refrigerators that utilize a heat source to operate the heat exchanger should be installed where they are free from draughts, with sufficient air space between the heating unit and the adjacent joinery. Overhead ventilation and flue pipe must be provided and, if the refrigerator burns liquid petroleum gas, it should be equipped with an automatic fail-safe that closes the gas line if the flame blows out.

Ice boxes are very easily made, and can be designed to fit into the curved sections of the lower hull. Access should be from the top, with a drainage pipe plumbed into the base to allow water to be emptied. Four inches (100mm) of insulation is necessary around and beneath the icebox, with 2 inches (50mm) of insulation on top, sealed with a rubber gasket. Instead of using ice cubes, an ingenious way of maximizing the ice box space is to stack frozen juice cartons or beer cans around the sides and bottom of the box, and pack the remaining space with items that need to be kept fresh.

Cooking stoves

A stove without gimbals must always face fore and aft. There should always be a metal fiddle rail around the top of the stove, with intermediates spaced across the top, to help retain the pans. A simple adjustable fiddle running on brass or chrome rod slides can easily be fabricated from brass rod, with a nut for a retaining screw soldered or tapped at one end.

Gimballed stoves are usually aligned fore and aft. The height of the gimbals varies. Those with the pivoting point level with the top of the burners have the steadiest movement, and are less likely to swing the cooking pots and spill their contents, but these stoves need to be ballasted to remain upright when heavy pots are placed on their burners. Those with higher pivoting points do not require the ballast, but take up more space.

In both systems there must be plenty of room for the stoves to swing freely. All cooking stoves must be securely fastened to prevent them from coming adrift during a knockdown or capsize.

Gas Stoves

The illustration shows a burner assembly and control knob unit of a typical small gas stove. Similar burners in the oven are controlled in the same way, except that the aeration control is often omitted.

Provided that the gas jet is kept clean, little is likely to go wrong with such a simple installation. The colour of flame will indicate the state of the burner: the flame should be blue. If it is yellow or smoky, the burner should be cleaned. After cleaning, if the flame is still unsatisfactory, clean the jet.

Gas stoves equipped with an automatic fail-safe switch-off device are ideally suited for use aboard ship. Do not tamper with the fail-safe unit, which is carefully adjusted to close the gas line when the sensor cools. The rest of the cooker is easily dismantled and the parts can be cleaned in soapy water.

Changing the gas cylinders

Units fitted with a cylinder immediately beneath the cooker should be taken on deck before replacing the cylinder. The

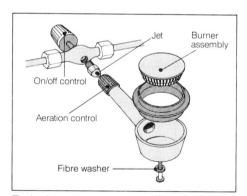

Typical gas burner assembly

operation is almost certain to cause a leakage of gas. It is sensible to make a rule that all cigarettes and any other lights are extinguished while changing the cylinder.

Paraffin stoves

Most paraffin stoves installed in small boats are of the pressurized type. Whether the fuel tank and pressure pump are integral with the cooker, or separate, the working principles remain the same. Tanks must be positioned where they can be readily topped up and pumped. It is very important that the pressure release vent, often incorporated into the filler cap, is always above the level of the fuel in the tank at all normal angles of heel. If it is too low, liquid paraffin will squirt out when the vent is opened.

A well-maintained paraffin stove, using clean fuel, burns with a hot blue flame. Accumulations of carbon and grease will collect on the burner causing the flame to turn orange, and burn smokily.

Dismantle the burner unit, and soak it in soda or washing-up liquid. Scrub and soak it until clean. Dirty fuel will block the jet, which should be blown clean, and then cleared with a pricker. It is sensible to carry a pair of spare prickers, sealed against the damp and covered in a light coat of oil, as they rust very quickly.

Pump washers, filler gaskets, etc. are all easy to replace. Carry a comprehensive selection of spare parts so that most servicing and repairs can be carried out at sea.

207

Pre-heating
A paraffin stove has to be pre-heated before it will start. This usually involves pouring a small quantity of methylated spirits on to the burner, and into a small pan beneath the jet. In rough conditions it may be impossible to prevent the priming methylated spirits from spilling out of the pan. Keep an asbestos clip soaking in a bottle of methylated spirits.

In rough weather this can be slipped on to the pipe above the pan instead and ignited. Remove the clip when the stove is burning.

Galley cleaning hints

Removing smells
Refrigerator An open tub of bicarbonate of soda, left standing in the refrigerator, will absorb unpleasant smells. Replace the tub every month.

Cutting boards, working surfaces
Make a paste of bicarbonate of soda, and rub on to the surface. Wipe clean with a damp rag. Alternatively wipe the surface with lemon juice, then dry it.

Plastic containers, tins, storage bins
Smells will be absorbed by newspaper, crumpled and packed inside the container. Leave overnight.

Cupboards
Place a bowl containing cat litter deodorizer in the cupboard.

Leave overnight, then rinse inside the cupboard with vinegar to prevent bacterial growth.

Cleaning
Ovens Some food is certain to be spilled, and it is never easy to scrape away once it has burnt on to the inside of the oven or the wire trays.

Instead of scraping, coat the sides, bottom, and door of the oven with a paste of bicarbonate of soda and water. Wipe the paste over the interior of the oven, and then bake in place. With this barrier between the oven walls etc. and the burnt food, cleaning is simplified. By washing with a brush and warm water, the interior will be left clean and fresh.

Grill, racks, trays, burners Remove from the oven and drop them into a large polythene bag. Empty about half a cup of household ammonia into the bag and close it carefully, taking great care not to puff the fumes into the face. Leave the bag until the burnt food is loosened, then open the bag outside and remove the contents. Wash them in plenty of cold, fresh water.

Caution Do not soak brass or alloy fittings in ammonia. Do not breathe the ammonia fumes or even look into the bag. Take care when closing it, as the ammonia escapes if the bag is closed too quickly. Walk with the open bag behind, rather than in front, of you.

Cabins

Some simple and useful techniques are described below to help the boat owner keep his cabin accommodation tidy, clean and shipshape.

Cupboards and drawers
Cupboards for small items must always be sited athwart-ship, so that when the door is opened, the contents won't fall out. Cupboards with sliding doors should always be sited fore and aft, unless a positive means of keeping them closed is incorporated. Prevent drawers from sliding open when the boat heels or rolls by screwing a turnbuckle to the framework over the drawer. A more convenient method is to notch the drawer side rails so that the drawer remains closed when the notch rests across the front of the framework. Where cabin joinery makes this kind of alteration difficult, screw and glue two wedges to the underside of the drawer. Whichever method is used, it will be necessary to cut away the top rail to allow the drawer to open.

Strips of elastic, stretched across the inside of the drawer, will keep the contents from sliding about.

Upholstery repairs
Repair torn mattresses or seat coverings as soon as possible, otherwise the fabric will stretch and later repairs will be impossible to disguise. Cut a backing patch of suitable thin cloth and use a spoon handle to help insert it behind the covering material. Gently lift the torn material and brush a thin coat of latex adhesive over the backing piece. Lightly press the tear against the backing piece, taking care to align the fabric correctly.

Anchor the repair with long pins. Remove when the adhesive is dry.

Heavier covering fabrics must be sewn after they have been glued into place.

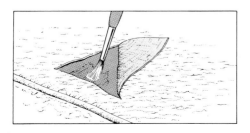
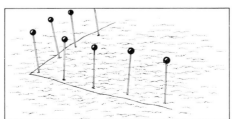
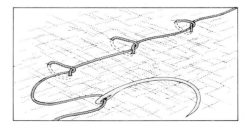

Removing stains

Fabric
Clean all stains or spillages as soon as possible. Avoid soaking the area, as this will spread the mess. Use the minimum amount of liquid, or foam if available (shaving foam makes a good fabric cleaner). Try to blot the stain. Rubbing will make it more deep-seated, and harder to remove.

Tar Remove as much as possible by scraping away any solids. Check that paraffin does not damage the colour of the fabric. Dampen a soft rag with paraffin and dab the stain until the tar is lifted off. Wash with water and detergent. Alternatively, use Oil of Eucalyptus instead of paraffin.

Mildew Brush away mildew and air the fabric. If mildew is well established, dampen the area with a mixture of lemon juice and salt. Wash plastic curtains in salt water to prevent mildew.

Rust marks Carry out simple tests to see if the recommended cleaners alter the colour of the cloth. Wash the area with lemon juice and leave to dry. Whites can be cleaned by bleaching with oxalic acid. Alternatively, dampen the rust mark with hot water, cover it with a sprinkling of cream of tartar, dip the stained part in hot water, then launder as normal.

Blood Biological washing powder and cold water will remove bloodstains. Soak overnight if necessary. Alternatively, make a paste of cornflour and cold water, cover the bloodstain with the paste, and allow to dry. Clean off with a stiff brush, and launder if necessary.

Alcohol and drink stains These should be dealt with quickly, as they are far more difficult to remove when dry. Sprinkle with salt while the fabric is wet, and rinse in cold water before washing.

Wax, crayon, candle wax, hot grease Place the fabric between blotting paper, or clean absorbent brown paper. Press with a warm iron. Repeat with fresh blotting paper.

Oil, grease, wet paint Dab the the stain with a clean rag moistened with turpentine. Sponge clean using a sponge dampened with soap and water.

Dry paint Paint spots can often be lifted off fabrics with the point of a sharp knife. Otherwise, cover the stain with a small quantity of paint remover and clean when the paint is softened. Neutralize the paint remover as recommended.

Urine Sponge the area with a weak water and vinegar solution, and wash as soon as possible.

Treatment for special fabrics
PVC fabrics should be cleaned regularly, or they will begin to smell. Wash with mild soap and fresh water. Very dirty fabric can be cleaned by rubbing with a cloth dampened with vinegar, or with water and baking soda. Do not use strong detergents or waxes as they tend to harden the fabric

Treatment for cloth that is yellowing after prolonged exposure to sunlight

Nylon Mix six tablespoons of dishwasher detergent and three of bleach into a gallon (4.5 ls) of hot water. When the mixture is cool, soak the cloth for half an hour. Rinse in cool water, in which a little vinegar has been added to neutralize the bleach.

Polyester Leave to soak in a gallon (4.5 ls) of water into which a cupful of dishwasher detergent has been added. Then wash the fabric.

Floor areas
Carpets Clean stains as soon as possible. Fresh stains can be removed quickly by dabbing the area until most of the marks are lifted off. A dash of soda water is an efficient stain remover. Otherwise use foam (if necessary by whipping soap powder into a small quantity of water), as this tends to limit the spread of the stain. Difficult stains can often be removed by sponging them with a mixture of two tablespoons of detergent, and three tablespoons of vinegar, mixed in a quart (l litre) of water.

Mud Sprinkle salt over wet mud marks and vacuum when thoroughly dry.

Floors Remove tar from floors or woodwork by rubbing with a soft paste wax, or by soaking them with linseed oil.

Windows
Glass Clean with a mixture of half a cupful of vinegar, half a cupful of domestic ammonia, and two tablespoons of cornflour. Wipe the outside of the windows with horizontal wipes and the inside with vertical strokes. It is then easy to see whether the marks that remain are on the inside or the outside.

Perspex or acrylic Clean with a liquid metal polish. This is a fine abrasive. More serious scratches can be removed by rubbing the area with fine abrasive paper, using progressively finer grades until the mark is removed and the perspex is once again smooth and clear. Finish with metal polish.

Metal Aluminium window frames can be cleaned with a liquid silver polish. Brass can be cleaned with any metal polish, then rubbed with a soft cloth dipped in petroleum jelly to prevent tarnishing. Polish with a soft, dry cloth.

Chapter 9

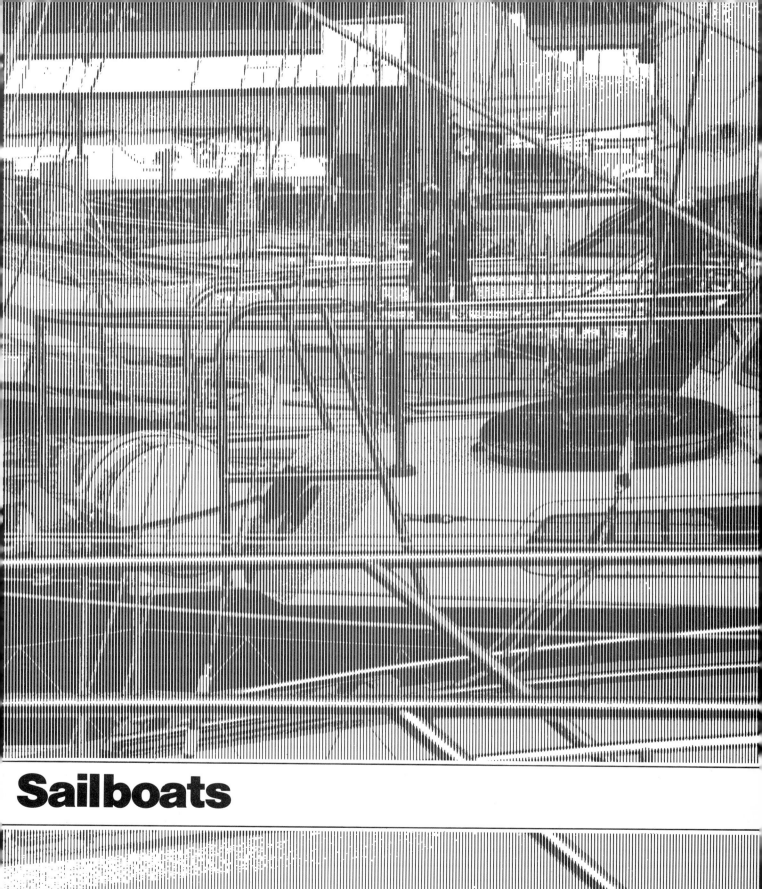

Sailboats

Sailboats

The notes on the illustration name the principal features of the deck plan, rigging, and sails of a typical small cruising yacht.

The rigging lines support the mast. Known as the standing rigging, they are often made from wire rope or stainless steel rod. Standing rigging is tensioned and, if correctly positioned and tightened, rarely needs adjustment during the season. It is, nevertheless, subjected to continual vibration and frequent severe stresses, and is prone to metal fatigue.

Sails are controlled by the running rigging. Running rigging is usually made from wide diameter, easily handled rope, To reduce stretch, halyards are often spliced to a wire rope, which passes through the bottom sheave in the mast and up to the masthead.

The example shows a boat with an extruded aluminium alloy mast stepped on deck. Hollow wooden and pole masts are also common. Carbon fibre masts have a higher strength-to-weight ratio than any of the above and are often unstayed.

Sailcloth is either Terylene (Dacron in the USA) or nylon. Both of these materials are stronger than cotton and present a smoother surface to the wind. After an initial slight change, neither stretch or shrink appreciably, but, as with cotton, they will lose their shape after several years. Terylene and nylon are not subject to rot, but will degrade after prolonged exposure to sunlight.

The illustrations depict a, right, variety of other sail plans. Older wooden yachts and barges are still to be seen in coastal waters and the outlines of their rigs are also illustrated.

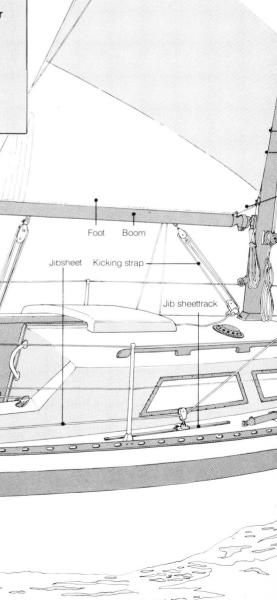

Leech

Mainsail

Topping lift

Backstay

Clew Outhaul

Foot   Boom

Sheet winches

Jibsheet   Kicking strap

Jib sheettrack

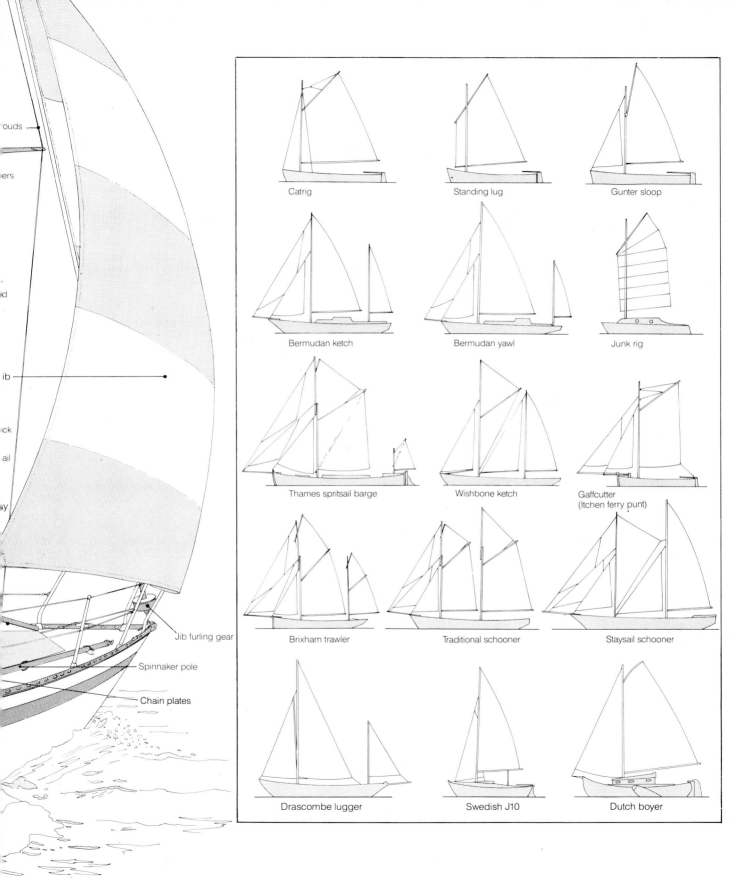

ouds

ers

jib

ck

ail

ay

Catrig

Standing lug

Gunter sloop

Bermudan ketch

Bermudan yawl

Junk rig

Thames spritsail barge

Wishbone ketch

Gaffcutter
(Itchen ferry punt)

Brixham trawler

Traditional schooner

Staysail schooner

Drascombe lugger

Swedish J10

Dutch boyer

Jib furling gear

Spinnaker pole

Chain plates

Hollow wooden masts

Wooden masts are usually made from close and straight-grained sitka spruce. This is a light, irridescent pale wood which varnishes to a rich golden yellow colour. Hollow masts are made from two or more matching lengths of spruce and some of the sections are illustrated below. Older masts are glued with casein glue, a waterproof organic adhesive, which loses its strength unless it is thoroughly protected by paint or varnish. Urea-formaldehyde and epoxy resin glues are used for making new masts; heavier woods such as Oregon pine are glued with resorcinal glue.

Wooden masts must be well maintained and stored with care. They should be varnished or painted annually, stored horizontally, and supported so they lie perfectly straight.

The varnish on a wooden mast should be clear and smooth. Flaking or opaque patches indicate poor maintenance or the use of inappropriate varnish. Greying or blackening beneath the varnish points to damp penetration and possibly rot. The luff groove should be smooth and varnished. Roughened edges show lack of maintenance. A gap of ¼ inch (6mm) at the sides of the groove is ample space for most sails. Gaps in excess of this may indicate that the mast is nearing the end of its useful life.

A well-made hollow mast should not crack, unless it has been poorly maintained or left outside for several winters. Check the mast head for cracks that might allow moisture into the mast. It is usually impossible to repair a crack caused by shrinkage, but matters can be made worse by the insertion of brittle stopping compounds to fill the gap.

Cracked varnish and blackening at the glue line are a prelude to joint failure. In its worst form, sections of hollow spars separate and are held only by the metal fittings screwed or bolted through them. Very little can be done to cure this problem, apart from dismantling the spar and re-glueing it.

Compression shakes are transverse irregularities in the grain caused by sudden and concentrated loading of the spar. Such loads may be imposed if a shroud parts, or if the mast strikes bottom during a capsize. If they are present, they will be found just above the spreaders of a stayed mast, and at deck level in an unstayed mast. A slight kink in the mast might be caused by a compression shake, and should be inspected closely. Masts weakened by a compression shake should not be used.

The condition of a painted mast is difficult to assess. Distortions and kinks can be seen by sighting along the spar. Probe the wood with a very fine bradawl at the mast bands to check for rot, filling the indentation afterwards.

Mast top

The mast head should be inspected for rot where fittings are screwed into the end grain. Seal cracks in the mast with a mixture of linseed oil and oil-based varnish. Remove any rot surrounding wood screws and, when the timber has dried, re-fit the screws and bed them in a paste of colodial silica and epoxy resin.

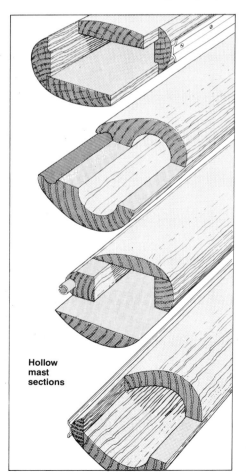

Hollow mast sections

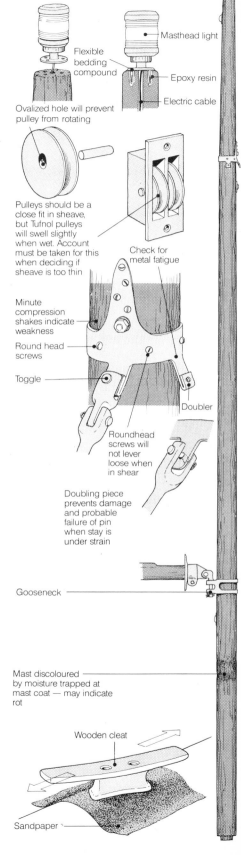

Masthead light

Flexible bedding compound

Epoxy resin

Electric cable

Ovalized hole will prevent pulley from rotating

Pulleys should be a close fit in sheave, but Tufnol pulleys will swell slightly when wet. Account must be taken for this when deciding if sheave is too thin

Check for metal fatigue

Minute compression shakes indicate weakness

Round head screws

Toggle

Doubler

Roundhead screws will not lever loose when in shear

Doubling piece prevents damage and probable failure of pin when stay is under strain

Gooseneck

Mast discoloured by moisture trapped at mast coat — may indicate rot

Wooden cleat

Sandpaper

Sheaves

Relieve the load from the halyards and check for wear in the sheaves. Sheaves are usually retained by screws and can be removed for inspection. Enlargement of the pivot hole will eventually cause the pulley to jam. Replace worn sheaves, and wash those in good condition in fresh water. Dry, and lubricate them with thin oil.

Look for evidence that the halyard runs are fair. Note signs of wear at the side of the sheave or against the mast and re-run or protect the wires or ropes.

Mast strap

The fastenings holding a mast strap come under severe strain. All fastenings must be secure. Loose screws can be re-bedded in epoxy resin mixed with colodial silica as described above, and should be clamped into position while the resin cures. Some masts are blocked solid at the hounds, and here longer screws can be used successfully instead of the epoxy resin. Always use round head screws.

The spur straps holding the fork terminals of the shrouds should be aligned with the shrouds, and the terminal and clevis pins must be the correct size. Check the straps for metal fatigue. Fore stays must always have a toggle or shackle at the head to allow for movement.

Mast track and luff groove

Clean the mast track with fresh water, dry, and then rub with candlewax. All screws securing the track must be tight and closely spaced. A distance greater than 4 inches (100 mm) between screws will result in distortions in the track and over-stressed fastenings. Loose screws cannot be replaced with longer screws. Instead they will have to be bonded into place with epoxy resin.

Gooseneck

Bolts and screws holding the gooseneck should be tight and the wood above and below the mast band inspected for rot. Clean and oil the roller reefing gear. At the end of each season, it will be necessary to dismantle, clean, and regrease them.

The anchorage points for the kicking strap and the cleats should be secure. If any movement is detected, they should be removed, and properly bedded against the mast.

Plug old screw holes with tapered pegs dipped in epoxy resin.

A wooden mast is particularly vulnerable to rot at the point where it passes through the deck. Probe suspected weak parts. Rot occurs at the top edge of the mast coat and at the wedges. Compression shakes may also be found just above the wedges. The heel of the mast should be clean and in good condition. There should be functioning drain holes in the mast step. Where necessary, a new mast heel tenon can be cut and the step adjusted. The procedure for doing this is described on page 224.

Winter maintenance

Remove the fittings from the mast and sand it back. If the mast is sanded right to the wood, prime the mast with a thinned varnish (15 per cent white spirit, 15 per cent linseed oil and 70 per cent varnish). Sand smooth, and build a high gloss with two or three coats of the same, unthinned, oil varnish, sanded between coats. The wood beneath mast fittings should be protected by paint, and then bedding compound.

Store wooden masts horizontally, and support them so that they do not bend.

Metal masts

Extruded aluminium masts are made in a variety of different sections, some of which are illustrated below. The choice of section, size, and wall thickness depends upon the size and type of craft.

Compared to wooden masts, those made from aluminium are largely maintenance free. The minor chores needed to keep the mast in good condition are described below. Some of the problems that occur are outlined, and should be remembered when inspecting or working on a metal mast.

Aluminium masts are light and easily handled. Their thin sides can, however, be kinked if they are dropped or leant against a sharp corner. A kink, especially at a highly-stressed area, will weaken a mast. Badly kinked masts are immediately noticeable, but smaller depressions in the surface of the mast can be felt. Look for signs of fatigue at the point of the depression. These will be revealed as minute cracks and localized bleaching in the anodizing. Seek professional advice where there is evidence of fatigue or serious weakening.

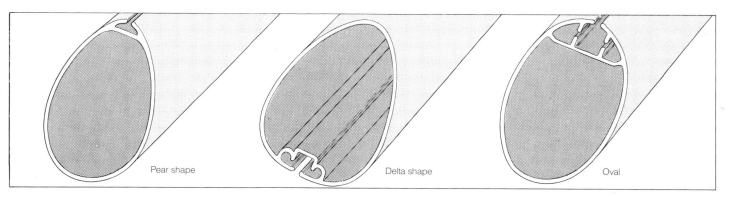

Pear shape

Delta shape

Oval

Metal masts (continued)

A mast will also be weakened by a row of fastenings. The degree of weakening is difficult to estimate, and there is little that the owner can do to restore the strength of the mast, other than return it to the manufacturer to be welded. Before planning additions to the mast, check for other fittings close by, and stagger the rivets or screws.

Although some mast fittings are welded in place, many are tapped, and screwed or pop-rivetted. Both methods are satisfactory. Self-tapping screws, which remain with their points protruding through the inside mast wall, will foul or chafe against the halyards or mast head wiring, and should not be used.

Mast head

The headbox is welded or bolted into a slot cut in the end of the mast. Halyards should have a free run over the sheaves, which must revolve easily. Mast head lights, wind speed indicators, etc., must all be properly fastened, and insulated where necessary.

Where a mast strap is fitted, inspect the tangs that hold the fork or eye terminals for metal fatigue, and the fastenings for tightness and corrosion. 'T' fittings are sometimes associated with distortions in the mast wall or covering plate, but the use of internally fitted plates has, to a great extent, overcome this problem.

Looseness in the spreader bracket may be caused by the rivets or screws pulling out or stretching when the cap shrouds prevent the spreaders bending forwards with the mast.

Accumulations of dirt, grease and salt crystals will impede the movement of the slides. Wash the sail track with fresh water, dry, and rub with candlewax. A stopper should be fitted at the top of the mast track. Clean and lubricate the gooseneck fittings. A wipe with light oil or a spray with an aerosol lubricant will usually suffice.

Cleats and all other mast fittings must be well bedded against the mast. File a badly seated fitting to the correct profile, or clean its bedding surface and set it in thickened epoxy resin.

All sheaves should be in good condition, and turn freely. Rope runs from the exit

sheave to the winch, and from the winch to the cleat, should all be direct and well-planned.

Deck-stepped masts are best secured with one bolt, so that the mast can rock without weakening the deck structure. Where masts pass through the deck, the mast coat should be lifted and the mast inspected for corrosion. Drain holes above the mast coat should be clear.

Keep the mast step clean and the drainage holes unblocked.

Aluminium spars are subject to corrosion, and to galvanic corrosion where fittings are rivetted or screwed to the mast. Anodized masts are usually well protected, and it is not until the anodized aluminium surface is worn away that corrosion will occur. The surface of the aluminium oxidizes rapidly and the oxide film prevents further corrosion. The volume of grey-white dust present on the surface of the mast bears little obvious relation to the quantity of metal actually lost, which is usually very slight. More serious pitting will occur where water rests against the aluminium, as at the mast coat, mast strap, spreaders, etc., and corrosion can be quite serious when it occurs in conjunction with chafe or abrasion, perhaps caused by a badly run wire. Mast steps can corrode completely due to a combination of moisture and abrasion.

Most mast fittings are made from aluminium or stainless steel. Fastenings are either from stainless steel or monel. A small degree of galvanic corrosion will occur between these metals, but it is not usually serious. However, fittings of bronze or other metals should be insulated from the mast with a Neoprene, PVC, Delrin or cast epoxy resin barrier. Zinc chromate paste can be smeared against fittings and screw threads, etc., to help insulate them.

Winter maintenance

Undress the mast, wash and coil the standing rigging wires. Remove as many mast fastenings as possible and check those that are rivetted to make sure that they are secure.

Hose fresh water down the inside of the mast, and lean it at an angle to dry. Hose the outside of the mast to wash off the

T fitting

Radiused corners to reduce risk of stress cracking

deposits of salt and dirt. Leave the mast to dry.

Wax the mast with a hard, quick-drying wax. Burnish it by hand and store the mast horizontally, supporting it at suitable intervals.

Running rigging **Sailboats**

Most of the ropes used aboard cruising and racing boats are made from synthetic fibres. The list outlines the main qualities of the man-made fibre ropes commonly available.

Stretch and flexibility are affected not only by the type of fibre used, but also by the angle, and type of lay, of the rope. Three-strand laid ropes which have the strands laid at a steep angle to the centre-line of the rope are stiffer to handle, but stretch more than the stronger soft lay rope. Three-strand rope chafes, but after initial roughening resists further wear. Braided ropes are easier to hold and coil, and wear and kink less than three-strand ropes, but they are vulnerable to chafe, and once the outside case is cut the rope is useless.

Material	Characteristics	Chemical and UV degradation	Specific gravity	10mm minimum strength
Nylon	Very high dry strength. Reduced by 15 per cent when saturated very elastic — stand clear of nylon ropes under load. Tends to work harden, and becomes harder to handle when under load	At normal temperatures nylon is resistant to most alkalis, but it has limited resistance to acids. Good UV resistance Does not rot	1.14	2.08
Polyester	Performance un- affected by water. Durable and less elastic than nylon. Easy to handle, but with slight work-hardening	Resistant to most chemicals and rot. Exterior fibres slightly affected by UV	1.38	2.02
Spun polypropylene	Similar appearance and handling texture to natural fibre ropes. Remains flexible whether wet or dry	Water and rot-proof. Resistant to most common acids and alkalis. Low melting point reduction in strength as temperature increases	0.91 floats	1.43
Split film polypropylene	Cheaper, with lower stretch than above	Deteriorates after prolonged exposure to sunlight. Resistant to rot, etc.	0.91	1.43

Safe working load

The safe working load of a rope is generally up to 20 per cent of its guaranteed minimum strength. Nylon ropes, in particular, have great load-absorbing characteristics and will stretch about 20 per cent within their safe working load, and revert to their original length when the load is released. As synthetic ropes do not rot or suffer from mildew, strength loss is only the result of wear, heat fusion (caused by friction over a winch or seized pulley) or ultra-violet degradation. Nylon and Terylene are not significantly weakened after prolonged exposure to sunlight, but the outer fibres

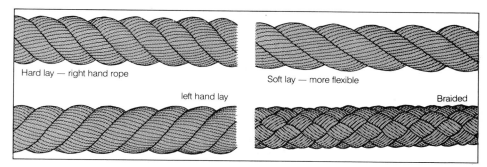

Hard lay — right hand rope

left hand lay

Soft lay — more flexible

Braided

of polypropylene ropes become brittle and frayed. In most ropes this superficial deterioration will cause a significant loss

of strength only where the rope diameter is small.

Handling and maintenance

The strands of a synthetic rope will untwist very rapidly, unless they are whipped or heat sealed to prevent them from unravelling. The simplest method is to hold the rope end over a cigarette lighter or candle until the yarns blacken or shrivel. Press these ends together to form a solid seal. Synthetic ropes can be

effectively heat sealed in this way, but for a permanent ending, rope should be whipped, as well as sealed.

Wear

Although the strength of synthetic ropes is unaffected by rot or mildew, they remain vulnerable to chafe, and weaken

through being kinked. In order to minimize chafe on the running rigging, every effort should be taken to protect the rope and make sure that the rope runs are direct and do not pass across or around sharp edges, etc. Some particular points to note are illustrated.

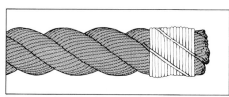

Heat seal and whip rope ends

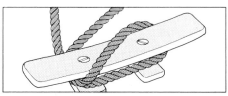

Methods for securing a rope to a cleat

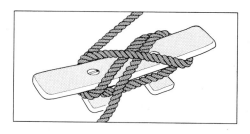

Running rigging Sailboats

Cleaning a synthetic rope
Most synthetic ropes are resistant to oil, grease, and mild acids. Rinse them in warm water to remove salt crystals. Wash in soapy water and rinse thoroughly.

To check the condition of a rope, back twist it and inspect the fibres. A worn and weakened rope will be frayed and abraded between the strands. Chafe on the outside of the rope is often much less serious than inner deterioration.

As with the standing rigging, where corrosion and fatigue weakening are usually concentrated at the terminals, the wear on running rigging is often limited to a relatively small percentage of the overall length of the rope. Because of slippage between rope fibres, rope tends to deteriorate and weaken under constant load. Halyards are the most obvious example of a rope under permanent tension, yet the only part under strain is the length between the peak and the cleat or winch. Where a wire rope is spliced to the tail of the halyard to reduce stretch, the length of rope which is under tension, and therefore liable to deteriorate, may be no more than three or four feet (approximately 1 metre).

The same is true of the mainsheet tackle, where the end third is disproportionately subjected to wear, while the remaining rope is rarely under much strain.

All running rigging can be turned to distribute wear evenly over its length. If the ropes are purchased rather longer than necessary, weakened parts can be cut out and discarded, and the rope reversed.

Recovering a lost halyard
This frustrating task can be made a little easier if the exit box at the bottom of the mast can be removed. Tighten the halyards and topping lift which remain in the mast, so they present as little hindrance as possible to the light chain messenger. Take the burgee halyard, or a similar light line, and attach a length of thin chain to it. Tie the rope halyard to the other end of the line.

Heel the boat slightly, to help the messenger keep to the side of the mast, and prevent it from snagging on halyards or wires. Lower the chain through the sheave and down inside the mast until it reaches the bottom, where it can be recovered with a wire hook. Continue to pull until the halyard is rove through the top sheave, and accessible at the mast exit block.

Coiling
Braided ropes are less prone to kinking than laid ropes. When coiling, a laid rope should be given a twist in the direction of the lay as each coil is made. Make sure that the rope end is free to prevent the twists from accumulating at the rope end and kinking it.

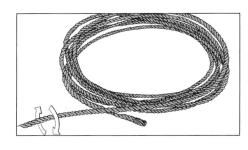

Thimble
Inspect the condition of thimbles that have been in use. Cracking at the crown of the thimble is an indication of fatigue. Thimbles that are distorted or cracked should be replaced with new thimbles fitted and seized into place.

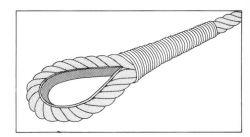

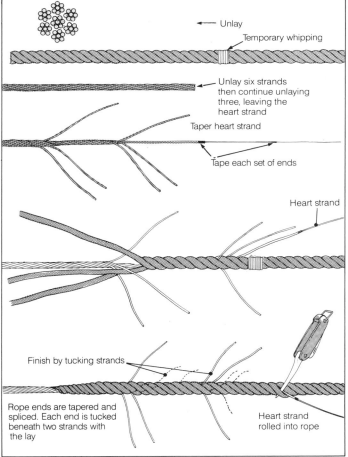

Joining flexible seven-strand rigging wire to a laid terylene halyard

Unlay

Temporary whipping

Unlay six strands then continue unlaying three, leaving the heart strand

Taper heart strand

Tape each set of ends

Heart strand

Lay back over wire, leaving ends protruding through lay. Snip out several strands from rope once second row of wire is passed

Roll end of wire into rope by opening lay with spike and inserting tapered wire end. Finish with sailmakers whipping

Finish by tucking strands

Rope ends are tapered and spliced. Each end is tucked beneath two strands with the lay

Heart strand rolled into rope

Sheaves

The pulley diameter should be sufficiently large for the rope to pass over the pulley without distortion. The rope should lie snugly into the pulley groove, and not be flattened or compressed by it when under load.

When a kinked rope is strained around a sharp corner or pulled up tight into a knot, the lay is distorted, and parts of the rope bear excessive strain while the heavily compressed fibres are rendered inoperative. This uneven load distribution is likely to cause the rope to part well before its guaranteed minimum strength is reached. This weakening is in addition to that caused by wear, which may have already reduced the strength of the rope.

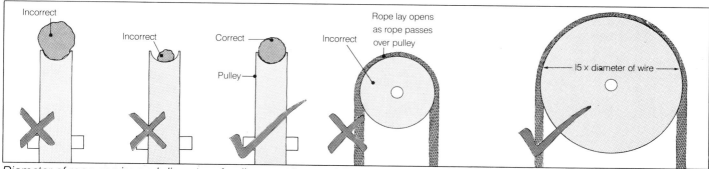

Diameter of rope or wire and diameter of pulley must be carefully matched

Pulleys

A variety of simple purchases is illustrated. The approximate mechanical advantage of each can be found by counting the number of ropes at the moving block. True mechanical advantage will be significantly less as energy is lost at the sheave bearings and in the distortion of the rope as it passes over the pulley. Note that the fixed block (standing block) imposes a strain on its attachment point equal to the sum of the loads at each end of the tackle.

The minimum size of sheave for a wire rope is 15 times its diameter. A slightly smaller size can be accepted if the wire has a rope heart, and the wire is only deflected up to 120°.

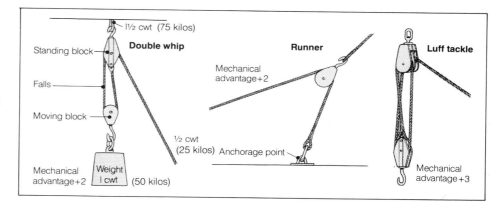

A smaller but similar arrangement to the luff tackle is known as a 'handy Billy'. This is a general purpose tackle that can be set up for hauling in anchor lines, etc. (in conjunction with rolling hitch) or for lifting weights aboard

Blackwall hitch

Blackwall hitches are quick and easy to make, but do not withstand heavy loading. The Midshipman hitch is more secure than the Blackwall hitches, and is made by first forming a Blackwall hitch. The loop is then lifted and pulled around the shank, and slipped over the point of the hook.

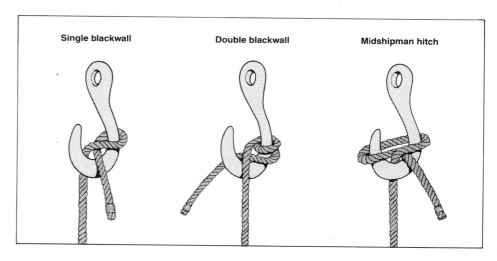

Standing rigging Sailboats

> The standing rigging supports and braces the mast. For maximum sailing efficiency, the mast should remain straight, and any curve that is induced should be carefully controlled by the crew.
>
> The mast and rigging are subjected to extremely high stresses. The compressive force of the mast can be in excess of twice the displacement of the boat. All individual wires and their fittings should have a designed breaking load higher than the total weight of the boat. All parts of the rigging should be correctly fitted and well maintained.

Wire

In theory, an absolutely rigid mast is desirable, but in practice a certain degree of flexibility in the standing rigging is necessary. Nineteen-strand stainless steel wire is commonly used for standing rigging as it combines great strength, low stretch, and adequate flexibility. Galvanized wire, which for the same diameter is slightly weaker, is also used and has the advantage of being cheaper, less prone to work harden, and gives a clear warning of corrosion and weakness.

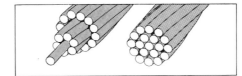

As the diameter of the steel wire increases, its tendency to stretch for a given weight is reduced. There may therefore be an advantage in using two or more diameters of wire rope in the standing rigging. Terminals and fittings should always be as strong or stronger than the breaking strain of the wire.

There are a number of terminal fittings, many of which involve the use of specialist, and often expensive, equipment. The screw clamp terminals can be fitted with no more than a pair of sharp wire cutters and two spanners. The Norseman and Sta-Lock type of screwed clamp terminal has a variety of end fittings that can be used, which permit shortening at a later date.

All wire runs should be straight. Kinks in a stainless steel wire will initiate localized corrosion, and, because of the uneven distribution of load over the section of the wire, will reduce its strength.

Like any other metal fitting, wire is subject to fatigue. Once the wire begins to deteriorate, small broken strands will spike out from the wire. When this occurs, the wire should be replaced. Wire ends are most subject to fatigue, particularly where they enter a ferrule or terminal. Check for fraying and signs of corrosion. Galvanized wire will stain with rust before failing. Stainless steel wire does not give such a clear warning. Although it may last for 10 to 20 years, it should be checked regularly. Replace wires that are suspected of being weakened by corrosion or wear.

Wash stainless steel wire in fresh warm water at the end of the sailing season. Dry, coil, label it. 1 x 19 stainless steel wire can be taped to a batten and stored with the mast. Galvanized wire should also be washed, and rubbed with warm linseed oil before storing.

Rod rigging

Strength for strength, wire rigging has more stretch and more windage than rod rigging. Weights are approximately the same but rod rigging work hardens more quickly. Terminals are cold forged to fit into cupped sockets in the rigging screws and terminals. Kinks will seriously weaken rod rigging and carefully designed sleeves are fitted to ensure that terminals remain in direct line with the steel rod. Rod rigging is easy to clean, as the rod presents no crevice in which salt crystals can form and corrode. Rigging should be removed, washed, and stored in large diameter coils or on a batten, to prevent kinks.

Because of its greater rigidity, rod rigging is vulnerable to metal fatigue, kinking and associated corrosion, and should be replaced at least as regularly as steel wire.

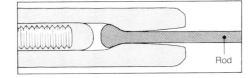

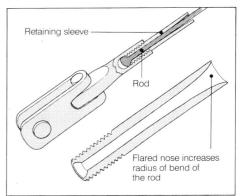

Retaining sleeve

Rod

Flared nose increases radius of bend of the rod

Rigging screws

Rigging screws and all other standing rigging fittings must be of at least equal strength to the rigging wire. Many manufacturers will supply wire complete with terminal ends and rigging screws, which should ensure compatibility. Where fittings of differing makes are used together, a rough indication of suitability is that the diameter of the

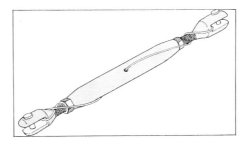

threaded bolts of the rigging screw should be nearly twice the diameter of the wire it is to tension.

Rigging screws must be locked to the correct setting. Unless a positive locking device such as a split pin is used, lash the fork with stainless steel wire, and then bind it with insulation or Armet tape to prevent chafe.

Rigging screws must be in direct line with the rigging wire. Fork terminals should be shackled to the chain plate or mast band fitting. Where there is excessive sideways movement of the mast, or where chain plates are not aligned accurately with the angle of the rigging wire, fit a toggled rigging screw which will adjust itself to the angle of the wire without weakening or bending.

Head fittings and chain plates
The same general remarks apply to these as to the rigging screw. The clevis pins in fork terminals must take a direct pull. Toggles should be used where circumstances make this impossible.

Shorter spreaders, and the reduction in distance between chain plates and mast step in modern boats, necessitate

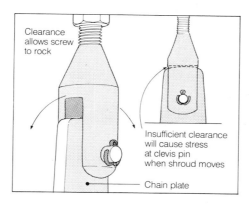

Clearance allows screw to rock

Insufficient clearance will cause stress at clevis pin when shroud moves

Chain plate

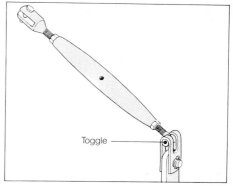

Toggle

greater rigging tensions, which cause increased compressive loads on the mast step. Chain plates are often through-deck mounted, and carried to reinforced floors and sides. These may include tensioning screws below deck

to anchor the deck plate. Check round the deck fitting for evidence of lifting or stress cracking and tighten the anchorage screws where necessary.

Spreaders
The angle made by the bend in the rigging wire, where it passes round the end of the spreader, should be bisected by the centre-line of the spreader. The spreaders must tilt upwards slightly, and be retained in this position by end clamps or, if necessary, by a bulldog clamp tightened just below the spreader.

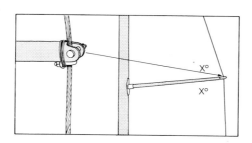

X°

X°

Chafe
The standing rigging presents many surfaces against which sails or running rigging may chafe. For those who are more concerned with saving expense than achieving the utmost speed, the roller protection for the shrouds and the traditional baggywrinkle are illustrated. The technique for making baggywrinkle is described on page 23l.

Climbing the mast
Many of the masts on large sailing boats are fitted with steps rivetted to the side of the mast. Where these are not fitted, a sling or bos'n's chair must be used. A variety of arrangements is available, from a simple webbing band to sewn harness and seat. When working aloft use a clip

and line to reduce the pendulum effect caused by the movement of the mast. Where work is needed at the end of the cross trees, it may help to have an additional light line to help restrain the seat. All the extra lines should be fastened to the suspension point of the chair, and released prior to lowering.

Lowering the mast
If the boat is rolling, do not attempt to lower the mast to reach a part that needs servicing. As the deck-mounted mast is lowered, the sideways support of the shrouds is eliminated, and severe and damaging twisting strains are imposed on the tabernacle and mast pivot.

Emergency wire repairs
A temporary eye can be formed in a length of steel wire by clamping the wires together with bulldog grips. Two per eye is the minimum necessary and three is better. Grips tend to weaken and distort the lay of the wire, and should be aligned with the flat bridge of the grip on the standing part and the U-bolt over its tail end. Space the grips well apart, and cover them if they are in the way of running gear. A stronger, temporary eye is the Flemish eye illustrated.

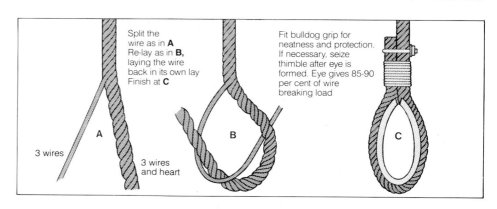

Split the wire as in **A** Re-lay as in **B,** laying the wire back in its own lay Finish at **C**

Fit bulldog grip for neatness and protection. If necessary, seize thimble after eye is formed. Eye gives 85-90 per cent of wire breaking load

3 wires

A

3 wires and heart

B

C

Reef knot For joining ropes of equal thickness. This knot pulls very tight, is difficult to undo, and will slip if used to tie greasy, slippery and some synthetic ropes.

Timber hitch This holds well under a constant load, but will work free when not under strain.

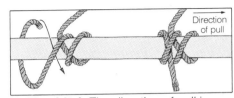

Rolling hitch The direction of pull is always from the side with the two turns. This knot may loosen under intermittent loads. It is used whenever a sideways pull is needed.

Clove hitch Two half hitches are formed which jam together. Under heavy loading becomes very difficult to release.

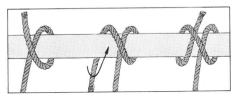

An alternative method of tying a clove hitch.

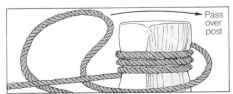

Towing hitch Will bear the strain up to the breaking point of the rope but can be released instantly.

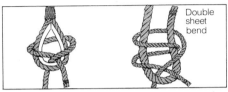

Sheet bend A strong knot, easy to make and easy to release. Can be used around an eye or to join ropes together. Where added strength is needed, a double sheet bend should be used.

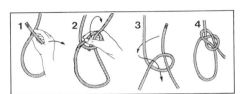

Bowline This knot forms a very secure eye that will not slip. Cross rope to form loop (1). Hold cross between forefinger and thumb (2). Roll wrist to the right, flicking the end through the loop and over the top (3).

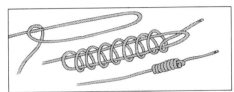

Heaving line knot This forms a heavy knot at the rope end which helps carry the line when it is thrown.

Whipping

Synthetic ropes should be whipped with waxed nylon line. Use natural fibre twine for whipping ropes made from natural fibre.

West Country whipping
This whipping is formed by tying an overhand knot on opposite sides of the rope. Work towards the rope end, lining the knots to keep the whipping neat. Finish with a reef knot.

Sailmaker's whipping
1 Select twine and suitable sailmaker's needle. Pass needle through the lay of the rope, leaving a short tail of twine held against the rope.
2 Bind the twine around the rope. The first few turns cross the tail end and secure it in position. Subsequent turns can be pulled tight without difficulty.
3 Finish the first stage by passing the needle between two strands of the rope,

angling it to emerge between two strands on the opposite side.
4 Pull the twine tight and wind it around the whipping following the lay of the rope. At the top, pass the needle through the rope between the two strands. Continue sewing and winding the twine until each part of the whipping is retained. Finish by forcing the needle behind the whipping.

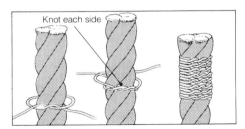

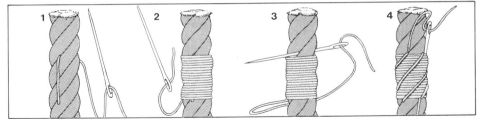

Splicing

1 Unlay more rope than is likely to be needed for the tucks. Prevent the rope from untwisting further by wrapping tape or twine around it. Seal the strand ends to prevent the yarns unravelling.
2 Tucks should be against the lay of the rope. When working the tucks, disturb and distort the rope as little as possible.
3 In each round of tucks, each tuck should be beneath a different strand. Work the tucks in order.
4 Once the splice is complete, roll it between the palms of the hands or between two boards to smarten it up.
5 Only three and two half tucks per strand are necessary with natural fibre ropes. Splices in synthetic ropes should have at least five tucks per strand. Taper

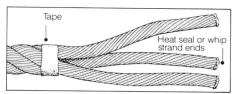

strands and continue. The more gradual the taper, the stronger the splice.

Eye splice

Splice the eye into and not across the rope. Prepare the rope for splicing, wrap it round the thimble, and tuck the first two strands. Turn the rope and pass the remaining strand under the unoccupied strand. This tuck must emerge in the same direction as the other two. Pull them tight, and smooth slight distortions in the lay by pulling the tucks, and then rolling the splice between the palms of the hands.

Continue working the tucks against the lay of the rope.

After five tucks have been completed, taper the strands by scraping the strand with a sharp knife, or by separating the

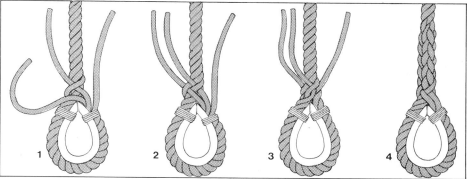

strand and cutting away some of the yarns, before re-twisting and continuing to work the tucks.
Scorch off the remaining hairs on the surface of the splice (taking care not to damage the rope) and finish the splice with a whipping. Secure the thimble with two short seizings.

Short splice

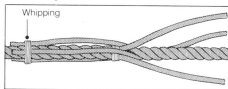

This is easier than the eye splice, although there may be difficulty in starting the second set of tucks once the first set of strands has been fully tucked. This difficulty can be avoided if the tucks are pulled up tight.

1 Prepare both ropes as described above.
2 Marry the ropes and carry one set of strands down the side of the opposing rope. Lash them in place.
3 Complete the first half of the splice.
4 Release the lashing on the other part and work the first row of tucks into place. These, like the others, must first pass over a strand before being tucked below the next.
5 Complete the splice, fair down the strands, roll the splice to round it up. Whip it if necessary.

Long splice

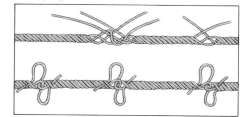

A long splice is used for joining or repairing ropes that pass through sheaves or tackles. It does not increase rope diameter or reduce its strength.

1 Unlay the strands of each rope a distance of approximately 30 times its diameter, or 12 times its circumference. Tie a light line around the ropes to prevent unravelling.
2 Slip both ropes together as for short splice.
3 Tie an overhand knot between the first two adjacent strands. For right-hand lay, the knot should be left over right, as this will help the knot to conform to the lay.
4 Unlay a strand, and twist the adjacent strand from the other rope in its place.
5 Do the same in the other direction and tie each pair with an overhand knot snugged down into the lay of the rope.
6 Cut off the excess strands at each knot, leaving enough strands at each knot to make about three tucks.
7 Pull and check the rope for evenness. The lay of the rope must remain regular. Loosen or tighten the overhand knots where necessary, and then give each strand a tuck as for the overhand knot.

Haul the rope tight, check it for distortion, tighten the strands, and trim them back. Press them into the lay.

Stepping and adjusting a mast Sailboats

This is a two-stage operation in which the mast is stepped and the rigging is set to the correct tension. Final tuning is carried out after the boat has been sailed, and the rigging has settled in. Wire rope, and to a lesser extent rod rigging, will stretch when under load. New rigging should be tuned and then re-checked after several days sailing, when tensions can be re-adjusted.

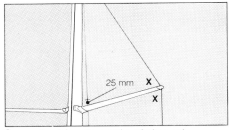

Spreader bisects angle of shroud

Preparation

Before attaching the standing rigging to the mast, check that the halyards and all the other parts of the running rigging, as well as the mast head fittings, are in good order. Run the halyards down the mast and knot their ends together so that they do not work loose when the mast is being stepped.

Clip or shackle the standing rigging to the mast. Wire and tape shackles; clevis pins should be secured with split pins opened to 30°, and wrapped in insulation tape. Pull each cap shroud in turn, and angle and clamp the spreader so that it projects at an angle of

approximately 85° to the upper mast. If there are no slight kinks in the wire to indicate the previous position of the spreader clamps, hold the stay against the mast and mark a point on the stay approximately 1 inch (25 mm) above the spreader bracket which is fixed to the mast. If the clamp is fastened at this point the spreader should bisect the angle made by the shroud as it passes around the spreader clamp.

If some of the rigging wire has to be renewed, remember that the new wire will stretch and that the original wire will also have stretched. Unless Norseman or Sta-Lock terminals are fitted to enable the wire to be shortened, measure the original shroud and estimate a slight additional length owing

to stretching. This rarely amounts to more than 1 or 2 diameters of wire. Subtract this from the terminal to terminal measurement when ordering the new wire. If necessary, fit an extra toggle or shackle between the rigging screw and the chain plate to make up the distance until the new wire is stretched and re-tightened.

Diamond shrouds can be tightened before the mast is stepped. These usually have a slightly higher tension than the other shrouds.

Connect the rigging screws and tighten them at an equal rate. Test the tension as the wires become taut by tapping each with a backward flick of the hand. The fingernails should just strike the wire, which will resonate with a singing sound as adequate tension is reached.

Sight along the luff groove or track to ensure that the mast is perfectly straight, before wiring and taping the rigging screws.

Fit the lower and intermediate shrouds and tape their ends to the mast. If the mast is stepped in the keel, slide the mast coat over the heel of the mast.

Preparing the boat

Mast wedges and rubber chocks should bear against clean flat faces at the mast partners, which ought to be cleaned prior to fitting the mast. Do not step a mast when the boat is pitching or rolling. If the water is troubled by passing ships or fast power boats, wait until their wash has subsided before stepping the mast.

Fit the lifting strop just above the balancing point of the mast. Pull it tight and prepare to lift the mast into position. Ask an assistant to watch the mast head while the heel is lowered between the

partners and into the step. Fasten the stays as quickly as possible to free the crane from the mast.

Wedge the mast, following the supplier's instructions, or described on page 188. Once the wedges or rubber chocks are in position, the stays can be slackened off. The mast should stand plumb with the centre-line of the boat. This can be checked by fixing a light line to a heavy shackle, connected to the mainsail halyard. Haul the line to the mast head, and swing the line across to the chain plates or toe rail. If the mast is plumb, the

touching point of the line under moderate tension will be the same for each side. Adjust mast wedges or mast step to correct a bias to one or other of the sides. Leave the line so that it can be used later, after the remaining standing rigging has been tensioned.

A deck-stepped mast is retained with the mast step bolt, and supported by shrouds. Do not slacken off the shrouds, check that the mast is perpendicular to the boat, adjust it with the rigging screws.

Dockside tuning

Tighten the shrouds, fore stay, and back stay, until they are taut but not under significant load.

Tighten the cap stays first. Unless the previous year's settings are marked on the rigging screws, an estimate of the tension can be gained by strumming the wires as described above.

Sight up the mast after adjusting each pair of shrouds. The mast must remain straight in the athwartships plane and any slight rake or hook is controlled in the fore and aft direction by tensioning the jumper strut stays (if fitted) and the after lower shrouds.

Tighten the fore lower shrouds. These need not be as tight as the upper

shrouds, otherwise the mast will kink when under sideways pressure. Tension the intermediate stays so that their tension is less than that of the cap stays, but greater than the lower shrouds.

Tighten the fore stay and the back stay, and the after lower shroud to control the hook. The tension on the fore stay is usually higher than all of the others.

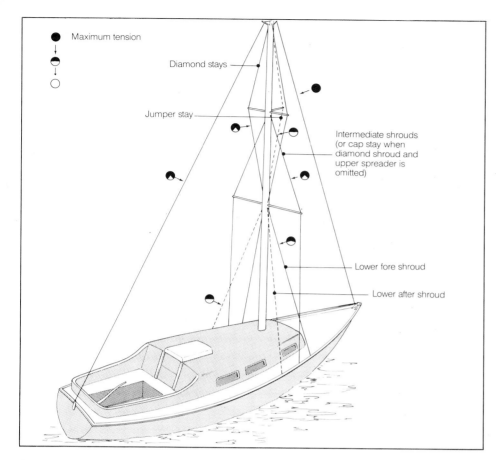

Maximum tension

Diamond stays

Jumper stay

Intermediate shrouds
(or cap stay when
diamond shroud and
upper spreader is
omitted)

Lower fore shroud

Lower after shroud

rigging is set, alterations to the tension on one side must be compensated by an opposite and equal number of rigging screw turns on the other. Note that the forward hook of the mast is controlled by the jumper strut and the after lower shroud, neither of which should be used for athwartship corrections.

The mast should form a regular slight curve when the boat is heeling at about 20°, and the lee rigging at this angle should be very slightly loose.

Reef the mainsail and with the sail pressure now working at a lower point on the mast, check its curvature again.

When all of the adjustments are made and the mast stands straight and plumb when the sails are lowered, lock, wire and tape the rigging screws.

Balancing the boat

As a result of these procedures, most masts will be set up well, and the sailing performance should be satisfactory. However, the rake of a mast affects the balance of the boat. The amount of weather or lee helm can be altered by raking the mast or inclining it forwards. Since this will involve altering the tension on some of the stays, correct the handling characteristics of the boat before tuning the mast. See page 232.

Undressing the mast

At the end of each sailing season, mark the rigging screws so that their location and setting are recorded. This information will speed up the rigging process the following year.

Check again that the mast is straight and that the rigging is at the same tension at each side.

Once the mast is set up, it is possible to test its deflection by heaving on the lee shrouds and sighting up the mast. Correct unfair bends in the mast by loosening the appropriate shroud.

Fine tuning

With the rigging set up and tensioned correctly, the final corrections are made

when the yacht is sailed in a fresh breeze, and the performance of the boat and the curvature of the mast can be studied and improved if necessary. New rigging should be given time to stretch and the slack should be taken up before final adjustments are made.

The mast will curve or distort in two planes, which are corrected separately. The drawings below illustrate the main faults and the wires that need adjustment. Once the tension in the standing

Adjust rigging until mast forms slight regular curve at about 20° angle of heel

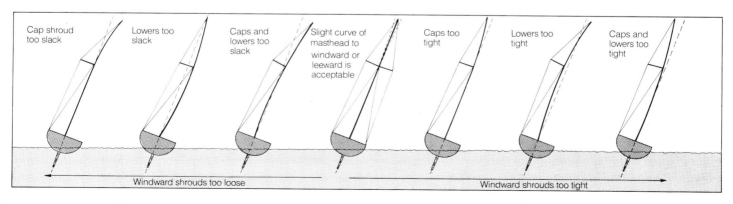

Cap shroud too slack

Lowers too slack

Caps and lowers too slack

Slight curve of masthead to windward or leeward is acceptable

Caps too tight

Lowers too tight

Caps and lowers too tight

Windward shrouds too loose

Windward shrouds too tight

Sails Sailboats

Yachtsmen will be alert to the condition of their sails even when preoccupied with running the ship, making a landfall, or training the crew. Sails should be checked constantly, to see that they are setting well, and to identify faults so that these can be repaired before the sail is harmed. The time to check a sail is when it is set and drawing. It is then that its condition and efficiency can best be judged.

The illustration shows the sails set on a sailing dinghy. Parts of the sail and areas that most frequently need attention or repair are indicated.

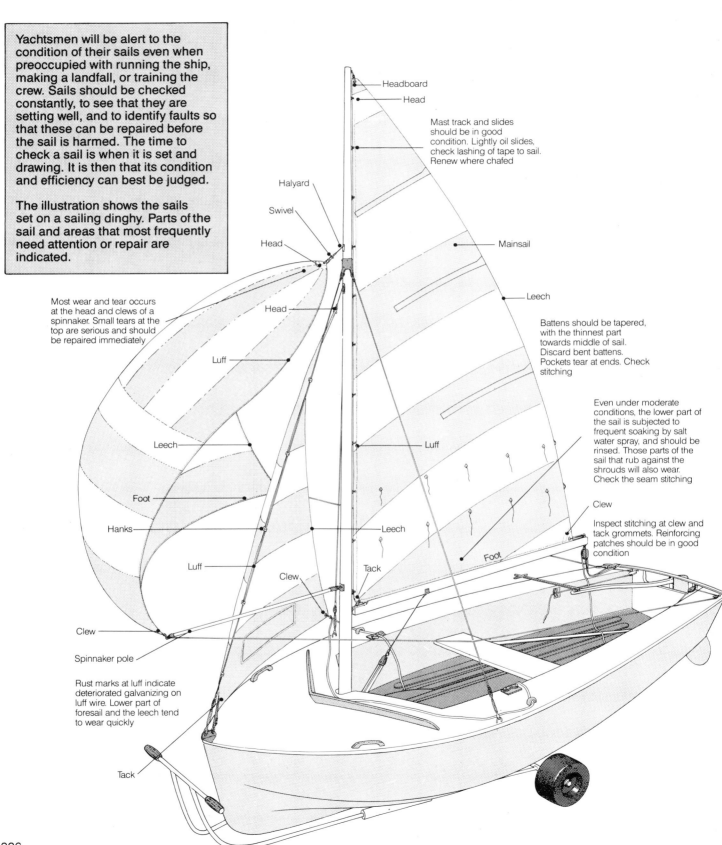

Headboard

Head

Mast track and slides should be in good condition. Lightly oil slides, check lashing of tape to sail. Renew where chafed

Halyard

Swivel

Head

Mainsail

Leech

Most wear and tear occurs at the head and clews of a spinnaker. Small tears at the top are serious and should be repaired immediately

Head

Battens should be tapered, with the thinnest part towards middle of sail. Discard bent battens. Pockets tear at ends. Check stitching

Luff

Even under moderate conditions, the lower part of the sail is subjected to frequent soaking by salt water spray, and should be rinsed. Those parts of the sail that rub against the shrouds will also wear. Check the seam stitching

Leech

Luff

Clew

Foot

Inspect stitching at clew and tack grommets. Reinforcing patches should be in good condition

Hanks

Leech

Luff

Tack

Foot

Clew

Clew

Clew

Spinnaker pole

Rust marks at luff indicate deteriorated galvanizing on luff wire. Lower part of foresail and the leech tend to wear quickly

Tack

Headboard
Inspect the seams and stitching at any part of the sail where there is localized stiffening or stress. Stitching around a solid headboard often frays. Check also for chafe at the leading edge.

The leech
Handle as rarely and as gently as possible, to avoid stretching the leech or the sailcloth adjacent to it. A stretched leech will flutter when reaching or close hauled, and a leech that has stretched less than the rest of the sail will be tight, and backwind the trailing edge of the sail. Both conditions detract from the sailing performance, and have to be corrected by a sailmaker.

Sailcloth

Mainsails and headsails are generally made from polyester fibre (Terylene, Dacron) and spinnakers from nylon. After four or five years' use, or prolonged exposure to direct sunlight, both types of fabric will harden and lose their strength and flexibility. Once sailcloth has been weakened by ultraviolet light, it will be difficult to repair, as even the individual stitches may tear the brittle fabric. Where the sail can still be used, perhaps as a light weather sail, stagger the stitches to avoid forming a weak line in the cloth.

Both the sailcloth and the seam stitching are likely to chafe. Headsails are often chafed at their leech, and at the foot, spinnakers at the swivel, and mainsails wear when they rub against shrouds and runners. A topping lift will also chafe the mainsail unless it is wrapped in baggy wrinkle.

Chafe is most serious at the seams. Polyester fibre has very little give, and stitches do not bury into the sailcloth but remain prominent and vulnerable to wear. Inspect the seams of the sails for evidence of wear. Polyester sail twine is extremely strong. If it is worn to the extent that it parts when rubbed or snagged, resew the seam.

Many polyester sailcloths are treated with a resin filler to improve the wind flow over their surface. In time, the resin sealer will begin to separate from the sailcloth. This will first be evident at the creases in the sail and at the headboard. Once the resin begins to fall away, there is nothing that can be done to replace it or to restore the sail to its former efficiency. The sailcloth, however, may be perfectly sound and have many years useful life left.

Sail maintenance
Although polyester and nylon are not vulnerable to rot, etc., it is very important that sails that have been splashed or soaked in seawater should be rinsed with fresh water. Modern sails can be stored wet without harm, but they should be clean, because the grit or salt crystals that form on the sailcloth can work into the weave and weaken the fibres.

Hose down dinghy sails while they are still set. Larger sails can be laid across a lawn or suspended by the luff from a washing line and washed clean.

Store sails in their bags. When changing headsails, for instance, store the lowered sail in its bag, and carry it below where it will be protected and not subjected to ultra violet degradation.

Each sail should fit easily into its own bag, marked for easy identification. Store the bags loosely where they will not be compressed, flattened and creased. Every effort should be taken to avoid creasing, as creases reduce the sails' efficiency, particularly in light airs.

Folding and storing sails
The illustrations show several methods of rolling and folding a headsail and a mainsail. It is good practice to vary the method used to pack dinghy sails so that permanent creases do not develop. The sails of cruising and racing yachts, however, should be rolled and bundled in an established and practised order, so that they can be handled with speed and confidence.

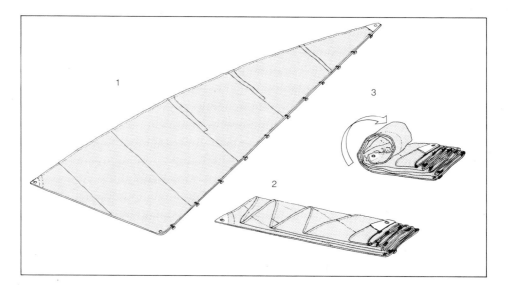

Folding a mainsail
Lay the sail flat. Gather sail and flake it down. Roll up sail from leech to luff

Folding and storing (continued)

Sails taken ashore after the weekend sail, or at the end of the sailing season, should be cleaned and stored loosely, or rolled. A convenient lightweight roller can be made from a long cardboard tube (obtainable from carpet manufacturers and carpet fitting specialists) suspended from the rafters of a garage or workroom. Sails can be inspected while they are still on the roller, and repairs carried out without the inconvenience of a large sail cluttering a small room.

Flake down sail, ending with the leech. Roll the sail

Starting at the head, roll up luff wire until sail forms tube. Fold tube, starting at luff wire

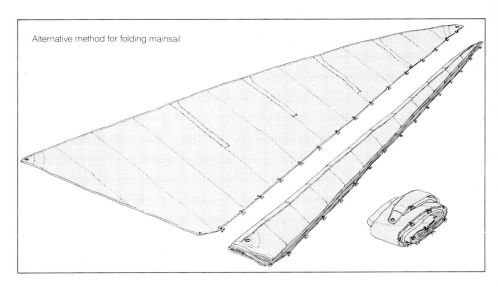

Alternative method for folding mainsail

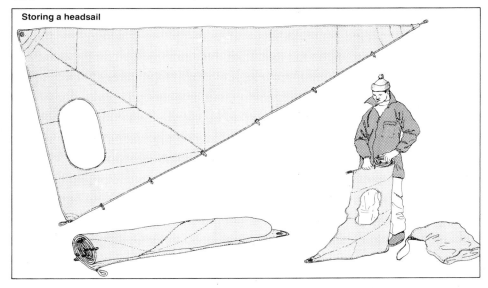

Storing a headsail

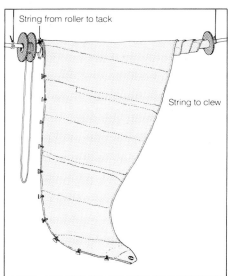

String from roller to tack

String to clew

Cleaning sails

One of the problems with washing a large sail is to find a large or clean enough surface on which to spread the sail. A wet sail is likely to pick up more dirt and grit from a dusty floor than it had in it before being washed. For this reason, it is often best to scrub and wipe the sail over a clean, flat table, then take it outside for rinsing.

Most marks can be removed with a vigorous scrubbing with soap and lukewarm water. Smaller stains, grease, oil and wet paint can be removed with white spirit or carbon tetrachloride.

Scrubbing will not harm the sail, unless the surface beneath is uneven or rough. Wash off solvents with soap and water before rinsing with fresh water.

Awkward stains must be removed after experiments with solvents over a small part of the stain have proved successful. Do not use acetone to clean polyester or nylon. If in doubt, seek expert advice.

Rust stains may be removed by washing the affected part with a mild solution of oxalic acid. This is a bleach, which may alter the tone of a coloured sail, and

should only be used on white sails. Rust marks which may appear at kinks in the luff, at the tack, and where bronze hanks are lashed to a galvanized luff wire suggest it is dangerously near the end of its useful life.

Stainless steel wire which is unprotected by a thin plastic coating will react with polyester fibres. Staining of the sailcloth will indicate that the plastic insulation has failed. Replacing luff wires is a task for a professional sailmaker.

Sail repairs

Handle sails with great care, make sure your hands are clean and the working area is free from patches of grease and dirt. Because of their flimsiness, light nylon ghosting sails and spinnakers should be handled very gently.

Sails are made from lengths of polyester or nylon cloth, cut into strips and sewn together. The shape and configuration of the strips will control the shape of the sail and its fullness. Although modern sailcloths are stable, they will stretch if pulled diagonally across the weave. Stretch is not only affected by the direction of the pull, but also by the age of the cloth. Old sailcloth stiffens and stretches less than new. When repairing a sail, match the weave of the patch to

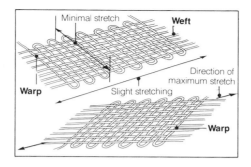

the weave of the sailcloth, and use old sailcloth to repair an old sail.

The sail and the patch are likely to stretch when the sail is in use. Arrange the stitches that hold the patch so that they give slightly. This is achieved by

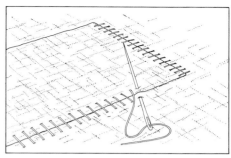

working the stitches at an angle to the weave of the cloth.

Equipment

A selection of sailmaker's needles, a palm, a block of beeswax, and some polyester thread will be needed for repairing Terylene or Dacron sails. Nylon sails should be sewn with nylon thread, and cotton sails with cotton thread. Needles should be large enough so they part the weave sufficiently for the thread to pull through. A needle that is too large will cut the sailcloth fibres. If too small a needle is used, the cloth may be damaged by the thread. Most modern sailcloths can be sewn with 14-17 gauge needles.

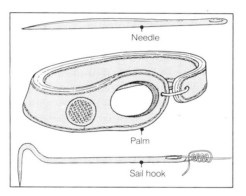

Needle

Palm

Sail hook

Cutting

Because of the manufacturing processes involved, modern polyester and nylon sailcloth can be cut without the need for heat sealing at the edge, or turning and sewing a seam. Both of these methods of preventing fraying, tend to distort the sailcloth and may impair the sail's performance.
Older sailcloth which is likely to fray should be cut with an old knife heated over a stove until it is red-hot. As it cuts it melts the end of the fibres and prevents the cloth from unravelling.

Holding the sailcloth

One of the problems with sail repairing is that the areas of sailcloth are so large that it is difficult to keep the parts to be sewn in their correct alignment. Small patches can be glued with a few spots of Bostick Clear Adhesive before sewing. The glue will dirty the sail if it is used on

long seams, and pins are likely to cause the seam to pucker. Sailmakers use a double-sided adhesive tape with which they glue the sailcloth before sewing. Rolls of this are commercially available and those planning to undertake extensive cruising should carry some of this tape with them.

The only other item of equipment that may be needed is a sailhook. This is a strong sharp hook tied to a lanyard, which in turn is fastened to a convenient post or fitting. It is used to hold the cloth while it is being sewn. In the absence of a hook, a woodworking clamp or similar simple device will serve instead.

Stitching

Starting a seam

Tie an overhand knot an inch (25mm) from the end of the twine. Make the first stitch passing over the tail of the twine, which should then be laid in the direction of the seam and held down by subsequent stitches (A).

Joining new twine

Knot and thread the new twine. Re-sew

the last stitch and tuck the end of the twine between the pieces of sailcloth that are being sewn together (B).

Finishing off

Make a double stitch at the end of the seam and then back-stitch up the seam. Pass the needle beneath a couple of stitches and cut off the thread (C).

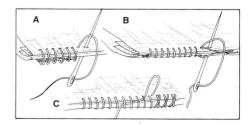

Sailmaking Sailboats

Tears

The herringbone stitch is used to repair tears in canvas or sailcloth. The cloth is laid flat and tensioned as illustrated. The repair is started a short distance back from the rent, with the tail end of the thread laid along the edge of the tear. Each pair of stitches is pulled tight before making the next. If the cloth is weak, or tears easily, stagger the stitches.

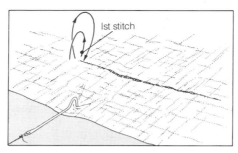

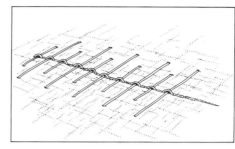

Seams

A round seam is sewn by holding the edges of the seam together and passing a series of fairly loose stitches over the edge and through the sailcloth. The stitch must be loose, otherwise the twine will tear the cloth when the seam is rubbed flat. A double seam is made by reversing the cloth and folding a new seam. A second seam, similar to the first, is then sewn.

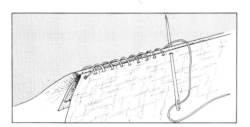

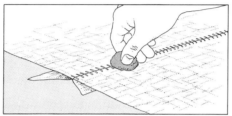

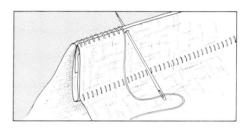

Patches

Patches are sewn with a flat seam. These are sewn with the cloth lying flat, and the tension in the stitching can be adjusted as the sewing progresses.

When a new length of twine is needed, the tail end of the old piece is withdrawn through one layer of sailcloth so that it lies inside the stitch and is sandwiched between the cloths.

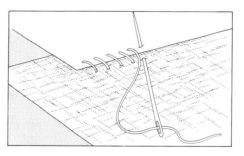

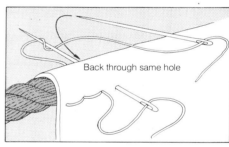

Sewing leather or canvas reinforcements

Where additional strength is needed in a sewn seam, a saddle stitch is used. A needle is threaded at each end of the thread, a sailmaker's needle at one end and a round-sectioned needle at the other. Both needles pass through the same hole, a twist of thread being hooked over the sailmaker's needle as it emerges from the seam. As the thread is tightened, it forms an overhand knot inside the cloth.

Patching a sail

The repair patch must have similar stretch characteristics to the sailcloth, otherwise it will distort the sail, reduce its efficiency and cause stress to the new seams.

Cut a new patch to size, position it carefully over the rent in the sail, tape it and sew with a flat seam. Turn the sailcloth over, cut back the torn fabric so that it has a margin with the patch seam of approximately 1-2 inches (25-50 mm). Mitre the corners to allow for a ¼ inch (6mm) fold and sew the inner seam.

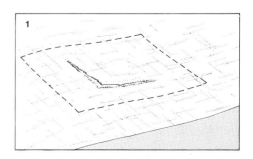

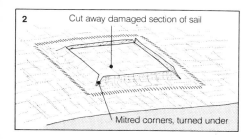

2 Cut away damaged section of sail

Mitred corners, turned under

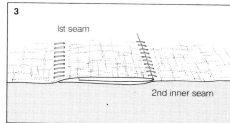

3 1st seam

2nd inner seam

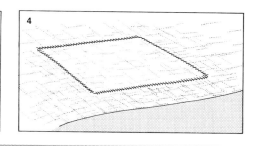

4

Grommets

Beneath the thimble lining the hole is another ring sewn to the sail. Fitting the outer ring requires the use of a powerful press, and for this type of repair the assistance of a professional sailmaker is needed. It is possible to reinforce a thimble that is loose by fitting a leather or sailcloth strip through the thimble and sewing it to the sailcloth. If hide is used, soak it in water to soften it before fitting and sewing it in place.

Where the old thimble and grommet are loose and badly worn, prise the thimble free and cut out the inner grommet ring. A new bronze or nylon ring, larger than the previous ring, should be fitted against the side of the sail and sewn into position with a round seam. Protect the stitching with hide or sailcloth.

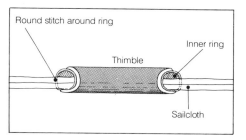

Round stitch around ring

Inner ring

Thimble

Sailcloth

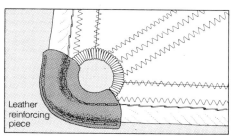

Leather reinforcing piece

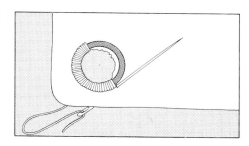

Cringles

Unlay length of rope so that one strand is long enough to make a cringle. Whip both ends

Work with roped edge closest. Pass strand through left hand cringle. Leave one end longer than the other. The lengths will depend upon the size of cringle being worked, but in general, A needs to be about 6-12 inches (150-300mm) longer than B

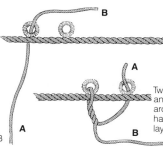

Twist B in direction of its lay, and wind it four turns around A. Pass A into right hand grommet. Twist A and lay it into cringle

Splice A and B into the cringle. Splice with the lay of the rope. Each end should pass beneath two strands, over one, then beneath two more. Taper the strands before the last two tucks. A thimble is inserted by stretching the cringle open with a tapered spike, and then slipping the thimble into position. It is usually necessary to hit the thimble to get it to slip behind the sail edge

Baggywrinkle

Baggywrinkle is wound around shrouds, topping lift, or the ends of the spreaders to prevent the sail chafing. It is made by weaving unlaid strands of rope between two lengths of line, stretched between two points. Each short length of rope strand is knotted in the manner illustrated and pushed up hard against the previous strands. These should all hang downwards, and once sufficient baggywrinkle has been made up, and the ends are seized, the strands are frayed out and trimmed to length.

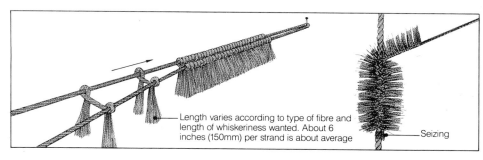

Length varies according to type of fibre and length of whiskeriness wanted. About 6 inches (150mm) per strand is about average

Seizing

One end of the baggywrinkle is seized to the shroud and the rest is wound around, until it forms a complete whiskery cover. Seize the other end.

Tuning Sailboats

Small alterations to the rigging and hull can make a considerable difference to the performance of a sailing boat. Some of the recommendations listed below will increase the speed of the boat in any wind or water conditions, others are more specific and the type of tuning will depend upon the strength of wind, weight of crew etc.

The most satisfactory method of tuning a sailboat is to race it competitively with another boat of the same type but of superior performance. Sailing to windward highlights the shortcomings of the boat, helmsman and crew, and this is the point of sailing where tuning adjustments are generally made. A fairly analytical attitude is necessary as there are many different factors that combine to create an efficient hull and rig. Adjust and test each element in turn, noting the alterations to help identify the reasons for improvement and the causes of the poor performance.

Class rules will forbid a few of the changes and alterations listed here, and before undertaking them, it is wise to check that the changes planned are within the scope of the measurement etc., rules for that class.

Light weather sailing
Heel boat to help sails adopt efficient profile

Hull finish
Paint should be smooth, clean, and polished with a hard wax. Fair the centreboard and rudder to reduce their resistance through the water. Lighten the hull as much as possible. Hull weight plays no part in the stability of the dinghy, but unnecessary weight will slow her down. This is not true of crews, where weight (and nimbleness) can be an advantage. All tracks, pulleys, pivots, etc. should be greased or lightly oiled for quick and easy adjustment. Grease or wax the sides of the self-bailer so that when it is needed it can be lowered without difficulty.

Handling
One or two pairs of light woollen tell-tails sewn to the luff of the mainsail help the helmsman to know if his sails are set efficiently. The tell-tails stream in the direction of the air flow, and if the foresail and mainsail are trimmed correctly, will lie against the sail, parallel to the boom. Once they flutter, or point away from the leech, the sails will need adjustment.

Lee and weather helm
Excessive use of the rudder causes turbulence and drag which will slow the boat. Rudder corrections of over 30° from the centre-line will act as a break. The boat should handle with very little lee or weather helm. Lee helm is where the boat veers off course to run down wind when the helm is released. Weather helm is the opposite — at every strong puff, the boat tries to turn into the wind. In both cases, valuable forward energy is lost in trying to compensate for these tendencies. There are a number of causes of both characteristics, which can be corrected by altering crew position, adjusting the centreboard, or raking the mast.

The diagrams show that as the horizontal distance between the centre of effort of the sails and the centre of resistance increases, the turning moment of the boat will become more powerful, and increasingly difficult to correct. Weather helm is where the centre of effort is too far back, or the centre of resistance is too far foward. Lee helm is the opposite. Alterations to the disposition of the crew or the position of the centreboard may help balance the boat. If these changes are insufficient, adjust the fore stay and shrouds, so that the mast is raked forward to reduce weather helm, and raked aft to eliminate lee helm. When the correct balance is achieved, lock the shroud rigging screws and in future, tension the rigging by the fore stay rigging screw.

Sailing in strong winds
Crew and helmsman lean out and use their weight to counteract the heeling effect. A planing hull sails faster when the mast is as near vertical as possible. As planing speed is reached, the crew should shift their weight aft in a rocking

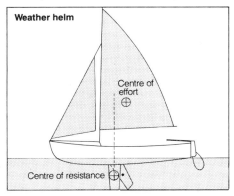

Weather helm
Centre of effort
Centre of resistance

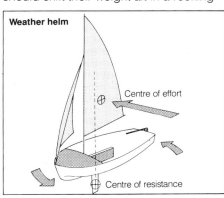

Weather helm
Centre of effort
Centre of resistance

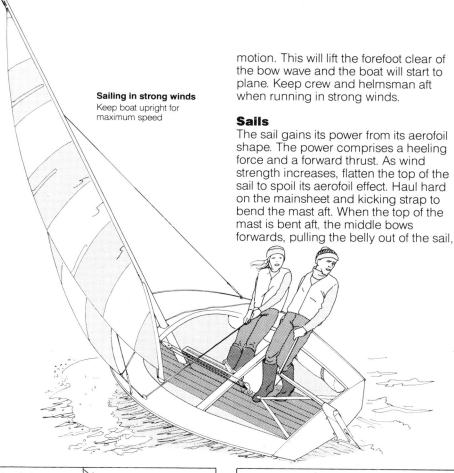

Sailing in strong winds
Keep boat upright for maximum speed

motion. This will lift the forefoot clear of the bow wave and the boat will start to plane. Keep crew and helmsman aft when running in strong winds.

Sails

The sail gains its power from its aerofoil shape. The power comprises a heeling force and a forward thrust. As wind strength increases, flatten the top of the sail to spoil its aerofoil effect. Haul hard on the mainsheet and kicking strap to bend the mast aft. When the top of the mast is bent aft, the middle bows forwards, pulling the belly out of the sail, and flattening it. This reduces the heel and thrust from the top of the sail — but the lower part remains sheeted in hard and driving effectively.

Cunningham tensioner

As wind force increases, the sails change profile, and the power points of the sails will move aft. This increases turbulence at the leech, and forward drive is wasted. By heaving down the lanyard which passes through the grommet in the luff, the sail is gathered at the luff, and the power point is moved forward again.

Sheeting

The slot between the leech of the foresail and the mainsail should be wider in strong winds than in light winds. This can be achieved by positioning the sheet fairleads close to the sides of the boat, or by allowing the mast to bend to leeward by tightening the lee side shroud. A foresail that is sheeted in too closely will backwind the luff of the mainsail.

Rolling

The reason for downwind rolling (which is often unnerving and very difficult to control) is excessive sail twist, which allows wind to spill from the upper part of the mainsail. By hauling in on the mainsheet, tightening the kicking strap to bring the boom down hard, then letting out the mainsheet, the rolling will be eliminated or at least reduced.

Fair weather — very light breeze

The movement of the crew and helmsman about the boat should be slow and deliberate. Sudden movements shake the wind out of the sails. Heel the boat so the sails sag into an aerofoil shape by their own weight, and every breath of wind is utilized for forward motion.

Tell-tails and burgee will give very little useful information about wind direction or the set of the sails. Keep a close eye on the water to windward and watch for the darkening of the surface, caused by a slight breeze. Sails should be full, with the mast kept straight, outhauls and Cunningham tensioner all slack.

In all weather conditions make the best use of the tides and currents, etc. In near calm conditions a longer route that utilizes a strong current or avoids an adverse one, may be the quickest.

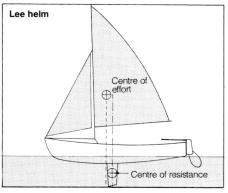

Lee helm

Centre of effort

Centre of resistance

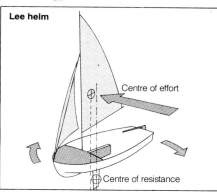

Lee helm

Centre of effort

Centre of resistance

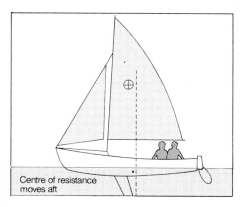

Centre of resistance moves aft

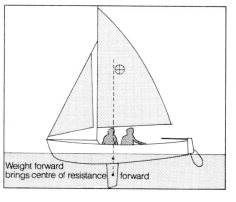

Weight forward brings centre of resistance forward

Chapter 10

Motorboats and Auxiliaries

Diesel inboard motor

The illustration shows a typical inboard diesel motor. Like most marine engines, this unit has been marinized to make it suitable for use in the confined space and often hostile working conditions onboard a small boat. Mounting points have been raised so that the motor is suspended on brackets, level with the crankshaft, and arrangements are made to drain the sump by hand pump rather than by the customary means of unscrewing a drain plug in the base of the sump. Cooling and lubrication filtering arrangements are also slightly altered.

Diesel engines are heavier, slower-revving and more reliable than petrol engines of the same power. Unlike the latter, they do not depend upon external carburation, or an electrical spark for ignition. Instead, spontaneous combustion occurs when the fuel is injected into the cylinder as the piston reaches maximum compression. Assuming that the cylinders provide adequate compression, and that the fuel is clean and injected at the correct moment of compression, very little will go wrong.

This section points to the maintenance and running procedures that the owner should follow to ensure a satisfactory service from his motor. It is not recommended that he undertakes any mechanical repairs to his diesel, unless they are obvious and straight-forward. Fault-finding and repair should be left to an engineer.

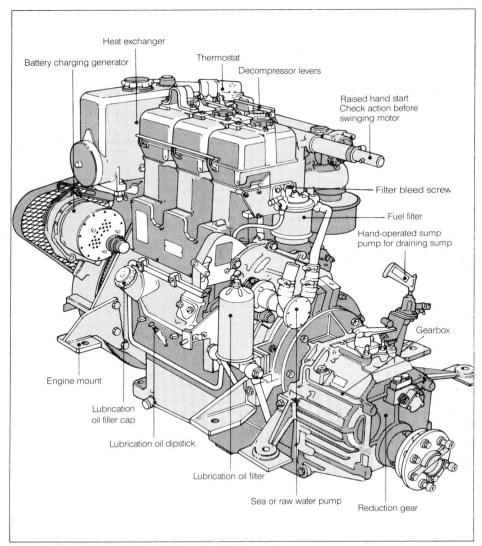

Lister HRW3 water cooled propulsion engine

Lubrication

Most marinized diesel engines can be mounted at an angle of up to 15° from the horizontal. Where a greater angle of propshaft is required, constant velocity joints have to be fitted between the engine and the shaft. Provided that the motor is installed permanently within these limitations of angle, the motor will be unaffected by heeling.

A diesel that is working normally will burn lubrication oil in a quantity equivalent to approximately ½ per cent of the fuel oil consumed. Check the engine oil levels daily and top up with the correct grade of lubrication oil whenever necessary. Oil should be changed and oil filters renewed every 250 running hours, or every 4 months (whichever is sooner). An engine with a working speed of 3,000 revs should have its oil and filter changed more frequently. On these higher revving engines oil types may differ — check your handbook.

The sump pump is shown in the illustration, and also the lubrication oil filter. The filter is often installed horizontally, or even upside down, and when the filter is changed there is usually a likelihood of oil spilling. Spread rags around the engine to catch the drips and spillage as the filter is removed.

Oil pressure

Most diesel installations are equipped with an oil pressure gauge, warning light, and sometimes an audible alarm as well. Operating pressure can vary considerably. Initial oil pressure is often about 70-80lbs p.s.i. which drops in some engines as low as 15lbs p.s.i. as the motor warms. Provided that there are no other obvious signs of malfunctioning and that the oil pressure warning light or audible alarm do not come on, there is little reason to be concerned.

Fuel

Diesels must be supplied with clean fuel, uncontaminated with water. A system of filters and water traps should ensure that an adequate supply of clean fuel reaches the engine. A supply of spare fuel filter elements should be carried. In normal conditions with clean fuel, the filter should be replaced every 1,000 running hours. Watertraps in the base of the oil tank and fuel filters, should be drained regularly, as well as the centrifugal water separator, if fitted.

Once the fuel filter has been changed, it will be necessary to bleed the fuel line to clear it of air locks. There is a special order in which this simple procedure is carried out, which is illustrated below.

There are two main types of fuel injection system. In figure 3 below, a pump is fitted as an integral unit with the injectors. The alternative is the inline (figures 1 and 2).

When bleeding the fuel line, especially when the starter motor is used to operate the fuel lift pump, wrap rags around the venting unit to collect excess diesel fuel that splashes out.

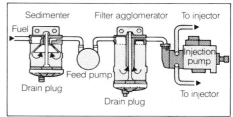

1 Diesel fuel filter system

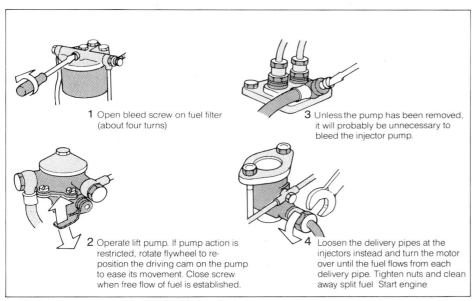

1 Open bleed screw on fuel filter (about four turns)

3 Unless the pump has been removed, it will probably be unnecessary to bleed the injector pump.

2 Operate lift pump. If pump action is restricted, rotate flywheel to re-position the driving cam on the pump to ease its movement. Close screw when free flow of fuel is established.

4 Loosen the delivery pipes at the injectors instead and turn the motor over until the fuel flows from each delivery pipe. Tighten nuts and clean away split fuel Start engine

2 Bleeding procedure for typical inline fuel pump system

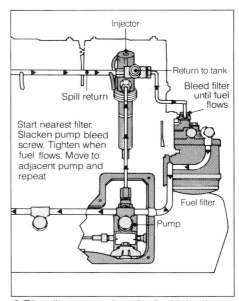

3 Bleeding procedure for fuel injection pump

Air

The diesel needs copious quantities of clean air for satisfactory combustion, and in the case of air cooled units, an additional volume of air is needed to dissipate the heat.

Combustion

The air inlet should be situated so the supply of air is fresh and clean. It must not be positioned near the exhaust outlet or close to the water-line. A variety of paper element air filters are fitted which should be inspected and replaced regularly. Every 1,000 running hours is a suitable interval in clean air conditions, but daily inspection is necessary where the air is sandy or polluted.

Some diesels are fitted with an oil bath air cleaner, in which a gauze element is moistened by the oil in which it rests. However, oil bath filters are not recommended in small boats if there is a possibility that in rough conditions the oil will spill into the induction system and cause the motor to race. If this happens, block the air inlet to choke the motor.

The efficiency of the filter can be retained if the oil bath is drained, but the element is washed and dipped in oil each day, before being replaced in the air cleaner.

Engine cooling

At least 33 per cent of the fuel consumed by a diesel is converted directly into heat, which has to be dissipated by the engine cooling system. Engines should be well-ventilated with sufficient air flow to supply the engine with cool air for combustion and to prevent a build-up in temperature in the engine space. Ducting both for the inlet and the outlet of the engine must be of adequate size and cross-sectional area.

Inadequate air supply will result in a black exhaust, and tail-off in engine performance at higher engine revolutions.

Cooling

Cooling systems are described in more detail on page 255.

The exhaust will give a good indication of the condition of the engine and the state of the fuel air mixture. An engine at full throttle that is working well will have an exhaust that is clear and just visible.

Diesel inboard motors Motorboats and auxiliaries

Fault-finding chart

Problem	Cause	Remedy
Engine is difficult to start	Overload trip not lifted	Lift to give extra fuel for starting in cold weather
	Unsuitable lubricating oil	Drain and refill with correct grade
	Incorrect grade of fuel	Drain, refill and bleed system
	No fuel	Fill tank, bleed system
	Choked fuel filter	Clean and bleed system
	Air lock in fuel line	Bleed fuel system
Black, smoky exhaust	Engine overloaded	Oversize propeller fited, reduce load
	Inlet air temperature too high	Install ducting to draw air from cooler source
	Choked air filter	Clean
	Unsuitable fuel oil or water in fuel	Drain fuel system and refill with correct fuel
		Bleed fuel lines
Smoky blue exhaust	Piston rings worn, cylinder bore worn	Seek expert assistance
Engine stops	No fuel	Fill and bleed
	Air or water in fuel	Drain off water and bleed system
	Choked fuel filter or blocked nozzle	Inspect and rectify
	Overload	Allow engine to cool slowly, turn it over by hand to ensure moving parts are free. Restart and check load
	Overheating	Air temperature too high, hot air may be re-circulating
Loss of power	Choked air filter	Clean
	Choked fuel filter	Clean and bleed system
	Choked exhaust system	Dismantle and clean
	Fuel injector pump out of order	Seek expert assistance
Failure to obtain normal speed	Engine started on overload	Reduce load
	Fuel system not properly primed	Check and rectify
	Insufficient fuel supply	Clean fuel filter. Fuel pump may be out of adjustment
Low oil pressure	Low oil level	Check dip-stick and rectify
	Oil strainer choked	Clean
	Fractured pipe or leaking joint	Inspect and rectify
	Badly worn bearings	Seek expert assistance
	Oil cooler choked	Clean
Overheating (air cooled)	Cooling air is re-circulated	Deflect outlet from inlet
	Fins on cylinder head are blocked with dirt	Clean
	Cooling air inlet obstructed	Check installation manual
	Outlet obstructed	Check installation manual
Overheating (water cooled)	Overloaded	Reduce load
	Lubricating oil or water pressure is low	Check level and replenish
	Waterpump belt is slipping	Adjust
	Blockage in water cooling system	Check and renew hoses, remove cylinder block, inspection doors. Clean out water channels and blockages in cylinder head

The illustration shows a typical drive shaft, coupling, and propeller configuration. The propeller is fitted on a taper turned at the end of the prop shaft, locked by a key, and retained by a castle nut and split pin. The shaft is supported by a hull-mounted bracket, which incorporates a water-lubricated bearing. The stern tube conducts the shaft through the hull. At the inboard end, the tube is sealed to prevent leaks, but is sufficiently free to allow the prop shaft to revolve. The stern tube (or log, if it is made from wood) is often filled with waterproof grease, unless a rubber water-lubricated bearing is fitted at the end. In this case it is flooded right to the packing gland, with more

water sometimes injected into the tube from the engine cooling system.

At the inboard end of the tube is a watertight packing gland (or stuffing box), perhaps combined with an oil- or water-lubricated bearing. If the bearing is omitted, the gland is clamped to the tube by a couple of jubilee clips and a short length of reinforced hose. The gland comprises a set of grease- or graphite-impregnated fibre washers that wedge against the shaft as the tightening nut is adjusted. Intermediate bearings are spaced along the shaft between 30-40 shaft diameters apart, the spacing dependent upon the shaft's flexibility.

The shaft coupling flange is connected to a similar flange on the drive side of the marine reduction gearbox. This usually incorporates a thrust bearing, in the absence of which a suitable bearing will be fitted on the shaft between the flange and the packing gland.

This is a simple and efficient system of transferring the power from the motor to the propeller. The Z drive, inboard/outboard, or hydraulic drives, have the advantage of versatility and compactness, but they require specialist servicing and maintenance which is beyond the scope of this book. Procedures for maintenance and alignment are described below.

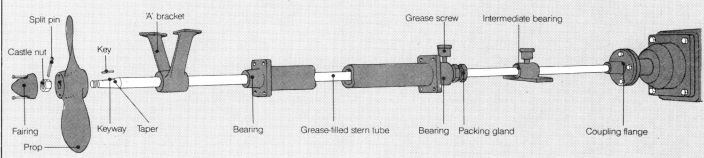

Split pin · Castle nut · Key · 'A' bracket · Grease screw · Intermediate bearing
Fairing · Prop · Keyway · Taper · Bearing · Grease-filled stern tube · Bearing · Packing gland · Coupling flange

Leaks

Some of the leaks commonly associated with propeller shafts that are caused by poor initial construction, lack of maintenance and vibration, are described together with some suggested remedies on page 293. A very common source of leakage is at the packing gland. The compression of the fibre washers is adjusted by releasing the locking nut and turning the packing nut. By tightening, the sealing washers are pressed hard against the prop shaft. This will reduce seepage through the gland, but may also bind the prop shaft so that it does not turn freely. To set the pressure

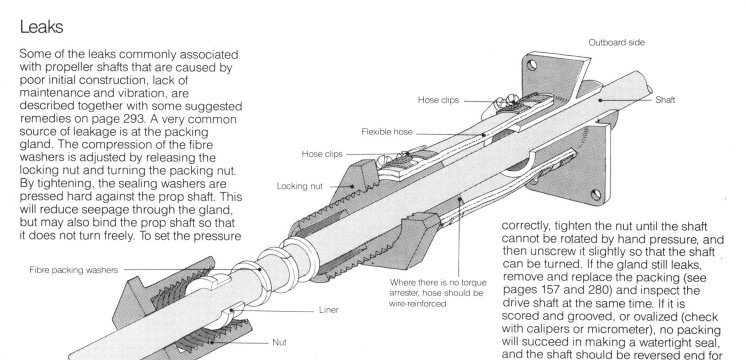

Outboard side · Hose clips · Flexible hose · Hose clips · Locking nut · Shaft · Fibre packing washers · Where there is no torque arrester, hose should be wire-reinforced · Liner · Nut

correctly, tighten the nut until the shaft cannot be rotated by hand pressure, and then unscrew it slightly so that the shaft can be turned. If the gland still leaks, remove and replace the packing (see pages 157 and 280) and inspect the drive shaft at the same time. If it is scored and grooved, or ovalized (check with calipers or micrometer), no packing will succeed in making a watertight seal, and the shaft should be reversed end for end or replaced.

Vibration

Vibration is always a problem with internal combustion engines, but it diminishes as the number of cylinders is increased. The engines on most yachts and motor cruisers have between 1-8 cylinders, single cylinder engines perhaps, causing the most vibration. The likely causes of vibration in an engine and prop shaft unit can be divided into the following components.

Engine
Faulty, worn or misfiring engine.

Vibration caused by the inherent imbalance in its form of operation.

Vibration caused by the torque of the crankshaft and flywheel trying to rotate the motor against the resistance of the engine mountings.

Vibration caused by the equal and opposite force of the propeller trying to thrust the engine forwards (when under power).

Prop shaft
Vibration caused by parallel or conical misalignments of the prop shaft.

Vibration caused by torsional stress as prop shaft 'twists' under load.

Vibration caused by bent prop shaft or misaligned intermediate bearings.

Vibration caused by an ovalized prop shaft bearing.

Propeller
Vibration caused by the propeller cavitating.

Vibration caused by damaged propeller.

Vibration which is a result of misalignments of the drive couplings causing the propeller to flail.

Vibration of a rudder with worn bearings shaking in the turbulence caused by the propeller.

Where vibration is a problem, some and perhaps most of these elements will be present. To a certain degree they are interlinked: the motor transmitting its vibrations down the prop shaft, while the propeller does the same in the reverse direction. An additional problem is that once a particular resonance is established, other fittings, not directly connected, may resonate in sympathy, contributing to the overall noise level. Vibration has a fatiguing effect on all materials. Once the causes have been identified and remedied, check all fastenings subjected to vibration, to ensure they are tight, and check the hull structure to see if it has been weakened.

Engine beds and mounts
Marine engines are usually suspended by feet or brackets fixed to the crankcase. The feet are normally level with the crankshaft in which position they help reduce the turning moment of the engine. Bearers rest against the hull or framing and are longer than the engine so that its weight and stresses are dissipated over a wide area. Intercostal bracing pieces, shaped to fit below the sump, hold the bearers in alignment, and tie the bearing assembly into one unit to equalize loading on the hull. Engine bearers are usually wooden. Soft wood bearers should be capped with iron channelling or a hardwood strip, with large steel plate washers set beneath each foot. Bearers are bonded into place in a fibreglass hull, and bolted in a wooden hull. The problems associated with de-lamination of the bonding are described on page 77. Holding bolts often work loose, particularly where the engine bed shrinks. Vibration will result, and if the bolts are carried right through the frames and fasten against the outer skin, they will leak as well.

Engine
Excessive vibration will occur if a motor is functioning badly, misfiring, or overloaded. When the engine performs normally in neutral, slight movement at the engine mounts or between bearers, frames or the bonding will be evident. If all the bolts etc. are tight, and there is no evidence of excessive shaking, it is likely that the vibration emanates from another part of the drive train.

Resilient mountings
A motor will be quietest if it is clamped directly on to solid beds in a substantially framed heavy boat. The noise and vibration caused by the motor fitted into a lighter hull can be reduced by the

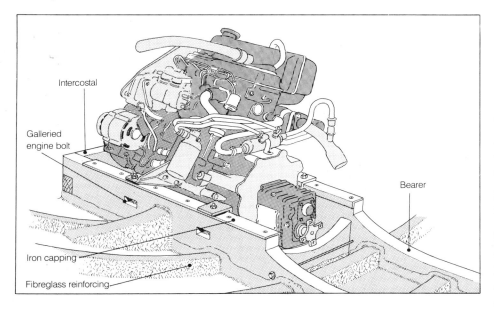

Intercostal

Galleried engine bolt

Bearer

Iron capping

Fibreglass reinforcing

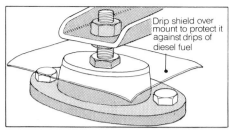
Resilient mount

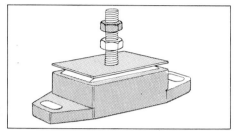
Flexible engine mounting

use of resilient mountings. These are designed as fail-safe fittings that will

hold the motor even if the boat is capsized, or if the rubber shears. The rubber in the bearings cushions the boat from engine-induced vibrations. It is important that the correct type and size of mounting is fitted to the motor, and that all other pipework and the drive connections to the engine should be flexible as well. A shield should be fitted above each resilient mount to protect it from drips of diesel oil which will degrade its synthetic rubber components.

Prop shaft vibration

If the engine beds are secure and the motor is bolted tightly so that it is unable to move (apart from the small degree of movement permitted by the resilient mounting blocks) it will be safe to assume that the cause of the vibration is either in the drive train or the propeller. The most common causes of vibration in the prop shaft are misalignments between engine and shaft, and poorly positioned or insufficient intermediate

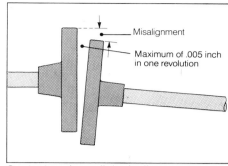
Conical and parallel misalignment

bearings between drive flanges and packing gland.

It is usually the motor that moves out of alignment. Use the procedures described below to test its alignment at the drive flange. There is very little tolerance to spare: alignment should be within .002 inches (.005cm) at any point between the flanges, with a total maximum of .005 inches (.013cm).

Flexible coupling

Engine prop shaft misalignments cannot be taken up by fitting flexible coupling. These will absorb some engine induced vibration, but they are not designed to cope with conical or parallel misalignments in excess of the figures quoted above. At low shaft speeds they may operate quietly and without trouble. Misalignments however will still be present, and at higher shaft speeds will cause the shaft to whip and the bearings to wear and loosen. Where misalignments are inevitable — perhaps

where the prop shaft angle is greater than 15° from horizontal, a constant velocity joint such as Hardy Spicer or 'Scatra' Coupling should be installed between the motor and shaft, with shaft supporting bearings at each end of the coupling. Seek professional advice before starting work of this kind as it may be necessary to incorporate an additional thrust bearing. In most installations, marine engines can be tilted to the appropriate angle, and all that is required is care and patience in aligning the drive components.

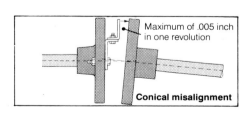
Flexible shaft coupling

Checking and aligning

Final checking will have to be carried out with the boat afloat. The major part of the work, however, can be completed with the boat hauled out.

Both conical and parallel misalignments can be measured with a dial gauge, which can also be used to test if the shaft between intermediates is bent or distorted. In the absence of a dial gauge, feeler gauge or even slips of thin paper can be used to measure conical misalignment, a bracket and feeler gauge will measure parallel misalignment.

Parallel misalignment is when the motor

shaft and the propeller shaft are parallel to, but not in line with, each other.

Parallel misalignment

Measure this first, using the dial gauge and flange (or feeler gauge and flange) as illustrated. Horizontal adjustments are difficult to make, as the engine holding bolts will have to be removed and re-positioned, and the original bolt holes may have to be plugged with dowels soaked in epoxy resin and sawn off flush before new ones can be bored. Use a crowbar or jack to move the motor into the correct position. Once lateral adjustments have been made, check for conical errors caused by the motor

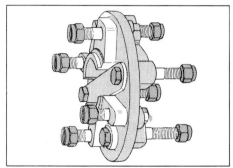

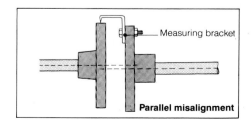

Propeller shaft and engine mountings Motorboats and auxiliaries

Parallel misalignment (continued)

being angled away from the centre-line when viewed from above. Check this with a dial gauge, or with feeler gauges slipped between the flanges. Correct before fitting the bolts.

Drill through the mounting feet into the bearer. Where the hole has been ovalized by the drill to allow slight lateral movement, the bolt will have to be cast into position.

Insert the nut and washers into the galleries in the side of the engine bearers, and hold them in place with a bolt tightened from above. Pack Plasticine or modelling clay beneath the nut and then withdraw the engine bearing bolt. Grease the bolt and the sides of the engine bearers. Make a thick epoxy resin and colodial silica mixture, and press it into the bolt holes.

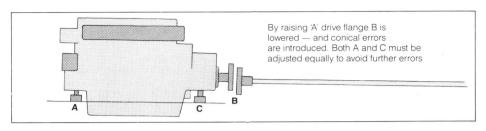

By raising 'A' drive flange B is lowered — and conical errors are introduced. Both A and C must be adjusted equally to avoid further errors

Gently insert the bolts so that only a small proportion of resin is displaced, then tighten the bolts. Clean away the excess epoxy resin and leave the resin to cure.

Conical misalignments

The remaining adjustments involve raising or lowering the motor until the prop shaft and drive shaft are parallel and in line. An illustration showing how conical errors are measured features on the previous page.

Since adjusting the bolts of the resilient mountings or shimming the engine bearers may result in further conical and parallel errors, both checks should be carried out as the packing or adjustments proceed. Once the flanges seem in almost perfect alignment, the holding bolts should be secured with lock nuts. If wedges are used to raise the motor while shims are added, check after the wedges have been removed, in case the motor settled as its weight came on to the shims.

Problems in alignment

If it is found to be impossible to eliminate conical misalignments, check that the propeller shaft is running true. This is tested by placing the dial gauge against the shaft which is rotated by hand.

If, after the two flanges have been aligned, and bolted together, there still seems to be excessive vibration from the drive shaft, check to see if it is whipping. A dial gauge is too delicate an instrument for this. Instead, position a pivoted batten (as illustrated) beneath the shaft, with one end clamped to a frame or floor. Rest the batten against the prop shaft and tie a restraining lanyard to its end.

Shaft misalignment is exaggerated by the length of the batten, but movement indicates a distortion or inbalance in the drive train. Pull the batten away from the shaft once the source of the vibration

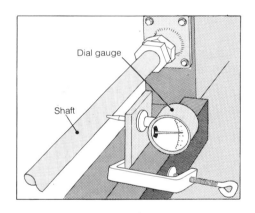

Dial gauge

Shaft

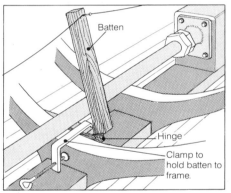

Batten

Hinge

Clamp to hold batten to frame.

has been identified. The causes of movement in the prop shaft may be one of the following.

Intermediate bearings are too far apart: This will not be the problem if the intermediates are spaced less than 30 shaft diameters apart. Seek professional

advice before fitting additonal intermediate bearings.

Tests for other causes will have to be carried out with the boat out of the water, when the condition of the propeller and the alignment of the shaft can be checked as described below.

Propeller

Inspect the propeller. Kinks or bends at the edges will cause vibration. Surface pitting at the forward side of the blades, suggests that the propeller is cavitating. Check the location of the propeller: the hull immediately forward of the prop should be nicely faired (abrupt edges will cause turbulence and cavitation).

The propeller should be well below the surface of the water and clear of the rudder. Remember that clearances with the boat pulled out of the water and when the motor is stopped will not be the same as when the boat is afloat and travelling under power. The whirling effect of an unbalanced propeller,

coupled with a slight hull flexing, may reduce clearances by at least half an inch (l2mm), and this reduction may bring the propeller too close to, and perhaps touch the rudder. The minimum clearance between the propeller and any obstruction is $1/12$ propeller diameter. It is better to have more clearance, particularly when sternpost or rudder are poorly faired.

Remove the screw cover and inspect the propeller shaft fitting. A poorly fitted propeller can cause vibrations that are very difficult to trace.

With the fairing and nut removed, a key will be visible preventing the propeller from rotating on the shaft. If this is inserted incorrectly, it will offset the propeller. Remove the propeller by easing it aft, tapping it with a hammer and a block of wood if necessary. Remove the key,. Clean all parts of the propeller, shaft, nuts etc., and grease

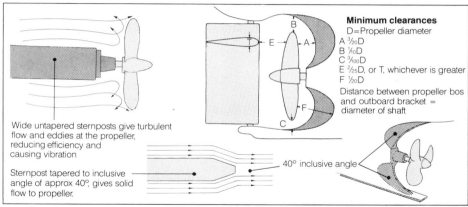

Minimum clearances
D=Propeller diameter
A $\frac{3}{20}$D
B $\frac{1}{10}$D
C $\frac{3}{100}$D
E $\frac{2}{25}$D, or T, whichever is greater
F $\frac{1}{20}$D

Distance between propeller boss and outboard bracket = diameter of shaft

Wide untapered sternposts give turbulent flow and eddies at the propeller, reducing efficiency and causing vibration

Sternpost tapered to inclusive angle of approx 40°, gives solid flow to propeller.

40° inclusive angle

Recommended practices for hull fairing and propeller clearance.

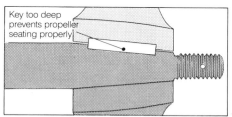

Key too deep prevents propeller seating properly

Oversize key offsets propeller.

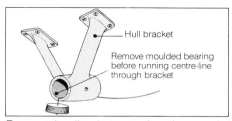

Hull bracket

Remove moulded bearing before running centre-line through bracket

Run a string line between bearings and drive flange and check intermediate bearings.

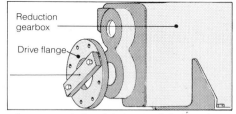

Reduction gearbox

Drive flange

them. Replace the propeller, making sure that it is seated properly on the tapered end to the propeller shaft. Line the keyways, and insert the key. If it is too tight, change it for a smaller one, or grind it to size on a plate of glass covered with grinding paste. The key should be a smooth fit — too tight, and it will be difficult to remove at the end of the season, too loose, and the propeller will snatch on the shaft. With the key in place, fit the washer nut and split pin.

Shaft and bearings
Withdraw the prop shaft, after releasing the packing gland and drive flange. Remove the water lubricated bearing from the hull bracket, and run a string line or wire through the 'A' bracket, and up through the stern tube. Attach it to a batten bolted across the drive flange fitted to the reduction gearbox. Pull the line tight, and measure the offsets for each bearing. Adjust their position where necessary.

As the shaft is removed, take the opportunity to check the condition of the bearings and replace where necessary. If there are signs of excessive, or uneven, wear in the bearings, take the propeller shaft to a marine engineer, and ask him to check it for longitudinal distortions and ovalizing.

Corrosion

In order to control corrosion and eliminate shaft-generated electrical interference, couple the shaft to the electrical bonding system of the boat via a brush which remains in electrical contact while the shaft rotates (see pages 268-290)

The choice of metals used in the propeller shaft, stern tube, and propeller will vary, according to the construction material of the hull, as well as other factors such as cost, and weight. The table below outlines some satisfactory combinations of materials.

Fibreglass and wooden hulls
Stern tube bronze with gunmetal castings
Shafts and propellers from stainless steel or bronze

There are many different alloys of all of these metals, and their exact type and compatibility should be checked by a marine engineer if there are corrosion problems.

Steel hulls
Stern tube steel or cast iron
Shafts and propellers stainless steel or monel.

Both the propeller and tube should be protected by zinc spraying.

Aluminium
Tube — aluminium alloy.
Propeller — aluminium alloy (both of marine standard).
Shaft — stainless or monel. If the alloys are used, the combination of stainless and aluminium alloy is compatible. If a manganese bronze propeller is fitted instead of an aluminium one, a zinc sacrificial anode should be fitted to the hull or prop shaft bracket.

See pages 121 and 290.

Petrol inboard motor

The petrol-driven inboard motor will hold few mysteries for those reasonably familiar with the power unit of a family car.

In contrast to diesel engines of similar weight, petrol engines generate greater power at higher engine revolutions.

These qualities make them ideally suited to stern drive installations where a diesel motor of similar power output would push the boat out of trim. This is why outboard motors are invariably petrol-powered.

It is, however, the cold and damp conditions on board boat, coupled with irregular use, that make a petrol motor so much more temperamental than a diesel.

Petrol engines also present a fire hazard. Unlike diesel fuel which needs to be heated to a high temperature before it will ignite, petrol has a low flash point, and evaporates to form a heavy, highly explosive vapour.

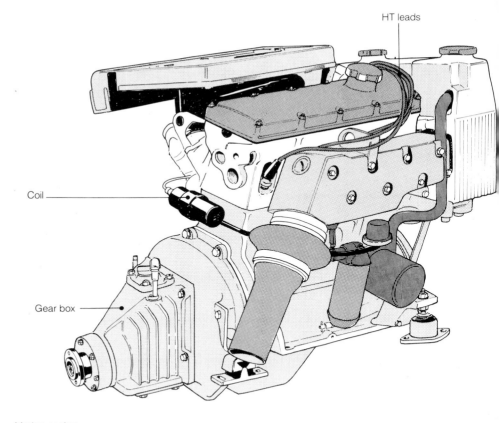

Marine engine

Safety
Petrol is a highly volatile fuel which vaporizes to a heavier-than-air gas which when mixed with air forms an explosive vapour. Thorough precautions have to be taken to avoid fire on board. Fuel leaks must be repaired immediately. Fuel pipes should be made from steel or copper or fire resistant flexible hose, not flexible plastic (which will melt or burn through in the event of an engine room fire). Pumps and filters should be fitted with metal sediment sumps, not glass or plastic, as these are easily broken.

Petrol vapour, particularly in the engine compartment, presents a serious potential hazard, due to the electrical equipment associated with the engine and the other appliances installed there.

Very careful attention must be paid to the design and installation of the ignition system, starter motors, alternators and other ancillary devices. In the United States of America, such protection against the ignition of surrounding flammable gasses is referred to as ignition protection.

Servicing and maintenance
As with the diesel engine, it is recommended that repair of the engine unit should be left to a professional marine engineer. There are, however, some essential adjustments that can be successfully tackled by the boat owner. Occasionally professional help may not be available; it is sensible, therefore, to carry a complete set of tools, a spare set of air and oil filters, and a comprehensive stock of electrical components.

Lubrication should be checked frequently and the oil topped up when necessary. Oil and oil filters should be changed regularly.

Petrol tanks
These should be installed away from the engine compartment and arranged with the filler cap positioned so accidental fuel spillages do not trickle below decks. Tanks are fitted with baffles to prevent excessive movement of the liquid in the tank. Each part of the tank and the fuel lines etc., should be connected into the bonding system of the boat. Petrol must be clean and free from sediment or dirt. Filters in the tank and also in the pump ensure that the fuel reaching the carburettor is clean. Inspect them regularly.

Regular replacement of filter elements is the best insurance against contaminated or dirty fuel.

If excessive deposits of sediment or dirt are found in the fuel line, take the first opportunity to check and replace the filter elements. It is often in the roughest conditions that sediment in the fuel tank is stirred and drawn into the pipe lines.

Tuning the engine

Adjustments to the idling and high speed jets must be made when the engine is warmed up and with the ignition set correctly.

The screw on the throttle arm should be set so that the motor idles in neutral with a smooth and regular rhythm.

Turn the knurled idling or low speed jet clockwise. This will reduce the quantity of fuel in the fuel/air mixture. As the jet is turned, the motor will begin to fire irregularly. Gently turn the screw in a clockwise direction until smooth running is restored.

High speed adjustment
This has to be adjusted with the engine under load. The adjustment of the low speed jet will not affect the performance or setting of the high speed jet.

Open the throttle and take the boat out into open water where she can gather speed. When the motor is warm, turn down the high speed jet or adjustment screw, until the motor begins to misfire and run roughly. This is the lean fuel setting. Turn up the adjustment and the boat should accelerate as the power output of the motor increases. Gradually and slowly increase the proportion of fuel (by turning up the adjustment) until further turning results in no additional increase in performance. Turn back the adjustment slightly for an economical but efficient setting.

Ignition timing
Although there are several elements in a petrol-powered motor that can go wrong, most faults with new or well maintained installations originate at the ignition.

A precondition of trouble-free operation is that the motor should be kept clean and dry. Accumulations of dirt and oil or moisture on the engine or wiring will cause trouble and may prevent engine ignition.

The chart on page 248 can be used to trace faults in the fuel and ignition system of petrol-driven engines. If the ignition system is clean, with all connections tight and insulation in good condition, the following tests can be carried out to identify the reasons for the lack of spark. The procedures also describe how to set the points and time the motor correctly when a spark has been re-established.

The wiring diagram of the ignition system sets out clearly the sequence and mode of operation of the ignition system.

Starter switch
This breaks the low voltage wiring to the coil and distributor. In its fairly exposed position in the wheelhouse or cockpit, it is frequently a source of trouble caused by dirt or moisture entering its mechanism. Oil the switch or the key, and provide the switch with a cover.

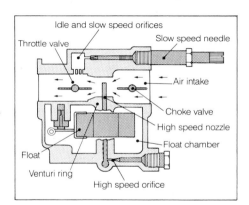

Idle and slow speed orifices
Throttle valve
Slow speed needle
Air intake
Choke valve
High speed nozzle
Float chamber
Float
Venturi ring
High speed orifice

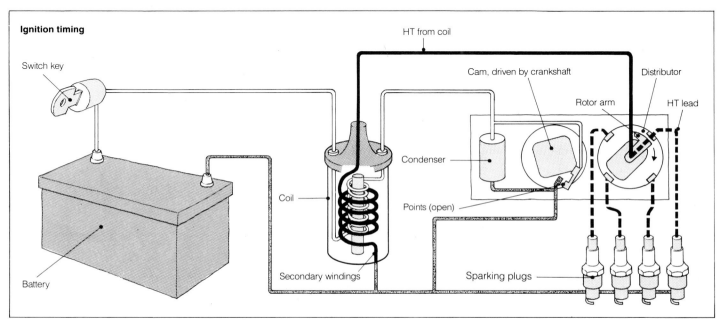

Ignition timing
Switch key
HT from coil
Cam, driven by crankshaft
Distributor
Rotor arm
HT lead
Condenser
Coil
Points (open)
Battery
Secondary windings
Sparking plugs

Ignition coil

The coil employs the principle of electro-magnetic induction (as in a transformer), which produces very high voltage in the secondary winding, as a result of interruptions of the low voltage, primary coil current. The high voltage current comes from the centre terminal of the coil and goes to the distributor cap.

Distributor

In series with the coil and starter switch in the primary low tension circuit are the points and the capacitor. These are usually installed in the distributor, which also houses the separate circuitry of the HT distribution system to the sparking plugs. If it is remembered that the high tension and the low tension circuits are related but distinct, fault-finding and timing will be much easier.

The points form a switch which is activated by the rotating cam in the centre of the distributor. Although marine systems vary in their distributor layout, it is normal for the cam to have as many flat faces as there are cylinders. When the cam, which is rotated at half the speed of the engine (on a four-stroke engine) opens the points, the low tension circuit is broken, and by electro-magnetic induction, a very high voltage is produced in the secondary windings of the coil.

The condenser/capacitor absorbs the energy present whilst the points are opening, thereby protecting them from damage caused by arcing.

The points have to be adjusted so that they open and close sufficiently to make and break the low tension circuit, and are synchronized to induce the spark at the moment the piston reaches close to the top of its compression stroke.

The high voltage current goes straight to the distributor, where it makes electrical contact with the rotor arm, attached to the top end of the rotating cam, which makes contact with the spark leads as it rotates in the insulated housing of the distributor cap. The timing of the spark is related to engine speed and occurs at some point before the piston reaches TDC.

For full power to be obtained from a petrol engine over its entire speed range it is necessary to vary the time at which ignition takes place. Normally a spark would occur just before the piston reaches the top of the cylinder, but with increased speed, better performance is achieved if the spark occurs even earlier in the cycle. The amount by which the spark is advanced must be carefully controlled, as an over-advanced ignition may be detrimental and cause loss of power. If the spark occurs too late, the engine can become overheated. The automatic advance and retard is obtained mechanically by a centrifugal device and additionally by a vacuum-operated distributor advance mechanism.

Fault finding

The chart on page 248 enables the general cause of the malfunction to be identified. If, after checking cables and connections, it is found that there is still no spark at the outlet of the coil or at the plugs, change the coil, condenser, leads and plugs. Always carry new tested spares aboard, as it is much easier to replace parts that might be faulty than it is to check their working characteristics in all engine operating conditions.

Replace the coil and leads first, then condenser and points. Check between each operation to see if a healthy spark has been re-established.
If sparking is erratic, inspect the HT wiring. Wires should not be bunched together or run through conduit. As far as possible, run them separately, without touching either the engine block or any other wiring. Arcing across the HT leads is dangerous (because pockets of heavy petrol vapour may be ignited by the spark) and causes intermittent firing.

If no spark is visible, lift the cap of the distributor and look inside. Grease or oil deposits on the inside capping, traces of soot, or cracking may lead to tracking and shorting to earth. Clean the inside of the cap, and replace it if it is cracked, or if the terminal points are corroded.

Setting the points

If the points are poorly adjusted, the spark will be weak or erratic. To adjust the points, switch off the ignition, and remove the distributor cap. Lift off the rotor arm, and crank the motor slowly. Watch the points until the cam pushes them apart.

Inspect the surface of the points. If the points are clean and flat, rub sandpaper between their faces to clean them. Arcing across the points leaves them pitted or singed. Remove and replace them, taking care that the new set is installed correctly.

Slip a feeler gauge between the points. This should measure about .015 inches (.038mm). Check with the workshop manual to find the correct setting, and adjust by releasing the setting screw and altering the position of the stationary terminal. Lock the setting screw and turn the motor a few times before re-checking to make certain that the setting is correct.

In the absence of a workshop manual, the correct points gap can be approximated as half the maximum opening of the points when they are adjusted so that when the breaker is resting against the flat of the cam, the points barely touch.

In this setting, electrical connection between the two points is poor, and the additional pressure of the spring is needed to ensure a good contact. Crank the engine until the cam lifts the points apart. Measure the distance and halve it. This new setting provides satisfactory contact pressure when the points are closed, and sufficient gap when they are open.

Replace rotor arm and distributor cap.

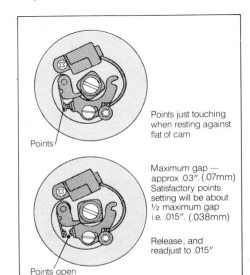

Points

Points just touching when resting against flat of cam

Maximum gap — approx .03". (.07mm) Satisfactory points setting will be about ½ maximum gap i.e. .015". (.038mm)

Release, and readjust to .015"

Points open

Timing

This is a simple operation requiring a few tools and, if possible, the guidance of a workshop manual.

Timing is usually set and checked with the piston of number one cylinder at top dead centre on its compression stroke. Cylinder numbers may be stamped on the engine casting or on the manifold, but if they are not, seek advice.

Once the cylinder is identified, follow the HT lead to the distributor, note which it is, and remove the cap. The piston is approaching top dead centre when the rotor arm nears the HT contact position for the number one cylinder.

A series of small marks will be stamped on the flywheel or on the drive pulley at the other end of the crankshaft. These indicate the top dead centre position of the piston and degrees in advance of TDC. As the piston reaches top, the marks on the flywheel align themselves with an arrow or short pointer fixed to the flywheel casing. Timing is set so that the sparking plug ignites the fuel/air mixture in the cylinder as the piston is about to reach the top of its stroke. To adjust the timing, the body of the distributor is rotated slightly. This moves the point in the distributor cap relative to the rotor.

Release the distributor clamp which is usually just below the body of the distributor, and turn the distributor. The spark is retarded when the distributor is turned in the direction of the rotor arm. When it is turned against the direction of the rotor arm, the spark is advanced. An advanced spark will ignite the fuel mixture earlier in the piston stroke than a retarded spark.

To discover the precise moment at which the points open, and generate the spark, connect a light bulb across the low tension terminals of the coil. When the light goes out, the contact breaker has opened.

With the light indicator connected, and with the distributor cap and spark plugs removed, switch on the ignition. As number one piston reaches top dead centre the light should go out. (It will also be extinguished as the other pistons reach TDC as well, so keep the distributor cap off and watch the alignment of the rotor arm). Position the flywheel in the correct relationship to the

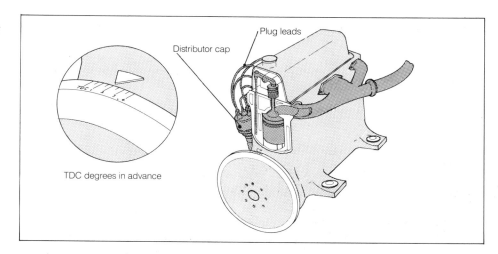

TDC degrees in advance

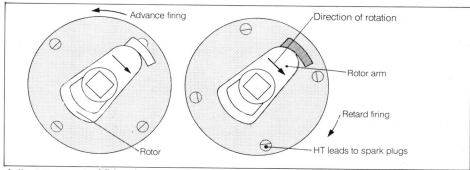

Adjust moment of firing by carefully twisting distributor housing

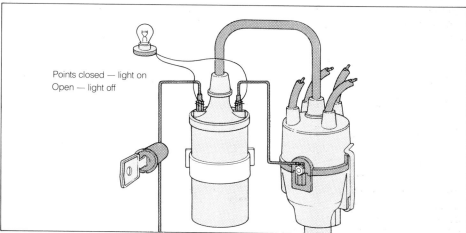

Light extinguished at moment of ignition

marks on the crankcase, (approximately 8° before TDC) and twist the distributor until the light just goes out. Lock the distributor at the base clamp, and replace plugs and distributor cap.

Timing is checked by running the engine under load. If the motor takes up easily and accelerates well, the timing is probably satisfactory, if it hesitates as it accelerates, and does not run happily at full speed, the timing is insufficiently advanced. If, on the other hand, it knocks, or misfires at high revs, and idles roughly when in neutral, the timing will be too far advanced.

247

Petrol inboard motors Motorboats and auxiliaries

Fault-finding chart

The chart can be used to isolate the causes of many of the common faults that bedevil petrol engines.

Inboard motors are usually fitted with a car-type ignition system.

Methods of tracing and rectifying common faults are descibed below. Some modern units are equipped with electronic ignitions. Problems with transistorized ignitions must be left to a marine engineer to rectify.

However, many of the same problems remain. The chart will be useful in isolating and identifying the reasons for poor engine performance.

Engine cranks but does not fire
Ensure there is good ventilation with no evident accumulation of petrol vapour. Remove the HT lead from the spark plug or the distributor cap, and hold it ¼ inch (6mm) away from the engine block. Crank the motor and watch for a spark.

No spark

Spark will be present if all tests and replacements are carried out.

Spark present Remove the spark plug

Check the low tension circuit Lift off the distributor cap, and prise the points apart with a screwdriver. With the ignition on, a small spark should crackle across the points. If the distributor is fitted with two sets of points, wedge one open with a slip of card or plastic and check the other. If the points spark when they are prised apart, the low tension circuit is functioning.

Wet plug A wet plug that smells of petrol means the engine is choked. Replace the plug and the HT lead, and open the choke and the throttle. Crank the motor a dozen times. This will clear the cylinders and the engine will probably start. If it starts, turn the throttle to idle to prevent damage to the engine.

Dry plug Check fuel line, filters and tanks (see page 260).

Dirty plug This will cause uneven firing and poor starting. Remove all the plugs, and clean or replace.

No spark Trace round the low tension circuit with a test lamp.

Switch Connect the coil side of the switch to earth. Via the test lamp, switch on. The bulb should light. If not, the switch is faulty.

Engine runs roughly This may be caused by a combination of factors, including the setting of the carburettor, a blocked fuel line, damaged pistons or valves. Electrical reasons will be one of the following:

Poor connections Check all the wiring, and clean all the wires, both in the HT and the LT circuit. Check the points at every position on the distributor cam. Old motors often wear their cam, so that the points open more in one position than in another.

Check the sparking plugs They should be clean and reasonably new. Change them if in doubt.

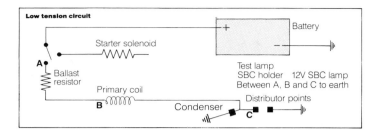

Low tension circuit

Battery

Starter solenoid

A

Ballast resistor

Primary coil

B

Condenser

C

Test lamp
SBC holder   12V SBC lamp
Between A, B and C to earth

Distributor points

Spark at the end of the HT lead from the coil, but not from the distributor Clean the distributor cap. Inspect for cracks, dirt, scorch marks. Soot inside the cap suggests that there is too much lubrication oil in the distributor. Dismantle and clean it, taking care to replace all parts in their correct position.

Cap is clean, but no spark at the plugs Check the runs of the HT wiring. Keep them apart and away from ground. Change the sparking plugs and HT leads if necessary.

When the low tension circuit is functioning, check the high tension circuit. Disconnect the HT lead from the centre of the distributor cap, and hold it about ¼ inch (6mm) from the engine block. With the ignition on, prise the points apart. A bright blue spark should snap across to the engine. If the spark is weak, or orange rather than blue, change the condenser. If there is no spark, change the coil and re-test.

Coil Check the coil in the same way. First, check the battery terminal of the coil. If the light comes on, this circuit is working. If not, the ballast resistor (which controls the flow of low voltage electricity to the coil) is faulty, or there is a broken wire or loose connection in the circuit. Check.

Connect up to the distributor side of the coil. If the light does not come on, the primary winding of the coil is broken. Change the coil.

Distributor If the power is not reaching the distributor, look for loose connections and broken wiring. Check connections at the contact breaker and at the condenser. Points should be clean and smooth. Replace and reset if they are at all corroded or burnt.

Condenser Disconnect the condenser from the distributor, retaining its wiring to the points. Connect the test lamp between ground connection on the condenser and earth. If the lamp lights, the condenser is faulty. Since condensers cannot be thoroughly tested in isolation from the engine, replace with a new one if possible.

Misfiring If the engine fires in a rhythmic, imbalanced manner, a cylinder may be functioning badly. Hold an insulated screwdriver across each plug, so that the HT charge is shorted to the engine block. If there is a persistent fault in one of the cylinders, the rhythm of misfiring will not be altered when the offending cylinder is shorted, and its plug prevented from sparking.

If none of the faults seems to account for the engine's performance, only the timing remains to be tested.

Retarded The engine will backfire when hot.

Too advanced When the timing is too advanced, the engine will idle roughly at low speeds and knock at high speeds.

Outboard motors Motorboats and auxiliaries

A well maintained outboard will provide reliable and economic power while occupying a fraction of the hull space needed for an inboard motor. Outboards are compact, light, and easy to maintain, and have the great advantage over the inboard motor that they can be taken ashore and serviced in the convenience and relative comfort of a garage or workshop.

The outboard motor must be suited to the boat size and the kind of work expected from it. Planing hulls are normally powered by an engine of a specified horsepower, below which the hull will not accelerate to a planing speed. The speed of a displacement boat, however, is limited by its water-line and, under many circumstances, equal speeds through the water will be achieved by motors of very different power

output. When choosing a motor, select one that has sufficient power for day-to-day use under normal conditions, and adequate reserve power to push the boat against wind and current when conditions are bad. A small motor worked at the limit of its output for long periods will not only be noisier, smellier and thirstier than a larger one pushing the boat at the same speed, it will also wear more quickly.

Mounting the outboard

A variety of clamping and bolting devices is used to mount an outboard motor. The type of fitting will depend upon the stern shape, height of the transom, position of the rudder, etc. Outboard motors are designed to operate with the anti-cavitation plate or exhaust outlet about 2-3 inches (50-75 mm) below the surface of the water. At a depth less than this, the outboard will vibrate, race as the stern lifts to a wave, and overheat. If the mounting bracket is too low, the motor will operate below its optimum speed, power output will be reduced, and fuel consumption will increase. A selection of clamps, alternative lengths of propeller shaft 15-19 inches (380-480 mm) and a choice of propellers of different pitch and diameter enable motors to be tailored to the boat.

Outboards are designed to withstand the occasional splashing and the ubiquitous spray. They can, however, be seriously damaged if submerged. To prevent this, and as security against theft, it is sensible to chain the outboard motor to the boat.

Stern mounting

In many boats the outboard motor doubles as the rudder. The motor is clamped at the centre of the transom and the boat is steered by the tiller fitted to the outboard. This works very well, provided one remembers that steerage is lost once the motor is cut or slipped into neutral.

The propeller should turn in water that is as free from turbulence as possible. It is often impossible or undesirable to mount the motor so that the propeller is deep below the keel. In such a position it

would be vulnerable to damage. The normal mounting point for the outboard is on the centre-line immediately aft of the skeg. In this position, the motor may tend to vibrate, and the forward motion relative to the output of the motor may seem disappointing. The likeliest reason for this is that the turbulence created by the skeg causes the propeller to cavitate. Move the motor to one side, or trim the skeg to reduce turbulence.

As a propeller turns in the water, it produces forwards motion and slight sideways thrust. This is because the lower part of the propeller is operating in deeper (and therefore denser) water than the upper half — and the stern is pushed sideways in the direction of rotation. A propeller turning clockwise will thrust the stern to starboard — altering the heading to port. The bias which is the result of the offset mounted engine position can therefore be compensated for by mounting the motor on the appropriate side of the boat.

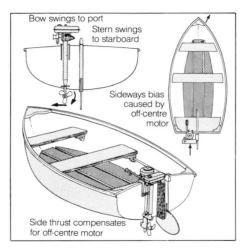

Bow swings to port
Stern swings to starboard

Sideways bias caused by off-centre motor

Side thrust compensates for off-centre motor

Fuel

Most outboard motors are two stroke and use a petrol/oil mix. The proportion of oil to petrol varies between 25:1 and 50:1. Within certain limits the proportions are not critical. The oil is necessary to lubricate the crank case, connecting rod bearings and cylinder linings. Excessive oil in the mixture will make the motor difficult to start, and produce a blue or smoky exhaust. Too little oil will cause the engine to overheat and seize.

An outboard will run best on low octane petrol. If the petrol/oil mixture is allowed to stand, a gummy deposit will form on the walls and passages of the carburettor. Carry spare petrol and oil, but mix them when needed.

Mix the petrol and oil in the petrol can, and shake it vigorously before filling the outboard motor petrol tank. If the petrol and oil are not thoroughly mixed, the sparking plugs will oil up, and the engine will not fire.

If the tank has been left to stand for a while before it is connected to the engine, lean it to one side to integrate the petrol and oil. Shaking will stir up sediment in the tank, which might find its way down the fuel line and block the carburettor.

If the fuel tank is usually only part- filled, the moisture in the air above the petrol will condense and a layer of water will accumulate beneath the fuel. To prevent this accumulation, disconnect the fuel line, and drain the tank. When the last few inches of fuel remain in the bottom, open the filler cap and tip out the remainder. Flush the tank with petrol , connect the fuel line and refill the tank.

Care and maintenance

Most motors are supplied with an owner's handbook which gives concise directions for the maintenance of the motor. Manufacturers will supply a handbook for those who do not have one.

Although motors vary greatly in their complexity, the following maintenance guidelines will have a general relevance to most types and makes.

1 Fuel tank. Keep this clean, both inside and out. Check that the air inlet screw is functioning — it should be able to seal the cap and also be opened to allow air into the tank. Fuel filters at the outlet point should be washed clean

2 Fuel lines should be in good condition, without kinks or evidence of perishing

3 Power head. Keep the power head clean. Electrical wiring should be wiped clean. Inspect HT leads for cracking, tracking (often revealed by black lines on the insulation) and arcing. Rinse all castings with fresh water to remove salt deposits. Wipe with oil to preserve the finish. Sparking plugs should be free of carbon deposits and correctly adjusted

4 Check the lower drive unit; replace oil occasionally and frequently drain and top up with oil. Water seepage in to the lower gear shaft assembly may be normal, but it should not be allowed to remain there, otherwise the steel gears and shaft will corrode. Check that the propeller is free to rotate and can be withdrawn once the sheer pin is removed. Grease the drive shaft before replacing the propeller

5 Tighten all loose nuts (except the spring-loaded adjustment nuts on the carburettor)

6 Inspect the condition of the starter cord, and replace it before it becomes too frayed

Motoring

Make certain that the motor is securely mounted, and that the chain or lanyard fastening the motor to the boat is connected. After five or ten minutes running, re-tighten the clamps. Check that the unit will tilt if it hits an obstruction. This safeguard against damaging the

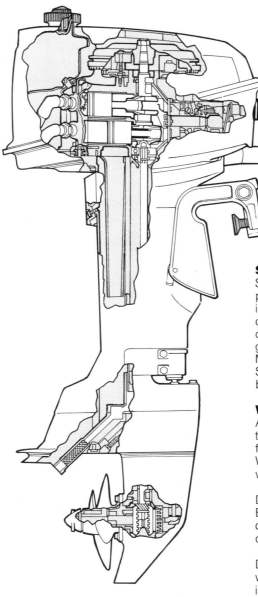

propeller is not available when going astern, so take extra care. Try to avoid using the motor in weedy or very shallow water. Ensure that cooling water is circulating through the unit. If the motor begins to overheat, turn it off, and clear the water inlet pipe.

Look after the motor when it is not in use. Fit a canvas or PVC hood over the power head. Store the motor upright and carry it so the power head is higher than the propeller, to prevent trapped cooling water entering the cylinders and causing considerable damage.

Spares and tool kit

Spark plug, length of HT lead, shear pins, starter cord, small and large insulated screwdrivers, socket set. Set of small spanners or sockets for dismantling the carburettor. Funnel with gauze filter, spare petrol can and oil. Mixing tin.
Safety — disconnect spark plug lead before working on propeller.

Winter lay-up

Attach a hose to the water exhaust outlet tube and flush the cooling tubes with fresh water. Leave the motor to drain. Wash all outer surfaces, rub dry, and wipe or brush them with thin oil.

Drain the fuel tank and carburettor. Empty the fuel tank by tipping out the contents. Rinse the tank with paraffin or petrol and leave it empty.

Drain the lower gear unit, and replace it with fresh oil. Inspect the propeller. If it is bent or damaged, send it to the manufacturers for repair or replacement. An unbalanced propellor will vibrate, and wear the shaft bearings and gears.

Remove the sparking plug, and inject a little oil into the cylinder heads. Turn the motor to spread the oil over the cylinders. Inject more to lie on the piston heads, and clean and replace the spark plug.

Clean all wires, check that the connections are sound and tight. Replace.

Oil the screw clamps, the throttle control, and the tilt mechanism. Store the motor vertically, in a dry place.

Fault-finding chart

Is the fuel fresh? If in doubt, discard fuel, and use freshly mixed petrol and oil.

Is the mixture correct? Mix the ratio of oil to petrol to suit the motor. Increase proportion of oil to petrol if the motor has poor compression or if the weather is cold.

Is there water in the fuel? If in doubt, discard the fuel by emptying it out of the filler cap.

Is the fuel tap on?

Is the fuel pipe blocked? Release pipe at the carburettor and blow it clear. Use compressed air if possible — remove filler cap when doing so. Remove petrol filter and clean it. If the cause of the trouble is dirt in the fuel tank, flush the fuel tank and pipe, and clean the carburettor.

Is the weather very cold (at or below freezing)? Increase proportion of oil to petrol by 25 per cent. Remove spark plug, and increase gap very slightly. Warm plug with blowtorch, or over gas burner or cooker, and replace it while still hot. If the motor is not equipped with neutral gear position, change oil in drive gear for thinner oil. Remember to check oil level frequently, and replace with thicker oil when the weather warms.

Poor carburation The motor will be difficult to start if the fuel/air mixture is incorrect, or if the carburettor is blocked. Switch off fuel and disconnect fuel line, throttle, and choke controls. Dismantle carburettor on clean, white paper. Lay out the parts neatly. Blow through the holes in the casting, and remove gum deposits by cleaning each part in solvent (obtainable from garages or auto spares shops). Needles and seating should not be worn, and float assembly should function freely. Re-assemble the carburettor. Tighten the low speed needle valve with a minimum of force, otherwise the needle may be bent, or its seating damaged. Set the jet by turning it counter-clockwise 1½ times. Reconnect fuel and control lines.

Flooded Plugs wet with oil and petrol. Switch off the fuel tap, screw in the low speed jet, close the throttle, and spin the motor. Dry the plugs, re-set the low speed jet (1½ turns counter-clockwise) and spin the motor. Open the fuel tap. Start the motor.

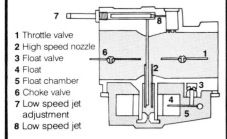

1 Throttle valve
2 High speed nozzle
3 Float valve
4 Float
5 Float chamber
6 Choke valve
7 Low speed jet adjustment
8 Low speed jet

Motor will not turn Power head or drive unit is rusted or seized. Take the motor to a specialist company, or return it to the manufacturers.

Propeller will not turn or motor will not spin Check that the propeller is not fouled with rope, wire, etc. Check that the water inlet and outlet ports are clear. Overheating of power head is usually caused by blocked or congested cooling water passages. Back flush the cooling system (see page 255) where the motor has overheated and seized, spray light oil in the cylinders and free them by rotating the flywheel before starting the motor.

Test
Spin the motor a few times. If the motor does not start, remove spark plugs. Plugs should be damp with petrol vapour. Inspect and test each plug in turn for spark. With the plug still connected to the HT lead, rest it against the engine casing, spin the motor. If there is a good earth connection to the metal engine casing, a spark should crack across the plug.

No spark Loose or wet wiring. Check all wiring. Connections must be tight and wires should be clean and dry. Clean dirty wiring in carbon tetrachloride or methylated spirits. If necessary use a rag moistened with washing-up liquid to clean the wires. Dry them thoroughly.

Fuel flow may be impeded. Intermittent faults are difficult to trace, and can be located only by rigorous checking and cleaning of all parts.

Poor compression/induction

Remove spark plugs and squirt some light oil into each cylinder. Rotate the motor a few times to lubricate rings and improve compression. Replace plugs and swing the motor again.

1 Intake port
2 Fuel-air from carburettor
3 Leaf valve closed
4 Exhaust port

Poor crankcase compression

Crankcase compression is necessary in order to induct fuel into the cylinder head. On the compression stroke, fuel is inducted into the crankcase from the carburettor, where it is compressed by the exhaust stroke until the inlet port opens, and the mixture enters the cylinder head. Check for compression by disconnecting HT leads. Turn choke control to maximum, and spin the motor. After several pulls on the starter, remove the plugs, which should be thoroughly flooded with fuel. The valves controlling the induction of the air/fuel mix are situated between the carburettor and the crankcase. It may be possible to inspect them by removing the carburettor and the leaf valve unit. Broken or bent leaf valves should be replaced.

Motor is carbonned up. This is a normal consequence of use, exacerbated by a rich oil mixture. Carbon deposits form on the exhaust ports and piston crown and cylinder head. The condition of the plug may indicate the general condition of the cylinder head. The motor will have to be stripped down and cleaned.

Pistons may be worn or distorted. This entails major work. Initial indications are loss of power when running and poor compression when spinning. Repairs must be carried out by specialist companies.

Engine has fuel, carburation and ignition, but power output is diminished or erratic

Propeller cavitation. Make sure the propeller is turning in unaerated, clear water. If it is too close to the surface, the engine will race and the propeller will vibrate. Remember that when you peer over the stern, the extra weight aft will lower the propeller deeper into the water.

No spark Remove the spark plug from the HT lead, hold the lead against the engine case and spin motor. If there is no spark, replace with a new lead and try again. If there is still no spark, seek professional advice. For those motors that are fitted with a distributor, etc., carry out the checks described on page 248.

HT lead has a spark, but the plug does not The most likely cause is that the porcelain insulation on the plug has been cracked and a new plug of the correct type with the correct gap should be fitted. Where the hot end of the plug is covered by thick carbon deposits, clean the terminals with a penknife and wire brush. Slip sandpaper between the points of the plug, then blow it clean. Adjust the gap before testing it against the engine casing.

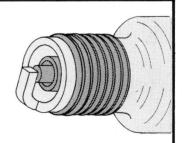

Engine overboard

A chain or lanyard secured to a ring bolt in the transom and made fast to the propeller shaft will prevent the motor from being lost altogether if it shakes loose and falls overboard. Before starting the motor, tighten the holding clamps. After about l5 minutes' continuous running, re-tighten them, and continue to check them while the outboard is in use.

Despite all efforts, an outboard motor may occasionally be submerged, and no time should be lost before it is recovered and dried. Small outboard motors, such as the 'British Seagull' can be dismantled and cleaned at home. All that is needed is a modest tool kit, some spare HT wire, a new sparking plug and a quantity of carbon tetrachloride or methylated spirits to wash the magneto, carburettor, cylinder walls and crank case. Larger motors may have to be taken to a specialist service centre for immediate dismantling and cleaning. Refer to the owner's manual for advice.

Service stations are not always nearby and it is not always convenient or possible to reach one. The best treatment for the motor in this situation is to clean it as well as possible, and then to start it, so that it dries itself. The only occasions where this might harm the motor are when grit has entered the drive shaft bearings and has not been properly cleaned away, or where water has been inducted into the running motor, and the momentum of the crankshaft and flywheel has bent the con-rods and wrist pins as the water was forced into the cylinder head.
In either case, the motor will be seriously damaged if it is restarted before a thorough overhaul.

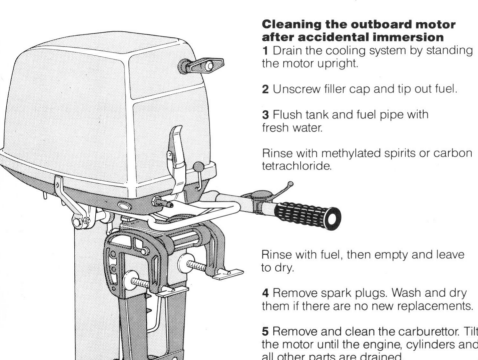

Cleaning the outboard motor after accidental immersion

1 Drain the cooling system by standing the motor upright.

2 Unscrew filler cap and tip out fuel.

3 Flush tank and fuel pipe with fresh water.

Rinse with methylated spirits or carbon tetrachloride.

Rinse with fuel, then empty and leave to dry.

4 Remove spark plugs. Wash and dry them if there are no new replacements.

5 Remove and clean the carburettor. Tilt the motor until the engine, cylinders and all other parts are drained.

6 Wash the motor with fresh water and dry it. If access to the magneto is difficult, remove flywheel, wash the coils, leads etc., and rinse them as in **3** and dry. Remove and replace HT lead.

7 Squirt oil into the cylinders, rotate the engine by hand by turning flywheel or propeller (plugs should be out). Squirt light oil into the fuel inlet manifold. Check the movement of the pistons: the action when turned by the propeller or flywheel should feel free and smooth. If the motor was running when it fell into the water, and there are now slight tight spots as the motor is turned, send it away for a thorough check and overhaul.

Larger motors should also be sent away once the carburettor has been cleaned, and all parts re-assembled. However, the following routine can be adopted to restart the motor, provided that the possibility of damaging the bearings has been considered and accepted as either an insignificant risk, or a necessary risk in order to remain mobile.

8 Replace the flywheel and cleaned carburettor, spin the motor and check for a spark. If there is no spark, check for loose connections and dry the magneto assembly again.

9 Heat the spark plugs. Hold them over a gas torch or burner, or put them in the oven until they are really hot, and have to be handled with pliers or an oven cloth. Oil the threads, and insert the plugs and screw them tight. (Do not overtighten spark plugs. Half a turn after the plug is seated is sufficient.) Connect HT leads.

10 Fill the fuel tank with fresh fuel, with double the quantity of oil mixed in.

11 Start the motor. Although most motors can be run for about half a minute out of the water without being damaged, it is better to clamp the motor on to the stern of a boat and work it quite hard until it is hot and running well. Prolonged running in a water tank may cause the motor to overheat as the turbulence caused by the propeller will starve the water inlet of cooling water.

If the motor fails to start, check all work to make sure it has been cleaned, dried, and replaced correctly.

Engine cooling

Between 20 and 40 per cent of the fuel consumed in an internal combustion engine is converted into heat which has to be dissipated by the engine cooling system. The air supply and cooling systems of the engine room must be very efficient and balanced by the heat output of the engine. Whether the engine is water or air-cooled, adequate ventilation of the engine compartment is essential. For every 1° rise in ambient engine room temperature, the exhaust outlet temperature will rise by about 7°. This may not seem very significant in a temperate climate, but in the hotter parts of the world, and where engine cooling air is re-directed to the air inlet ducts, this can have a serious effect both on engine performance and safety.

An engine that overheats will seize or catch fire. If the cooling system is too effective, the engine will run cold. Performance will be noisy and rough.

Cooling is achieved by ducting cool air or water around the engine block, sump and exhaust manifold, and by using the lubrication oil as a coolant.

The normal operating temperature of diesel and petrol engines is about 93°C (200°F). Petrol engines tend to run a little hotter. Temperatures at the exhaust manifold can be very much higher and require efficient cooling. A diesel exhaust is approximately 650°C (1202°F), and petrol engine exhausts 750°C (1382°F) Considerable quantities of heat are generated. Cooling systems are

designed to cope with the engine working at maximum power in most air and seawater temperatures.

In an effort to raise the engine running temperature of a water-cooled engine, owners will often partially close the water inlet valve of the cooling system to restrict the flow of water to the engine block. In a water-cooled exhaust system that incorporates rubber or plastic components, this practice might have disastrous results. Only restrict the flow of cooling water where the entire exhaust system is metal, and is thoroughly lagged and shielded from the hull.

Air-cooled engine installations

The drawing illustrates a typical air-cooled marine engine installation. Ducting should be of sufficient cross-sectional area to carry air for cooling (including dissipating the radiant heat from the engine) and for combustion. Inlet and outlet ducts are situated to minimize the possibility of cooling air being re-circulated by the engine fan. Outlets should be louvred or fitted with a grill. Volumetric losses, due to constrictions at the outlet grills and friction in the ducting, must be compensated for by fitting ducting of greater cross-sectional area. Adjustments to ducting and grills, etc. are made during engine trials.

Maintenance
Air-cooled systems are relatively trouble-free and simple to maintain. Ducting

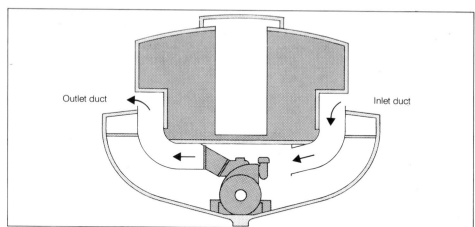

Outlet duct

Inlet duct

ports should be unobstructed; a cat basking in the hot air of the outlet duct will cause the engine room temperature to rise. Vanes in the cylinder head and

the light steel ducting around the engine should be cleaned and inspected for accumulations of dust.

Raw water cooling

In this system, raw seawater is piped from outside the hull, around the engine and exhaust manifold, then discharged overboard.

Only motors designed for such a system should be cooled by seawater. Engine

castings need to be heavier, with open waterways and thicker walls. Because of the considerable temperature differences at different parts of the engine casting, expansion stresses are set up, which will distort an engine that is not designed to cope with them.

Water is circulated by a powerful pump. A valve or stopcock is usually fitted in the inlet and outlet ports to prevent the engine from draining when at rest. This should be checked occasionally to ensure that it moves freely.

Raw water cooling systems are vulnerable to erosion, congestion, and clogging. An obstruction at the inlet will starve the jacket of cooling water, and the engine will rapidly overheat.

Maintenance

It is essential that waterways, thermostat, pump, and water filters are kept clear. Some boats are fitted with water inlet filters that can be removed and cleaned from inside the hull. These should be checked when the engine is in use, and a careful watch kept on the engine temperature gauge when motoring in shallow or weedy water.

Cleaning a raw water system

These are prone to congestion owing to the entry of sediment and organic matter into the waterways, and, because of the presence of salt in the water, to corrosion as well. Raw water circuits are also hard on the pumps and impellers should be changed regularly.

Cleaning

Most raw water systems can be back-flushed by inserting a cold water hose into the outlet pipe. After an initial clean, drain the system, disconnect as many hoses and units of the cooling system as possible, and scrape out the accumulations of rust and silt. Many waterways will be inaccessible unless the cylinder head is removed, but some parts can be reached and stirred with a flexible wire. When the heat exchangers are fitted with inspection ports, these should be opened every two years, and the insides de-scaled.

Scraping and flushing will only partially succeed in cleaning the cooling system. Commercial engine cleaning solutions are available from most garages and can be used provided that they are compatible with the metals in the cylinder block and cooling system.

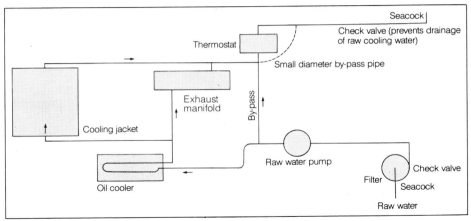

Typical raw water cooling system

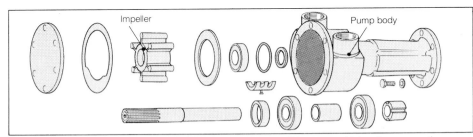

Exploded view of the popular Jabsco water pump. It is a good idea to renew the impeller at fitting-out time

In the absence of a suitable cleaner, a solution of 1 ounce (28g) oxalic acid to 1 gallon (4ls) of water will clear away rust. Flush with a solution of bicarbonate of soda. A solution of hydroflouric acid (10 per cent) and water left in the engine for about 12 hours will clear deposits of sand. Flush clean with bicarbonate of soda.

Flushing will not be effective unless the fluids are allowed to stand in the engine and are then pumped out under pressure. To gain the maximum benefit from the chemical cleaners, arrange a temporary water reservoir from an old drum, fitted with plumber's waterpipe

connections. Connect the inlet and outlet hoses to the tank, and allow the engine to circulate the cleaning fluid. Arrange a strainer over the inlet pipe, and continue to flush the cooling system until the water coming from the outlet pipe is clear of rust and sediment. Flush the system immediately with the neutralizing solution, then with fresh water. Replace the hoses. Check the condition of the flexible hoses, and replace those that are weak or worn. As engine revolutions increase, a weak-walled inlet hose will collapse and constrict the waterpipe and lead to overheating. Hoses should be secured by stainless steel worm screw-type clips (two clips per pipe end).

Keel cooling

This indirect system is totally enclosed, except for a small header tank positioned above the engine. Fresh cooling water is circulated around the engine, cooling the manifold, oil, engine block and exhaust, before being channelled through pipes bolted to the side of the keel or the underside of the hull. The cooled water is then returned

to the engine. A flexible impeller pump circulates the water at the required rate. No secondary water circuit is involved, and there are no problems with choking, seaweed congestion, etc.

Apart from the annual inspection of the pipework to check for corrosion, wear and pipe damage, no maintenance is

required. Keep the header tank topped up with the specified quantity of anti-freeze, and change the impeller of the water pump at the start of each session.

Indirect — heat exchanger system

This is a more easily installed alternative to the keel cooling system. It is also less vulnerable to damage when grounding. In this system both primary and secondary cooling circuits pass through a heat exchanger fitted to the engine. The primary circuit cools the engine and manifold and transfers its heat to the raw seawater at the heat exchanger.

The size of the heat exchanger and the capacity of the pump must be matched to ensure an adequate flow of seawater to remove the heat from the primary circuit. A centrifugal engine waterpump circulates the primary cooling water, while a powerful self-priming flexible impeller pump provides the flow for the secondary circuit.

Because of the need to achieve a satisfactory heat gain over a relatively short interface with the cooling system, the oil cooling heat exchanger is plumbed into the raw water circuit. In both indirect systems described above, the maintenance of the primary circuit is straightforward, and usually entails keeping the header tank topped up with a mixture of fresh water and anti-freeze. The raw water circuit is prone to congestion and should be cleaned as described above.

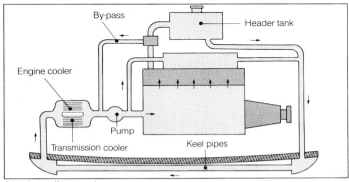

Keel cooling system

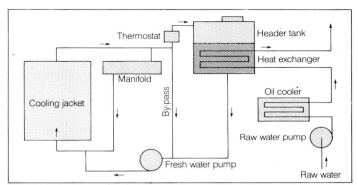

Typical indirect cooling system

Thermostats and corrosion

The flow of cooling water to the manifold and engine block in both raw and indirect cooling systems is controlled by a thermostat. The thermostat will require periodic renewal. Before discarding the old one, inspect it closely, and compare it to the new one. It is often found that the installation engineer who installed the original thermostat has drilled a $^3/_{16}$ inch (5mm) hole through the valve. This hole allows a small quantity of water to circulate through the manifold when the engine is started, and prevents the engine water boiling and overflowing the header tank. If in other respects, the new thermostat is identical to the previous one, and engine start up has always been satisfactory, copy the previous example and drill the small hole in the valve.

If Admiralty brass water pipe is used, sacrificial zinc anodes are placed inside the heat exchanger. When topping up, check the zinc pencil and replace whenever necessary.

Anodes should not be installed if 90/10 (cunifer 10) or 70/30 (cunifer 30) cupro-nickel tubes are used, as the protection film which builds up inside the tubes will break down and corrosion will result.

Causes of engine overheating

Sudden overheating
Water inlet blocked

Congested water piping
Insufficient water or oil

Gradual overheating
Constriction in the water cooling circuits

Worn, poorly functioning impeller pump

Oil cooler not working

Engine overloaded

Poor valve timing, ignition timing, or injector timing

Fuel/air mixture out of adjustment

Propeller is too large

Shortage of lubricating oil, or wrong type.

If the engine overheats and it is impossible to clear the system, and it is dangerous (because of sea conditions, manoeuvring, etc.) to switch the engine off, run the motor at minimum revs and add more oil. This will help to control the temperature until the motor can be switched off and the problem solved.

Exhaust systems Motorboats and auxiliaries

The exhaust system's primary task is to convey the engine exhaust gases away from the engine, with a minimum of noise and vibration, and the least possible back pressure. As many small boat engines are tucked away below the water-line, several practical difficulties arise.

If the exhaust is not cooled or insulated, the heat build-up in the manifold and exhaust system will be sufficient to melt the rubber engine mounts and electrical cable insulation and produce a serious fire hazard to adjacent woodwork.

The exhaust outlet has to be arranged so that even when the boat is heeled, there is no danger of water backing up the pipe and damaging the engine. Finally, there is the difficulty of firmly supporting the exhaust pipework without transmitting its noise and vibration to the hull.

Wet exhaust
Most small boats with water-cooled engines have a wet exhaust system.

The illustration shows a simple installation where the engine is situated above the water-line. The vacuum valve is to prevent water being sucked back into the engine. Note that the cooling water is injected at an angle into the exhaust pipe as close to the engine as possible. A flexible steel hose is used to connect the manifold to the exhaust.

Water from the cooling system is injected into the exhaust pipe and this lowers the gas temperature to below 100°C (212°F).

The gas and water mixture can then be run through a silencer and a pipe and hose run to the outlet.

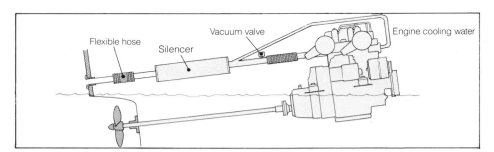

The illustration shows the engine manifold less than 10 inches (250mm) above the water-line. A watertrap is used to prevent the back flow of cooling water and seawater from entering the engine. A condensation trap and drain plug should be fitted at the manifold, and the length of hot pipe insulated.

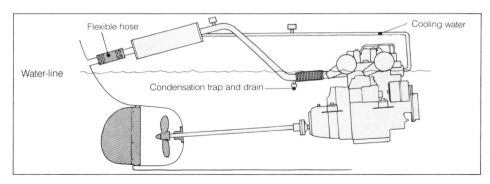

Dry exhaust
The dry exhaust system vents to the air, often with a 90° bend to prevent rainwater from entering. A condensation trap with a drain plug is fitted at the manifold.

The silencer, pipe and through-deck fittings should be thoroughly insulated. Engine units which use a sealed fresh water cooling system sometimes pipe the water through specially made water jackets which surround the exhaust pipe and silencer. The pipe will be made in several sections, with water connections between each.

Checking the exhaust system
Inspect for accumulations of carbon and salt in the pipe. Disconnect flexible hoses and remove any deposits in the pipe. The most serious congestion will occur where the water coolant is injected into the exhaust pipe. Hoses and gaskets should be checked for deterioration. Replace them before they leak dangerous gases into the boat. Inspect the exhaust outlet fitting for water leaks. Clean, remove and re-seal. If the exhaust system is badly corroded, it should be replaced.

Dismantling the exhaust system

The best time to dismantle the exhaust is after the engine has been used and the exhaust is thoroughly hot. This is not always possible, so a blowlamp may be needed. If the pipework is in a very bad state, then it may be best to saw the pipes into lengths and recover the re-usable fittings later. Flexible hose connections should be easy to release. If necessary, saw through the hose and clips. Problems arise at corroded flange and gasket connections.

Method for releasing pipe joins

Great care should be taken to avoid damaging the engine manifold. Soak fittings in penetrating oil and leave overnight. Gentle pressure with a wrench and light tapping may release the nuts. Alternatively, heat the nuts with a blowlamp and apply sudden pressure with a wrench. If these methods fail, drill into the nut, using the largest drill possible, and split it away, using a cold chisel and hammer. Once nuts have been removed, tap thin metal wedges between the flanges to separate them. If the nut sheers off, leaving studs still holding the flange, drill the stud, and withdraw it with a screw extractor.

To remove threaded pipe from flanges

Cut pipe at about 5 inches (127mm) from the flange. Cut the side of the pipe right down to the flange. Place a small piece of angle iron against the cut in the pipe, and press with a vice. Free the pipe from the flange. Rotate the pipe in the vice, and squash it until the pipe is released. Do not discard the pipe until you have noted its internal diameter.

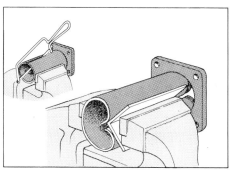

Method for releasing pipe joins

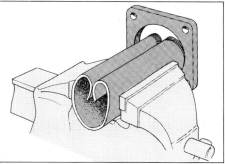

To remove threaded pipe from flanges

Replacement

The exhaust run should be as straight as possible to avoid back pressure. Right-angle bends must be avoided (except at the top of a dry exhaust outlet). Pipework should never be smaller than the diameter specified by the engine manufacturer. If the exhaust run is long, or unusually complicated, use a larger size of pipe than specified. Plan to allow a sufficient fall in the pipe run to prevent water accumulating in low spots. Use copper piping for small petrol engines and steel for larger ones. The exhaust and water mixture from a diesel engine is corrosive of these metals, and either specially made rubber hose, or ceramic clad steel piping should be used. The vacuum valve at the watertrap should be at least 24 inches (600mm) above the water-line and if a second loop is installed just before the hull outlet, this should not rise to less than 14 inches (350mm) above the water-line.

Support the exhaust system at least every 4 feet (1200mm). The engine manifold should not bear the weight of any part of the exhaust system. The silencer must be self-supporting. Smear the threads of pipework, studs etc., with graphite grease before assembling.

Use flexible hoses secured by two clips per pipe end, to break up long pipework runs in a wet exhaust system. Bond across the hoses to keep each part of the exhaust piping at the same electrical potential (see page 290). Pipe supports should be secured to the side or bottom of the boat, never to the deck, otherwise engine vibration will be transmitted throughout the hull.

If the run of uncooled exhaust pipe is more than 17 inches (430mm) it should be insulated. A short length of uncooled pipe can be left to act as a moisture barrier, and it helps the engine to run at its optimum working temperature. If a hot pipe passes through a bulkhead, insulated supports will be needed.

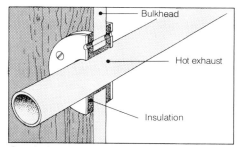

Steel plates held by bolts

Rubber hose connections

By using short lengths of steel pipe connected by car radiator or steam hose, the exhaust can be made to follow the side of the hull. Two clips per pipe end should be used to fasten the hose. Position clips with screws readily accessible for tightening or release.

Insulation

A ceramic fibre blanket carefully wrapped around the hot exhaust, and protected from splashes of oil etc. by a thin sheet of copper or foil secured with wire, makes an excellent insulator. The ceramic fibre blanket, which is easy to remove and does not crack or disintegrate when subjected to vibration and temperature extremes, is available from insulation engineers and suppliers.

Ventilation

While working on the exhaust system, you will become aware of the quality of the ventilation the engine is receiving. It is important that air should circulate freely around the engine, and it is good practice for the engine to have its own ventilation cowls. If the engine compartment smells or becomes very hot, fit additional ventilators.

Fire hazard

Always ensure that all the tanks, pipework, vents and connections are in good condition, and do not leak. Check the fuel system regularly, while the engine is running, and when it is at rest.

Petrol is a highly volatile fuel. The following safety measures and installation advice is directed particularly at those with boats powered by petrol engines, but it is also broadly relevant to those with diesel engines.

Precautions when refuelling

Keep a powder-type fire extinguisher close at hand ready for immediate use. Extinguish all naked lights, and switch off the engine and electrical equipment. Hold the nozzle of the petrol filler hose against the inlet pipe to prevent sparking. To avoid confusion the filler cap should be clearly marked either 'petrol' or 'diesel'.

When refuelling is complete, close the filler cap, wipe away spilled fuel, and go below to sniff for fuel leaks.

Re-start the engine after the engine space has been checked for accumulations of petrol vapour and for fuel leaks.

The illustration shows a petrol fuel tank and feed pipe arrangement. Small installations are fitted with a gravity feed fuel tank, sometimes with the tank mounted on the engine. In larger boats, the fuel tanks are positioned lower in the hull. Fuel is lifted to the engine by fuel pumps working in parallel.

On a diesel installation, it is necessary to have a spill return to carry unused low pressure fuel oil from the injectors to the fuel tank. The return pipe should continue almost to the bottom of the fuel tank to prevent the possibility of aerating the fuel, and subsequent failure of the engine when the level in the tank gets low and hot fuel, returning and dropping on to remaining fuel creates bubbles.

Tanks

In many fibreglass boats the tank is incorporated in the hull structure, or is foamed into position when the hull moulding is complete and before the boat is fitted out. Prefabricated metal

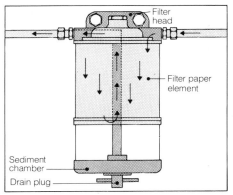

Fuel filter — CAV agglomerator

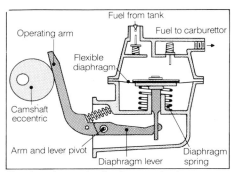

Section through diaphragm fuel pump

tanks are usually retained by metal straps or tensioned steel wires.

Holding arrangements must be very secure as considerable weights of fuel are involved, which can exert great strains on the tank fastenings. Tanks must be secure. Straps or wires must be capable of restraining the tank without movement (which might fatigue the fuel pipes) even when the boat is heeled or capsized.

Baffles are built into the tank to reduce the de-stabilizing effect of the free surface liquid in the tank. Where several fuel tanks supply the engine, levelling pipes of small diameter are plumbed between them to equalize the levels and to help trim the boat. These pipes should be fitted with shut-off valves to isolate the tanks.

Tanks are made from a variety of materials, the most common being copper, stainless steel, and monel. Fibreglass tanks are made from a special resin, which has been mixed with a water-and-petrol-resistant additive to prevent fuel contamination.

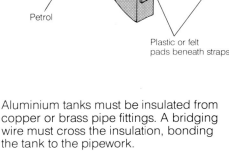

Aluminium tanks must be insulated from copper or brass pipe fittings. A bridging wire must cross the insulation, bonding the tank to the pipework.

A filler cap should be chained or wired to the filler pipe, so that every part of the fuel system is wired to the earthing system of the boat.

Vent pipe

This should be no less than a quarter of the diameter of the filler pipe. The vent should lead over the side, with its end covered by a fine meshed flame arrester, and protected with a clam shell fitting. A small drain plug is sometimes screwed into the base of the tank to drain water from the fuel. The fuel outlet and filter leave the tank from the top.

Pipework

Piping is usually copper, or fire resistant flexible hose. Steel or chromium plated fuel lines are sometimes used instead. The latter two should not be used in conjunction with a diesel engine. Both are prone to corrosion. The diameter of the pipework should not be less than the diameter of the feed line between the carburettor and the fuel pump. A valve,

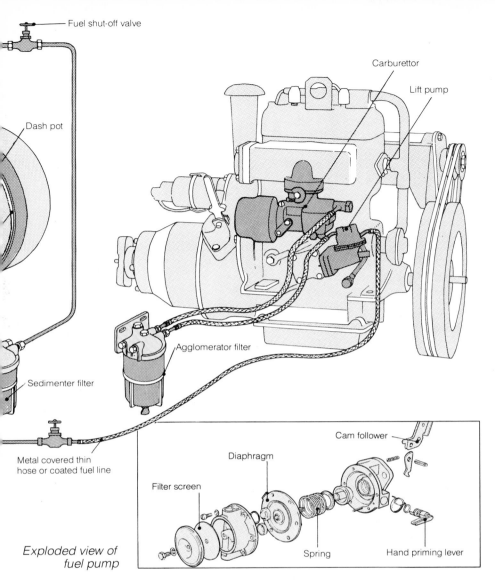

Fuel shut-off valve

Dash pot

Carburettor

Lift pump

Sedimenter filter

Agglomerator filter

Metal covered thin
hose or coated fuel line

Cam follower

Diaphragm

Filter screen

Spring

Hand priming lever

*Exploded view of
fuel pump*

which is easily accessible from the outside of the hull, should be fitted close to the outlet pipe. This enables the fuel tank to be isolated from the engine in case of fire.

Pipework should be kept out of the bilge water and protected from damage by knocking or abrasion. It should be supported by clips or grommets at regular intervals.

Filters

Two types of filter may be incorporated into the fuel line. A sedimenter filter to remove larger particles of dirt and water droplets from the fuel before it enters the fuel pump. An agglomerator unit fits in the pressure line between the pump and carburettor or injection pump, and filters out the smaller impurities. Water traps in the base of each filter unit

should be drained at regular intervals. When fuel flow is greater than can be handled by agglomerator and sedimenter in series, additional filters are fitted and piped in parallel.

Fuel filters should be bolted to the hull in a position where they are easily visible, and the fuel pipeline should carry none of their weight. Glass or plastic water-traps should not be used in a marine installation.

Pumps

A valve should be fitted between the pump and the end of the fuel line to the tank. Where the feed pipe is 'T'ed into the pump from two or more tanks, each feed line should be fitted with a valve to isolate the tanks. Pumps should not leak. Dismantling and cleaning is usually straightforward.

Carburettor

A flame arrester should be fitted to the carburettor of a petrol engine. In some installations a drip pan, covered with a fine gauze mesh, and drained by a small pipe tapped into the inlet manifold is fitted beneath the carburettor.

Safety

Before starting work on the fuel system of a petrol engine, extinguish all naked lights and switch off electrical equipment. Remember that even a spanner that drops against a metal fitting may strike a spark that could ignite petrol vapour. This is equally true if the tank is full or empty. In either case the tank and fuel lines are highly dangerous, until they have been flushed clean and aired.

Removing water from petrol

Water is heavier than petrol or diesel and can be drained from the tank or from the filters by opening small low level drain plugs. Less water will be condensed in a fuel tank that is left full than in one that is left only partially full.

Fuel blockages

These are usually simple to trace and to remedy. Disconnect the flexible hose from the petrol pump and blow down it. This should clear the line back to the tank, where the debris, and then air bubbles, will be heard gurgling in the fuel. If a filter is fitted between the pump and the tank, disconnect the filter, and blow back each section of the fuel line. Change the filter element.

Vapour locks

These occur when the engine room temperature rises and vaporizes fuel standing in the piping. It does not occur when the engine is running, as the flow of fuel is sufficient to prevent adequate heat build up. To cure a vapour lock, either blow back the fuel line or, if there is no hurry, wrap cold, wet rags around the fuel line to condense the vapour.

Fire fighting

Aim a dry powder or BCF extinguisher at the base of the flames of an oil or petrol fire. Turn off a diesel engine before operating a dry powder extinguisher, (see page 297).

Cool the fuel tank by throwing water over it. Do not throw water at the flames, as this will spread the fire.

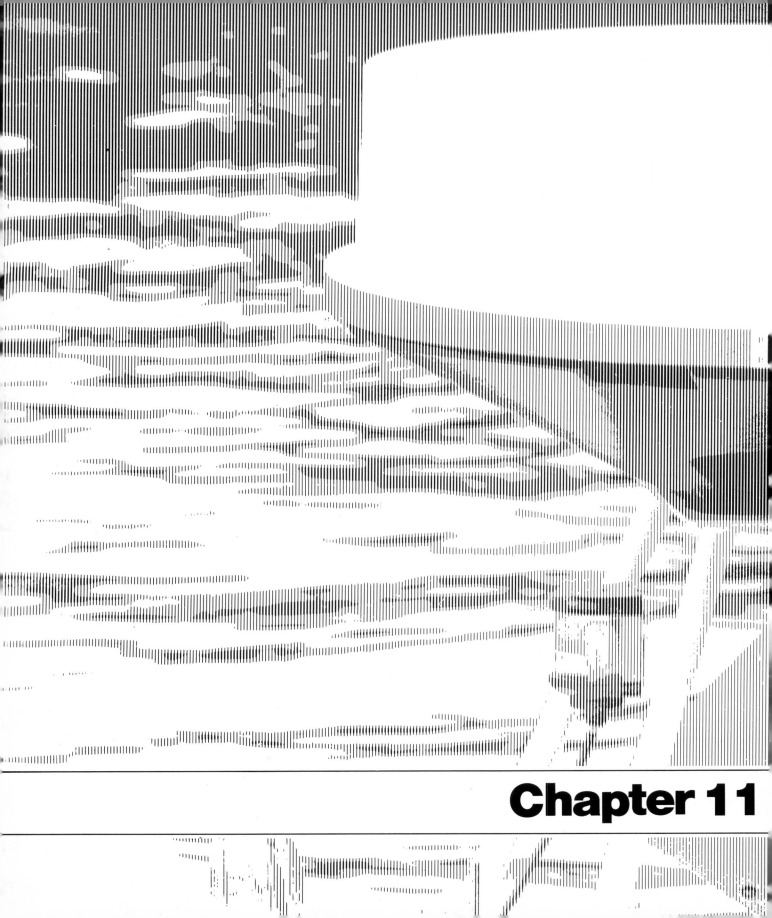

Chapter 11

Navigation and Communication

The International Regulations for Preventing Collisions at Sea include specifications for the installation of navigation lights for small craft. Those who do not show these lights not only take the risk of being run down, but, since July 1981 when the regulations came into force, also risk nullifying their insurance cover.

The Regulations specify minimum requirements which even small yachts should have no difficulty in meeting. In some circumstances tri-colour and bi-colour lanterns are authorized which help to reduce battery drain. These are minimum requirements. Even a range of three miles in good visibility is barely sufficient when a small boat is sharing a shipping lane with fast-moving but unmanoeuvrable bulk cargo carriers. Lights of greater intensity can be fitted which will increase the chances of being seen, provided that their location complies with the Regulations.

The categories are divided into boats under sail and those under power. There is another section for all boats at anchor or aground. Yachts under both sail and power are regarded as power boats. Yachts with auxilliary motors need to be equipped with lights appropriate for both sailing and motoring. This may involve duplicating some lights especially in boats under 40 feet (12m) long, where a tri-colour masthead light fulfils all the requirements when under sail. However, the duplication of the lighting systems may be considered as an additional safety factor should the tri-colour masthead light burn out, but only the appropriate combination should be used in accordance with the mode in which the vessel is actually operating.

Positioning lights

Provided they are not masked by sails or other gear, the higher the lights are placed, the more easily visible they will be. Measure the wiring runs, and consult the manufacturer's installation instructions concerning the size of wiring. In low voltage circuits heavy section wiring is necessary to prevent voltage drop (see page 274). Position the lights where they will not be confused with cabin light filtering through curtains etc. The masthead light of a power-driven vessel from 40-65 feet (12-20m) must not be less than 8 feet (2½m) above the uppermost continuous deck. On shorter boats it may be lower, as long as the navigation lights are above other lights and obstructions. In no case should the combined side lights be less than 39 inches (1m) below the masthead light.

In some positions, the lights will be shrouded by sails, or obstructed by ventilators and other fixtures. In many boats, the optimum position for the lights if they are not fixed to or near the masthead, is on the pulpit, or fixed to a vertical staff welded to the pulpit. Where traditional wooden or steel sidelight screens are used, their masking faces must be painted matt black. Other lights which are not in continuous use may be permanently installed, or hauled to the masthead when needed.

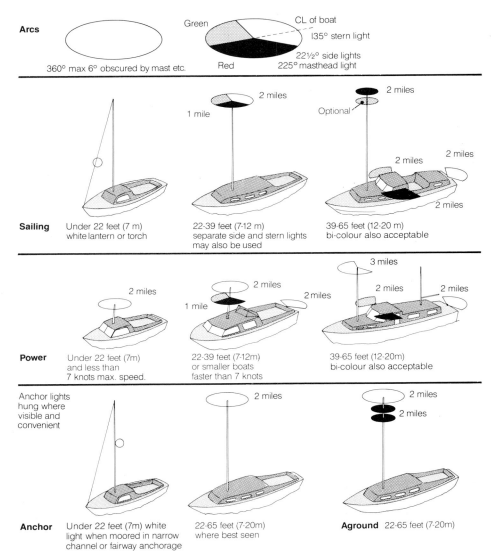

Arcs 360° max 6° obscured by mast etc.

Green CL of boat 135° stern light 22½° side lights 225° masthead light Red

Sailing
Under 22 feet (7 m) white lantern or torch — 1 mile, 2 miles

22-39 feet (7-12 m) separate side and stern lights may also be used — 2 miles

39-65 feet (12-20 m) bi-colour also acceptable — Optional, 2 miles, 2 miles, 2 miles

Power
Under 22 feet (7m) and less than 7 knots max. speed. — 2 miles

22-39 feet (7-12m) or smaller boats faster than 7 knots — 1 mile, 2 miles, 2 miles

39-65 feet (12-20m) bi-colour also acceptable — 3 miles, 2 miles, 2 miles

Anchor
Anchor lights hung where visible and convenient

Under 22 feet (7m) white light when moored in narrow channel or fairway anchorage

22-65 feet (7-20m) where best seen — 2 miles

Aground 22-65 feet (7-20m) — 2 miles, 2 miles

Compass, charts, sextant

The prime consideration when installing a compass is that it is easily visible. It should also, consistent with a convenient cockpit location, be as remote as possible from magnetic and electro-magnetic interference.

The typical navigation compass carried aboard small boats is filled with paraffin or alcohol and distilled water. For the method of topping up fluid see page 280. The bearings taken will be affected by any ferrous, magnetic or electrical equipment or wiring close to the compass. Deviation thus caused varies in accordance with the ship's heading. The deviation at a single bearing may alter owing to intermittent operation of adjacent electrical equipment.

Checking compass deviation

Compass deviation alters relative to the ship's heading, and will be changed both by the re-positioning of mechanical and electrical gear, and by transient factors such as a steel wristwatch, or spectacle frames too close to the compass card. Compasses mounted in steel-hulled or ferro-cement hulled craft should be frequently checked for deviation, as the overall magnetic effect of the hull seems to vary.

The simplest means of establishing deviation is to swing the boat, taking bearings of a distant object of a known magnetic bearing. A buoy or dolphin will supply the fixed position, but greater accuracy is obtained if, instead of taking bearings from a known point to a charted and easily visible building etc., a bearing is taken of a pair of leading marks, when they are in line. Any pair of conspicuous and charted buildings will do and the farther away they are, the more accurate will be the reading.

Take a number of readings, altering the heading of the boat each time. Check the results both against the magnetic bearing taken from the chart, and between bearings taken from the boat. A compass totally unaffected by shipboard magnetic influence will give the same magnetic bearing whatever the boat's heading. A compass adjuster should be asked to eliminate or reduce deviation in excess of 3° if long sea passages are planned. For coastal sailing greater errors can be accepted, provided a deviation chart is kept, and corrections made each time bearings are taken.

In many wooden and fibreglass boats, there is no difficulty in finding a suitable and easily visible location clear of magnetic interference. The site can be checked before installation, by moving the compass a foot or so around the proposed position. If compass deviation is imperceptible, the proposed mounting position is likely to be satisfactory. In steel and ferro-cement hulls, and in boats with a lot of electrical equipment and associated power cables in the deck house, it may be impossible to find such an interference-free site and it may be necessary to re-route cables and to call in a professional compass adjuster to fit compensating bars and magnets around the compass mount to negate the shipboard magnetic influences.

A form of deviation that cannot be detected by the above tests is caused by ferrous or electrical fittings above or below the compass. These operate when the boat heels, usually preventing the compass from settling to a steady heading. This form of deviation is normally noticed only when the boat is moving through rough water, and the unsettled motion of the compass card may be attributed to sea conditions rather than shipboard magnetic influence. It will still however, be present in smooth water, where the compass might settle to allow satisfactory but nevertheless inaccurate readings to be taken. Magnets placed beneath the compass will eliminate this effect, but should be fitted by a compass adjuster.

Charts

Keep charts dry and flat. Before a voyage, sort the charts into groups which cover specified sections of the route. Store them in canvas or calico folios marked with the relevant way-points. This makes storage simpler and makes it easier to find the right chart. Use soft pencils for drawing on the chart, and keep them up to date with the Notices for Mariners.

Sextants

If the sextant needs servicing, or adjustment, it should be sent away to the appropriate national organization. No maintenance is required apart from cleaning mirror and lenses, and wiping the framework, index arm, and micrometer screw with machine oil. Protect the sextant against spray, which corrodes brasswork and destroys the mirror silvering.

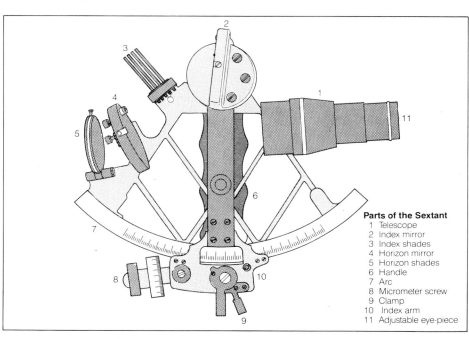

Parts of the Sextant
1 Telescope
2 Index mirror
3 Index shades
4 Horizon mirror
5 Horizon shades
6 Handle
7 Arc
8 Micrometer screw
9 Clamp
10 Index arm
11 Adjustable eye-piece

Echo-sounder

Regardless of type and cost, echo-sounders are susceptible to two main operating conditions which affect the clarity of their read-out and their accuracy.

External factors, such as the type of seabed, as well as variations in the salinity and temperature of the water, affect performance.

Signal frequency is gauged to give the best possible echo response from the seabed. Higher frequency signals might be less affected by changes in salinity etc. but the echo from a sandy, silted or weedy seabed would be weaker and less reliable. All that can be done is to become familiar with the way in which the reading changes owing to the variables mentioned above.

Installation-induced faults however can be overcome. These are essentially of two types:

1 Poor positioning of transducers
The transducer must be positioned below the water-line, in clear water, parallel to the sea level. If the transducer is placed too near the water-line, propeller keel or bilge keels, turbulence will result, and the echo response will be lost. If the transducer is placed too close to the keel, it may also be masked from the echos and give a maximum depth reading irrespective of the true depth. To avoid these problems, the transducer is usually situated slightly forward of amidships, just below the turn of the bilge. Prominent fixtures should be streamlined with fairing-in plates.

2 Wiring and interference faults The coaxial cable from the transducer to the echo sounder unit should be kept well clear of other wiring which might generate interference (see page 268). Sheathe the cable if necessary. Ignition systems and strobe lights are often the cause of inconsistencies in the read-out.

Maintenance
Echo sounders are virtually maintenance-free. Weed or barnacles growing on the transducer will impair its performance. Scrub away weed, and remove barnacles by squashing them with a pair or pliers or a 'mole' type wrench. Make sure that the coaxial lead in the bilges is protected against damp.

Radios
In contrast to the normal reception when listening to a radio at home, the performance of a marine ship-to-shore radio is often disappointing. There are many reasons. Some are related to the transmission frequencies and the quality of the received signals, but a significant cause of poor performance is often found to be in the installation itself.

The fitting of the radio and erection and tuning of the aerials should be left to a professional marine electrical engineer. However, the following points may help to improve the radio's performance.

1 Power leads should be short and of ample capacity. 50 per cent excess capacity will ensure that voltage drop is minimal. Bunch the leads together, and shield where necessary. If there is excessive noise, remove the aerial lead at the radio. Noise conducted through the power cables may remain, and should be suppressed. (See page 268).

2 Make sure the radio is thoroughly earthed. Over half the power of the radio can be lost if the ground connection is poor. All ground terminal connections should be clean, soldered or clamped, and protected against corrosion. Fit several earthing leads, including one to the earth plate of the bonding system. (See page 290). A separate copper mesh, soldered around its edge and fitted outside the hull, in addition to the earth plate, should improve radio reception.

3 Fit a suitable aerial. In small sailing boats the most satisfactory aerials are of the 'L' type, utilizing the rigging with strain insulators wherever necessary. Shipboard-radiated sound will be picked up both by unsheathed power lines and by the aerial. The distinctive sounds made by the boat's equipment might help to identify and suppress the interference sources.

Popping regular, synchronized with engine speed — ignition system

Popping but not synchronized with engine revs — fuel depth gauge

Howling pitch varying with engine — generator

Whistling varied with engine revs — alternator

Sizzling crackling — voltage regulator

Pulsed tone regular and monotonous — digital read-out from adjacent equipment

Prop shaft similar to alternator

Loran C

These units should be professionally installed and adjusted. Poor performance is usually the result of shipboard-generated interference or aerial location. The latter can be reduced to a tolerable level by measures described on page 268. If these do not succeed, check aerial and ground lead. The ground wiring should be heavy and well connected.

Loran C and radio ground leads should be kept separate. Improved performance can often be obtained by moving the aerial away from metal structures, horizontal wires and other aerials. Position the aerial temporarily, and check the signal, both with other equipment turned off and with each item of equipment turned on before making a permanent installation.

Radar

The microwave energy emitted by a radar scanner at close range can be dangerous. Avoid looking directly at the scanner while the radar is switched on, and do not come within 39 inches (1m) of a small yacht scanner, or 8 feet (2½m) of a larger commercial unit, while they are working.

If the scanner is enclosed in a radome, make sure it is switched off before venturing close.

The installation and care of a radar system should be left to the manufacturer or his agents. Do not tamper with the installation and seek advice before siting any other electronic equipment near the radar.

Faults

Faults can be inherent in a system through poor installation or subsequent alteration to power lines aboard ship. They can also develop because of poor maintenance.

Blind spots

These occur when the scanner is situated close to an obstruction. Often this will be only a small, perhaps 1° loss, and the motion of the boat will eliminate the blind spot. If the blind spot persists move the scanner or the obstruction.

False echoes

These reveal themselves by a double echo on the display. Usually the ranges of the two echoes are similar, the false echo generally the more transient of the two. The false echo occurs when a transmission is deflected by rigging or part of the superstructure, and returns from the target by the same route. Fitting deflector plates which will absorb or scatter the signal will remedy this problem.

Loss of performance

Loss of power, brilliance or range is often caused by a faulty or overheating power unit. Power units should be situated in a cool place where heat can readily be dissipated. Cable runs should be kept to a minimum to prevent voltage loss.

Poor definition

When the scanner becomes dirty and encrusted with salt, loss of definition results. Switch off and clean it.

Display misaligned

This might be an obvious fault, or show itself in continual variance between compass bearings and bearings taken from the radar. The radar display is sensitive to external magnetic influences. Compass, electrical equipment or power cables which distort radar alignment, may have to be moved. Occasionally the scanner bearings fail. This causes a slop as it rotates, which is noticeable on the scanner as a variable heading line. Seek expert help.

Scanner does not revolve

Check for obstructions around the scanner. Remove and replace blown fuses. Check all wiring connections.

Radio direction finders

RDF sets are either hand-held or permanently installed in the boat. If you own a portable set, then it is worth while checking it for accuracy. Hand-held sets however, cannot be properly calibrated. Their accuracy varies according to the bearing of the beacon relative to the centre-line of the boat. In steel-hulled boats, and where there is a steel superstructure or wires and aerials, these deviations can be quite significant.

It is virtually impossible to eliminate all factors which affect the accuracy of the RDF set on a small boat, but the following suggestions may help in obtaining satisfactory readings with a hand-held or fixed RDF set.

The aerial of a fixed RDF should be on the centre-line of the boat, and clear of any obstructions. It should be easily accessible with a minimum run of cable to the receiver. Always keep the aerial away from metal window frames. When choosing a site for a fixed RDF aerial, or taking a bearing with a hand-held unit, choose an area as free as possible from large metal objects, aerial leads or rigging.

Calibrating a fixed unit, and checking a hand-held RDF set

Calibration or checking should be carried out in calm weather, away from structures which may cause interference or deviation (e.g. large sheds, wire fences, railway tracks, cranes). The beacon should be at least one mile away, and preferably visible. If it is not, a chart will give the correct bearing.

Choose a middle frequency signal for initial calibration. Begin at 0°, and swing the boat, taking compass and DF readings at 10° intervals. Take several readings at each point. These bearings should correspond to the compass bearings and form a regular curve when plotted on a deviation graph. Sudden distortions in the curve will be caused by shipboard equipment interfering with the radio beacon signal. Try to track down the source of serious irregularities in the RDF reading.

Swing the boat back to the compass bearings which show most variance from the RDF bearing and try to identify the item which is picking up the beacon signal and re-radiating it to the receiver.

Use a pair of jump leads as a temporary bond between stanchions and other metalwork. Since the fault may be intermittent, caused by the movement of gear making contact with the rigging, etc., it may be difficult to locate. When the cause has been found, bond it or try to eliminate the effect with insulators. Record remaining errors on a deviation graph. Make graphs for higher and lower frequencies.

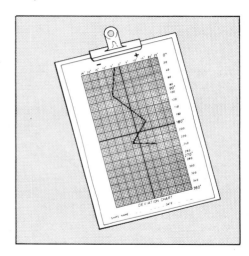

An extensive range of sophisticated, relatively low-powered domestic and navigational equipment is designed and manufactured for use in small boats. Sometimes after installation the owner may discover that the close juxtaposition of the equipment, the additional wiring it entails and the existence of other inadequately suppressed equipment, results in electrical interference which impairs the efficiency of sensitive electronic navigational and communications equipment.

Although the owner is quite likely to install cabin and galley electrical appliances and re-run wiring, installation and maintenance of navigational and other electronic equipment is a task for a professional marine electrical engineer, who has the knowledge and the necessary tools and testing equipment to ensure that it operates and functions correctly.

Any interference in the distress frequency (500, 2182 khz) and RDF wavebands (200, 400 khz) must be identified and eliminated.

Sources of interference

Electromagnetic interference is caused by changes in the electromagnetic field, associated with fluctuations, interruptions, or reversals of current flowing through a conductor. The more powerful the current, the more abruptly it is interrupted and the faster its rate of repetition, the greater will be the interference.

Most electrical units are a potential nuisance. Electrical motors, fluorescent or strobe lights, thermostats, petrol ignition systems, refrigerators, pumps, windscreen wipers, power generators, and many other items may cause interference. Unless it is filtered and screened, the electronic equipment itself may generate and radiate interference.

Identifying and eliminating causes of interference

Shipboard-generated interference usually covers a broad spectrum of frequencies, and within its normal ranges is likely to interfere with most of the electronic navigation and communication equipment carried on board. Tracking down the source of the interference is often difficult. It will help to carry a hand-held RDF or four-channel portable radio tuned to the interference frequency to avoid having to return to the deck house every time an appliance is turned off to check the interference level.

With the exception of the RDF or radio, turn off all electrical equipment. If the interference continues, it is likely to originate from a source other than the boat. If not, try each item in turn, and operate it in all its usual modes until the offending equipment is identified.

If the interference is caused by a hair drier, television, or cabin heater, for instance, these items, (provided that they are non-essential) can be switched off when navigation or communication equipment is in use. In these circumstances, nothing further need be done, and the problem is solved. However, interference is likely to be generated by several sources, and some at least will be essential equipment.

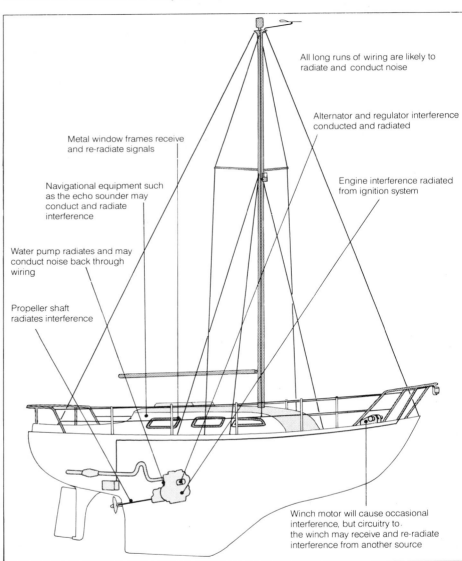

All long runs of wiring are likely to radiate and conduct noise

Alternator and regulator interference conducted and radiated

Engine interference radiated from ignition system

Metal window frames receive and re-radiate signals

Navigational equipment such as the echo sounder may conduct and radiate interference

Water pump radiates and may conduct noise back through wiring

Propeller shaft radiates interference

Winch motor will cause occasional interference, but circuitry to the winch may receive and re-radiate interference from another source

Some of the sources and means of propagation of interference

Propagation of interference

Radio frequency interference is introduced into the receivers in various ways — the two most important of which are conduction and radiation. The conducted component flows through the wiring system directly from the source to the receiver and may, in so doing, also produce radiation from the source and its associated wiring, in which case the wiring network effectively becomes a complex of aerials radiating the unwanted signals.

Conducted interference can also be propagated by inductance or mutual coupling between cables or equipment in close proximity to a receiver aerial, then the unwanted interference is passed to the receiver even though the conductors are not electrically connected to each other. The radiated interference may, in turn, act as aerials and be re-radiated by metal fittings, wire stays and the like, which then add to the sum total of radiated interference. Indeed, if the cabling is of the correct length, harmonics of particular frequencies may be generated so that the unwanted interference is increased in magnitude.

Suppression

The three main ways in which shipboard generated interference is suppressed are by shielding, bonding and filtering.

Shielding

A wire which carries a fluctuating current will radiate interference. The larger the loop formed by the wire, the more powerful its signal. If the source of the current fluctuations is shielded by a metallic case, and the wire itself is covered with a steel or copper braid or metal conduit, interference from the source will be contained within the wire, which in its turn is protected against externally radiated interference. When fitting a shielded cable, it is most important that the connections between the conduit or sheathing and the metal case shielding the appliance are electrically sound (clamped and soldered) and also that all parts of the wire and the case shielding are connected at fairly close intervals to the bonding system of the hull. Otherwise, the sheathing itself will become a very active aerial, capable of receiving and re-radiating interference signals.

Bonding

In most marine electrical systems (with the exception of those in steel hulled vessels, but including ferro-cement hulls) the bonding circuit provides the ground connection for appliances and also serves to bring all metal fittings and appliances to the same voltage potential. The circuit terminates at an anodic hull plate, fixed amidships below the water-line, away from gear vulnerable to corrosion.

Bonding, by bringing all appliances and metal fittings to the same voltage potential, reduces the chance of intermittent electrical contact which may otherwise cause interference.

Fixed appliances, not clamped directly to the bonding wire, should have an earthing wire connecting them to the bonding circuit. All bonding connections must be in good electrical contact, and protected against corrosion. The use of tinned copperbraid wire is effective in inhibiting corrosion at the joints. The bonding circuit should be kept clear of damp and bilge water which might provide an alternative lower resistance path to earth.

Filtering

The measures mentioned should help in eliminating the propagation of radiated interference, but do not suppress the interference at source. Electric motors, generators, the ignition system of a petrol motor and many other appliances all generate strong signals which must be suppressed or filtered at source.

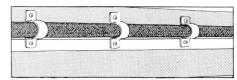

Screening harness bonded to earth tape

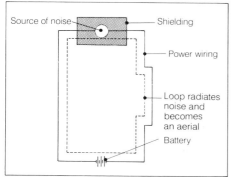

Although appliance is shielded, which prevents it directly radiating interference, extensive loop circuit supplying power to appliance will radiate noise conducted from appliance and may also conduct received interference into appliance

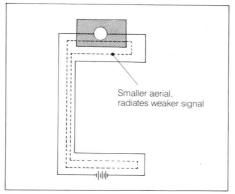

By running power leads together aerial effect is reduced, and interference is diminished

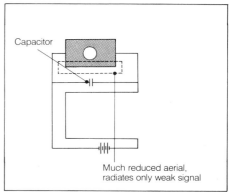

Reduced aerial, and capacitor fitted across power lines should eliminate interference

Petrol Engines

Check that it is the petrol engine, not the alternator or dynamo driven by the engine, that is causing the trouble. Stop the engine, mark, and disconnect the main output and field leads from the generator. Engine-caused interference will persist, and corresponds with engine revolutions. Reduce it by bolting the ignition coil directly to the engine block, or (if the coil is not capable of withstanding the increased temperatures) by bonding it to the engine block. Shorten the HT leads where practical, and fit suppressors to the spark plug and distributor end caps of wire cored leads, and screened plug and screened distributor end caps to resistive HT leads. Sheathe the lead to the instrument panel from an electronic engine revolution counter if fitted. A capacitor connected into the low tension wire (as illustrated) and bonded to the coil or common earth will assist in reducing interference.

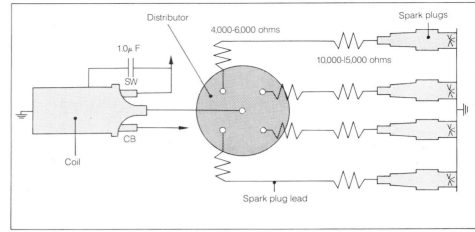

Interference suppression for petrol ignition system

Generator equipment

The 'noise' generated by a dynamo-type generator can sometimes be reduced by dismantling and cleaning the commutator and re-bedding the brushes. However, the dynamo or alternator, and also the regulator are likely to introduce serious interference into the output circuit, which may have to be screened and filtered.

Use sheathed electrical wiring, and keep the wiring runs as short and as close together as possible with the sheathing effectively bonded.

In addition, a suppression unit, or a large capacitor, capable of absorbing the ripple voltages and of withstanding the high temperatures involved can be fitted into the circuit to filter the variable voltages in the power generation circuit. Seek manufacturer's or an electrical engineer's advice before installing one of these units.

Electric motors

Electric motors which cause a high level of interference require individually formulated suppression measures. Low output motors can often be effectively suppressed by fitting capacitors between the power leads and earth (see diagram), but for larger motors, and those which are in close proximity to a receiver, specialist help will be needed.

Electronics equipment

Those which generate serious interference can be suppressed by connecting a capacitor between the power leads, but before doing so, it is advisable to seek professional advice.

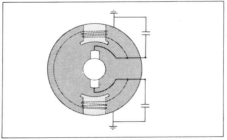

Use of capacitors for suppression

Otherwise, to ensure that there is minimum interference, keep power leads from different pieces of equipment separate, and take them directly to the

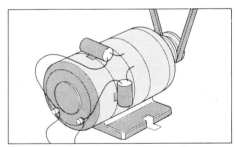

Capacitors bonded to motor casing

main switchboard. Make sure that all appliances are earthed, either to the grounded power wiring or to the common earth on the switchboard.

Other forms of radiated interference

Most interference signals are generated by electrical equipment and are propagated through the wiring, and radiated from unsheathed wiring. Until the more obvious causes are eliminated, other more devious sources of interference are difficult to identify. Any source which creates sufficient electrical energy is a potential source of interference. A rotating propeller shaft is a common cause, particularly when the bearings or brackets are made from metals with widely different voltage potentials. This effect is eliminated by connecting the shaft to the bonding circuit, via a bronze brush, pressing against the prop shaft. Other similar sources will be found in pumps, and other power-driven rotary and reciprocating gear. The noise signals emitted can be identified by the intermittent loud crackles, which correspond with the electrical discharge. Suppression measures usually involve dismantling and the provision of an electrical connection between the moving parts and earth.

Batteries

Lead acid and alkaline batteries on charge emit hydrogen, which will present a potential fire hazard if it is permitted to accumulate.

Battery compartments
Battery compartments must be fitted with high and low vents. The outlet should lead overboard, never into a space where the lighter-than-air hydrogen gas can collect. A spark-proof fan which ducts air into the bottom of the compartment can be installed to boost circulation. The battery compartment is usually close to the engine space and it is sensible to provide some means of maintaining a relatively cool environment for the battery. No switches or electrical appliances should be located within the battery compartment.

Lighting	10 lights at 12 watts =	120 watts
Navigation lights	4 lights at 10 watts =	40 watts
Vent fan	1 at 24 watts =	24 watts
Sundry loads	at 60 watts =	60 watts
Total maximum load		= 244 watts at 12 volts = 20.3 amperes

Possible maximum loading for small boat (12V) installation

Lighting	6 lights at 20 watts for 6 hours	= 720 watt hours
Navigation	4 lights total 80 watts for 4 hours	= 320 watt hours
Radio telephone	1 at 60 watts for 2 hours	= 120 watt hours
Refrigerator	1 at 180 watts for 8 hours	= 1440 watt hours
Radar	1 at 350 watts for 4 hours	= 1400 watt hours
Vent fans	2 at 48 watts for 4 hours	= 384 watt hours
Pumps	3 at 48 watts for 1 hour	= 144 watt hours
Sundry loads	at 120 watts for 1 hours	= 120 watt hours
Total power consumption = divided by 24 volts =		**4648 watt hours 193 ampere hours**

Calculation to show average requirements during typical 24 hour period

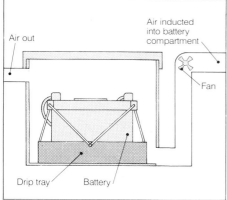

Tight, sealed, hatch gives overhead access to batteries for testing and removal

The bracing clamps must be stout enough to hold the batteries in the event of a capsize or knockdown. When designing a compartment, or installing a new battery, ensure there is adequate space for the batteries, and that it will be possible to remove them.

Where there is no room for a separate compartment, batteries should be protected with a fibreglass box, pierced at the top and sides for ventilation. Clamps which retain the box and those securing the battery should be independent.

The wiring should be at least equal to the theoretical maximum load it might carry. This is calculated as follows.

Although it is unlikely that all the equipment will be running simultaneously, it is best if the general wiring circuits have a minimum rating equivalent to the maximum possible loading. The engine starter cables should be rated to avoid excessive voltage drop, and one volt is normally the maximum recommended in order to reduce resistance and avoid the consequent danger of overheating. In cold weather, the starter current will be higher than that required during warmer weather, and discharge rates may sometimes be as high as 1000 amps over a very short period. Refer to the engine handbook for battery specification.

Battery selection
The choice of battery will depend upon the electrical consumption of appliances in normal use. The energy consumed by an appliance is measured in watts. A watt hour represents the amount of energy used by the appliance in one hour. To calculate the normal loads that the battery will have to meet, list each appliance, and multiply its wattage by the total number of hours it is likely to be used during a typical 24 hour period. Add the totals together.

Where only a single battery is fitted, the engine manufacturer's specification should be added to the general requirements. It is also worth while fitting an alarm which will indicate the state of charge of the battery. This can be particularly useful in indicating stray battery discharge currents. A separate starter battery is an insurance policy against a flat battery and the inability to start the main engine when there are no facilities for manual starting.

The inference from the above calculation is that as long as battery capacity is sufficient, there is no limit to the number and variety of electrical appliances that can be wired into the electrical system. But however many batteries are installed, the energy used must be replaced. The drain on the batteries is invariably greater than anticipated, partly because if equipment is there it will be used, and also because the owner invariably adds to the installation.

The selection of the batteries will be determined by many factors, including first cost, space and type and condition of the other batteries in the installation. Lead acid batteries nowadays require virtually no maintenance, and can be left aboard during off season lay up without losing their charge. Alkaline batteries are larger and more expensive, but they last longer. It is not advisable to mix acid and alkaline batteries as damage may occur to the batteries. Sulphuric acid and potassium hydroxide are not in any way compatible and a small amount of either in the wrong battery can result in irreparable damage.

Battery charging

In general terms, particularly for sailing boats, there is never enough motoring time for really effective battery charging, and it is often necessary to run the motor while sailing or while at anchor to maintain the batteries at full charge. The amount of electrical power required and the quantity of fuel that will be needed to convert to electricity to sustain this minimum requirement will have to be closely considered. The calculation and chart illustrated showing the charging characteristics of the battery should be of assistance in balancing the need for charging the battery with the additional fuel required.

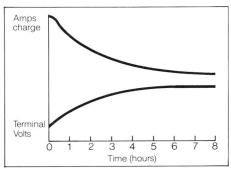

Battery charging characteristics

With shore supply facilities available in a large number of marinas, it is common practice to install a mains charging unit in the boat, and it is sensible to install a charger especially designed to protect batteries from excessively high charge rates, with the consequent loss of electrolyte. Care should be taken in terminating the shore supply on board and there are a number of suitable multi-pin water-tight insulated sockets and plugs for this purpose.

Acid and alkaline batteries emit hydrogen during the charging cycle and it is necessary to ensure that there is good ventilation since a stray spark may trigger an explosion.

Batteries are rated by the current they can deliver. In the case of lead acid batteries, it is usually a 10 hour rate, and for nickel cadmium, a 5 hour rate is normal (250AH=25 amps for 10 hours continuous running).

The efficiency of both types of battery is 70 per cent, which means that for a nominal battery rating of 250AH, the recharge rate must be calculated to provide 250 x 1.4 amps=350 amps. This means that the charging facilities must be able to provide in excess of 35 amps, since the time charge curve will show a rapid reduction in the charge rate as a function of time.

Higher charge rates are unlikely to harm a battery in good condition, so long as the electrolyte temperature does not exceed 43°C (110°F).

The specific gravity of a lead acid battery will give an indication of its state of charge. Low specific gravity readings after refilling with distilled water should be expected.

The state of charge and condition of the cells of the lead acid battery are tested with a hydrometer. Average readings are 1.280 fully charged; 1.200 half discharged; 1.115 fully discharged; taken at 16°C (60°F).

It is sometimes thought that continuous charging will result in a higher specific gravity than is indicated. It is not sufficient simply to recharge until the ammeter falls back to a charge rate of about 10 amps, and then to shut down the engine, believing that the power consumed has been replaced. The only real indication of a full charge is to charge until the specific gravity remains constant for three consecutive hourly readings, after which no further improvement of specific gravity reading is possible.

Alkaline batteries

Alkaline battery discharge capacities are given at a 5 hour rate for normal resistance cells and at a 2 hour rate for high performance cells.

Normal charge rate is calculated at 0.2 of the total battery capacity for a period of 7 hours. For example, a battery of 250AH capacity would normally accept a charge rate of 50 amps for 7 hours, i.e. 0.2 of 250=50 amps.

Higher charge rates may safely be used but batteries must be kept as cool as possible. The maximum temperature of the cells should not exceed 45°C (113°F). Both normal resistance and high performance types are available in plastic containers up to 120AH capacity per container.

The specific gravity will vary with temperature changes but not with the state of charge. A specific gravity of 1.200 at 20°C (68°F) is usual but will gradually fall as the electrolyte deteriorates. Renewal of the electrolyte is essential in order to restore the efficiency of the battery and the manufacturers should be consulted.

Gassing should not be taken as an indication that the battery is fully charged. The charge to discharge ratio is 1.4, as for lead acid batteries; that is to say, after a discharge of 100AH, a charge of 140AH is needed to restore the full battery capacity.

There are a variety of voltmeters specially scaled to give an indication of the state of charge, but they are generally most effective if a load is taken from the battery by switching on some electrical appliance while the reading is being taken. A rapid drop in the reading indicates that the battery needs charging. The specific gravity of the electrolyte only indicates the condition of the battery cells. Never use the same hydrometer for testing both lead acid and alkaline batteries. The installation of an automatic battery discharge warning device will give protection against the inadvertent discharge of the batteries which might result in poor starting performance.

Battery faults

Battery fully discharged
Electrical equipment has been left on.
Earth leak in wiring system.
Shorting across battery terminals.
Fault in wiring circuitry between batteries.
Cells are old or damaged.
Generating equipment is faulty.

Battery uses excessive water
Battery compartment is too hot.
Charging rate is too high.

Generators
Marine engines and auxiliaries usually mount a belt-driven generator on the engine frame. Additional generators may be attached to the prop shaft or powered by a separate motor and should be installed in accordance with manufacturers' instructions.

Check V belt tightness. Normal belt deflection between pulleys should be about half an inch (12mm). In small, high speed engines it is essential to fit a good quality belt, because the pulley ratio generally does not permit adequate wrap, and the section of the belt that drives the pulley is therefore less than ideal.

Always make certain when installing the battery that it is connected in the correct polarity; + to +, − to −. Reverse polarity will immediately destroy an alternator, and it is for this reason that some manufacturers will provide a fast fuse, the function of which is to rupture in advance of the rectifying diodes, when the battery is connected in reverse to the normal polarity. Under no circumstances should any other fuse be used as a replacement, other than that specified by the manufacturer.

A running alternator must not be disconnected from the battery. Should this occur, very high transient voltages will, unless reduced by a surge suppression unit, irreparably damage the transistors in the voltage regulator.

There are some complete systems available which include a self-regulating alternator, reverse polarity protection and surge suppression.

For most marine applications it is possible to obtain voltage regulators with alternative voltages. In the case of the Lucas marine system, the type 440 regulator has three settings — low, medium and high.

Include a tested dynamo or alternator with matching regulator and suitable spare V belt in the spares locker. Keep them well protected against damp. Complete replacement is, in most instances, the easiest way of overcoming problems with the generating equipment.

Dynamo faults
Some boat engines are still equipped with a conventional dynamo, and apart from cleaning the dynamo's commutator to reduce interference, no maintenance other than occasional brush replacement is required.

If the engine is laid up for a long period, the residual magnetic field in the winding fades, preventing the rotating armature from generating electrical power. By connecting a jump lead from the positive pole of the battery to the positive output terminal of the generator, via a test lamp, the magnetic field is reactivated in its correct polarity **A.** If, despite this, the dynamo still does not register a charge it will help to discover whether it is the regulator or the dynamo at fault. Stop the engine, and disconnect both the field and the positive terminals from the dynamo. Clip a test light across the positive output and negative terminals **B.** With the engine running, touch a jump lead via a test lamp from the generator negative terminal to the field terminal **C** and hold it there for a short while. If the bulb lights, the generator is working and the fault will be in the regulator circuit. Replacement of the regulator or cleaning the contacts will be necessary.

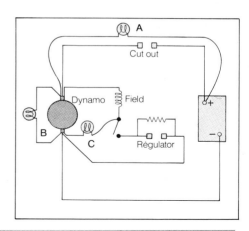

Alternators
Alternators are more compact than a conventional dynamo, and are able to generate greater power at low revolutions and have a higher maximum revolution limit. Like the dynamo, they require a small initial current in order to excite the alternator into generating. This is achieved by connecting the field system wiring to the battery, via a small warning light, which fulfils two functions. First, as already stated, it provides an excitation current, and it will also indicate that the generator is operating when the warning light goes off.

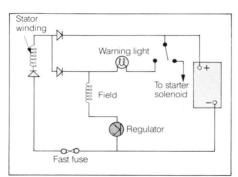

3 phase self-limiting alternator (one phase only illustrated) warning light providing external source of excitation

If the alternator does not charge, replace the warning light, or temporarily bridge its connections to provide excitation current.

Alternator control systems are now solid state, transistorized, and are not normally repairable. In the event of the alternator failing to charge, seek advice of a qualified electrician or remove both machine and regulator and return it to the manufacturer's servicing agent.

Electrical wiring

Apart from navigation and working lights, and the cabin lights below deck, electricity is used to start the main engines, and to power winches, refrigerators, pumps, showers and many other appliances. In addition, many items of electronic navigation and communications equipment require separate circuitry and considerable amounts of power.

Conditions aboard small boats are not ideal for the installation and maintenance of electrical equipment. Damp is pervasive and, in time, breaches the insulation of cables and corrodes terminals. The continual movement and vibration of the boat also tends to harden copper wiring, which if it is incorrectly installed, will fracture or burn through.

For most purposes the two-wire insulated system similar to domestic wiring is the most satisfactory method of wiring a boat (figure 3). An alternative system is the two-wire, with one pole earthed (figure 1). The wiring diagrams illustrated show examples of both wiring circuits. The earth return circuit is also illustrated (figure 2).

The two-wire insulated system is preferable, as the engine frame, hull fittings and outer skin, can be insulated from the electrical wiring of the boat, and this reduces the danger of stray leakage currents which are a common source of corrosion.

Wiring of the correct rating should be installed. Cable that is too small will overheat and cause voltage drop. The gauge of the wiring should be chosen with reference to the current it is to carry and the length of the cable required. For long runs of cable, much heavier wire is needed. The table and calculation below illustrate this and can be used to calculate the size of wire required. If the correct gauge is not available, fit slightly oversize wires.

Cable can be run in galvanized, or plastic conduit, or clipped to a batten. Conduit should be purpose-made for marine use, with waterproof closures at the ends and at the junction boxes.

All but the engine starting circuit should be fused or embody circuit breakers. Two-wire insulated circuits are normally fitted with fuses or circuit breakers on both the negative and the positive cable, but it is also common practice to fit either fuses or circuit breakers in the positive pole of the system with common negatives throughout. Circuit isolating switches should be installed at the switchboard to break both the positive and negative cable, so totally isolating the circuit. Elsewhere single pole operating switches are positioned where convenient.

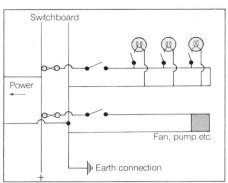

1 Two-wire with one pole earthed circuit. Only one cable need be broken in order for earth leak to occur

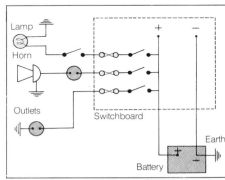

2 Earth return circuit. All circuits are earthed. Different earth potential at widely separated parts of boat can cause electrolyte corrosion

Appliance 240 watts, 24v – current= $\frac{240}{24}$ =10 amps

Measured length of cable (there and back) 30 m

Resistance of cable with maximum permissible voltage drop of 1.0 volt= $\frac{1.0\ V}{10A}$ = 0.1 ohms

For l metre, maximum resistance $\frac{0.1\ ohms}{30\ m}$

Converting to l000m $\frac{0.1\ ohms}{30\ m}$ ×1000=3.33 ohms

Using cable guide most suitable= 6.00 mm²

If the cable was chosen by amp rating (ie 10 amp=1.5 mm²) voltage drop would have been above 1.0 maximum permitted.

ie voltage drop

=10 (amps)× $\frac{12.57}{1000}$ (ohms)×30 =3.77 volts.

Nominal cross-section mm2	General purpose rubber and PVC		'High temperature' or heat-resisting		Butyl		Ethylene propylene rubber		Resistance ohms per 1000m at 20C
	Single core	2 core	Single core	2 core	Single core	2 core	Single core	2 core	
	Amps		Amps		Amps		Amps		
1	8	7	13	.11	15	12	16	13	18.84
1.5	12	10	17	14	19	16	20	17	12.57
2.5	17	14	24	20	26	22	28	23	7.54
4	22	19	32	27	35	30	38	32	4.71
6	29	25	41	35	45	38	48	40	3.14
10	40	34	57	49	63	53	67	57	1.82
16	54	46	76	64	84	71	90	76	1.152
25	71	60	100	86	110	93	120	102	0.762
35	87	74	125	105	140	119	145	120	Q.537
50	105	89	150	127	165	140	180	155	0.381
60	120	100	175	150	185	160	200	170	0.295
70	135	115	190	161	215	183	225	191	0.252

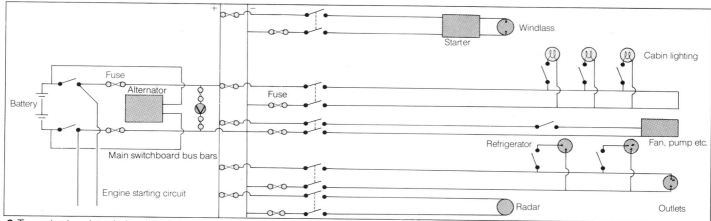

3 *Two-wire insulated circuit requires two breaks in insulation before earth leak is established*

Fault finding

Faults in electrical wiring and fittings are likely to be of three kinds.

Intermittent working
This fault indicates poor connections in the circuitry, or the failure of the cable. Tests for locating the latter are described below. Before testing for wire failure, inspect all the terminal connections that are not soldered. Clean the connections of the fuse, switch gear, and other terminals, and re-test.

Complete failure of the appliance
First check that the appliance is working by connecting it to an alternative power supply.

Wire failure
Failure in the appliance is more common than the failure of the wiring; however, as wiring gets old, and damp penetrates the insulation, total failure and perhaps short circuiting will result. Check the fuse or circuit breaker, clean the wires and connections and re-test before checking for wire failure.

Locating a broken or fractured cable
For the purposes of illustration, let us suppose that the cabin light **1** fails to work and that **2** and **3**, which are connected in parallel with **1**, are working normally.

Remove the light bulb and check its connections. Replace the bulb after cleaning the terminals and checking that

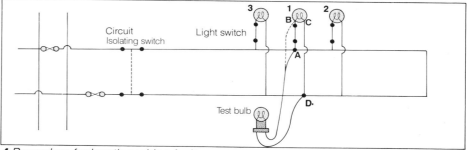

4 *Procedure for locating wiring faults*

the bulb works. If the light still does not work, but other lights controlled by the same isolating switch do, attempt to establish the following: that all three lights are wired into the same circuit; which part of the circuit is likely to be at fault; where the junction boxes that need to be opened are situated.

These can all be deduced from the switchboard and wiring layout. Before removing any connections, label the wires, or draw wiring diagrams of each junction box, noting the colouring of the wires to help identify them when testing and re-connecting.

Make a test lamp, using a spare lamp socket and suitable bulb. Attach two leads to the socket with a crocodile clip at the free end of each. Clip one end of the wire at **D** and the other end to position **A**.

If the test lamp lights, this will confirm that the correct subcircuit has been

identified. Move clip **A** to position **B**. If both lights glow dimly, then the fault has been bridged by the test lamp, and lies between points **A** and **B**. If the test lamp lights, but lamp **I** does not, then the fault is between the light socket and **D**. Check the light socket terminals and replace the bulb before moving the lead to **C**. Both lamps should light. The faulty cable is **C-D** and this should be replaced.

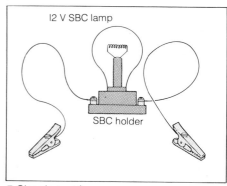

5 *Simple test lamp*

Short circuits

A different test is used for locating a short circuit. The first indication of a short will be that the fuse blows or the circuit breaker opens, and the appliance ceases to function. Changing the fuse or closing the circuit breaker may cure the fault, but if not the cause of the failure which will have to be identified.

Short circuits in low voltage wiring are often associated with burning and scorching and are easy to identify. However, where the wiring is hidden, detective work will be needed to pin-point the wiring fault.

Remove fuse and connect crocodile clips of the test lamp to the fuse holding clips. Switch off main circuit isolating switch. If test lamp lights, short is between fuse and main switch. If not, but the light comes on when the isolating switch is closed and all appliances in

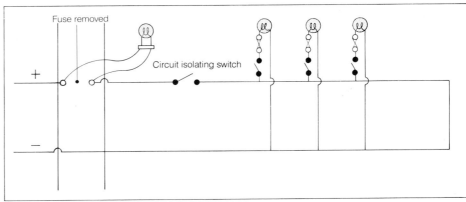

Procedure for locating short circuit

sub circuits are turned off, isolate each sub circuit in turn. When the light goes off, the faulty sub circuit has been identified.

If it is impossible to locate any faulty fitting, then perhaps one of the cables has worn through its insulation and is causing a short circuit. Move the wires around until the light flickers or goes out. This will be the wire to replace.

Replacing an electrical cable

Select wire suited to marine use. Stranded rather than solid copper wire should be used. Refer to the chart for guidance in selecting the right size.

If the cable being renewed has shorted or burnt through, withdraw and inspect adjacent cables for damage.

Cable held by clips should be well supported and laid neatly. Do not loop cable through holes in the deck beams, etc. without clipping and holding the cable at intervals of about 8 inches (20cm). Insert grommets where cables pass through metal or other hard-edged

fittings which could damage their insulation. Outlets on deck should be sealed to prevent water entering.

Replacing a conduit enclosed cable

Release closures at the ends of the conduit. Wind the ends of the new and the damaged wire together, and pull gently on the old cable. Extra help will be needed to feed the new wire into the conduit and to prevent it from scoring and damaging its insulation at the edge of the junction box. Cut the cable to length after the connection and springing has been completed at one end, and allow sufficient for the connection and springing at the other.

Where the cable has been burnt inside the conduit, attach its end to some nylon lanyard, which can be pulled through easily, and used to draw the new cables along the conduit. If more than one cable needs to be replaced, make a loop in the centre of the lanyard so that it can be withdrawn and used again from the same end without re-threading.

If the cable has been totally burnt through, withdraw the remains and disconnect an existing wire and attach the end of the nylon lanyard to it and pull it through.

Temporary repairs

These repairs need to be quick and simple to complete, and yet should have the same high degree of insulation and water resistance as the rest of the circuitry. Once the damaged sections of the cable are identified and withdrawn, a new section of cable can be temporarily installed and connected to complete the circuit and restore power.

Before joining the new and the old stranded cables together, slip a short length of polythene tube over the old cable insulation. Twist and press the

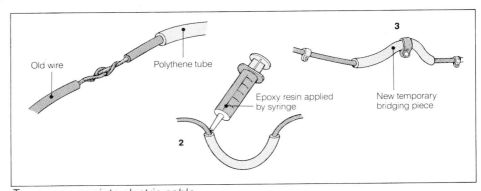

Temporary repair to electric cable

wires together to make a satisfactory electrical contact.

Bend the tube downwards and pour epoxy resin glue down both ends of the tube. Warm to accelerate drying. Once the resin has cured, clip the wire into position in the boat, with the centre point of the tube's arc uppermost.

Earth leaks
The smallest earth leak from a battery to any part of the boat in contact with seawater may cause electrolytic corrosion. Very small currents are difficult to detect and may result in serious damage to the battery, hull fittings, propeller or shaft.

It is possible to test for some leaks to earth especially those from the power supply circuits on the boat, but others, for instance from a faulty radio, can be difficult to detect.

Electrical wiring and installations should be kept clean and as dry as possible. Wires can be cleaned with carbon tetrachloride. Any black residue left when a wire is tracking should be scraped from the insulation and the wire replaced at the earliest convenience. Insulation should be in good condition, and terminals clean and secure. Earthing should be to a common, specially fitted, earthplate via the bonding system. Earth wires should never be attached at random points about the hull.

Earth leaks from the battery and wiring can be measured with a multi-meter, capable of measuring milli-amps. A high-resistance ohm-meter (megger) is then used to check the value of the insulation of the wiring system, using the methods described below.

Switch off the battery isolating switch and with the multi-meter set on the highest scale setting, connect it in series in the main positive connection to the battery. If no deflection is seen, progressively reduce the multi-meter setting down to the lowest level before there is any deflection. The meter should give an accurate indication of the rate of leakage.

If there remains a measurable current with the battery isolating switch turned off, the fault must be located in the wiring and equipment between the battery and the isolator switch. Clean the battery top, terminals and switch. Clean the wires with carbon tetrachloride, re-connect the battery and smear the terminals with petroleum jelly. Re-test for current flow. If the problem appears to be solved, complete the testing procedure described below, as there is often more than a single fault to be found.

If the current ceases to register on the meter when the switch is off, the leakage is from the wiring circuits. Again, leaving the multi-meter connected in series with the main battery connection, but with it set on the highest scale setting and with all circuits (except for the main battery

isolating switch) turned off, check the meter through all its settings for current flow. Return it to its highest setting, switch on individual circuits to indicate satisfactory operation. Do not switch on the heavy duty circuits such as the winch motor circuit which will carry a current outside the capacity of the meter, and will damage it.

Turn off every appliance and progressively reduce the multi-meter setting to the lowest level before there is any deflection. This will give a clear indication of the rate of leakage, and it is then only necessary to isolate each circuit in turn to establish the source of the leak.

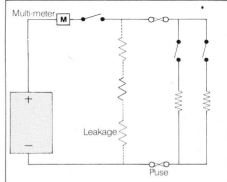

When circuit is made, leakage reading will show on both positive and negative connections, although two separate wiring circuits sharing same conduit etc, may be involved in single leakage

Insulation test
This can only be carried out after first having disconnected voltage-conscious solid state devices (such as the regulator in an alternator system) which are highly susceptible to the higher voltages generated by an insulation testing unit.

Carry out the insulation test in each circuit, working from the main switchboard. With the megger, test across each pole to earth, and then between poles. For the between poles test, all motors, lamps etc. must be switched off. In damp conditions the

starter motor will give a low reading, which may be below 5000 ohms, all other circuits should be at one megohm at 250V. (1 megohm=1 million ohms.) Failure in insulation will be revealed by low resistance reading, the causes are usually discovered by inspection.

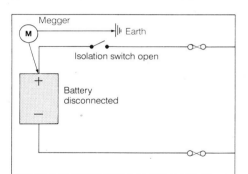

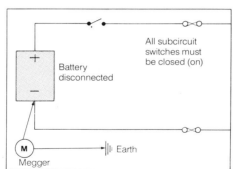

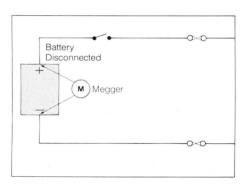

Chapter 12

Routine Maintenance

Pre-season check list   Routine maintenance

A carefully planned fitting-out procedure will help to ensure that everything is remembered. Once the boat is launched, and the propeller shaft connected, and one or two last-minute jobs completed, the boat should be ready for sea. Fitting-out should be virtually completed by the launch date. Try not to leave jobs for completion during the first spring cruise — it might spoil the work, and it will almost certainly spoil the cruise. The first condition of the check list is that all the maintenance tasks undertaken during the winter are finished. Use the check list to help review the progress of fitting out.

Inside

Engine
Refit carburettor, coil, alternator. Remove rag from distributor cap, tighten spark plugs and connect HT leads. Check alternator and waterpump belt tension. If engine was protected by corrosion-inhibiting oil, fill sump with correct grade lubricating oil. Ensure that suitable spares, filters, sparking plugs etc. as well as the owner's maintenance and operating manual, are onboard.

Stuffing boxes
These should be sufficiently tight to prevent leaks at the prop shaft or rudder stock, but free enough to allow them to rotate. Make sure that the locking nuts are tightened. Stuffing boxes that leaked the previous season after glands were re-packed, can be sealed using a pair of untanned leather washers, cut and slipped each side of the fibre washers in the stuffing box.

Tanks
Petrol tanks that contain stale petrol should be flushed with clean, fresh petrol. Clean filters etc. but do not fill tanks until the boat is in the water.

Diesel tanks should not require flushing, but drain water traps in the tank and filter after the first hour or so at sea, when any condensation on the tank top will have washed off and separated out at the bottom of the tank. Water tanks should be flushed before filling. This can also be done with the boat afloat. Remove one outlet pump hose, connect a hose to its feed pipe, and drain it overside. Fill tanks with fresh water, and keep flushing before turning off the water supply and re-connecting water outlet pump.

Control wires
Oil wires and sheaves. Check wire tension, and tighten where necessary. Ensure that spare wires and some bulldog grips are available in the spares locker in case of wire failure.

Steering wires
Treat as above.

Bearings
Grease white metal rudder and prop shaft bearings. Do not grease water-lubricated cutlass-type bearings.

Toilet
Re-connect toilet unit.

Seacocks
Re-connect hoses to seacocks. Make sure that each hose end is secured by two worm screw hose clips, set at least ½ inch (12 mm) apart. Grease seacocks and close them.

Drain plugs
Close all hull drainage plugs.

Chain and anchor
Bring anchor and chain aboard. Shackle end to long rope tail made fast to strong point in chain locker. Stow chain, and lash anchor to chocks on deck. Check that hardwood pin is in place in the anchor shackle.

Cabin
Clean cabin interior, windows, woodwork, and all working surfaces.

Galley
Bring aboard and stow crockery and cutlery, cooking utensils, can opener, etc. Make sure that there are sufficient items for all crew and guests. Flush ice box and clean refrigerator.

Upholstery
Bring aboard mattresses, cushions. Re-hang curtains. Douse shower curtain with salt water before hanging.

Batteries
Clean battery terminals and clamps. Connect battery and smear petroleum jelly over the terminals. Check all electrical appliances. Terminals are likely to be corroded and may need to be scraped with a penknife and blown clean. Ensure that power supplies are disconnected when doing this.

Gas
Connect gas cylinder and check all pipework for leaks. Leave gas turned off at cylinder.

Compass
After several years an air bubble will form in the compass. Remove the compass and place in the refrigerator with the refilling liquid. When they are really cold, take out, and invert the compass. Open the filler cap on the underside and top up the compass fluid.

Spares
Organize the spares locker. Know what it contains, and add and replace pieces where necessary. Experience will tell which spares are most commonly needed. Fuses, light bulbs, shackle pins, bolts, nuts as well as engine parts, should all be included.

Outside the Hull

Anti-fouling
This is usually the last painting job. After anti-fouling, bolt the protective anodes on to the studs fixed to the hull. Before fitting, make sure that the anodes are in good electrical contact with the items they are placed to protect. This connection should be with a bonding wire inside the hull, or, in the case

of a steel hull, grind clean the bolting surfaces of the anode plates before bolting. Paint the steel holding bolts etc. after fitting the anodes, but do not allow any paint on to the zinc anode.

Deck, mast and standing rigging
Check all mast fittings, in particular the gooseneck, cleats, winches etc. for security and corrosion. Grease roller reefing gear. Check all rigging wire. Feel for stranding, particularly at terminals. Rigging screws should be tight and wired. Rock the screw to test for worn threads. Tighten locking nuts. All clevis pins should be fitted with retaining clips, and rough surfaces should be covered to prevent chafe or injury.

Handholds
These should be bolted into place, and lifelines tensioned with locked rigging screws. All fastenings must be tight.

Hatches
Rub hatch slides with candle wax and oil hinges and catches with light oil.

Fenders
Clean fenders and renew their ropes if worn or too short.

Sails
Shake out and air sails. Inspect stitching in case tears or worn seams escaped notice during winter maintenance. Each sail bag should be painted with the name of its sail, and the head and tack of each sail should be marked.

Battens
These should be smooth and unfractured, and marked 'top', 'middle' and 'bottom' as appropriate. Keep spare ones in the sail locker.

Running rigging
Glance over the running rigging. This will have been checked during the winter, but inevitably some faults will be missed. Re-do worn or frayed whippings and splices. Replace weakened ropes. Reverse those with uneven wear. Grease or oil blocks, pulleys, and cam cleats. Spray hanks with light lubricating oil.

Safety

Check all paperwork necessary prior to launch date. Check that insurance premiums are up to date and that the boat is fully covered. Test lifejackets unless they have been sent away and serviced professionally. Inflatable lifejackets should be left inflated for approximately 48 hours during which time they should not appreciably deflate. Repair leaking lifejackets and re-test, then place in cockpit lockers ready for use. Make sure that there are enough safety harnesses and lifejackets of a suitable size for all those likely to be aboard. Fire extinguishers should be in position, with recent service sheet attached or pinned nearby. Attach a fire blanket in its container to the bulkhead in the galley.

All flares and other survival equipment should be taken aboard having previously been checked or serviced. Stow boarding ladder in a cockpit locker.

Once the boat is afloat

Ballast
Install inside ballast and batten down securely.

Prop shaft
Align engine to prop shaft. Check alignment after a couple of weeks, as some craft take a while to resume their shape.

Lines
Check mooring lines, fenders, and anti-chafe gear.

Tender
The tender should be fully equipped with oars, paddle and buoyancy, and with the name of the mother ship clearly painted on her transom.

Ready to sail

Supplies
Take adequate provisions, tinned as well as fresh food, and water. Toilet and kitchen provisions will also be needed, also matches, bulbs, life raft, charts and navigation equipment. Calibrate RDF and compass before embarking on the first voyage.

Ground tackle

An essential part of the boat's equipment. At least three anchors are required, two main and one kedge anchor, each with sufficient chain or rope, separately stored. Areas of maximum wear will be towards the end of chain or cable. Check galvanizing and assess loss of strength due to corrosion or abrasion. Back-twist ropes to check for hidden severing of strands inside lay.

Bitter end should be shackled to synthetic rope, which reaches to the deck and is made fast to a strong point in the chain locker. The locker should be ventilated and drained.

All deck gear, winches, chain grips, etc., should be in good condition. The bow roller should incorporate a chain retaining pin.

Wet berths

Your boat will not look after herself. If she is left afloat during the winter months, take every reasonable precaution to ensure that she is well-secured and protected, not only from rubbing against the pier, but also from damage that might be caused by other boats.

Maintenance work will be limited. Most of the jobs on the exterior of the hull must be left. Interior work is more difficult when the boat is afloat than when she is propped in a boat-yard with power supplies and motor transport nearby.

However, many boat owners, particularly those who own fibreglass boats, consider that a dry winter berth is unnecessary and, instead, haul out on alternate years. If the boat winters afloat, do not expect to carry out a full maintenance programme, and remember that corrosion and fouling will continue throughout the winter. An early beaching and cleaning at the start of the new season may be necessary.

Preparing to winter afloat

The illustration shows a satisfactory arrangement of fenders and mooring lines. Fenders are hung around the hull, to protect her against accidental damage as well as from spoiling her paintwork against the pier. Fore and aft springs prevent her surging.

- Breast rope
- Fore spring
- Aft spring
- Stern rope

Where there is a choice of moorings, choose one where the set of the tide or the prevailing wind keeps the boat away from the pier, and ensure that there is sufficient slack in the mooring lines to allow for the tidal ranges expected over the winter. A few well-placed mooring lines will be more satisfactory and more easily checked than a badly planned, makeshift arrangement.

A simple awning will protect the brightwork in the cockpit and coamings. Ample ventilation is ensured by leaving as many windows and hatches open as possible (consistent with security) and by opening all ventilation cowls.

Checking the ground tackle

If a permanent mooring is used, make sure there is sufficient chain, and that it is in good condition. An iron chain will corrode more slowly in cold weather. In many coastal parts, onshore winds will increase the height of the tides, flood water will tend to run faster, and carry with it flotsam, and perhaps other boats, that may strike your craft, placing additional stress on the mooring line.

The maintenance of the permanent mooring is usually the responsibility of the owner of the mooring, who should have a map or chart, on which the position of the anchors and weights are marked. This enables him to lift them for inspection or removal. Moorings attached to a single heavy weight or mushroom anchor can be lifted by pulling on the mooring chain. Those with two or more anchors must be lifted by dragging a grapnel across the line of the ground arms, and lifting each anchor in turn. When lifting a two-legged

Haul in anchors at low tide

arrangement of ground tackle, only the first anchor need be lifted by grapnel. Once it has been recovered the second one can be lifted direct.

Locate the anchor cables at low water, and pull in as much chain as possible before the tide turns. Make the chain fast over the stern of the boat, and wait for the rising tide to lift the anchor. Heavy anchors may have to be lifted from a beam supported by two boats. In areas where the tidal range is small, a boat-

Grapnel

yard winch or derrick barge will have to be used instead.

Bring anchors and chain ashore, and inspect their condition. Those that are weakened by corrosion can be partially protected by bolting zinc anodes to the chain at intervals of no more than two feet (60cm). Use steel bolts and roofing zinc, hammered into small lumps for the anodes. Clean the touching surface of the link with an electric grinder prior to bolting, to ensure a good contact. Re-lay the mooring, charting the position of the anchors, and their relation to buildings and other points ashore.

When at a permanent mooring, ensure that there is enough room to allow the boat to swing, and sufficient space between boats riding at moorings.

Mud berths

A mud berth can provide a satisfactory winter berth for round and flat-bottomed boats. The site should be tidal, allowing the boat to float on an average high tide.

It is best if the site for a mud berth is away from public rights of way, or is close to a house owner who can be persuaded to keep a sympathetic watch on the boat during the winter.

Prepare the mud berth by excavating a depression to suit the boat. Only a rough approximation is necessary, as tidal water will scour the mud until the boat sits happily. Bury a couple of mud weights or 'deadmen' at each end of the boat for anchorage points. 'Deadman' must be buried across direction of pull sufficiently deep to prevent it being washed out. 3 feet (1m) is usually deep enough.

Make sure that there are no rocks or piles buried in the mud that might damage the boat. Sail her in on a high tide, arranging the springs and mooring lines to hold her over the trench. Food

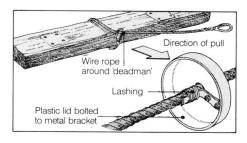

and fabrics that might attract rats should be taken ashore. Fit barriers on the shore ropes to stop vermin climbing aboard.

Legs

Where legs are to be used, the sea shore should be fairly level and hard. Only boats with long, fairly straight, keels are suitable. These can be fitted with a pair of wooden beams, bolted to a reinforced part of the hull amidships. A couple of guy ropes from the foot of each leg to the ends of the boat will hold them in position, and prevent them from twisting and collapsing.

The pivoting point of the legs should be just below the beam shelf on a wooden hulled boat, and a little below the hull and deck join and as close to a structural bulkhead as possible in a fibreglass boat. Inside reinforcements will have to be made to spread the loading on the bolt. Notch the top, so that when the leg is vertical, its top rests beneath the rubbing strake.

Shape the top inner side of each leg, and fit a pad to give sideways support to the leg a little below the pivot. The distance from the bolt to the bottom of the leg should be slightly less than from the same point to the bottom of the keel. This ensures that at no time will the main

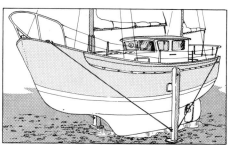

Brace each leg with two guy ropes

part of the boat's weight be taken by the legs.

Preparing to leave the boat

The following check list will help ensure that the boat will pass the winter and come to little harm. Heavy condensation should be expected in a boat that winters afloat. Everything removable should be taken ashore, to ensure the maximum possible circulation of air.

Paint and varnish

Choose a fine, dry day to scrutinize the exterior brightwork, and look for lifted varnish and exposed wood. Varnish bare wood to protect it during the winter and to prevent it from blackening from exposure. Use a thick varnish, brush it on or apply with a rag, working the varnish well into the grain.

Treat paintwork in the same way, with an oil-based undercoat. For boats riding at moorings, place a marker on the hull at the water-line, in a position visible from the shore. This will give a reference point from which the amount of bilge water can be assessed.

Preparation for laying-up

Remove the running rigging, reeve a light nylon messenger in place, and make fast away from the mast to prevent chafe. Wash all deck fittings, rigging screws, etc. with fresh, warm water, and coat them in petroleum jelly for winter protection.

Inside

Shut all seacocks, disconnect and drain water hoses. These should include the toilet, engine water jacket, heat exchanger etc. Plug seacocks or refit hoses for safety.

Disconnect the batteries, and take ashore (see page 270). Smear the battery leads with petroleum jelly.

Empty water tanks, top up diesel fuel tanks. Remove the gas cylinder. Brush paraffin over the jets and burner of the stove. This will leave a thin protective layer of wax over their vulnerable brass and steel parts.

Clean and rub brasswork, then wipe with a cloth dipped in petroleum jelly.

Ventilation

Remove cushions, mattresses, curtains, carpets, drawers, all other movable and valuable pieces of equipment and take them ashore.

Lift cabin floorboards, and pump the bilges dry. Ensure that all waterways and limbers are clear.

Open cabin and locker doors and wedge to allow air to circulate. Prevent them from swinging.

Open ventilators and as many portholes as possible (it is particularly important to arrange for air circulation at the ends of the boat). If possible, lock the forehatch slightly open. It is better for cold air to circulate, perhaps bringing with it a little rain or snow, than to lock stale air in the boat over the winter. All ventilation arrangements must, however, be consistent with protection against thieves and vandals.

Rig an awning over the cockpit. One that covers the entire boat is more satisfactory and will protect varnish and paintwork on wooden coach roofs, hatches, etc. Awnings must be secure and completely weather-proof, while allowing air to circulate between cabin and awning. Arrange an entry point to allow people to come aboard. Leave handholds or ropes at the entrance to help those boarding from a dinghy.

Check all mooring ropes, making sure that they are well-secured and protected against chafe. If ice is expected, take suitable precautions.

Ice
Boats are badly damaged or sunk by ice, both by the pressures that ice can exert on a steep-sided hull, and also from the abrasive effects of the floes as they grind past the hull in the spring thaw. If it is necessary to leave the boat afloat where it will be iced in, equip the boat with a bubbler beneath the hull, and fabricate and suspend light plywood defences against the outside of the fenders, which will deflect ice floes from the hull. Pump all water from the bilges and visit the boat regularly. Open the cabin whenever possible to increase the ventilation, and arrange with a local resident or boat-yard to keep a watch from the shore.

Supervision
The mark on the side of the hull will be an inch or two (50mm) above the water-line once the tanks are emptied and movables taken ashore. A watcher will be able to assess the quantity of water in the bilge at a glance, by gauging the reduction in distance between the mark and the water. Go aboard as frequently as possible to open the hatches and ventilate the cabin. Keep the bilges clear, and pump when necessary.

Dry berths

Preparation for hauling out
Hauling out can be left entirely in the hands of the boat-yard. The owner's only responsibility is to leave the boat in an accessible mooring close to the yard, and to pay for the work when it has been completed.

Most craft, except perhaps small steel boats, will flex as they are lifted out of the water and are manoeuvred and propped ashore. To minimize damage, the following simple precautions are necessary.

Disconnect the drive flanges on the propeller shaft and separate them by about ½ inch (12mm). This is necessary even if flexible couplings are fitted, and avoids harming the prop shaft and engine mountings.

Remove loosely stored items. Pump the bilges dry. If there are troublesome leaks that are difficult to locate, leave some water in the bilges, in the hope that the leakage will be spotted once the boat is ashore.

Remove internal ballast (see page 141). If it is necessary to remove the mast, assistance from the boat-yard may be needed. The process of stepping the mast is outlined on page 224. For its removal the procedures are reversed.

Lifting the boat out
Many modern yards are equipped with a self-propelled travel lift that enters the water and lifts the boat, suspending it from two web slings. The lift is then driven to the designated site, where yard staff will prop the boat. The operation is quick and efficient, and the owner does not need to help or advise. Other yards will be equipped with a winch and a carriage which runs on rails into the water. It will be the boat-yard's responsibility to operate this equipment, and only boat-yard workers are likely to be allowed in the vicinity of the operation.

There is little left for an owner to do if he plans to pay for the services of the boat-yard. However, if his boat is unusual, or has non-standard underwater fittings it will be a great help to the boat-yard staff to have a blueprint of the plans, or a reasonably accurate drawing of the boat's profile.

Lifting the boat out of the water
The following section will help the owner who plans to organize the lifting and propping of the boat himself.

Hoist or cradle
It is usually cheaper and easier to hire a crane to lift the boat to its trailer or dry berth, than to construct a cradle and pull the boat out of the water on improvised plank ways. The latter is an arduous, skilled and difficult operation, which can be carried out only where there is a suitable hard-shelving shoreline, and considerable tidal range. The cost of fabricating the cradle from wood or steel is likely to be greater than the cost of hiring a crane. If the crane hire is shared between several owners, the cost per boat can be reduced and the difficulties of the alternative method avoided.

Before lifting, remove heavy items from the boat. Take out all inside ballast, marking each piece with its exact location on a carefully drawn chart.

Make sure that each pig is marked with a clearly identifiable colour (green for starboard, red for port) before stacking in a safe place. Removal is easier with the boat in the water, and the additional weight of the ballast might otherwise cause the boat to hog.

When the internal ballast is removed, remember that the longitudinal centre of gravity of the boat is likely to move aft, towards the engine. This will affect the position and length of the straps holding the webbing beneath the hull.

Use the crane to help unstep the mast before lifting the hull.

Choosing a site
The site should be fairly level and firm as considerable weights are involved. If it seems poorly-drained, and likely to turn into a quagmire during the winter, find somewhere else: the cost of adequately supporting a boat in these conditions will far outweigh the saving in rent. A

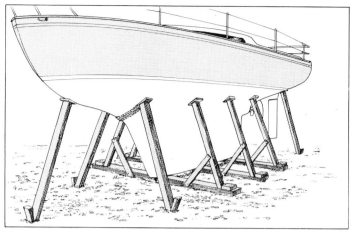

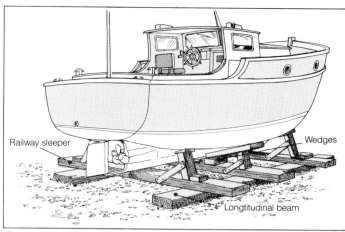

Transverse beams support the keel and provide a foundation for the props at the sides

Ensure area beneath engine is well-supported

drained concrete hard-standing area is ideal. Asphalt may be thin, and unable to support the weight of the boat unless horizontal load-spreading bearers are placed beneath the keel. If bearers are used, fasten the props to them, to equalize the downwards thrust of the boat, and to prevent the side props pushing into the ground.

To ensure that a mud or gravel site will not subside in the winter (ground subject to heavy frosts will swell when frozen, which can have disastrous consequences for the boat), prepare the foundations for the berth with care.

Movement in the supports might distort the hull, and perhaps threaten the safety of adjacent boats.

Lumber is expensive, and considerable quantities are needed to support a heavy boat that winters on an unprepared mud or shingle site.

Propping the boat

The suggestions given below relate to propping boats of all types of construction. Wooden boats, especially those with large overhangs, require more supports, and they need to be positioned with care. Fibreglass boats, which have most of their weight concentrated at the ballast keel, require fewer props. If the boat is berthed on a concrete or well-made tarmac park, some of the precautions described will be unnecessary. See what others do, and copy the examples set by the boat-yard or the owners of the smartest boats in the park.

Lay the transverse keel beams in preparation for the boat. A length equivalent to at least two-thirds the keel length should be supported. If the ground is wet, or likely to subside under the weight of the boat, they should be supported with levelled longitudinal bearers. If the boat has a straight keel, all transverse beams can be placed, levelled, and spiked, prior to lifting the boat. Otherwise, spike two transverse bearers and add more once the boat is resting on them.

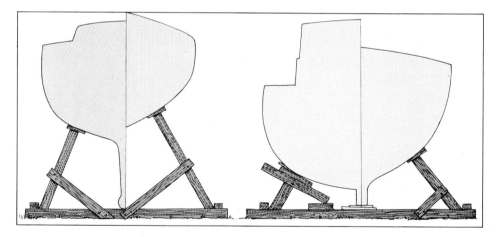

Lift the boat on to the prepared supports, and wedge additional transverse supports beneath her keel. Tap them with a sledge hammer; the resonance and movement of the bearers will indicate the proportion of weight each is taking. Equalize the distribution by wedging beneath the keel.

Ensure that the water-line is level in both planes before propping. Even with the inside ballast removed, the resolved hull weights give a centre of gravity on the longitudinal centre-line, a little above the water-line. A boat with a fixed ballast keel will have its centre of gravity lower than this. Support the hull with the props appearing to radiate from this theoretical point. Place a pad against the hull, and if necessary wedge and cleat the lower end of each prop to the bearer.

Tap each prop to ensure that it supports the hull. Brace the overhangs in the same way with props positioned on the centre-line and angled towards the hull.

It is sometimes difficult to prop a fibreglass boat firmly because of the thin, frameless, skin. The harder wedges are pressed, the more the hull gives. Prop at the bulkheads. These can be found by tapping along the hull and listening to its resonance. The note hardens and sharpens as a bulkhead is approached.

Fasten the props athwartships, with webbing or rope. These ties are particularly important with a fibreglass hull, which will shiver and might loosen the props in a strong wind. For boats under 25 feet (7m) four per side will be adequate. Longer boats should have at least five per side. This density allows sufficient spread along the length, to prevent the craft trying to twist in a cross wind.

First jobs after hauling out
The following jobs must be done as soon as possible after the boat is hauled out.

Clean the bottom. This is much easier when the hull is wet. Scrub the bottom with an old broom dipped in sand and gravel. Hose off the loosened marine growths, and scrape away barnacles. A high pressure water hose is ideal for this work, but take care not to wash away paint and wood fibres. Clean topsides and apply a coat of boat polishing wax for protection during the winter. Arrange an awning. This involves getting on deck. Take great care, particularly if the ballast has been removed. Move cautiously, and ask a friend to watch the props for the first few minutes, and to warn you if they move.

The more protection afforded by the awning, the less work there will be in the spring. This applies to all boats, and particularly those with varnished or painted topsides, decks and cabins. Arrange the awning over a strong back supported at each end, or from a series of tubular hoops dropped into the stanchion sockets. Whatever framework is used, it is essential that the awning should not work loose.

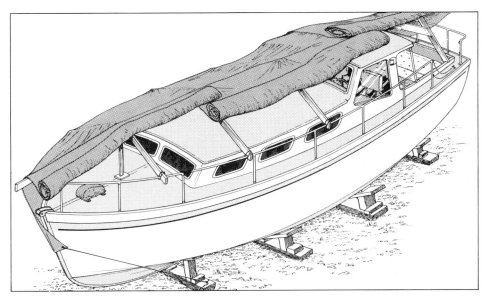

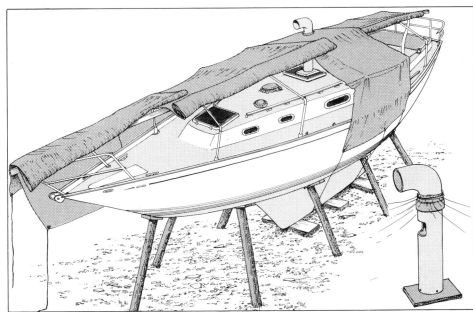

Arrange access points into the awning. It can be an advantage to use several overlapping strips of awning to enable sections of the deck to be exposed without uncovering the entire boat.

Ensure the boat is thoroughly ventilated. If necessary, use large diameter plastic drain pipes through the awning to duct fresh air into the bilges. The air outlet should be at the top of the awning.

Before leaving the boat for winter
Remove all items that might be stolen. This includes the propeller, which, if it looks bent or corroded, can be sent away to the manufacturer for checking. Stop holes in the hull after cleaning out any marine growths that might have accumulated over the summer.

Prepare the cabin for winter by removing floor boards, drawers etc. as described on page 283. Make a check list of all the jobs that need to be done. Divide the page into two parts: one for essential maintenance tasks, the other for essential jobs.

Rot and worms

A wooden hull will not rot, unless the temperature and moisture conditions are favourable. Moisture content needs to be above 20 per cent, and the optimum temperatures for rot are between 24-35°C (75-95°F). There must also be some wood, unprotected by paint, varnish or preservative where the fungus can grow. If any of these conditions are absent, fungal decay will not occur.

The most important rot prevention measures are taken by the boat-builder. The selection and careful seasoning of durable timbers, coupled with construction techniques which avoid the creation of damp and badly ventilated areas in the hull, provide a good foundation for successful rot prevention.

A regular programme of winter cleaning and drying, combined with spring repainting, with perhaps an application of suitable preservatives beforehand, will safeguard the boat against future attacks.

Although virtually every part of a wooden boat is at risk, rot is most frequently found at the ends, limbers, frameheads, bulwark ends (next to the frames) and deck beam ends. Areas that suffer intermittent soaking are more likely to rot than those that are continually beneath the water.

Decay may be present without any obvious evidence of fungal attack. The indications may be a subtle shrinkage inwards of the surface of a piece of timber, longitudinal or cross grain cracking, localized darkening, or simply peeling paintwork.

The extent of the decay can be discovered by probing with an awl, or penknife blade. The ease with which the tool penetrates will reflect the condition of the timber, although it should be remembered that wood that is wet is softer than dry wood.
Plywood cannot always be so easily tested, as decay often affects the inner laminates leaving the outer plies in good condition. A light blow with a hammer should, by its dull report, indicate the presence of rot.

Techniques for the successful treatment of the rot will depend upon accurate recognition of the rot. The severity of the attack will depend upon the type of timber affected, its temperature and moisture content. Some woods (notably teak, oak and iroko), are resistant to decay and even where dry rot fungus is present, its impact may be quite minor compared to its effect on more vulnerable woods. Although both forms of rot will travel and contaminate other timbers, the spread of the fungus is greatly influenced by temperature; low temperatures will inhibit their growth, and may even cause them to lie dormant until they are re-activated by warmer weather.

Both wet and dry rot require a moisture content higher than 20 per cent before they develop, although their spores will remain dormant until these conditions occur. Wet rot will cease growing once the moisture in the wood drops; the dry rot fungus grows a root like network of rhizomorphs which are able to extract the moisture necessary to support continued growth from dry wood. It is this latter quality which makes the dry rot fungus more feared than any other form of fungal wood decay.

Identification

Wet rot (coniophora cerebella)
This is very much more common but less serious than dry rot. The wood darkens and softens, is weakened and lightened. A steel spike will pass through the infected timber without resistance. When dried, the wood splits into cuboid sections, with clear cracks across and along the grain. There is a slight musty smell, but without the lingering sweet smell associated with dry rot. Sometimes a black vein like a network of mycelium covers the surface of the wood.

Attack is usually limited to damp wood. It will not spread unless the paintwork is damaged, and allows moisture into the timber. Wet rot occasionally travels inside the timber, leaving the surface sound, though fragile.

Remedial action
The first priority is to cure the leak, and ventilate the hull. Inspect the timber and assess its loss of strength. Replace where necessary with wood treated with a fungicide and insecticide.

Dry rot (serpula lachrymans)
Only rarely are boats damaged by dry rot fungus (serpula lachrymans). When it does occur, it is usually where unsuitable house-building woods have been used in the construction and conversion of the boat, and it is most commonly found in boats moored in fresh water.

Dry rot usually attacks above the water-line, in deck houses, or behind cabin partitions, etc. In warm and damp conditions it will spread rapidly.

Wood darkens and softens, and in severe cases, dries out, leaving a flimsy shell, riven by longitudinal and transverse fissures. Considerable loss of weight and strength results, and the wood will offer little resistance to a steel spike driven through. The similarity with wet rot ends here. Dry rot has a distinctive and unpleasantly sweet odour reminiscent of mushrooms. The fungus (sporophore) which spreads across the surface of the timber is flat, ridged or corrugated at the centre, with white edges, tinged with purple, brown or bright yellow. Where the fungus is growing rapidly, the mycelium appears as cotton wool, which collects between timbers, on to ironwork, and over any other obstructions in its way. In drier conditions, where growth is slower, the mycelium appears in white or grey sheets.

Associated with these very obvious signs are the thick vein-like rhizomorphs which carry the moisture from adjacent timber to decayed wood. These are thicker than those of the wet rot fungus and are lighter, often white.

If dry rot is found, then immediate action should be taken to inhibit its spread. If the boat is hauled up, precautions should be taken to prevent contamination of other boats by careless littering of decayed wood around the yard, and inadvertent spreading of the spores on the soles of the feet, etc.

Remedial action
Seek professional advice. The first priority is to discover the extent of the decay, and for this extensive dismantling may be necessary. This is essential, as the entire area infected by the dry rot fungus must be treated or removed, otherwise decay will continue unabated. Remove all infected wood and burn it, taking care not to scatter the spores of the fungus as the decayed wood is taken from the boat and carried to the bonfire.

Remove all wood inside, and at the margins of the infected area. This is the only sure way of eliminating the fungus, but where this involves the removal of large quantities of planking, and perhaps parts of the central frame members, it may be satisfactory to remove the decayed wood, and scorch the rest with a blowlamp, before treating with liberal quantities of preservative.

It is probably preferable to avoid painting internal timbers since this retains moisture.

Treatment with wood preservative will be just as effective as paint in protecting wood against renewed attack, and will not have the disadvantage of acting as a moisture barrier. If the wood is to be painted, use a rot-inhibiting (i.e. zinc oxychloride) paint

Improve the hull ventilation, and cure the source of dampness that contributed to the initial decay. Particular attention should be given to prevention of drainage of rain water on to hull timbers.

Poria
Often confused with wet rot, and sometimes erroneously referred to as 'dry rot'. Infested wood does not turn as dark as wood attacked by wet rot. Wood is laced with a network of whitish surface strands and sheets of tissue. Surface fruiting bodies (brackets and plates) will be present when attack is well established, and are without the purple/brown tinges typical of dry rot. Untreated, poria will spread, and its attack will be more extensive than that of wet rot. Infected wood splits and cracks into cuboidal segments. Treat as for dry rot.

Electro-chemical decay
Most hardwood planking suffers from this form of attack around the fastenings and through-hull fittings on the outside of the hull, as a result of electrolytic activity. This is noticeable by localized darkening of wood, and the accumulation of white crystals around the fastenings. (See Corrosion, page 290.)

In normal circumstances, the insertion of graving pieces is usually all that is required to make good the damage. In severe cases it may be necessary to replace planks and fastenings (see pages 30, 46 and 70).

Preventing rot
With the exception of steam bent frames (which require a thorough soaking with preservative after bending and fitting) all boat-building and repair wood should be seasoned. When replacing pieces choose a durable wood, resistant to fungal attack. Shape and fit all pieces before removing them, and soaking them in preservative. Tributyl tin oxide, which is effective against fungal and worm attack, is probably the most widely used preservative. Take particular care to soak end grain, cracks and openings in the wood as they are difficult to seal adequately with paint. The timber should be left dipped in the preservative for as long as possible, to ensure a satisfactory penetration of the fluid.

If the timbers are too long for soaking, stand the ends in a basin of preservative for about 10 minutes, then brush or spray several coats on to the sides and face, making sure that each crack or hole is well filled. Once the woodwork is repaired, give it an additional soaking with preservative, this time applied with a garden spray.

Wear a breathing mask and gloves, and avoid skin contact with freshly treated timber. Adjust the nozzle to give a coarse spray. Leave to dry, paint if necessary.

These procedures should be followed whenever replacing timber in a wooden boat. The additional cost and labour involved is negligible compared to the time it takes to repair damage caused by rot. When additional holes are made in the hull structure, apply preservative to the hole. Stop one end of the hole with a cork, and inject preservative from an oil can filled with preservative, before driving the fastenings.

The guide-lines above will help in eradicating the wood decay, and should help prevent problems developing. Decayed wood attracts wood-boring beetles. Do not delay treating areas of wet rot, just because it is, compared with dry rot, fairly benign.

Marine borers

Unprotected wood left in seawater for more than a few days is likely to be attacked by shipworm or gribble. These marine borers are active in most salt waters. Although the destruction they cause is most dramatically illustrated by their depredations in warm and tropical seas, many of the species remain active (although their activity is reduced) in colder waters. Several species will survive immersion in fresh and polluted water. No wood is entirely safe, but afromosia, iroko, jarrah, kapur, opepe, and teak, and some other tropical hardwoods are fairly resistant to attack. The only long-term safeguards are to sheathe, paint or impregnate the wood with preservatives.

The minute size of some of the marine borers, when they first attack, makes even the most carefully protected wooden hull vulnerable. A partially opened plank seam, a crack, a scratch in the paintwork, or the inside wood of an unprotected hull opening, is all they need to enable them to enter the wood, and begin their destruction.

Teredo navalis and Teredo norvegica (Mollusca)

Damage These enter wood through pin-sized holes, which give little warning of the 1 inch (25mm) diameter tunnels that may be bored inside the timber. Holes are lined with a white calcareous deposit. Affected planks often leak.

Conditions Teredo (or shipworm) are tolerant to salinity conditions as low as 1 per cent (less than $\frac{1}{3}$ normal seawater salinity), and survive periodic immersion in polluted or fresh water for periods up to approximately two weeks. They are most active in temperatures between 15-25°C (59-77°F) and will survive freezing. Reproduction is inhibited in lower temperatures. The length and size of the worm depends on the density of the infestation — the length of the adult varies from 4 inches to around 4-5 feet (100mm-150cm).

Life cycle The larvae (which in the early stages of their life are free-floating) lodge in minute cracks in the paintwork below the water-line, and bore a narrow tunnel into the plank. As the worm grows, the tunnel is enlarged to about 1 inch (25 mm) diameter. After two months, the teredo is able to reproduce, and reaches full growth in about a year.

Bankia (Mollusca)
Similar to Teredo, active in warm waters where they grow larger than teredo.

Martesia (Mollusca)
The body of the Martesia is encased by its shell, and in this respect more closely resembles the typical mollusc than the others described above. The entrance hole is larger than the teredo's, approximately $\frac{1}{8}$ inch (3 mm) diameter, or slightly less. Martesia grow inside the wood, but are rarely larger than 1 inch by 3 inches (25 mm by 75 mm). Martesia attack wood only in tropical waters.

Xylophaga dorsalis
Similar to the teredo, often found in temperate waters. Unlike the burrows of the teredo, and the others described, the tunnel is rarely more than 2 inches (50 mm) deep and is without the shell lining found in the tunnels of the others.

Crustacea
The second group of marine borers belong to the crustacean family. In their appearance and manoeuvrability, they resemble wood lice rather than worms. The main types include Limnoria, Chelura and Sphaeroma species.

Limnoria (Crustacea)
There are several types of Limnoria (or gribble). Limnoria lignorum up to $\frac{3}{16}$ inch (5mm) is a cold water species that will not survive temperatures above 20°C (68°F). Limnoria tripunctata and Limnoria quadripuncta are shorter $\frac{1}{16}$ inch (2mm) and less sensitive to temperature variations. Where salinity is below 1.5 per cent, the limnoria is unlikely to survive, although they survive regular drying-out for up to eight hours at a time.
Unlike the Teredo, the Limnoria do not burrow deep into the wood. Tunnels are about $\frac{1}{20}$ inch (1 mm), diameter, and do not penetrate more than $\frac{1}{2}$ inch (12 mm). However, the surface of infested wood is rapidly reduced to a weak sponge-like consistency, which washes away, exposing timber for continued attack.

Life cycle Limnoria are usually found in pairs. They are able to swim and will attack any unprotected wood. The females hatch their eggs in a brood pouch, and when the young are liberated, they bore tunnels of their own, which branch off the parents' tunnel. In warm weather full development takes place between 3-4 weeks.

Chelura and Sphaeroma (Crustacea)
Two other types of crustacean borers similar in appearance to the Limnoria also cause serious attacks on marine timbers. Chelura is similar to the Limnoria in habits and life cycle, but a little larger. Sphaeroma which is even larger (from $\frac{1}{4}-\frac{3}{4}$ inch (6-19 mm) long and $\frac{3}{4}$ inch (19 mm) diameter bores larger and deeper holes up to about $\frac{1}{2}$ inch (12 mm) wide and 3-4 inches (75-100 mm) in depth. Chiefly found in warm waters, these will survive for a while in fresh water.

Remedial action
Regular hauling-out and drying will kill both mollusc and crustacean borers. The same result can be achieved by moving the boats into fresh water, but this method is effective only where the saline content of the water is below 1 per cent. In estuaries and tidal rivers, these conditions will be fulfilled if the boat is moored a considerable distance upstream.

The most satisfactory defence against attack is to sheathe the hull with copper, glass fibre or nylon fabric, or to regularly coat it with anti-fouling paint. Resistant woods are sometimes used to clad the keels and underside of the bilge keels where frequent grounding is likely to tear away copper sheathing, and score paintwork.

Where marine borers are active, extensive internal damage to the structure of the wood can be expected. Planks and frames should be tested ruthlessly with a long steel spike for evidence of weakness.

The only other method of protecting wood is to treat it with preservative. A brushed, dipped or sprayed application will not give lasting protection, as the preservative will be leached out by the water, leaving the wood vulnerable to attack. Only pressurized treatment seems to succeed, but here, the woods normally used for the construction of boats often have a natural resistance to impregnation. Cracks that open later will allow marine borers to enter.

When repainting a wooden boat, the shores and keel blocks are likely to cover part of the hull surface, and arrangements must be made to ensure these patches are properly treated prior to launching. This is not difficult when using a hoist, and the use of twin keel bearers and additional bilge shores allows access to every part of the hull.

The wharf beetle
The larva of the wharf beetle attacks rotting timber, and once established, will move on to eat adjacent sound wood. Damage is recognizable by the large oval flight holes and the wide diameter tunnels burrowed along the grain by the larva. Beetles will later emerge from the wood, and in suitable weather conditions they all emerge together in a swarm. Eggs are laid in the cracks and crevices of rotting wood into which the larvae burrow and where they grow to a length of about $1\frac{3}{4}$ inches (44 mm). Tunnels are usually bored with the grain, and are about $\frac{1}{8}-\frac{3}{8}$ inch (3-9 mm) diameter. The grey-white larvae turn into red-brown beetles ($\frac{1}{2}-\frac{3}{4}$ inch (12-19 mm) long) which emerge from flight holes.

Once established, affected wood usually needs to be replaced with new wood, treated with preservative.

Most metals corrode if they are immersed or occasionally soaked in seawater. To a lesser extent, those in fresh water will also corrode. Although the rates of corrosion are different, the descriptions of the corrosive processes and the measures taken to counter them are applicable to both.

Seawater is an efficient electrolyte, and it is through the activity of small electrical cells immersed in the water that corrosion occurs. Apart from small local variations, seawater carries the same ingredients in similar proportions throughout the world. Concentrations are higher in seas where there are high levels of evaporation and corrosion proceeds more quickly.

Oxygen is one of the elements dissolved in seawater, and it is a primary factor governing the rate of corrosion. In general, oxygen-starved metals corrode faster than those which are better ventilated. Without oxygen, however, corrosion will not take place. The rate of corrosion is affected by temperature, the concentration of the electrolyte, the type of metals immersed in it, and the proportion of oxygen present in the corrosive environment.

The list below places the various metals used in the manufacture of fittings and fastenings and in boat construction in order of voltage potential. Metals high in the list (gold, silicon, bronze, and stainless steel) are less likely to be damaged by corrosion than those with lower voltage potentials. Where other factors are equal, it is the difference in voltage potential between metals or within the structure of the metal, which determines the rate and severity of corrosion. In general, where the voltage potential difference between metals is greater than .25V inside the hull and .20V outside the hull, corrosion is likely to take place, and methods to prevent it should be taken. Below this figure, and in the absence of aggravating factors (stray electrical currents, stress, high velocity water) corrosion is unlikely to be a serious problem.

Before corrosion occurs, the metals involved need to be immersed in an electrolyte. An example of a simple cell is illustrated. The zinc, which is anodic to the copper, is corroded, while the structure of the copper is unaffected.

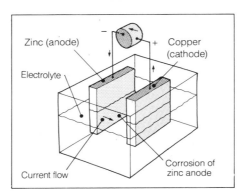

Zinc (anode)   − + Copper (cathode)

Electrolyte

Current flow

Corrosion of zinc anode

Dry wood is an insulator, but when soaked with seawater, electrolytic activity may take place. Any porous material thus saturated will provide the necessary conditions for an electrical circuit. On its own, seawater is a good electrolyte, enabling currents to pass between hull fittings and plating some distance away, and also between boats moored in close proximity.

No metals used in the manufacture of boats, fittings, or fastenings are absolutely pure. Corrosion will occur between metals or impurities in alloy. The voltage potential of a piece of steel hull plate, for example, will vary across its surface. Mill scale, minute impurities, and even areas of stress or heat treatment (around rivetting and welding) cause differences in voltage potential, making it vulnerable to corrosion. Although there are some brass alloys which are reasonably durable in marine conditions, most brass screws and fittings are made from an alloy of copper, with more than 30 per cent zinc, without the addition of a corrosion inhibitor. The considerable potential difference between the two metals used in the brass alloy (.85V) ensures that they will corrode, leaving behind a copper shell of greatly reduced strength. Small accumulations of grey green dust on its surface, indicate that de-zincification has occurred. Stainless steel and other more durable alloys are also vulnerable to this type of corrosion.

The corrosion products of aluminium, copper, stainless steel, cast iron, and some other metals, form a corrosion-inhibiting oxide on the metal's surface. This is most noticeable on the surface of unanodized aluminium masts, where considerable quantities of white powder seem to suggest serious and active corrosion. The appearance of the protective coating varies with the metal, but its volume bears little resemblance to the quantity of metal actually corroded. However, once the protective oxide is brushed or rubbed away, corrosion recommences. Typically, this occurs where wire rubs against an aluminium mast, dislodging the protective film of oxide, and also where high velocity water passes through copper tubing. In both, the surfaces are cleaned, and corrosion is renewed.

Corrosion also takes place where there are different levels of oxygen at different parts of the metal. Corrosion, which may start in any minute surface irregularity, commences slowly, until the crevice deepens and the metal in the depths of the crevice becomes starved of oxygen. Owing to the difference in aeration between the surface and the inside of the crevice, corrosion accelerates, and provides increasingly favourable conditions for corrosive attack as the pit grows deeper. Because of the difficulties of identification, crevice corrosion presents a serious hazard, especially

Metal	Voltage	potential
1 Magnesium	-1.60	
2 Magnesium alloy	-1.60	
3 Zinc	-1.10	
4 Galvanized iron	-1.05	
5 Cadmium	-0.80	
6 Aluminium	-0.75	
7 Mild steel	-0.70	
8 Cast iron	-0.70	
9 Lead	-0.55	
10 Tin	-0.45	
11 Manganese bronze	-0.27	
12 Yellow brass	-0.26	
13 Admiralty brass	-0.26	
14 Aluminium bronze	-0.26	
15 Red brass	-0.26	
16 Copper	-0.25	
17 Monel metal	-0.20	
18 Stainless steel (passive)	-0.20	
19 Silicon bronze	-0.18	
20 Nickel (passive)	-0.15	
21 Silver	0.0	
22 Gold	+0.15	

when stainless steel fastenings and fittings are used, and it illustrates the importance of sealing all cracks and joints with bedding compound to prevent initial establishment of the galvanic cell.

A similar form of corrosion may occur below the water-line where a hull fitting or the propeller causes the differential aeration of the water, thus creating suitable conditions for corrosion. In low speed pleasure boats the area at risk is around the propeller, but with high speed craft, any bracket or hull protrusion may have the same turbulent effect.

Water is drawn towards the suction face of the propeller and accelerates past as the propeller rotates. Some water in the low pressure area vaporizes, or cavitates. When this happens, the cavitation caused by the propeller will cause smooth surface corrosion on the suction face of the propeller blades. Cavitation, however, is associated with other problems, particularly those of vibration and metal fatigue and, at higher revolutions, the edge of the blades on the pressure side are damaged by high velocity water, causing disintegration of its surface, which becomes rough and pitted.

These complex erosive, corrosive, and mechanical forces operate together to reduce the efficiency of the propeller, and will ultimately destroy it. If corrosion is noticed, or if the propeller vibrates, there is little that the amateur can do, apart from smoothing sharp edges, ensuring that there is sufficient space between the propeller and the deadwood, checking engine alignment, and ensuring that there is a suitable cathodic protection device fitted to the shaft or propeller to eliminate the most common forms of deterioration. Seek professional advice.

Stress corrosion

Stress corrosion is a common problem at welds and fastenings and also a hazard in fastenings and stainless steel wire, which occasionally break without warning or any obvious indication of fatigue failure. Parts that are stressed through flexing, hammering, or heating, will be at a different, lower, voltage potential to parts which are un-stressed. Localized corrosion will develop between stressed and un-stressed parts. Solutions are not always easy to devise, and depend upon many circumstances. It is best to keep a close watch for signs of pitting and corrosion, particularly at welds. The life of a stainless steel tackle may be prolonged using larger diameter sheaves and wires, but in some cases it might be better to replace the wire with a light chain or a polypropylene rope.

Poultice corrosion will occur where metal plating or pipework is masked with wet, porous material, which traps moisture and denies oxygen. Lagged exhaust systems must be kept dry if corrosion is to be prevented. A similar effect may be seen in the bilges or on the decks of steel or aluminium hulls where accumulations of debris prevent ventilation of the metal surface. To forestall this often serious form of corrosive attack, bilges and exposed metal surfaces should be kept scrupulously clean.

Fastenings which are embedded in wooden planking may also deteriorate through electrically-induced corrosion. This is often a problem with wooden boats and may develop undetected, producing a hazardous condition which is extremely costly to remedy.

Wood is an insulator until it is saturated with water. The wood then retains the electrolyte and corrosion cannot be stopped until the boat is taken from the water and allowed to dry out. Most woods contain acid: oak and western red cedar are very acidic. Two part urea-formaldehyde wood glues use an acid as a hardening agent. In these conditions, fastenings might be corroded both by the galvanic current between metals embedded in the wood, and also by the acid present in the timber, or painted on to it when glueing.

The wood also decays, owing to the high concentrations of alkali (in the form of caustic soda) which collect at the cathode. The alkali first destroys the paint and varnish, then the wood itself.

White deposits around the fastenings, lifted paint, rust stains, and blackened wood, (emphasized perhaps by cracked paintwork between planks and loosened fittings) are signs that indicate corrosion in the fastenings of a wooden hull. In minor instances, the remedy may simply be to change affected fastenings and coat new ones with epoxy resin. Where the hull is left to deteriorate, planks, as well as fastenings, may have to be replaced.

These forms of corrosion illustrate the destructive effects of small currents between areas of different voltage potential. Once the galvanic cell is established, its circuitry is simple and the voltages involved are usually low. All these effects are enhanced if stray electrical currents from the boat's electrical or power generation system leak to the hull. Then extensive corrosion can occur within a very short time.

This hazard is eliminated by bonding together the hull and all metal fittings to bring them to the same electrical potential. In addition, all electrical systems used aboard the boat should be of the insulated return type, described on page 274.

Bonding must be thorough, with thick copper bonding straps clamped in good electrical connection with the pieces being bonded. Connecting faces must never be painted. All fittings, including the through-hull fittings, stanchions, standing rigging, engine, and propeller shaft must be bonded. The propeller shaft is connected by fitting a brush which bears against the rotating shaft. If bonding is thorough, the potential difference between parts of the hull will be low enough to eliminate most forms of stray current-induced electrolysis.

Corrosion Routine maintenance

It is most important that all metallic parts of the hull and its equipment should be bonded, as corrosion will occur in the unlikeliest places. For example, a magneto-hydrodynamic current is produced when high velocity exhaust gases are mixed with the cooling water from a powerful engine. The strong current which is generated may not cause any problems if the engine, exhaust, and hull fittings are connected in the bonding system described above. Where fibreglass exhaust chambers or rubber hoses are incorporated in the exhaust system, it is important that the metalwork between engine, water inlet, and exhaust system are bonded.

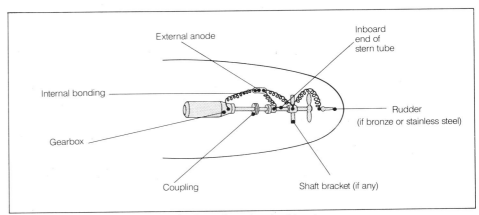

Cable connects metal work to the bonding circuit of boat

Other measures must be taken to control or eliminate the various forms of corrosion described above. Two methods are used. The first is to impose a current on to the hull, using a separate electrical supply from a separate battery, which transforms the entire hull into a cathode, with a durable, inactive terminal as the anode. This method is used to protect large commercial vessels. Smaller boats (including those that are less than 60 feet (18 m) long) are usually protected by sacrificial anodes installed outside the hull, and wired to the bonding circuit of the boat. Pure zinc cannot be used, as it protects itself with a layer of corrosion — preventing residue only weeks after it is immersed. The anodes used are normally alloys of zinc or magnesium, and are anodic to all of the metals used in the construction of the hull, propeller shaft and rudder. They corrode at a controlled rate and are replaced regularly.

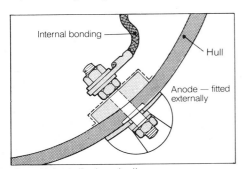

Anode installed on hull

Seek advice before positioning sacrificial anodes. Their size and position depends upon the construction material of the hull and fastenings, and the expected interval between replacement. Anodes must be placed in close proximity to the item being protected. It is wasteful and often ineffective to place them indiscriminately. They should not be painted, as the paint film will protect the zinc from corrosion, rendering them useless. While the sacrificial anodes are being corroded, the hull and fittings are protected. Anodes should be replaced when more than 80 per cent of the zinc has been corroded.

A typical installation of anodes fitted to protect the stern gear of a fibreglass boat is illustrated.

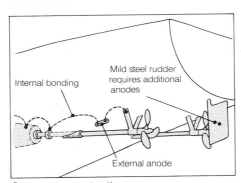

Stern gear protection

Metals that are periodically immersed in seawater are best protected with a surface coating. Painting schedules for painting metal hulls are described on page 303.

Galvanizing (coating with a thin protective layer of zinc) is a traditional method which will protect steel in the absence of other more noble metals, but when a galvanized chain or centreplate is placed in close proximity to a copper fitting, rapid corrosion of the zinc will occur, leaving the steel exposed to corrosion. Aluminium coatings are also used and are effective in protecting steel bolts used above the water-line. However, sprayed, electroplated or hot dipped metal coatings are satisfactory only where there is an adequate thickness of protective deposit. Always use marine quality fittings and fastenings, and remember that the protection provided is effective only as long as the coat remains intact, and is not in close proximity to other metals.

Corrosion between metals is inhibited by interposing impervious insulating materials between the different metals. Neoprene polythene, rubber Delrin and some flexible sealants are suitable. Avoid more porous substances such as Tufnol, leather, nylon and wood, as they absorb water and allow electrolytic activity to continue.

It is not always possible or desirable to rely on an electrical insulation between different metals used in the construction of a boat; there are many situations where such a practice is inappropriate. In these circumstances, it is important to choose the fastening material with care, and attempt to match voltage potentials. However, many of the metals with lower voltage potentials are unsuitable for use as stressed fittings. Fastenings higher in the scale can be used, provided that there is sufficient bulk of anodic metal being fastened. The bulk of the item being fastened has to be taken into account, as well as its relative position on the voltage potential scale.

Most boats, if they are kept at moorings, will have water in the bilges. The state of the water will provide a clue to the condition of the boat. Some water will certainly have trickled in from the deck, cockpit, and awning etc. but the bilge water in a badly leaking hull will tend to be plentiful, clean and, in estuary and sea boats, salty. Often the cabin furniture, the bottoms of the bulkheads, and the inside planking at the turn of the bilge, will be stained with one, or several high-water marks.

In well-maintained boats, persistent and elusive leaks are more annoying than hazardous. Locating the source of small seepages of water is often very difficult and may involve far more disruption to the crew than the leak itself. Having found the leak, there are very few instances where the remedies can be successfully accomplished without access to the outside of the hull.

However, before the boat is hauled out for the winter lay up, every effort should be made to pin-point the source of the leaks, so they can be attended to as part of the winter maintenance programme.

Locating the leak

For some, notably double skinned wooden hulls, where the ingress and the apparent leak in the inside are often some distance apart, the only means of finding the leak is to haul the boat out of the water, and wait for several days for the hull to dry off. Inspect the inside and outside seams carefully.

Wood that is saturated with water will appear as a dark patch, evident even behind several layers of paint and anti-fouling.

In single skin hulls, leaks can be located while the boat is still in the water. Choose a bright, dry day. Lift the cabin floorboards, pump the hull dry and, if possible, vacuum or sponge it clean. Block each waterway, or limber hole, with Plasticine or other waterproof putty compound, and watch for the accumulation of water in the spaces between the keelson and the frames or floors. This method will indicate the approximate position of the leak, narrowing the outside area to a frame space on one side. Fixed cabin furniture etc. will probably prevent the exact location being established on the inside.

It is quite likely that the hull will not show any evidence of leaking, and it might be necessary to ballast the boat so that she heels first to one side and then to the other before the leak is discovered.

The hull, despite being tilted, still may not leak. There are several probable reasons for this. The first is that it only occurs when some machinery or through-hull fitting is in use. Start the motor, and allow it to idle for a while. The vibration may expose the leak: If it doesn't, slip the moorings and gently motor around the anchorage. Any leaks in the water seal around the propeller shaft, at bolt heads holding the prop shaft 'A' brackets, and at the rudder stock should become evident.

If these tests fail to identify the leak, then it is usually safe to conclude that it occurs either at the ends of the boat that were not immersed when she was heeled, or that the hull planks move when she is being driven hard. Whichever is the cause, the condition of the caulking and the plank fastenings must be inspected once the boat is hauled out of the water.

A traditional, if temporary, cure for a leaky hull is to moor the boat over a mud bank. At low tide a pole can be dropped over the side and used to stir the mud, some of which will be sucked into the openings and crevices in the hull, stopping the leaks. This is a haphazard and, at best, provisional cure, which nevertheless works, provided that the hull comes to no other harm at her new mooring.

Wooden hulls

Wood that is saturated with water turns black, and becomes soft. Paint or varnish will tend to lift or discolour over wet spots. Although these spots do not necessarily indicate the presence of a leak, they should be investigated with care, dried, and adequate drainage provided for the future.

Leaking seams
Minor seepage at joints between planks will require re-caulking from the outside. Also check the state of the caulking in other seams. Never attempt to caulk from the inside.

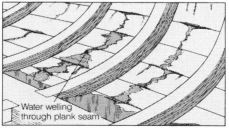
Leakage through seams

Leaking planks
This can be a very serious problem. Where water wells up from the plank itself, the likeliest cause is that the plank

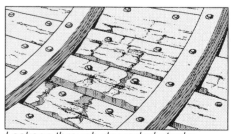
Leakage through degraded planks

is badly worm eaten. The boat will have to be hauled out, and the worm-eaten planks removed and replaced.

Leaks at the fastenings

This may be caused by nail sickness or by the degradation of the metal fastenings, or where the timber becomes degraded as a result of electro-chemical decay, emanating from a fastening. Usually, there is a tell-tale ring of whitish deposit in the vicinity of the offending fastening, but this may be obscured by internal fittings etc. New fastenings should be fitted and the wood surrounding the original fittings raked out, dried, and filled with epoxy putty. For repairs at the stem and stern see page 68.

Leaks at the keel bolts

First check that the keel bolt is sound. Place a ring spanner on to the bolt nut, add an extension bar for added leverage, and tighten it. Badly corroded bolts will sheer, and need to be replaced (see page l38). If the bolt is sound, loosen it (with an extension bar on the socket spanner if necessary), and make several turns of cotton wicking around the underside of the washer. Cover the cotton in bedding compound and re-tighten the bolt. Where washers seem to be too small, or are distorted, fit larger ones of the same metal. Bed the new washers in cotton and compound before pulling them tight.

Split shaft logs

One-piece shaft logs are particularly vulnerable to splitting. Where they are accessible, the splits should be covered with a lead or copper tingle and the nails bedded in cotton and compound. This can be supplemented by injecting waterproof grease into the shaft log.

Drill into the log, until the drill passes into the prop shaft cavity. Tap a small diameter threaded pipe into the hole, and screw in a grease nipple. Pump waterproof grease into the prop shaft space, until it seeps out of the small cracks in the log. Pumping with a gun has to be done with patience. When back pressure is achieved the gun must be left, and the handle screwed down, only when there is no resistance and then only till resistance is met. In a particularly large cavity this process may take quite a few hours but, if done in this way, the possibility of damage is minimized. Instead of waterproof grease, white lead bedding compound, or polysulphide rubber bedding compound for underwater use are equally good.

A simple means of judging the progress of this operation is to bore a small hole at the opposite end of the shaft log. When grease or compound begins to exude from this hole, you will know that the log has been filled to that point. Plug the hole, before removing the filling nipple and fitting a blanking screw.

Occasionally the stuffing box itself comes slightly adrift from the end of the shaft log. As the fastenings are usually set into the log end-grain, it is difficult to gain a satisfactory pressure with longer replacement screws. In these circumstances, make a covering plate to bear against the flange of the stuffing box, and bolt it to angle brackets screwed to the side of the shaft log.

Leaking stopwaters

Stopwaters are fitted to prevent the seepage of water along a scarf join from entering the hull (see page 43). These are subject to rot, and cannot be replaced. It is impossible to install new ones unless the planking covering the old stopwater is removed. If a keel scarf is leaking, both the garboard and the plank above will probably have to be

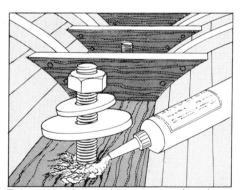
Twist cotton beneath washer and seal

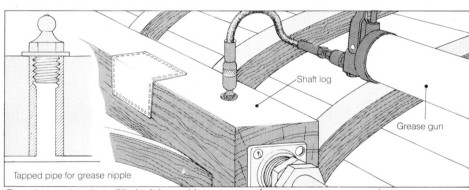
Repair cracks, then fill shaft log with waterproof grease or compound

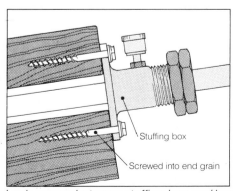
Leak occurs between stuffing box and log

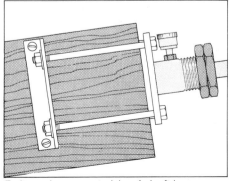
Bolt anchorage at side of shaft log

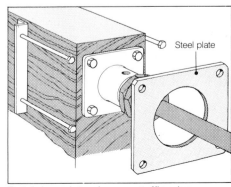
Retaining plate clamps stuffing box

removed, and a new hole drilled through the scarf rabbet intersection. Stop the drill before it passes through the opposite garboard plank.

Make a stopwater from straight-grained, seasoned pine. Bore a hole, the diameter of the stopwater, in a sheet of flat steel. Trim the ends of the pine stick, and chamfer its edges. Hammer the stick through the hole in the steel plate. This will shape and compress the stick into a dowel of the correct diameter, which will swell both as a consequence of its earlier compression and from water absorption.

Do not paint, varnish or glue the stopwater. It should be driven into the hole dry, and allowed to swell, until it seals the passage through the scarf joint. If only one garboard is removed and the stopwater is driven blind, trim its end to fit against the plank before hammering it in place.

Fibreglass hull

Unless it has been punctured, this type of hull is unlikely to leak, except where there are fittings that pass through the hull near or below the water-line.

A common source of leakage is at the stuffing boxes (see pages l57 and 239) and also where the shaft log passes through the fibreglass hull. These are difficult leaks to locate, and the latter can be cured only when the hull has dried out completely. The procedure is to cut back the surface of the log and the surrounding fibreglass laminate, and lay up extra reinforcing layers of glass fibre matt, bedded in epoxy resin. Flanges should be added to the shaft log to help it withstand vibration and, to complete the repair, the engine prop shaft alignment should be checked and, if necessary, a floating gland fitted to relieve the log fastenings from engine induced loadings.

Other through-hull fittings can also be a source of leaks, particularly where the inside screw thread assembly is difficult to reach. Such fittings are sometimes installed rather badly, with inadequate bedding compound in the inner face of the flange to take up the surface irregularities of the hull.

Another area for leaks in fibreglass hulls, both of conventional configuration and fin and skeg type, is the attachment

of the rudder heel fitting. It is seldom much of a problem in the fin and skeg boats, as the skegs tend to be filled in solid at the top, and so the voids in the lower end are simply unintentional ballast tanks. In the conventional hulls the form of the moulding tends to leave the fastening area neither solid nor wide

enough to get access to ensure that bolts passing through are properly watertight. Leaks through these bolts can be difficult to locate, and can only be cured by removing the heel fitting, and refitting it with adequate water-proofing safeguards both inside and outside the hull.

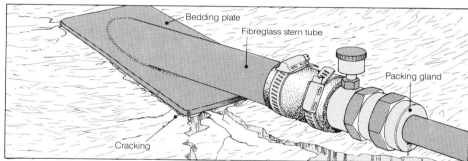

Vibration induced fatigue cracking at stern tube bedding plate

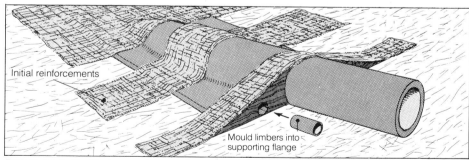

Reinforce hull with layups tapered over a wide area

Steel hulls

Steel hulls will leak where welds are fractured, and at points where the hull has worn or has rusted through. A more common source is at points where through-fittings are welded into the hull. Places that are difficult to reach are more likely to leak than parts of the hull that are more easily inspected.

Welding repairs in these circumstances are very difficult, and the solution is often to cut out the pipework and remove the hull flange, and then to cover the area with a repair plate bolted or welded to the hull, with a new hull pipe outlet, screwed and properly bedded, already fixed to it. The connection to the new

outlet can be made from steam hose or, if the pipe is conducting uncooled exhaust gases from the engine, new pipework will have to be screwed to the outlet and a new connection made inboard (see page l09).

Emergency repairs at sea   Routine maintenance

Holes below the water-line
Stay with the boat, and try to prevent her sinking. Locate and stop the flow of water. From the inside, wedge rags, cushions, or a mattress against the hole. Heel the boat to bring the hole closer to the water-line. Drive in a tapered wooden plug to stop the leak, or drape a sail over the bow, and position it across the hole, making it fast to cleats on deck.

A more permanent repair can be made later by covering the hole with canvas or copper sheeting, tacked, taped or pop-rivetted into place, or by filling the hole with epoxy putty. This latter is ideal for stopping small punctures, as once the two components are mixed and applied, it will harden, even under water.

Rigging failure, dismasting
Change tacks to relieve stress on mast. Join wires with two or three bulldog grips. Make up length with synthetic lanyard lashed between chain plate and thimble. A broken alloy mast can either be used shortened, or re-assembled with a wooden plug forced inside the alloy moulding, and supported on each side with splints lashed above and below the break. Halyards will have to be re-run outside the mast to avoid the plug.

Steering
Emergency steering arrangements should be part of the boat's equipment. A spar lashed to the stern will act as a sweep. A bucket or drogue, run from the side or quarter, will alter the direction of the boat in high winds.

Towing
Use the anchor-rope for towing, and protect it against chafe. Make the rope end fast to the mast where it passes through the deck. If the mast is deck-stepped, rope together strong points (winches, chain plates, cleats) to form a strop running around the deck. Fasten the tow-rope to the strop, leading it over the bow roller.

More small boats are lost when under tow than as a result of the original damage, because of the stress imposed by the snatch of the towline. If possible a rubber tyre or length of chain should be worked into the towline to help eliminate snatch in a seaway.

Emergency equipment
Lifejackets, with whistles
Safety belts (for each crew member) with clips at each end of the lifeline.
Life raft with following equipment:
sea anchor or drogue, bellows, pump or compressed air supply for maintaining inflation. Signalling light, 3 hand flares, baler, repair kit, paddles and knife.

Stored separately in waterproof plastic containers: 4 red parachute flares, 4 red hand-held flares, 4 white hand-held flares for boats up to 30 feet (9 m) and 2 orange smoke day signals for larger boats.

Heaving line at least 50 feet (l5 m) long stored within reach of helmsman.

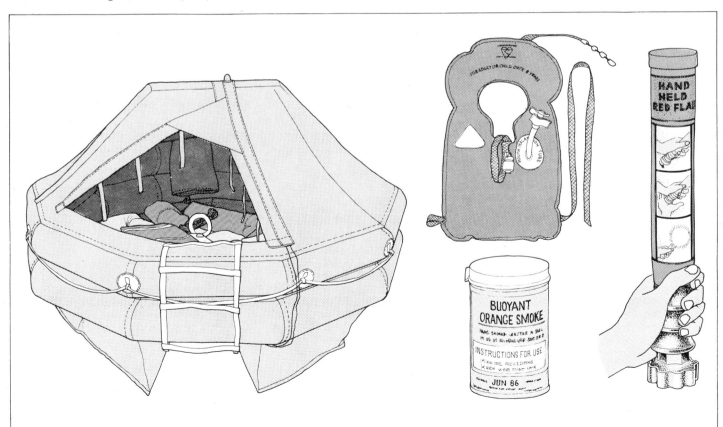

Think safety. One does not have to venture far from shore before the boat becomes essential for one's survival. Discount swimming ability — it is a useful skill, but unlikely to be much help if the boat sinks. The safety of the crew is inextricably bound up with the maintenance of the boat as a self-supporting and buoyant unit. From fitting out to laying up at the end of the season, think safety: anticipate trouble, and take appropriate measures to safeguard the crew and the boat. Ensure that the boat's equipment is suitable and serviceable, and that the crew know how to use it.

Spares and tools

Experience will help to decide which items to stock in the spares locker. Consult the engine manufacturer for a list of suitable engine spares and tools. For more general use, the following items may be useful: shackles, bulldog grips, toggles, rigging screws, clevis pins and split pins, adjustable extension plates, stainless steel hose clips of various sizes, and suitable replacement flexible hoses, tapered wooden plugs, fuses, bulbs, spare electrical cable and insulating tape, bolts, screws and nails, epoxy putty. There are plenty of other useful items which can be included. Make a regular survey of the stock, and replenish whenever necessary.

Carry a selection of tools and include a heavy duty pair of bolt croppers capable of cutting through stainless steel rigging wire or chain links, and one or two small hacksaws, with plenty of spare blades. Apart from their ability to cut through most materials, they will also cut steel rigging wire, enabling mast and gear to be cut free in the event of a dismasting.

Fire

Fire is one of the greatest hazards aboard ship. Areas most at risk are the engine room, fuel pipeline, and galley. As a precaution, fire retardant paints can be used in these areas. In poorly maintained boats, wiring may also present a fire hazard. Carry at least two dry powder fire extinguishers, and for engine rooms where access is difficult, a BCF extinguisher is useful. Position the extinguishers where they can be reached both from inside and outside the cabin. Familiarize the crew with their location and use.

Emphasize the need to act quickly, and aim extinguisher at the base of the fire. Hang a carton containing an asbestos fire blanket in the galley. Tack a notice outlining fire precautions and fire fighting recommendations to a cabin bulkhead. It should include safety precautions when refuelling. Cultivate the habit of sniffing the air in the cabin and bilges. Even if a gas and vapour detector is fitted, this habit will be an additional safeguard and may help detect fuel and gas leaks before they become dangerous. If at all possible, dry powder fire extinguishers should not be discharged into the engine compartment while the engine is running. The result of quenching a minor fire could damage the machinery. This is particularly true of diesel engines, and as diesel burns and does not explode, it is worth the two seconds' delay to close down the engine before tackling the fire.

See and be seen

Organize regular watches. Radar should complement and not replace keen visual observation of sea conditions. Hang a radar reflector from the cross trees, mast head or back stay. They should be at least 9 feet (3 m) above the water-line and of an approved design. For additional safety, and particularly where this height is difficult to obtain, use a Firdell-type reflector. Ensure that navigation lights are working and check them regularly. A fog-horn should be kept close at hand, and used to signal position and course in conditions of reduced visibility.

Man overboard

Move about deck on the windward side — if you lose your footing, or the stanchions and lifelines give way, you will fall inboard. Approved and tested safety harnesses should be available for all members of crew and children. Suitable attachment points should be provided. If lifelines are not stout enough, replace them. Fit a jackstay to run the length of the deck, to facilitate movement along the deck. Lifejackets should also be available, and worn whenever it is thought necessary. Practise man overboard drill, making sure every crew member knows the boat-handling procedures necessary to turn about and recover the person in the water. At least one horseshoe-shaped lifebuoy should be within reach of the helmsman, and also a floating lifeline in a canister. Arrange duties and devise techniques to ensure that the man overboard is not lost in the waves. It may be necessary to throw a paper trail and perhaps other items into the water to mark the course back to the man in the water. Have a boarding ladder or scrambling net or some other means of lifting heavy members of crew aboard.

Abandon ship

This must only be the very last resort. Lives are lost because of premature abandonment. Do not regard the life raft as a means of escape. It is only a means of keeping the crew above water when the boat is gone. First, try to repair hull damage. Secondly, bail out. If the boat has lost its rudder and all means of propulsion and control, it is still likely to be a safer refuge than the life raft.

An inflatable life raft capable of holding the crew should be carried on deck, or in an accessible place. The life raft should be sent away during the lay-up period for annual maintenance and repair by the manufacturer or an approved service agent.

Familiarize the crew with their duties in the event of having to abandon ship. These duties should include collecting food, water and blankets, valuables, papers, passports, signalling gear, flares and radio, and inflating and securing the life raft.

Never inflate the raft in anticipation of trouble. Once inflated, it is difficult to control, and the painter may break under shock loading. Pull the raft alongside, and encourage the crew to scramble into it as quickly as possible. The more people inside it, the more stable it becomes.

The tender may also assist in abandoning ship, but should never be considered as an alternative or a supplement to the life raft.

Planning a winter maintenance programme may work, but very often there is less time available and the weather conditions are worse than anticipated, and the schedule is disrupted.

Instead of working out a maintenance programme, have a clear sense of priorities, and keep to them. When the weather is too cold for outside work, complete the top priority jobs inside the cabin. Tackle the outside work whenever weather conditions permit.

The criteria by which the maintenance work is first organized are those of seaworthiness and safety. Once the high priority tasks have been completed, the order of the remaining work can be decided using other idiosyncratic criteria chosen by the owner.

However the first jobs are almost always the same (see page 286). They do not take long and until they are completed, it will be impossible to obtain a clear idea of the condition of the hull.

It is very important to make a careful note of maintenance tasks, as soon as they are identified. The preliminary work described below gives an ideal opportunity to survey the boat. While cleaning is in progress, note down the jobs as you notice them.

A small notebook will be needed. The type of book that opens into a double page is ideal. Keep one page for the essential work, and the opposite for non-essential. Never confuse the list by placing incidental cosmetic jobs in the essential list.

Describe faults and problems clearly, so that they can be recognized, and readily identified several months later.

First maintenance jobs

The following tasks are listed in their order of precedence. When carrying out these jobs, keep alert for indications of rot, leaks etc. that need attention and note them down. By sniffing the stale air in the bilges, beneath the cock-pit and in other poorly ventilated areas it is possible to sense troubles even when they are not apparent.
Investigate suspected problems as the cleaning and winterizing procedures are being undertaken. Do not be diverted from the initial task of cleaning and preparing the boat for winter work.

Winterize the engine

The details on the following page give suggestions for doing this. Engine repairs in all but the largest and best planned motor boats cause a considerable amount of disruption and mess; if work is needed on the engine, have it done at the earliest opportunity.

Clear out lockers and drawers

Empty all of the lockers and drawers. Discard any rusty or unserviceable items. It is rarely worth while storing worn or used spare parts. If it is thought that the part or fitting may come in useful, replace it with a new one.

Brush or vacuum the drawers and lockers

When all the lockers and drawers and other stowage holes have been cleared, checked and aired, remove the bottom boards and clean the bilges.
Hook and scrape out accumulations of mud, dust and other debris and scrub the bilges with a strong liquid detergent. Oil around the engine compartment must be scrubbed away. This should not be allowed to accumulate as it constitutes a fire hazard. Heavy accumulations of grease or dirt can be removed with paint stripper or carbon tetrachloride. Ensure excellent ventilation, as the fumes of both products are toxic.

The close scrutiny of the bilges that accompanies a thorough scrubbing will reveal any problems that might be developing. As the work progresses, the bilge smell should disappear. If the smell persists (especially if, in a wooden boat it is the sweet distinctive odour of dry rot) watch for decay and fungal growth. Inspect poorly ventilated areas, particularly those parts that may occasionally be soaked in fresh water. If drainage bungs are found in the bilge, open them to improve ventilation, and drainage.

Outside work

After the initial scrubbing, inspect the skin fittings for corrosion. Those that are fastened from the outside can often be detached and removed for inspection. Fastenings and fittings should be in good condition, evidence of corrosion should be noted, and remedial measures taken (see page 290).

With the outside skin fittings removed, probe into the pipework to remove obstructions and at the same time inspect the condition of the hull skin where the fitting passses through. In wooden boats, this is often an entry point for shipworm. Localized de-lamination or osmosis may be apparent in a fibreglass hull. Steel and aluminium hulls tend to corrode faster at these heavily welded areas than at other parts.

Replace the fittings, but leave them unblocked to allow air to enter the hull. The thorough scrubbing and scraping the boat received when she was first lifted out will reveal faulty seams, blistering etc. Because the wood behind the paint is saturated with water, the anti-fouling around a leaking seam in a wooden hull will appear darker than the surrounding paint. Hook out the sealing compound and the caulking if that too has also deteriorated (see page 40).

If osmosis blistering is revealed, note it down, and seek professional advice. Its seriousness will depend upon the size and extent of the blistering, which may itself be partially dependent upon the length of time the boat has been in the water since her previous winter ashore. Repairing the blistering is not a winter task unless a covered workplace is available. Wait until the weather is warm, and the boat has had an opportunity to dry out before resealing the blisters with resin (see page 76).

Inside the hull
Scrub the paint and varnish in the cabin with warm soapy water. Cabin decorations can usually be revived by cleaning off the grime that collects during the season. Study the brightwork as it is washed. If faded or discoloured varnish revives when wet, all it will need to bring the varnish to its former beauty is a light sanding and a single coat of varnish. If the varnish remains opaque when it is wet, it will have to be scraped away, and new finish built up. Take a note of these things, but do not try to varnish at this stage.

Rinse out the bilges. By this time there should not be any unattributable smells in the cabin. If there are hunt them out and remove the source. Make sure that they are not caused by incipient rot, or decaying matter in a hull crevice.

Water tanks
Connect a fresh water hose to the inlet pipe, and fill the water tanks. If the water has been tainted with an unpleasant taste, add some bicarbonate of soda to the water as it enters the filler pipe.

Replace the filler cap when the tank is full, and leave the water to stand. The following week, disconnect each fresh water outlet in turn and attach the hose to its feed pipe. Open the other taps, until clean sweet water runs from them all.

Drain the tank, using a siphon tube if necessary. Remember to repeat this operation during fitting out, to clean away any odours that might have clung to the tanks during the winter.

Dismantling and servicing seacocks
Prepare the seacocks by leaving penetrating oil on the bolts and valve of each. Dismantle and grease them where necessary. If they are worn, apply a little grinding paste to the touching faces. Bed them by turning them off and on. Clean thoroughly, grease and reassemble. Leave the seacocks open, removing their flexible hoses where possible, to help ventilate the hull.

Winterizing the engine

Before hauling out
Drain oil sump, and refill with recommended lubricating oil. An oil which incorporates a rust-inhibiting additive is ideal when laying up a motor for very long periods. Add anti-freeze to the sealed water cooling system. Run motor to ensure that the anti-freeze is thoroughly mixed. If the motor has been overheating, the cooling system will need to be drained and cleaned.

Petrol
To protect cylinder head and valves, mix a small quantity of petrol with oil, in the proportion of 3:1, and feed it into the fuel line; to coat the carburettor and cylinder head, pour a little thin oil into the air intake with the engine running.
Clean or replace filters and strainers (fuel, oil and water). Remove rocker cover, oil rockers and springs, and replace. Clean the engine, wire brush rusty parts, and then clean with a rag dipped in methylated spirits. Remove carburettor, bung air inlet with an oily rag, remove spark plugs, and pour about one teaspoonful of oil into each cylinder. Replace the plugs finger tight, and rotate the flywheel several times to distribute oil.

Remove the distributor cap, and place a rag moistened with thin oil over the rotor arm and points.

Remove HT leads, and replace cap. Disconnect starter, alternator and coil. Mark all wires clearly to prevent confusion in the spring. Store carburettor and all electrical parts in the dry.

Diesel
See manufacturer's recommendations concerning use of inhibiting oils etc.

For normal lay-up periods, all that is usually required is to top up the diesel fuel tank, change the lubrication oil and filters, and ensure that the proportion of anti-freeze to cooling water is correct.

For a lay-up period of more than five months, drain the sump and fill with a heavy grade engine protection de-watering oil. Drain the fuel and pour a small quantity of a higher grade protection oil into the fuel tank. Run the engine until the fuel oil reaches the injectors. Exhaust and smoke will change colour, and the engine noise will change. Stop the engine, drain the sump, and tape over all ports and inlets.

At the end of the lay up period, heavy oil can be flushed out with a thinner flushing oil, or it can be left and dissolved into the normal lubricating oil.

Check oil level in clutch and gearbox housing. If there is emulsified oil on the filler plug, or on the dip-stick, drain the gearbox and refill with fresh oil.

Brush oil on all exposed threads and bright metal (prop shaft, control wires, holding bolts, etc).

Draining to cooling system
Open seacocks and check valves, and drain the engine cooling system.

Release upper-most flexible hose and blow down it, until air can be heard gurgling out of the water inlet and outlet. Shut seacocks to exclude the seawater. Open all other pet cocks and drain plugs to ensure that water is completely drained from the system. Close drain plugs etc., and flush the system with a fresh water hose inserted into the water inlet.

Open all drain plugs in turn, and make sure that they are clear. Poke with a stiff wire if necessary. Blocked pipes can usually be reached by disconnecting hoses. Bung the exhaust and keep the seacocks closed if the boat is to winter afloat.

If there is any possibility that water is trapped in the raw water cooling system, fill it with a mixture of water and anti-freeze pre-mixed before pouring it into a top hose. Bleed drain plugs, and pet cocks and top up if necessary.

Paint rusted engine parts

Prepare a list of lay up procedures, and tape it to the engine to ensure there is thorough preparation in the spring.

Winter and spring are not ideal times to paint or varnish out of doors. Weather is unpredictable, and changes quickly. However well prepared and executed, work will be spoilt if the weather is too cold or damp. Paint and varnish manufacturers give specific recommendations for the use of their products, and these are always worth while following.

Planning

Impose control over the order of work. Plan ahead and try to prevent work getting out of step. Do not start too early in the year. Work progresses swiftly in warm weather, and the resulting finish is better.

First complete the varnishing and painting inside the boat. Adequate ventilation and a low output electric heater left on during preparation and drying time should ensure satisfactory results even if there is frost or rain outside. Leave the exterior until the weather moderates. After completion, allow seven days to elapse before handling and launching to avoid damaging paint coatings.

By working from the top, the finished work is rarely spoiled by nearby sanding or painting. When weather permits, work from the mast downwards, sanding and varnishing spars and masts, (whether they are on the boat, or stored in the spar loft of the boat-yard). Prepare, varnish or paint the coach roof, then the cabin-sides, before working on the decks, bulwarks and topsides. Except when using conventional yacht enamel, carry topside paintwork below the boot top, and the boot top below the anti-fouling to prevent paint starvation where the colours and different paints meet.

Weather conditions cannot be planned, but if the boat is berthed in the open without a satisfactory awning, do not remove more paintwork than can be prepared and protected by a coat of primer applied the same day. As weather improves, prepared surfaces can be left overnight without coming to harm.

The success of the entire paint job depends upon careful and thorough preparation. Surfaces must be dry, clean and with sufficient texture to enable paint and varnish to adhere. Unless the weather is particularly dry, do not apply top coats or varnish before midday. Morning and evening mist will spoil new work, paints tend to lose their gloss, and varnish will bloom and may have to be removed before more coats are added. In addition, the bond between the new coating and the substrate will be impaired if the prepared surfaces are damp. This is a particular problem with steel or fibreglass hulls, which in comparison to wood, are cold surfaces upon which moisture readily condenses.

Surface preparation

Scrub all grimy surfaces and all those that need re-painting. Use a commercial yacht-cleaning fluid or strong detergent. Rinse and leave to dry. If a high pressure hose is used to wash away the dirt on a wooden hull, take care not to damage the wood surface.

Repair all structural damage

Much of this work can be completed before painting is scheduled to begin.

Note that if an epoxy filler is used, stringent temperature and humidity controls have to be met. Dig out rot spots in a wooden hull and grave or fill them. Leave surfaces level and smooth, and protect them with suitable varnish or primer prior to painting or varnishing in warm weather.

The finish of a well-maintained hull rarely requires complete stripping and re-finishing. For many years the paintwork can be touched in and waxed, perhaps occasionally sanding back one layer of top enamel, and giving a new top coat. Do not remove paint because it is old. Re-painting or re-varnishing is an expensive and lengthy operation, and is necessary only when the original scheme is detaching or generally breaking down.

Removing old finishes

Blowlamp

Never burn off paint from a plywood, fibreglass or steel hull, or in preparation for a varnished finish. Ensure that the paint scrapings do not ignite the other debris that accumulates beneath the boat. Take stringent fire precautions at all times, and in particular when working inside the hull. Do not burn off anti-fouling.

A pressurized paraffin blowlamp is more convenient than a gas torch and is less likely to go out when held close to the paint, but a heat gun is probably best if an electrical supply is close at hand.

Whichever is used, play the flame over the paintwork, and use a flat, slightly flexible sharpened paint scraper to remove paint once it bubbles, and before it burns and becomes brittle. Take care when burning off black paint, as it is not always easy to distinguish between paint and charred wood.

Stripper

Work with good ventilation as the fumes are toxic and irritating, and may cause nausea and headaches or even collapse. Wear an air-fed breathing mask if working in a confined space. Protect eyes and skin, and dispose of the accumulations of dissolved paint and saturated wire wool safely. Do not pile them together with shavings and rags, as spontaneous combustion may occur.

Use strippers for removing finishes on fibreglass and metal hulls, and where varnish is to be used. Areas that need protection should be masked with tape and newspaper. Apply stripper generously, adding more and agitating with a short, stiff-haired brush until the finish softens and lifts. Try to remove the entire paint finish in one operation, periodically agitating and then covering the stripper with damp hessian or polythene between applications. Remove with a paint scraper and coarse wire wool. Neutralize the surface with suitable spirit, and/or fresh water as recommended by the manufacturer.

Sanding
Use sandpaper in preference to a cabinet scraper, as it is less likely to mar the surface beneath the finish. Start with coarse grit paper, backed by a cork or felt backing pad. Work at an angle to the grain of the wood or to the finish lines on the hull until the surface is smooth. Use progressively finer grades of paper to remove sanding marks. Change the sanding angle with each grade of paper, each angle being slightly more acute than the previous, until all scratches are sanded out. 180 grit and finer can be fitted into an orbital sander to speed surface preparation. Never use a disc sander for smoothing and levelling.

Do not oversand. Texture is needed to improve the bond between the finish and the newly prepared surface. Wet and dry paper (used wet, and continuously lubricated by a hose dribbling water from above) cuts swiftly, but the wet slurry fills the small pores and cavities in the surface, and impairs the adhesion of the primer or undercoat. After using wet and dry paper, wash the surface thoroughly and wait for two or three hours for the surface to dry, then sand lightly with 220 garnet paper. Vacuum or brush the dust away.

Fillers
Filling should keep in step with the sanding. Fill large cavities with epoxide filler and level them as well as possible to minimize the heavy sanding necessary once the resin cures. As a finish builds up filling will be limited to smaller and smaller holes and scratches that become obvious as larger blemishes are eliminated. Do not, however, fill caulking

seams with sealer until after the priming coats are applied (see Wooden boats, painting, page 303).

Paint or varnish do not adhere to a greasy or oily surface. Grease and oil stains, and naturally oily woods such as teak, iroko or afromosia, should be washed and scrubbed with white spirit, or a suitable de-greaser prepared by the paint manufacturer, immediately prior to finishing.

Surfaces must be clean and dry. Wood and other porous surfaces will not dry if they are saturated with salt. Salt crystals must be thoroughly flushed with fresh warm water, and dried before re-finishing. A useful guide for re-painting is that if the surface can be sanded to produce a fine dust or scraped to produce fine shavings, the surface is probably dry enough for painting.

Paints and varnish

Paints
Always follow the manufacturer's instructions when using paints, and if in any doubt consult them. Manufacturers and suppliers are happy to specify a painting scheme for a particular boat and fixed budget. Use their skills and benefit from their experience by asking them to specify the best possible finish for a given cost.

Storage
Paints should be stored in a warm dry cupboard, or brought slowly to room temperature before use. Part-empty paint cans should be stored with their lids hammered tightly in. Shake them to seal the top.

Re-opening
Remove paint skin before stirring, and strain the paint into a clean tin before use. A piece of clean wood without loose fibre makes a good paint stirrer.

Paint left standing for a long time may separate, the pigment forming a heavy sediment in the bottom of the can. To reconsitute the paint, pour the surface liquid into a jar, and stir the sediment into a smooth paste. Then add the fluid, and continue stirring until the paint is restored to its previous consistency.

Selecting the right paint
The paint must be compatible with the surface it is to adhere to. Do not coat a hard epoxide or polyester finish over a flexible or conventional paint. To identify the paint that has been used before, check by pressing a thumbnail against the existing paint finish. Hard two-pack paints will be brittle and impossible to dent, whereas a conventional or urethane finish will be slightly flexible, and give beneath the pressure of the thumbnail. This test is not always conclusive, and one may be best advised to consult the manufacturer. A hard, stable, groundwork (fibreglass, steel or ferro-cement) should be protected by a hard and abrasion-resistant epoxide scheme, overcoated with a two-pack polyurethane or an enamel. A conventional wooden hull will be better protected by a more flexible paint film, which will permit the wood to move and breathe. Cold moulded and large plywood hulls are suited to epoxide schemes. Unfortunately, epoxies, despite their excellent protective qualities, do not make good cosmetic finishing coats, due to a tendency to chalk when exposed.

Varnish
Varnishes should never be shaken before use. Bubbles in the varnish will

be impossible to brush out, and the resulting slight depressions will mar the finish unless they are thoroughly sanded. Store varnish in a cool place, and bring it slowly to room temperature.

Brushes
Always use the largest possible paintbrush for the work in hand. A 2 inch (50mm) brush is an excellent all-purpose size. Anti-fouling is usually applied with a 3-4 inch (75-100mm) brush, and delicate paintwork can be touched in with a chisel-edged brush. Paint seams with a round brush. Use masking tape to ensure straight edges and to protect brightwork when painting close to varnished woodwork.

Do not use brand-new brushes for varnish. Instead, choose an old soft-haired brush that is thoroughly clean and dry. Use new brushes for priming and undercoating, until they are worn into shape and shed no more hairs.

Paint or varnish will dry on the upper hairs of the brush close to the ferrule, and as the brush is used, small particles will work down the hairs and spoil the finish. Clean the brush every twenty minutes, and immediately after use.

Re-painting Routine maintenance

Apply paint with horizontal strokes, leaving a small space between strokes. Spread the paint evenly with vertical strokes, and then lay it off with a final long light horizontal brushstroke from right to left. (Left handed people will be happier working in the opposite direction.) Once the area has been laid off, do not return to it. Wait until the next coat to remedy a blemish.

Varnish should not be brushed across the grain. Brush on with slow steady brush strokes (unless a two-component varnish is used, in which case speed of working is essential), then lay it off with the brush held at an angle of 45° or less to the surface of the hull, and dragged lightly across the surface.

Clean paint or varnish brushes in clean turpentine or recommended thinners.

Rinse them in soap and water, then fresh water. Shake dry and form the bristles neatly. Wrap them in brown packing paper, retained by an elastic band. If the brushes are left to soak in thinners or turpentine during a break, make certain they are dry before use, otherwise the finish will be marred by small spots and depressions where the thinners have diluted the finish.

Waxing
A wax coat applied three times a year will revive and protect old paintwork, and keep the new paintwork looking clean and bright. A thorough scrubbing with boat cleaning fluid or strong soap and water will clean and revive a finish.

Rub away blemishes with abrasive paste before waxing the surface with a hard, non-silicone polishing wax, which must be kept away from the anti-fouling at the boot top. Previously, boat waxes tended to make surface preparation for repairs or re-painting difficult, but the new waxes are easily removed with de-greasing

fluid, and do not have this disadvantage.

Varnish will be revived by washing it in a mixture of equal parts of turpentine, linseed oil and methylated spirits, with a dash of vinegar added. Apply with fine wire wool, and leave for half an hour before wiping off and waxing.

Touching up paintwork
This can be done at any time during the season, provided that the surface is dry and the weather suitable. The sooner exposed surfaces are protected, the easier it is to re-finish and the better the bond between new paint and substrate.

To provide a key for the new finish, cut back the surrounding paintwork with sandpaper. Dust, then re-finish with paint, the first coat with a short stiff-haired brush. Where damage has completely removed the finish, re-build with the correct types of paint in their

correct order. Read instructions before touching in epoxide and polyurethane two-part paints. Priming coats for these need great care, and should not overlap surrounding paintwork.

Touching in varnish
Prepare the wood carefully as blemishes are highlighted once the varnish is applied. Smooth the wood surface with 220 garnet paper. Wood that has been exposed often darkens or bleaches. Restore its colour before varnishing.

Bleach darkened timber with a saturated solution of oxalic acid, (brushed on and allowed to soak) before neutralizing with sodium bicarbonate solution. Household bleach has a stronger action and is neutralized in the same way. Stubborn stains can often be removed by dripping

domestic bleach on to the mark and leaving it to take effect. Rinse the wood with fresh water, then stain and varnish.

Staining
Rub the wood with fine wire wool or abrasive paper and then apply a suitable oil or spirit stain. The latter is quicker-drying, and will not interact with the solvents of the varnish. Oil stains have less bite and are easier to apply over large areas. Ensure that the stains are

thoroughly dry before varnishing, otherwise the solvents in the stain will prevent the varnish drying.

Rub the stained area with a dry rag, and then follow with a thinned coat of varnish (30 per cent white spirit) applied with a rag, making sure that all the pores in the

wood are filled. Build on this with more varnish applied with a brush, and reduce the proportion of thinners. Sand between coats. Burnish the final coat with polishing paste to help it merge into the surrounding varnish, and then wax.

Health and safety
Wear protective clothing when using stripper or epoxide two-pack polyurethane and anti-fouling products. Wear a breathing mask when machine-sanding, or hand-sanding anti-fouling. Read and follow instructions for use on

paint, fillers, etc. Follow and take the precautions recommended.

Wear an air-fed hood when spraying in a confined space, or where ventilation is poor. Where there is good ventilation, wear a simple dust mask to prevent

inhalation of spray. When spraying two-pack polyurethane or anti-fouling, an air-fed hood must be worn at all times. Ensure good ventilation when stripping, or wear air-fed hood. Protect hands with barrier cream or polythene disposable gloves. Do not wash skin with thinners.

Wood

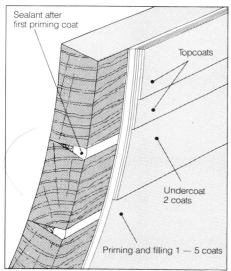

Conventional wood finish

Washing
Equipment Hose, broom, sand, scraper, wire brush for metalwork.

Technique Work quickly, wash off marine growths as soon as possible after hauling out.

Note Leaks, opened seams, loose paint, and areas where paint is discoloured by water trapped behind.

Paint removal
Equipment Blow lamp, gas torch or heat gun, 60 grit wet and dry, sanding block, paint scraper and mask.

Technique Burn off paint. Hold lamp about 4 inches (100 mm) from wood, and play heat over small area. Scrape when paint lifts and bubbles. After burning off, sand down to wood. Clean back keel and metalwork with disc sander or wire brush. Soak wood with preservative, and leave to dry before sanding and filling.

Note Do not burn off paint from plywood hull. Wear suitable breathing mask when removing anti-fouling with sandpaper or stripper.

Sanding and filling
Equipment 60, 100, 180, 220 wet and dry, sanding block, orbital sander, epoxide filler, trowel, knife, rag, brush, masking tape, face mask, graving tools.

Technique Mask around depressions, and fill with epoxide filler. Level with trowel. Sand with 60 grit wet and dry. Add more filler if required. Work down to 220 grit, leaving only the finest sanding marks. Wipe clean with stiff brush.

Note Do not use an electric sander with wet and dry paper used wet. Wear a mask if machine-sanding. Do not sand if boats downwind are being painted or varnished. Do not fill cracks that are likely to close when the boat is in the water. All filler must be sanded flush with the hull before continuing.

Priming
Equipment Primer, thinners, 2-3 inch (50-75mm) flat brush, seam brush, masking tape and newspaper, rag and stiff brush for dusting.

Technique Wipe with rag dipped in thinners. Follow manufacturer's instructions, thin the first coat. Paint seams. Rub rag along seams to remove excess paint and runs. Paint from top downwards, after masking varnished work. Primer can usually be applied on top of wet paint.

Note Choose dry weather. Priming restores oil to dried-out wood, and hardens surface, in preparation for top coats. Do not skimp priming. Always ensure that there is a barrier of primer covering bare wood, otherwise adhesion and durability of finish will be poor.

Filling
Equipment 180 and 220 grit wet and dry, sanding block, orbital sander, filler, trowel, primer, brush and thinners.

Technique Priming coat is touch dry, fill cracks and depressions with suitable paint fillers. Sand and dust and repeat with filler, until surfaces are smooth. Sand and prime as soon as filler dries. Seal caulking seams and prime prior to applying undercoat.

Note All surfaces must be smooth and level, with dents and scratches filled. Sand lightly, and prime exposed filler and wood. Use flexible fillers to stop cracks likely to close when the boat is in the water.

Undercoat — 2 coats
Equipment Undercoat, thinners, brush, 220-280 grit wet and dry, block and orbital sander.

Technique Apply paint generously, using long slow brush strokes, with the grain. Clean brush every 20-30 minutes. Sand between coats. Mix final undercoat with 50 per cent top coat enamel.

Note Do not allow drips or runs to form. Keep surface clear of dust, hairs, grit etc. Sand between coats, but do not cut back to bare wood.

Re-painting over old finish
Wire-brush metal work first, then prepare finish for repainting

Equipment 220-280 grit wet and dry, block, orbital sander, scouring powder, stiff brush, paint brush, hose, yacht cleaning fluid.

Technique Clean back and wet-sand surface. Mouldings and awkward spots can be scoured by abrasive powder applied with a brush or rag. Surface must be completely clean and matt finish to ensure good adhesion of top coat. First top coat should be mixed with 50 per cent undercoat to obtain easy coverage and good initial bond.

Note Work into all corners. Brush away or vacuum sanding dust. Wipe surface with rag dampened with thinners prior to applying top coats.

Top coat — 2/3 coats
Equipment Oil-based enamel yacht finish, thinners, brush, 280-320 grit wet and dry, sanding block, masking tape.

Technique Work from the top downwards, thin the first coat. Use long even and slow strokes. Clean brush every 20-30 minutes. Sand gently between coats. Final polish with burnishing cream and polish with wax.

Note Warm, dry weather. Pick off flies, insects and hairs with pointed stick. Do not overbrush, but take care to prevent runs and drips forming at the hard edges of the planking. Mask varnished work prior to painting.

Inside the hull of a wooden boat

Cleaning
Equipment Scraper, wire brush, old chisel, 60 and 180 grit garnet paper, dust pan and brush, or (preferably) vacuum cleaner.

Technique Remove debris with scraper, and old chisel. Scrape and sand finish. Remove all old loose paint. Dry then brush preservative on to all exposed woodwork and leave to dry.

Note Ensure plenty of ventilation when applying preservative, and during the drying time.

Finishing
Equipment No 2 wire wool or abrasive pad, 180 grit sandpaper, sanding blocks, disc sander or orbital sander, red lead, linseed oil or bitumen paint, with brush and rags.

Technique Thoroughly prepare surfaces, then paint with red lead or bitumen. If linseed oil is to be used, warm in a double boiler and apply when hot. Raw oil penetrates deeper, and gives better protection, but takes longer to dry. Overcoat wet on wet, until the wood seems unable to absorb more.

Note Thorough preparation is difficult, but essential. Work from the ends of the boat to the middle. Try to avoid getting the interior wet, as drying out is slow and often incomplete.

Steel hulls — topsides

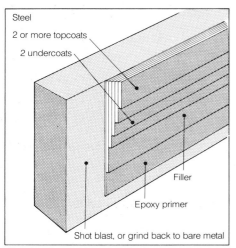

Steel
2 or more topcoats
2 undercoats
Filler
Epoxy primer
Shot blast, or grind back to bare metal

Paint scheme for steel hull

If considering entirely re-painting the boat, consult paint manufacturers for suggested specification. Many finishes are available, and the choice will depend upon cost and working conditions.

Preparation
Equipment Wire brush, electric grinder with wire brush or abrasive disc, shot blasting equipment if it is available, epoxide resin and thinners, brush.

Technique Thorough preparation is essential. Remove all rust, scale, loose paint etc., and paint immediately with suitable epoxy primer, or thinned epoxy resin.

Note Surface must be ground down to steel. Burnished scale and rust will make a poor foundation and lift shortly after painting. Work quickly to prevent corrosion occurring on areas previously cleaned. Brush dust and grit from surface before painting.

Touching in existing paintwork
Ensure painted surfaces are thoroughly sanded, and free of dust or grease. Match new paintwork to existing paint.

Filling and sanding
Equipment Low density epoxide filler, palette knife or trowel, 180 grit sandpaper, sanding block, orbital sander, brush and primer.

Technique Fill and level. Add more coats and level until surface is smooth and fair.

Note A thorough filling, after the first coat, will obviate further work. If filler sweats after curing, wash with water.

Undercoat — 2 coats
Equipment Primer, brush, thinners, 240 grit sandpaper.

Technique Conventional, single-pack polyurethane, or two-pack paints can be used. Choice depends on cost and usage. Two-pack paints are more durable and abrasion-resistant, and cost more. When re-painting over painted surface, ensure paints are compatible.

Note Temperature and humidity conditions — both are critical for successful re-painting. 65 per cent humidity is the acceptable maximum, but if working close to the limits of temperature or humidity, ensure that weather conditions are not going to turn while work is in progress, and spoil it.

Top coats
Equipment Suitable paint, brush, masking tape.

Technique See notes for top coat application, fibreglass.

Steel hulls — bottoms

Preparation
Equipment Grinder with abrasive discs, wire brush, epoxide primer and brush.

Technique Grind down to bare steel, brush away dust, and prime within 1½ hours. Follow with another four coats, allowing suitable drying time between each coat.

Note Hull must be clean and dry. Do not work during early morning or late afternoon, unless boat is in a sheltered workshop with adequate heating. Anti-foul as for fibreglass hull.

Aluminium, zinc or aluminium sprayed steel or galvanized iron

Preparation
Equipment 220 and 230 grit wet and dry, abrasive paste or scouring fluid, water supply, brushes, yacht cleaning fluid, de-greaser, rags.

Technique Clean surfaces carefully: wire brushing or shot blasting may injure or disfigure metal finish. Wash and then de-grease hull. Lightly sand surface and wash prior to primer.

Note Ensure a good bond between paint and metal. Entire surface must be rubbed or abraded to remove loose paint, and to give texture.

Self-etch primer
Equipment Primer (self-etching), brush.

Technique One thin coat of primer. Read instructions for preparation before applying.

Note Temperature conditions must be right for self-etching primer, and the surface must be dry and clean. Self-etching primer usually changes colour when conditions for application are satisfactory.

Finish with three metal primer coats, then two undercoats and two gloss coats as for fibreglass.

Ferro-cement

Preparation
Equipment 180 grit wet and dry paper, sanding block, orbital sander, hose, stiff brush.

Technique Brush surface with dry brush to sweep out loose dust. Previously finished surfaces should be sanded back to sound paint.

Unfinished cement must be left for at least one month before painting. See ferro-cement (page 122) for supervision of curing.

Priming — 4 coats
Equipment Epoxy resin, thinners, mixing can, brush.

Technique Brush one thinned coat of resin, 15 per cent, followed by three unthinned coats.

Note Follow manufacturer's recommended drying times between applications (usually between 16-24 hours). Temperature and humidity conditions are critical.

Filling
Equipment Epoxide low density filler, trowel, filler suited to fairing between coats, 220 and 320 grit wet and dry paper, brush, and rags for cleaning.

Technique Fill and level surface. Re-paint exposed cement with primer.

Note Fillers should be applied carefully to reduce amount of sanding after curing. If filler sweats after curing, rinse it with fresh water, then dry it.

Varnish

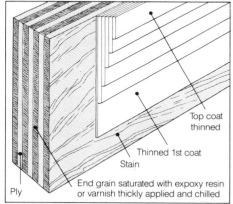

Varnish scheme

Top coat thinned
Thinned 1st coat
Stain
End grain saturated with expoxy resin or varnish thickly applied and chilled
Ply

Stripping
Equipment Marine stripper, brush, paint scraper, hessian or polythene, thumbtacks, neutralizer, no.2 and 00 wire wool, 180 and 220 grit garnet paper.

Technique Strip in areas; complete one part before starting the next. Use plenty

of stripper, cover with damp hessian or polythene while stripper is working. Lift off varnish, and clean with 00 wire wool dipped in neutralizer.

Note Protect eyes and skin, ensure excellent ventilation when working inside boat. Wear breathing mask in confined spaces. Mask off areas with tape and newspaper to limit spread of the stripper.

Brush cleaned surface with preservative, and leave to dry. Do not brush preservative on to marine ply or teak or where two-part hard varnish is used.

Filling and sanding
Equipment Epoxide filler, or resin with suitable filling dust i.e. ground coconut shell, palette knife, masking tape, 180, 220 and 240 grit garnet paper, orbital sander, and sanding blocks.

Technique Match filler to wood colour. Final colour of re-varnished wood can be checked by damping bare wood

with water or methylated spirits. Fill depressions and sand until surface is smooth and all old varnish is completely removed.

Always apply filler neatly, so that later sanding is minimized. Remove all excess filler from around blemishes. Sand mouldings with a block shaped to negative profile of moulding.

Touching-in or re-varnishing
Equipment Varnish (warmed before use), thinners, mixing jar or tin, 220, 240 and 320 grit garnet paper, sander, blocks, brush, stain, rags, epoxide resin for sealing end grain on plywood panels and absorbent woods.

Technique Stain if necessary. Apply stain with grain, in long smooth strokes with wet absorbent rag. Wipe off excess stain before drying. Thin first varnish coat (10-15 per cent). Dry, then sand. Wipe clean, then wipe with rag dipped in thinners. Saturate end grain with varnish,

Technique (continued)

or epoxide resin if very absorbent. End grain varnish can be built up more quickly if the varnish is chilled before use, and applied with the tip of a finger.

Note Varnish in dry, warm weather. Do not shake varnish. Follow manufacturer's instructions for re-coating and sanding times. After sanding, wipe with hand, or with rag moistened with thinners. Clean brush every 30 minutes, or more frequently if varnish is drying quickly.

Take care when rubbing down not to cut below hardened finish. Urethane varnishes, and some others, dry from the surface inwards, and it is possible to tear up varnish by sanding too hard or too soon.

Finish coat

Equipment Varnish, thinners, brush, rag, 320 and 500 grit abrasive paper, sanding blocks and orbital sander for large flat areas, polishing paste and wax.

Technique Rub down varnish very lightly. Apply thinned 15 per cent varnish coat and leave to dry. Polish with fine paper, then abrasive cream. Wash off before waxing.

Note Only the very lightest sanding is necessary. Change paper regularly to prevent build-up of dust scratching surface. Do not use old worn paper if a good finish is desired.

Hard finish — suitable for fibreglass, thick plywood and ABS hulls

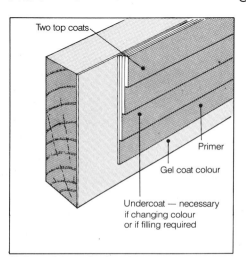

Paint scheme for hard finish

Preparation Sanding and stripping as for the above. Take care when prising away marine growths from fibreglass hull, as gel coat can be damaged. Never apply two-part hard finish over conventional or new one-pot polyurethane. For best results and maximum durability, all previous finishes should be cut back until a smooth and dust-free surface is obtained.

Primer

Equipment Correct primer for two-pot paint, epoxide filler, mixing knife.

Technique Thorough surface preparation. Fill opened seams and cracks, level depressions otherwise hard high gloss will emphasize surface irregularities. Paint primer on to surface.

Note Overcoat within recommended time. Note temperature and humidity conditions (65 per cent maximum).

Moisture will condense on cold surfaces such as fibreglass, and spoil the paint adhesion or finish. Work only when the weather is set fair.

Repainting and touching-up

Equipment Yacht cleaner, de-greaser, rags, bucket and brushes, 180 and 320 grit wet and dry.

Technique Sand down damaged paintwork. Entire surface must be thoroughly prepared with no shiny spots. After using wet and dry, leave to dry and then sand lightly with 320 used dry. Brush or vacuum dust.

Note Primer must be applied only to bare surface, never to existing paintwork. Overcoat within recommended time.

Undercoat

Only necessary if changing colour of top coat or filling.

Equipment Suitable two-pack undercoat, mixing stick or knife, brush, masking tape, thinners.

Technique Follow mixing instructions. Mask off varnish work, boot top line, and then paint.

Note Choose warm dry weather. Work quickly. Do not overbrush. Observe temperature and humidity conditions.

Undercoat and fillers

Equipment Suitable epoxide filler, palette knife, 220 grit wet and dry, undercoat, brush and thinners.

Technique Fill all holes and crevices. Leave to cure, and rub down with 220 used wet. Add more filler and smooth

before second coat of undercoat is applied.

Note Try to avoid cutting back to hull surface. If surface is exposed, prime with the correct primer, (only on the surface, not on the paintwork). Follow with undercoat within recommended time.

Topcoats 1 and 2

Equipment Top enamel, mixing stick or knife, masking tape.

Technique Arrange all staging prior to applying paint. Work with steady brush strokes, from right to left (if right-handed). Do not re-work areas already covered with wet paint. Pad and spray also recommended — see manufacturer's instructions.

Note Ensure temperature and humidity conditions are satisfactory. Do not paint downwind from someone burning off or sanding. Mix paint thoroughly. Apply second coat at recommended drying interval. If this is impossible, re-sand with 320 used wet, and then dust. Change brushes every 20 minutes as paint begins to dry on the hairs. Leave finish for one week to harden, and a month before polishing or waxing.

Anti-fouling protects the immersed part of the hull from worm and marine growths, and is applied over a primed and painted finish. A variety of anti-fouling is available. Traditional paints are generally cheaper, but apart from the advantage of lower cost, there is little advantage in using them. The new, self-activating anti-fouling paints are easier to apply, require less surface preparation, and their efficiency is not impaired as the biocides are leached into the water.

Dinghies and small boats that are hauled out daily do not need anti-fouling. Those kept in the water need protection. Marine organisms will attach themselves to the hull whether the water is fresh or salt, and they flourish in warmer waters.

Anti-fouling is not applied evenly. The illustration shows which parts of the underwater hull require most coats of paint. If the boat is to be used in warm or polluted waters, a more powerful anti-fouling is required.

Forefoot

Water-line zone

Extra coats of anti-fouling

Leading edge of rudder and keel

With all types of anti-fouling, the effectiveness is dependent upon the thickness of the paint layer. Sufficient paint should be applied at the start of the season to provide protection until hauling out. The relative thickness of the paint is illustrated. If the paint is sanded smooth, allow for the loss of thickness by applying an additional coat. If paint is thinned or padded on, apply an extra coat. Traditional anti-fouling becomes porous as the biocide is leached from the paint, and the small crevices and pores fill with silt which inhibits the action of the remaining biocide.

Increase their effectiveness by washing the water-line once or twice during the season to remove the silt and dirt, and to re-activate the biocide.

Preparation
Conditions for painting anti-fouling are the same as for painting other finishes. Avoid painting on damp or humid days. Take particular care to ensure that cold surfaces (steel or fibreglass) are completely dry before painting. Protect a stripped hull with suitable priming coats before painting on the anti-fouling. Check the instructions before the first coat is applied, as it may adhere better if the primer is only partially cured. Steel and alloy hulls must be thoroughly primed before soft and hard anti-fouling paints which contain heavy metals are applied. This prevents hull corrosion once the boat is returned to the water.

Painting over anti-fouling
Correct preparation is very important. Soft and hard anti-fouling finishes should be scrubbed and washed clean, and then wet sanded, dried, and primed before applying a new coat. If the priming is omitted and the new anti-fouling is painted on to the smooth but porous previous coat, the biocides will work into the previous paint layer, and the period of protection will be shortened. Self-activating anti-fouling paints can be applied over most types of anti-fouling, but for maximum benefit, soft anti-foulings should be sanded or stripped back, and an appropriate priming finish applied, before the new anti-fouling is brushed or padded on. In subsequent years, it will only be necessary to wash, sponge, rinse, and dry the surface of the old self-activating anti-fouling before repainting.

Equipment
Hose, scrubbing brush, scraper, (paint stripper and neutralizer if necessary), wire brush for metal work.

Masking tape, 180 grit wet and dry paper, sanding blocks.

Priming and anti-fouling paint, thinners, 3-4 inch (75-100 mm) brushes, pad or roller.

Some additional props, pads and wedges to support the boat as shores are moved to a new location to allow previously masked areas to be painted.

Canvas decks

Preparation

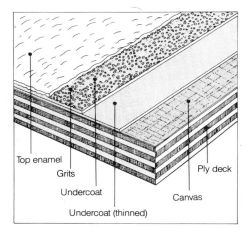

Equipment Sandpaper (60 grit), sanding block, orbital sander, paint stripper or heat gun, neutralizer, wire wool, paint scraper.

Technique Remove top coats from canvas deck. Sandpaper where paint coating is thin. Thicker coats must be removed with heat gun and scraper or paint stripper (take care to mask adjacent paintwork and varnish). Sand and dust after cleaning.

Note Sanding should be very carefully controlled to avoid cutting into the canvas. Stripping and stripping with a heat gun must also be carried out with care so as not to damage the canvas. Strip or burn back to the undercoat. It is not necessary to reach canvas provided that the foundation for the new paint is firm and clean.

Foundation coat
Equipment Undercoat, brush, thinners, top coat, pearls or grit, sieve or sugar shaker, brush.

Technique Apply one thinned undercoat and one unthinned undercoat. Follow the instructions for the use of the textured surface. Some manufacturers specify that the texture be applied with the paint, others recommend use of a fine sieve to scatter grit over the surface.

Some manufacturers recommend a sieve to scatter grit

Note Do not spread too many grits over the surface. Quantities are usually specified in relation to the quantity of top coat.

Finish coat
Equipment Paint roller or brush, dusting brush or vacuum cleaner.

Technique Clean away dust and loose particles with a brush. Then roll or brush final coat of enamel over the deck.

Fibreglass deck with moulded tread

Preparation
Equipment Belt sander and dusting brush or vacuum cleaner, epoxide filler or yacht cleaning fluid, 60 grit sandpaper, sanding block.

Technique Grind down raised deck pattern until it is smooth and level. Then fill and re-finish with epoxide filler, or sand across the top of the raised pattern. This will be successful if the pattern is in the form of raised flat diamonds or squares, each with a surface area of more than one square inch (25mm^2).

Note Take care that the levelling is carried out carefully, otherwise the new flat, textured surface will look uneven.

Wear a face mask and goggles when sanding fibreglass. Wear polythene gloves when handling epoxy resins.

Finish
Either as for canvas decks using one-pack or two-pack paints instead of yacht enamel, or use epoxy resin.

Where raised deck tread remains
Equipment Roller, epoxy resin colodial silica added, pearls or grit, shaker, brush, top coat of finish paint.

Technique Roll epoxy resin over the raised part of the deck pattern and scatter grit over deck. Leave to cure. Re-cover with resin (unthickened) applied with a brush or roller, after vacuuming the surface to remove excess and loose particles. Brush on top coat of paint.

Bright decks

Equipment Stiff-haired scrubbing brush, soft-haired scrubbing brush, sponge, sandstone block, scraper, scouring liquid, de-greasing fluid or detergent, mat or knee pads, bucket.

Technique Scrape away tar, paint and other deposits. Wash deck and then scrub the surface across the grain with a brush, or with the grain with a flat sandstone block. Lubricate the block or brush with abrasive cleaner. Deck oil or sealer can be applied to the deck once it is completely dry.

Note Regular applications of deck oil or teak sealer will keep the deck looking bright and clean. Avoid a built-up finish that will be slippery when wet. If a bleached, scrubbed finish is desired, regular cleaning is essential. Do not scrub the deck with the grain. For more details see page 170.

Painting a water-line and boot top

Unless the boat has had all its paint removed, there should be some indication of the water-line and boot top and re-painting will be straightforward.

Topsides paint should be brushed below the boot top. When the topside paintwork is dry, mask off the boot top line with 1 inch (25 mm) masking tape, ensuring the tape adheres firmly.

Paints
The hull at the water-line is prone to heavy marine growth. Choose an anti-fouling paint for the boot top.

Painting
Paint below the water-line, and avoid running over the masking tape on to the new topside paintwork. Remove the tape before the boot top paint is quite dry.

With the boot top dry, mask off the water-line, and apply anti-fouling up to the masking tape, which should then be removed.

Marking in a new water-line
Take measurements from the plans (measuring down from the stem head and stern and perhaps amidships, too, if a suitable station can be identified) or take measurements from an identical boat. If there are no plans, and no similar boats from which dimensions can be taken, try to sight the water-line by

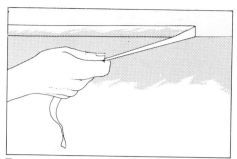

To remove tape, pull directly backwards.

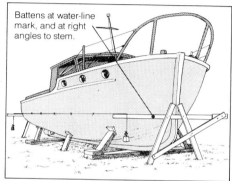

Battens at water-line mark, and at right angles to stem.

Battens set up for marking water-line.

eye, or seek professional assistance. With marks for the stem and stern, set up battens at each end of the boat.

Water-line
Run a string line, weighted at each end,

Inclined battens for marking boot top.

and move the line against the hull, pencilling in the mark where the string touches. Repeat on the other side.

Boot top
Pin a couple of inclined battens to the levelled battens at each end. Amidships, the boot top line should be about 1½-2 inches (37-50mm) above the water-line. At the bow it is closer to 3-3½ inches (75-88mm), and at the stern it will be between 2½-3 inches (62-75mm). The angled battens can be adjusted until the string line meets the boot top marks at each end, and lies parallel and a little above the water-line for most of the boat's length. Mark in the line and mask and paint the boot top. Remove the masking tape before the paint dries.

Gold leaf

Lettering is a highly skilled art, and unless there is a clear outline of the boat's name and port of registration visible beneath the new paint, leave the lettering to a professional sign writer. If the writing is still visible, choose a warm, dry, windless day for the gold leaf and lettering work. It is important that the weather is calm, or the boat will vibrate and shudder and make neat brush work impossible.

Equipment
Gold leaf (available in book form, or loose) each sheet of fine gold is gummed to a sheet of thin tissue paper, gold size, talcum powder, a wad of cotton wool, 600 grit sandpaper and sanding block. A pencil eraser, handrest, good quality yacht varnish, brush, and

perhaps some contrasting yacht enamel to outline the lettering.

Technique
Sand the surface very lightly. Shake talcum powder over it, making sure that it is evenly distributed by wiping it with cotton wool. The fine dust prevents the gold from adhering to the flat paint or varnish surface of the hull.

Mark in the lettering with a pencil, then use an artist's fine watercolour brush to paint the gold size over each letter.

Wait until the gold size begins to gel. It should be almost dry, but wet enough to bond the gold leaf. Too wet, and the gold will be impossible to burnish. Too dry, and it will not bond. Experiment to find

the right moment to apply the gold leaf. Open the first page of the book, and press the gold against the sized letters. The gold adheres to the size and separates from the rest of the gold on the sheet. If the gold refuses to come away, it can be assisted by pressing against the back of the tissue with a thumbnail.

Overlap the sections of gold leaf. When the work is completed, rub the lettering with a mop of dry cotton wool. This will burnish the gold and remove excess gold that clings at the edges of the letters. Highlight the letters with good quality paint. Coat the entire lettering and surrounding area with a single coat of conventional yacht varnish when the paint has dried.

Index